D0594077

TREASON IN
THE BLOOD

ANTHONY CAVE BROWN

TREASON IN
THE BLOOD

———

H. St. John Philby, Kim Philby,

and the

Spy Case of the Century

———

A Marc Jaffe Book

HOUGHTON MIFFLIN COMPANY

Boston · New York

1994

For information about permission to reproduce
selections from this book, write to
Permissions, Houghton Mifflin Company,
215 Park Avenue South, New York,
New York 10003.

Library of Congress Cataloging-in-Publication Data
Brown, Anthony Cave
Treason in the blood : H. St. John Philby, Kim Philby,
and the spy case of the century / Anthony Cave Brown.
p.   cm.
"A Marc Jaffe Book."
Includes bibliographical references and index.
ISBN 0-395-63119-X
1. Philby, Kim, 1912–   . 2. Spies — Great Britain —
Biography. 3. Espionage, Russian — Great Britain.
4. Philby, H. St. J. B. (Harry St. John Bridger),
1885–1960. I. Title.
UB271.R92P432   1994   94-26189
327. 1'2'092 — dc 20   [B]   CIP

Printed in the United States of America

Book design by Robert Overholtzer

MP 10 9 8 7 6 5 4 3 2 1

FOR MY DEAR JOAN
who has kept my wicket so well
these past twenty-five years

Contents

TREASON IN
THE BLOOD

1

The Approvers

1885–1915

THIS STORY BEGINS in England, in Norfolk, a rich county with a long low coast on the North Sea. The Danes landed here over the centuries, and Harry St. John Bridger Philby liked to believe that his family came from such folk in the sixteenth century. The original causes that drove the Northmen from Scandinavia were overpopulation, internal dissension, quest for trade, and a thirst for adventure. They were a hairy, hardy, and cruel lot, and they made much trouble for the English — as did St. John in his time. But by Queen Victoria's reign they had calmed down and become assimilated and known as energetic, independent, practical men, often prosperous in fishing and farming. The name of one of the clans became Anglicized into Filby, of Filby Broad in the county of Norfolkshire; they had the reputation for being steady and loyal men in politics, the salt of the earth. They thought a lot of their origins and formed the Filby Society, which met every so often at the church hall in Filby Broad, where they compared notes about their family trees, took tea together, and sang old hymns: *And did those feet in ancient times walk upon England's pastures green.*

By then, of course, nothing of their politics suggested that any of them would embrace such alien causes as Wahhabism, the most austere of the Moslem fundamentalist sects of Islam, or Bolshevism, the sternest of the socialist credos; and doubtless the Filbians would have been offended were such suggested, especially when a branch of the Filbys became the Philbys, bourgeois folk, solid men — as solid as their silver, they liked to claim. They had moved south into the county of Essex in the seventeenth century, the better to follow the trade produced by London. They came to reside at Chigwell, a small town in the agreeable countryside then to be found around the capital. There they were known locally as worthies, esquires in trade, the law, the church. Some went to the empire in the service of the crown. But it is well known in genealogy and in that fashionable science of the twentieth century, genetics, that praiseworthy people of old lineages produce regrettable throwbacks to the past. One such was St. John Philby, who proved to be a brainy man but with a good deal of villainy in him. Another was his son, Harold Adrian Russell Philby, Kim, who became quite possibly the greatest unhanged scoundrel in modern British history.

Furthermore, it is explained, when you mix the blood, complicated persons are produced. And that was certainly the case in the 1870s, when Harry Montagu Philby — Montie, as he was known — went to Ceylon, one of the fairest of the crown colonies, to seek his fortune as a coffee planter. Montie bought a share in the Cocoawall and Galoola estates in the highlands at Badulla, near Nuwera Eliya, and worked hard, clearing bush, cutting trails, planting the coffee beans, building his bungalow, and laying its lawns and its fringe of shade trees. Good fortune sometimes smiles on dutiful and industrious men, and at first so it did with Montie. In 1883, while on business in Colombo, he met May Beatrice Duncan, born in 1885 at Bangalore, a tidy city in south-central India. The Duncans were Scots and a more intricate lot than the Philbys of Chigwell. They were of a military caste whose regiments had stood behind the Raj, the body of laws by which the Indian Empire was ruled but which by now had come to be used for the rulers themselves. The Indians called her memsahib, "the lady of the sir" or "lady-sir." By report, she was a strapping body, resourceful, kindly, wise in money, a real imperial lass.

Her grandfather had been the commanding officer of the Burmese Rifles at Rangoon in British Burma and rose to become a lieutenant general. Her father, Colonel John Duncan, commanded the Dublin Fusiliers at Colombo. He too succeeded mightily, becoming an instructor at the Staff College in Camberley, Adjutant General in Ireland, and deputy Adjutant General at the War Office in London. When he died, in 1898, he commanded in the Bombay District, an important post in the British Indian Army, the backbone of the Second British Empire, which was established in the 1780s and lasted until the 1970s. The men who made it up were part of an extensive web of politicos, soldiers, and diplomats in British imperial society.

It speaks much for Montie that when he and May decided to marry, Colonel Duncan approved of him. After the wedding in Colombo, the couple returned to the highlands, where, between 1884 and 1889, May Philby produced four sons. Harry St. John Bridger Philby, her favorite, was her second; and it is with "Sinjun," as his name is pronounced, that we are at first mainly concerned. St. John was an odd bird from the first moment he became aware. He noted with pleasure that on the day of his birth, April 3, 1885, a comet had blazed, considered a portentous event. St. John himself believed that its passage across the heavens between the Bay of Bengal and the Arabian Sea endowed the day with mystical and notable connotations. It was, he noted, Good Friday and therefore the anniversary of Christ's Crucifixion. He made fetishes of Friday and the number thirteen, what he called "the small beginnings of a career spent almost entirely in opposition to, or, as I prefer to think, in advance of the conventions and fallacies of the era."[1] It was St. John Philby who became the Wahhab, his son the Bolshevik. After the two of them, twentieth-century English politics were never quite the same.

Treason was in their blood; they possessed the "wild trick" of their ancestors, as Shakespeare wrote of Henry IV. Both rose high in the crown service; both turned traitor to escape it. St. John became known in Whitehall as more trouble than all the other Britons in foreign parts put together. It was he who arranged that the Saudi oil lease, which came to be known as "the richest commercial prize in the history of the planet," went to the Americans even though King Ibn Saud of Saudi Arabia wished it to go to Britain.[2] And it was his son, Kim, a high officer in the British Secret Service, who worked against his English masters in the interests of the Soviet Union. The Regius Professor of Modern History at Oxford thought him to be "one of the most remarkable double-agents to have been exposed in our time."[3] The Central Intelligence Agency called him "the most remarkable spy of our generation."[4] The KGB considered him "a unique spy, one of the most important men of the century."[5] The head of the KGB, Yuri Alexandrovich Andropov, who later became head of the Communist Party of the Soviet Union, knew him as "esteemed Comrade Kim."[6] Prime Minister Harold Macmillan called the Philby case "an almost historic affair."[7] And in the view of John le Carré, Philby's story resembled "a great novel, and an unfinished one at that."[8]

Montie Philby's good fortune failed him in the year of St. John's birth. His coffee caught the blight, for which there was then no cure, and by 1890 he was ruined. The banks would not lend him the money he needed to switch to tea. The region's entire coffee industry collapsed, and so did Montie's spirit. He went to seed, taking to drink and the Tamil girls who flitted about the jungle. Montie and May separated once, twice, thrice, and in 1891, May took her four boys to London, where her father, Colonel Duncan, was at the War Office, living in fine style in Prince's Square. Montie reappeared only rarely in his family's life. He spent his last years as a gamekeeper on a gentleman's estate at Sandford Orcas in Devon, his only legacy being a medal he had won during the Boer War. He left no money, no securities, and no property, in an age when the worth of a man was judged by the estate he bequeathed his family.

St. John regarded his father as worthless. May Philby became the breadwinner. With her father's help, in 1903 she took out a mortgage and established a residential hotel at 102a Queen's Gate, a good address, for persons of the officer class on leave or business from the empire. But it was never quite a success and gave much anxiety and little security; from time to time the bailiff called, and there was trouble over tradesmen's bills. It is in these debts, that struggle, that an essential element in Philby's character can be found. He became a man of grudges, especially against those who were richer, more privileged than he was. The constant theme of his large correspondence was that he would have succeeded to a far greater extent if only he had had a private income.

May struggled on, much encouraged by her sons' promise. They were charming children, by all accounts; and of the four, St. John was the bright spark. From the start, May decided that he should become a member of the Political and Secret Department of the Indian Foreign Office. The age in which Philby was educated was of importance in what came to be called the Philby Case, that story of revolt, conspiracy, and treason that lasted for most of the century. His was, in fact, a revolt against British imperialism, the very "ism" that nourished his career and that of his only son, Harold Adrian Russell (Kim) Philby.

Throughout the period of St. John Philby's early manhood, the British Empire expanded enormously; it became the largest geopolitical entity in the history of the planet. The opportunities before Philby were proportionately large, the spirit of his time inspired by a speech made by John Ruskin, the English social theorist, at Oxford in 1877: "Will you youths of England make your country again a royal throne of kings, a sceptered island, for all the world a source of light, a center of peace? . . . England must found colonies as far as she is able, formed of the most energetic and worthiest of men . . . their first aim to be to advance the power of England by land and sea."[9] By the turn of the century Ruskin's advocacy of imperialism and others like it had been almost generally accepted in Britain. A small group of early socialists rejected the policy, and Little Englanders spoke of England assuming the too vast orb of her fate, but the anti-imperialists had little following, and certainly there were none in the Philby clan — until St. John Philby.

British imperialism found powerful rivals abroad, principally Kaiser Wilhelm II, Tsar Nicholas II, and the American anti-imperialists. Powerful British financial interests took steps to protect what was known in Whitehall as "the imperial interest." Private capital reformed the British Secret Service and placed it at the service of the crown. The Round Table was formed by such men as Dr. D. G. Hogarth, Keeper of the Ashmolean Museum at Oxford; John Buchan, the Scottish author and statesman; Lord Milner, the statesman and colonial administrator who later took an interest in St. John Philby's career; and the Marquess of Lothian, Britain's first ambassador to Washington in World War II. Its object was to create the imperial ideology. Associated with the Round Table was John Cecil Rhodes, who was close to Milner and was reputed to earn a million pounds a year from his corner on African diamonds and gold. He endowed his fortune to Oxford University for the Rhodes Scholarships, to create what he called "the best men for the world's fight" and thereby established an educational doctrine, a spirit, for the era.

Philby was raised in Rhodes's spirit. To prepare him for the Raj, he received superb grounding at a tiny school, Henfield House in Sussex, to which he went in 1894. Here he developed a taste for the classics, for bird-watching, and cricket. May Philby then sent him to a preparatory school at Westgate-on-Sea, whose headmaster was J. V. Milne. Milne's son, Alan, was there, too. In later life A. A. Milne became famous as the creator of Christopher Robin, the well-mannered boy of the imperial ideal, and there was debate about who inspired Milne. His son? Philby? Kim? Or was Christopher Robin a combination of them all?

St. John did very well at Milne's school. One might say he was outstanding. In 1898, when he was thirteen, J. V. Milne thought it worth his while to sit for the Westminster Challenge, the royal scholarship by which boys of the middle-middle class could become King's Scholars at Westminster School. St. John won the challenge, a large personal achievement, and marched to the top in his studies. In 1903 he became captain of the school and of the King's Scholars, which he thought "the most illustrious post in the most illustrious school in the world."[10] His name went up in gold with those of the others who had been captain since the refounding of the school by Queen Elizabeth I in 1560. He became a member of the meritocracy in a day and age when such an achievement was greatly admired by the Whitehall mandarins across the road. It was an era "of the tyranny of the classics," Latin and Greek, when it was held that the best administrators for the empire were to be found among those whose minds had been polished by the Vulgate. He proved to be less successful in the exercise of his powers as captain, which were large in many matters of administration, including discipline. He was now eighteen, beginning to display something of his personality.

According to Percival Waterfield, his successor and the man responsible for making the final report on Philby's year in office, it was a "mixture of good and evil." St. John began a campaign to cleanse the morals of Westminster from what he called "the low estate into which they had fallen." Waterfield recorded of him:

> that he restored order and discipline where before had been little less than chaos, I do not deny. Nevertheless, although his system will I trust bring forth good fruit, at the moment it was not a success. Autocracy was his aim and autocratic rule his avowed intention. He meant to rule with an iron hand and he had not the good sense to conceal it in a velvet glove. The result was that his year was conspicuous for internal dissensions.

And so he remained for the rest of his life. Waterfield told how Philby had been more concerned for the King's Scholars than for the well-being of the school as a whole; he appeared to "despise" the town boys; he had worked against rather than with the masters; and he had failed to "wield the enormous influence that was available to a captain combining top-class scholarship with excellence at games." Philby's own account of his captaincy showed him to have been what his biographer called "stiffly conventional," "long-winded," and filled with controversies that "convulsed" the school. Masters were forever "meddling" in his affairs. His biographer concluded that "his aim was honest and righteous, but his judgment about how best to fulfill it was faulty."

Moreover, while he was brilliant in his studies, he did not entirely succeed in them. He claimed that it was the prejudice of a master that resulted in his name not appearing on the list of those who were to take the examination for a scholarship to Trinity College, Cambridge, in December 1903. But he did win an exhibition to Trinity in the following March. He had survived therefore as a man for the fight, but perhaps only just. His brains had saved him, and so he went on to Trinity College, founded in 1546 and the most distinguished of all the Cambridge colleges, Trinity men liked to think.

By then he was confirmed in his decision to make his career in the Indian Civil Service. The king had just been proclaimed Emperor of India, an event in the history of the empire of which the *Illustrated London News* recorded, "From every part of our Indian empire came a long array — ninety-eight feudatory chieftains in all, representing nearly one-fifth of the entire human race — to tender their allegiance to the Imperial Sovereignty."[11] Furthermore, his imagination had been captured by his reading of the two volumes on Persia by George Nathaniel Curzon, First Marquess of Kedleston, Viceroy of India; and he copied into a notebook a paragraph of that work, one that had significance in the light of the career he followed:

> Turkestan, Afghanistan, Transcaspia, Persia — to many these words breathe only a sense of utter remoteness or a memory of strange vicissitudes and of moribund romance. To me, I confess, they are pieces on a chessboard upon which is being played out a game for the domination of the world.[12]

Philby arrived at Trinity in October 1904, at a time when the college was passing through what has been called "an extraordinary philosophical brilliance." G. E. Moore was ascending to the philosopher's throne. In 1903 he had finished writing *Principia Ethica,* and Trinity was bathed in its reason and light when Philby passed into Great Court. But as Philby himself wrote of the changing spirit of Trinity, "Criticism and controversy were the salt and savour of Cambridge life," and "the established laws of philosophy, politics, economics and everything else were beginning to be challenged or brought under review."[13] Fabian socialism — Marxism without the blood — had taken hold there under the advocacy of Hugh Dalton, the son of the Canon of St. George's Chapel at Windsor Castle and thereby chaplain to Edward VII.

Yet the established laws remained the law of the class Philby proposed to enter. He was careful not to reveal too much about his responses to those changes, especially in religious and political matters. The code of the Raj was stern in regard to convention, and he took pains to display himself as the champion of orthodoxy. He joined the Sunday Essay Society, at which theological subjects were discussed — an important step, for Trinity was bound closely to the Church of England. He argued for the government at the Cambridge Union against liberal criticism of a grave decision in Egypt that had led to several hangings. He made powerful friends, men of importance, for Trinity men formed a power web in imperial society, and the trust and friendships there made most often lasted for life and sometimes into the next generations. He proposed Jawaharlal Nehru, who would become prime minister and foreign secretary in the first postimperial government of India, for membership in Trinity's debating society, the Magpie and Stump — a proposal that showed he might be more radical than he appeared. Cambridge had not yet reached the stage when "western Oriental gentlemen," "Wogs," were fully accepted in select society. But radicalism, which in political terms was defined then, as it is still, as "the most advanced views of political reform on democratic lines," was not an offense, although to display too much of it was, for a man with Philby's ambitions, imprudent. Many men were considered radical, but their opinions were tolerated as long as they accepted the conventions and the code by which the Raj ruled. Even so, men who displayed too much radicalism in Edwardian society were likely to be excluded from the places — especially Tory places — where high policy was made.

But Philby's ability spoke for him. He became secretary and then president of the Magpie and Stump, where such subjects as the abolition of the ordinary male dress of the day, the immorality of war, the iniquities of tobacco, and the education of the masses were proposed and carried or rejected. Here he came to know well two men who would become friends for life. Donald Robertson had been with Philby at Westminster and would become Regius Professor of Greek at Trinity. Claude Elliott, whose family had connections in the Raj, became headmaster and then provost of Eton College, the training ground for the aristocratic branch of the official class.

But there is something to be said about Philby's true regard for his friends. In the privacy of his letters he was occasionally scornful, even contemptuous of them, especially if they had money or position or both. Furthermore, he was not as candid with them as he seemed to be. They may or may not have known that Philby became a Fabian; he did not join the party for sixteen years, by which time it mattered no longer. In religious matters, too, his record was ambiguous. At the Sunday Essay Society he came down openly heavily in favor of the importance of religion, declaring it "of all conventions the greatest — so universal, so fundamental a part of the human system . . . so strong in its resistance to all opposition."[14] Much less publicly, and almost immediately after that declaration, he became an unbeliever and for the first time found himself, so he claimed, challenging the canons of his age. From that time forward, he recorded, his life became marked by what he called "a gradual agnosticism, atheism, anti-imperialism, socialism, and general progressive revolt against the philosophical and political canons in which I was brought up."[15] In its place he developed what he called "an uncompromising passion for the truth."

But he was an ambitious man, and it would not do to show that he had begun to doubt the very basis on which the Raj worked. And so the man of Rhodes's ideal prospered. He worked hard and won a brilliant first in modern languages. He showed also great promise in Oriental languages and in the first phase of his career he developed a command of six in about six years: Arabic, Baluch, Hindi, Persian, Punjabi, and Urdu. Undoubtedly he felt drawn to the East and the "great game" that had called Curzon. He went on to win a place in the Indian Civil Service by competitive examination. He accepted the code by which the Raj ruled:

> An officer must be loyal to his service and to his country. He may hold whatever political opinions he likes but as long as he is serving he must not allow politics to affect his loyalty to his service or to the Government which is in power, even if he thinks that it is not the right form of Government.

It was then not the practice to test a man's loyalty. His acceptance of the code meant that he accepted the established order, the monarchy, the body of laws, Parliament, the system. Later on there were men who asserted that in making Philby a member of the Raj the crown had clasped a viper to its bosom. But to the end of his life he maintained that he was loyal to the British government, but perhaps not so loyal to its establishment.

Whether this was true is a matter of judgment. Philby spoke of his "progressive revolt against the philosophical and political canons" in which he was brought up. Yet it was laid down in the seventeenth century in the History of the Pleas of the Crown that "because as the subject hath his protection from the King and his laws, so on the other side the subject is bound by his allegiance to be true and faithful to the King." This legal contention was binding on all Britons at all times during their lives. Whether Philby was entirely loyal was, and will remain, a major consideration in the life of conspiracy on which he now embarked.

St. John Philby sailed for India in November 1908. The voyage took three weeks, and the *Persia* arrived at Bombay on December 2, 1908. By December 5, Philby and his Cambridge companion, Gerard Young, were installed in the Gymkhana Club in the Punjabi capital, Lahore.

They could have had no better introduction to the life of the Raj. Christmas was a time of breathtaking festivities. The Raj gathered from the north, the south, the east, and the west of the Punjab. The cricket season opened; the Lahore Hunt, which wore blue coats with gold buttons, held its ball at Lawrence Hall and everyone danced until four o'clock in the morning. The races began, and the governor arrived in a carriage drawn by his Omani camels; the Indian princes came, too, riding in a Rolls-Royce built in the shape of a swan. The polo started. As the newest young officer, Philby dined at Government House with the lieutenant governor, Sir Louis Dane, who had been where St. John Philby hoped to be, in the Political and Secret Department of the Indian Foreign Office. Dane sat at one end of the table in the great dining room, the badge of a Knight Grand Commander of the Most Eminent Order of the British Empire on his left hip, suspended by a broad ribbon of imperial purple, and, on the left breast, a star of gold and silver rays bearing a portrait of Queen Victoria and the legend *Victoria Imperatrix*. At the other end sat her ladyship, Edith, a Lady of Grace of the Grand Priory in the British Realm of the Most Venerable Order of St. John of Jerusalem. And as they dined and talked a piper circled the cloisters playing Celtic laments.

A career in the public service of India lay at Philby's feet. He set out for Jhelum on the Grand Trunk Road at the end of the Salt Range, there to take up his first appointment as a district officer. Arriving six days later, he found a town on the map through which passed the commerce between the Punjab, the Northwest Frontier, and Kashmir, and, beyond, Afghanistan and Russian Central Asia. It had not changed much since the Mutiny of 1857. The bungalows — still called *daks* — were the same as they were in Kipling's time, and in one of them the furnishings were so unchanged that a colleague found a set of the five original bound volumes of Charles Dickens's magazine *All the Year Round*. Six months of the year was perfect cold weather, and for St. John the Salt Range and the Kashmir snows beyond were paradise. A bird watcher since Westminster, he saw hill birds he had not seen before and would not see again, the flash of the chirchaman, the great tragopan or argus with its red ruff, and, when he was above the snow line and fortunate, the purple-violet *moonal* planing down a snowy slope. His pay was four hundred rupees a month (£30 or $150), ample in a place where he could live and eat for £4 a month. He had ten days' leave each year at some pine-clad hill station of the Himalayas, where, as in Kipling's day, all the girls were lovely and the young Raj picnicked with them on weekends in the cool under the deodars.

Philby began his settlement training: six months of Urdu, revenue collection, treasury, and judicial procedures; the arts and crafts of keeping the peace between the Sikhs, the Jat, and the Dogra; how to clip the claws of the moneylenders; and learning what his mission in India was to be. He became one of the "Heaven-born," as the Indians called their rulers, one of the hundred and forty-one Britons who ruled the forty-two million Indians in the Punjab. Again he excelled. There was the secretary's instruction:

> The Punjab, when we took it about sixty years ago, was a ruined country. It had less than twenty million inhabitants. Except near the five great rivers it was mostly desert and camel thorn, and such cultivation as existed was liable to devastating floods and long droughts. Famine was endemic. It was the road by which every conqueror, Mongol, Persian or Afghan, entered India, and their armies lived on the land and carried off the women. Finally a small but fanatic Hindu military sect, the Sikhs, established their rule on the debris of the Mogul Empire. They were more destructive than the long series of Moslem conquerors who had preceded them. From them we conquered the Punjab after a series of battles when we were more than once near to defeat. Look what it is now. The great rivers harnessed — no longer famine but a great wheat-exporting country. Peace between the Sikhs and Moslems . . . the Hindu Dogra of the foothills and Jat of the plains prosperous. But all remembering their bloody rivalries of the past. Do you think that if we removed our hand the Moslems of the West would tolerate the rich Sikh landowners of the new Canal colonies, or that the Sikh, the Jat or the Dogra would tolerate the Moslems in the East? We have changed the economic face of the country, and we rule over these races which would do their best to exterminate each other if it were not for us. The Punjab as we have made it is artificial — there is no compromise between our personal rule and chaos — however liberal-minded you may be. The rest of India is different. You will see.[16]

The secretary added, as he did usually, "Do not think that you were born to reform the Government of India. You would be mistaken, let me tell you now."[17]

In his first two years Philby proved to be an exemplary officer. He seemed to fit in. He kept his politics to himself. He sat on the bench at the local courts, empowered to award up to two years in jail to an Indian, three months to a European, floggings, to settle tax questions, and generally to keep law and order in his district. He ranged widely, his stamina was extraordinary, his health was excellent, and he seemed immune to disease. Where others were laid low, he was a glutton for work. In five months he passed a higher examination in Urdu with credit. His performance, every inch of which was watched by his masters, pleased all. But it was not long before he again felt himself to be an odd man out, again over money, although he was well paid and his living was inexpensive. He could afford to help support his mother, whose hotel in London still had not produced a living for her, and he did so. But as his letters to his mother show, his resentment was against those of his colleagues who enjoyed private incomes.

Late in his second year Philby made one or two statements that reflected something of his Fabianism at Trinity, and there was talk about his attitudes in the messes where he stayed during his travels. This was dangerous in a small society such as that of the Raj in the Punjab. As dangerous was his irritation with the Raj itself, its meticulous clerkly ways, its ponderous machine, its stern doctrine. This was an uncertain time in Indian politics. Revolt was in the air. While the Raj had been reforming itself, the Sikhs in the golden temples were stirring. Their leader, Lala Hardayal, spoke not of reforming the Raj but of "reforming it away, leaving, if necessary, only nominal traces of its existence."[18]

By his third year, at the cavalry mess he frequented, he came to be known as "a redhot radical."[19] There was talk about his socialist opinions, and this was still a time when to be known as a socialist could be dangerous to a man's career. Such statements set a man apart from the rest. In 1909 he began to flout one of the conventions on which the Raj was founded. This concerned marriage, about which there were well-known rules that a young officer was required to obey.

At the Rawalpindi Club at Christmas of 1909, he had met Miss Dora Johnston, a daughter of Adrian H. Johnston of the Public Works Department, and not, therefore, of Philby's status. It was said that Johnston had a touch of Indian blood in him, and these were times when such people, termed Anglo-Indians, were regarded as unacceptable and even undesirable, both within the Civil Service and in society. With her great mane of red hair and her young Elizabethan looks, Miss Johnston was a striking woman, twenty-four to Philby's twenty-four and the toast of the Cavalry Brigade at Rawalpindi. "Miss Johnston is one of the belles of Pindi," St. John wrote to May in February 1910. "A beautiful dancer and I have been honoured with several dances at all the dances I have been able to attend." She "does not play bridge or smoke and I have never heard her say a nasty thing about anyone." May expected that the romance would wither. It did not.[20]

The news that St. John wished to marry Dora provoked the only serious row he had with his mother throughout their lives. The intention was not only unwise for a man so young but was also against the Civil Service regulations, which Philby had accepted when he appeared before the commissioners. Nor did the marriage sit well on the lieutenant governor, for cadets in the service were not expected to marry until they had been in India for five years, and St. John had been there only two. Philby's good judgment was called into question, for the Raj wished its cadets to be as wise in their personal lives as they were required to be in their official duties. Quiet words of advice were offered. But Philby was a prickly man, and the advice, well meant as it may have been, served only to make him determined. His personal life was his own affair. He proceeded with his courtship on the grounds that, as he wrote about himself in later life:

> From the earliest times I have ever had a comfortable feeling of adequate intellectual, physical and spiritual equipment and a definite consciousness of my individual right to think for myself and to act or speak accordingly.[21]

He made the mistake of being right. The opposition to his marriage became official and it led to antagonism between him and his master in the Raj, Lieutenant Governor Dane.

The banns were called for Murree Cathedral in September 1910, and the marriage proceeded despite all advice that he should bide his time, wait a little to see whether he was sure about it. The best man was a relative of Philby's on his mother's side, Lieutenant Bernard Montgomery, of the Royal Warwickshire Regiment, later to become land forces commander in chief at the Normandy landing in June 1944. They were married in accordance with the Form of Solemnization of Matrimony of Canterbury, his atheism notwithstanding, They were then driven off by carriage for their honeymoon at a hill station, Changli Gali. Then, after no more than a week in the highlands, he and Dora returned to Sarghoda. There the Hindus, Philby's champions, pelted their carriage with roses and jasmine petals. Dane sent his congratulations, but after the marriage, and perhaps because of it, so St. John Philby complained, he began to get what he considered second-rate posts. Administrative rebukes came his way, and Philby began to believe that his chief was trying to force him to resign.

Here Philby erred; there is no evidence that Dane did more than try to whip this able but difficult man into the mold of the Raj. But for all Dane's interest in him, Philby became ever more certain that the Raj as constituted was incompetent. He began openly to advocate socialism for India. As he wrote to his mother in 1913: "Why we don't all plump for socialism is a mystery, but England is very dense and conservative and cannot see reason." Those who were reasonable, like himself, "are considered mad and argumentative and generally impossible."[22] Yet he prospered through his marvelous command of Oriental languages. But for these gifts Philby might well have found himself transferred to some lowly agency like the Customs Service or even sent home. His grudge — that those with private incomes and their accompanying influence in London were being favored by Dane — became stronger. This he began to cloak in all manner of modern causes — antiestablishmentarianism, anti-imperialism, and more advanced socialism, which at times made it seem that he was none too far from Marxism. A colleague, Sir Ronald Wingate, a son of Wingate Pasha of the Anglo-Egyptian Sudan, felt that "he became the sort of Englishman who would have been much happier as a pioneer in Teddy Roosevelt's America."[23] Administrative action taken against him served only to convince him that he was right about Dane.

But his marriage prospered; and so, really, did his career. In 1911, St. John and Dora found themselves at Ambala, a pretty town near the frontier of the United Provinces, his rank that of revenue assistant. St. John welcomed his new tasks as a way out of civil and criminal judicial work, which he disliked. Here, Dora and he had a bungalow on the Civil Lines, and it was here that their firstborn arrived on January 1, 1912. They named the child Harold Adrian Russell Philby, after various members of their families, and St. John took a determined step to ensure that his son did not become contaminated by the Christian doctrine he himself had renounced at Cambridge. He refused to allow "Kimbo," as he first nicknamed his boy, to be christened.[24] May warned St. John about the conventions: "It's all very well being peculiar but peculiar people don't always get on, and at school the boys will very soon find out that the child is a Heathen, and give him a time of it." May held Dora to blame because "she never goes to church."[25] Dane, the canon of Lahore, and the wife of the secretary to the Punjab government, Heather Rudkin, all advised St. John to follow the convention, but he listened to none. He did, however, allow his son to submit to that other imperial ritual, circumcision. As he wrote to May on October 26, 1912:

> I suppose Dora has told you of Baby's little operation! Poor little child he was much upset about it for several days but Dora says he is alright

now. It is a good thing to have had it done — I hope he will not be such a wet little boy in future. Really he is a perfectly sweet child and I do hope he is going to develop an intellect as I hope he will do all that I would have liked to do myself.[26]

Kimbo the boy remained until about 1914, when St. John gave him another nickname, a famous one, Kim, after the orphaned son of an Anglo-Irish soldier in Rudyard Kipling's greatest novel, *Kim,* which was set in the Punjab and Lahore, where Kipling had lived and worked a generation before Philby. The name touched the British heart; it meant something in the Raj and other official classes: the young man on duty on the frontiers of the empire; the subaltern working for the common good, that of the Occident and the Orient, in the foothills of the Himalayas. It had something imperial and admirable about it. No other name of the period had such resonance, for it bespoke romance and adventure in distant parts.

But that is not all. After its publication in 1901, eleven years before Kim Philby's birth, the book became associated in the public mind with England's imperial primacy and the dangers to that primacy coming from the "great game" of espionage and power politics between England and Russia for the control of Northwest India, the gateway into India — the game played out by the Raj's Political and Secret Department with the Russian secret agents of Tsar Alexander II.[27] The eponymous hero was in the British Secret Service. Four lines in *Kim* express the unsure loyalties of both Kims:

> Something I owe to the soil that grew
> More to the life that fed —
> But most to Allah Who gave me two
> Separate sides to my head.

In May 1912, soon after Kim's birth, an incident took place that set Philby's career backward. He had been required to go to Jagadri, a large village that, as Philby wrote, possessed "a bad reputation as a hot-bed of intrigue and sedition" that gave the stranger "an inexplicable and uncomfortable feeling that he was surrounded by watchful enemies."[28] It was a place where, as Philby witnessed, some of the natives could will themselves into a state resembling death so convincingly that on occasions death was pronounced by the Raj doctor, only to have the corpse return to life, thus discrediting Raj medicine.

But there were other ways in which the Jagadrites sought to embarrass the Raj, and this was through a subtle campaign of disdain. Philby encountered just such a case. While on a narrow path leading to Jagadri, he met a party of schoolboys led by an Indian schoolmaster who carried an open umbrella as protection against the sun. Because the wearing of an umbrella in the presence of a superior was regarded as a mark of disrespect, Philby reprimanded the schoolmaster and the boys. The Indian did not furl his umbrella. This annoyed him; he felt that the schoolmaster "was trying to be insolent — perhaps to show off before the boys." This might be a sign that times were changing "as a result of the new spirit of independence of which I approved so wholeheartedly," but nonetheless the schoolmaster had gone too far. Philby snatched the umbrella and then boxed the man's ears. In that moment he committed what the Raj regarded as a most serious offense, striking an Indian.

The incident got into the local press. The India of 1912 was a tinderbox in which the slightest slip on the part of an Englishman was likely to spark flames, and somebody sent the clipping in the press to Sir Louis Dane. There were already two marks against Philby — marriage against the wish of authority, and a case in which he had jailed two Indians who he believed had committed perjury in a murder case. Dane took a serious view of the incident, for it might well have led to rioting, and proposed to punish Philby by permanently reducing him by two places in the list on which promotion was based. The punishment could have placed his career in jeopardy.

While Dane's finding was on its way to the government of India for confirmation, and on the advice of a friend, Philby requested and was granted a personal interview with Dane. Dane knew that Philby's relations with Indians had been excellent. He knew, too, that the schoolmaster had been insolent. He did not withdraw punishment, as Philby hoped, but he did recommend to the government of India that its severity be reduced. The word *permanent* was removed, although it was decreed that Philby must not be promoted in any way for a year. This hit Philby hard, and, in the belief that he had been wronged by Dane, he decided to take a major step. He decided to petition the Viceroy of India, Lord Hardinge, as was the privilege of officers who felt they were being wronged by a superior. In the first draft, he alleged that Dane was attempting to punish him cumulatively for not one but three instances of misdemeanor. He did not doubt that he had behaved badly in hitting the Indian but pointed to his good record in dealing with Indians and asked the viceroy to forgive a stupidity that, he claimed, was the result of overwork in hot weather.

Only Dane could forward an appeal to the viceroy, and Philby was warned by a colleague that he would do himself no good by complaining about the lieutenant governor. In the final version, therefore, Philby confined himself to a statement that he "sincerely regrets and has never ceased to repent of his hasty action, yet he would most humbly urge that the circumstances in which he found himself were such that a sudden loss of temper was inevitable though the practical result of it was inexcusable."[29] More than a year later, Philby learned that his punishment had been reduced to a stoppage of promotion for nine months, a modification that served merely to intensify his dislike for Dane.

From that point forward Philby did not cease to mutter and grumble about "the rottenness" of the government and his dislike for the Raj and for Dane in particular. "I have worked well and where I could show my merit, for instance in my languages," he wrote to his mother in 1913. "I have beaten all my contemporaries," but "never had a word of recognition from Louis Dane," who had "gone out of his way to keep me down." St. John's dislike for the man and the system dated from these incidents. What was no more than resentment grew in his mind until it became a cause. He might have left but for Dane's retirement in 1914, just before the outbreak of World War I. Philby emphasized his dislike for Dane by declining publicly to contribute to his farewell present and welcoming his departure, in a letter to his mother, as being the end of what had been the "egotistical and tyrannical rule of a most unworthy Lieutenant Governor." Philby's last sally was in the queer dialect of English and Urdu affected by educated Indians at that time: *"Affability to bahut hai lekin true sympathy"* — "Very affable indeed but entirely lacking in true sympathy."[30]

With Dane's last ride in his camel carriage, a new lieutenant governor appeared at Government House, Sir Michael O'Dwyer, an Irishman from Tipperary who had been at Balliol in Oxford. He was not, however, a man of the old guard like Dane, having married the daughter of a French Catholic. They were a gayer couple than the Danes; O'Dwyer was more supple, more aware of the realities of the Indian political situation; and with the O'Dwyers' arrival, the attitude of Government House changed toward St. John in particular and the internal security situation in general. Probably because war was in the air, O'Dwyer realized that men of St. John's language ability would be invaluable.

Philby's career flourished. O'Dwyer sent him as acting district commissioner at Lyallpur, an important industrial town in the Punjab, a company town created by the Raj. He acknowledged that Lyallpur was a "difficult" post, with what he called "a large and very independent Sikh element and a permanent undercurrent of sedition." Philby thought the appointment a step upward and plainly enjoyed the attributes of personal power. "It does one good to talk 'high,'" he wrote to his mother, adding, "The feeling of real power and importance is of course very pleasant," although he had not yet "got used to seeing my police guard do sentry-go over me as I sleep." He was, he said, "tasting the wine of life." And he tasted more of it when World War I broke out, in August 1914.

O'Dwyer advised that he had a special job for Philby. Would he take charge of the Press Section of the Criminal Investigation Department? Philby was delighted. He was to put a stop to sedition in the press throughout the Punjab. As he wrote to his mother in England, "I sit upon the slightest flicker of sedition." This was amusing, he confessed, for "if I were a journalist I would be a most seditious one and a constant thorn in the side of government." As part of his duties, he prepared a daily bulletin of war news for the press and public. The object, he recounted later, "was to prevent the dissemination of alarm and despondency among the population of India by emphasizing all successes and minimizing any reverses" of the British Army in France. He was required, too, to review the Indian press in order to "safeguard the people against the reversing of those processes by less responsible publicists."[31]

This work he did so capably that when the Viceroy of India and O'Dwyer were both established with their administrations at Simla, the summer capital of India, O'Dwyer again appointed Philby to his staff. The Raj was busying itself with affairs in the arc of Asia from Aden on the Red Sea, through the Trucial Coast of Arabia, across Mesopotamia, across Persia, across Afghanistan, Nepal, Tibet, Baluchistan, and down through British Burma and Siam to Malaya and Singapore.

With the Belle Époque being extinguished as if by forest fire, St. John hastened up to Simla, that other Eden nestled high in the Himalayas, to find that Dora and Kim had arrived and were staying at the villa (called World's End) of Dora's father, who was still with the Public Works Department. Called into audience with O'Dwyer at the end of August 1914, Philby got what he called "the chance of my lifetime." The lieutenant governor wanted St. John to work with the countersedition section of the Special Branch, a police and security agency of three sections, which concerned itself with counterterrorism, countersedition, and the activities of the Indian National Congress, which was considered to be subversive. St. John thereupon became the radical whose job it was to hunt radicals. This was also his first direct encounter with that mysterious body in imperial lore, the British Secret Service. He formed an association with a number of its officers, particularly with Captain Valentine (Veevee) Vivian, who would figure in the lives of both St. John and Kim.

Valentine Terrell Patrick Vivian, willowy with carefully dressed crinkly hair, a monocle, and a kindly but official manner, was born in 1886, a year after St. John Philby. He was the son of Comley Vivian, a portrait painter. Veevee, as he was known to the secret circle for the rest of his career, was educated at St. Paul's School in London at the same time St. John's cousin and best man, Bernard Montgomery, was there. He entered the Indian Police in 1906 and in 1911 married Mary Primrose, a daughter of the canon of Lahore Cathedral — the cleric who had made trouble for Philby over Kim's baptism — and joined the Special Branch, which was responsible for protecting the safety and dignity of the Raj. Veevee was, like St. John, a leading light of the Lahore and the Simla Clubs, where they played bridge together.

In late October 1914, both became engaged in a brief flash of serious violence among the Sikhs in the Punjab, who revolted in the expectation of receiving guns and gold from German agents. An intelligence report mentioned the Sikhs' intention to "murder all Europeans and loyal Indian subjects, overthrow the existing government and form a republic." But they were not a match for the Raj, with its methodical but irresistible ways of maintaining imperial power. The machine began to work as silkily as a Rolls-Royce. Proclamations were issued; the press came under Philby's control, Vivian's "approvers" — the police term for informants — brought in more and more of the Sikhs' plans. To prevent the overseas Sikhs from landing in India at all, O'Dwyer introduced, on September 5, 1914, the Ingress into India Ordinance, to provide for the control of all persons entering British India, whether by sea or land, "in order to protect the State from anything prejudicial to its safety, interests, or tranquillity."[32]

By February 1915 the Sikhs' revolt was over. Their tricolor — yellow for the Sikhs, red for Hindus, and blue for the Moslems — had flown over a handful of Punjabi villages on February 19, the day on which the Second Indian Mutiny was to have begun with the general massacre of British troops at the Artillery Cantonment in Lahore and of all European subjects in the capital. The British guns were to have been seized and turned against the British component of the Indian Army by the 23rd Cavalry Regiment in Lahore and the 26th Punjabi Regiment at Ferozepore. But the British, the official report claimed, had been "in possession of the plans of the movement." And as the Raj also noted with satisfaction, "The result of all this, coupled with the complete failure of the plot and the punishment which they saw overtake the more reckless members of the party, had the effect of causing them to abandon their revolutionary views and to return to more level-headed ways of thinking."

From the Raj's point of view the Sikh revolt had been an impressive exercise in imperial power, in India and throughout the world. Philby went to Calcutta to sit for his language examinations and won the Degree of Honor in Urdu, a high achievement by the standards of any linguist or scholar of the day. He was appointed as the invigilator at the language school, another fine post for a young officer albeit a wearisome one. But he did not stay long. His services were requested by Sir Percy Cox, chief of the Political Mission to the commander in chief of the army in Mesopotamia, which had been landed there to counter the move of a Turkish army toward the great British oil fields and refinery at Abadan in southwest Persia. Did Philby wish to accept? At last he had been proposed for the Political and Secret Department. Joyfully, he wrote to Dora in Simla from Calcutta:

> I don't know whether I am standing on my head or my heels. Yesterday afternoon I was awoken from my slumbers by a Govt. of India wire enquiring whether my services are available for Mesopotamia [Iraq] . . . My chance at last . . . I am sure you will be delighted darling for my sake as it is just the thing I have been clamouring for for ages.[33]

He urged Dora to leave Simla immediately, bringing Kim with her so that he would be able "to give him my parting counsel!" Philby asked whether it was not "all too splendid," and ended, revealing Persian ambitions for the first time, "I have been in a dream ever since I heard the news & now old girl my firm intention of spending the rest of my life in Persia." He declared his final attitude toward the Supreme Government: "Wild horses won't drag me back to India!"

Dora and Kim descended from the Himalayas to make their farewells, and Kim was in a flood of tears as his father boarded the S.S. *Lhasa*, a steamer of the British India Company, and the liner drew out into the Hoogly River and set its bow toward the Sea of Bengal. Although he too was saddened by the parting, Philby noted with satisfaction — it still tickled him to challenge the Fates — that his steamer left from berth 13 on November 13, 1915. But Kim's reaction to the parting was serious. In the view of his grandmother, May, it was Kim's sudden separation from his father amid the tumult of a looming campaign (combined with the perils of the voyage that now confronted him and his mother) that resulted in the severe stammer that would afflict him in varying degrees for the rest of his life. Dora and Kim sailed for England in the S.S. *City of Glasgow.*

Many years later, when he attempted to write his biography, Kim Philby remembered nothing of his life in India or of St. John except that English was their "second language," that they talked in Hindustani, that they had lived in a bungalow under the Himalayas at Darjeeling, and that his father required him to give him a weather report each morning. St. John, "who in many ways was as conversational as only an eccentric can be," instructed him to use one of two formulas: "either 'Daddy, the mountains are visible,' or 'Daddy, the mountains are invisible.' If the formula was the first, he would join me on the verandah; if the second, he would go back to sleep."[34] At St. John's departure, Kim was within two months of his fourth birthday and it was to be almost three years before father and son were reunited.

Dora and Kim's journey was neither calm nor comfortable. The liner was packed; the seas were rough into the Red Sea; U-boats were rumored in the Indian Ocean and the Arabian and Red Seas; German commerce raiders were in the eastern Mediterranean; U-boats were off Gibraltar. The captain therefore zigzagged into Marseilles, where Dora and Kim disembarked to make the rest of the journey to England by rail. The trains had been badly damaged by the troops which the French had been moving to the front, the track was poor, the train rattled the bones, and some of the carriage windows were out. Kim caught a cold. Then came tonsillitis and adenoidal problems, and finally pneumonia; and by the time Dora reached her grandmother's home, "The Crossways," a big Victorian villa on the military cantonment at Camberley in Surrey, Kim seemed more dead than alive.

Here, through the many absences of St. John and Dora in Asia, Kim Philby spent almost all the next eight years, until he was almost thirteen, in the care of his grandmother, May Philby. In some unpublished reminiscences found in Moscow in February 1992, Philby had something to say about the matriarchy in which he found himself. May ran the Crossways, a house large enough to benefit the suite of General Duncan. But she was not the head of the family. May's mother, Emily Duncan, was seventy years old. Philby remembered a "pale, frail, white-haired" lady from the Indian Empire who "spent the mornings in her bedroom, the afternoons in her drawing-room, and the evenings, when it was fine, mucking about in the herbaceous border, shredding pair after pair of mittens." She was attended constantly by Kate, the cook-general, Mr. Bishop, the gardener, and, as befitted

> the home of one elderly lady in those days, the regime, while not too harsh, was well defined. Just as Kate's place was in the kitchens and the backyard, mine was the nursery and the garden, with strict injunctions against treading on flower beds. I was kept in order by a succession of young nursemaids who shared my bedroom and gave me a vague awareness of sex, presumably because they were sexually aware themselves.

Granny Duncan's drawing room, he remembered, "was forbidden territory," which he had no wish to visit, any more than he wished her to visit his domain, the nursery. At her house, "it was recognised that both children and adults had an equal right to their own ways of life." The earliest books he remembered were at about the time of his fifth birthday: the children's edition of *Sinbad the Sailor* and Arthur Mee's *Children's Encyclopaedia*. There was also a book of short stories, the title of which he had forgotten but which he remembered because it concerned

> an attack by a pack of wolves on a sledge in Siberia. The wolves announced their presence by "a long, low melancholy howl": the traces of several horses were cut to delay the pursuit and the story ended happily with the twinkling lights of a village. But that phrase about the howl stuck in my mind and caused me many a nightmare. With other stories, illustrated by pictures of snakes and sea-monsters, it gave me a fear of the dark that lasted two or three years.

His fears were "completely eclipsed" by Granny May's love.

Through Kim's parents' absences in Asia, May Philby had principal charge of the boy between the ages of three and twelve. His affection for May, he went on, endured "undiminished until, with appetite and sense of fun undiminished, she died at the age of 85." When Kim arrived at the Crossways, May had lost one son killed in action at the First Battle of Ypres in 1914. In 1916 she lost a second son at the Second Battle of Ypres. For the rest of her life she wrote all her letters on stationery with black borders, and Philby thought, "My presence must have helped close the gap in her heart: her preference for me is otherwise inexplicable."

Otherwise, the Crossways was not the sort of house to encourage an influx of little boys, and so it was that during those years "my grandmother, Kate, Mr. Bishop, my books and my atlas monopolised my vision." Also, before he was five, he was put into a kindergarten, run by a Miss Herring and a Miss Crisp, where, he claimed, he became interested in the atlas, in cartography, in atheism, and in rationalism. He formed the opinion that there was no God and revealed as much to his grandmother, which "scandalised her." As he wrote in his recollections:

> My scepticism owed its origin to the kindergarten where the miraculous element stressed was supposedly attractive to small children. In my case, the result was the opposite. This I contradicted in frank disbelief, repelled in particular by the wide gap between the powers attributed to Christ and the trivial use to which he put them. Why cure one leper? Why not all lepers? and so on.

Thereafter no argument dented his belief; he could remember then and afterward "not the slightest twinge of religious experience," and he came to the belief that "the senses are far more genuinely 'miraculous' than any flight of faith." By the time he left kindergarten, he claimed toward the end of his life, he had begun to repudiate the ethos of England — God, King, and Empire — and became "a godless little anti-imperialist before I reached my teens."

2

The Ride to Fame

1917–1919

ST. JOHN PHILBY ARRIVED off Basra on November 20, 1915, wearing the British Army's khaki uniform, Sam Browne belt, soft cap, and the white lapel tabs of a major in the Political and Secret Department of the Indian government. His orders directed him to place himself at the disposal of Sir Percy Cox, of the Political Mission to the commander in chief of the British Army on the Iraqi front. Cox was to bind the sheikhs, presently the myrmidons of the Turkish Empire in southwest Asia, to the Raj's direction as firmly as he had created the British hegemony in the Persian Gulf over the past quarter of a century.

In India St. John had learned much about state fiscal work — how to keep the tax rolls, how to collect taxes and get money out of delinquents, how to curb the public-monies spendthrifts — so his first task was to rewrite the Turkish tax code to provide revenue for the military and political campaigns. It was important work, but remote from that of high policy and grand strategy, and Philby found himself no more than a medium-level official in a large machine. He did the job in six months, producing the excess of revenue over expenditure of £100,000. He polished his Arabic by translating the New Testament aloud in Arabic to his Arab manservant and by conversation with the nautch girls in the nightclubs of Basra. And then he was noticed by the Oriental Secretary, Miss Gertrude Bell, one of the leading Arabists of her time and the British Secret Service's representative at Basra. St. John's Arabic, his charm, his vigor, his bearing — all, in Miss Bell's view, should be put to a higher task. This she arranged, and Philby owed much to her.

Miss Bell — as she was usually known — was born in 1868, a daughter of one of the richest British ironmasters, a man who was well connected with the Whitehall establishment. She was seventeen years older than Philby, but handsome, striking, and able. She had had an enchanted youth at Lady Margaret's Hall, in what she called "that Oxford garden among the roses and the scarlet robes."[1] She too was outstanding as a student of Oriental languages, and afterward her allowance was large enough to allow her to travel where she pleased, which was usually in Turkey and the Levant. She was feminine — "Paris frocks and Mayfair manners," they said of her at that place of boots and spurs, Cox's headquarters — and tall and graceful. The Viceroy of India, Lord Hardinge, thought her "a remarkably clever woman with a man's mind."[2]

Miss Bell's involvement in British political and secret work had begun in November 1915, when she received a commission from Captain Sir Reginald (Blinker) Hall of British naval intelligence in World War I. As "Major Miss Bell" she became the first woman officer in the army. Then she went out to Cairo to join the Arab Bureau, one of the two political and secret missions in the Middle East, the other being Cox's. Such was her eminence in society and as an explorer that at Port Said she was met by the archaeologist Leonard Woolley, the chief of the British Secret Service in that city, and at Cairo a few days later was greeted by the man who would become her chief, Commander David Hogarth, the head of the Arab Bureau and until lately the Keeper of the Ashmolean Museum at Oxford. There, too, was a young political officer whom she had known when she explored the ruins of the Hittite city of Carchemish on the Turko-Syrian frontier — T. E. Lawrence, a scholar of Jesus College, Oxford, another archaeologist who became famous (and, to some, illustrious) as Lawrence of Arabia.

The Arab Bureau was a small group of Oxford and Cambridge men (leavened with army officers) who called themselves "the Intrusives," after their official telegraphic address, INTRUSIVE CAIRO.[3] While in Cairo, between November 1915 and February 1916, Miss Bell learned of the Arab Bureau's plan to raise what would enter history as "the Arab Revolt," the stirring by the bureau of the tribes of Hussein, Sherif of Mecca, a direct descendant of the Prophet and the head of the leading family in the Near East, the Hashemites, against the German-led Turkish army in Syria, Palestine, and the Sinai Desert. If the revolt succeeded, then the British government would recognize Hussein as the Caliph of the Arabs and would rule the new Islamic dominion (with all its oil fields) through him and his four sons. Then Britain would secure the air and sea communications that connected Britain with India, Asia, and Australasia; and would produce religious tranquillity among the large, passionate Moslem population of the Empire. There was, too, a second aspect of the Intrusives' plan, which was largely the brainchild of Lawrence but which became the cause of most and perhaps all the other members of the bureau: to obtain the support of world Jewry for the war. In order to further this, the Intrusives gave thought to the establishment of a Jewish national home in Palestine, one that would again be under the jurisdiction of Whitehall.

In due course Gertrude Bell became an important disciple of the plan; indeed, she became one of the great power brokers of the Orient. In March 1916 she arrived at Basra as Hogarth's representative at Cox's headquarters and there met St. John Philby, who had recently been elevated to the high rank of revenue commissioner, an official with his own aircraft and his own launch. They became good friends. Philby was thirty-one, able, vigorous, virile, vituperative, and destined for high places if only he held his tongue; Miss Bell, forty-eight, equally brilliant and equal to Philby in her knowledge of the Iraqi and Persian tribes and causes, and handsome. She was five feet, five and a half inches tall, slender, with a good figure, sharp-faced, and crowned with graying hair.

From the first she regarded Philby almost as a brother, never a lover. She became the key to his advancement, and soon acquired real power when Cox made her his Oriental Secretary, his right arm in Iraqi and Arabian affairs, the officer whose duty it was to provide Cox with the information he needed on local politics and personalities. She advised, too, on the affairs of neighboring Middle Eastern countries, and she was required to write knowledgeably on the incoming papers, draft Cox's dispatches and telegrams, and advise him in that most important aspect of diplomatic affairs, protocol and custom in his dealings with notables. No work was more important; no member of the staff came to possess greater access to and influence over Cox in his political and social activities. So well did she perform her duties that she remained Oriental Secretary at Baghdad for almost all the last decade of her life, through the fall of Baghdad, the Turkish surrender, the establishment of the state of Iraq, and the installation — as she had intended — of one of the Sherif of Mecca's sons as king. Her role was the more extraordinary since the Mesopotamian Arabs, like all Arabs, were unaccustomed to dealing with women in any sphere save the harem; and they knew her as Katoun, which an early State Department spy in the Middle East defined as "a lady of the Court who keeps an open eye and ear for the benefit of the State."[4]

Though Miss Bell was the woman who made his career, Philby came to dislike her through her fondness for king making. She referred to him always not as "Jack" or "St. John" but as "my dear Mr. Philby." They traveled much together in the Shatt-al-Arab and spent the Christmas holiday of 1916 together there, in his launch, meeting the sheikhs and merchants. She was well aware of Philby's dangerous habit of laying down the law and his tendency to say one thing when he really meant another, but when the British Army captured Baghdad in March 1917, she worked in subtle ways to persuade Cox to make Philby his personal assistant there, a post that placed him in line for high position. From that time forward Philby's career in crown service began to prosper mightily. Miss Bell did not exaggerate the importance of St. John's Arabic; in full blast Philby was a wonder to hear and a lesson to every Englishman in Iraq on how to deal with suspicious or unwilling Orientals. He could curse, converse, cajole, in colloquial and classical Arabic, as well as speak the elegant Turkish-Arabic dialect affected by the notables. Philby became Cox's devoted clerk. He was good at his work of looking after Cox's secret mail with Whitehall, Cairo, and Simla, and for the first time he became familiar with higher policy pertaining to the British interest in Arabia.

Having gained the trust of Cox and Miss Bell, he began to display another of his characteristics, deceit. Without the knowledge of either Cox or Miss Bell, as he himself admitted in a memoir, he began to go through Cox's files with "parental solicitude" to create "my own separate files . . . with papers purloined from the files of political and other departments."[5] He never declared his reason for "purloining" these papers, but whatever it was, his action was entirely in contravention of the Official Secrets Act, the instrumentation by which the government secured its files. The penalty for such action was severe; fourteen years in prison was the maximum sentence in cases where the theft had occurred in the interests of a foreign power. At the least, the act would have cast doubt on his loyalty to Cox and thus would inevitably have led to his dismissal from the crown service. As his official record shows, this incident was not the only suspect one in Philby's crown service.

His purpose in stealing Cox's and Miss Bell's papers is clear: he intended to use them to further his career. In October 1917 he learned from the files and through his talks with Miss Bell — they shared the office outside Cox's — that Lawrence and the Arab Revolt intended to march on Jerusalem and Damascus but were vulnerable to a stab in the flank from Rashid, the Sherif of Hail, one of the triangle of princes who ruled Arabia. His capital, Hail, a place of twenty thousand souls, was in northwestern Arabia, he was an ally of the Turks, and his was a most murderous regime; all in the male line of the succession for as long as anyone could remember had been murdered, even in the cradle. The sherif and his two rivals for the power of Arabia, Ibn Saud of Riyadh and the Hashemite king at Mecca, had been at war with him for as long as anyone knew. He was a thorn in Britain's side. Here was an opportunity for Philby to acquire what he so deeply desired — fame. As he wrote of himself: "My ambition is fame, whatever that may mean and for what it is worth. I have fought for it hard . . . If my ambition had been to make money, it would have been easier to understand."[6] Miss Bell proposed and Cox disposed. Might Philby not go to Riyadh and, with the help of Britain's half-ally, Ibn Saud, eliminate the Sherif of Hail and thereby remove the threat to Lawrence's flank? He had just the qualities necessary to make that dangerous and difficult journey and to deal with a strong prince like Ibn Saud: his presence was commanding — St. John was only of medium height but he was built like a dolmen — and he was resolute, fit, and gifted with unusual diplomatic skills.

Cox did not agree, at least at first. He sent another official on that long camel ride to Riyadh, but that traveler collapsed of heat stroke, so Cox had no other choice. In October 1917 Philby received his instructions. His business at Ibn Saud's court, other than to remove Rashid, the Sherif of Hail, was to establish a political agency, the first official British presence at Riyadh, and to report on relations between Ibn Saud and Britain's nominee for the rule of Arabia, Hussein, Sherif of Mecca, who now began to call himself King of the Arabs.

Miss Bell was able to give Philby an idea of the man that he would deal with. In 1916 she had talked with Ibn Saud and left this brilliant pen portrait of him in the files of the Political and Secret Department:

Ibn Saud is now barely forty, though he looks some years older. He is a man of splendid physique, standing well over six feet, and carrying himself with the air of one accustomed to command. Though he is more massively built than the typical nomad shaikh, he has the characteristics of the well-bred Arab, a strongly-marked aquiline profile, full-flesh nostrils, prominent lips and a long narrow chin accentuated by a pointed beard. His hands are fine, with slender fingers . . . and in spite of his great height and breadth, of an indefinable lassitude . . . the secular weariness of an ancient and self-contained people, which has made heavy drafts on its vital forces and borrowed little from beyond its own forbidding frontiers . . . Nevertheless report credits him with the powers of physical endurance rare even in hard-bitten Arabia. Among men bred in the camel saddle he is said to have few rivals as a tireless rider. As a leader of irregular forces he is of proved daring, and he combines with his qualities as a soldier that grasp of statecraft which is yet more highly prized by the tribesmen . . . Politician, ruler and raider, Ibn Saud illustrates a historic type. Such men as he are the exception in any community, but they are thrown up persistently by the Arab race.[7]

With gifts of guns and gold, perfumes and aphrodisiacs, Cox controlled Ibn Saud through a treaty that was intended to be binding in perpetuity:

TREATY WITH IBN SAUD
In the Name of God, the Merciful and Compassionate

The High British Government on its own part, and Abdul Aziz bin Abdur Rahman bin Faisal al Saud, Ruler of Najd, El Hasa, Qatif and Jubail, and the towns and ports belonging to them, on behalf of himself, his heirs and successors, and tribesmen, being desirous of confirming and strengthening the friendly relations, which have for a long time existed between the two parties, and with a view to consolidating their respective interests — the British Government have named and appointed Lieutenant-Colonel Sir Percy Cox, K.C.S.I., K.C.I.E., British Resident in the Persian Gulf, as their Plenipotentiary, to conclude a treaty for this purpose with Abdul Aziz bin Abdur Rahman bin Faisal al Saud.[8]

The treaty was signed, sealed, and ratified in December 1915, with Britain acknowledging the extent of Ibn Saud's territories in Arabia. In return Ibn Saud pledged not to be "antagonistic to the British Government in any respect." He

hereby agrees and promises to refrain from entering into any correspondence, agreement, or treaty, with any Foreign Nation or Power, and further to give immediate notice to the Political Authorities of the British Government of an attempt on the part of any other Power to interfere with the above territories.

By this parchment Ibn Saud was bound to recognize Britain's interest in whatever treasure lay under the deserts he controlled; oil was thought to be in Hasa province, and King Solomon's gold mines in the mountains of Hijaz. There was much else besides, written and spoken, that bore upon the question of Ibn Saud's participation in the war between Britain and the Turko-German alliance, but in general the document conceded to Ibn Saud his right to the territories he now held while conceding to the British hegemony over the foreign aspects of his affairs. It was an important treaty, more important than anyone knew when it was signed — and Ibn Saud's signature contributed to the British imperial power along both coasts of the Persian Gulf and around the Arabian coast as far as the imperial coaling port of Aden. Cox policy — gold and guns in return for imperial protection — was farsighted from the Great Government's viewpoint. It established the Royal Navy, the British banks, and the British merchant houses as the main governing power in those oil-rich and politically useful parts for six decades or more. He who held this parchment held the riches of Arabia.

In all, the mission to Ibn Saud shaped the course of Philby's entire life. Philby was authorized to take with him a substantial sum to ensure that he retained Ibn Saud's support for British policy. Two advisers were to accompany him, both senior, but he allowed neither to play a part.

Purposefully he kept his mission small and, preferring camels, declined to take motor vehicles with him, or even a wireless, for the dangers presented by the tribes along the way, even though they might be under Ibn Saud's control, were great. As he explained in a report: "Useful as a wireless installation would have been, the presence of a considerable number of British operators in this inhospitable and fanatical country would have been a constant source of anxiety." As for a doctor, one would "certainly have been a most valuable asset in assisting to allay the fanatical attitude of the people toward all things foreign except food supplies, piecegoods, arms and medicine." However, the doctor offered to him would have been an American divine with the Dutch Reform Church who had displayed "a certain unmistakable tendency in the direction of the extension of Missionary activities in Arabia." He would not therefore have been acceptable to Ibn Saud and his subjects. Philby wrote: "It can never be absolutely necessary to wrap up pills and powders in Christian tracts." All this may have been true, but it was also true that Philby was by nature a lone wolf, preferring to do his business without interference from the radio. The camel post to Baghdad through Kuwait would be quite fast enough for his purposes.

Cox adjured him to use his good sense and judgment at all times, for much would depend on both, including Philby's career, and so, at the age of thirty-two, St. John became an imperial agent, an appointment that filled him with pride. As he wrote to May, he had become "the selected representative of our government to carry the prestige of Britain into the unknown lands of Central Arabia which have never before been visited by an official British mission."[9] He left Baghdad by river launch to Basra on October 17, 1917, but just before he left he received a telegram announcing the death of his second brother, Tim, in action against the Germans. Paddy had been killed in action at Ypres in 1914. St. John scribbled a letter to the Philbians, which, in the circumstances, may be thought to have constituted a spasm of grief, but with one eye on the censor, was rather a reflection of his politics and loyalty to the Raj.

The world had become "a blank for me. One realises what one has lost and I feel very sad and weary of the whole business of this empty world." He could only "scarcely realise that we shall never, never see those two little brothers again." Then St. John made a passionate declaration of fidelity to the established order of which in the past he had been so dismissive:[10]

> They have gone from us for ever to be numbered among the glorious dead who died for their country in a noble cause & we remain to serve that country and that cause a little longer — knowing that we cannot serve them better than they did & hoping that we may do so half as well.

St. John addressed himself to Kim:

> Poor little Kim he will be so sad about his gallant uncle but tell him that he must follow in that uncle's footsteps and even make it his aim to serve his country bravely and faithfully as his uncle Tim did. That after all is the lesson we learn from the lives of the two brothers who have died so nobly. Let us all put that lesson above all things and strive to do each our little best in that direction. That is the only path worth following.

Philby landed from an Arab dhow at the little pearling port of Uqair on the Persian Gulf coast of Arabia. The journey before him — across the Central Arabian desert from the Persian Gulf to Riyadh and thence to the Red Sea at Jidda — was largely unknown territory, the *terra incognita* of the ancients. His predecessor at Ibn Saud's court, Captain W. H. S. Shakespear, had been murdered in late 1914 by the Sherif of Hail's forces, and Philby's only guarantee of safe passage was Ibn Saud's assurance that he alone controlled the tribes of the interior.

Philby's reward for making such an uncertain journey would be the fame he so ardently desired; he would come to rank with Lawrence as one of the great figures of modern Arabian history, and the Royal Geographical Society would acknowledge his courage and his stamina with its Founder's Medal, which had last been given to Scott of the Antarctic.

Philby started from Uqair by camel on November 15, 1917. Two weeks later the mission had crossed the 360 miles of winding trail across the Dahna, using the compass and the stars for direction, topped the escarpment of the Arma plateau, to look down on Ibn Saud's fortress-capital, Riyadh. It was a Friday, the Wahhab Sabbath; the fortress gates were locked, the city seemed deserted, and the population was at prayer. But then, Philby recorded in his sweat-stained notebooks, "Suddenly there was a stir as of rustling leaves; somehow it was known that the gates had been flung open; life resumed its sway over the world that had seemed dead." The mission entered the city.[11]

At the Murrabba Palace, Ibn Saud emerged from shadows. Each age of Arabian history has produced a great leader, and he was as impressive as any of them. He spoke with a hoarse whisper. His Semitic face was adorned with a henna-dyed beard that, in the fashion of the Ikhwan — the swordsmen of the Wahhabis — jutted outward. He received Philby and his colleagues most cordially. As he would explain from time to time, he liked the island people because "you find them all over the world, serving their king, whereby he may sit quietly at home." Then he would add: "I have nothing in common with the English. They are strangers to us, and Christians. But I need the help of a Great Power and the British are better than the other Powers like France and Italy."[12]

From the start Philby was impressed with Ibn Saud, and the prince with Philby. Ibn Saud's manner was paternal. He seemed benevolent, although Philby did not forget that this benign prince in the service of God had employed massacre to rise to power, and the Ikhwan were at his disposal to use more massacre should the patriarch's interests require it. As Ibn Saud explained the philosophy of his rule to Philby later on:

> We raise them not above us, nor do we place ourselves above them. We give them what we can; we satisfy them with an excuse when we cannot. And if they go beyond their bounds we make them taste the sweetness of our discipline.[13]

This first audience constituted no more than an elaborate, cordial Arab reception, which ended with Philby and his colleagues withdrawing backward and bowing thrice. Then there was a great banquet. Ibn

Saud, Philby, his colleagues, the court, and Ikhwan by the score dined from mountains of rice crowned by whole roast sheep, followed by a whey of camels' milk. Philby noted that the prince ate little except bread dipped in gravy. The feast ended only when each guest's hands had been anointed with fragrance and the servants had wafted censors of frankincense under the guests' beards. Ibn Saud then departed for the harem, as he did each night, it was said. The business began the next morning, and so did a friendship between the two men that was to last for thirty-six years.

The talks lasted ten days, each day broken by five calls to prayer. There was regal entertainment for the mission — a gazelle hunt, a splendid affair of swooping falcons, racing hounds, and death. There was hare hunting with the rifle. There was much hard bargaining, which left Philby impressed by Ibn Saud's intelligence and his discipline in devotions. The prince was tireless and slept little. His virility, Philby again noted with approval, was large; in all, during their association, Philby estimated that Ibn Saud had a hundred and twenty-five wives. He acknowledged producing forty-three princes, and it would be said he produced three hundred others whom he could not, for tribal political reasons, acknowledge. There was also an unknown but very large number of princesses. Ibn Saud's object was, through procreation, to bind the tribes dynastically to his person. As to Ibn Saud personally, Philby reported to Cox by camel post:

> I found an indefatigable worker and, in spite of a tendency to be carried away from the point of his argument by the waves of his [Koranic] eloquence, a man of good business capacity, moderately well versed in the affairs of the world, fully conversant with but by no means a disinterested spectator in the intricasies of Arab politics and above all genuinely convinced of the British alliance as the only secure safeguard of the interests of his country and people both now and hereafter.

At the root of the troubles in the region was, he advised, that

> Ibn Saud was actuated by consuming jealousy of the Sherif [of Mecca] and genuine apprehension in respect of the latter's unveiled pretensions to be considered the overlord, if not the actual ruler, of all Arab countries by virtue of his position [as the only direct descendant of the Prophet and therefore] as de facto supreme spiritual head of Sunni Islam.[14]

As to his conduct of business with Ibn Saud, since Philby was accompanied by two other members of the Political and Secret Department, he was, evidently, careful to show himself during the first phase of the negotiations to be the entirely dutiful British political agent with the national interest in mind at all times when dealing with this crafty and beguiling prince. As he reported to Cox, it was evident that besides England's friendship and protection, he wished for guns and gold for use, after the war, to fight Hussein for control of Arabia. In pursuing the question of the campaign against the Turks' ally, Rashid, the Sherif of Hail, Philby noted that Ibn Saud had promised to march in the spring of 1918, but his price was large, far larger than the campaign would require: four field guns, ten thousand modern Lee-Enfield rifles with the necessary ammunition, £20,000 in gold to buy food and transport animals, and £50,000 monthly out of which to pay ten thousand men during the three-month agreement. Further, Ibn Saud required that England transmute his present £5,000 stipend into a permanent subsidy. These were large commitments, Ibn Saud agreed, but they were far less than what Lawrence paid to the Sherif of Mecca's three thousand men — more than $1.2 million.

As Philby further advised Cox, he had done no more than assure the prince that he would transmit the demands to Baghdad for Cox's agreement. In the meantime, he had handed over to Ibn Saud £10,000 of the £30,000 he had brought with him as a token of the high esteem in which he was held by the Great Government. There was, therefore, nothing exceptional in Philby's assurances to Ibn Saud, at least while his two colleagues were at court. Shortly after the military aspects of the conversations had ended, however, they left Riyadh, and Philby found himself alone with Ibn Saud. It was at this point that he entered into private conversations with the prince, the nature of which he did not report fully to Cox. For a crown agent on official business this was unusual, but nothing more.

These conversations, held at the instigation of Ibn Saud, proved to be the first of hundreds of private audiences Philby would have until Ibn Saud's death in 1953. Again, this was not undesirable except that the official policy of Philby's government was to support Ibn Saud's enemy, Hussein, Sherif of Mecca. Imperial politics were bound up in this policy: most of the world's Moslems were subjects of the British Empire, and since Hussein was the only direct descendant of the Prophet, it was intended that he be confirmed by Britain as King of Arabia and that Whitehall would rule the Middle East and the empire's Moslems through him and his sons. In short, Whitehall's policy was a Hussein policy, not one calculated to further Ibn Saud's Wahhab aspirations. The undesirable element in these private conversations was enhanced further by the personal relationship that quickly arose between the two men during that protracted period in which they waited for Cox's response to the prince's terms for the march on Hail.

A strong and genuine friendship and admiration developed between them, one that lasted for both their lifetimes. In some respects this relationship came to resemble that of Kipling's poem when the strong man from the Occident met the strong man of the Orient. It assumed almost immediately a bond in which Philby, as his correspondence shows, began to transfer his allegiance from the crown to Ibn Saud. And since this element emerged also in the relationship between Kim Philby and the Bolsheviks, it is important to understand how and why this transfer of fealty occurred between Philby, the imperial agent, and Ibn Saud, the Wahhab prince.

It is evident that Philby had become disaffected in the crown service, although not wholly so. That was to come a little later. There were several reasons for that disaffection, as we have seen of his career in India and Iraq. But the main one was ideological and political. Through his socialism, Philby had found the conservative ways of the Raj onerous. While the Raj was a good deal more tolerant of liberal ways than Philby ever acknowledged, he felt that his ambitions could not prosper in the Indian Civil Service, and by the time he met Ibn Saud he wished for a measure of power, fame, and freedom that he could never acquire with the Raj. He found in the prince a man he could admire deeply, for in several senses Philby's brand of socialism and Ibn Saud's Wahhabism were not far apart. More, there was the question of fame. Philby's was an age of great explorations, and the way to fame lay in the Hima, the holy land of Arabia, a region then all but unknown in the Occident. Only Ibn Saud possessed the absolute theological power Philby required if the objection of the Wahhab priesthood was to be overcome and Philby the infidel was to be allowed to enter the Hima.

But there is more. Also involved was a perverse, powerful, and austere streak in Philby, and he found much that was agreeable about Ibn Saud's primitive and savage dominion. A sensual element in Philby's makeup may also have played a part, for the sap rose very strongly in the Briton, and Ibn Saud's harem contained the most beautiful concubines in Arabia. But beyond all else was the personal power to be obtained at Ibn Saud's court. No doubt Ibn Saud revealed something of his personal ambitions. He would destroy the Hashemite dynasty of Hussein; he would take the holiest cities of Islam, Mecca and Medina, which were adjacent to Ibn Saud's polity in the Nejd; he would seize the Hijaz, Hussein's province along the Red Sea. He may well even have discussed himself as the future Caliph of Islam, a position that would make him not only lord of Arabia but also of all the Prophet's dominions beyond the seas, including those of the British Empire in Asia. There were rumors of oil, then becoming as desirable a resource as uranium became after World War II. There was still gold in King Solomon's mines.

Philby left no record of what was said in these conversations. But it is evident that whatever it was, it affected him as powerfully as the young crusader was in the poem of Walter de la Mare: Philby's wits were stolen away. At first, therefore, his ambition may not have been exceptional. He would not abandon the Raj, his hearth, his home, his family. He may well have restrained his ambition to simply becoming the first resident British agent at Ibn Saud's court at Riyadh, a prospect that Cox mentioned to him when they talked over his mission in Baghdad. If that was so, then it would suit the course his actions took from this point forward.

What Philby did record in his reports to Cox was that Ibn Saud discoursed openly about his hated rival, Hussein of Mecca. Who was the sherif? An upstart provincial governor of the Hijaz for only a few years, and that by the dispensation of the Turks. Who was he to call himself King of the Arabs? Why did Hussein receive a subvention of £200,000 from the British government when he, Ibn Saud, the ruler of all eastern and central Arabia, received no more than a pittance — £5,000 a month? Would nothing convince the British that Hussein was corrupt and inept?

At one stage during Ibn Saud's tirades someone mentioned Sir Ronald Storrs, the brain behind Lawrence and the Arab Revolt. He had received advice that shortly Storrs was to visit Hussein at Taif. Storrs did not, however, intend to visit Ibn Saud and Riyadh. Why not? If he did, would he not then be satisfied that one man alone ruled Arabia — Ibn Saud? In that outraged moment Ibn Saud conveyed an idea to Philby, and during what followed Philby did not become disloyal or disobedient, but he did begin to exceed his orders in an interest other than that of the Raj — his own. He called on one of his gifts — the ability to make others think for themselves what he wanted them to think.

He proposed subtly that he, Philby, should ride across Ibn Saud's lands into those of Hussein, traveling on Ibn Saud's grant of safe conduct and without Hussein's knowledge or permission. He would meet Storrs at Taif and bring him back to Riyadh. If it was seen that Philby was traveling over Hussein's territory on Ibn Saud's safe conduct, surely that would demonstrate to all, including Cox, that only one man ruled Arabia — Ibn Saud. Philby would demonstrate that

Hussein's claim to be King of the Arabs was false. In making this proposal he exceeded Cox's orders. At the least he could be accused of using his mission to further his ambitions. Also, he showed himself disposed to work against the accepted policy of his government, which was to give its strongest support to Hussein, the Sherif of Mecca, the holiest city in Islam. As a British agent he was "requested and required" not to engage in any activity contrary to established policy. But there was another aspect to his action.

In seeking to demonstrate that it was Ibn Saud's writ that controlled the Hijaz, he might find that that writ did not run as far as he thought it did. The tribes in those parts were known for their attitude toward infidels. At the least, he was liable to arrest; at the worst, to murder. What then? If he was captured, would Cox be required to send a force to rescue him? If the tribes were under the Sherif of Mecca's control, would his journey not cause a serious eruption in the politics between Cox and the sherif? If the tribes were under Ibn Saud's control, would Philby's capture or death not compel Cox to use armed force against Ibn Saud? The capture or the death of British officers at the hands of Arabs usually provoked punitive reactions; and part of the Foreign Office's and the Government of India's suspicion of Wahhabs was that in the distant and the near past they had killed Britons.

But Philby was careless of all this; he wrote in due course, "I should confess, that my motives in making the proposal were of a mixed character, and not wholly based on the actual requirements of the situation, but that is a trifle and I have never regretted my action."[15]

Philby's ingenuity greatly pleased Ibn Saud, appealing to his humor as well as his politics. He gave orders for Philby to be given the use of his best camels and to have escorts of good men of every tribe along the way. St. John then settled down to the task of explaining what was in his heart. The occasion was a letter to his wife on Kim's sixth birthday, January 1, 1918. In it St. John recalled that this was the ninth anniversary of his appointment to the Raj. His ambitions were now very different from what they had been. He tried to explain what he had felt at Ibn Saud's court:

> Why anybody consents to live in this arid tract of endless desert of sand and bare stony hills and ridges must remain a mystery except perhaps that liberty as an end in itself has charms which overcome the disadvantage of endless wandering where water and food are scarce. What will come of it I can scarcely say as I have only just begun my work here.

He added:

> I needn't say that I am very happy — in fact probably happier than
> ever I have been before and I only long for letters to tell me of your
> doings and how my little son is getting on — bless his little soul . . .
> Many happy returns to the little boy on his birthday . . . and much
> love to you all. You can think of me passing my time very pleasantly
> in the great deserts of Central Arabia & perfectly happy and content
> with my lot and the great prospects before me.[16]

Ibn Saud placed Philby in the care of God and instructed the escort
to obey his every command. Philby, his bodyguard of thirty-six swordsmen, and his camel train set out from the Jidda Gate on December 8,
1918. Guided by the Southern Cross, he took the route — marked by
the remains of hundreds of pilgrims' fires — of 450 miles; he made
the traverse in fifteen days in the teeth of the vast storms that, at this
equinox, struck the Arabian highlands. His energy and his endurance
were extraordinary; so was his nervelessness — a quality he bequeathed
to his son. The dangers were real and became still more so in the
Nadji-Hijazi borderlands, where the shepherds wavered in their allegiance between Ibn Saud and Hussein. For the first time he was in the
hands of Wahhabi led by an Ikhwan. If Philby respected Arabs, he
distrusted his bodyguard. They were, he thought, inclined to treachery; their leader had accepted Ibn Saud's mission only under protest;
he belonged to the inner circle of the Ikhwan and he was, notwithstanding Ibn Saud's command, unwilling to defile himself by eating
with an infidel, even with one acceptable to Ibn Saud. There were long
stops five times a day, when the men unrolled their prayer mats in a
line and bowed to Mecca. He suspected a plot to murder or abandon
him, as the bodyguard wished to advance only by night. Philby refused,
as he wished to see the lay of the land and to collect specimens for
the British Museum. Each evening, having collected a packet of rocks
and bugs, he drank in lore about social customs and tribal pedigrees,
and heard folktales about stones that walked, angels who beat drums
to make thunder, and sands that sang. Yet if Philby distrusted his
Wahhab escort, they protected him well.

By Christmas Eve of 1917, Philby was out on the moonlit plain four
thousand feet up in the lands of the Buqum, inside Hussein's kingdom
and without challenge from Hussein's riders. Here he made camp with
his bodyguard, and, dining on dates and camel flank, surrounded by
scores of Arab shepherds' camps, each with its own fire burning brightly
in the moonlight, settled down with his map case on his knee to write

his third Christmas letter to the Philbians. In it he revealed much of himself. All the "gold in India would not tempt me back into that fair land," which might be "fruitful and prosperous in itself" but which was "blighted by an effete administration," one that had "long outgrown its vigor and originality." What St. John now wanted was to be the "first representative of Great Britain at the Court of the Great King, the monarch of Central Arabia."

On Christmas Day Philby arrived in Taif, a place of queer Turkish houses, and reported to the Sherif of Mecca's governor. There was much fuss that Philby had entered the sherif's kingdom without a by-your-leave. Why had he come? Where was he going? On whose authority had he entered the Kingdom of the Hijaz? When Philby announced that he had come from Riyadh on imperial business to see the great and noble Storrs, the fuss subsided while the governor inquired by telegraph to Mecca to locate Storrs. He learned that the sherif had refused Storrs safe conduct to Taif but that he might be at Jidda, the port of entry to Central Arabia from the Red Sea.

Philby rode on, still beset by rainstorms coming off the Red Sea, down from the mountains to the pilgrims' port of Jidda, a place of such antiquity that it seemed to Philby he had stepped back into the time of Genesis. There, at Lawrence's rear headquarters, Philby heard the latest news. Lenin had seized the power of Russia and, to the great embarrassment of the British government, had published the secret text of the Sykes-Picot Treaty, through which Britain, France, Italy, and Russia had intended to carve up the Turkish Empire in Arabia as the booty of war. The British government had made public the Balfour Declaration, promising the Jewish people a national home in Palestine. Prime Minister David Lloyd George had proclaimed the entitlement of "Arabia, Armenia, Mesopotamia, Syria, and Palestine" to recognition of their "separate national conditions." Woodrow Wilson had listed his Fourteen Points, which, besides much else, assured the Arabs of their right to national self-determination, of the "unmolested and autonomous development for the nationalities under Turkish rule." Everyone had now promised everything to the three rival faiths, the Christians, the Moslems, and the Jews. Did it not mean that the British had promised the Jews what they had already promised to the Arabs?

Storrs was not at Jidda, but Philby learned that D. G. Hogarth, a senior political officer at the Arab Bureau in Cairo, was on his way by sloop to see King Hussein to explain what the three treaties meant to the Hashemites. Hogarth arrived in Jidda on January 6, 1918, on H.M.S. *Hardinge* and was surprised to find Philby. He had received no advice at Cairo that an officer from Baghdad would be present at his talk with Hussein. Nor could Philby show him orders other than those to conduct business with Ibn Saud at Riyadh. What was Philby's business in Jidda? When the answer developed into a discourse by Philby about the merits of an Ibn Saud policy as opposed to the Hussein policy of Hogarth, Hogarth gained Philby's measure. "Mighty intelligent," he wrote in his diary, "but very impracticable from an imperial point of view."[17]

King Hussein arrived two days later from Mecca. Philby found the little king "old, small, calm, and the pink of courtesy," but not for long. When Ibn Saud's name was mentioned, his bulging eyes flashed. He rejected the notion that Hogarth or Storrs or anyone, including Philby, would be allowed to cross his domain to see the prince at Riyadh. He rebuked Philby for his discourtesy in entering the Kingdom of the Hijaz through the back door, unannounced, "like the sun in the sky," and declared that if Philby intended to return to Riyadh, he would have to do so by sea, by way of India. As for Ibn Saud, Hussein said that the prince of Riyadh had "sold his country to the English" and that the Arabs would "come to accept Hussein's estimate of Ibn Saud's unworthiness."[18]

In his reply, Philby displayed none of the tact expected of an imperial agent. "I was sent to Najd by the British Government to see with my own eyes," he told the king, "and it is my misfortune that I have arrived at conclusions widely differing from those of Your Majesty."[19] When Hussein complained that Philby's action had given weight to the Turks' warning that Britain intended to annex Arabia and that Hussein was no more than a British agent, a representative of the Arab Bureau reported to his headquarters that he had been much struck by "a certain lack of respect in Mr. Philby's manner."[20] Philby's charm had deserted him, and thereafter he was excluded from the discussions. And if Hussein had planted a kiss on Philby's forehead at the end of their exchange, this display of affection did not facilitate Philby's plea to be allowed to return to Baghdad by the short route. No, the king told him evenly, he would have to return through Bombay. Philby would have to go to Saturn in order to land on the Moon. It would be late spring of 1918 before he reached Riyadh.

Philby invited Hogarth to accompany him to Riyadh for an audience with Ibn Saud, but Hogarth declined, although he did invite Philby to accompany him back to Cairo in order to present his views on Riyadh conditions to the high intelligence authorities there. Hogarth and Philby then sailed on the *Hardinge* for Ismailia on the Suez Canal.

There, having shed his Arab clothes to return to uniform and having shaved his beard, Philby disembarked. Traveling on to Cairo by train, he made the largest mistake of his career to date. He gave Hogarth a long lecture on the superiority of Ibn Saud over Hussein and the amorality of a war policy in which the Arabs and the Jews alike had been promised the moon in return for their assistance, thereby expressing his dissatisfaction with the imperial order. He clearly offended Hogarth, the most purple of imperialists. Philby had more than met his match, and Hogarth reported adversely on his attitudes to Baghdad and for his own files when they reached his headquarters, the Arab Bureau at the Savoy Hotel in Cairo.

In a world where a whisper and even a nod could be made to tell, Philby had shown himself to be disloyal. But he was well received by Cox's rivals, the Intrusives. All in authority wished to hear about Ibn Saud, about his ride across Arabia. Wingate Pasha, the High Commissioner for Egypt, called Philby to the residency to hear him out in regard to Ibn Saud's requirements in gold and guns for his attack against Rashid of Hail. But if Philby was well received personally by Sir Reginald Wingate, his enthusiasm for Ibn Saud received no encouragement. British policy, intoned Wingate, was a Hashemite policy. Now that the army was taking Jerusalem, and Lawrence and Hussein's men were nearing Damascus, what need was there for Ibn Saud? All that Philby could tell Ibn Saud, therefore, was that the £10,000 "loan" could be considered a gift. Also, Britain would send Ibn Saud a thousand rifles, not ten thousand. But, Wingate added, he could not guarantee that the rifles would be the Lee-Enfields that Ibn Saud admired so much — weapons that would have made him King of Arabia. Nor could the British spare any pack guns. The attack against Rashid could proceed, and Ibn Saud would receive British support, but he must not interfere with Hussein. Whitehall, Philby was told, regarded Ibn Saud as a blackmailer.

Philby prepared to return to Riyadh with Wingate Pasha's dismaying instructions. He went briefly to Jerusalem, where he arrived as the Turks' guns still boomed across the Mount of Olives. There, his desire to enter Ibn Saud's service was overtaken by his ambition to become the military governor of Damascus. When news of Philby's ambition reached Baghdad, Miss Bell, his patron, dealt with his proposal firmly:

I do not think it likely that you will get a job in Syria, and enclose a letter from Mr. Hogarth which will I fear be a surprise to you. It is

well from time to time to see oneself as others see you . . . but it is
seldom pleasant, especially when this revelation comes from a man
as fair-minded and liberal as Mr. Hogarth. You know how difficult it
is for me to judge of you in a detached manner, for you have always
been so delightful with me, but I cannot, nor could anyone, disregard
such an arraignment as this. It is in the hope — is it a vain one? —
that it may as he says put the fear of God into you, that I send it. And
if you are wise you will be grateful to me. And now be very wise
in your dealings with [Ibn Saud], and do your best to make things
easier.[21]

Philby stood rejected. He left for Arabia as quickly as he could,
beginning the long journey back to Ibn Saud by way of the Red Sea,
Aden, Bombay, the Persian Gulf, and Kuwait. It was the spring of 1918
before he reached the edge of the Dahna sandbelt, where he found
Ibn Saud hunting gazelle. His welcome was warm, at first anyway. As
St. John wrote to the Philbians, Ibn Saud gave him "almost a feeling
of homecoming."[22] In a public speech, he invited Philby to stay in the
royal camp, and soon the two men talked privately. What St. John
Philby had to report did not sit well with his host. All he could say of
a favorable nature was that he had personally tested the range of
Hussein's sovereignty of the desert and had found it far from complete; he himself had ridden from Riyadh to Jidda and had encountered none of Hussein's representatives until he was at Taif.

In all, Philby's report brought only cold comfort to a prince who
intended to make himself King of Arabia with the guns and gold he
would receive to conquer Hail. Philby needed all of his diplomacy to
make his report without permanently damaging his standing. Ibn Saud
received it graciously enough but not without complaint. If this was
all "Feel-bee" could bring him, then Hussein had done his work well
with the British, who seemed to favor Ibn Saud's enemies. How could
he attack Hail when he was surrounded by enemies and denied the
help of Britain? He would be defeated if his enemies attacked him in
concert. Nor did he have the gold necessary to buy the rifles from the
arms merchants. In view of Britain's lack of support, he would be obliged
to withdraw his agreement to attack Hail, a position that Ibn Saud
maintained throughout the next four weeks. During that period Philby
could offer Ibn Saud only the pleasure of his company. But if this was
acceptable to Ibn Saud, it was not to the Ikhwan. They shunned the
prince when news of the poverty of Philby's offerings reached them.
They did not acknowledge Philby's *salaam* and hid their faces in their
hands to avoid seeing him pass. "I call God to witness my hatred of

you,"[23] hissed one of them in the royal tent lines. The sullen hostility depressed Philby, who had expected more from his long, risky ride across Arabia; and he wrote home, "It should be realized that the vast majority of the people spend half their day in prayer and other religious exercise, and should not be dealt with as fully reasonable beings." Their vision was "hopelessly limited and their souls sour with fanaticism."[24] The prospect of his becoming the British political agent at Riyadh, the post that only recently he had wished for himself so ardently, had vanished, largely because Whitehall and Simla were no longer interested in Ibn Saud.

Philby offered to pay Ibn Saud's treasury the £20,000 balance of the gold he had earlier brought with him from Baghdad and buried in the desert as a precaution against theft, provided Ibn Saud agreed to attack Hail. Would Ibn Saud attack? Yes, as soon as Ramadan, the great fast, was over. For the moment, Ibn Saud was placated. As Ramadan reached its twenty-eighth day, Philby again wrote in his notes that through the fasting, the heat, and the intensity of the prayers, the people had approached the point of physical exhaustion and cried out for the appearance of the new moon, which would mark the end of the fast. Such indeed was their condition that on the twenty-ninth day Ibn Saud asked Philby if he thought the moon would appear that night. He consulted his nautical calendar and announced that it would. But the moon did not appear, for clouds obscured its rising. That evening great crowds assembled on the roofs to watch for the young crescent, including women, whose eyesight was supposed by the Arabs to be keener than that of men. Yet "strain as we might, we could not see the moon and there were doubtless many who rejoiced that the prediction of the infidel had been falsified though it meant an extra day's fasting for them."[25]

Very uneasily, for the Ikhwan were likely to become unbalanced toward the end of the rite, he "retired to bed with a feeling of discomfiture" and was helped to sleep by "the anguished intonations of the congregations gathered for the all-night prayer." St. John liked to claim that he was more often right than wrong, and in this incident that proved to be the case. He was startled from his sleep in the early hours by

the firing of the guns announcing the end of Ramadan. Two Badawin [Bedouin] had come in from the desert with the joyful news that they had seen the moon. An ecclesiastical council was immediately summoned to take their evidence, which was accepted without hesitation, and the order was sent down to the kitchens to prepare the feast which should usher in the Id [the feast held at the end of every fast] at dawn of the next day.

Ordinary life began again, the Faithful assured they had taken another step toward Paradise. Great bowls of rice, mutton, rosewater, and cold, curdled camel milk were served to the hollow, fiery-eyed assemblies; the palace returned to its politicking, the Wahhabi to their wives, and Ibn Saud and Philby and the tribal army assembled and set out for Hail. But Ibn Saud dealt Philby another blow: he would not accompany the army for the attack on Hail but must remain at Anaiza, a town noted for its hospitality and the beauty of its women. Ibn Saud did not wish to be accused by the Faithful of acting on British orders. So as Ibn Saud's camel army moved on, Philby found himself marking time at Anaiza, which, in a poetic moment, he reckoned to be "the Paris of Arabia." During the daytime he poked about for beetles and rare flowers; during the evenings he spent time on the roof of his lodgings, watching through his field glasses the famous virgins cavorting in the last gold-green rays of sunset. St. John's record of these scenes reveals something of the strength of his sap:

> We dined at 4.30 P.M. at the Emir's special request and ate enormously in spite of the hour and the heat, but we were glad to creep away to the solitude of our quarters, and settled down in the hope of an undisturbed evening in the cool of our roofs. "Come and look!" called Dr. Abdullah to me, and as I followed his eyes out across to a neighbouring roof, lo and behold! a trio of young women of great loveliness. Mere girls they were indeed, virgins ready for the marriage market . . . they disported themselves without bashfulness before our eyes and flinched not even when Abdullah brought my binoculars to bear on them.

Here, following this and the other agreeable pursuits of falconing and gazelle hunting on camelback, Philby waited until September 21, 1918. Ibn Saud's army then trickled back. There was evidence, Ibn Saud claimed, that his intentions had been betrayed to Rashid Ali. His camel corps had reached the walls of Hail but, as Philby reported to Miss Bell, they had "missed by dilatory tactics a providential opportunity of capturing Ibn Rashid and his bodyguard in the open."[26] They found him again at the fort at Aaiwij Baqaa, but he proved too strong, so instead, Ibn Saud's army fell upon the Shammar shepherds outside Hail. They killed thirty of them and, Philby reported, "came away with a rich booty including 1,500 camels, 10,000 rounds of ammunition, many sheep and much camp furniture."[27] The operation to bring Ibn Saud into the war with Turkey had failed. The best that Philby could report to Miss Bell was that Ibn Saud remained "very confident of bringing Ibn Rashid to his knees by the efforts he intended to keep up at high pressure until that object was attained."[28]

But now it was nearly November 1918, and the war was ending. Philby's masters lost interest in Hail as the Turkish Empire collapsed, and in Ibn Saud, although not completely. The British government canceled all supplies, especially the consignment of Lee-Enfields, which would have given Ibn Saud primacy over the King of the Arabs. Baghdad then terminated Philby's mission and ordered him to return. When that news reached Ibn Saud, he sent for Philby and asked, in regard to the rifles, "Who after this will put their trust in you?" Philby had held him "up to the ridicule of my own people" and "if your government declines to modify its policy, it is of no use your coming back."[29]

Ibn Saud presented Philby with a ceremonial sword in a gold filigree scabbard and a white stallion of eighteen months, which would have a distinguished career both as a racehorse and as a stud. Then, still wearing not the uniform of a "political" but the gold-embroidered robes and tasseled headdress of an Arab notable, Philby bowed and replied. "God willing," he declared, "all will be well, or I won't come back to you as the envoy of Britain."[30] Philby left the camp, with his long retinue of bodyguards and servants, for Kuwait and then Baghdad. All over the Orient the Red Crescent came down, the Union Jack went up, and British forces seized the great oil deposits of the region, including Kirkuk in northern Iraq and Maikop in what was becoming the Soviet Caucasus. Cairo, Jerusalem, Damascus, and Baghdad all became centers of British political power.

When he reported to his masters at Baghdad, Philby found that Cox had gone to Persia to become high commissioner and Gertrude Bell to London, there to discuss with the authorities her establishment of a Hashemite prince, Feisal, as king of the new state of Iraq. There was no one in Baghdad with the authority and knowledge to look into Philby's unauthorized journey to Jidda at the end of 1917. Arnold T. Wilson, temporarily in charge at Baghdad, was no friend of Philby's. But he wanted no trouble with a man who tended to argue a point for weeks on end. What he wanted was Philby's report on Riyadh conditions; then he could go on leave to England. This Philby prepared and a masterly report it was. He marked time at Baghdad until his orders came through.

At the end of 1918 he set out for his first home leave since sailing for India in 1908. He was reunited with his wife, Dora, who had been in India since 1917 nursing the wounded, his mother, May, and his blessed son, Kim, who was now almost seven and, being bright and cheery and good at cricket and football, had emerged as the personification of that Edwardian ideal, Christopher Robin.

3

Revolts

1919–1924

IN JANUARY 1919, Kim Philby received news that his parents would arrive in England shortly, and that he would go to London and stay with them. This news was troubling to Kim. He would record that he had thought that his only parent was his grandmother; his father and mother were strangers to him. He had become content with Granny Philby at the Crossways. Later he remembered:

> As the boat train steamed in, a tallish woman in a black and white striped dress leaned out of a window, waving to us. But when she tried to gather me up, I resisted, clinging to my grandmother's skirt. And when we returned to Camberley and my mother announced her plans, I was guilty of my first act of conscious rebellion against authority. Like most rebellions, it was very short-lived.[1]

The cause of the lad's rebellion was that his mother intended to take him to London to be on hand when St. John arrived from Baghdad. They would stay at a hotel, and Kim would love it. Kim replied that he did not want to go to London and wished only to stay in Camberley with Granny May. But they went to the Tudor Court Hotel, where "mysteriously my father was among us." Kim's only other recollection of his father's arrival was that shortly he

> took me across Kensington Gardens to the Royal Geographical Society where in an upper room, he sat on a stool beside a huge table, covered with large sheets of blank paper. There were several notebooks, coloured bottles, the slimmest of pens and a lot of pencils

sharpened to the finest of points imaginable. My wonder grew; but
when my father started what he called "work," I was amazed.

   He was drawing a map, and, as far as I could see, an imaginary
map at that, for he had no atlas to copy from. I remember two distinct
and contradictory reactions. First admiration at the wonderful neatness of my father's map; second, disappointment that he should
describe as work an occupation I knew all about.

Thereafter, it seems clear, Kim Philby regarded his father with love
and admiration and as a rival. Kim's great passions of the period were
to study his atlas and to emulate and surpass his father.

   He recorded nothing of the fame his father had acquired by his ride
across Arabia; perhaps he remembered nothing. His parents moved
into a leased house, the property of the secretary of the Royal Geographical Society, on St. Petersburg Place, just off Moscow Road and
Bayswater Road. His parents placed him in a day school in Orme
Square, around the corner.

   At the breakfast table on the first day, my father remarked casually
   that I would be beaten once a week as a matter of school routine.
   When I looked doubtfully at my mother, she confirmed it; oh yes! I
   would have to learn to take my medicine like a man in this life. I was
   not surprised, as I had read many stories about tough schooldays,
   and it was a week before I realized it was a joke. It was not a very
   good joke, and would doubtless be considered cruel today, but I did
   not think so at the time.

Having known only his grandmother,

   My mother's attitude to my upbringing has always puzzled me. She
   was incapable of conscious cruelty. Yet she never tired of telling me
   that life was a desperate struggle for survival, and that only unremit-
   ting work and fearsome drive would pull me through. Sometimes,
   during my adolescence, she would induce panicky thoughts of early
   death from starvation and exposure. Where she got such ideas from
   I do not know; but in the very long run, it helped. When I found
   from experience that life, for a product of the British middle classes,
   was not so very difficult after all, my confidence was boosted in proportion to the groundless fears that my mother's homilies had induced.

At the school in Orme Square, where he spent one term, Philby "came
out top of the bottom form, but only, I think, because my most serious
rival fell ill during the exams and failed to complete the course." The
result "confirmed my father in a resolution that he had made on the

day of my birth: that I should get a scholarship to Westminster and another to Trinity, just as he had done."

When St. John Philby arrived in London in January 1919, the Second British Empire was at the pinnacle of its political power. It had suffered a million men dead and two million wounded, but now, Prime Minister David Lloyd George declared in Parliament, "the German enemy lies prostrate before us. Advance Britannia!" It did. Even as the triumvirs — David Lloyd George of Britain, Georges Clemenceau of France, and President Woodrow Wilson of the United States — arrived at the Versailles Peace Conference, the future of the Ottoman Empire had been decided secretly (and without the knowledge of the United States, so it was claimed at the time) between Lloyd George and Clemenceau. Neither intended to accept Wilson's Fourteen Points, at least for the Middle East. Nor did Lloyd George intend to give Clemenceau very much. The British, not the French, had fought for the Middle East. The British now held it all, and Queen Victoria's dictum had been "What we have we hold." Whatever Wilson may have desired, Lloyd George had decided already what he was going to get for the British Empire. Arnold Toynbee, the historian and a member of the British delegation, recorded a visit to Lloyd George's office, where he overheard the prime minister musing aloud as he read some state papers Toynbee had delivered to him: "Mesopotamia . . . yes . . . oil . . . irrigation . . . we must have Mesopotamia; Palestine . . . yes . . . the Holy Land . . . Zionism . . . we must have Palestine; Syria . . . h'm . . . What is there in Syria? Let the French have that."

So it happened.

The British expansion sat quite well with St. John Philby, who was thirty-four, noted for his work in Iraq and Arabia, and with the best part of his career before him. His family had indeed showed itself to be as solid as its silver. He examined the records and noted with pride that a hundred and forty-one Philbians had served the armed forces of the crown. Thirteen had been killed in action, including two of his brothers and two of Dora's; twenty-six had been wounded; three were missing; two listed as prisoners of war; one had received a knighthood; one was made a Commander of the Bath; three had become Commanders of St. Michael and St. George; one received a Distinguished Service Order; one a Distinguished Service Cross; two, Military Crosses; and twenty-three were mentioned in dispatches. There was, he concluded, no more constant family in all England. He himself went to Buckingham Palace to receive the Order of the Indian Empire by King George V for his work in India against the Sikhs and for his revenue work in Iraq among the sheikhs of the Shatt-al-Arab. Dora, May, and Kim were with him at the palace in their Sunday best to see him receive the honor, which consisted of a gold five-petaled rose, enameled crimson and mounted with an effigy of Queen Victoria and the legend *Imperatricis Auspiciis*. Now he became H. St. John B. Philby, C.I.E., I.C.S. From time to time, in his personal and official mail, he used that style. On other correspondence, even personal, he signed himself "H. St. John" and added "Political Department."

More recognition followed, although his exploit was overshadowed by the adventures of Lawrence of Arabia. He went to the Royal Geographical Society to lecture on his ride of twenty-six hundred miles in and across Arabia and to receive its Gold Medal. He lectured at the Central Asian Society on Wahhabism, Ibn Saud, and the Ikhwan. Bearing letters of introduction from Miss Bell, he met the mandarins of foreign affairs of his age — Sir Arthur Hirtzel at the India Office, Sir Eyre Crowe at the Foreign Office, Sir Valentine Chirol at *The Times* — and told them about Ibn Saud and Arabian conditions. He went on up to the great mandarins of Whitehall, Lord Curzon at the Foreign Office and Sir Edwin Montagu at the India Office. Curzon invited him to give his opinion on Ibn Saud to the first meeting of the Eastern Committee of the Foreign Office, which advised the cabinet on its policy in the new empire in the Middle East and southwest Asia.

Philby spoke vigorously to the admirals, generals, and other policy-makers that England's best horse in Arabia was not Hussein but Ibn Saud and that the Ikhwan could take Mecca and the Hijaz whenever Ibn Saud gave the order, that Hussein's army was no match whatever for Ibn Saud's. He had seen both and he knew. His gospeling could not prevail, however. He gathered a small constituency, but Lawrence's voice was the more powerful. Lord Curzon declared that Britain's policy must be a Hussein policy. Hussein's sons, Feisal, the leader under Lawrence of the Arab Revolt, Abdullah, and Ali would provide Britain with a dynasty through whom the British would rule or guide in their new empire, along with all the sheikhs who had signed Cox's treaties. And behind it all, Philby convinced himself, was oil. The Eastern Committee had been persuaded that Ibn Saud had no oil, that there was none in the Saudi province of el-Hasa, and that if there was oil in the peninsula, it was in the Hijaz, on the Red Sea. The reverse proved, of course, to be true; and in any case it did not matter. Britain had control of Persia, Iraq, and the Persian Gulf. Cox had seen to that.

Because the Eastern Committee decided that Britain would continue Ibn Saud's gold subsidy, to keep him and his Wahhabi quiet, and to fulfill its engagement with the Jews, a British high commission under Sir Herbert Samuel would sit at Jerusalem. This was quite contrary to Philby's personal vision for the Middle East. St. John had shown little interest in oil — at least in his files of the period, although the word *oil* was then as secret as *uranium* became after World War II — and spoke little about the Jewish question. His only interest was in advancing Ibn Saud's claims to the sovereignty of all Arabia and in effecting the Anglo-French Declaration for the Arabs, uttered four days before the Armistice with Germany. Since this document became the foundation of all Philby's quarrels and, ultimately, of his revolt against the establishment, its text may be quoted:

> The object aimed at by France and Great Britain in prosecuting in the East the War let loose by the ambition of Germany is the complete and definite emancipation of the peoples so long oppressed by the Turks and the establishment of national governments and administrations deriving their authority from the initiative and free choice of the indigenous populations.
>
> In order to carry out these intentions France and Great Britain are at one in encouraging and assisting the establishment of indigenous Governments and administrations in Syria and [Iraq], now liberated by the Allies, and in the territories the liberation of which they are engaged in securing and recognising these as soon as they are actually established.
>
> Far from wishing to impose on the populations of these regions any particular institutions they are only concerned to ensure by their support and by adequate assisting the regular working of Governments and administrations freely chosen by the populations themselves.[2]

When Philby withdrew from the first meeting of the Eastern Committee and went home to the family's lodgings in St. Petersburg Place, he was none too sure that Curzon would invite him again, as the administration was not interested in Ibn Saud, except to keep him quiet. Hussein was its only interest, and all involved in policy shared this view. Philby, only on leave from the Government of India, felt he would have to return to the Raj, which he disliked as much as ever. He set about family business. Kim must receive the best start in life possible, and to that end St. John and Dora set out to look for a preparatory school that would give the boy a good classical preparation for Westminster and then Trinity but would not insist on religious instruction. Then, it had been decided even at that early date, he would go to the Foreign Office, not the Indian Civil Service, which Philby thought had become old-fashioned.

Thus a dynastic seed took root. St. John and Dora Philby found the school they were looking for at Eastbourne, a resort on the English Channel, where, they felt, the air would be beneficial for Kim's weak chest. St. Aldro was a small, expensive school that produced Christopher Robins. They all went off to meet Dr. Browne, the headmaster, and his sister, Miss Mary Browne, the matron. The motto of the school was in the tradition of the English establishment, *Suivez Raison,* Follow Reason. Dr. Browne had a reputation for producing healthy minds in healthy bodies, minds able to win the Westminster Challenge. The curriculum included Greek, Latin, French, English, history, geography, art, algebra and geometry, sport, and deportment. There were about sixty boys, all of the middle-middle class, all earmarked for the better schools, then the better colleges, and most from the better squares in London.

Kim duly mounted the high stone steps into the hall and was received by Dr. Browne, a portly man in a black parson's suit and white collar, a little gold cross hanging from the watch chain over his ample belly. Philby delivered his son to the Establishment for his education. St. John and Dora moved into rooms on the Royal Parade to be on hand should Kim need help in settling down to the disciplines of his new school. St. John made a start on his first book, *The Heart of Arabia,* an account of his march from Uqair to Jidda. It was an uneasy, anxious period not only in his domestic life but also in general politics; a fresh war was in the air, this time between the Allies and Russia. And as Churchill, the new war minister, related, "The poise and balance even of Britain was deranged" by the tumult of revolutionary politics. It was almost a mystical period in which everywhere, even at Eastbourne, in the distant reaches of provincial England, the streets seemed to be filled with women in black and purple mourning.

In these circumstances, while working on what he called his "epic in embryo," a telegram came from the Foreign Office. The crown still had need of his services. There was trouble at Khurma Oasis in the desert on the frontier between Ibn Saud and the King of the Arabs. Would he come to London for a meeting of the Eastern Committee without delay? Hastening to London, he learned that in the small hours of May 19, 1919, Ibn Saud's Ikhwan army had attacked the British-trained, British-equipped, and British-paid army of Hussein at Khurma Oasis — Hussein, on whom rested the rock of England in the Orient. Philby's presentation at the first Eastern Committee meeting had been proven correct. The troops had been butchered and their commander, Prince Abdullah, a son of Hussein, had fled the battlefield in his nightshirt. The war by Ibn Saud to capture the holy places of Mecca, where the Prophet was born, and Medina, where he died, had begun, just as St. John had predicted in his report at Baghdad and just as he had told the admirals, the generals, and the Foreign Office men.

Curzon presided. The reports at hand, he announced, showed that with Wahhabism on the march there was panic at Mecca. The Pilgrimage to Mecca was in progress when the Ikhwan attacked, and consequently a multitude was in flight from the holy places to the coast, including some eleven thousand British-Indian Moslem subjects. The British political agent at Jidda had reported that the Wahhabi cavalry and swordsmen were swarming eastward in pursuit of Abdullah and were expected at Mecca immediately. An epidemic was likely among the refugees at Jidda, where water was scarce and sanitary arrangements primitive. He appealed for military protection of the refugees and for ships to carry them away to their homes as soon as possible. There was a suggestion that British troops should be landed to protect those in flight from the Wahhab scourge.

Britain's ability to impose tranquillity on Arabia had been challenged by Ibn Saud. Curzon had wanted Lawrence to go out and mediate, but he was at the Peace Conference in Paris, escorting Prince Feisal, the leader of the Arab Revolt and another of Hussein's sons, and could not be found. Consequently, Curzon asked Philby to go at once to Jidda and put a stop to the war. Philby accepted, and Curzon ordered an aircraft to carry his agent out to the Near East. There he was to take instructions from the high commissioner, Lord Allenby, conqueror of Jerusalem. Curzon provided Philby with credentials as a "Foreign Office representative traveling to Cairo on urgent business," and Philby and Dora sped to Lympne, an airfield near Eastbourne. Philby returned to St. Aldro to kiss Kim goodbye and to give him a bottle of sweets; then Kim watched his father disappear again on business of state.

Philby flew to Cairo, a five-day journey, by way of Paris, Lyons, Istres, Pisa, Rome, Taranto, Patras, Athens, and Crete. At Crete he encountered Lawrence, who had been found and dispatched in a Vickers Vimy, which had crashed with casualties. The two men knew each other's names but had never met; when they did, Lawrence simply said, "So, you're Philby." Philby offered Lawrence passage in his plane; Lawrence accepted, and the aircraft flew on across the Mediterranean to Sollum in Libya and thence to Cairo. There Lawrence vanished to make contact with his Hashemites. Philby wrote to Dora on June 28, 1919:

> Tell my little Kim to write to me often & I will write to him. He is a dear child but why oh why is he the only one? That is a great disappointment to me as I believe it is to you but others are in the same box. Don't spoil him and remember the need of discipline![3]

Plainly Philby expected to be away for a long time. He had the highest hopes that once in Jidda he would be able to "fix things up" in the Arab war, for he wrote from Cairo to the Philbians on July 9, 1919, that this would give him "a wonderful chance of really making my name." Then India would not see him again, "except perhaps some day as a Governor!" Alas, politics can be only rarely predicted in Arabia. After taking instructions from Allenby Pasha, he went on to Jidda by steamer, the *Baron Beck*, into which had been crowded Hashemite regulars for the defense of Jidda against Ibn Saud's Wahhabi. During the passage from Port Suez into the Red Sea he sent yet another note to the family, saying how pleased he was that Kim was at St. Aldro, which was "a first-rate school," and St. John did not think "we could possibly have given him a better start in life." Also, "the sea air should completely cure his little ailments" — Kim's weak chest again — "and he ought to be hale and hearty enough by the time he has to go to Westminster."[4]

But at the moment of landing at Jidda on July 21, he received a letter from the British political agent that the Foreign Office had settled the trouble between Hussein and Ibn Saud and that he should return home. Lawrence had stolen his thunder. Cursing his luck and the Foreign Office at having wasted so much of his time, he turned around and went back to England, to take Dora and Kim up to Cape Wrath in Scotland for a holiday. That did not last long either, for the Foreign Office found another task for him; he was to escort the fourteen-year-old prince royal of the Saud dynasty, Feisal, during a state visit to England. St. John leaped at the prospect; it would strengthen his links to Ibn Saud. Feisal might help his chances of becoming the British agent at Riyadh. One of the potentates escorting Feisal did ask the Foreign Office to consider "our dear loving friend, Mr. Philby." The Foreign Office avoided a commitment, but the prince's visit was a success, one that began with a presentation of swords between King George V and the prince royal and ended with a visit to St. Aldro to meet Kim.

There is a photograph of that meeting. The future King of Saudi Arabia is in royal robes with a cloak of Damascus camel hair. There is a dagger at his belt, a sword at his side that was half the length of his plump little body. Kim is to his right wearing the school uniform, awkward and shy. To his left is Dr. Browne. Above him is St. John, hard, stiff, erect, military, official — astonishingly similar to the KGB's official portrait of Kim Philby taken fifty-four years later in Moscow. The portraits made the men look, as his doctor said of Hindenburg, as if they had "never seen a rose bloom or heard a bird sing," as if each "needed treatment for his soul." Dora is there, the perfect *memsahib* in a long dress and a floral hat, and so is the head boy and Kim's house prefect. Around the group are members of Feisal's bodyguard, also in robes. At the ceremony, the prince gave Kim a twenty-carat diamond as a keepsake. But that was not all. The royal visit established Kim at Feisal's court in later years. There would always be a visa for him to enter Saudi Arabia, even when the kingdom was closed to infidels. Feisal's visit, combined with his ability, ensured that Kim would become a schoolboy success. Which other boy could bring an Arab prince to Aldro? The school rang with admiration and envy. Other boys' fathers did no more than make money in the City. Philby's was a man of *Deserta Felix*.

With Prince Feisal's departure and the restoration of peace in Arabia between the Hashemites and the Saudis, Philby looked for a post in the new empire. In the immediate aftermath of the war the Fertile Crescent of the Middle East had been divided, with tidy, British colonial administration terminology, into four separate zones, each called an Occupied Enemy Territory Administration. Two of these, covering what was becoming Iraq and Palestine, were controlled by Britain. A third, covering the Lebanon and coastal Syria, went to the French, while the Syrian interior was assigned to the Arabs. At the Paris Peace Conference, however, the British, in order to secure French approval for Britain's control of the oil-bearing regions around Mosul, agreed to the French occupation of all Syria and Lebanon. These zones thereupon became League of Nations mandatory states, and Britain and France became the mandatory powers. In July 1920 the French Army seized the formerly Arab-controlled Occupied Enemy Territory Administration. In 1921, in an attempt to give some substance to their promises to the Arabs, the British transferred the eastern part of Palestine to the Hashemite prince Abdullah. This area later became known as Jordan.

Philby had begun to look for work anywhere in the new administrative system in the Middle East but did not find a suitable post; India and its clerkly bondage seemed to beckon yet again. There were few prospects for him in Whitehall, which is where he might have remained but for his argumentative side, his certainty that he alone was right. Men with such confidence often prosper in London. But Philby did not. The vigor of his advocacy of Ibn Saud and his opposition to the government's Hussein policy gave him a weird whiff. His vocal support of that obscure dynasty earned him the reputation for being a monomaniac, a derisory and damaging term for "a form of insanity in which the patient is mad on one subject." He denounced the Balfour Declaration as "an act of betrayal for whose parallel, the shekels and the kiss and all the rest of it, we have to go back to the garden of Gethsemane."[5] This did not sit well with the Zionists in the Establishment, who had great power. In another statement he announced that every British government should reaffirm the Balfour Declaration, because Jews had a perfect right to settle in Palestine at will "on a basis of equality with the existing population." In a third ambiguity he declared that he could accept the notion of a Jewish homeland only if Ibn Saud was made head of an Arab-Jewish state, as he was the "only great and outstanding figure" in Arabia. In due course he would announce that Jordan would be "only too happy" to accept "the boon of Jewish immigration and investment."*

On two points Philby, however, was consistent: that the Jews had it in them to benefit the Arab world if they would forgo the Zionist wish for dominance; and that only Ibn Saud had the power to rule a Palestine that was so divided. A man as forthright as Philby could not succeed in gaining a place at the India or Colonial Office, for few there could determine his real attitudes. But he did make powerful friends during his year in London. He sat on a League of Nations Union committee of politicians, dons, lawyers, and Zionists charged with producing a "model mandate" for Palestine. He joined a deputation collected by Lawrence to rescue the Middle East from the "pernicious grasp" of the India Office and the Foreign Office and what the group called "a semi-diplomatic, semi-administrative clearing house" that would put an end to clashes over British policy in the Arab world between rival governments. With some of the leading names of Arabian policy — Lord Robert Cecil, D. G. Hogarth, Lionel Curtis, Arnold Toynbee, T. E. Lawrence, Aubrey Herbert, and politicians of all three parties chosen for what Philby called "weight reasons" — Philby called

---

*At its formation, the new state was known as Transjordan. For the convenience of the reader, however, it will be called Jordan, its modern name.

at the Foreign Office to lobby for the Arab Declaration. But all too soon he found himself enmeshed in silken bonds that allowed no freedom of movement for the deputation unless it undertook to support the British-Arabian and Zionist policies.

Philby and Lawrence became firm friends during this time, although they did not agree on Arab affairs. As Lawrence wrote of St. John in a private letter dated 1921, he was "rather a 'red'; but decent — very."[6] Philby despised the Hashemites, whereas Lawrence was at work to get thrones for them in Iraq and Jordan. But in that passionate topic of the time, the Jewish national state, they saw eye to eye in the belief that an injection of Jewish brains and money into the Arab world would improve Arab chances of successful independence. Philby went so far as to lobby at a League of Nations committee for a post in Palestine.[7] But again he found himself thwarted.

Until 1920, Philby had given little thought to the question of a Jewish national home in Palestine. But he felt the need for employment other than in the Indian service, and when the government appointed Herbert Samuel, a Liberal banker, as high commissioner to Palestine, Philby wrote to an acquaintance, Leonard Stein, a barrister-at-law whom he knew to be a prominent Zionist, that he hoped "a satisfactory arrangement with the Arab states" would be a prelude "to the development of Palestine on reasonable lines in the spirit of the [Balfour Declaration]."[8]

Aware of Philby's brains and capacity for hard work, Stein mentioned these sentiments to Chaim Weizmann, who in 1920 became the leader of the World Zionist Organization, and Weizmann passed Philby's name to Samuel, who was looking for assistants to work with him in Palestine. Philby's reputation had reached Samuel already, so he sought a second opinion from Major Hubert Young, with whom Philby had worked on the Eastern Committee. Young replied that in Philby, Samuel would get a glutton for work and a clever man, but "I fear you will find his argumentative turn a nuisance to you. He is liable to take a side and stick to it."[9] The side was likely to be that of Ibn Saud. Samuel had enough bias to deal with already, and he rejected Philby. Philby reacted as usual under such circumstances; equipped with a well-concealed vindictiveness and a long memory, he decided the hand of Zion had been raised against him and that Samuel wanted not trained British administrators for Palestine but British Jews. He said so in terms that thereafter marked him, rightly or wrongly, as anti-Zionist.

Again he had begun his preparations to return to India when his patron, Sir Percy Cox, appeared in London in August 1920. Since the end of the war with Turkey, Cox had been stamping Whitehall's imprint on Persia, where what would come to be called the Anglo-Persian Oil Company was emerging as one of the largest oil producers in the world. But in July 1920 violent rebellion broke out in Iraq. *The Times* declared, on June 19, that it was being financed by Standard Oil of America. There were many British casualties, including the murder of one of Philby's colleagues, Colonel Gerald E. Leachman, a famous British agent in India and west Asia. The British garrison in Iraq had to be increased to sixty thousand men.

Cox was recalled from Tehran to London to advise the British government on its Iraqi and Arabian policies. When he was appointed the high commissioner, he began his work by seeking out Philby. Would St. John take over the work of adviser to the interior minister — the security minister — at Baghdad? He would be the man responsible for law and order. Philby accepted. "I have had my long-awaited orders to go to Irak," he wrote to his friend Donald Robertson, who was soon to become Regius Professor of Greek at Cambridge. "Needless to say I am overjoyed at the prospect of my work out there. I escape from India, and the Arab government of which I have dreamed is to have a fair trial."[10] Dora, heavily pregnant, packed her trunks for Baghdad, and once more St. John went down to Eastbourne to make his farewells to Kim, now into his eighth year and doing well and acquiring that most desirable of all schoolboy appellations, "a good egg."

Late in August 1920, St. John set out with Sir Percy and Lady Cox down that now familiar route to Baghdad by way of Bombay and Basra. But while in the Persian Gulf — which Ibn Saud had begun to call the Arabian Gulf — Sir Percy decided to stop for two days of meetings with Ibn Saud at Uqair, the pearling port where Philby had landed in Arabia for the first time in 1917. The meetings took place in one of the port's date gardens. Whitehall still had a Hashemite policy, so Ibn Saud was regarded as a second fiddle to Hussein, Sherif of Mecca, King of Arabia, and, Hussein prayed, Britain's nominee in the future as Caliph of Islam. Whitehall considered Ibn Saud as no more than a princely zealot who carried his treasury in the saddlebags of his camel, but who nonetheless had to be listened to. Who could tell when his Wahhabs would again spill out into the Hashemite kingdom or into the British protectorates that lined the Gulf and the Arabian Sea as far as the great imperial coal port of Aden?

There were desert politics to attend to. Would the Great Government continue to pay Ibn Saud's wartime subvention of £5,000 a year?

What were Cox's views on the reports, which Ibn Saud found most troubling, that the Great Government was considering the establishment of the Sherif of Mecca's oldest son, Feisal, as King of Iraq. Was the sherif not thinking of making another of his sons, Ali, the King of the Hijaz and the third, Abdullah, the king of a new state to be called Jordan? Was Ibn Saud not being ringed by hostile princes? Was the Wahhab kingdom not being surrounded by the Hashemite polity? Could such a state of affairs assure tranquillity in the deserts? Would there not be trouble? According to Philby's account, Cox gave Ibn Saud a "high assurance" that this was not the intent of the British government, although he may not have known that Miss Bell, who was shortly again to become Cox's Oriental Secretary, did have just such a plan in mind.

Did the Great Government intend to establish a political agent at Riyadh? Who would he be? When would he come? Would "our dear Mr. Feel-bee" be nominated for that high task? There were many such questions. Few could be answered while the nature of the postwar imperial system was being considered by the three departments involved: the Foreign Office, the Colonial Office, and the India Office. Cox promised to keep Ibn Saud advised of developments as they occurred. But little was settled with the Emir of Nejd and al-Hasa, except that the Great Government would continue to pay Ibn Saud's subvention as long as he played his part in ensuring the tranquillity of the desert. There must not be a second Battle of Khurma Oasis. In one direction, however, Philby was able to render Ibn Saud an important personal service, possibly and even probably without the knowledge of the Great Cockus, as Cox was generally known throughout the Gulf.

Well aware of Ibn Saud's intent to bring the entire Arabian Peninsula under Wahhab rule, at some stage the conversations between Philby and Ibn Saud, of which there were several when Cox was aboard his ship, turned to the question of Rashid Ali, Sherif of Hail, whose elimination by Ibn Saud was sanctioned by Cox when he sent Philby to Riyadh in 1917. But now that the war was over, times had changed, and imperial politics with them. That powerful voice in British councils, the Sherif of Mecca, now saw Rashid Ali and his murderous family as a counterweight to Ibn Saud and his swordsmen, the Ikhwan, and wished that the Rashid dynasty be preserved. Miss Bell, too, now favored Rashid's survival as a "balancing factor" against Ibn Saud should she succeed in establishing a Hashemite prince as King of Iraq. But Philby had other ideas.

He did not share Miss Bell's or Lawrence's passion for kings. Believing as he did in the worth of the Arab Declaration, he wished to see only self-governing republics arise from the League of Nations mandates through which Britain and France would rule the Middle East. His conviction that only Ibn Saud could rule Arabia had remained, along with his desire to find a place at Ibn Saud's court. In all this, his personal ambition played its part, as did his desire for the fame he would achieve if he could become the greatest of all the Arab explorers. Also, it seems to have begun to dawn on him that should Ibn Saud seize Mecca, as Philby believed to be well within the power of the Ikhwan, then Ibn Saud, not the Sherif of Mecca, might well become the Caliph of Islam, the supreme theological authority in the Moslem world and presently more or less in abeyance. What would Philby's position as counselor in foreign affairs to Ibn Saud then become?

According to Philby's account of those private sessions in the date garden beside the Persian Gulf, Philby began to press Ibn Saud to take "immediate steps" to "eliminate Rashid as a political factor in Arabia." In a world where a nod was as good as a wink, Rashid was now under sentence of death. Within the year he was duly killed and his successors contrived to murder each other, as they usually did following a regicide. Ibn Saud felt compelled to intervene and impose his peace on that bloody little feudatory, using pack artillery to hasten the process. And a year later Philby was able to record with satisfaction that "the Rashid dynasty had ceased to exist; and Ibn Saud ruled unchallenged in desert Arabia, as his ancestors had done a century before."[11] Hail became Wahhab. Another obstacle had been removed from the process by which Ibn Saud might reach Mecca.

Such was Philby's influence at Cox's court. Philby had shown himself to be indispensable to both Cox and Ibn Saud while serving both in his own interest. The meetings with Ibn Saud were now over. The party sailed for Basra, where in due course they arrived to a popular welcome and a seventeen-gun salute. Sir Percy Cox, splendid in his white and gold uniform and Cawnpower tent club sun helmet, was joined by Miss Bell, who had come down from Baghdad in her river launch to meet her chief, Cox, and her friend Philby. Now fifty-eight and tall and cool as ever, she had the measure of Iraq, that new piece in the imperial chessboard through which the Great Government acquired eighty million new subjects. And as she noted of the temperament of the Iraqis among those new subjects:

Men who have kept the tradition of a personal independence, which was limited only by their own customs, entirely ignorant of a world which lay outside their swamps and pastures, and as entirely indifferent to its interests as to the opportunities it offers, will not in a day fall into step with European ambitions, nor welcome European methods.[12]

They never did.

At first, again, Philby's career owed much to Miss Bell, but their relationship could not prosper. Philby could not countenance Iraq under an alien king. It must, he insisted, be for the Iraqis if the Anglo-French Declaration was to have meaning. Neither Cox nor Miss Bell agreed with him, for without a foreign king under British control, the tribes and the races would prove ungovernable and therefore endanger the Anglo-Iraq Oil Company, which was by way of becoming the largest such combine in the world. Nor was Miss Bell able to be such a sister to him as she had been during the war. Philby was older now, he was succeeding, and Dora arrived from England, having just produced a daughter, Diana. He had rented a house on the Tigris, entertained on the grandest scale, and made Dora pregnant yet again. Patricia was born in the midsummer heat of 1921. In his work Philby seemed content. He was writing a third volume about his experiences in Arabia, although the first had yet to be published, and he regularly raced the stallion Ibn Saud had given him in 1918. It was a lovely animal and won many purses on the Baghdad racecourse. "Do you realize," he asked Dora one day, "that we shall probably be here — possibly in this very house, for there is no better in all Baghdad — for the rest of our lives? I cannot see anything interfering with that prospect and I could wish for nothing better."[13]

Philby was wrong. They would not spend the rest of their lives at Baghdad, for something had begun to interfere with his prospects; and that had to do with Miss Bell's passion for a king in Iraq. She was secretly king-making with her friend Winston Churchill, who in January 1921 moved from the War Office to the Colonial Office and thereby found himself in charge of what he called "these thankless deserts" of the Middle East and, in particular, "this odious Mesoptn embarrassment."[14] Even before he kissed hands, Churchill had been considering Feisal the King of Iraq. Lawrence had spoken of Feisal in warm terms. In appearance he was "tall, graceful and vigorous, with the most beautiful gait, and a royal dignity of head and shoulders." His training in the entourage of Abdul Hamid, the Ottoman leader at Constantinople, had made him a "pastmaster of diplomacy." As Lawrence had commended him to the Arab Bureau in Cairo:

> His military service with the Turks has given him a working knowledge of tactics. His life in Constantinople and in the Turkish Parliament has made him familiar with European questions and manners.

He is a careful judge of men. If he had the strength to realize his dreams he would go very far, for he is wrapped up in his work and lives for nothing else; but the fear is that he will wear himself out by trying to seem to aim always a little higher than the truth, or that he would die of too much action. His men told me how, after a long spell of fighting, in which he had to guard himself, and lead the charges, and control and encourage them, he had collapsed physically and was carried away from his victory, unconscious, with the foam flecking his lips . . . here, as it seemed, was offered to our hand, which had only to be big enough to take it, a prophet who, if veiled, would give cogent form to the idea behind the activity of the Arab revolt.[15]

Few men believed much of this, but Churchill and Miss Bell did when, in the wintry, gray world of the Paris Peace Conference, Feisal appeared with Lawrence at his side among the old men in chesterfields and astrakhans. Both wore pure white silk robes and Damascus cloaks and gold and white headdresses. The theatrics did not escape the War Office, which ordered Lawrence back into British Army uniform, with its Sam Browne belt and hanging sword. Feisal was then in his early thirties, and what Lawrence called "his dark, appealing eyes, set a little sloping in his face," charmed Miss Bell. Lawrence thought her "not a good judge of men . . . always the slave of some momentary power: at one time Hogarth, at another Wilson, at another me, at last Sir Percy Cox. She changed her direction each time like a weathercock: because she had no great depth of mind. But depth and strength of emotion — Oh Lord yes."[16]

From the time of their meeting in Paris, Miss Bell saw this slender prince of Mecca as the future of Iraq, of the Hashemites. Here, as Lawrence had told the bureau, was the spirit of the Arab awakening. At the end of the war, Feisal became King of Syria, but when he began in 1919 to intrigue against his masters, the French, they ejected him at bayonet point. He then became available to Cox and Miss Bell — and Churchill — for the post of King of Iraq. In July 1920 Miss Bell's intrigues caused her chief, the formidable Arnold T. Wilson, to recommend to Cox that she was becoming dangerous:

If you can find a job for Miss Bell at home I think you will be advised to do so. Her irresponsible activities are a source of considerable concern to me here and are not a little resented by the Political Offices.[17]

But it was Wilson who went home, not Miss Bell. Cox took little notice of Wilson; he knew Miss Bell of old and saw use for her. So did Churchill. There might be oil in Iraq, big oil, and Churchill knew its value. It was Churchill as First Lord of the Admiralty who had seen to it that the British government obtained a half-share in the Anglo-Persian Oil Company, and he was well aware of the importance to the empire of British rule in the Middle East. Churchill enjoyed the entire support of Prime Minister Lloyd George, who declared a little later on, with an eye on the Turko-Franco-American oil interests' activities against the British position in Iraq, that a "policy of scuttle" in Iraq would hand over "some of the richest oilfields in the world" to the Americans and French in return for no more that "one derisive shout from our enemies."[18]

In January 1921 Lord Curzon introduced Feisal to Churchill personally as a man who had "behaved like a real gentleman & with a fine sense of honour & loyalty." Churchill agreed and advised Cox accordingly, adding that "Western political methods are not necessarily applicable to the East and a basis of election should be framed."[19] That is what occurred to produce Philby's revolt against the imperial system. Not only did this election fail to honor the Arab Declaration of 1919, in which the Arab nation was guaranteed its freedom in return for the part it had played in the Arab Revolt of World War I, but also the British government was imposing an alien monarch on a country that wished to become a republic. Nonetheless, Cox began to "frame" the basis of Feisal's election.

Miss Bell and Philby once again formed the core of Cox's secretariat. No doubt as before Philby created his own files with "parental solicitude"; for even with the successful termination of the Iraqi revolt, the situation remained dangerous and murderous. Philby earned Cox's praise by devising the rules for relations between Iraqi ministers and their British advisers. When this was done, Philby assumed the task for which Cox had selected him, to advise Sayed Talib Pasha, the minister of the interior, the police minister, the keeper of the peace. As with Ibn Saud, so with Sayed Talib. Here was another of the seeds of Philby's revolt against the crown service.

A son of the religious and political leader of Basra, Talib was in his middle years, a man with a long record of political conspiracy. In 1915, Cox had deported him to India for activities in the Turkish interest that were "inimical to the safety and dignity" of the crown service in Mesopotamia. There was at least one political murder in his dossier; he had carried out numerous extortions; Miss Bell thought him a *"succès de crime."*[20] Philby agreed, declaring Talib "an accomplished villain." Yet on his return to Baghdad in 1920, he came to regard Talib as the ablest man in the Council of Ministers; at one stage, when Miss Bell despaired of convincing Whitehall of Feisal's suitability, Philby mentioned to Cox that Talib would make a fine King of Iraq. He said too that he would cut a fine figure at his coronation. Philby told others that Talib would make a fine first president of the Iraqi republic — an advocacy that caused Philby's downfall.

To settle the question for good and, it was hoped fervently, for all, in March 1921 Churchill called a Middle East conference at Cairo. Cox and Miss Bell attended, but not Philby. Either he was not invited by Cox, or Miss Bell had recommended his exclusion on account of his bias toward Ibn Saud and his championship of Talib. Or Philby declined to go. During the conference Churchill announced that he favored a Jewish state in Palestine, and he spoke lyrically about Zion's "splendid open-air men" and beautiful women who were making the "desert blossom like the rose."[21]

As to the Arabs, he declared, his policy was "to run both Ibn Saud and Hussein" and to "dole out benefits of various kinds to each on condition they play our game & don't bite each other."[22] Miss Bell found rare opportunities to put a word in for Feisal with Clementine Churchill and with Churchill personally while riding camels around the Sphinx with the minister and Lawrence, Feisal's other champion. With another ear for intelligence reports of the Russian Bolsheviks' attempts at sedition in Turkey, Persia, and Iraq, at one stroke Churchill created two kings, Feisal for Baghdad and Abdullah for Amman. Miss Bell, triumphant, remarked to a colleague after Churchill's decision was announced: "We've pulled it off!"[23]

So Iraq was made. Its name meant "the cliff," and so it proved to be. St. John was among the first to fall off it. From the start it was amenable only to military rule, but even with eighty thousand Anglo-Indian troops there, Iraq revolted. Cox warned Churchill on April 11 that Talib's father, the illustrious and revered Naqib of Baghdad, the chairman of the Council of Ministers, had declared in the presence of his son that he "could not agree that [Feisal] or his family had the slightest claim to concern themselves with Iraq and he was confident that [the British government], with its well-known sense of justice, would be of his opinion."[24] Churchill, taking a Machiavellian view, suggested several candidates so as to split the vote. The Machiavellian view did not prosper. A fresh crisis arose and, aware that his minister was making trouble everywhere, Philby asked Talib not to do or say anything that would "let me down now." But Talib ignored the appeal. On April 16, 1921, he gave a dinner for a British newspaper correspondent, several members of the foreign diplomatic corps, and some Iraqi notables, and, in the sure knowledge that what he said would reach the ears of Cox, he made a fiery speech. If Cox placed Feisal on the throne, Talib would raise the tribes in rebellion. He hinted that Feisal would be assassinated if he set foot in Basra. He asserted that "certain officials" were "predisposed" toward Feisal and were trying to exert "improper influence" in his favor, and he intended to appeal to King George V, with a view to the officials being removed. The Naqib of Baghdad was well aware of the scheme afoot and was prepared to appeal to the Islamic world.[25]

Cox learned of the address within a few hours and advised the Colonial Office that his position would become intolerable were he to overlook it. As Miss Bell wrote to her parents, Talib's statement "was an incitement to rebellion as bad as anything which was said by the men who roused the country last year, and not far from a declaration of *jihad*" — of holy war against the British. Since the 1920 rebellion had taken many British lives and the immense sum of 20 million pounds sterling, Cox could not afford the risk. It is unclear whether Churchill was aware personally of what now followed, but it is evident that he knew and approved of Cox's action, at least after the fact. Lady Cox invited Talib to tea at the residency, an invitation she knew he would accept. They met in Cox's drawing room at half-past four. Afterward, as Talib crossed the nearby Tigris bridge on his way home, a British Army officer arrested him. Cox reported to Churchill that the deed was done and that "I do not anticipate any trouble as I think the great majority of people are relieved." He trusted that Churchill would "be able to support me in my action and authorise me to send him to Ceylon." Churchill replied that Talib's speech had been seditious and that he must be exiled.[26]

Talib was spirited from Iraq to Ceylon. Certainly Miss Bell was party to the plot. But equally clearly Philby, Talib's adviser, was not. During the operation the telephone line to his residence was cut, and he learned of Talib's arrest only by chance, at the bar of his club during a dance. When he heard what had happened, he was "breathing maledictions and in a tearing temper" and went to Cox to resign.[27] Cox had always liked and admired Philby and, aware that he might lose a good man, succeeded in calming his brilliant subordinate with the statement that he had long intended to suspend the Iraqi Council of Ministers, pending their choice of a ruler, and replace them temporarily with their British advisers. Would St. John not review his opinion? Philby did so and returned to his home an hour after leaving it. More concerned with his career than his philosophical views, he told Dora that he had been appointed acting interior minister, perhaps the second most important post in the Council of Ministers. He was now in charge of the law and order of Iraq.

But not for long.

In the hope that Philby would accept Feisal, Cox sent him to Basra to receive the Hashemite prince when he arrived in Iraq on June 23, aboard a British cruiser, accompanied by one of Cox's most distinguished officers, Kinahan Cornwallis, who had been the Intrusives' director during the war. The hope, Miss Bell recorded, was that "Feisal will make a conquest and that Mr Philby will come back an ardent Sharifian."[28] That hope was misplaced. Cornwallis noted that Philby made it clear that Feisal was unwelcome in Iraq; that the Iraqi people wished for a republic, not a monarchy. When Feisal complained about his poor reception, Philby replied that he must not think that the support of all British officials could be regarded as a foregone conclusion — a clever implication that Feisal was no more welcome among the British than among the Iraqis. Unused to such rudeness, Feisal complained to Cox personally, and when Philby returned to Baghdad, Cox sent for him: Feisal would stay and he must go.

Philby, "bristling with righteous indignation," replied that he was "quite ready to hand over."[29] He could stay only if free elections were held, as Cox had promised the Iraqi Council of Ministers when they met in 1920 to put down the rebellion. With what was perhaps a deft reference to Churchill's instruction to "frame" Feisal's election, he declared that "a rigged choice of Britain's candidate was against his principles and he would be glad to leave."[30]

His session with Cox at an end, St. John went home to give Dora the fresh news. She realized that he had been caught in a nasty conspiracy, and she recognized too that if he were to remain in crown service, as she hoped, he must leave Baghdad with his reputation intact. As they talked, Miss Bell arrived from her house nearby to say she was sorry. Dora upbraided her for the part she had played in engineering Feisal's acceptance. No, Dora said, Gertrude was not sorry. And she may have been right. At any event, Philby never talked to Miss Bell again. A letter about his defeat to his mother, May, has survived. It said:

> I have always been considered a straight and honest man and my giving up my comfortable job rather than partake in the Government's breach of faith has enhanced my reputation in that direction. All my old [Arab] friends have been flocking to see me . . . and it is clear that the country is heartily sick of Feisal and his entourage though the people are too much afraid of the British to do anything. However it seems to me only a matter of time before some sort of crash comes and then I will come into my own again but for the time being I am out![31]

The reality was different. The crash visualized by Philby did not come until 1958, thirty-seven years later. No other Iraqi government, before the arrival of the Hashemites or after, lasted as long. For all the conspiracy that attended Feisal's selection, in the light of what is now known about Philby's attitudes, it may be considered that Cox and Miss Bell's judgment was better than his. Certainly from the imperial point of view Feisal's appointment was a triumph, for it ensured British command of Iraqi oil for almost four decades.

On the morrow of his dismissal Philby left Baghdad for a holiday in the mountains of Persia, plainly to avoid being identified with the maneuvers over the appointment of Feisal as King of Iraq. He wrote an essay entitled "A Persian Holiday," in which he dwelt upon socialism, the ills of imperialism, and a Persian theologian called Bab. Babism, he thought, had "entirely admirable features," like "political socialism of the democratic type," except that "it seemed to be afraid of some of its more revolutionary ideals."[32] Every statement Philby made about politics, however indirect, had a meaning — as, later, did those of his son. He was moving farther and farther to the left as he fished for the famous trout of the Lar Valley. He climbed the nineteen thousand feet to the peak of Damavand and obtained satisfaction for Cox's deportation of Talib. Encountering a *Times* correspondent, Arthur Moore, Philby, although bound by the official code to silence regarding the press, related to him "the story of Mesopotamia in detail." He also let Moore read his proofs of *The Heart of Arabia* and, Philby recorded with satisfaction, "a month or so later his paper ran a series of special articles by him on the [Talib] affair, which scandalised the official world."[33] As Philby added, "Besides him only Cox and Gertrude Bell had read my proofs, and of course they had no difficulty in identifying the source of [Moore's] information." Leaks were then much rarer than they became, and Philby found himself in the soup again when he returned to Baghdad after ninety days.

The Iraqi opposition to Feisal had rapidly melted under Cox's lordly glare, and on July 11, 1921, the Council of Ministers decided simply to proclaim him king. This was not done publicly but in the courtyard of the palace on the bank of the Tigris. Philby was not present when Talib's father, the Naqib of Baghdad, read a proclamation written by Cox that Feisal had been elected king by 96 percent of the people. The naqib, who until that moment had been one of Feisal's most determined opponents, cried, "Long live the King!" and, Miss Bell recorded, those present — "English and Arab officials, townsmen, Ministers, local deputations — stood up and saluted him." The national flag was broken out and the band played "God Save the King." There followed a salute of twenty-one guns and it was, Miss Bell recorded, "an amazing thing to see all Iraq, from North to South, gathered together. It is the first time it has happened in history." Feisal looked along the front row of dignitaries, his glance caught the eyes of Miss Bell, and "I gave him a tiny salute."[34]

Such was the manner in which the state of Iraq was created. It was not long before Churchill began to deplore the entire affair and to complain about Cox and "all these bitter people, each with his Arab pet, tumbling over each other fighting for power."[35] As Feisal bit the hand that nourished him and demanded complete freedom, Cox swamped Churchill with telegrams about the new king. Churchill wearied of "all these telegrams about Feisal and his state of mind." He complained to Cox:

> There is too much of it. Six months ago we were paying his hotel bill in London, and now I am forced to read day after day 8oo-word messages on questions of his status and his relations with foreign Powers. Has he not got some wives to keep him quiet?[36]

The entire Iraqi scene was "an ungrateful volcano," and the throne to which Feisal had been hoisted was "a monstrous burden to the British Exchequer." Could not Feisal develop his country and pay his own way? Until then, Britain would retain final control of Iraq, and liability for both internal order and external defense, until such time — perhaps fifteen years distant — when the "independent Islamic state of Irak can stand alone."[37] Before long, however, Churchill found that Feisal was "playing a very low & treacherous game with us," and he asked that Lawrence, his agent to Abdullah, be withdrawn from Amman to help the minister deal with these tricky princes. But who should replace Lawrence? Who had the skill? Philby believed it was Lawrence who proposed him for the succession. This may have been so, but it was a telegram from the assistant secretary of the Colonial Office, Hubert Young — who earlier had warned Samuel against employing Philby in Palestine because of his bias in favor of Ibn Saud — that gave Philby another run for his money. "What is really required," Young wrote of Abdullah and his muddled and troubled kingdom, "is someone of [the] calibre of Philby."

Philby was at home when Cox called to say that he had received a telegram that might interest him. Would he come over and read it? Lawrence had proposed Philby as successor; if Philby wanted the job, he should proceed immediately by air to Amman to consult with Lawrence and Abdullah. He should see the high commissioner at Jerusalem, Herbert Samuel, and then go on to London for an interview with Churchill. Did Philby want the job? He accepted with pleasure, thereby winning another reprieve from the Raj. He hastened to Amman and was taken by Lawrence straight to Abdullah's tent. "We got on famously from the beginning," Philby claimed, recalling that Abdullah said to him, "We know what you have done for Ibn Saud; if you do as much for me, I shall be grateful indeed." Abdullah, wrote Philby, was "charming — a brilliant talker with intellectual and literary tastes."[38] Abdullah wrote of Philby, "He is very sincere in serving the country where he lives." Philby passed the regal inspection and so proceeded to Jerusalem and Samuel, whom he found to be in a receptive mood; he wanted only to get Abdullah off his hands. So, Philby wrote, "the third hurdle was easily jumped and I proceeded to London to see Mr. Churchill."

By Philby's own account, Churchill proved to be as eager to have him in Jordan as Samuel was, and perhaps for the same reason: Philby "was at least marked as an uncompromising champion of Arab independence." Churchill, Philby claimed, "gave me the assurances I needed." Philby's task, the minister assured him, would be to further the promises of independence to the Arabs, without supervision. Palestine and Jordan would be administered separately, with Samuel acting only in a supervisory role. He could keep or sack the king as he saw fit. As to the Balfour Declaration:

> The Zionist clauses of the mandate would on no account apply to Trans-Jordan. And, so long as that country refrained from being a nuisance to all its neighbors, as it certainly had been of late, the British Government was prepared to let it develop as a self-governing entity. Under the general control of Sir Herbert Samuel, but entirely independent of the Palestine administration, I would be the Chief British Representative, with a free hand to advise the Emir Abdullah and his Government as I thought fit in the working out of their salvation. I could not have improved on the policy propounded to me by Churchill, and he was duly satisfied of my competence.[39]

Churchill had inserted the round peg in the square hole. "Philby was always a good and attractive talker," his biographer recorded, and "he propounded his ideas so lucidly that he won [Churchill] over."[40]

His Whitehall work done, Philby prepared to return to Jordan immediately. But first he spent the weekend with Kim at St. Aldro. To his delight, he found that the boy was emerging as he had hoped: cheery, clean, bright, upright, a good batsman, fast at football, a good fly half at rugger. He was popular and fit. He seemed happy. But, as Kim would

recall in reminiscences nearly half a century later while in the hands
of the KGB in Moscow, the school was not distinguished either in
learning or in sports, due to the personality of the Reverend Browne.
He was a fifteen-stone clergyman "with an uncertain temper. He was
never cruel; just too big, too awesome and too remote."[41] He had a
spinster daughter "who once gave me an electrifying sight of her knick-
ers, but there was no follow-up." The service Dr. Browne did him was

> to reinforce my atheism by an active dislike of religious observance
> and a distaste for the person of Christ. He presided over the 15-min-
> ute tedium of daily chapel, the Sunday morning service with its long
> and incomprehensible sermon, the Sunday evening service held in
> deepening gloom, with Monday looming nastily ahead. A little relief
> came in my last year, for it was the duty of the senior boys to man
> the bellows for Mary Browne's organ. That meant standing in a hid-
> den niche, where we could suck sweets and think of knickers.

His master, F. E. Hill, liked Kim, and Kim liked him, but he was

> a conservative, and naturally an imperialist. He renamed our dormi-
> tories after British dominions and possessions. The British Empire,
> he told us, was unique in one simple particular: it would last forever.
> As I digested this thought, my scepticism again surfaced. Why? Why
> should the British Empire be so different — except for the accident
> that Mr Hill and I were both British? I couldn't take it, any more
> than I could take Christ's conjuring trick at the marraige [sic] feast
> at Cana.

He became ever more, he confessed, the "godless little anti-imperialist."
But he presented a very different picture to his father. As St. John
wrote to Dora on November 4, 1921, he was able to see "a lot more
of Kimbo than I would have done if I had stayed at a hotel & just taken
him out at fixed hours." He had had "breakfast each day with the
school & went round with Mr. and Miss Browne each night to see the
boys in bed & at odd moments I used to go into the big schoolroom
& play billiards with Kimbo or watch him play with others."[42] On Saturday, Philby took Kim and two friends, Petrovich and Loxton, to
lunch at the Grand Hotel and then to the pier, where "there was an
excellent performance of 'The Tempest' which they all thoroughly
enjoyed." On Sunday he took Kim and Petrovich to see Kim's friend
Ernest Green, an entomologist who later became president of the
Royal Entomological Society. Green "enthused over Kim's marvellous
knowledge of entomology & said he hoped one day Kim & I & he
might be able to do a caravan tour of collecting in the New Forest."

Kim Philby, too, would have something to say about his friend. In his recollections written in old age, he recalled how Ernest Green taught him the "most efficient way of capturing moths," with a mixture of treacle and beer. And as St. John remembered, Mr. Green showed him the *Entomologist,* in which was printed Kim's letter announcing his capture of a rare moth. As St. John wrote to Dora, this "must have been Kim's "first printed contribution!" It was so well written, Philby felt sure, that "I bet the editor did not realise that his correspondent was a boy of 9½!'"

Kim and his father walked in the sand, on the pier, lunched at the Violet Rooms, played billiards, and talked. St. John was content. His son was in the pink, although there were tears when the time came for St. John to return to Amman. As he reported to Dora:

> I can't think of any time for years which I have enjoyed so much, it was all so quiet and nice and my memories went back to my own school days long gone by & I felt a thrill of pride to see my own son going through it all and wondered what joys & troubles lay ahead of him.

St. John's parting words to the son he adored were: "Goodbye, my boy, work hard and play hard; don't do anything you are not allowed to, but, if you do, don't mind owning up." He ended his letter:

> Sweetheart, I think we may be justly proud of our son, who is well in advance of boys of his age in every way & seems to be popular & full of life & mischief while at the same time being very serious over his work & hobbies. That's the right stuff & I think the spirit of the school is splendid.

Within the week Philby was with Lawrence in Amman. Lawrence began to hand over to Philby a piece of the Arabian Desert and the Fertile Crescent that everybody wanted but none knew what to do with. The process took ten days, and Lawrence transferred, with much else, his personal, initialed files, which covered 1914 to 1921. All related to high British policy in the Middle East in the period before, during, and after the Arab Revolt and included a record of the British government's dealings with Hussein, Feisal, Abdullah, and Ibn Saud and matters concerning the Balfour Declaration and the Sykes-Picot Agreement. Parts of them were still confidential as late as 1939, especially the correspondence between Sir Henry McMahon, the British high commissioner, and Hussein, Sherif of Mecca, leading to the Arab Revolt. These Philby made his own, transferring them to the private files he was still acquiring with the "parental solicitude" that he had displayed as Cox's personal assistant at Baghdad in 1917.

Also, Lawrence handed Philby a sheet of notepaper recording how he had spent £100,000 gold during his incumbency, which had lasted only a month when Philby replaced him. One item read: "£10,000 — lost, I forget how or where."[43] Later, when Philby found a locked safe containing £10,000 in gold buried in the sands at Aqaba, he surmised that Lawrence had camped there, buried the gold for safety, and had then forgotten about it.

Philby gave Lawrence a note of quittance and, with the gold and the files now in his possession, began his career as a crown servant afresh, in no way daunted by the the past or by a problematic future. Before him lay all Jordan, a country that had not existed a short while earlier, one populated by tribes armed to the teeth, where there were but vague frontiers, and one whose sovereignty was contested by the Syrians, the Iraqis, the Saudis, the Palestinians, and the Jews, many of whom maintained that it belonged to the descendants of the tribes of Reuben and Gad. Its capital, Amman, was no more than a village in a mountain fastness. In theory the country was under the tutelage of the British high commissioner in Jerusalem, Herbert Samuel, and such was the tribal turbulence there that he had wanted to occupy it militarily. But when Churchill said no, Britain could not afford these little military enclaves, Samuel turned away, and left the law, order, and administration to six young British officers. Their ages ranged from nineteen to thirty-five; their orders were to encourage local self-government, to advise only when asked, and to make themselves scarce if it seemed that they might fall into hostile hands. Samuel did not wish to pay the price of a hostage. When Philby arrived, he found the country, consequently, divided into six little territories.

Abdullah, the second son of King Hussein of the Hijaz and the younger brother of King Feisal of Iraq, had been washed up at Amman when Ibn Saud's Ikhwan defeated his little tribal army at Khurma in May 1919. He had begun to prosper only when Churchill appeared in Cairo in 1921 as colonial minister, determined to use Hussein and his sons to "enable His Majesty's Government to bring pressure to bear on one Arab sphere in order to attain their own ends in another."[44] The importance of Abdullah at Amman, as Lawrence had said, was that he could be used as "a safety valve" to check anti-Zionism, and he was bound to allow himself to be so used, as he was dependent upon the British government for his throne, his kingdom, and his money.

As for his subjects, they were part of a complex of tribes who had been assured by their British advisers that there was no question of a Zionist government in Palestine. All religions would be equally respected; no land would be taken from any Arab. Churchill closed the 1921 meeting with the statement that Abdullah would be king on a trial basis of six months. He would have a British political officer as his chief adviser. Abdullah and the officer — Philby — would establish order in Jordan and "set the revenue of the country on a proper basis."[45] Churchill would be willing to support Abdullah in both money and troops. Abdullah accepted Churchill's proposal, asking only that "he be regarded as a British officer and trusted accordingly." Churchill agreed, thanking Abdullah "for his readiness to help" and assuring him "that he would be given as far as possible a free hand in the very difficult task which he had undertaken."[46] In return, Abdullah received £5,000 sterling a month for six months as a civil list and a grant-in-aid of £150,000, to be administered by Philby as the British political agent at Abdullah's court.

Philby's main task was to establish Abdullah as King of Jordan, as Cox and Miss Bell had established his brother Feisal at Baghdad. Philby set about the task with his usual energy; his dislike for monarchs notwithstanding. He was, at first, as impressed by Abdullah as Churchill. As he wrote during that first year in Amman, he liked Abdullah, who was a "vain but well-read man with excellent ideas" but "lacking in initiative or vigour of action."[47] Philby also found him hopelessly extravagant, which offended Philby's parsimony regarding the treasury. No taxation system had been established, and Abdullah borrowed money where he could, especially from his father and his brother, Hussein and Feisal. But in all, he wrote in February 1922, "time flies at an amazing pace . . . I frankly like Abdullah. Of course nobody here or in Syria wants him or any member of the Sharifian family, but what matter? He is here and is as good a figurehead as anyone else would be." But "his debts which amount to about £25,000 to date, are a problem the solution to which will not be without difficulty."[48]

The first year went well. Abdullah presented Philby with his own residence, a handsome building near the Roman baths in central Amman. This suited Philby well enough, but when Dora joined him, she came to dislike both the mansion and Amman. It was far too primitive, and she invited High Commissioner Samuel to inspect it. He agreed with her that it was "insanitary and infested with vermin." Unless the residence was improved, she would return to England. There was, too, trouble over Philby's pay. When he went to see Churchill he forgot to settle the terms of his employment; consequently, he did the work of a political agent but was paid at the scale of an assistant district commissioner, losing thereby about £500 a year on his £2,500 wage at Baghdad. Philby, who was businesslike with other people's money but less so about his own, did represent his case in Whitehall. He thought his complaint had been settled. But he was wrong, and when he began to entertain the many notables who called at his own expense, Dora went back to England. He implored her to return; she did; then she went back to England once again. He wrote to Dora, pleading with her to return, and let her know, "I am beginning to lose my patience with Government's shabby treatment of me in financial matters," and unless Whitehall "coughed up some more cash" to cover his large entertainment expenses, it would be a "bit of a shock to the next noble lord who wants to see the wilds of Jordan to be told that the Chief British Representative is unable to put him up."[49]

His remedy proved foolish. Philby began to pay himself what he thought his salary should be and to compensate himself for his expenses from Abdullah's £150,000 subsidy from Whitehall, which he controlled. This practice was not discovered for some time, but when it was, Samuel, who had a tidy mind and was distrustful of Philby for whatever he did and said, found his personal financial problems interwoven with local politics. The auditors argued, with some success, that his use of the subsidy for personal compensation constituted a breach of trust, and this had serious consequences at a time when the political complexities of the work, and Philby's sense of grudge, made the agent vulnerable to powerful local voices like Samuel's.

Inevitably, Philby began to fall out with all his regional colleagues, with Cox in Baghdad, then with Samuel in Jerusalem. Worse, suspicion developed that he was in correspondence with Ibn Saud. If this was so, it was foolish and dangerous, for the Saud and Hashemite dynasties were still virtually at war, and Ikhwan agents were known to visit Amman during their prowling about the desert. It could not be long before Ibn Saud and the Sherif of Mecca settled their troubles in their own way. By his public statements Philby did himself little good with the British, the Hashemite, or the Jewish interests. The main damage he did himself came, however, in December 1922, when, with Abdullah, he visited London. Having translated for Abdullah at a tea with Churchill and at a government dinner, he spoke to a private audience on British policy in Arabia and criticized strongly the British and French in Iraq and Syria for their failure to fulfill the Anglo-French Declaration of 1918. Samuel suspected, as did others, that Philby was hostile to Jewish settlement in Jordan and not more than lukewarm to the

Balfour Declaration. Then Philby offended the Hashemites with a statement that only Ibn Saud would be strong enough to deal with the Turks if they attempted to restore their empire, a matter that was in the wind. And he offended everybody when he declared:

> The Arab is a democrat, and the greatest and most powerful Arab ruler of the present day is proof of it. Ibn Saud is no more than *primus inter pares;* his strength lies in the fact that he has for twenty years accurately interpreted the aspirations and will of his people.[50]

The end of Philby's career approached. There was a happy glint in that tricky world of politics and ambition. Kim arrived in Amman on holiday accompanied by his grandmother, May, that summer of 1923. He traveled in style by train from London to Marseilles and thence by liner to Port Said. Afterward came the train to Amman, located three thousand feet up on the Moabite plateau of Jordan. St. John, approaching forty, was in the pink of good humor, despite the gathering storm. They set out from the residency on a rare holiday. Traveling by road, rail, boat, pack horse, and camel, Philby and Kim and the family crisscrossed the places of magic. They started at Damascus, a city half as old as time; went on to Baalbek and the temples of Jupiter and Bacchus; then to Beirut. Philby, an archaeologist, kept up a flow of rich information especially for Kim, who had himself already shown promise as an architect and would prove to be clever at sketching Roman and Greek antiquities.

The party went on to Sidon, one of the leading seaports of the Phoenicians, and Tyre, the Crusaders' chief port of entry into the Levant. They visited Tiberias, Nazareth, Acre, and Haifa and came at last to Jerusalem, where there was pie-in-the-sky about how Kim would become his father's deputy when Philby became the high commissioner of Palestine. The Philbians collected samples of Jordan water at the place where Jesus was said to have been baptized. The collection had a purpose. It was claimed that the water contained special properties, and for centuries it had been drawn at that point and sent to England for christenings; they would send the water to the British Museum to establish whether it really contained holy properties. Finally Philby's caravan returned to Amman in a stately and joyous fashion late in September. There was much blowing of Arab trumpets and thumping of drums as the family returned to the residency, which was near Hercules' temple.

Kim made his first flight in an aircraft when his father ordered the Royal Air Force at Amman to attack an Ikhwan band that was advancing toward Amman, gathering strength from Jordanian tribesmen who had become disaffected by the taxation policies of King Abdullah. That they were Ibn Saud's men made no difference to Philby. A few two-pound bombs were dropped, a few hundred rounds of machine gun ammunition were fired, and then the aircraft returned to Amman. Kim was wildly excited. But the fun came to an end. A few days later, the family went to the Jordan to collect more samples of holy water, Kim caught malaria, and before the week was out he found himself on the liner, bound for England and St. Aldro's matron.

But on St. John's return from the holiday it became evident that the end could not be long delayed. The matter of his pay came up again when an auditor found that Philby had drawn many hundreds of pounds from the Jordan subsidy without authority. Now Samuel had a reason to recommend his dismissal for what the Colonial Office in London called "serious irregularities" and "misuse of the Jordan grant-in-aid funds entrusted to your care."[51] That assertion implied that Philby had embezzled money in his charge. Instead of prosecution there was argument. It went on until 1925 and in the end the crown concluded that Philby owed it £567, a large sum at that time. Samuel asked London for permission to dismiss Philby, but Philby acted first.

The end began early in 1924 over a matter of high Arab politics. The British censor at Amman, who read all incoming and outgoing mail of importance, found Philby to be in "unauthorised correspondence" with Ibn Saud.[52] This was an administrative crime in itself, for crown agents were not expected to have secret mail with kings and princes who might become enemies. There could be only one punishment for such action: Philby's dismissal from the crown service. But Philby, one step ahead of the crown, formally resigned all his posts, declaring in a letter to Sir Herbert Samuel that he was "no longer able to discharge with enthusiasm or efficiency the functions of Chief British Representative in Jordan." Unofficially, as he wrote to Donald Robertson at Cambridge, he had

> resigned this job for many, very many reasons; the chief of them is that I can no longer go on working with the present High Commissioner who, being a Zionist Jew, cannot hold the scales even between Zionist and Arab interests. Besides this, Abdullah has rather let me down by his personal extravagance, which is on such a scale that he is simply inviting interference, and getting it in full measure from H.M.G., which means the Zionist element. So I am off.[53]

Philby elaborated in a letter to his mother: "One can't help feeling & being disgusted at the fact that the older (and more respectable!!)

parties" — Philby used exclamation marks as instruments of his scorn; the more there were, the greater the scorn — "are practically in the pay of the Jews and Germans. In Government service of course one sees only one's own little corner but so far as this part of the world is concerned I am absolutely convinced that the motives of our policy are dishonest."[54]

Philby's revolt against the government was complete when his resignations were accepted. In the interests of damage control, in which it was expert, Whitehall said and did nothing further about Philby. His boats burned, he left Amman after sixteen years in the service of the Raj and the Great Government. He had thirteen months' paid leave due to him, and then he would be in the cold.

4

Renegade

1924–1932

ARRIVING IN ENGLAND on May 24, 1924, with, he liked to say, but a pittance in his fob, St. John Philby found little to encourage him as he examined the horizons of his career. At Camberley, in Surrey, where his mother, May, still presided over the family, he announced that when his year's terminal leave was up, in May 1925, he would have freed himself from "official bondage."[1] He had resigned as a matter of principle so that he could "serve my country after my own fashion."[2] He could not serve a Britain that had betrayed its word to the Arabs, and he must struggle to undo a wrong that could not be righted without sacrifice. Dora and May understood and praised his honesty. He had sacrificed a brilliant career in order to expose the system being created by the British, the French, and the Zionists in the Middle East. He displayed that same honest glint that Kim would show later on. Perhaps the son learned the trick from the father, but whatever the case, it had the same effect: to create the appearance of a strength of character that confounded critics and enemies.

St. John was the model of convention about the professions suited to a gentleman, and in considering a new career for himself, he ranked the possibilities in the following order: a seat in Parliament, an academic post, and, third by a long shot, trade. He found much support for the second, and even Sir Percy Cox (who had sacked him) and Sir Herbert Samuel (who had been about to) spoke for him when he sought a place at Trinity. But not much happened in those first ninety days of energetic job seeking, and with Dora pregnant yet again, he felt the clammy hand of despair. His one bright gleam was Kim, who had become St. Aldro's star pupil, an outstanding all-rounder in both his studies and sport. Although he was almost a year younger than his classmates, he had been head boy, house prefect, and the winner of numerous prizes. A member of the cricket first eleven, one of its most reliable batsmen and its best fielder, that slender figure in whites on the school's greenswards fulfilled not only his father's and the school's hopes but, in a way, the country's. Britain, it was said, won her wars on the cricket fields, at that gentlemanly game of strategy and tactics. Skill at cricket still meant something in English society.

Always known as H. Philby, not Kim, he had been played in that key position, inside right, in the football first eleven and inside three quarter in the rugby first fifteen. When he was dropped from the first fifteen because of his lack of inches, young Philby learned to become a fullback and was accepted back into the team. He was the golden boy of the school. St. John's confidence in the school and Kim was well founded, for the Aldronian system brought out Kim's classical brilliance, the same brilliance St. John had shown at his preparatory school. Kim was now reading hard for the examinations that, his father hoped most earnestly, would win him a scholarship to Westminster.

On June 17, three weeks after St. John arrived in London, Kim began sitting for the Westminster Challenge. At the end of that same day, Philby wrote to May, Kim was very pleased with himself when he came to the East India Club to see his father. There was a dizzy moment when Philby considered putting Kim in for Eton, but in the end Philby's dynastic sense about Westminster prevailed. Kim *must* get in, Philby decided, pushing and prodding the boy unmercifully. Brimming with confidence, Philby wrote to May that there were seventy-six candidates, but he was sure that "Kim is the best of the bunch."[3] This was no more than paternal pride. Kim did win the challenge, a prize indeed for a boy of only twelve and a half, but only through happenstance. A place to Westminster fell open when another student decided to go to another school. Kim, whose scholarship was good enough, was offered and accepted the challenge, and arrangements were made for him to enter the school on September 18, 1924. And as Philby estimated his prospects, Kim would be "a good man — *if he works.*"

Kim's election was a triumph of scholarship, for Westminster's standards were high, the discipline stern. Only the select obtained places there, and even they needed a special toughness to survive. Such was Kim's accomplishment, and such was his popularity, that on hearing the news Dr. Browne gave the school a holiday to mark Kim's success. In the morning Kim and his friends watched a cricket match and in the afternoon they walked over the Sussex Downs to Wannock, where St. John and Dora entertained the school to a strawberries and cream tea party. A little later, St. John took his boy to his old school in the shadow of Westminster Abbey, dressed in the school uniform — mortarboard, Eton collar, white tie, and black gown. And as they went to the bursar's office they stepped into a place that had not changed much from medieval times and back into St. John's own youth there.

A. A. Milne's nephews, I. I. (Tim) Milne and his brother Tony, entered about the same time. "Westminster is wonderful," St. John wrote to Dora, "and I really think the proudest moments of my life have been when I heard he was elected after all and when I took him to the school the other day."[4] Kim's election to be a King's Scholar was a source of relief as well as pride to his father, who felt himself close to penury. St. John's pride can be understood. Westminster was still one of seven great public schools of Britain (the others being Eton, Harrow, Winchester Rugby, Charterhouse, and Clifton). St. John had prophesied that Kim's life would not be a bed of roses, and he was correct. Westminster's discipline was Spartan. Order was kept by the senior boys, not their masters; the discipline permitted the "tanning" of the bare buttocks. Kim's dormitory resembled a barracks; meals were eaten from bare tables that had been in place for centuries. The baths were of cold water. The school's task was to create English gentlemen, and it did not pamper weaklings or failure. Kim settled in well and was well received. That St. John had been one of his generation's leading scholars was there for all to see, on gold letters on the board that carried the names of the captains since the time of the Virgin Queen. Now came Kim's turn.

During this time, fortune smiled somewhat on St. John. While he was out and about in Mayfair, marking time and waiting for Kim's examination results, a familiar voice had hailed him: "Hullo! Philby, I was this moment wondering where you were — come and lunch with me."[5] The voice was that of Major Remy Ernest Fisher, an expert in Oriental agriculture whom Philby met first in 1917–1918 in Cairo. By now he had become British, had acquired important friends, and lived in grand style in London and Spain.

Philby's meeting with Fisher was of interest, for he was close to one of the richest and most influential power groupings in London. What now occurred undoubtedly involved Philby in that group's affairs. The two men lunched at the Royal Automobile Club, and Fisher mentioned his interest in concessions in the Hijaz. It was rumored (and the Bible mentioned) that there was gold and oil there. Fisher spoke of his desire to establish a company of merchant venturers in the Near East and spoke of his association with "a powerful syndicate." He invited Philby — and Kim, too — to a holiday on his estate at St. Jean de Luz on the Franco-Spanish frontier. So Philby moved up in the social world as he moved out of the official world. Delighted at the prospect of a free holiday in a rich man's house, St. John sped off with Kim, although Dora was expecting her third child — a daughter, as it turned out — at any time. They remained as Fisher's guests until the middle of September, fishing, bottling butterflies, attending bullfights, and talking about everything under the sun.

These were the days before network radio, so it was not until the holiday was over and they were passing through Paris that St. John learned that Ibn Saud had begun his war against Hussein for the crown of the Hijaz, a possession that would enable him eventually to establish his Kingdom of Saudi Arabia. The immediate cause for his sudden attack was Hussein's assumption of the title Caliph of Islam, the rulership of all Islam, that theocracy of perhaps four hundred million souls in the band of Moslem states extending from Morocco and the Atlantic Ocean to the Dutch East Indies and the Pacific. Ibn Saud's reaction had been to call to action the Ikhwan, which numbered perhaps eighteen thousand warriors, mainly cavalry with some pack artillery. To divert and split Hussein's army, which had British officers, Ibn Saud had sent one force against Abdullah in Jordan and another against Feisal in Iraq — actions that invited British intervention. Ibn Saud's main force had entered the Hijaz and was advancing against the holy cities of Mecca, Medina, and the Red Sea port of Jidda. Much slaughter was reported as the Ikhwan slew Hashemite Moslems in flight from the holy cities toward Jidda.

When Philby reached London, the news was almost complete. Ibn Saud, escorted by his bodyguard of Sudanese in scarlet and gold, had entered Mecca for the first time. King Hussein had abdicated in favor of his eldest son, Prince Ali, and was fleeing the port in his yacht, taking his treasury (British sovereigns soldered into petrol tins) with him. He was seeking sanctuary at Aqaba, Abdullah's port on the Red Sea. Here was momentous news for Philby. Would Ibn Saud not now proclaim himself the new caliph? In theory, at least, and perhaps also in fact if he wished, the caliphate would make him the most powerful figure in Islam. Indeed, he might now emerge as one of the most powerful spiritual leaders in the world. Philby saw his chance for personal fame and power in these developments, to say nothing of the trade and mining concessions he might obtain for Fisher's company of merchant venturers. On reaching London, he resolved to go immediately to Jidda to be on hand when his great friend — and Ibn Saud was a great friend — entered the city.

Philby's actions are now open to several interpretations. St. John was still a British official, subject to the discipline and the orders of his service. Above all, he was not to involve himself in matters of policy without the authority of the government; and at that moment his government considered sending a military force to Arabia to restore or support the Hashemite dynasty and to frustrate Ibn Saud in his attempt to impose his authority over the peninsula. In all his actions during his expedition to Jidda, therefore, Philby was acting contrary to the interests of his government. To prevent its taking action to restrain him, consequently, he acted in secrecy.

He had known Ali in Jordan, and so he proposed to the Hijazi agent in London that he go to Jidda and mediate between Ibn Saud and Ali. Despite pressure from the Foreign Office, the Hijazi accepted the offer and begged Philby to leave on the wings of speed. But he had no cash for such an expedition. Nor, it seems, did the Hijazi agent. To raise the money, Philby proposed to the famous explorer Rosita Forbes, whom he knew, that they jointly but separately go to Arabia to explore the Empty Quarter, the great desert of South Arabia, which had not yet been crossed by Occidentals. This, of course, was no more than a cover to enable him to reach Ibn Saud.

Miss Forbes, a woman who was game for any high adventure if it would provide her with money and material for a book, began to seek ways to finance the expedition; she succeeded. In those days of the Lawrentian saga, a woman adventuring into so dangerous a part of the world as Arabia was worth her weight in gold to the print, and a London press lord, Burnham of the *Daily Telegraph,* put up what Philby called "the magnificent sum of £4,000 for the venture." Departure: October 1924. The contracts signed and Lord Burnham's money in his pocket, Philby arranged with Rosita Forbes to leave England secretly and separately and meet on the Persian Gulf; she would travel by way of Syria and Iraq, he through Marseilles and Alexandria to the Red Sea.

In Egypt, half expecting to be detained by the British authorities, Philby boarded the steamer S.S. *Registan,* behaving as if he were a secret agent. "I wonder if the Foreign Office and all that crowd have got news of my movements," he wrote to May on October 24, from

Port Said. "I don't suppose they care very much now what happens out there, which is all to the good for me." Philby erred. The government did care what happened in Arabia, and its agents watched his movements. When the *Registan* reached Jidda on October 28, the captain took the ship as close to shore as he dared, and a boat sent by King Ali put out to take Philby into the port. As Philby felt able to tell May, "Ali was delighted to see me and fell on my neck and all the big men here have showed me very plainly that they expect great results from my visit." Burnham's expedition was forgotten for the moment, with Ibn Saud's Ikhwan, their war banners still unfurled, waiting outside the Meccan Gate of Jidda for Ibn Saud's order to take the port. Ali had seen to it that Philby was given what he described as "a lovely suite of apartments (three rooms & bathroom) on the third floor of the house next to the King's." It was the first time he had been back in Jidda since Yuletide of 1917. He wrote again to May on October 28:

> I feel very happy to be again on Arabian soil. A country so full of interest gets hold of one — one cant help it and I always feel miserable in England as, when there, I am of course kept strictly out of all Arabian news, etc. No! This is the country for me especially at such an interesting time as the present. You know I would make any sacrifice for you & Dora & the family but I would be miserable to give up my lifework and you all would suffer in the long run . . . After all it was an accident of fate that brought me into touch with Arabia & the best man is the man who makes best use of the chances he gets. Considering that Government has been against me all along I have really not done so badly & (with the possible exception of Lawrence) there is no man who has made a bigger mark than me in the Arabian sphere. It would be absurd to give it all up.

The British agent in the port, a Trinity friend of Philby's named Reader Bullard, received Philby unhappily. Fearing that Ibn Saud intended to conquer all Arabia whatever the British position, Bullard wrote to Philby advising him that the British government could not permit him "to go into the interior owing to the disturbed state of things in Central Arabia." On October 29 Bullard sent for St. John to ask what he was doing in Jidda. Receiving no satisfactory answer, Bullard became suspicious that Philby was a spy for Ibn Saud and raised the question of the "morality" of his business. Bullard reminded Philby that he was still a crown servant, but Philby dismissed these concerns by saying that the question of moral considerations did not "wash with me." Thereupon Reader Bullard presented Philby with a signal from London:

In the event of Mr Philby evincing any disposition to disobey orders
of H.M.G. you should inform him that the Secretary of State for India
is party to these orders and desires to impress upon him that . . . any
disobedience to orders will be viewed in serious light. Mr. Philby will
remember that the ordinary sequel to disobedience to direct orders
is dismissal.*6

Serious business. Moreover, when Ibn Saud himself realized that
Philby might attempt to get through the lines as a peace envoy, he
warned "our dear loving Mr. Philby," in a letter dated December 10,
1924, against trying that.

If there is something personal you are welcome to discuss it with me
personally. If however there is something that pertains to the Hijaz
and you wish to act as a mediator, I would suggest your holding aloof
from it. As you will observe, it is a purely Islamic problem in which
your mediation will be uncalled for.[7]

Philby's business in Jidda — his intention to obtain a peaceful settlement between Ibn Saud and Ali, negotiate permission for his expedition to enter the Empty Quarter, and introduce the matter of concessions for Remy Fisher's company — thus came to a dead end. But he
waited in hope and while doing so he encountered a familiar face at
King Ali's palace. Sayid Talib, Philby's minister at the Interior Department of the government of Iraq, appeared from nowhere as an adviser
in Iraqi affairs to King Ali. With a man like Talib, whom Philby had
called "an accomplished villain," anything was possible, and Philby
may well have had cause to regret having set eyes on him again. On
Christmas Eve, 1924, Talib gave Philby a pot of caviar; he devoured it
with relish and then collapsed. He attributed his illness to what he
called "a frightful attack" of dysentery, although there was a story that
Talib had poisoned the caviar as revenge for his arrest and deportation
after his tea with Lady Cox. Philby was prostrate for days on end,
sustained only by special food prepared for him in Reader Bullard's
kitchens. To make his condition worse, a local physician inoculated
him with what proved to have been a dirty needle, and Philby developed gangrene in his arm.

By the New Year Philby seemed more dead than alive, despite his
claim to an iron stomach. Bullard arranged his transfer to Aden, where

*Technically Philby was a crown servant until May 25, 1925, at which point his terminal
leave would expire. He could then do as he pleased, although in a real sense the crown
retained control over him for life. Since his pension was a royal gift paid to him by the
government of India, it could be withheld or removed should Philby give cause.

the British had a good hospital. Relieved to have seen the last of his troublesome friend, Bullard advised the Foreign Office of St. John's departure and noted that, in both sickness and health, Philby's hot rage against the British government was "a simple dualism in which the powers of darkness are represented by H.M.G."[8] At Aden, Philby recovered and, as had been arranged, was joined by Miss Forbes, who was still game to cross the Empty Quarter on behalf of Lord Burnham. But the British security authorities, always vigilant for adventurers at Aden, detected that they were preparing to enter Arabia by the back door. The governor "confronted" Philby with what St. John felt were "peremptory orders from the British Government" not to attempt to enter the Arabian interior, again on pain of dismissal and loss of pension rights. The expedition then collapsed, increasing Philby's already heavy debts by the £600 of Lord Burnham's money that he and Miss Forbes had spent.

When Philby returned to England, Dora was biting in her criticism of him: he had wasted five months of paid leave and still had no job. He had further damaged his reputation inside Whitehall by his persistent meddling in Arabic politics. To pay his debt to Lord Burnham, Philby obtained from Constable, the London publishers, an advance to write a book called *Arabian Mandates*. This might have given Philby some respite from Dora and his creditors, but the manuscript contained such intemperate language about the British government that Constable had to ask him to tone it down. By the time this was done in 1925, the work had fallen out of date, so Constable canceled the contract and demanded its money back. Philby had to find a a new Peter to pay Paul. Close to despair, he sought out Major Fisher, who had interesting news.[9]

By now — 1925 — Remy Fisher's plan for the establishment of Sharquieh Limited had developed substance. What Fisher wished was to interest another company, Midian Limited, whose origins lay in an exploration that Sir Richard Burton, one of the greatest of the Arabian explorers of Queen Victoria's time, had undertaken for Ismail Pasha, Viceroy of Egypt in 1879 in the Land of Midian, a region of the Middle East extending from northern Arabia to eastern Palestine. Burton had reported enthusiastically on the mineral possibilities of the region, but nothing eventuated, although there was much speculation about gold and copper deposits and some other oil and minerals.

Philby succeeded in introducing Fisher to Midian's directors, who agreed to take up two thousand ten-shilling shares provided that the company was represented on Sharquieh's board of management, and Philby was employed to obtain the concessions. Two Midian directors were appointed to Sharquieh's board, and Philby was appointed to the post of Jidda representative at a salary of £1,200 a year, a fairly good wage. His appointment would last for three years in the first instance, and he was awarded a holding of five thousand shares. These would become some of his most valuable assets, but not for a long time. Philby obtained an advance of £750 to enable him to go to Jidda "to spy out the land."[10] Fisher interested himself in Kim and offered, should he fail at Westminster, to employ him in agricultural scientific work on his estate along the Guadalquivir River in Spain.

No longer a civil servant, Philby arrived in Jidda in late October 1925 to establish Sharquieh. He wrote to May, "My own darling little Mother," on the twenty-ninth to give his views on the futility of the slaughter of World War I and to record the nature of his reception by the new British consul, S. R. Jordan, who was no more welcoming than his predecessors. As Philby wrote:

> The British Government has at last taken notice of my being here and yesterday sent me a message through the consul deprecating my discussing politics with the Arabs here and criticising British policy. The message also reminds me that the orders against my going into the interior, which were sent to me last year, still hold good! They don't seem to realise that I am now a free man. However I am not worrying much about the message & am only lost in wonder at the importance they attach to my actions and movements.[11]

Disregarding the consul, and occasionally making political war against him, Philby set about his plans to see Ibn Saud concerning Fisher's desire for concessions. These contacts were made as if they were secret matters, as they were. As Philby himself related in his memoirs, *Arabian Days*, contact with Ibn Saud was established through the agency of the leader of an official Persian mission to Ibn Saud's court. He sent "a secret message" to Ibn Saud asking for a meeting and received "an affirmative reply," suggesting that Philby go by sea to Rabigh, a fishing port farther up the Red Sea. There he would find an escort waiting to take him to Ibn Saud at Shumaisi, the point closest to Mecca that could be visited by an infidel.

By mid-November Philby's plans for his journey to Rabigh were complete, with the help of Arab friends and at least one of Ibn Saud's agents. The subterfuge was necessary evidently because Ibn Saud had not finished his desert war with the Hashemites. All he had done was to stop the campaign while he established whether the British would intervene against him and to allow the Ikhwan to rest and their camel corps to restore themselves with the sweet green grass of autumn. But the autumn equinox spelled the start of the cool season, the campaign season, and all knew that it would not be long before Ibn Saud struck at Jidda, thereby completing his conquests of the three main Arabian provinces. The British consulate feared that Philby would contrive to visit Ibn Saud and give away the secrets of Jidda's feeble defenses — to say nothing of what he knew about British capabilities and intentions — and so, as he remembered in *Arabian Days:*

> At dead of night on the date fixed, all the lights were left on in my rooms to create the impression that I was in residence as usual, while my baggage was being trundled or carried through the dark streets to the quay, whence I was soon sailing northwards under the very nose of a Dutch cruiser, which happened to be entertaining all the international rank and fashion of Jidda in honour of its visit to the port. My little *sambuck* — a sailing boat of some fifteen tons — did not disturb the festivities, and, after a somewhat stormy passage, the third day brought me to the jetty at Rabigh.

On November 28, Philby met with Ibn Saud alone for the first time since 1921 at Uqair, where they had arranged the demise of Rashid Ali of Hail. He found the Emir of the Nejd — as Ibn Saud now called himself, displaying something of the present Arabian fondness for royal titles — greatly changed. In 1922 he had contracted a severe form of St. Anthony's Fire, erysipelas, a streptococcal infection for which Arabian medicine had no remedy. The infection spread over his face and ended in his left eye, the sight of which he lost, and his handsome features were badly scarred. This was particularly marked when, as was often, he wore his grim look, but it was alleviated when he flashed his radiant, captivating smile. Nevertheless, Philby found his friend's appearance unnerving, for Ibn Saud had replaced his lost eye with a glass one, and its "stare was always disconcerting to strangers," the more so since Ibn Saud's "good eye was always hawk-like, but one never knew which way it was looking."

Philby found Ibn Saud determined to destroy what remained of the Hashemite dynasty in Arabia. To that end, Philby committed what was in any language an act of espionage in Ibn Saud's interest. He told Ibn Saud that King Ali had small armored and air forces manned by German and Russian mercenaries — important news. They were, he advised, "in a military sense, quite incapable of putting up any serious opposition, and the great majority of the people would be only too glad to see an end put to their sufferings and hopeless situation." Otherwise, Ali's army consisted mainly of destitute West African pilgrims and a pox-ridden battalion of Hashemite infantry brought down from Syria. They could not resist any determined attack, the more so since Jidda was so short of food that "the poor were reduced to begging for brackish water and sifting the dung of horses for undigested grains of barley."

Having dealt with the political and military situation, Philby then turned to the question of Sharquieh's concessions. He had been commissioned, he said, by a "powerful syndicate" to ask for preferment. When Ibn Saud asked what sort of concessions he had in mind, Philby replied that Sharquieh would like to establish a state bank, build the Mecca-Medina link of the Hijaz Railway, and develop certain minerals. Oil was not, it appears, mentioned specifically, for it was as yet no more than petroliferous traces in the desert and the sea. But the gold and iron deposits were mentioned, although in the event there was more of the former than the latter. Ibn Saud agreed to all this, according to Philby.

As they talked in their tent, a Hijazi Bristol Bulldog flew overhead on a reconnaissance, unloaded a few two-pound high-explosive bombs, wheeled, and flew back toward Jidda. Fearing that Ibn Saud's headquarters had been betrayed, the men left the meeting. Almost immediately afterward perhaps five thousand Ikhwan besieging Jidda suddenly attacked over the old walls of the port. King Ali sent in his armored cars, but the Ikhwan — "these mad fanatics," as one observer called them — attacked them barehanded, and they were stopped by the mangled corpses of the Ikhwan. The tank crews were dragged out by the mob and cut to pieces. The Bulldogs bombed the Ikhwan lines, not without success, but when some of them were brought down by rifle fire, their Russian pilots met the same end as the tank crews.

Philby did not return immediately to Jidda, for he did not wish to be there when Ibn Saud's army attacked the city, in case he was accused of having encouraged the attack, if not by the Arabs then by the Ikhwan, and if not by the Ikhwan then by Whitehall. Instead, he sailed for Port Sudan, on the other side of the Red Sea, traveling by *sambouk* laden with a cargo of shells for the Italian mother-of-pearl industry. Surviving a tempest that very nearly sank the fifty-ton boat, Philby reached his destination and celebrated Christmas with some English friends, lurking beyond the reach of the consul at Jidda until he received word that the green flag of the Wahhabi flew over the port.

That happened on December 17, when a party of Jidda notables rode from the port to Ragamah, a simple farm at the ten-kilometer stone outside Jidda, to negotiate an armistice with Ibn Saud.

It was the end for the Hashemites in the Hijaz. Ali left Jidda quietly on December 20, 1925, in the sloop *Cornflower,* to join his brother, King Feisal of Iraq. A tented pavilion was built outside Jidda's walls in the gardens of the Kandara Villa, owned by the Saggqaf family, rich traders in the Far East who had fled the Hijaz at the prospect of encountering the advancing Ikhwan. Here, on December 23, the notables of the Hijaz paid homage to the King of the Nejd, as Ibn Saud was now styled. The next day, Ibn Saud entered Jidda on horseback through the Medina Gate and went to the Nassif house, the home of the leading citizen of Jidda and a good friend of Philby's. There the constitution of the new kingdom was debated. The Hijazi were not willing to be incorporated into the Nejd, but they would accept Ibn Saud as the sovereign of a dual polity, Hijaz and Nejd. Thus Ibn Saud became King of the Hijaz and Nejd. A little later a wholly new political entity arose, the Kingdom of Saudi Arabia, with Ibn Saud as monarch.

On December 29, when the news reached Philby at Port Sudan that it was safe for him to enter Jidda, he sailed immediately. He met the Ikhwan, decked with the glory of their triumph against the hated Hussein; they controlled the port, and Philby was not welcome. They regarded him as *nasrani,* a Christian, a follower of the Man of Nazareth. Ibn Saud's administration, such as it was, was wholly Nejdi Wahhabi, who thought their mission divinely inspired by Allah's will. They had wanted to kill all *nasrani* and *mushriquin,* the lax Moslems of the Hijaz, but Ibn Saud, fearful of British intervention, intervened and directed them instead to teach the Hijazis their austere religious belief. Many of the Ikhwan became religious police to compel all in the province to strict obedience. All who were there then spoke of the need to speak with hushed voices. The Ikhwan were deadly serious. They did not laugh. Their law was the divine command, taken directly from God's revelation to the Prophet. Strict obedience would be the only rule in the country singled out by God as His Holy Land. Even Ibn Saud, their *imam,* their spiritual and temporal leader, began his reign under severe constraints, although the Ikhwan recognized him as the greatest Arab since the Prophet. The five daily prayers would be strictly performed in the mosque. Smoking tobacco, drinking alcohol, dressing up in fine attire, music — all was banned as sinful. All the Hijaz males were required to grow beards like the Prophet's. The Wahhab could not interfere with Philby and the rest of the minute Christian community at

Jidda as long as their behavior was seemly. But the rhythm of public life slowed to that of the Wahhab warriors, and puritanism governed it again as in the seventh century of the Prophet.

Little of this affected Philby at first. As *nasrani,* he was not allowed to attend the king's coronation at Mecca. But Ibn Saud did choose him to arrange the seating at the coronation banquet in Jidda. The small diplomatic, commercial, and political elect in that tiny enclave, to say nothing of the Ikhwan, interpreted this correctly as a sign of royal regard for Philby. Philby was beside himself with excitement at "my king's" triumph, for the capture of the Hijaz was indeed the greatest triumph of Ibn Saud's career, and undoubtedly Philby had facilitated victory without going as far as to provoke British intervention. Afterward St. John wrote a letter home, what he called "An Epistle to the Philbians," as if his family were a religious sect:

> The news of Ibn Saud's accession to the kingship was made official and the Wahhabi flagstaffs were all gay with bunting while the salute of 101 guns (just a little ragged it was) proclaimed to the world that Jack was right again. But of course he always is! In the afternoon there was a reception at the Government Offices, our friend, Dr. Abdullah, who arrived the same day to take up the post of Viceroy of Jidda (!), doing the honours on behalf of his royal master. From my point of view nobody could be better than Abdullah so I rejoice and he is very friendly. The other day he sent a huge basket of fruit (oranges, bananas and pomegranates) from Mecca and today he gave me almost a complete set of Wahhabi stamps, one each of 67 varieties. I believe the complete set is 75 varieties, so I have with me a complete set [of them] all except 8 and of these 8 you have 3 (the little yellow-brown Turkish 5 p. stamps with crescent).[12]

The business about the stamps was soon to be of some importance in the Philby family's life. As for the British government, the news of Ibn Saud's coronation "ought to give the Colonial Office cold shudders down the spine." It did, for the British fear of the Third Wahhabi Revival was much stimulated in Whitehall by Ibn Saud's quick victory. He was, Philby wrote, "delighted — step by step my views are slowly being justified before the world." He enclosed the stamps, which had value, for Dora to sell at auction in London. Seeking to give the impression that his future was bright, St. John reported that he had been asked to arrange the manufacture in England of the coinage of the new realm.

Thus St. John Philby became a merchant of Jidda, with a Royal Assent for concessions. Later, he would become the man who, through big oil and his influence with the king, would make America rich and powerful, or at least richer and more powerful. And remembering Kim's birthday just in time, Philby wrote triumphantly from Jidda on January 1, 1926:

> Very many happy returns of the day and a very happy New Year to you. You are fourteen today but it seems ages since that New Year's Day at Ambala when you first arrived on the scene and in your short life time the whole world has been turned upside down and inside out. It is still struggling to get straight again and I hope that by the time you have finished with Westminster and Trinity everything will have smoothed out a bit. I wonder what your career will be. It was easy enough when you were born to make plans for the educational part of your life and I am glad to say that so far those plans have been successfully carried out and I am sure that . . . you will do very well. But I wonder what you will be doing ten years hence!

What indeed.

In March 1926, Philby left Jidda for London to report to Fisher on commercial prospects in the new kingdom. He was not discouraging, despite the Ikhwan's rejection of all Western ideas and trade. As evidence of the prospects, he produced a contract of sorts from the Viceroy of the Hijaz for the manufacture of the king's new coinage, a contract that would be canceled by Ibn Saud at the demand of the Ikhwan. Nonetheless, Fisher proceeded with the formal establishment of Sharquieh Limited. By October he had raised £10,000 (about $50,000). The board included two directors of Midian Limited, who claimed title to King Solomon's Mines in the mountains of northern Arabia. And Philby accepted Fisher's confirmed offer to be the company's agent near the court of Ibn Saud. His salary was half what he had received while in crown service, but he thought he could manage — provided he obtained the king's permission to import telephone and telegraph systems, automobiles, and a postal system. Then he would receive important commissions. He may have judged that such contracts as these were not more than vapor, for the Ikhwan had not the slightest intention of letting in such unholy contraptions, but there is no record that he warned Fisher or the other members of the syndicate.

As if to rehabilitate him in the official London world, his friend Sir Alexander Kennedy, an archaeologist and a specialist in the Midian and the caravan trade of the vanished Nabateans, arranged Philby's membership in the Athenaeum, a club with connections with the Royal

Society founded in 1824 for, according to its charter, "the association of individuals known for their scientific and literary attainments, artists of eminence in any class of the fine arts and noblemen and gentlemen distinguished as liberal patrons of science, literature or the arts." Philby's double-quick membership in that august institution — most aspirants had to wait seven years to become members, some waited forever; Philby got in through a short circuit open only to "candidates of distinction" — represented a milestone in the Philby case. The Athenaeum was then an institution where a member could not be expelled for his views, only for disgrace or immorality. Kennedy is said to have told Dora Philby that St. John had had "more signatures on his paper than any other candidate balloted for." This statement would indicate that in the world beyond Whitehall, Philby remained well regarded, although at the Foreign, Colonial, and India Offices his name remained an anathema.

In these circumstances, Philby became something of a catch for Fisher, who was ever vigilant for influential Britons who might be of use to his aspirations for acceptance in high places. Philby became acquainted not only with Fisher's wealth but also his problems; these became important now that Kim was growing up. It emerged that Fisher's great burden in life was his wife, a well-to-do Frenchwoman he had married in Cairo and who had become a devout member of the Third Degree of the Benedictines, the female branch of that Catholic order, famous for its sung liturgy. There had been little in the way of marital relations between them, and Madame Fisher would not or could not bear him children. It further happened that Fisher had approached a friend, the wife of the Imperial Russian naval attaché in Cairo, and employed her to provide him with two children, a boy and a girl. The boy was born in November 1918, the girl in December 1920. Fisher had persuaded his wife to accept the children as her own, and this she had done. But by 1926 Madame Fisher had become ever more devout, and Fisher, believing that his wife was raising the children in bigotry, decided to remove them from her influence and bring them to England to be raised in a culture that Fisher admired.

Such was the relationship between Major Fisher and both St. John and Dora Philby that late one evening in May 1926 Philby heard a violent hammering on the front door of the Philbians' new home at 18 Acol Road, West Hampstead; he found Fisher on his doorstep with his children. Fisher explained that he had just removed them from the custody of his wife at their estate near St. Jean de Luz. Would St.

John kindly allow them to lodge at the Philbys' for a short time, as he was truly afraid of his wife's influence over them? St. John and Dora agreed immediately. The house was large, Kim was boarding at Westminster, and the two Fisher children would find companionship in the Philby daughters. The Fisher children moved in that night with their governess, a Miss Pattinson, and there they remained for seventeen months, until September 1928, when both entered boarding schools. All that Miss Fisher remembered of her long stay at the Philbys' was that when St. John was there "the place was like a bedlam, with noisy political arguments at table, and long discourses on life with the Arabs and British policy in the Middle East." These were of such a nature that when Kim was home, he "seemed to us to be enraptured by his father's voice, his accomplishments, his thoughts on society and Mr. Philby's unending denunciations of some of the more famous of his colleagues in the Middle East during the late war." Otherwise, "Dora Philby and her daughters were wonderful to us," but "Kim was perfectly beastly — a torment." The house was "furnished in ramshackle fashion and it had a long narrow garden at the back." At Fisher's request his wife was allowed to see the children only rarely, and Fisher asked that they should not be given any religious instruction at the Philbys' home. This suited St. John entirely, as, according to the girl, the household was "quite without religious atmosphere."

The Fisher children were still in residence when, in October 1926, Philby returned to Jidda as the agent for Sharquieh, abandoning his family to live the life of a sheikh. He never formally separated from Dora, nor did she divorce him, although he gave her much cause. Indeed, they remained devoted to each other for the rest of their lives. He continued to support his family as best he could, and he continued to adore his children, although for a time he regarded his son as a physical and intellectual weakling while forever busying himself with his education and career. Such became his financial predicament in Jidda that Philby did not return to England until, it seems, 1932. Between 1926 and 1929, Fisher, consequently, became a surrogate father for Kim and his sisters. He sought also to become the lover of Dora, not without St. John's encouragement, for as Philby said before he left, Fisher was so rich that such an arrangement would suit everyone's purposes. Fisher, it appears, fell genuinely in love with Dora when she became a grass widow. Had St. John shown any interest in leading a normal existence, there is no doubt that Dora would have remained loyal to him. But Dora saw more of Fisher than she desired. He named an island on the Guadalquivir River after her; and during

St. John's poverty-stricken years in Jidda, between 1926 and 1931, Fisher did much to relieve her trials. She, always in straits, accepted several family holidays at his expense and, once, a fee for furnishing a house for him. He may well have paid for, or at least subsidized, Kim's education. Writing to Philby in Jidda, Fisher conveyed something of his regard for Dora and his reasons for parking his children with the Philbys:

> The atmosphere of your house, the healthy ring of the children's mirth, the tact and ease of your wife in the performance of household duties, have, I think, drawn me a little closer to both of you. You have something very precious there and I, whose happiness is not of the same nature, would like to see my friends not make a wreck of theirs.

Remy Fisher's association with Dora and the Philby children extended almost the span of Kim's time at Westminster, which lasted until late 1929, when Kim was seventeen and ready for Trinity College. Dora seems never to have had the same affection for Fisher that he had for her, and in the period immediately before his sudden death in London, early in 1931, she found the relationship, as she wrote in a letter, "terribly trying." The reason for this irritation was, doubtless, that Fisher's marriage had come to an end; Madame Fisher had obtained a papal separation from her husband, and plainly he had Dora in mind as her successor, or at least his mistress. But that could not be: Madame Fisher was far too devout a Catholic to permit a formal divorce.

Fisher appeared ever more frequently at the Philbys', and they at his estate in southwestern France. His children believed that Dora became his mistress, although this is denied by St. John's biographer, Elizabeth Monroe. Dora did become a main beneficiary in Fisher's will, although it is evident that when she declined to divorce St. John and Fisher transferred his affections to the wife of the agent of Thomas Cook & Sons, he cut Dora out. This was by no means the end of the entanglement between the Fisher and Philby families. When Fisher did die, Dora's successor in his affections brought suit to enforce his will, and this led to an involvement in Fisher's affairs of that distinguished courtier at Buckingham Palace, Sir Alexander Hardinge.

No man could have acquitted himself of a more difficult task. Between 1931 and 1952, the Fisher estate was the subject of constant complicated legal and fiscal problems, and these Hardinge dealt with faithfully through his own private solicitors, Withers & Company. He accepted Fisher's children completely into his family, and they spent their holidays with Hardinge and his wife and family or, when his duties required his attendance upon the royal family, with the king and the queen and their children at Balmoral and Windsor. Queen Mary, the Queen Mother, took a great interest in their welfare, and France Farmer, Fisher's daughter, claimed that she became friendly with the royal princess, Elizabeth, the future Queen Elizabeth II, and her sister, Princess Margaret.

Beyond this, according to a daughter of France Farmer, Kim Philby and her mother "grew up together," although Mrs. Farmer was at pains to state that after she and her brother left Acol Road, in September 1928, she saw little of Kim. They did remain good friends even as late as 1963, thirty-five years on. And, as she stated, she went on holiday with the Philby children, once, she recalled, to the Isle of Wight. But she had not "grown up" with Kim, as her daughter said, and certainly Kim never visited St. James's Palace while they lived there between 1931 and 1941.

The actual facts are obscured by time, but they are important in the history of the Philby case of conspiracy against the established order — against the crown, the court, the administration, the intelligence, security, and police authorities, and the interests of the middle and upper classes, on which the power of the crown rested. If at the end of the century the crown's influence had diminished, in the 1930s and 1940s it dominated the social order and was important in Kim Philby's scheme of things. It represented the enemy that was to be destroyed. Between 1933 and 1941, France Fisher represented access to the political affairs and movements of the royal family if Kim chose to exploit it. In his political activities, the palace and its personalities provided names that could be dropped, gossip with which to spice talks with persons who might be of use to him. Above all it showed that he too had *connections* — in a day and age when such connections could be important.

This has its sinister aspects. As some young men interested themselves in the history of the American or the French Revolution, so young Philby, it is evident from his library in Moscow, studied the aspects of the Russian Revolution before Lenin. That revolution began with the murder of Tsar Alexander II in Petersburg on March 1, 1881, four years before St. John's birth, by the Narodnaya Volya (the People's Will), the leading extreme Russian movement before Lenin. This action ultimately provided Lenin with a body of clandestine doctrine that guided him as he completed the work of the People's Will in October 1917, with his capturing of the Russian power and the mur-

der of the Romanovs, the royal family. Kim Philby's maxim in politics
became that of the leader of the Narodniks, A. I. Zhelyabov: "History
moves too slowly. It needs a push."[13]

St. John Philby arrived in Jidda to take up permanent residence in
1926. In reward for his services to the Wahhab dynasty, Ibn Saud gave
him the Beit Baghdadi, the former residence of the Wali, the Turks'
holy man of the Hijaz. This palace had some sixty rooms, which Philby
guarded against prowling pilgrims with teams of baboons. The king
sought to honor his agreement for Philby to trade in Arabia, but it
proved worthless. Such was the power of the Ikhwan, their determina-
tion to prevent the importation of Western goods and ideas, and such
was the king's poverty — to say nothing of the Moslem law that forbade any trade based on usury — that Philby found himself reduced
to the status of a beachcomber. He was pinned to the little enclave of
Jidda by the Ikhwan. The king dared not command Philby to an audience at Mecca, forty-five miles away: even an absolute monarch was
forced to temporize with the Ikhwan lest they accuse him of being
tempted by worldly gain to neglect the interests of God. Philby did
have a telephone in the Beit Baghdadi, despite the Ikhwan's proscrip-
tion of such devices, and it enabled him to discuss matters of state with
the king at Mecca. But he could not undertake any real negotiation
or trade.

He received several notices that the king proposed to build a network of Marconi wireless stations by which to maintain the security
and integrity of the kingdom. This would have justified St. John in the
eyes of his backers, but nothing came of it, at least for the moment.
There was also talk about telephones, fire engines, harbor launches,
uniforms, machine guns, and airplanes. But again nothing came St.
John's way, again largely through the influence of the Ikhwan. For the
next five years Philby was permitted to import only trifles — biscuits,
aspirin, perambulators, secondhand cars, tires, a copy or two of *Encyclopaedia Britannica,* telephone wire, and used harbor boats. He had
commuted his pension so that he could take out a mortgage on the
house in West Hempstead, thus leaving Dora with only £375 a year
with which to pay the mortgage, heat the house, and feed the children.
It was not enough, Philby knew, and so, with little else to do except
sip coffee and twist his prayer beads with the Arab notables, he recalled
the incident at the coronation when the first vice-regent of Jidda gave
him some old Hashemite postage stamps. He began to look for more

to sell through Stanley Gibbons, a stamp dealer in London, and he found them. As he wrote to Dora:

> Stick to the Wahhabi stamps you have got. The stock is rapidly running out here and one can only get a few kinds in the Post Office. I fancy one or two wise people (including the Prime Minister) are making a corner of them.

A little later, in a further letter, St. John announced that he had had

> a great bit of luck in discovering a new series of Wahhabi stamps of which I don't think any of the Europeans here knows anything! I was in the Post Office enquiring about stamps when one of the clerks said to me: Would you care for any *used* Medina stamps? I thought he meant the "Commemoration of the capture of Medina" series and said yes. Well what will you pay for them? Oh said I what do you want for them? Anything you like he replied. So I said carelessly I will give you the face value. Very well said he and he produced the stamps about 13 of them for which I paid 23 pence and when I looked at them they were not the "Commemoration" issue at all but stamps actually overprinted *at Medina* with the words "The Saudian Sultanate of Najd"—just a temporary local issue of which nobody here yet knows anything and which is likely to be rare. Among the 13 stamps are 5 different kinds and I have asked the man to send to Medina for more, so I hope to get a complete set.

He did get a complete set, and the house and the children were safe for another year.

He then withdrew from stamps and turned to Red Sea and Persian Gulf pearls, the best of which had great value. There were many such transactions, most of them conducted secretly in order to escape the eagle eyes of the Ikhwan, to say nothing of the English excise. His first consignment, sent by the hand of the purser of a steamer that called at Jidda regularly on its way between Bombay and London, consisted of an odd lot of six pearls. These he bought in the Jidda market for about two shillings each; Dora sold them in London for between £4 and £5 each — a profit of 400 to 500 percent. A large part of the cost of keeping Kim at Westminster may well have been met by the proceeds of these pearl sales, for in all, Philby's correspondence shows, he sent 1,200 pearls which he bought for £50, 1,800 for £32, and two earrings at £10. But as he wrote to Dora on January 27, 1927, he had begun to understand "the state of mind of a beachcomber in the South Sea Islands."

There was a brief bright glint of trade early in 1927. The king again put out a tender for new small change in his kingdom when he found Hussein's head on the old coinage. St. John hoped to have the small change contract, but the king ruled this out, stating that the coinage was to be made by the British government. This puzzled and bothered Philby, and he saw Palestinian politics at work again:

> As [the king] is still at Mecca I can't understand why he has done it but I suppose he thinks that the British Government may ask him to be King of Palestine if he gives it a sop or two like this! However as I have said often [in dealings with Arabs] patience is the only thing.

St. John's self-confidence and self-esteem began to decline. The sullen silence of Kim, who now rarely wrote, the unending glare, heat, and flies, the severe and savage landscape, the Ikhwan, who shunned him, the British community, which blackballed him, the prospect that he might never get home and that if he did he would go as a Distressed British Subject, the pennilessness of his family in Hampstead, the silence of the king and his ministers — all produced self-doubt. Yet he never lost that air of effortless superiority of the Westminster and Trinity graduate. He always appeared in public with his heavy beard well trimmed, his Arab habit as white as the washerwomen could make it, the nails of his pink feet in leather sandals well cut. He maintained an exhausting correspondence with his family and his friends at home, his letters all written in that minutely neat Trinity script about everything under the sun — birds, the heat, bugs, flora, his servants, his consorts (of whom there were several), the arrivals and the departures of the Red Sea steamers, his bridge parties. It went on year after year, usually conveying the impression of a busy man in good heart. He would insist that he alone was right concerning the Arabs, and his optimism sounded boundless. In a town where everyone seemed to die young, he claimed his iron innards alone held up despite the assault of all manner of microbes. He became less diffident in the presence of the Ikhwan, who prowled the alleys in small parties, carrying long canes with which to beat the idolaters; he had violent, finger-wagging shouting matches with them about *their* misdemeanors. Yet his temper shortened, he drank and smoked his pipes heavily — in a town where alcohol and tobacco were forbidden. He made an English garden from marigold seeds and golden mohur trees from India. He spent much of his day in a dark room, to escape the flies, and he slept on the roof of his palace to catch the fair breezes of the Red Sea, which alone seemed to make life pleasant. He made war against the little British community in that silent, steamy, rotting, malodorous place, preferring the company of the Arab merchants and scholars at Jidda, although at first he did see much of the Dutch vice-consul, Colonel D. Van Der Meulen, a notable Arabist and student of Islam, who had arrived in Jidda just before Philby. His main work was to attend to the many Moslem pilgrims who came to Jidda each year from the Dutch East Indies. Meulen wrote:

> For me H. St. J. B. Philby was new. I had only known him as the author of *The Heart of Arabia,* but I was ready to meet him with respect, the man of such outstanding achievement as an explorer of unknown Arabia. I gladly took every opportunity to talk with this provocative person who seemed to go out of his way to oppose everything British and indeed, wherever Arab interests were concerned, openly scorned everything Western.[14]

Philby had just embarked on a triple career. First, he set out to serve the Wahhabi cause with all the means at his disposal. Second, he hoped to explore the unknown parts of Ibn Saud's expanding domain. Third, he wanted to lay a solid financial foundation for himself. Such endeavors interested Meulen, but what intrigued him most was St. John's propaganda on behalf of Ibn Saud, which entailed criticism of British policy. Meulen recorded:

> The tide of events was with Philby and made him bold. He was blessed with more conviction than is usually shown by official England. His open attacks, the retorts they provoked in the British press and the attitude of the British official representatives in Jedda provided a most interesting spectacle for me . . . The men who represented England in Jedda were no match for him. He was a very capable student of Arab affairs, and had seen more of Arabia's two leading contestants than anyone else. No English diplomatist knew more than Philby of that new source of power which had spread from the heart of Arabia until it reached the Red Sea and the Persian Gulf. Philby was the only one, too, who also had knowledge based upon long personal experience of the other, now retiring power. And Philby had freed himself from the shackles of officialdom. In the Jedda of those early days I saw him in full strength, a man free to speak and to write, armed with a wealth of information about the two-sided problem, and apparently determined to outrage English convention in dress, appearance and general social behaviour.

Weight to this statement is lent by Philby's letters to Dora. For all his dislike of the British official classes and his efforts to embarrass its officers wherever he encountered them, he admired conservative institutions whenever he felt they might benefit him personally. He lobbied unashamedly for honors, a knighthood, and even a peerage; he never abandoned his hope that one day the Labour Party would run him as a candidate for Parliament; and when his three daughters came of age, he ordered Dora to see that they were presented at Court. As he wrote from the deepest inferno of a desert in 1936, having just inflicted an almost mortal political blow upon the imperial interest:

> By the by I think you definitely ought to apply for an invitation to one of the July garden parties at Buckingham Palace. That counts as a presentation at court. So mind you arrange it to please me! And above all mind you go dressed in a fashion worthy of me!

In Meulen's view, the contrast between Philby and the British representatives was most marked. They "still lived in the glory of the declining light of British predominance in the Arab world." Philby had quit their ranks in order to attack them and what they represented. Yet

> the Arabs and we foreigners were agreed that Philby remained fundamentally very English although he tried hard to appear publicly in Jedda as a man who had cut loose from all those conventions and racial weaknesses he so insistently exposed. He doubtless convinced himself but did not entirely succeed in convincing us that he practiced what he preached . . . Philby fought against prejudice but was a most prejudiced man himself. He was a born controversialist who loved contradiction and opposition. Not understanding himself, he lacked the gift of understanding others and that may well have been the reason why he was always in conflict: with the Arabs of his caravan, with the [Saudi] government, with its policy, with his own personnel [at Sharquieh] and, I think, most of all with himself.

Meulen was uneasy that Philby might not be a wholly honest man and noted that "many onlookers" believed that "Philby was playing a double game and was in effect a British secret agent." He noted that Albert Londres, a prominent French journalist, reported to the *Petit Parisien* that Philby was "the mystery man of British Near East diplomacy, the man with the double face." Meulen and Londres were undoubtedly correct, up to a point. For as cooler heads noted in the entry on Philby in the *Dictionary of National Biography* many years later: "He firmly believed that friendship between British and Arabian governments was essential for the security and progress of the Middle East, but that the political support of Whitehall, which entailed, in his view, involvement in policies dangerous and irrelevant to Arabia and the Arabs, was fatal for an Arab." The root of Philby's ambiguity is right there, and there is good evidence that St. John replicated that same ambiguity in Kim when soon he began to deal with that dangerous band of zealots, Soviet secret agents.

Such duplicity does not make for personal popularity in remote outposts such as Jidda, where British officials were both afraid of his power and eager to hear what he had to report about Ibn Saud. Philby was frequently blackballed for his too-offensive, too-clever ways, so he spent much time in the company of the Soviet political and trade agent in the port, Hassim Hakimoff Khan, who was also a mystery man. Philby went to lengths to persuade Ibn Saud, who regarded Bolshevism as a godless ambition, to accept Hassim's credentials as a good Soviet Moslem at Jidda to help other good Soviet Moslems in the pilgrimage to Mecca. However, Hassim came to find little call for his services. He turned to trade and to the making of anti-British propaganda among the many Moslems from the empire who did make the pilgrimage. This suited Philby well. For perhaps a decade between 1928 and 1938, when Hassim vanished, a victim of the great purges in Russia, this odd couple — Hassim resembled Sydney Greenstreet in manner, bearing, and appearance, it was said — were to be found drinking sundowners together on each other's balconies overlooking the Jiddawi lagoons. These agreeable sessions may have been important politically, for in 1991 a KGB spokesman in Moscow, Colonel Oleg Tsarev, claimed that the Soviet secret service of that time, the OGPU, regarded St. John as "an Anglo agent but a Soviet asset — that is to say, a British intelligence officer who was prepared to assist Soviet causes."[15]

Given Kim Philby's later extraordinary record in the OGPU and its successors, this statement is startling but not improbable. It cannot be excluded that St. John became his son's inspirator and mentor in Kim's activities against Whitehall or that Kim's long trek to Moscow, now just beginning, started here in Jidda with Hassim. For as Tsarev also stated, he found evidence that there had been a small file on St. John tucked into Kim's personal file at KGB headquarters. This had been weeded out and replaced by an advice that showed this had been done in order to prevent anyone's concluding that St. John had been in league with Kim in his underground work for Russia.

Certainly, as Philby himself confessed in his *Arabia Jubilee* (1952), in the 1920s and 1930s he did all he could to undermine the British hegemony in the Middle East by encouraging a Soviet presence in Arabia and, later, that still more powerful anticolonial power, the United States, into the region. In the American oil industry's growing interest in the region, Philby found further opportunities for mischief against the British. He could do little for Ibn Saud until the 1915 treaty was negated. It provided specifically that Ibn Saud would refrain from entering into any agreement with any other foreign nation and would immediately notify the British government of an attempt at negotiation by any other power. Further, he would grant no concessions to any Foreign Power without the consent of the British government.

Philby began to work behind the scenes as a private individual to obtain amendments to the treaty that would permit American capital to examine Ibn Saud's mineral rights, which, Philby thought, were extensive. Perhaps there was oil; certainly there was gold and vast deposits of rich iron ore. In 1927, with Philby working behind the scenes, Ibn Saud succeeded in amending the treaty; the new version was signed by Ibn Saud and the British political agent, Gilbert Clayton.

With that abatement, Philby then went to work in 1928 in Cairo to win U.S. diplomatic recognition. This did not succeed, largely because the application might, it was believed, disturb other negotiations that seemed likely to admit the U.S. oil industry into the Persian Gulf. Also, the State Department took the view that there could be no recognition of Ibn Saud until he brought the Ikhwan under control. There was then a pause as Ibn Saud arranged to put down the Ikhwan, while Philby, acting as Ibn Saud's confidential man, left messages around the world inviting to Jidda an American multimillionaire, Charles R. Crane, who was known in high American capitalist circles as "the darling of the Arabs" and "a backer of great force."[16] This reputation derived from his sympathy for Arab nationalism, which he displayed in a report for President Woodrow Wilson on the Mandates question during a visit to the Middle East in 1920. Since then, Crane had made extensive visits to the region each cool season, and he had become especially interested in talking politics with Ibn Saud. In 1927, Crane visited Jidda, but in vain. Large elements of the Ikhwan had revolted against Ibn Saud and, Crane was told, he was in the distant deserts campaigning against the insurgents. Crane went on to Yemen, to see the imam about building a road and erecting windmills.

The American returned to the region later in 1929 but again suffered misfortune. Traveling by Chevrolets in the cool season from Basra in southern Iraq through Kuwait toward the Arabian frontier, his party was informed by an Iraqi shepherd on horseback that the Ikhwan was raiding along the Iraqi border. Crane ignored the warning. Near the Hamar Ridge, a dozen Ikhwan appeared and fired about thirty rounds at his party. The Reverend Henry Bilkert, a Christian missionary in the Kuwait area, was hit, and the Ikhwan vanished. When the group stopped, Bilkert declared calmly that he was paralyzed. The bullet had hit him in the left shoulder and passed through his spinal cord and right arm. He died as the caravan made its way to the hospital at Kuwait.[17]

Crane now abandoned any thought of trying to see Ibn Saud. Instead, he began to interest himself further in the affairs of the Imam of Yemen, Ibn Saud's rival and neighboring ruler on the Red Sea. Ibn Saud, who depended on the Christian missionaries at Kuwait to provide medical services for his people at Riyadh, denied that his Ikhwan had been involved in the incident. And he mounted a major military campaign against the very men who had made him king — the Ikhwan. Philby undoubtedly made him aware that as long as the Ikhwan placed foreign lives at risk, there could be no foreign investment in Saudi Arabia. Indeed, the United States, which had demonstrated that it might extend some form of diplomatic recognition to Ibn Saud's kingdom, indicated that, because of the Crane-Bilkert incident, it was not now prepared to do so.

Philby began to display all his political dexterity. At the end of December 1929, just after the incident, he wrote a long letter to Crane.[18] He advised that a socialist government had recently come to power in England and that relations with the new government had become "very cordial." The old British system of representation at Jidda had given way to the establishment of a British legation; Philby hinted that if the British felt Jidda to be safe enough to establish a minister there, why should the United States think otherwise? As a sign of its confidence in Ibn Saud's ability to control the tribes, the British were giving "very substantial" political and military support to Iraq, Jordan, Kuwait, and Bahrain to "mop up" the rebel Ikhwan leaders. So effective were these operations that the rebels were now "effectively surrounded by the King's forces and the various leaders are making desperate efforts to secure the King's pardon before they are finally rounded up and captured." The French and Persian governments evidently believed that the king alone ruled, for they too had established legations at Jidda.

Philby asked whether Crane would not reconsider his attitude. Would he not make another attempt to speak with Ibn Saud? He would "find a country which has gone steadily ahead with agricultural development and a Government which has really settled down to serious work to the great advantage of the pilgrims who come here yearly in ever-increasing numbers." If "I could tempt you with an invitation to come and stay with me on a purely private and personal" visit, he would find it very much to the advantage of all concerned, especially as the conditions here are greatly changed in relation to those obtaining at the time of your last visit," in 1927.

Philby was reopening the door of Arabia to Crane, but Crane did not accept the invitation. The attack on him and his friends was fresh in his mind. Moreover, he had doubtless learned that the king might be taking vigorous action against the Ikhwan but had yet to prevail.

In 1929–1930, at the time of the attack, the Ikhwan were in full-scale revolt against Ibn Saud, largely because they believed he had placed the desire for capital and the encouragement of infidels before the interests of God. The British government, the main foreign power in the region, had feared this ever since the Ikhwan had spread the Wahhabi Revival as far east in the British Empire as Malaya and the Dutch East Indies in the nineteenth century. Accordingly, with the stability of the region disturbed, the British government found itself in a position where it might have to defend Iraq militarily in a war with Ibn Saud. Something, Philby decided in consultation with Ibn Saud, must be done about the Ikhwan if Arabia was not to remain what it now was, a seventh-century kingdom in a twentieth-century world. If Ibn Saud would not move to break their power, he would. He took to his pen and invoked the power of the Trinity web, where, despite the hostility toward him, he still had friends. It was probably this correspondence that gave him the reputation among the Syrian Arabs at Ibn Saud's court for being a British spy.

On November 7, 1929, and again on the eighteenth, Philby wrote two important letters to Hugh Dalton, the parliamentary secretary at the Foreign Office and a Trinity man who had played a leading part in establishing Fabianism at Trinity a little before St. John's time. Dalton had come to power with the formation of the coalition government of the socialist J. Ramsay MacDonald in 1929. Philby felt able to do with Dalton what he had been disinclined to do with the conservative governments before and after — special business. In one of these letters Philby proposed himself to Dalton as a confidential correspondent and voiced his hope "to see something in the shape of practical results advantageous alike to Arabia and [the British government]." Dalton's reply shows that he accepted St. John's suggestion on December 28, declaring guardedly, "I shall look forward to hearing from you, from time to time, if you think it worth while to write to me privately."[19] In his second letter, Philby addressed himself to a matter of state of concern to both Britain and the kingdom — a joint Anglo-Arabian operation to kill or capture Sheikh Dawish, a leader of the rebellion against Ibn Saud. As Philby put it, Ibn Saud had determined "to finish with Dawish and Co. once and for all." Ibn Saud proposed to surround him at his home in Artawiya "in such a way as to force him to fight or flee." Since Dawish's only haven would be Kuwait, a British protectorate, there was danger of fighting between the Anglo-Kuwait forces and Ibn Saud's if the latter followed Dawish. This Ibn Saud wanted to avoid. St. John warned Dalton:

> Everything points to a rather serious conflict between Ibn Saud and Kuwait if the latter's ruler is not sharply bidden by Whitehall to refuse asylum to the rebels and, to be perfectly frank with you, the conflict might involve the occupation of Kuwait by the Wahhabis unless [Whitehall] intervenes.

Acting evidently as Ibn Saud's adviser in foreign affairs even though he was no more than a British merchant at Jidda, Philby recommended that the British government warn the Sheikh of Kuwait against granting Dawish asylum. The "future peace of the Iraq frontier demands the extermination of [Dawish] even if it involves, as it may, the disappearance of Kuwait as an independent state." As for Anglo-American lives in Kuwait, Philby assured Dalton, "you need anticipate no danger whatever. I.S. will see to that."

Dalton replied to both letters on Foreign Office notepaper on December 28 in "My dear Philby" terms, offering thanks for "much invaluable information." But he did not, it appears, reply to Philby's suggestion for joint operations against Dawish. It was the British high commission in Baghdad that authorized collaboration between the Anglo-Iraqi-Kuwait forces and Ibn Saud's army. Together they surrounded Dawish and his Ikhwan; after prolonged and severe disturbances the revolt collapsed, and Dawish and two other Ikhwan leaders were arrested and turned over to Ibn Saud by Major John B. Glubb, a British intelligence officer in Iraq.

With the successful end of the joint operation, in March 1930 St. John learned that Dora was to meet Dalton at a reception at the Egyptian embassy in London. Philby thereupon invited his wife to propose him for the office of British commissioner in Egypt, Iraq, or Palestine or one of the Indian governorships, although he acknowledged ruefully that such a grand opening was not likely to come his way even with men like Dalton in power, for he had, he agreed, "burnt my boats pretty badly." Dalton ignored the overtures. Philby persisted. He suggested directly to Dalton that "the best thing you could do with me would be to make me a peer," adding that that would be "at least

an amusing climax to a career of anti-imperialism." But Dalton ignored that hint too, so, instead of kissing hands with King George V,
Philby elected to bow at the black stone of the Kaaba at Mecca and
thereby become a Moslem. He professed to spiritual and therefore
praiseworthy impulses for his startling — to official Britain — decision,
but the real reason was his desire for the power, and thus the money,
to be gained through a place at Ibn Saud's court. Philby wrote to the
king in August 1930:[20]

> Peace. Mercy, and the Blessing of Allah be upon you. I have already
> had the honour to submit to Your Majesty's consideration my desire
> to become a Moslem and to abandon other religions.
>
> Now I once more beg to state to Your Majesty that Allah has re-
> joiced my heart to accept Islam and has shown me the right way to
> follow this religion with firm belief and perfect conscious satisfaction.
>
> I therefore "bear witness that there is no God but Allah and that
> Mohammed is His slave and Messenger," and I believe in all that is
> mentioned in the "Book of Allah," in the tradition of His Messenger
> and in what the good ancestors did. I also wish to express that I am
> convinced that all is true and that I desire to follow the same; and as
> regards the details that I desire to follow all that is written in the
> books of the good ancestors and more especially the statements of
> [the precentors of Islam and Wahhabism] Shaikh Ibn Taimia, Ibn al
> Qaiyem aj-Jowziah, and in the later ages those of Shaikh Mohhamed
> Ibn Abdul Wahhab, may God have mercy on him and all other Mos-
> lems.
>
> I beg you to accept my conversion to Islam which springs in me
> from grounds of belief, reflection, wisdom and good intention. Allah
> the Almighty guides to the right path.

Not often in Wahhab conversions has there been a more impudent
letter, but it worked. Ibn Saud needed St. John badly at Mecca and he
himself responded. The telephone rang at Beit Baghdadi on August
3. The king was at his summer residence at Taif, the hill resort in the
mountains behind Jidda. He said he had decided to permit the entrance of "the esteemed Mr. Philby" into Islam, but first he must go to
Mecca "for a ceremony." Could he be ready that afternoon? Philby
assured the king that he would leave immediately. "Farewell to all
that!" St. John declared in a note to Dora, Kim, and his daughters. On
August 7 he made his intentions seem as normal as ever, and he
attended Sunday tea at the British legation. He wore Arab habit and
announced that he intended to do a spot of hunting up on the border
with the Holy Land. But he really intended to do what few other men

contemplated: to embrace Wahhabism, a cause that was not only a religion but also a politico-economic autocracy.

He left Jidda after dark, his driver in attendance, and was driven up the pilgrim's trail to Bahra, about halfway along the forty-three rough miles to Mecca. There he was met by, among others, Fuad Hamza, one of Ibn Saud's advisers in foreign affairs. Hamza put a tent up for Philby, who performed the ritual ablutions and donned the pilgrim's habit, towels around his upper and lower body and leather sandals. Then the party continued, and reached Mecca during the early evening of August 10, while St. John's associates at Jidda awaited him for tea and bridge.

The nightlong ritual took place by moonlight that same night. Attended by a number of officials from Ibn Saud's court, St. John kissed the black stone of the Kaaba. He prostrated himself at Abraham's Station, prayed, chanted incantations, underwent the ritual shaving, and drank from the holy well of Zamzam. At sunrise, he turned to the east and made the holy pledge: "I therefore proclaim thus: I testify there is no god but God; and that Mohammed is His Servant and Prophet."

After prayers and a breakfast of melon, Philby went to Taif, where he and Ibn Saud kissed noses. At a little ceremony in those sun-blasted hills above Jidda, the king bestowed on Philby the name Abdullah, Slave of God, and made a speech to the privy council about Philby's services to Arabia, about how Philby had resigned his king's posts at Baghdad and Amman rather than work for the Hashemites. Philby, said Ibn Saud, had never accepted wages, a statement that may have been true; there is evidence that, despite his penury, he declined Ibn Saud's offer to pay £50 gold a month — a large sum by Philby's standards — into a Swiss bank account. Probably Philby knew that the king was impoverished and did not wish to embarrass him by accepting a promise that he knew the king could not keep. On the other hand, there is some slight evidence that Ibn Saud did pay the money into the account but St. John never used it. It may have piled up into a very large sum of money, which perhaps Kim Philby used for his special purposes.

The king went on to say that Philby had considered this step for years before he actually took it. He had read the Koran, had received advice from holy and learned men, and would continue his studies at Mecca. In short, Philby was a worthy man, and he would now, in consequence of his services to the Wahhab kingdom, be invited to share his great knowledge of foreign affairs with the privy council.

News of that appointment was received with surprise and disquiet in the British official world. An official of the Colonial Office sent a minute to the cabinet of Prime Minister J. Ramsay MacDonald that since he had

> retired from Govt. service 5 years ago, Mr. Philby has lost no oppor-
> tunity of attacking & misrepresenting the Govt. & its policy in the
> Middle East. His methods have been as unscrupulous as they have
> been violent. He is a public nuisance, & it is largely due to him & his
> intrigues that Ibn Saud — over whom he unfortunately exercises some
> influence — has given us so much trouble during the last few years.[21]

Similar unease attended Philby's call on the British consul in Jidda on August 30, 1930. The consul, G. C. Hope-Gill, reported to the Middle Eastern desk at the Foreign Office in terms that indicated his belief that the reason for Philby's conversion was not spiritual but political and commercial. Philby had been deliberating the step for four years, Gill wrote, "ever since the first hot moments of his rage against HMG's Arab policy." This had now cooled, but his dissociation from British ideals remained. He had become a Pan-Arabist, one who believed in the reestablishment of the Arab empire that had once extended from the Atlantic to the Indian Ocean under a single leader. Philby thought that leader would be Ibn Saud, but the latter wanted no trouble with Great Britain and would do everything he could "to avoid any conflict with her while she remains on his frontiers (and this point is always stressed)." Hope-Gill went on to advise that he thought Philby to be "a fanatic" about Pan-Arabism. He warned pro-phetically, "The man is undoubtedly a monomaniac, of a kind and now in a position to do us no good at all in our relations with Ibn Saud."[22]

Privy council business, Hope-Gill was able to report, "ranges far and wide"; the "King's Arabic being understood hardly at all, except by the Nejdis"; and he "generally seems to end up with women." Philby spoke freely of "corruption in high places," "royal extravagance, and such piffling matters as public finance and education," and relayed the menacing view that the Arabs thought their troubles arose through "the oppression exercised by Great Britain on their frontiers." This, Philby reported and Gill recorded, takes "all their attention and wastes all their energies."[23] Philby disclosed much else that was of importance to those concerned with maintaining British hegemony in the Middle East. That he did so served to strengthen the belief of his enemies that he was, whatever he said and did, Britain's spy at Ibn Saud's court.

And certainly, whether a spy or not, his information to the consul was of a type that could not be obtained elsewhere. That led to more speculation about what Philby was really about in Arabia. Fuad Hamza, the foreign minister who had acted as a guide during Philby's introduction to Islam, summed up the puzzlement. "Do you know what people say about you?" Hamza asked Philby, and gave the answer:

> What most people in Mecca and Jidda think about you and your rather special position with the King [is that] nothing will persuade them that you are anything but a British spy in our midst [and] that your apparently friendly attitude toward the Arabs is anything but a cloak for work in promoting British imperialist interests in this country.[24]

There were also those at court who thought that Philby was a Communist. Had he not arranged for Hassim Hakimoff Khan to trade in Arabia, making him therefore a friend of Bolshevik Russia? Further, through his statements that a Jewish state in Arabia would benefit the Arabs, had he not shown himself a Zionist?

About such prickly matters the king thought Philby to be "a little mad" — sunstroke, perhaps. Ibn Saud declared that he hated Russian Communism and feared the outcome of the migration of Jews into Palestine because "they will become one of the most powerful governments equipped with arms and wealth and everything else." But he and Philby were and remained true friends, and in any case Philby was useful at court as the king's agent, as an adviser in foreign affairs, as a sorcerer's apprentice, and as a future source of foreign money. After one of Philby's tirades, Ibn Saud remarked, "One good thing — although you talk through the top of your head at least you keep me awake."

As for Philby's sincerity in embracing Islam, many British officials suspected, as did Hope-Gill, that his motives were not pure. When Ibn Saud awarded him the patronymic Abdullah, the wits began calling him "Abdullah al Qirsh, Slave of Tuppence Halfpence." But, confident of himself as always, St. John dismissed allegations of humbuggery as the words of men who were themselves humbugs. But he did admit something of the truth when he wrote to Dora on April 1, 1931, "My general policy now is to stick as close as possible to the king, as I am sure that is the best way to get at the big business." He said much the same thing in a note to his principals at Sharquieh: "My coming to Mecca has entirely changed our position," he claimed, announcing that if they agreed, he would reside more or less permanently at the court, leaving the company offices at Jidda in the hands of his staff there. It was significant that one of the few people who wrote to him to applaud his conversion was Kim, as Philby noted proudly to his Trinity friend Sir Donald Robertson. It is certainly noteworthy that even as St. John became a Wahhab, Kim took his first steps toward becoming a Bolshevik secret agent.

5

At Court

1930–1934

WHEN PHILBY JOINED the privy council in August 1930, Ibn Saud had recently turned forty-two, or thereabouts — he did not know his birthdate himself. Philby was forty-five. The Ikhwan rebellion at an end, Ibn Saud was secure as the absolute monarch. The privy council then comprised five or six largely foreign Arabs who had been chosen carefully by Ibn Saud for their intelligence, their origins, and their acceptance of the Wahhabi Reformation. Also, as aliens, they were not likely to conspire against the king. There was one minister of the crown, Sheikh Abdullah Suleiman, the keeper of the privy purse. A Saudi Arab and a peremptory xenophobe, he had succeeded in making the largest private fortune in the kingdom. Also in the council was Shaikh Yusuf Yassin, chief of the political department, a Syrian Alawite from Latakia; Fuad Hamza, a Druze, who attended to foreign affairs; and Sheikh Hafez Wahba, an Egyptian who graduated from the al-Azhar University in Cairo, that mysterious and fanatical hotspot of anti-Western doctrine. Hafez was Ibn Saud's minister extraordinary and ambassador plenipotentiary to the Court of St. James's. Although he had been blacklisted for anti-British activities during the war, Hafez became the doyen of the diplomatic corps in London and, at great affairs of state, wore with pride the mantle and insignia of a Knight Grand Cross of the Royal Victorian Order. There too at the *diwan* were two others of consequence to Ibn Saud: Khalid el-Qarqani and Bashir Saadawi Bey, who came from the Mahgreb of North Africa. Last, but not least, there was Philby, a redheaded Englishman who wore Arab clothes and dyed his beard henna in keeping with the custom.

Philby's power in Arabia was great, of interest even to the U.S. State Department, which hitherto had shown little interest in matters Arabian. Who was this Briton at Mecca? Was he still not connected with the British Foreign Office, and if so, what was the nature and extent of his powers over Ibn Saud? Cloyee K. Huston, the American vice-consul at Aden, did not know Philby and had never visited Jidda; what information he knew was obtained from the British administrators of Aden, who knew Philby only too well. Huston reported that the intimacy between the king and Philby "is fairly close," but that

> it is, of course, an intimacy between an occidental and an oriental, between a nominal Christian and a puritan Mohammedan, between a merchant and a king; but it is to be remembered that they were host and guest over a long period, they have dined and sipped coffee together a very great number of times and they have traveled together over considerable distances in Arabia, they have exchanged presents, suggestions, comment, and advice on various subjects, and they have discussed at various times such questions as Arabian politics, religion, the social order, and others. Mr. Philby professed to discern a great future leader in Ibn Saud . . . and he remains loud in his praise of the King of the Hedjaz in his letter to the press to this day. Ibn Saud . . . has always given the appearance of respecting and esteeming Mr. Philby very highly.

But, Huston continued,

> no one but Ibn Saud himself actually knows the amount of confidence now extended to Mr. Philby. Mr. Philby believes, or at least claims, that it is a great deal, and many, including British officers, complain that he has become so pro-Arabian and pro–Ibn Saud that he is anti-British in many Anglo-Arab questions of today. It is, indeed, probably true that he is closer to Ibn Saud than any other white man and he does enjoy an unusual amount of confidence, but the heart of a shrewd and intelligent Arab who is playing a game of politics on the Arabian chessboard can rarely be read or understood.[1]

The reality was much more complicated.

In his affairs, the king was essentially anti-Western, anti-Christian, and anti-Jewish, but pro-American, or, rather, pro-Wilsonian idealism; he was also markedly interested in money, especially gold coin. His public attitude was one of friendship for Great Britain, but his private policy belied this. Ibn Saud flattered the main power on his borders in order to keep up relations with it, thus displaying respect for that imperial doggerel of Victorian time:

> Whatever happens
> We have got
> The Maxim gun and
> They have not.

According to Philby's own account, the council, over which Ibn Saud himself presided, met twice each day in Mecca except on the Sabbath and on holy days, but it was a rickety affair. There was as often talk of women, horses, hunting, aphrodisiacs, and perfumes as there was of business of state. Philby's letter to Dora on his first experiences at court could have done little to give her confidence:

> I am never idle, but life consists largely in attending the sittings of the king, morning, afternoon and night, while latterly I have spent most of my meals with him as he has no womenfolk with him and likes to have people about at all times. He often keeps us up late just chatting, generally about five or six of us . . . Altogether it is a very jolly party and rather reminds one of what one reads of the time of Henry VIII, though of course the women don't appear on the scene.[2]

Ibn Saud provided St. John with residences at Riyadh, Mecca, Medina, and Taif and reminded him that by Moslem law he was entitled to as many wives as he wished, provided he did not have more than four at one time. St. John further advised Dora, probably to prepare her for events soon to occur, that a woman was needed "to complete the comfort" of his place at court, but so far Ibn Saud had not "offered me any of the princesses in marriage," although "I understand he intends to present me with a lady (slave and mistress combined!!) to look after me as soon as a suitable and sufficiently beautiful one can be found." There was trouble here, he advised Dora, for the mistress would, under Islamic usage, "automatically regain her liberty if she produced a child!" That would be "a bit awkward, wouldn't it?" For the moment, therefore, he was doing no more than "let[ting] myself drift happily on the tide of life, which has certainly become very agreeable and interesting."[3]

To maintain his place among the privy councillors he observed carefully his religious obligations, which could be severe. His biographer, Monroe, noted:

> Islam is more than a religion. In the land of a devout ruler, all actions were governed by it, and no one could hope to belong to Arabia

unless he took part in the prayers and readings, rejoicings and fast-
ings, laws and personal habits, that, for an Arab, constitute a way of
life. The very language that Arabia speaks is bound up with it, for
Arabic is the tongue in which the eternal word of Allah was spoken
to the Prophet. Islam's spiritual inheritance, tradition, symbolism
and doctrine permeated the actions of every day, and reconciliation
of the first with the foundation and spread of Ibn Saud's temporal
and political power was a problem that he constantly thrashed with
the learned Ulema [the council of priests] at his court. The need for
this reconciliation has exercised thinkers for centuries, and still today
colours the life of Muslims, even of those to whom the spiritual
element in Islam appeals little. Conversion would wed Philby to Arabia, and would set him a pattern of life in which he must ponder
these problems; the explanations that he later wrote to friends show
that he admired Muslim ethics, and that he felt at ease when he made
the change.[4]

Philby frequently likened his new faith to a form of socialism, declaring at one place in *A Pilgrim in Arabia* that the "basic principles of
Islam" were "essentially a democratic and socialist creed." In another,
dealing with the Shia branch of Islam in Persia, he mentioned "its
socialistic ethics [as] an essential element in any effective religion." In
a third he spoke of Islam's "entirely admirable features" as being "like
political socialism of the democratic type," but it "seemed to be afraid
of its own more revolutionary ideals."[5] It is not hard to see that Philby's
becoming a Wahhab had philosophical as well as commercial and personal aspects. Nor is it difficult to understand why Kim Philby came so
completely to accept Marxist-Leninism; St. John had shown him the way.
    The daily routine was exacting and displayed how profoundly Philby
was prepared to accept hardship in return for fame and power — and
financial security. He recorded that they were wakened each day at
3 A.M., when the council rushed to the king's private oratory to perform a two-bow prayer before the king arrived. A light breakfast of
bread, honey, dates, and curdled milk followed. There followed a further two-bow prayer at sunrise. The council then returned to bed until 7 A.M. At seven-thirty the king's first audiences took place, usually
in the study where Philby had first met the king in 1917 and usually
with special visitors, clerks, and secretaries in attendance. From these
audiences the king went on to the daily public audience, the *majlis*,
notables visiting from the provinces. Those who desired a private audience, and had reason, were then seen. There followed audiences
with members of the royal family, the king's doctor, and persons such
as Philby, who had the right of what he called "private entrée." The

business of the day ended at about 10 A.M. The king usually departed for the Badia palace nearby, "where his favorite section of the harem was installed." This was the part of his household in which he lived permanently and ate his meals. At 4 P.M. he would be joined at the Badia palace by Philby and other intimates. At about four-thirty dinner, the only regular meal of the day, would be served. The rest of the afternoon would be spent, Philby recorded, "sitting round and chatting, generally rather emptily, or perhaps in a short outing in the palm groves, while the king retired to his women."[6]

At five there were sunset prayers and then more talk over dishes of dates. The king returned to Riyadh at seven o'clock in his Hudson motor car "to spend the night with one or other of his wives according to the turn of each." At eight came evening prayers, which Philby described as "two complete *taslimat* and preceded by one *taslim* of *sunna* and followed by another." The assembly proceeded to a small courtyard "for half an hour's reading of *Hadith* and *Tafsir*" by the royal precentor, "a youth with a good but monotonous voice which generally had a soporific effect on me and defeated my best efforts to follow the reading in detail." Just before retiring, "we generally consumed a large bowl of camel's milk each." This routine was unvarying, except on the Wahhab sabbath, which was on Friday, and at times of crises and the religious festivals that Philby found feats of physical endurance.[7]

He accompanied the king on the Haj, the great pilgrimage and Islam's main rite, in April 1931. For orthodox Moslems the Haj represented, and does still, the culmination of their religious lives. Few Westerners had made the pilgrimage before and those who had spoke of the ecstasy they experienced as they made the "sublime act of complete surrender to the Supreme Will of a merciful God." Philby's reaction was more mundane, although he did acquire the precious right — to use the title Haji, "one who has made the pilgrimage," before his Islamic name, Abdullah. As he wrote to Dora on April 27:

> We ride out on camels with the king and I am greatly looking forward to it though the actual ceremonies don't fill me with much enthusiasm. The crowd will be a wonderful sight and even now in the Great Mosque especially at the time of the sunset prayer it is a truly magnificent spectacle, the huge concentration all arranged in concentric circles with the women here and there forming solid wedges of softer colours and draperies. And then round the Ka'aba there is nowadays a regular and sometimes turbulent stream of human beings going round and round, a wonderful sight consisting of the regular kaleidoscope of all the races of the earth, the aged and infants carried on cushions, the blind and maimed and the halt.

Of the ceremony of "the standing," the central rite of the three days of devotions, which were intended to remind all of the Day of Judgment and of the Farewell Sermon of the Prophet at the Mount of Mercy, Philby was almost prosaic when he wrote to the family: "Six hours barehead and towel-clothed in the blazing sun of that afternoon sitting on a camel was quite a feat in itself but I was none the worse for any of it and in fact felt wonderfully fit at the end of the whole show. It was all very interesting and impressive." Philby's reaction was that of a rationalist who had been impressed by a pageant, not a man who felt, as Hajis were supposed to feel, that he had been close to God. This raised afresh the question of the degree of his commitment to Islam.[8]

Now known at court as Haji Abdullah, an appellation that came to be used by Dora and Kim and the rest of the family, he had forsworn liquor, he claimed. More accurately, he dwelt on his fealty to the laws and customs of Islam as proof of his acceptance of the Prophet. He had, he said, accepted obedience to the customs of his new faith, especially the severe fast of Ramadan, the ninth month of the Moslem year. He would and did undertake the month of prayer, penitence, and abstinence from all earthly pleasures, including wives and concubines and the imbibing of water, in order to purify his soul. St. John could not permit himself the slightest indulgence in case his delinquencies attracted the attention of the court priests and the Ikhwan. His survival depended on his most particular observance of the fast; and woe betide him if the priesthood caught him taking even a sip of melon water. Afterward, he wrote to Dora:

> Ramadan is at last over, having had its full complement of thirty days, and this afternoon at sunset we break the fast for the last time. Tomorrow is the Id [the start of the period of feasting and celebration after Ramadan] and the next three days are holidays which I suppose we have to spend in the dreary tasks of calling on each other, eating sweets and drinking tea, etc. Then we shall be free to resume normal life and hours once more. The fast, which I have taken very seriously by attending all or most of the extra services, etc., has not been a very serious ordeal but just at present I feel a bit tired, probably as a result of the three midnight services each lasting about three hours with very prolonged prostrations, which are very trying to a heart like mine.[9]

His devotions — along with the Raj's training in such matters of earthly competence as revenue collection, administration, population control, and communications — helped him in becoming Ibn Saud's grand vizier, the power behind the throne. That was where he wished to be, and he was content. But the same could not be said for Philby in his relationships with his family.

In the seven years between 1926, when Philby settled at Jidda, and 1933, when his business began to prosper, Dora experienced considerable financial hardship. Her basic income was £700 a year, from St. John's Indian government pension, plus what she was able to earn from Major Fisher in the way of house decoration. Otherwise she made ends meet through her sale of the old Saudi postage stamps and pearls that Philby bought in Jidda and sent to her in London. With a house to maintain and four children to raise, her plight at times was such that she was hard put to know where the next shilling for the gas meter would come from. Her only contact with St. John was the stream of seamail, which came and went every ten days.

An efficient and dutiful woman, and a loyal one, Dora never wholly accepted St. John's absence and wished only that he would return to his senses and find another, more conventional way of providing for his family. Also, she deplored St. John's becoming a Wahhab. She asserted again and again that he was wasting his time in Arabia, that he had not done an honest day's work in years, that he had gone native. She began to drink gin more heavily, but she was as handsome as ever and moved in a widening circle. It is claimed that she remained faithful to her marriage vows, resisting all the importunities of Major Fisher. In all this St. John behaved shamelessly, encouraging her to develop her own life, a phrase that for St. John included expeditions with other men. This she could have done quite easily. She remained well connected to the official and upper middle class of London life and was well entertained by her friends. She was not active politically and seems to have been a Liberal in the British sense; that is, she looked to the state to provide the conditions necessary for decent individual existence while not supporting the socialist goal of complete equality imposed by state control. Like most such people, she strongly opposed communism. In the early 1930s Kim did succeed in converting her to a mild form of socialism, but beyond that she did not go. She was alarmed when Kim's own socialism, which developed while he was still at Westminster, assumed what she thought was an extreme form of communism, which he did not conceal from her. In all, Dora was a mother who took a keen interest in the well-being of her home and children.

Dora's underlying discontent emerged when St. John discussed the other women in his life in Arabia. One of his peculiarities was that he would meet an Occidental woman once or twice and then maintain a correspondence with her that lasted their lifetimes. This correspondence was usually quite open, and in it St. John freely discussed his life at court and his political and philosophical interests. Dora knew of this but did not, it seems, object; what she did find tiresome and irritating was St. John's discussion of his sexual adventures. This was always framed in an unobjectionable manner, but by reading between the lines Dora could see that St. John had a very active sexual life.

Between 1927 and 1930 the correspondence shows no animus between them except when it seemed to Dora that her husband had installed a mistress in his palace at Jidda, the Beit Baghdadi, while continuing to fail to provide properly for his English family. When Dora wrote to him sternly, he responded in self-assured fashion; his place at court assured them that he would become rich through the commercial advantages he had gained by being close to the king. He had, he claimed, something to be proud of politically as well. His ideas had triumphed in Arabia. He was "really still the only one who really understands Arabia!" It might take fifty years for British policy to take shape along Philby's lines, but his place as a prophet was assured. That, he told Dora, "ought to be a great consolation to you." Dora replied that this was no consolation at all, for she was worried about her home and children, not the empire in Arabia. She wanted, she said, her independence. The last straw seems to have been a letter about his lovelife early in 1930, at about the same time as his conversion.[10]

A Polish count, Malmignetta, had arrived in his yacht to sell machine guns to the king. While the king and the count were in audience, Philby took the countess, an Englishwoman by birth, into the Jidda market to buy pearls. As Philby remarked, he was much taken with her "dreamy, violet eyes." Would Dora make inquiries about her in London? The fat hit the fire and sizzled for a long time. She was damned if she would ponce for him. Philby replied on February 27, 1930, much on his high horse: "I wish, Dora, you would not always harp on your passion to be independent." He pointed out that this type of row did little to provide Kim with the security he so badly needed at this critical time in his education. He went on to tell Dora that she could "do a good deal better for yourself than by sticking to your profession as mistress of my hearth and home." He asked her "to turn your heart inside out and have a look at it" and then answer the question: "Would you at any time during the last, say, eight years have been able to say that you were in love with me?" St. John answered for her in terms that showed Dora was quite right in assuming that he was being unfaithful to her on a large scale, and at the same time he gave her a long lecture on his sexuality:

> I think you have a certain respect and perhaps admiration of certain sides of me and you have tried to do your duty by me, but you have not been in love with me for years, and you have never realised how very much I need love. I don't think I really realised it myself until I had experience of it but I do think it has done me a lot of good all round. I have worked better for it and I have felt better. It is easy enough for a man to be in love if he is inclined to have strong feelings, sexual and emotional, but real love probably depends entirely on the woman's reaction to the feelings she stirs in a man. Of course I suppose I did not trust you properly (owing to want of experience) at the beginning of our married life and that may be the ultimate cause of our final failure; but then and indeed now my first love was and is my work. Love to me is a relaxation and an inspiration from my work and I don't think the person one loves has any real ground of offence in that. She might even take a pride in the fact that she is an element of inspiration and not merely a toy.[11]

He wanted her "to believe that I feel a very great liking and friendliness for you and that I have never even considered the possibility of changing the partner of my life and fortunes." That was "the gospel truth and I have always made it very clear to my few very dear friends that I do not regard marriage as the necessary or even the desirable climax of love." Unfortunately,

> I have to spend most of my life in a sort of exile from the world but I get a very great pleasure from quite an extensive love-letter correspondence! and I get just as much pleasure from my correspondence with you, as you can readily see by the regularity and length of my letters. I assure I don't write to you from any sense of duty but simply because it gives me great pleasure to do so.

This cat-and-mouse game went on for years. In a mid-April letter of 1930 Philby declared to Dora that it was "high time really I had somebody to love," and as he would not be home in England much before mid-July, he had begun to hope that, despite all that he had said, the female explorer Rosita Forbes might come through Jidda. As he admitted, he fancied Rosita, although "she is no more in love with me than I with her." What Rosita wanted was an introduction to Ibn Saud, he declared, and therefore "if we were both feeling lonely we might be able to pretend." After all, she was "a nice creature," although he preferred women "whose sex is obvious," and he had never "felt that Rosita came in that category, despite her salacious novels." Philby ended his letter in the most seductive fashion he could manage, for he had not been able to say very much that was seductive to Dora for donkey's years:

> Well I must go to bed as it is late but such a lovely moonlight night that I might even be affectionate to you if you were here! However I send you my love wafting across three thousand miles or more of perfect moonlight, and there is a lovely light breeze. So goodnight, take care of yourself and be prepared for my return in July or there-abouts.[12]

In the late fall of 1930 Philby returned again to their personal lives when Dora claimed to know that her husband's latest love was the wife of the young British engineer who managed Jidda's desalinization plant, Dorothy Ousman. Philby wriggled his way out of it:

> I think I am probably the best judge of how to direct my destinies; and, in so far as Dorothy is linked with them, I really don't think it at all reasonable to suggest my conduct should be influenced in the very slightest degree by the tittle-tattle of worms!! Ha! Ha! Anyway she is a dear though she has no sparkle of affection (certainly not of love) for me and merely likes being admired and entertained in the distinguished society that frequents my humble residence!! As I have told you before, I think, she is probably sexually defective as she has no feelings (and admits it) though physically she has all the attributes of attractiveness to the male and knows how to dress to the best advantage. However you really needn't worry about her as she does not reciprocate my affection.

By December, Philby had become bolder about his need for a woman in his entourage. He wrote at the end of his letter of December 2, 1930:

> I must go to bed now as I feel tired. I am really very fit these days and the climate is delightful but I am not so young as I used to be and this courtiers' life, with five or six hours a day in attendance on His Majesty (including both meals on most days, though I occasion-ally enjoy the luxury of a simple lunch of bread and cucumbers and cheese and tea) is very tiring for a man in the prime of life! Perhaps the absence of feminine society is also at times more tiring than one imagines. I need a woman to bring out the best in me. However I am advised that in Paradise I shall have 70 *houris* all to myself including

if desired one of my worldly wives. In the circumstances I have not a
wide field of choice, but it may flatter you to know that on mature
consideration I would like you to share the honour with the other 69.[13]

The atmosphere produced by these jousts and by poverty made the
house in Hampstead an uneasy place.

However, by 1931 Philby had begun to prosper. After his conversion,
he acquired the Ford dealership for Arabia and the concessions for
Singer sewing machines and Socony Vacuum oils and fuels, a connection that was to prove of importance. He also became so powerful a fish in that small pond, the king's court, that he felt able to resign from the privy council — in April 1931, eight months after his
appointment — as an expression of his doubt about the way the king
ran his kingdom. As Philby wrote of that daring and dangerous move:

> Without any official functions I was in effect an unofficial member
> of the Privy Council [but] I myself relinquished that position by
> refusal to attend an important meeting to discuss the currency posi-
> tion soon after the pilgrimage and by frequent absences from the
> King's evening audiences.[14]

The question of the Arabian currency was a technical and perennial
one in which Ibn Saud and his principal financial adviser, Abdullah
Suleiman, the head of the treasury, declined to accept St. John's counsel. But his resignation represented a stern act of independence and
courage that few men who valued their lives would have emulated. It
represented, too, Philby's general dissatisfaction with the way the privy
council conducted its business. Philby's first complaint against the
king concerned foreign policy, for Ibn Saud did not manage the kingdom Philby's way. As Philby wrote in a memoir:

> For all his personal charm, lavish hospitality, profuse generosity and
> deep integrity, he had no friends among the political entities of the
> world, while within his own realm he met with nothing but fawning
> and flattery simply because he had too often belayed the truth with
> the whips of his ill-humor.[15]

Under the king, the great cause of an Arab empire extending from
the Atlantic to the Indian Ocean "seemed to be drifting to the brink
of the worst form of disaster — moral and political impotence. There
was only one man capable of making the effort necessary to save it,"
and that was Ibn Saud. But he, in Philby's view, "seemed to be wrapped
in slumber and disappointment and inaction. Never before was reso-

lute action more needed in Arabia and never had there been less sign of it far and wide."[16]

These were remarkable statements, akin to treason, and it is interesting to note that Kim Philby would adopt just such an independence in his dealings with the Soviet government. St. John was the activist in Arabian imperialism, not Ibn Saud. Nor was his activism confined to the currency and foreign affairs. It arose too in the vital matter of wireless communications across those vast deserts. Hitherto, Ibn Saud had maintained his regime through the power of his penis, which he used on the grand scale. To Philby, the king was then "still in his physical prime, and still uxorious" and confessed to having married a hundred and thirty-five virgins whom he could remember and about a hundred "others," though recently he had decided to limit himself to two new wives each year.[17]

For all his burdens of statehood, the king still found the energy at forty to visit his harem twice each day, according to Philby, once during the afternoon siesta and once after the sunset prayer; the object was, through intercourse with the daughters of the sheikhs, to bind the tribes to his person, to establish a dynasty that would, until kingdom come, be loyal to the Sauds. But Philby recognized that the king's power could not last forever and that something else was required. — Ibn Saud's voice, speaking from the heavens to the distant and treacherous parts, was needed. Philby introduced the wireless to link the Wahhabi capital not only with the tribes but with the world. But when London came up, as it did, there was "not a word of royal thanks or royal congratulations or even royal approval." All that Philby encountered was a persisting "undercurrent of hostility to these inventions of the devil." Nor did the king pay for the stations until long afterward, thereby burdening Philby's company at Jidda with a debt that left it crippled until 1943, by which time Ibn Saud was receiving Lend Lease money from the United States and could pay his debts.[18]

Thus, as Philby also recorded, he left the privy council. During the season, he filled in the morning hours with "good bouts of butterfly hunting" in the Atna Gardens of the palace, an excellent place for blues and whites. But even this sport failed with the arrival at Riyadh of the Great Depression. More and more the king became addicted to indoor life, and this produced "a lack of energy to decide to do something different from the daily routine." Philby found that his own mind at this time "would ever recur to the failure of Ibn Saud's government to face and master its economic crisis." The result was that "trade and business became dead in the land." There were deep econo-

mies. The government declined to pay due debts and therefore became unable to purchase goods on credit. The economies went to the
bone. Even the royal kitchen fell on bad days; the food declined in
quality; the milk was often 50 percent watered; and "the dates that
came to our quarters were (quite inexcusably) the mere leavings of
slaves through whose hands they had passed."[19]

The jolly days at Taif, hunting the gazelle, lolling about in the mountain cool, eating the luscious prickly pear, gave way to a reality of a
kingdom approaching ruin even before it had become a kingdom. Ibn
Saud's treasury began to suffer a decline in the numbers of the faithful
making the pilgrimage, which provided the government with its main
source of general revenue. A hundred thousand Moslems came from
overseas each year to ensure themselves a place in Paradise; each spent
perhaps £50 gold while in the country. But in 1930 the number of
visitors fell to eighty thousand; in 1931, to forty thousand. The finance
minister, Suleiman, made dangerous economies. Money was available
to the departments administered by the king, charity, the household,
security, defense, the Ulema, but he began to defer paying the civil
service.

It began to demand *douceur* — bribery — for services that it should
perform without charge. Philby noted that "the trickle of corruption
developed into a steady stream as time went on," and it came to be
"regarded as a normal feature of the Arabian landscape." This he
deplored, especially when it was found in the princes, whom he considered "a lousy lot." A further loan was arranged, to the tune of about
£300,000, but only by defaulting on payments due to various commercial houses in Jidda, including his own, Sharquieh, which had provided
the palace with motor cars, aircraft, machine guns, and the wireless
stations, all on credit. Many other such practices were adopted to
conserve revenue, but by 1931 all failed to offer any solution to the
increasingly serious financial position. The merchants were reverting
to usury, which Koranic law forbade; those in government service
began to demand their pay; the sheikhs warned of civil disturbance;
and the government began to run on empty.

Philby approached the British consul for help, but, he wrote, "the
British system was too rigid for Arabia. It could offer no credit without
rules and regulations, guarantees and controls" — what he called "the
old-fashioned stranglehold over impecunious countries." Offers of assistance did appear from an unlikely quarter — the Soviet Union, which
had taken the lead among the powers in 1926 in recognizing the
Wahhab kingdom, even though it was a monarchy. The USSR's repre-

sentatives at Jidda, including Hassim Hakimoff Khan, provided cheap
Soviet paraffin, a main source for heating, lighting, and cooking, and
manufactured goods. It was rewarded in due course "with the scent of
honey in the emaciated carcase of an impoverished country." Khan
came bowing to Ibn Saud at his palace just outside Jidda in the wake
of the retiring British minister. The ensuing audience revealed what
Philby called "a complete identity of views, expressed in an atmosphere of great cordiality," although the king had always professed a
great distrust of communism.

Hassim offered petrol, then worth more than rubies to the kingdom. A tanker called and offloaded its cargo, although it was never
paid for. The Red Star became what Philby called "ascendant in Arabian skies," more especially in Yemen, the vital British victualing and
coaling port on the shipping lines between London and Bombay. But
what else could be done when the stark grimness of the economic
situation became more and more apparent in 1931? At the privy council, the king's mood appeared to worsen each day through a situation
in which, Philby wrote, "the Government could see no way of making
both ends meet, and was at the same time confronted by difficulties
with which it could not hope to cope." Ibn Saud became listless and
uninterested in any affairs except his economy. In the past, Philby
recorded, he had been "always debonair, optimistic, confident, adven-
turous, democratic." Now he was "inclined to be despotic and timid,
nervous and pessimistic, sombre-minded and laconic in speech." He
had lost much of his enthusiasm for what had been his cause, which
was to lead the Syrians, the Palestinians, and Iraqis from the rule of
Britain and France into the Wahhab kingdom. Only two members of
the council, Yusuf Yassin, the political secretary, and Abdullah Suleiman, the head of the treasury, possessed any of the abilities needed
to rescue the kingdom from bankruptcy, and they were, in Philby's
opinion, mere yes men. There were murmurs of revolt in the four
provinces, and as Philby recorded of the 1930–1931 winter at Mecca,
"Never had I felt so depressed about the prospects of Arabia." Until
then, a "sort of tacit optimism and hope based upon the slenderest
foundations had kept people alive and alert." Then the blow fell, and
the country and government suddenly collapsed as if paralyzed. The
king "allowed nobody to do anything and did nothing himself."[20]

Philby concluded that if the king would not help himself, he would
have to help the king. The opportunity arose one afternoon when the
king and Philby were alone in the Atna Gardens. Philby "made bold
to say" that the king and his people "were like folk sleeping over a vast

buried treasure, but without the will or energy to search under their beds." The Old Testament had spoken of gold in the Hijaz, and there had been mention of the use of bitumen (which sometimes implied the existence of petroleum) for caulking boats in the Persian Gulf province. The king exclaimed that he would give the infidel all manner of concessions in return for a million pounds gold. Philby responded that "no one would give him anything at all without having reasonable ground for believing that the minerals were there" and that "he would win far more than the sum he mentioned if they did in fact exist and were intelligently exploited." He must overrule the religious council, the Ulema, which had gained greatly in authority since the demise of the Ikhwan; he must overcome the fear of foreigners and let strangers into the country to see what was there. Would the Ulema permit infidels to visit at will about the holy land? Yes, said the king, he would see to it that this was permitted.

Philby then said he knew a man who was in a position to help if he wished. In the winter of 1926–1927, the king had declined to receive Charles Crane, the American millionaire. Would Ibn Saud permit Philby to invite Mr. Crane to make a state visit to Jidda now, in 1931? Yes, said Ibn Saud, he would receive the American, although "he disliked strangers at the gate." But Crane was different; he was an American who had denounced the Sykes-Picot Agreement, the Balfour Declaration, the Mandates, the British, and the French at the time of the Paris Peace Conference.[21]

Crane duly announced that he would be in Jidda in six weeks, for he had to cross the Atlantic, the Mediterranean, and the Red Sea; he would arrive on February 25. Three days before that date, Ibn Saud left for Jidda, something he did only rarely and with reluctance, because he disliked that malodorous town. Now the king, the privy council, the court, and the Ulema set out in a caravan of cars and camels across the stormy hills and steamy coastal plain to greet the American infidel.[22]

The first American capitalist stepped ashore at Jidda to be received in circumstances usually accorded royalty. The orator of Jidda welcomed Crane with verses from the Koran. There was much beating of drums, ululations, and banging of tambourines. Crane remained at Jidda for five days, staying with Sheikh Nasif, the great Najdi philosopher of the times. The visitor was an impressive man, almost as tall as Ibn Saud. Naturally, the king hoped that Crane would provide him with the necessary gold to secure his throne against bankruptcy and revolt. There were banquets, speeches, displays of horsemanship, and

tribal dances of the whirling dervish variety. Ibn Saud presented Crane
with two splendid white mares and a white stallion from his stud. Crane
had anticipated that Ibn Saud would seek a large loan — he had a
private intelligence service — and he surprised everyone. Allah, Crane
declared, helped him who helped himself. He rejected all invitations to
develop the gold, oil, and iron ore deposits in Arabia on the grounds
of principle. He believed, he said, that Arabian treasure should remain
Arabian and should not be exploited by foreigners. Crane repeated
this in writing:

> Although I am hesitant about offering advice on any particular pro-
> ject, on the basis of my own observations, I do feel that in general it
> is better for a nation to develop its own resources with its own talent
> and money, or, if those are inadequate, with a minimum of such aid
> from abroad. Certainly the granting to aliens of monopolies or ex-
> tensive concessions not infrequently leads to both internal and ex-
> ternal difficulties.[23]

Thus Crane passed on a project that would have made him perhaps
the world's richest man. To the surprise of Ibn Saud, and perhaps to his
disappointment, Crane instead produced only a box of dates, which,
he said, he had grown himself through dry farming at his estate in
California. He would put at the king's disposal two experts whom he
had himself trained. This Ibn Saud accepted with gratitude. The second proposal then followed.[24]

At a tea party for Crane, given by Philby at his palace and attended
by the king and his suite, the diplomatic and consular corps, and
Moslem notables, the American asked the king whether there were
underground rivers in the Nejd. There followed much talk about water,
of which there was more than Crane expected in a land so parched.
Crane again mentioned his date plantations in California and told Ibn
Saud that his sole means of irrigation was water drawn from two arte-
sian wells. Crane suggested that if Ibn Saud was agreeable he would
instruct Karl S. Twitchell, an engineer from Vermont whom he had
sent to Yemen, to visit Jidda on his way back to the United States and
look for water. Again Ibn Saud accepted readily, although Twitchell was
an American, an Occidental, and a Christian. This constituted Crane's
sole offer of assistance, and it would prove important. Twitchell was
the instrument through which Standard Oil of California was able to
bid for the Arabian mineral concessions, which, under Philby's direction, the king wished to sell.

Crane's visit ended on March 3. Attended by a guard of honor of
troops and a large assembly of officials, Crane went aboard the S.S.

Taif when it arrived from Port Sudan, northbound for Suez. He wished to be home in time for Easter. Shortly, Twitchell arrived. Within a month he found water at Ain Wazira, about seven miles outside Jidda, and within two months the fresh, sweet water was flowing to the town. Then Twitchell went on to look for gold and oil. When he found them, the American penetration of Arabia began.[25]

At Crane's departure, and with the thought at court that great financial benefits would derive from the visit, Philby saw an opportunity to realize his life's ambition — to become the first Occidental to cross the Rub-al-Khali, the Empty Quarter of Southern Arabia. The largest continuous body of sand in the world; at about a quarter of a million square miles, it was nearly the size of Texas. Ever since his arrival, Philby had sought Ibn Saud's permission to explore that waterless, arid, unpopulated region. Ibn Saud had agreed several times and had promised that he might go during the winter of 1930–1931. But nothing came of it. The king offered several reasons for withholding agreement. There was tribal trouble in the approaches to the desert. He was at war with the Imam Yahya of Yemen, and the Yemeni army was near Najran; Philby would at some stage have to pass through that desert town and become liable to capture. Further, the Ulema opposed Philby's entering a region that was part of the holy, the forbidden land. Fuad Hamza, the deputy foreign minister, whispered to St. John that the king was genuinely concerned to keep the services of his most valued friend at a time when he himself had to attend to great affairs such as the economy and the prospects for finding oil, water, and King Solomon's gold.

The king repeated his promise as a reward for Philby's part in arranging Crane's visit, but again he did not honor it; on January 11, 1931, Ibn Saud dealt his old friend "a crushing blow [by] very gently and very nicely breaking to me that the Rub al Khali is off." St. John took the news badly. "Curse!" he exclaimed in his diary. "There is nothing to do but drain the dregs of disappointment with a bitter heart. I shall be seeing Madina instead, but with me nothing counts but the Rub al Khali and I can find no peace of mind until that is over and done with." St. John took to nagging the king, but this annoyed Ibn Saud, who shouted, "Uskut" — "Shut up." His refusal even to talk about the exploration sat badly with Philby, the more so since it was now over a year since Ibn Saud had run up a debt of £30,000 with Sharquieh, and he still showed no signs of paying it. Philby had concluded that the king's attitude was rank ingratitude.

Then, in February, came the blow of blows. Bertram Thomas, one of Philby's assistants when they were together in crown service at Amman and now vizier and finance minister to the Sultan of Muscat and Oman, suddenly appeared at the head of a camel caravan in the Empty Quarter, on a march from Salalah on the Arabian Sea to the peninsula of Qatar, without even a by-your-leave from Ibn Saud. Beside himself that the king had let him down, that he had broken his most important promise to his faithful servant, on March 9 he wailed to Dora by letter: "Alas Alas! So the sword of Damocles has fallen at last on my hapless head and Thomas has borne off the laurels of the Rub' al Khali!" It was strange to think that "if only Ibn Saud had not ratted" on him, both he and Thomas would have been in the Empty Quarter as joint contenders for the Founder's Medal of the Royal Geographical Society. Now Thomas would get the great prize alone. And Philby would not be at all surprised if Thomas was knighted. If St. John regarded the British government as the source of human darkness and misfortune, that did not mean he did not yearn for that greatest of all British honors. As he lamented further: "No race can be run twice and the winner is forever the victor." He was, he told Dora, "full full of such envy, hatred and malice as a philosopher is capable of, for no one but myself knows how great is Thomas's achievement." He had won the "blue riband of modern exploration."

St. John was at a loss to know what he had done to warrant such treatment at the hands of the monarch he loved deeply and, it seems, genuinely. He had had several "friendly quarrels" with Ibn Saud during the three days since Philby learned of Thomas's feat. He complained vigorously that Ibn Saud had "let me down in spite of all my entreaties and his promises and my very clear warnings that Thomas would certainly be trying the venture at the very time I wanted to do it." But all that was left to St. John was to carry on with his own plans for crossing the Empty Quarter "so as not to leave Thomas solitary in his glory for too long."

The king sent him a royal *bhint,* as Philby wrote to Dora on March 9, "by way of solacing me for my great disappointment. She is a funny little thing, not beautiful by any manner of means but young and shapely enough and with a good elementary knowledge of cooking and housekeeping, which will solve my Meccan domestic problem." Her name was Miriam bint Abdullah al Hasan, and her arrival in Philby's household would improve his knowledge of Arabia and the Arabs and illuminate a side of Arabian life about which "up to date I have been completely and shamefully ignorant." Female company would help him "while away the long hours of my solitude," but nothing "could be done to solace the woe of my defeat. Time alone can do that," Philby declared, adding vigorously, "Damn and blast Ibn Saud and Thomas!"[26]

Immediately he canceled his plans for his first home leave to England since early 1927. He told the Dutch consul, Meulen, that Thomas had not really explored the Empty Quarter at all. What he had done was to ride a line so fast and so straight that all his march amounted to was a race with death. He, Philby, would do the real thing. He would explore the Empty Quarter and tell the world what that part of Arabia was like. Nobody would see him for a year. Perhaps two. Perhaps he would never be seen again. But if he did come back, he assured Meulen, he would have explored the Empty Quarter.

The supreme moment of his life as an explorer arrived, one that was to make him famous and infamous — and Kim, too. Ibn Saud agreed that the state would provide the escort, guides, camels, and stores, and pay the bills, although there was precious little in the treasury. Beyond himself with excitement, Philby set out for Hufuf late in December, and on January 7, 1932, the morrow of Kim's birthday, pausing only to send a telegram to Dora — STARTING, LOVE EVERY-BODY — Philby led his column of fourteen Arabs, thirty-two camels, and provisions for three months into the fogbound Empty Quarter. He was, he wrote, "gloriously conscious of physical well-being and spiritual contentment." At least Thomas had left him with a trial of magnitude.[27]

First he set off across a prehistoric sea. Ahead were four hundred miles of unmapped and trackless desert. In 1918, a guide had spoken of the castles in which a legendary king, Ad ibn Kinad, stabled his horses and "kept his women and eunuchs in a paradise of orgies." It was called Ubar or Wabar, and it had been destroyed by fire from heaven as punishment for the king's sins, a punishment mentioned in the Koran. The guide had told how Bedouin had found the blackened pearls of Kinad's ladies. As it happened, the old guide's directions were wonderfully accurate, as was Philby's understanding of the old Arabic in which he had spoken. But as soon as Philby set eyes on the scene, the legend was shattered: "I looked down not upon the ruins of an ancient city but into the mouth of a volcano, whose twin craters half filled with drifted sand lay side by side surrounded by slag and lava outpoured from the bowels of the earth."

He found little pellets and felt that the Wabar craters were the result of a shower of large masses of meteoric iron that, on falling, had created craters in which the kinetic energy generated heat, leading to violent explosions that threw fragments around; the "pearls" were grains of silica coated with carbon black. Most of these iron masses still lay as they had fallen. Some were large, and St. John removed one handsome piece of great weight to decorate the forecourt of what became Riyadh University, where it still remained in 1994, by which time in every other respect Philby had become a nonperson. However, all this was but the witty hors d'oeuvres before the main course.

The Empty Quarter became a fiery furnace, the nearest approximation to purgatory that existed on earth. Philby denied himself water for fifty-five days — so he claimed, but he did drink the sap of plants he found along the way — as the mercury reached 122 degrees and the sands began to sing, a phenomenon of the region. "Suddenly the great amphitheatre began to boom and drone with a sound not unlike that of a siren or perhaps an aeroplane engine — quite a musical pleasing rhythmic sound of astonishing depth." The Wahhabi spoke of djinns, but Philby provided a more earthly explanation. Plunging into the center of the singing sands, he noticed a deep, sucking sound as he pulled hand and knee out of the slope and felt a "curious but unmistakable sensation of a pulsing and throbbing below the surface, as in a mild earthquake."

He drove himself, his men, and his camels to exhaustion, and on the forty-fourth day of the expedition his escort devised a plot to murder him. He recorded:

> For many days now, I had endured the constant and inevitable friction engendered by the struggle between the insistent urge of my own fixed and unalterable purpose and the solid weight of the innate national inertia thrown into the balance against me by the united body of my companions.

Finding the daytime heat unendurable, the escort demanded that Philby change the pattern and direction of the march and ride by night, arguing that the heat imperiled their lives in this shadeless wilderness. They wanted to hunt oryx, not find answers to geographical and physical mysteries. But their complaints produced only a terrible fury. Philby had not come to sleep, he thundered at them, but to see. He knew what he was doing. He had the king's blessing and the royal protection, and what saved him was what had saved him from a cut throat before — the Arabs' fear of the king's wrath.

But the menace was real. The men looked evil and satanic. "Could one be anything but critical and on one's guard," he scribbled in his notebook, "with companions who would readily have sacrificed the whole object of our endeavour to their own miserable comfort." In such circumstances,

> the Arab does not show up to advantage. He clings frantically, desperately to life however miserable, and when that is at risk, loses heart and head . . . I could not, would not yield . . . A third of the journey was behind us and a steady effort would carry us through if only they would play the man. They were of course weak and disheartened with hunger, for we had had nothing but dates since Shanna. I was famished myself and could sympathise with their condition. I felt like Moses in the wilderness when the multitude clamoured against him.

Heavily bearded, sun-dried, and windburned, Philby displayed the titanic side of his character in this march; his sense of superiority demanded that he succeed where the Arabs would willingly lose. In a world so wild that the aristocratic Somali camels lost their plump beauty and forced him to ride on bone, he drove the escort on by staring them down and by allowing them to cut the throat of a newly born camel calf, which they roasted on a small fire. "In ordinary circumstances I do not think I could have brought myself to partake of such a meal," Philby excused himself later, "but our immediate circumstances were far from ordinary and I could have eaten anything, cooked or raw." Otherwise, in crossing a gravel plain called the Father of the Sea, to keep the camels going they poured water through the animals' nostrils while they themselves ate the prescribed number of dates. On one lap of the journey, circumstances required that Philby ride for eighteen of twenty-one hours, and he covered 70 miles without rest. At another the escort forced him to acknowledge that he was defeated and must turn back. "The Empty Quarter had routed us," he recorded. "At last sleep blotted out the nightmare of the day — the worst of the whole journey from beginning to end, and perhaps the most terrible of my experience."

The camels themselves began to fall. On reaching the foul, briny water well at Naifa, of which he drank three bowls and which tasted like nectar, he scribbled that this was "the first water I have tasted in 55 days." He divided the party into two teams: the fainthearted, who must turn back, and the resolute. To the fainthearted he gave his maps, diaries, and notebooks "so that these at least should not be lost to the world in the event of our failure to get across the desert." On March 5, strengthened by rest, water, and meat and traveling on the best remaining camels, Philby and the remnant of the caravan set out to cover the final 350 miles he had set himself.

Dora had fired a letter off to Philby at Hufuf, hoping to stop the ride, for she had no money and was at her wit's end to know what to do about creditors. It was still winter in England, and she had no money for either gas, electricity, or coal. "God knows where you are and what you are up to," she wrote, but "I have literally no one I can turn to." She might have been speaking to the grave, for there were rumors in London that St. John had died in that terrible wilderness. Then, to the relief of the Empire (save his enemies), St. John's party was sighted, alive and still marching. The sigh of relief whistled in the ionosphere, the *Daily Mail* claimed, and even Lawrence announced his thanks to Allah that Philby had survived. "Only vaguely I heard he was dead," Lawrence wrote. "Good he isn't, for Philby is a decent creature."[28]

For six days they traveled, three of which reminded Philby of life in a furnace. Steering by Jupiter, at last they reached a village called Bisha; the ride was almost over. Camel herders saw them as they came down from the dunes — some of them a thousand feet high — and activated the desert telegraph. The word leaked through the villages to the towns, and thence to Riyadh and London. There, in Hampstead, the telephone began to ring day and night with press inquiries, and Dora wrote another letter into the blue:

> The relief at hearing your news has completely gone to my head and in addition to this I ordered a bottle of sherry and we have all . . . drunk to your very good health. Kim is wild with excitement. His confidence in your success has helped me through the last fortnight. I was on the verge of a breakdown before he arrived. Now I could take on a tiger.

Philby replied that he was exhausted, his hands had been burned black, and he was suffering from huge inflamed hemorrhoids. It had been hard work on short rations of dates and raw, dried camel's meat, and he felt he had "done with desert exploration for good." As for money, there was not a bean in the till. The king had not paid him for the Ford cars he had supplied and the machine guns he had obtained from the Poles, and until he did so, St. John would not be able to send any money. Dora must ask his publishers, Constable, for an advance on the book he intended to write, for he was, he said, "bursting with my epic in embryo."

He set out for London, business, and cricket, and to visit Kim for the first time since 1926. Kim had by then arrived at his father's alma mater, Trinity College.

*

Kimbo was by now twenty-one. Six years had passed since 1926, when St. John moved to Jidda permanently.[29] On Kim's side was love and hate and a desire to emulate and even succeed his father. Only rarely had Kim corresponded with him — a sign of his dissatisfaction with St. John's treatment of Dora, the poverty the family had endured, and the nagging that Kim had received about his progress at school.

So ambitious had St. John been for Kim that he studied the performance of his son and his peers at Westminster as a bloodstock dealer studies form. From time to time St. John's mail gives the impression that he considered his son to be a weakling, likely to fail. He suggested that it might be better if Kim went to work for Major Fisher on his experimental agricultural estate on the Guadalquivir River, as Fisher himself had proposed. On another occasion St. John cast doubt on whether Kim had the ability to get into Trinity. "Of course there is no telling," Philby wrote hopelessly, that Kim "might suddenly pick up at Westminster sufficiently to make it worth while his going to Cambridge but I am not holding any hopes of that now." His next remark reflected his extreme disappointment:

> It is a tragedy that we should have only had one son but it can't be helped and as one gets older one feels more and more that after all it doesn't matter very much. If one is foolish enough to have ambition "the worldly hopes man sets his heart upon, turn ashes!"

In the event, Philby's doubts were unjustified. Kim became an excellent student at a school that set exceptional standards. In the sixth form, where he studied history, he began at the bottom and finished at the top, winning the Marshall Memorial Prize. Yet his achievements evoked no more than sporadic applause from Philby. Kim doubtless found it discouraging to have his record compared constantly and unfavorably with his father's at Westminster. Homosexual encounters added to Kim's distress. In later life Kim admitted that he had "buggered and been buggered" at Westminster, although he was not a homosexual. Indeed, in his private life the sap rose in him as bountifully as it did with his father, perhaps even more so. Still, Kim's stutter had become so serious that in 1928, when his academic record entitled him to a part in the school's annual Latin play, Kim was given only two brief statements to make, whereas St. John had made an entire speech. Also, Philby had so strongly impressed atheism on Kim that the boy was badly mauled when the school put him through its stern curriculum of religious observance. In later life, Kim said he had suffered something akin to a nervous breakdown through Westminster's unending Christian instruction. St. John found his son's sporting performance equally unsatisfactory. Kim showed little of his early interest in sports until 1927, when he began to excel. Philby was overjoyed to learn that Kim had regained his sporting prowess as well as scholastic ability. He wrote to Dora from Jidda:

> I am glad to hear about [Kim's] junior House colours which is excellent and shews that he can stand up in the rough and tumble of school life. I have of course written to congratulate him and have lectured him mildly on never writing to me — only twice since I left. I don't want to take up his work time but I feel he must have a certain amount of spare time. Try and make him a little unselfish and thoughtful of others . . . Encourage his writing essays etc. I think he has that gift and nowadays journalism is not a bad career — professional journalism I mean and not the freelance kind with a bee in one's bonnet that I do. But even I am among the prophets now — a regular and very ill-paid contributor from the Near East!!

But the disquieting aspect of Kim's conduct at Westminster came in April 1927. He was newly turned fifteen and therefore just into his "awkward age." The charge by Luce, one of Kim's tutors, was a serious one. Kim had begun to show an insufficient regard for the truth. The episode that produced Luce's letter must have been serious, for Luce would not have raised such a matter at all with a man so eminent in the school's modern history as St. John. But the legal maxim pertained: false in one thing, false in all. St. John dealt with the warning mildly enough in a letter of instruction to Dora:

> Mr. Luce wrote recently about him and does not seem altogether satisfied about his truthfulness. I have certainly noticed myself this tendency in him and I think it due more to a desire not to be in the wrong! But in any case it ought to be impressed on him (and I know you will do it if you get a chance) that he should always be careful to be truthful whatever the consequences.[30]

Forty years on, after the Philby case had run its course, one of Kim's closest friends and colleagues, Nicholas Elliott, a son of the headmaster of Eton, would see in Luce's letter the first evidence that Kim Philby was a clinical case, someone who needed medical treatment to protect himself and society. In Elliott's personal judgment, Kim Philby was "a schizophrenic with a supreme talent for deception."[31] Kim's reaction to his father's instructions was indicative of this, and guileful. No doubt aware that he was in trouble at Westminster, Kim wrote an essay on chivalry and sent it to his father. In it, for the first time it seems, Kim displayed an interest in socialism; as doubtless he intended, it had the desired effect on St. John. Philby wrote to Dora:

> I was exceedingly interested in Kim's essay on Chivalry and was pleasantly surprised to see that his views are quite unorthodox and controversial. Both in that respect and in his style his work has a strong family resemblance to mine, and I think his writing has a great deal of merit . . . Every line of it might easily have been written by me and he certainly shews no tendency to accept the ordinary dogmas of the Conservative school. Both his essay and his answers to the History questions shew a great capacity for thought and expression, and if he continues as he has begun he ought to do very well.

Kim did do well. He won two scholarships, to Christ Church, Oxford, and to Trinity College, Cambridge. St. John ordered him to accept Trinity, he did so, and there he went late in 1929, at the age of seventeen — young for Trinity but right for politics. His mother installed him in his rooms at 8 Jesus Lane and he began to read history.

At first Kim proved to be a solitary and spent much time reading, playing Beethoven sonatas over and over again, and joining in football games. But as he approached his eighteenth birthday, he decided on a political career. He was intelligent and dutiful and he might succeed, except in one respect — his stammer. At times it was so severe that he seemed to strangle himself in his efforts to speak. At other times he could speak normally and well. In his second year he met and became friendly with a Hungarian artist, Szigetti Szucs, a man who played an important role in his conversion to communism.

Szucs had been a member of the Expressionists, a postwar art group in Berlin that reflected the joyless disillusionment that reigned between the end of World War I and Hitler, a world where, as Otto Friedrich has written,

> there were no pretty girls, just apathetic whores, or matrons with sagging breasts, who stand and wait for paunchy husbands in suspenders and underwear to finish brushing their teeth. There is nobody, as a matter of fact, who looks as young and eager and cleancut as Grosz himself, only middle-aged businessmen with bristling mustaches and bald heads and thick cigars; and officers with monocles and ruthless jaws, and, often, no trousers; and, over and over again, sex murderers, real or potential, brandishing knives and hatchets. Even the buildings of Berlin become sinister . . . hard towers of stone,

usually tilted at threatening angles. And there is rarely any sunshine, just the pale light of a crescent moon glowing thinly outside the apartment house where some horror is occurring . . . They may not represent all Berliners, but those figures of hatred did walk up and down the streets of Berlin in the 1920s, and in the days of Hitler.

What Szucs did in that world of bitter misery has not been established; he remains a shadow, but an important one. Kim referred to him by his nationality in his letters to his father, not mentioning Szucs's name. They traveled together on Kim's motorcycle to the Black Country industrial towns of central England during the winter of 1929–1930. They lodged with poor industrial families; they ate what the unemployed ate; and they saw for themselves the misery being created by the Great Depression. This resulted in a striking letter from Kim to his father about the effects of the depression on the working class — the letter disappeared from St. John's files, but its contents were so vivid that it was well remembered by those who read it.[32] During the summer vacation of 1930 Kim traveled with Szucs to Hungary and Yugoslavia, and he sent a postcard to his father from Sarajevo, where in 1914 the assassination of Archduke Ferdinand of the Austro-Hungarian Empire had touched off World War I.

This seemed indeed a strange association for Philby, who looked and talked so conventionally — tweeds, pipe, gown, mortarboard on occasion, ties, brogues; he was clean-shaven, with a peaches and cream complexion; he was eager, earnest, and, it seemed at the time, as indeed throughout his life, decent and virtuous. But as he explained to his Soviet secret masters, the Black Country changed all that. *The rich had become far too damned rich, the poor far too damned poor.* This statement, which he made repeatedly throughout his life, became his watchword. Fifty years later he would say the same thing about the poor of Leonid Brezhnev's Moscow. His experience in the Black Country was reinforced by what he called the political bankruptcy and cowardice of the Ramsay MacDonald Labour government in dealing with what he believed was the root cause of the Black Country calamity: to maintain Britain's credit in the New York money exchange, MacDonald cut the workers' dole, for millions the sole means of support, by 10 percent. There is no doubt that Philby was sincere in this contention, which, he said, resulted in his conversion to communism. The socialists could achieve nothing against the "alien bankers." Only the communists could do that. His stammer prevented him from entering overt politics. He decided therefore on a career of covert politics. But there was another factor in this decision: he became possessed of a lifelong idée fixe that was quite similar to that which infected St. John when the British government did not honor the Arab Declaration. Kim Philby, too, became a monomaniac against Whitehall. The only difference between father and son was that St. John displayed his whereas Kim concealed his new passion from almost everyone except St. John for the obvious reason that to be effective, a secret communist in those times must not be seen as a secret communist.

St. John became aware of his son's communism from its start. As he wrote to Dora about a letter he had received from Kim in April 1931, he was "glad to think" Kim was "developing on advanced lines" politically, "quite independently of me."[33] That Philby had also realized that Kim might be somewhat extreme seems evident from his remark that "excesses can always be toned down afterwards in the light of experience." What was important was Kim's understanding, Philby declared, "that salvation lies to the left rather than to the right," that the "rising sun is more important than the setting sun." Their meeting of minds was complete. Kim Philby himself wrote of this period:

My decision to play an active part in the struggle against reaction was not the result of sudden conversion. My earliest thoughts on politics turned me toward the labour movement; and one of my first acts on going up to Cambridge in 1929 was to join the Cambridge University Socialist Society . . . But the real turning-point in my thinking came with the demoralisation and rout of the Labour Party in 1931. It seemed incredible that the party should be so helpless against the reserve strength which reaction could mobilise in time of crisis. More important still, the fact that a supposedly sophisticated electorate had been stampeded by the cynical propaganda of the day threw serious doubt on the validity of the assumptions of underlying parliamentary democracy as a whole.[34]

The impotence of British socialism was undoubtedly one of the reasons Philby became a revolutionary of a novel and dangerous type — a member of the bourgeois assigned by the Soviets to enter Whitehall with the object of destroying the system from within. Many men felt as did Philby, and almost all sought to change the system through due process. Philby, however, decided to go underground, a decision, it was true, that he did not make quickly. With his father's campaign against the ruling class as a model, and disposed by character toward the clandestine life, Philby moved steadily over the coming two years toward the vigorous underground world the communists were creating in order to capture the allegiance of men with a future, especially university men. Again, Philby's course was not unique; many of the undergraduates and graduates at the great universities were enrolled in the clandestine wing of the party. What made the Philby case unique was the task that the party set him to gain a place within the British Secret Service, the citadel of the security system of the empire, and, at the direction of the Soviets, capture that citadel for use by the proletariat in the Leninist world revolution.

In this task, the Trinity society played its part. Because Kim performed poorly in his first history examination in 1930, he decided to read economics instead. St. John approved and said he would write to his friend from Cambridge days, John Maynard Keynes, the leading economist of his time and a fellow and lecturer at King's College, about Kim's decision. This again became a fateful development, for through it Kim found himself in the homosexual reaches of Trinity life. Whether St. John's letter had any effect on Keynes we do not know (although it was well known that Keynes had been a homosexual himself) but one of Keynes's closest associates at Cambridge, Dennis Holmes Robertson, a distinguished classicist and economist, became Kim's director of studies. Robertson was also known to St. John. Nearing forty and a bachelor when Kim came under his wing, Robertson was, by repute, an outstanding don but overcivilized and overtutored. Each inch of him was that of a figure in the English Establishment.

A son of the headmaster of Haileybury, a product of Eton, he was a Craven Scholar, a Chancellor's Medallist for English Verse, a Cobden Prizeman, a Fellow of Trinity. Robertson's name appears in the leading modern encyclopedia as one of his generation's top economists. His *Banking Policy and the Price Level* of 1926 foreshadowed some of Keynes's later work. Some have contended that he was the real brains behind Keynes and that Keynes was the real figure behind Franklin Roosevelt's New Deal. He would handle the Anglo-American financial relationship during World War II, and he played a major role at the Bretton Woods Conference, at which the International Monetary Fund, to promote international cooperation, and the International Bank for Reconstruction and Development were established. He served as an adviser to the British government in its financial provisions for World War II. During the war, he became an adviser at the treasury, a member of the Royal Commission on Equal Pay, president of the Royal Economic Society, and a member of the American Philosophical Society. In 1953, Queen Elizabeth II made him a knight.

Robertson was a homosexual, and though there was never a complaint against him, he seems to have been so tortured by guilt that at some stage while Kim was at Trinity he went to Vienna to see Sigmund Freud. Whether Kim was sexually involved with Robertson is not known, but he did become a member of Robertson's circle. Through that group he met an extraordinary figure in Cambridge life, Guy Burgess, the most dazzling homosexual of his time, one at the center of homosexual activity even in Whitehall.

Guy Francis de Moncey Burgess was at once one of the most witty, most beautiful, most clever men and the most amoral undergraduate to come to Cambridge since, it was said, Lord Byron. He was amoral to the point of evil. As his former headmaster at Eton discovered when he called on Guy in his rooms by appointment during the summer term of 1931:

> Of course Guy wasn't in when I arrived so I entered his room in New Court and waited. There were many books on his shelves, and I'm always drawn to other people's taste in reading. As I expected, his taste was fairly wide and interesting. I noticed a number of Marxist tracts and text-books, but that's not what really shocked and depressed me. I realized that something must have gone terribly wrong when I came across an extraordinary array of explicit and extremely unpleasant pornographic literature. He bustled in finally, full of cheerful apologies for being late as usual, and we talked happily enough over the tea-cups.[35]

History underestimated Guy as a lout and a buffoon. Kim believed him to be the outstanding historian of his time, and this may have been true. Born in 1911, Guy was a year older than Kim, and his wit and his beauty made him a darling of Eton as it did at Trinity. He was a man of two worlds, the Marxist-homosexual underworld and the British Establishment. As one student of him wrote, he "loved the relics and memories of England's nineteenth-century greatness. He loved the Reform Club, *Middlemarch*, Lord Salisbury . . . and the British navy." He kept models of Britain's great ships-of-the-line in his flat. He was a dandy, a rogue, and a sodomite, and he claimed — whether in jest or seriously we do not know — that he had become "that way" through an unpleasant incident involving his father. As he told the story, Commander Burgess died while *in copula* with Burgess's mother. Guy, at home on holiday, heard his mother's cries for help and, so he claimed, had the gruesome task of disengaging his dead father from his frightened mother. In sexual matters, he declared, he was not the same again.

Guy bemused Cambridge society. In due course another homosexual, Anthony Blunt, "fathered" Guy as an Apostle, a member of a debating society so exclusive and certain of its excellence that it called itself simply "the Society." Its members saw themselves as a "conspiracy of the self-elected, answerable only to each other," and they termed their version of Platonic love "the High Sodomy." Apostles stood against the Establishment of England and the church, and members were required to swear an oath to secrecy in perpetuity. John Maynard Keynes was still a member. The Society regarded itself as others saw it, an elite within an elite. Their political statement during the 1930s was that since they had been chosen to make a bad society better, they had to join the Communist Party, the only force with the power to fight Nazism and fascism.[36]

Whether Guy and Kim became lovers is not known. Their contemporaries thought not, but even so it is not impossible, for Guy invariably attempted to establish an ascendancy over men who interested him sexually and politically, and he certainly dominated Kim for the next thirty-five years. It seems unlikely that Guy and Kim remained as interested in each other as they were without sex obtruding, for Guy had little interest in anyone unless the association culminated in a sexual act. Also, Guy was a relentless blackmailer, who usually completed his conquest with a reminder to his partner that male sexual relations were a criminal offense and that participants usually went to prison for long periods at hard labor. Certainly, Kim's association with Guy "dogged Kim's whole life, possibly shaping it more than any other human contact"[37] — a possible exaggeration, for there were others who shaped Kim, including his father and his first Soviet controller. But it contained truth.

Perhaps while Robertson was seeing Freud in Vienna about his homosexual guilt, Philby and Burgess came into contact with Cambridge's card-carrying communist Maurice Dobb, who lectured in economics. Dobb, who was born in 1900 and came from Gloucestershire squires, had been educated at Charterhouse and Pembroke College, Cambridge, and came to Marxism through his study of the British shipbuilding industry and his reading of *Das Kapital,* which he thought the most important book in history. His message was that of the classless, scientifically run society offered by Marx, the decline of capitalism, the high superiority of the very fashionable dialectical materialism. This, in theory, was meant to provide both a general worldview and a specific method for the investigation of scientific problems. It was the official philosophy of communism.

Dialectical materialism captured many men with Kim's disposition; and it is said that when he understood it, he experienced the blinding light of reality and certainty about life, a light similar to that experienced by some religious believers when they first sense the presence of God. In its physical aspects, this of realization was more powerful than a youth's first sexual experience and much more lasting in its consequences. As the gleaming Star in the East had shown the way to mankind, the beacon of dialectical materialism showed mankind the way, according to its theoreticians, to Utopia, that ideal state where all is ordered for the best and where the evils of society, such as poverty and misery, have been eliminated — the sort of world the Wahhabi thought they would find when they reached Paradise. Dobb spoke convincingly of dialectical materialism, as one who attended his classes remembered:

> Until the end of his life, Maurice Dobb steadfastly played commu- nism's John the Baptist, preaching the Decline of Capitalism to suc- cessive generations of undergraduates. In 1965, when I attended his classes, he was white-haired and weary after nearly half a century in his self-appointed role. But he still mustered the persuasive enthusi- asm of the true convert who is also an inspiring teacher. Unlike some of his younger colleagues in the Economics Faculty, whose ferociously statistical arguments were virtually impossible to follow, let alone take notes on, Dobb's twice-weekly classes were a breath of common sense to a confused newcomer to the Economics Tripos. His plausible ren- dering of the serpentine twists of Soviet economic policy were models of clarity and memorability.[38]

Kim became a member of Dobb's little group, called the Red House, after Dobb's tall, narrow house in Chesterton Lane. This was a center of Marxian thought and talk, "the nucleus of the University commu- nists," as many as forty young men who held an important part of England's future in their hands and who talked about a Soviet Union of Great Britain. Yet the security authorities were not unaware of Dobb's activities. After reading one of the 1925 Home Office reports on com- munist subversion, King George V wrote to Lord Balfour, then the chancellor of Cambridge, asking why such a well-known Marxist as Dobb was permitted to indoctrinate undergraduates. In making his inquiries, Balfour was misled by the high academic authorities who advised him. Dobb's influence, he was assured, was no more than academic.

All the same, Dobb came under the eye of the Security Service, which kept an eye on Cambridge politics, known since the Middle Ages as antiestablishmentarian. Still, there seems to have been no breath of suspicion, not a single document, on Kim when, in due course, an important authority in the Philby case asked whether there was "anything recorded against" him. This despite the fact that his communism was well known not only at Cambridge but also at Oxford. And this despite the events of early 1933, that year when history changed its tune.

Between late 1932 and early 1933, there began the last process that led to the assumption of supreme political power in Germany by Adolf Hitler. The death struggle between the Nazi Party and the powerful left-wing parties began. Kim Philby left England with A. A. Milne's nephew Tim, riding across Europe on Kim's motorcycle — a formidable journey in midwinter — and arrived in Berlin in January. In all, they appear to have spent eight weeks in Germany, Kim ostensibly to improve his German in preparation for his foreign service examination. In March, Kim was seen at the Hegelhof, a student pension where a bed could be had for a mark a night, soon after the Reichstag fire, the event Hitler used to outlaw the Communist Party. He was there for one of the main steps that led to the establishment of the Third Reich, on March 5, 1933, an event that led to the triumph of fascism in Austria, an attempted fascist coup d'état in France, to the consolidation of fascism in Italy, Poland, and Hungary, and open or hidden fascist dictatorships in all the Balkan states. It hastened the emergence of the Fascist Party in Great Britain.

We know nothing about Kim's personal reaction to the fearful and rapid march of events while he was in Berlin. No record has survived, if one existed in the first place, for his movements were shadowy. Milne may have had a record, but if he did, it was suppressed by the Thatcher government when he attempted to publish a memoir in the mid-1980s. What is sure about Philby's reaction is that the ignominious collapse of the German Communist Party again strengthened his commitment to Stalinism. Philby was back in Cambridge by June of 1933, to sit for his final examinations that month. At the time, in answering a friend's question about whether Stalin betrayed the Communist Party to Hitler and whether Stalin was really on the left, Kim replied with finality, "What Stalin does *is* left."[39] This reply convinced the friend — Richard Clarke, who became a third secretary of the treasury — that Kim had finally crossed over to the Communist camp. There were some who had no doubts about his politics, and two of them had no doubt that he had become a disloyalist. One was his tutor, Dennis Robertson, and the other, not a relative, was Sir Donald Robertson, the Regius Professor of Greek at Cambridge University and a close friend of St. John's.

Against this background, St. John arrived at Trinity in 1932 to meet Kimbo for the first time in seven years.

6

Little Son

1932–1934

IN APRIL 1932, St. John Philby arrived in London an authentic hero, his triumph in the Empty Quarter in the class of Scott's voyage to the South Pole or Lindbergh's Atlantic flight. The Royal Geographical Society gave him a dinner, and Philby gave a lecture afterward to an august audience. The Central Asian Society booked him for a lecture; newspapers commissioned articles and sent reporters to see him; and the publisher Benn commissioned a book. The British Broadcasting Corporation put on a series of talks; the British Museum asked to know more about the rare birds Philby had seen; and, his biographer wrote, "strangers levered themselves out of armchairs in the Athenaeum to wring his hand."[1] But no one was more delighted than Kim: the triumph increased his own worth at Cambridge and in the party. In the first of three articles for *The Times* Philby explained, "For fourteen years I have followed a will o' the wisp through the Arabian deserts with a fierce and relentless devotion. And now I am at rest."[2] But he was not at rest, of course.

There was a party at the family home in Hampstead, and St. John distributed marvelous presents. For Kim there was a pure white silk robe known as an *aba*. For each of the women there was a silk princess's shawl; for May a collection of tear bottles and the pilgrim's cooking utensils, or *kholpots*. As for "the jools," as Philby called the little treasure trove of pearls and emeralds, they were first to be valued, then made into ornaments for his daughters. Philby's signet ring was for Kim "as I can no longer wear it for very obvious reasons"; it was a christening ring, given to him at birth by May to signify his Christianity. In the eyes of the Wahhabi purists at Ibn Saud's court, to continue to wear the ring would be idolatrous. No such restraints existed in Kim's world. He wore the ring for life, and perhaps for death. There was talk of big money: Sharquieh had landed the Marconi contract for, at first, eleven stationary and four mobile wireless stations. The order was worth £17,000, the entire enterprise around £500,000. Sharquieh's commission was, Philby claimed, 20 percent of the principal, £100,000, although that figure seems very high. Here at last was something to celebrate, a benefit that flowed directly from Philby's new association with the Oneness.

St. John was in high good humor. One of his political enemies had died recently. Another had disgraced himself in some fashion. He was "delighted to find all my old enemies" were tasting "the bitters of life" — Sir Herbert Samuel, the former high commissioner at Jerusalem; Chaim Weizmann, the leader of the Zionist movement; Winston Churchill, who was having hard times as a politician and as a writer; the British imperialist statesman Leopold Amery; Sir Alfred Mond, founder of the huge Imperial Chemical Industry and a liberal politician, and what St. John called "the rest of them, a formidable list!"[3]

He hastened away to join Kim for three days at Trinity, in his new lodgings at Whewell's Court, the Victorian Gothic apartments across Trinity Street from Great Gate, prized and more convenient than Jesus Lane. It was a joyous reunion amid those noble buildings with their green lawns, the candlelit high tables laden with boiled beef, old Madeira, old silverware, port wine accents, the murmuring, nodding dons, caped and cowled in the medieval gloom. Here St. John had come to Fabianism, the anathema of his time; Kim was discovering communism, the new one. Kim was nineteen, gowned, fresh-faced, earnest, decent, it seemed, and quiet. A budding intellectual, a breed then defined as "a person of superior reasoning power." St. John met Kim's friends, notably Guy Burgess, of whom Rebecca West would write:

> It could be seen that he belonged to the world of the favoured, who have wealth and respect by right of birth; but it was certain that in his time he had wakened up in some very queer rooms. He had many friends. These included some of the most unpleasant Englishmen and women now living.

And she noted of his character, in a way better than others:

> Sometimes in a home for children . . . there is a small boy who always catches the visitor's eye. The brooding darkness of the child's face

lights up with such an enchanting smile, his response to strangers is so quick and gay, he has such a quaint turn of phrase. Surely, the visitor says, there cannot be anything very much wrong with this delightful little boy. Well, yes there is. It unfortunately happens that wherever he goes, fire breaks out. By constant watching it has been established that the only toy he cares for is a box of matches; and up the houses and barns and hayricks go, in crackling flames. That was Burgess's distinguishing mark: the flashing smile of the fire-raiser, full of secret pleasure in mischief and destruction.[4]

St. John felt that way about him. He and his friends were, Philby wrote, "pretty second rate."[5]

There was Donald Duart Maclean, the son of a lesser Liberal minister. Maclean read modern languages and was making a name as a speaker, reviewer, and propagandist. There was Anthony Blunt, who was reading mathematics. All belonged to the Marxist-Leninist group around Maurice Dobb. St. John could have had little doubt about what was occurring. Some doggerel appeared at about this time in a Cambridge journal:

WE'RE THE TRINITY SOVIET-SKI

You bet-ski! Just let-ski
Us sing u our little song-i-vitch
Not longi-vitch
But strong-i-bitch.

Down with law and order-ski;
Represented by the Porter-ski;
'Tis our intent to shoot-i-vitch
Don, Fellow, Dean and Tutor-vitch.[6]

The important matter about Kim was that he had remained the solitary, the odd man out. Whatever he did, he did mainly alone, using Burgess, a rogue with the means and the will to rove about, as his messenger. It seems Kim Philby never quite understood that Burgess might be using him and his father's name. For the most part, Kim had no contact after Trinity with the rest of the Cambridge Marxists, except to recruit them as Soviet agents. And of them all, only Kim made spying for the Soviets his life's work.

His father was not quite satisfied with what he found. Kim seemed to be doing not much better in economics than in history, and his tutor could offer no explanation for the failure. Nor could St. John. It was, he wrote to Dora, "quite unworthy of him." He was not gadding about with girls, and on this subject, St. John noted, Kim seemed not at all "disturbed by sex influences, which is fortunate for him."[7] So why was he not doing better in his studies? "Kim has all the brains you like to get Firsts on his head," St. John wrote, "but it is clear that he has not been attending to his work, and he must really take that more seriously."[8] For one thing, Kim would not get a place in the foreign service if he continued in this fashion; for another, St. John could not afford to support him at Trinity any longer than was necessary; the higher education of Kim's three sisters had now to be considered. Kim had announced his intention to learn German, which pleased his father, for until now Kim had shown no interest in foreign languages. It was therefore "gratifying to hear that he now realises the importance of learning languages; and he must be regretting his chances of learning without tears I threw in his way in his youth!"[9]

When Kim said he wished to make socialist politics his career, his father pointed out that the young man's stammer would prove to be an impediment. Kim changed course and said that, after all, he might try for the foreign service. His father encouraged him in this and agreed that Kim should spend more time in Germany to brush up his German. He gave Kim £50 — a large sum — and with this money Kim entered the communist underworld.

St. John's time with Kim came to an end. It is noteworthy that not long after St. John's departure, the Cambridge communists seized control of the Cambridge University Socialist Society, of which Kim was the treasurer. Then they captured the Heretics, an antichurch society founded to offer an alternative to compulsory chapel. Lastly, the communists won the Apostles. There could have been no greater political triumph for the communists, who had now acquired a base for their expansion throughout both Cambridge and Oxford.

When St. John left Cambridge, a serious matter affecting him arose in London concerning some secret papers that had been found recently at Cairo; they were in the possession of one of Ibn Saud's clerks at the foreign ministry in Mecca, Mohammed Tamini, who had been trying to sell them.[10] According to the Foreign Office docket on Tamini, he had eighty-eight files on British affairs in the Middle East between 1914 and 1922. There could be no more sensitive documents than these, for they showed what had been promised to whom, the reality of Whitehall's intentions in the Middle East, and who had paid what to whom. It was assumed that they had been given to Philby when he took over the Amman post from Lawrence and that he took them with him when he resigned in order to give them to Ibn Saud. This, it was believed, took place in 1927, a year after Philby took up permanent residence at Jidda.

St. John, of course, declared that he knew nothing of Tamini or that he had held such delicate papers — but his signature was on the note of quittance he had given to Lawrence at that time. Also, the Foreign Office had discovered that Tamini had been given the task of translating the files and of making one copy on an Arabic typewriter. He worked under supervision, but the supervisor had absented himself for some of the time, thus enabling Tamini to make a carbon copy of much if not all of the most important parts of the documents. In 1931, suspicion fell on Tamini, and he was dismissed by the Saudi deputy foreign minister.

He then fled to Jidda, where, the Foreign Office's questioning of him showed, he claimed to have spent a month with Philby. The report did not say what business they had together, but the implication was that Philby winnowed out the less important documents and then facilitated Tamini's "escape" to Beirut to spread them among the Arab nationalist and secret societies in Istanbul, Damascus, and Cairo. When Tamini was arrested in Cairo by the narcotics police, some of the papers were found on him. Norman Mayers, the official directing the investigation in Cairo, wrote: "Taminy's [*sic*] story, if true, is extremely injurious to Philby." Having read the reports, the high commissioner for the Anglo-Egyptian-Sudan, Sir Percy Loraine, wrote to Sir Lancelot Oliphant, an under secretary at the Foreign Office, that the affair "makes very unpleasant reading" and that other copies of the documents "in all probability are in the wrong hands." But, displaying the customary reluctance in high British circles to believe an Oriental's word against that of an Occidental, and the usual unwillingness of the Establishment to risk scandal, Loraine described the accusations against Philby as "implied." He was therefore sending his report to Oliphant "privately rather than to embody them in an official despatch," which would have been distributed to every embassy and consulate. Loraine added that any guilt of the part of Philby rested only on Tamini, "who is a rogue and is shown to be a liar." That statement reveals for the first time in the history of the Philby case the disposition of high officials to deploy the code of fair play rather than call in Scotland Yard. An Arab could easily be a rogue and a liar, and so might Philby be, but the code of inscrutability must be maintained if the crown was to continue to be seen as efficient and incorruptible.

Oliphant carefully did nothing that might embarrass St. John, perhaps because a charge that a Briton had committed treason would reflect on other members of the ruling generation. It is equally possible that Oliphant had no desire to lose an informant at Ibn Saud's court. Yet the existence of the files and Philby's connection to them was indeed good reason to call in the Special Branch of Scotland Yard. Someone somewhere, "together and with other persons unknown, for purposes prejudicial to the safety or interest of the state [had communicated] to other persons information which might be directly or indirectly useful to an enemy." But in the interests of discretion, the case was handled informally, which meant that the papers were not placed in Philby's file at the Foreign Office. Had it been otherwise, the Philby case itself might never have occurred.

And so St. John sped on. He now had to meet a representative of Standard Oil of California, which since 1919 had been in the forefront of the U.S. oil industry's attempts to break the British grip on Middle Eastern oil.

The full power of the British political system, staffed by its best men, guarded not only the Middle East but all the approaches to it around all the points of the compass. The system was backed by military and commercial power; each component state of the Middle East was bound to Britain, and, to a lesser extent, France, through subsidies paid in gold or treaties in which the rulers of all the oil-bearing states of Arabia and the Persian Gulf placed their foreign affairs in British hands in perpetuity. The only airline in the region was British, as were most of the shipping lines. Telecommunications were also in British hands. American diplomatic and consular missions in the region were no more than a nominal presence.

American nationals were admitted only on the sufferance of the British and the French, though mainly the British. And there was a sense that yesterday's ally — in fact, the United States had never officially recognized Britain as an allied power in the war, only as an "associated power" — had become today's rival. For its part, the United States had become ever more pessimistic about its future as a great oil power and, consequently, as a great political power. There developed a fear that the United States was running out of oil. The U.S. oil companies freely predicted a calamitous situation in which the nation might be forced into a form of economic colonialism by the great British and European oil companies, all of which were regarded as no more than instruments of colonial power. Through the oil lobby in Washington there developed what a congressional committee would call a "case of national jitters" in which "oil supply took on a vital national defense complexion."[11]

Accordingly, the State Department came under pressure to compel the British to observe Wilson's "open door" policy, particularly in regard to Middle Eastern oil. But the door remained shut — until Philby's visit to London in 1932. Charles R. Crane may have advised Standard Oil of Philby's disaffection for the British government and of his power over Ibn Saud. The State Department had its file on Philby and his attempts to win U.S. diplomatic recognition for the King of the Nejd. Philby's animus for the British government was common knowledge. Standard Oil was interested in buying the rights to explore for oil in Arabia; and Karl Twitchell, the American engineer employed by Crane who had found water near Jidda, gold near Medina, and signs of oil near Hofuf on the Persian Gulf, was now in New York, trying to interest Standard Oil in an exploration project.

But Twitchell could not guarantee Ibn Saud's approval for an American contract. Only Philby possessed the influence to win that. It was sensible therefore to approach Philby while he was in London, for a word from him to the king about Standard Oil's interest might gain the king's attention and the exploration contract. The approach had its official aspects. The U.S. consul general in London, Albert Halstead, in a letter to Philby dated May 26, 1932, introduced "the Honorable Francis B. Loomis, formerly Under Secretary of State of the United States, and a gentleman whom I have known most favorably for many years. Mr. Loomis has been impressed with your work in the desert in Arabia, and would like to meet you . . . With apologies for this intrusion, and thanks in advance."[12]

Philby rejected the invitation, believing that Loomis was interested in talking about Philby's conquest of the Empty Quarter, as were so many others. But on July 7, Philby heard again from Consul General Halstead. Mr. Loomis would be in London shortly and remained interested in speaking with Philby. Would lunch at Simpson's suit? This time it did, and Loomis disclosed his interest in oil over a roast beef luncheon. Philby recorded:

> [Loomis] was particularly anxious to know whether it would be possible to obtain a concession in Ibn Sa'ud's territory. Knowing the King's attitude in the matter, and his dire need for money, I responded positively, with a warning that the obtaining of such a concession would involve a satisfactory arrangement regarding the price to be paid for the privilege of investigating the resources of the mainland. Mr. Loomis said he would first have to consult his col-

leagues in America on the matter before committing himself to anything definite, but that he would be glad of my cooperation in the
event of the company being desirous of proceeding with the business.
I told him that I would be glad to help in any scheme which would
contribute to the prosperity of Arabia.[13]

Philby was himself rather pro-American. He believed the United States
to be an anti-imperial power, interested only in business, not, like the
British, in obtaining political control of the region where they invested
money. This attitude was to change later, but at the time it was an
important factor in the events that now developed. There were several
more letters and an exchange of commercial codes to enable Standard
Oil's officers to establish confidential correspondence with him when
he returned to Jidda. All this was agreeable news, and Philby splashed
out and bought a new silver Ford Phaeton, a purchase that occasioned
much speculation about his true financial state. But there was money
about. On October 19, 1932, he and Dora left England to journey
together overland to Jidda.

First they went to a quiet farm near the Whistling Sands of the Lleyn
peninsula in Denmark. There they were joined by Kim and his sisters,
Diana, Patricia, and Helena, for what was their first holiday together
as a family. It was a happy time, the last for many years. Since Philby
had a contract with Benn, the publisher, for a book on the Empty
Quarter:

> I burned the midnight oil with my writing, and my wife typed my
> script on a broken-down typewriter! It was all great fun, and I had
> not a care in the world, having achieved the peak of my ambition [in
> crossing the Empty Quarter], and little dreaming that another quar-
> ter of a century of Arabian exploration still lay before me. Oil cer-
> tainly played no part in such dreams as I had.[14]

Then St. John and Dora drove on in the Phaeton to Hamburg and
Berlin, where, according to the KGB, Philby met with Hitler, whose
party had recently become the largest in the Reichstag. They traveled
through Dresden, Prague, Vienna, Budapest, Belgrade, Sofia, and Adri-
anople. At some stage, according to the KGB, Philby met Mussolini,
whose blend of fascism appealed greatly to St. John; he admired particularly the "manly" and militaristic spirit Mussolini had bred in the
Italian youth.

They reached Jidda on December 3 to find two urgent telegrams
from Standard Oil. The great game over the Saudi oil concession
began. And at its center was the intricate relationship between Philby

and the first British minister to the court of Ibn Saud, Sir Andrew Ryan, lately His Britannic Majesty's Chief Dragoman to the Sublime Porte at Istanbul.

When Philby had entered into correspondence with Dr. Hugh Dalton of the Foreign Office in 1929, he mentioned the need to improve the "unsatisfactory relations between London and Riyadh."[15] The way to do it, he felt, was to replace the present consulate with a legation, which the Russians had already done. That is what happened. The Foreign Office named its first minister plenipotentiary to Arabia, Sir Andrew Ryan, a man of the finest imperial timber. Learning of his appointment, Philby wrote again to Dalton on January 17, 1930:

> If you can hint to [Ryan] . . . that he will not do ill to consult me I can assure you that all my knowledge and efforts will be unreservedly at his disposal. I have no personal axe to grind and seek no office or reward, while on the other hand I have placed my cards on the table before you as regards what I think the British Government should do to secure the by no means negligible goodwill of the Arabs. So far as I have a mission in life it is to secure complete harmony between Great Britain and Arabia; and it is not really a very difficult task if we concede the Arabs' right to complete independence.

Yet from the moment Ryan arrived, Philby began to make political warfare against him. When Ryan reached Jidda on May 6, 1930, in the small British warship *Dahlia*, Philby appeared in a boat off *Dahlia*'s quarterdeck, where Jidda notables were gathered to welcome the new minister. He had heard something of Ryan's celebrity as a poet at the Foreign Office. Holding a loudspeaker, he interrupted the quiet proceedings with an ode he had written for the occasion, which he read out in its original Latin and which, subsequently, he sent in English to Ryan as a memento. It reflected all the elegance of Trinity, something of Philby's attitude toward official Britons, and a good deal in deft form of Philby's warfare against Whitehall:

> Our greetings warm receive, Sir Andrew Ryan,
> A poet thou, 'tis said, from poetaster's hands.
> Hail! worthy envoy of the British lion!
> Hail! harbinger of peace to Arab lands
> After long discord and dissension! Fie on
> Those so long denied that Arab sands
> Could yet produce a really worthy scion
> Of that great chivalry that still commands
> The admiration of the world! But why on

Earth should we suppose that impious rebel bands
Or Hashim's rivalry or greedy Zion
Could cut inexorable Fate's sure strands
Wove on the loom of Wahab's creed. Orion
Himself, with belt and buckler girt, forth stands
To warn with dire destruction all who'd try on
The game of war with one whose doughty hands
Have wrought an empire, though he oft die lie on
An exile's bed, forlorn, near coral strands
Of Parsic Gulf far off. Amphitryon
Of the seas' lords, of Britain's sons demands
To leave henceforth the Arabs to rely on
One who has clearly shewn that his commands
Within his sphere of rule on lamb and lion
Alike impose the peace, that British hands
Alone were wont to guard, though they might die on
Far paynim shore, relieving robber bands
Of smuggled arms and captive slaves that cry on
Their God or England's might. She reprimands
All evil-doers her roaming sailors pry on;
But God decrees: the torch to other hands
Must pass; 'tis time and thou, Sir Andrew Ryan,
Art come to land the "white man's burden" on these sands
And win Arabian love and thanks for Albion.[16]

  The ode caused surprise and even consternation among those privileged gathered on *Dahlia*'s quarterdeck. Ryan, in later correspondence,
expressed his desire to put the matter behind them; Philby was evidently too important as a privy councilor, and perhaps as an informant, for Ryan to make a serious issue of what was an insult to him
personally and Whitehall generally. The sequel to the surprising scene
was testament to Philby's ability to deliver a telling insult to a high
officer of the crown and then to turn the victim into an admirer. Over
the next four years, the men became, it seems, good friends, sipping
their cocktails at sunset and talking together learnedly and amiably on
Ryan's balcony overlooking the Red Sea. Ryan called Philby "Sinjallah"
(a clever pun on the names St. John and Allah; one that reflected
Ryan's mild disapproval, as a practicing Roman Catholic, of Philby's
conversion), and their relationship became "a Red Sea friendship."[17]
Such associations were agreeable but susceptible to the double-cross.
  As Ryan recorded of Philby: "Whatever his peculiarities of character
and outlook, he was far and away the most conversable person in our
circle, and my wife and I were on the best of terms with him."[18] He

himself did not resent "the dash of bitters" in Philby's references to Ryan in his memoir, and "certain inaccuracies in his account of my arrival in Jedda" were "of too little importance to need correction in detail." Philby was too powerful in Saudi Arabia for Ryan to dismiss him.

If Ryan knew about the Tamini case, he said nothing. Although he and Philby were both Cambridge men, neither doubted that the other would double-cross him if the need arose, and Philby was aware that Ryan would not hesitate to employ any measure if the British hegemony in the region was threatened by Philby. Relations between the United States and Great Britain since World War I were described as "friendly but not cordial"; each had made plans for war against the other, a practice that was not abandoned until 1933; and the United States made little secret of its ambition to succeed Britain as the world's leading political power. In commercial matters the rivalry was intense, and relations between the great republic and the great monarchy would have become a great deal worse had Ryan realized what Philby was up to in Arabia.

The game began in mid-February 1933; the prize was Arabian oil (if there was any) and British control in the Near East. The issues:

1. The king had said he wanted a loan of £100,000 gold, recoverable from royalties, along with £5,000 gold yearly as rent. Standard Oil had said it would find such a sum "burdensome" but was prepared to consider it. Ibn Saud made Philby his principal agent in the negotiations.

2. "Confidentially" Philby revealed these terms to a friend in the Anglo-Persian Oil Company, the main British contestant and rival to Standard Oil. He told Anglo-Persian, in order to lure them in, that Ibn Saud was "right up against it" financially and would be "bound to accept any reasonable offer."[19]

3. Philby approached Ryan and assured him that he had not committed himself to either Standard Oil or Anglo-Persian and that he could therefore act as Ryan's informant. Ryan accepted and informed the Foreign Office accordingly. Anglo-Persian, which was closely connected to the Foreign Office, then entered the field.

4. In fact, Philby had accepted an honorarium of $1,000 a month for six months from Standard Oil to act as its confidential adviser and intermediary with the king and the finance minister, plus what Philby called "substantial bonuses on the signature of the concession, and on the discovery of oil in commercial quantities." He did not advise Ryan of this arrangement.

5. Ibn Saud said he would prefer doing business with the British if they would meet his terms in gold. Under no circumstances would he accept paper money. Philby thought Ibn Saud was, in his relations with Ryan, "like a bird mesmerized by a snake." Philby was determined to prevent the concession going to Anglo-Persian while encouraging their representative to believe that it might do so.

6. Philby's private position, as he also explained, was: "In the event of both parties being willing to go all the way, and in so far as my advice might be of any avail with the Government, I should, for purely political reasons, have been inclined to favor the Americans, whose record at that time was entirely free of any imperialistic implications. Otherwise I should favor the highest bidder."

As for Philby's acceptance of the secret honorarium, he was candid enough — but only thirty years later, in a small book called *Arabian Oil Ventures,* published in 1964 by the Middle East Institute in Washington, D.C. The "prospect of this windfall of some eighteen hundred pounds sterling eased the problem of bills for a son at Cambridge and three daughters at first-class schools."[20] He did not, however, withdraw from his relationship with the British minister, Ryan, and continued to advise him, with heavy emphasis on the fact that the information was the minister's exclusively.

What Philby did not know was that Karl Twitchell had been hired by Standard Oil as a confidential adviser. He had been offered 10 percent of the company's royalties if he would represent the company with the Saudi finance minister, Abdullah Suleiman. Twitchell had rejected this offer and instead asked for a one-time payment of $75,000 to collaborate with Suleiman in reopening the Cradle of Gold, as he called the Solomon gold mines. Standard Oil accepted this, the papers were signed, and thereby Twitchell gave away a chance to become perhaps a multibillionaire.

The die was cast. Two Americans, Lloyd N. Hamilton, a lawyer, and Twitchell, who had now been retained by Hamilton as an adviser, arrived at Jidda, and the negotiations began. Philby began to play the three parties against the middle — the king's interest and, to a lesser extent, his own, with a hidden bias toward Standard Oil. As Philby wrote of Ryan, he was "essentially a Conservative in his political outlook with a strong flavour of the old-fashioned imperialism," while Philby was, as he described himself, "an iconoclast with marked leanings to the Left" and one "generally regarded in Jidda society as something of a Bolshevik."[21]

After much complex negotiation over four months, Philby won the game by steering Hamilton into paying the right price in the right form — gold. Gold alone was what Ibn Saud wanted. He had no use for paper money; it disintegrated when it was exposed too much to the sweat of the palm. Philby gave no such advice to the British representative because he was led to believe that Ibn Saud might accept the paper rupees of India. Standard Oil gained the concession to what proved to be the richest oil field in the world in return for a loan of £35,000 gold, with a further £20,000 at a later date, an annual rent of £5,000 gold, and a royalty of four shillings per ton of production. It became worth hundreds of billions of U.S. dollars. Indeed, it became worth more than the British investment in the empire.

The agreement between Standard Oil and the Saudi government was ready for what Philby called "the expression of the King's pleasure" on May 8, 1933. It consisted of fourteen foolscap pages containing thirty-seven articles of agreement; the finance minister, Sheikh Suleiman, read them out, clause by clause. As the proceedings lengthened, Ibn Saud fell asleep. The meeting was adjourned until the next morning, when the council reassembled to hear the rest of the text. As Suleiman droned on, again clause by clause, again Ibn Saud fell asleep, to wake with a start when the reading ended. "Must have been asleep!" he exclaimed. "What do you think about it?" All expressed their satisfaction. And what did Philby think? He expressed his "pleasure at the successful termination of negotiations, which seemed to spell great prosperity for his people." "Very well," said the king, turning to the finance minister. "Put your trust in God, and sign." The document was signed, and Philby telephoned Hamilton with the news. The document was signed formally by both parties on Thursday, May 11, 1933.

The following evening the privy council resumed its ordinary business in no spirit of celebration. It devoted itself to what Philby called "a long and interesting discussion of women and their ways: the King did not sleep on this occasion, and was the life and soul of the party." Otherwise the privy council devoted itself briefly to a decision that the Kingdom of Saudi Arabia should be established out of the cumbersome title that had existed hitherto, that of the Dual Kingdom of the Hijaz and Nejd and its Dependencies. The council approved a decree appointing the king's eldest son, Saud, as heir to the throne and the crown prince; the formal proclamation of the existence of the new kingdom and the office of crown prince was made in the Great Mosque of Mecca. Philby recorded this a miracle that had "opened with developments fraught with great promise for the land, which the years to come would see realized in a manner exceeding the wildest dreams of those who had the good fortune to be eye-witnesses to these events."

Philby's personal reward was an invitation to become a permanent adviser to Standard Oil at an honorarium to him — not to Fisher's company, Sharquieh — of £1,000 sterling, or $5,000, a year. There was also a reward from Ibn Saud: Philby was granted a virtual monopoly of the motor transportation of pilgrims between Jidda and Mecca. This might not make Philby a rich man, but it would enable him to live in considerable comfort for as long as the monopoly existed.

Standard Oil of California was renamed, in due course, the Arabian American Oil Company. The consignment of gold sovereigns reached Jidda by steamer in August 1933 and was stored at the Netherlands Trading Society at Jidda, which acted as the state bank. There the finance minister, the manager of the society, and Twitchell counted each sovereign and consigned the £30,000 to the new Saudi Arabian government. The moment passed in which the British oil companies might have overturned the U.S. contract, and they made no attempt to do so — possibly because, with the emergence of German Nazism, Italian fascism, and Japanese militarism, Whitehall welcomed a stronger commercial presence in the Middle East. The flag followed trade.

Philby's adroitness had made a great impression upon the Americans. They believed Philby was a British spy, and continued to do so for the next twenty years.[22] But Hamilton and Standard Oil formed a very high opinion of him, and as Fred A. Davis, who became chairman of the board of directors of the Arabian American Oil Company, would write in testimony to the importance of Philby's role in the negotiations:

> His honesty, frankness, and sense of balance enabled him to act as liaison or go-between without either side then or since having the feeling that he was unduly favoring the other. A truly remarkable performance!
>
> I first had the pleasure of meeting Philby in 1937 on his home grounds in Jidda. He was a raconteur of great wit and charm, but it was for more substantive reasons that I came away from our first meeting, and our many subsequent ones, with a greater respect for the man and his accomplishments. His integrity and wholehearted devotion to the purposes he had set for himself in life made a deep impression. Saudi Arabia is better for his having been a part of it.[23]

Sir Andrew Ryan felt no such admiration for Philby. Philby's biographer, Elizabeth Monroe, observed that "Philby recorded this result with more than mere personal satisfaction; it struck him as a just reward to the Americans for their anti-imperialism, and to the British for their sharp practice." Not until the agreement was actually signed did Philby tell Ryan, and then, as Philby wrote,

> We talked about everything under the Arabian sun; but it was only when I got up to take my leave that I said to him: "I suppose you have heard that the Americans have got the concession." He was thunder-struck, and his face darkened with anger and disappointment . . . Our final leave-taking was somewhat strained.[24]

Philby had dealt the empire a heavy blow. He was satisfied with his victory, to say nothing of the new money, for, as Dora was to comment, St. John had been "getting very jumpy about the money problem."[25] But his satisfaction lasted only a short time. St. John and Dora received disquieting news from Kim in Vienna.

On January 1, 1933, Kim Philby reached his majority and thereby became responsible for his actions. He was already a dyed-in-the-wool communist — in the language of the times — and he had made little secret of his politics with his mother; Dora had seen much of him since he went to Trinity and was concerned about his communism. He had converted her from her apoliticism but only as far as the Labour Party. In several places his passions were a cause for distrust, for communists owed their loyalty not to their country of birth but to Moscow. Since Dora hoped that Kim would follow in the family tradition of crown service, she knew that he might be endangering his future in the Foreign Office.

Such were his passions in that passionate year — Hitler became chancellor of Germany, having declared in his testament, *Mein Kampf,* that he intended to destroy Bolshevism — that he spent much more time in communist politics than he did in preparing for his final examinations. Trinity awarded him an upper second in economics, a decent show but a long way from his father's glorious first. His father was greatly disappointed in his son's performance and never mentioned the subject again, in his letters at least. But Trinity gave Kim a cash award for his economics degree — £14 ($70) — which he spent on the complete works of Karl Marx. After the graduation ceremony, which Dora attended, he claimed that during his last week at Trinity he spent an evening in his room, reflecting on his future. What was he to do with his career and life? He decided to serve Soviet power.

Philby could have served it with his labor, but he decided to take another course, an intellectual one. He would enter the Bolshevik underground to serve the world revolution of the proletariat. What he would do in the underworld was not quite clear to him at first, but he saw in it a certain nobility, that of the revolutionary Zhelyabov, the man who killed Tsar Nicholas II. "History moves too slowly," Zhelyabov, now a Hero of the Soviet Union, had said. "Sometimes it needs a push." It is not probable that he knew much at this stage of his political development, except that conspiracy was more fun than hard work. He took the first steps then and there. On his last day at Cambridge he went to see Maurice Dobb, his tutor in economics, to ask his advice about how to get in touch with the Communist Party. It is not clear that Philby asked how he might contact the communist *underground;* but there are reasons to believe that Dobb did not send him to the party in London, which was under surveillance, but to the Comintern agent in Paris, who is thought to have been a certain Louis Gibarti.

At about this same time Kim went to dine with Sir Dennis Robertson, his father's friend and the Regius Professor of Greek. There he discovered that his politics, which he thought he had concealed from his colleagues, were widely known at the college. When Robertson asked Kim what he wanted to do when he went down, Kim replied that he had just completed the application form for the Foreign Service. Robertson, taken aback, said, "It's a pity you didn't consult me first. They will surely ask me for a reference." Kim said that he had indeed given Robertson's name, at which Robertson said, "But I think you quite unfit for government service: you are far too far to the left."[26]

So Philby stood exposed as a secret communist from the moment he set out to enter the Soviet underground. Nonetheless he did set out. Robertson's statement represents the earliest known suspicion about Kim's loyalty; it would not be the last. To polish his German for the Foreign Service examinations, Philby went to Vienna late in 1933, a time of severe disturbances between the right and the left in Austrian politics.

Through an arrangement with the communist-front Austrian Relief Fund for the Victims of German Fascism, he lodged with Israel Kohlman, a minor civil servant, and his wife, Gisella, at their home in Latschka-gasse 9, a workers' street in the ninth district of Vienna. In the house, too, was the Kohlmans' daughter, Alice, a comely girl of twenty.[27] Vaguely plump and leggy, wearing a dirndl and ankle socks, she had no known occupation except that of what came to be known as a "honey trap," a female employed by a secret service to recruit or compromise men for intelligence purposes. When she met Philby, she had married and just divorced Karl Friedman, a member of the Zionist Socialist Movement. She had recently been recruited into the Viennese communist underground by, it is supposed, Peter Gabor, later the police minister of Stalinist Hungary.

Alice took up with Kim as he neared his twenty-second birthday. His previous experience of women was not large, in the opinion of both his mother and his father, for he had been raised in a matriarchy and educated in a monastic system. He had had homosexual experiences at Westminster and may have done so again at Trinity, with Guy Burgess. Even as late as 1992 it was far from clear in the mind of one of Philby's closest associates, Nicholas Elliott, who was also a Trinity man, whether he was not a practicing homosexual even when, later in life, his sexual interest in women became vigorous.[28] As it emerged, he did select his women with care, according to the needs of his cover, and he abandoned them ruthlessly when they were no longer useful. In all, Kim would have four wives and numerous other mates, and all were, it seems, content.

Alice hooked her man; and she hooked him not only in her own interests but in those of the Soviet intelligence service, which had recently evolved a definite espionage doctrine. Part of that doctrine was that "in capitalistic countries lucrative appointments and quick promotions are usually assured to young men who are sons of political leaders." A young man of "this background, fresh from college, passes the civil service with the greatest of ease and is suddenly appointed private secretary to a cabinet minister and in a few short years assistant to a member of the Government." Then he becomes a member of the government, and therefore the Soviet service must assist them in their careers and in obtaining promotion.[29]

Such a policy had just become fashionable when Kim Philby appeared in Vienna in 1933, the son of St. John Philby, Ibn Saud's political adviser, a product of Westminster and Trinity, and a communist, and amenable by nature to a clandestine's career. He thought he was working for the party, and it seems that no one told him that he was marked down for the work of obtaining what the Soviets called "true intelligence," information "procured by undercover agents and secret informants in defiance of the laws of the foreign country in which they operate." This work was now to be directed against the "main enemy," England, and Philby was to become the first recruit. The instrument was Alice, who has been described as a "tremendous little sexpot."

Sharp eyes were about Philby when, on chivalric — and sexual — impulse, Kim married Alice to provide her with the protection of his passport and nationality from the Austrian political police. He took no steps to ensure that the marriage was not a public affair. He married her at Vienna's City Hall on February 24, 1934, declaring himself on his marriage lines to be a student "without religious faith"; Alice declared herself to be who she was, Alice Friedman, born on May 2, 1910, in Vienna. All who were interested heard about it and gossiped about it, and the British community in Vienna was astonished. One of those who knew was Hugh Gaitskell, later the Chancellor of the Exchequer and a leader of the Labour Party. He knew the Philby family and would play some part in its affairs as the Philby case matured. He and his wife may even have attended the ceremony or the celebrations afterward. Also present at the wedding was Teddy Kollek, the future mayor of Jerusalem, who knew Philby and Alice in Vienna. His recollection of the marriage would be important when Philby's career took him into the secret circle of Washington in 1950. There Kollek and Philby would meet again, with consequences.

Letters flew everywhere, particularly to Cambridge. St. John and Dora Philby were "horrified." Kim explained to his parents in a letter, which arrived while the Standard Oil men were moving into St. John's palace at Jidda, the Beit Baghdadi, and Philby was moving out to Ibn Saud's more modern residence, the Green Palace near the Mecca Gate. Alice, Kim wrote, was "interested" in communism, "she from the practical side and I from the theoretical." This interest in "practical communism" had brought her to the attention of the Viennese security service. Kim said he had become concerned for her safety when she was placed under restriction by the police, an order that required her to report at regular intervals to her police station. If she did not do so, she was liable to arrest. He advised his parents that he loved Alice and could not let her suffer; "in short, we were married last Saturday and [Alice] obtained the British passport that was the object of the step."[30] He added that the marriage was a temporary affair and could be dissolved once the emergency was over — ignorant, it seems, that the issuing authority, the Passport Control Office at the British Embassy, was also the cover organization for the British Secret Service in the city. There can be little doubt that the Passport Control officer, Thomas J. Kendrick, was aware of the circumstances in which his office issued the passport; if he was not, he was derelict in his duties.

The only son of St. John, a foe of Zionism, had married a Zionist, and St. John, dismayed, sent Dora back to England to inspect their new daughter-in-law. Whatever danger Alice thought herself to be in, she and Kim did not flee Vienna immediately, even though rebellion flared into the full-scale bombardment of the workers' housing developments on the outskirts of the capital by the forces of the Austrian right. Philby was given work with a machine gun crew (although he fired no shots) and as a messenger between the proletariats' outposts. He went to Prague and Budapest on courier assignments. There were many witnesses to his underground work, and some of them wrote about him. Muriel Gardiner, a young American heiress, met him under clandestine circumstances. A Wellesley graduate, Miss Gardiner was involved with the Viennese *Iskra, The Spark,* Lenin's underground newspaper back in 1903, and Kim had dangerous work for her, the more so since she was partly Jewish. She remembered Philby in terms that hint at his charm and animal spirits:

> My visitor arrived punctually, an extremely handsome dark-haired man, probably younger than I, dressed in hiking clothes and boots and carrying a rucksack. He spoke impeccable English, and I felt he must have been educated at an English school. But I was not certain of his national origin, for his occasional German phrases also had an authentic ring. We talked cautiously at first as we drank our coffee and as he smoked or played with his pipe. He got into a rather theoretical discussion, which gradually led into broader areas of history, sociology, philosophy. I was fascinated by my guest's intelligence and charm. After about two hours' talk neither of us showed an inclination to stop, so I made some sandwiches and more coffee and we continued our discussion well into the afternoon. I remained mystified as to who this man was, his nationality and party, whether he was living in Vienna or simply passing through, and whether he would want some service from me after he had explored my attitude sufficiently. I was of course reticent about my underground work and connections but frank in stating my socialist affiliations . . . He did not commit himself. I had not met with such complete secrecy before, and it made me somewhat uneasy. In all other respects my hours with this curious visitor were very enjoyable and I hoped to get to know him better.[31]

Both Alice and Philby continued to circulate among the British press corps in the city. Invited to visit them, the British author Naomi Mitchison found them "not very domesticated" at the Pension Schulhof, Alice "a dark, untidy comrade," while Kim struck her as "too gentle to be a good politician." A London reporter, Eric Gedye, remembered being taken by Alice to a forest to witness the martial arts training of a guerrilla band called "the Kirov Brigade"; and he remembered, too, that Kim was the leader of the brigade.[32]

But then, fearing that Alice's arrest was imminent, the couple left Vienna on May 2, 1934, sixty-seven days after their marriage. On their police form they stated that they were traveling to London. They wrote down Alice's maiden name and her address in Vienna, thus providing a permanent record for the Austrian police — which sent such names to the headquarters of all police forces in Western and Central Europe, on guard against the Communist International. With Alice riding pillion on the motorcycle, Philby rode to Paris, where they had a little holiday among the comrades. They arrived in London in the middle of May. With Dora Philby still on the high seas, St. John had asked his mother to inspect Alice. She found them not at the family home in Hampstead but, as she advised St. John, "pigging it" at the home of a comrade. The room occupied by Kim and Alice, May reported, was furnished only with a mattress, there being no toilet or bathing facilities; and there was a third person in the room, a male Hungarian whose name May could not recall.[33] This may have been the Comintern agent Peter Gabor, who had introduced Philby to Alice Friedman.

May took a rather favorable view of Alice. But Dora, when she arrived, felt otherwise. As she wrote to St. John, she found Alice "hard, pert and managing" and believed that she had "caught" Kim. "Just you wait till you see her," she went on. As for Kim, "I do hope he gets a job to get him off this bloody communism. He's not quite extreme yet but may become so if he's not got something to occupy his mind."[34] He made an attempt to join the Communist Party through its headquarters in King Street in Covent Market, but he was not accepted on the grounds that he was a bourgeois. He argued and implored them to listen, but he remained to them a bourgeois and perhaps even a police spy. He telephoned the Civil Service Commission to see what had become of his application to the Foreign Service. Then he received a message from a certain Edith Tudor Hart, a children's photographer in London and a former member of the Austrian Communist Party who was known to Alice. Mrs. Hart was an Austrian Jew who had married a physician, Alex Tudor Hart, a communist. Would Alice and Kim care to come to tea?

They did. Mrs. Hart was appalled to hear that Kim had gone to the headquarters of the Communist Party of Great Britain, which was under the permanent surveillance of the security authorities. There was an interlude of perhaps a week — long enough to see if there were any police reaction to his visit — after which Mrs. Hart took him to meet "a very important man." They went by a roundabout route, changing taxis, buses, and tubes, and he found himself at midday in Regent's

Park, sitting beside a man on a bench by the lake. A conversation took place, but none of it concerned the man, his business, whom he represented, or his status. All Philby learned was that the stranger's name was Otto.

Many years later, in Moscow, Philby used to celebrate a number of anniversaries each year. One of these was the first of June, the date in 1934 when he was approached by Otto to work for the Soviet Union. He wrote of Otto in an autobiography that he never completed:

> My stranger was a man in his middle thirties. He was rather below medium height, and the breadth of his shoulders was accentuated by his general stoutness. He had fairly curly hair and a broad clear brow. His blue eyes and wide mouth were highly mobile, hinting at rich possibilities of mischief. We spoke in German, in which he was completely at home. I took him at first to be an Austrian, but one or two later indications, so slight that I have forgotten them, suggested he might be Czech.[35]

Otto proved to be one Arnold Deutsch, an Austrian who had had contact with Alice in Vienna before her marriage to Philby. Eight years older than Philby, Deutsch had himself recently been recruited into the Soviet Secret Service in Moscow while working in Vienna as a psychologist and sex therapist. He was a proponent of a weird sexual theory known in Vienna as "the sex-pol movement." Founded by Deutsch's tutor at Vienna University, Wilhelm Reich — known locally as "the prophet of the better orgasm" — the movement provided sexual therapy to the proletariat in the belief that a poor man's sexual performance led him to fascism.[36]

In April 1934, just ahead of Kim and Alice, Deutsch and his wife fled Vienna for London when the Viennese vice squad began looking into the sex-pol movement. At the British frontier Deutsch claimed successfully that he was a political refugee and was given temporary residency. He obtained work as a part-time lecturer at London University and waited for Kim and Alice to arrive. There is a belief that he had been behind their marriage; and it seems evident that Philby was personally interested in psychology, for in his library in Moscow in 1992 was a volume on the subject in German. It had been signed but the signature had been cut out; Philby often wished to conceal the identity of a colleague in the Soviet service. There is also a belief that Deutsch had gained a thralldom over Philby, and certainly he came to regard Deutsch with a devotion reserved otherwise for his father and Guy Burgess.

At that first meeting in Regent's Park, Philby recorded in his incomplete autobiography, he told Deutsch that he wished to join the Communist Party, but Otto felt "he might do more elsewhere." If he joined the party he "would be one of many, but with my possibilities and capabilities I was qualified for a service for which recruits were few and far between." Otto then intimated that the work might be highly political. There was the rise of fascism and "the equivocal attitude" of the Western democracies toward the Soviet Union. It was "desperately important" to know what was occurring between those democracies and the fascist powers. An avowed communist "would never get near the real truth," but "somebody moving as a real bourgeois among bourgeois could." Long before Otto finished, Philby realized that he was being recruited as a spy, and he decided to accept; as he explained elsewhere, "One does not look twice at an offer for employment in an elite service."

But Deutsch was in no hurry to recruit Philby. He wished to study him more closely before formally recruiting him. He instructed Philby to meet him again in two weeks, to set his watch by a clock at Victoria Station, and to be at the rendezvous *precisely* on time. Before they separated, Deutsch asked Philby how he proposed to return home, and Philby said he would take a bus. Otto suggested a taxi and asked how much money he had with him. Philby said he had no more than a shilling, at which Otto said they would talk about money when next they met. Meanwhile, here was a pound — one ten-shilling note and the rest in silver. That, said Otto, would enable Philby to take a taxi. In parting, Otto told Philby, "If I don't turn up at the rendezvous, just go ahead and join the party," a statement that did little to reassure Philby, whose confidence at this stage was at ground zero.

Meanwhile Dennis Robertson, Philby's director of studies at Trinity, had received an official letter from the Civil Service Commission concerning Kim's application to sit for the Foreign Service examination. The letter invited Robertson to supply his opinion of his former student. Robertson found that he was, as he put it, quite prepared to vouch for Philby "on the personal side" but could not give him a political reference.[37] This distressed Robertson, for he knew that a failure on his part to supply such a reference might damn Philby's career for good.

Anxious about the implications of his decision, Robertson had contacted Donald Robertson, the professor of Greek. Donald Robertson, Philby's second referee, had also received a letter from the Civil Service Commission and also had concerns about giving Kim the necessary political reference. The two Robertsons met and decided to call Kim to Cambridge to discuss their concerns. Fresh from his meeting with Deutsch, Kim met with his referees on June 4 or 5. He of course said nothing about his wish to work for the Soviet Union as a spy. But he did admit that, should he find himself in a crisis with his loyalties divided between the British government and his own belief in communism, he might support the communist position. Thereupon both Robertsons told Kim that they could not give him the references. They warned him that any evasions on their part about his politics might prove fatal to his prospects for any sort of career. Both recommended that he withdraw his application, and Philby agreed. The system had worked. Donald Robertson then wrote to St. John at Jidda:

> Kim was quite definitely & clear-headedly conscious of divided loyalties, & that he could not give any guarantee, even in the most generalized way, that he would sacrifice the unofficial pull to the official one, nor yet, alternatively, that he would resign if it came to such a conflict, rather than remain in a false position. He was perfectly frank about all this, & I admired his courage and truthfulness very greatly.

He went on to say that he "could not help personally being glad, however disappointing the situation is at the moment, that K[im] is *not* going for the [Foreign Office], as the strain on him, considering his temperament, of such a divided position, would have been almost intolerable."[38]

Only rarely had St. John been more irate than he was when he received Robertson's letter. He never replied to it; instead, he sent his views to Dora:

> I have always held that he is entitled to his political views and I have never doubted that he is perfectly sincere in his leanings towards Communism. I disapprove personally of bloody revolutions, whether Fascist or Communist, but I cannot help thinking that some form of Communism is likely to establish itself as a reasonable political faith in this next generation just as Socialism, which was anathema in my youth, has made good in our generation. And, be that as it may, I hold strongly that no one should be victimised (least of all the young) for political or religious opinions honestly held. And, more than that, I think that a young man with serious views is more likely to be a valuable asset in Government service than the golf or football playing nincompoop with a vague tendency to Fascism, whom Dennis Robertson would probably have vouched for as a suitable Government of the future without wincing.

St. John turned to the graver question of Kim's loyalty:

> The only serious question really is whether Kim definitely intended
> to be disloyal to the Government while in its service. If that was his
> intention he should not have wasted his time (to say nothing of other
> things) in preparing for the exam. Some people may think (and they
> are welcome to think what they like) that I was disloyal to the Gov-
> ernment, but that was never the case. I was in opposition to its policy
> and always made that clear and I resigned in order to have freedom
> to express my views more publicly. And I do not doubt that today
> there are hundreds of Government servants who hold views strongly
> in opposition to Government policy but who do their daily work
> quietly and loyally. That I think would have been Kim's position and,
> if he did not think so, he should have withdrawn without being ad-
> vised to do so.[39]

St. John closed the matter with a thump. He was much occupied
with the oil negotiations in Mecca and Jidda. Declaring that Kim "has
been exceedingly silly," he wrote of Alice's claim to be "independent
of Kim financially" and asked Dora to see to it that she went back to
Vienna in order to "let the future work itself out without the added
complication of her obviously rather irksome presence." As for Kim,
his father was "sorry for him," both in his marriage "and the shock of
the exam business," but he was "clear-headed enough to see that in
both he has no one to blame but himself."[40]

Kim, in a letter to his father, set down the only words we know that
amounted to a hint that he had become a secret communist:

> The ideal would be for people of extreme views to keep them dark
> from everyone, their own families included. But it is very difficult to
> hide views when they are in the process of formation, and indeed
> unless they start extreme there is no incentive to do so.[41]

There it was, as plain as a pikestaff. He had made his commitment
as a clandestine even as Moscow Center was cutting orders to a senior
agent in Europe to proceed to London to undertake the "penetration
of the [British] intelligence service for illuminating the ways this establishment works on our territory." Mention was made in these orders
of the need for the "cultivation, surveillance and penetration into the
work of the English intelligence organs" in London and on the pe-
riphery of the USSR, in Latvia, Finland, and Estonia. The orders were
signed by Artur Krystianovich Artusov, the Soviet chief of foreign intelligence between 1930 and 1936.[42]

Under Deutsch's direct guidance, Philby was to take the first step
in that penetration, a major one. At some stage that June, Deutsch's

chief in London, Ignace Reif, advised Artusov that he was confident they had made contact with "a potentially very useful and trustworthy recruit" for "the organisation." This man had arrived in London with his wife, a "former Austrian Party member," and he was known to "Arnold" and recommended by "Edith." Together with Arnold and Edith, Reif advised, he had worked out a plan to meet with the man. The meeting had taken place "with all precautions," the candidate had declared "his full readiness to work for us," and Reif was announcing that he had decided "to recruit the fellow without delay, not for 'the organisation,' as it is too early for that, but for anti-Fascist work."[43]

Philby was formally recruited at his second meeting with Deutsch, on or about July 14, 1934. Being without means, Philby accepted a small sum of money from Deutsch "for expenses," probably not more than £5 ($20). His code name in Soviet communications became Synok, but to Deutsch he was Söhnchen, "Little Son." Artusov, aware of his recruitment, announced in a letter in July that the London group "has recruited the son of the Anglo-agent Philby, Ibn Saud's counsellor."[44]

Gennady X,* a retired KGB colonel who worked with Philby for more than ten years in the 1970s and 1980s, claimed that Kim said Deutsch became "father and tutor" to him in London — "the father he had never had." Philby spoke of Deutsch in terms of "great reverence and affection."[45] At first Philby believed that Deutsch represented not the Soviet Secret Service but the Communist International, "the general staff" of the world revolution of the proletariat. The discipline he began to experience was what Lenin had called "an iron discipline bordering on military discipline"; the subject worked under "the absolute control of an invisible, strictly secret, central body composed of intellectual leaders."[46]

Philby's enlistment into the Soviet Secret Service resembled his namesake Kim's into the "legion of the lost," as the British Secret Service was known in one of Kipling's poems. There was a reason for it. Philby believed that only the Soviet Union possessed the spiritual and industrial power necessary to defeat the rising power of Nazism. There was of course the romance and adventure offered by Deutsch, equal to

---

*Exceptionally in this book, this is not the individual's real name. The man concerned was a KGB colonel who was Philby's liaison officer with KGB headquarters for about a decade between 1970 and 1980. He became one of Philby's intimates in the last twenty years of Kim's life. The author interviewed this man extensively in Moscow in February 1992. In November 1993 he visited Washington on commercial business, and at a further meeting he requested that his name not be used on the grounds that there would be "complications" if it was. Such were the political uncertainties in the Moscow of Boris Yeltsin that the author assented, if very reluctantly. In all other cases, the true names of the KGB officers involved with Philby have been used.

that attendant on his father's position of power at the Wahhab court. Kim, too, was now a man of affairs. He would work for those affairs not only for an occasional evening, or a week, or just for the holidays. The step he had taken was for life. The perils in which he stood were made quite evident to him very shortly when officers of the Special Branch of Scotland Yard called on Ignace Reif, who had just supervised Philby's recruitment. They wished to know of his plans to leave the country. Reif fled. All Kim's Soviet masters would be compelled to take flight over the next decade.

But this was not all. Most of the Soviet officers who had control of him during most of the next decade were Jews of Eastern European origin. They too had an agenda. They had been recruited because, as a CIA study noted, they had "nothing to fight with except their brains." Only "by supporting Stalin and the Communist cause could the Jewish demands be realized." These demands mainly concerned the establishment of a Jewish state in Palestine. Further, "the war against Fascism and Nazism could be successfully waged only under the guidance of Communism and that support of the Soviet anti-Fascist movement was obligatory for the Jewish masses."[47] Young Kim Philby could assist the Jews in their struggle against Hitler and in their other struggle, against Whitehall for Jewish causes in Palestine. Before Reif fled, he wrote a letter to his superiors that the "important factors in the recruitment of SYNOK were: 1. Position of his father. 2. His intention to enter Foreign Office service."[48] There is, incidentally, no evidence that even Deutsch was aware that Philby had withdrawn his application to the Foreign Office. The reason is evident; his worth to the Soviets would be considerably diminished if they knew that the Robertsons had forced his withdrawal on loyalty grounds. If the Robertsons knew about his communism, who else knew in British society? Was it not possible that everyone knew? Beyond that was the value of St. John to the Soviet service. As the political adviser to Ibn Saud, he was at the very center of Arabian politics. His power of advice was great. What was decided at Ibn Saud's court might be important to the security and integrity of the Soviet Union. Could young Philby be relied on to use his father as an informant? Would the son really spy on his father? Here was a vital question. The answer: behind the patrician and kindly mask of Deutsch was a ruthless amorality. The ends justified the means. That is exactly what they expected of Kim, and that, as will be seen, is exactly one of the services that Philby now rendered to the Soviet Union. He began to spy on his father.

Deutsch's view of Kim is therefore of importance in this story:

Söhnchen comes from a peculiar family. His father is considered at present to be the most distinguished expert on the Arab world. He has command of several Arabic dialects and has himself become a Muslim. He is an ambitious tyrant and wanted to make a great man of his son. He repressed all his son's desires. He has a bit of a stammer and this increases his diffidence. He is a typical armchair scientist, well read, educated, serious and profound. He is a clumsy person emotionally and does not easily get close to people. Often he is simply afraid to talk because of his speech defect, unwilling to make a fool of himself. It is difficult for him to tell lies. Söhnchen has studied Marxist teachings thoroughly and he generally studies everything thoroughly, but he would always say that he knows little. He has a profound knowledge of history, geography and economy — and at the same time he likes and understands music. He is undoubtedly a sentimental person, but, owing to his upbringing and the whole life of the English bourgeoisie, this side of his character is rather corrupted. He is a shy person and does not know how to handle money in the sense that he does not know how to arrange his own budget. However, he handles our money very carefully. He enjoys great love and respect for his seriousness and honesty. He was ready, without questioning, to do anything for us and has shown all his seriousness and diligence working for us. He is a kind and mild person. His temperament inclines him to pessimism and that is why he needs constant encouragement.[49]

At the start of Philby's employment as a Soviet spy, Deutsch set him a routine but important task. He was to write short biographies of all he knew and met, including his father's associates. Philby proved excellent at such work; his ability to sum up the character of persons he met was altogether rare. So skilled was he that making the summaries became a regular task during the next twenty-four years, the span of the first phase of his career as a Soviet agent. An example of that gift was his neat paragraph on Lawrence of Arabia, written on the occasion of Lawrence's death in 1935:

Lawrence misjudged both the balance of power in the Arabian Peninsula and world interest in the Middle East. He was sent to Arabia to perform a concrete task, and performed it to perfection. But the surprising success of his operation and the brilliance of his personality lent a false glow to the material he had at hand. He was himself certainly deceived as to the permanence of his achievement. The dominant figure in contemporary Arabia is not Lawrence, still less Faisal, but Ibn Saud.[50]

As usual, his father speaketh. Everyone Kim encountered during his career was likely to be in his notes. These became what he called "a thick bundle of papers," which included "every detail, however trivial, I could remember about each." It was, he said, "awesome to think of the libel actions that would lie against me if the Moscow archives ever saw the light of day." Through these notes, Deutsch selected those who came to form the Cambridge Five, which Philby called "a pretty little espionage network."[51]

Philby's first recruit was Donald Duart Maclean, a son of a former education minister. Their meeting took place in August 1934, about eight weeks after Philby's own enlistment. Deutsch thought highly of him and wrote for his superiors that Maclean

> is a very different person in comparison to [Philby]. He is simpler and more sure of himself. He is a tall, handsome fellow with a striking presence. He knows this, but does not make too much use of it because he is too serious. He was an active member of the Communist Party at Cambridge . . . He came to us out of sincere motivation, namely the intellectual emptiness and aimlessness of the bourgeois class to which he belonged antagonised him. He is well read, clever, but not as profound as [Philby]. He is honest and at home became accustomed to a modest life because, even though his father was a minister, he was not a rich man. He dresses carelessly like [Philby] and is involved in the same Bohemian life. Like [Philby], he is reserved and secretive, seldom displaying his enthusiasms or admiration. This to a large degree is explainable from his upbringing in the English bourgeois world . . . He lives without a wife, though it would not be difficult for him to find someone. He explained it to me by the fact that he had an aversion to girls of his own class and so could only live with a woman who is also a comrade.
>
> Reif once told him a dirty joke and [Maclean] told me afterwards of his astonishment that a Communist could speak so shabbily and mockingly of women. [Maclean] is ambitious and he does not like anybody telling him he has made a mistake. He is a brave person and is ready to do anything for us. In money matters he is irreproachable. He did not want to take money from us, but in some cases he needed it . . . Neither he nor [Philby] knows for certain which organisation he is working for. We simply told them that it was for the Party and the Soviet Union . . . Our revolutionary cause has an absolute hold and authority over them.

In short, Maclean was "unconditionally a very prospective source."[52]

The second to be considered was Guy Burgess, who by then had become a Fellow of Trinity College. Deutsch was, Philby recorded, "anxious to recruit him; his potentialities were very tempting." But, he also recounted, "I had to insist on the dangers he represented. I was not so worried about discipline, since his sense of political discipline would probably look after that. His drawback was his unfailing capacity for making himself conspicuous." But as Philby and Deutsch deliberated at the third meeting, which took place late in June 1934 or early in July, they reckoned with Burgess himself.

> While we were talking, he was drawing conclusions and acting on them. He had convinced himself that Maclean and I had not undergone a sudden change of views, and that he was being excluded from something esoteric and exciting. So he started to badger us, and nobody could badger more effectively than Burgess. He went for Maclean and he went for me. Doubtless he went for others as well, for Theo and Otto became increasingly worried that, if he got nowhere, he might try some trick — perhaps talk about us to people outside our circle. He might well be more dangerous outside than inside. So the decision was taken to recruit him. He must have been one of the very few people to have forced themselves into the Soviet special service.[53]

It remained for Deutsch to commend Burgess to the Center. In a psychological report in 1939 he noted that Burgess was well educated and well read but superficial. He spoke well "and a lot" but was "a very temperamental and emotional man and he is easily subject to mood swings." The party and its purity and discipline had been "something of a salvation for him." Unlike Philby and Maclean, he was homosexual. He had taken to party work with great enthusiasm. Deutsch continued:

> Part of his private life is led in a circle of intellectual friends whom he recruited among a wide variety of people, ranging from the famous liberal economist Keynes and extending to the very trash of society down to male prostitutes. His personal degradation, drunkenness, irregular way of life and the feeling of being outside society were connected with this kind of life, but on the other hand his abhorrence of bourgeois morality came from this. This kind of life did not satisfy him. His homosexuality he explains as not inborn because he can also live with women. He learned it at Eton because everyone is engaged with homosexuality there, so he simply joined in. The pupils there lived several to a room and the class masters use their superior position to seduce the young boys.[54]

Burgess's homosexual associations constituted the "most exploitable assets" he brought to the Soviet service. In a four-page letter he named more than two hundred people, many of whom were moving up the rungs toward "the upper reaches of the British military, academic and governing establishment." Deutsch felt that in "relations with us he is honest and does everything without objections and sometimes produces an impression of a person who is too readily subdued. Though he dresses very scruffily, he still likes to attract attention."

Burgess was a weak link, and Deutsch had to consider how his personality might provide the British Secret and Security Services with an opportunity for countermeasures and whether Burgess would expose the members of the ring, in particular, Philby and Maclean. Deutsch's reservations were justified. In due course, Burgess made contact with the deputy chief of the Political Section of the British Secret Service, David Footman, an associate of St. John's in the old Levantine Consular Service. Through Footman, Burgess met Colonel Valentine Vivian, St. John's old friend in the Political and Secret Department of the Government of India during the Sikh Rebellion at the outbreak of World War I. As will be seen, Vivian would try to recruit Burgess as a penetration agent for work against the communist rings at Oxford and Cambridge, which Vivian knew existed, and against the Soviet service in London and Moscow.[55]

By late 1934 or early 1935, Deutsch judged Philby to be ready to penetrate one of the inner sanctums of Whitehall as a step toward penetration of the British Secret Service. In his surveys of his friends and associates he had written of Tom Wylie, who was about the same age as Philby. They had been together at Westminster, and Wylie had "enjoyed some distinction as a classical scholar at Oxford." But Wylie was known too as a heavy drinker with homosexual inclinations. Deutsch's interest was stirred when Philby found that Wylie had become private secretary to the permanent head of the War Office, Sir Herbert Creedy, and therefore one of the most powerful figures in the Whitehall establishment. Furthermore, Wylie also became the resident clerk at the War Office, which meant that he had an apartment there in order to deal with the after-hours business — telegrams from abroad, telephone messages, press inquiries, and the general administrative duties involved in running a great department of state.

The Wylie case proved to be the *fons et origo mali* of the Philby scandal, which lasted intermittently from 1951 until 1989, with frequent echoes thereafter. According to Philby, there was no question of recruiting Wylie as a Soviet spy; he did not specify why except to say that "there were more ways than one of using a contact in a sensitive position." But Philby did see much of Wylie in 1934 and discovered that he "was given to heavy drinking and tried to counteract its effects by violent exercise at week-ends." He had played Fives, a game like squash in which the hand is used as a bat, at Westminster; Philby had also played Fives there. They both began to play for Old Westminster on weekends, after which they would, as Philby put it, "settle down to convivial evenings in which I would tempt Wylie into indiscretions." The difficulty was "that he was not interested either in politics or the War Office." But

he was good at his job, not because he was interested, but because he combined a good mind with practical sense. Until the blue snakes [liquor] got him. Deutsch and I were soon discovering ways of prising more out of him. We considered blackmailing him on account of his homosexuality, but I advised against it; Wylie was not a person to be pushed around. We also discarded the idea of bribing him; he had private means and was comfortably off.

Philby then discovered that Wylie lived at the War Office and that in his sitting room there was a safe that held his whiskey supply.

I had often seen him open it and toss the key back into the middle drawer of his desk. We agreed on a course of action. [Deutsch] would give me a pill guaranteed to knock Wylie out for an hour or two. When I was quite certain that he was out I would open the safe and look at its contents. I was on no acount to remove anything. On the contrary, I must put everything back, including the key, exactly as I had found it.

Two or three Saturdays later Philby met Wylie for their weekly Fives match, Philby with Deutsch's

pill carefully wrapped in tissue paper, tucked into my waistcoat pocket. I need not have bothered. That afternoon we won and we returned to London in high spirits. Our pub crawl from the London terminus to the War Office was very thorough indeed. By the time we got to Whitehall, he needed support. Back at his flat, he opened the safe and poured us each a half tumbler of whisky. He drained his at a gulp, tottered to his couch and was snoring within seconds. The door of the safe was wide open.
  Wylie was out, without benefit of knock-out drop. But now for the safe! It contained unused stationery, some bits and pieces of office equipment; also a tray on which lay a single sheet of paper. At last I was looking at a secret document. But my excitement was followed by bitter disappointment. The paper was a communication from the British ambassador in Italy to the Foreign Office, reporting a talk

about Soviet policy with a colleague in Rome. Like many such reports, as I was to learn later, it was of depressing unimportance. With care, I replaced the paper; Wylie was still snoring. I left a flippant note and despondently boarded a homeward bus.

Deutsch was "disturbed by my report. What preoccupied him most was the ease of the operation. Was I sure that Wylie was really asleep? Couldn't it have been a trap? My reassurances failed to reassure him: Most foreigners at that time exaggerated the astuteness of the British; members of the Soviet service were not an exception." Afterward Philby tired of Wylie: "His homosexuality never obtruded itself directly. But it often meant that I met friends of his whom I would have preferred to avoid. It was for these personal, rather than professional, reasons that I suggested to [Deutsch] that the Wylie affair should be transferred to Burgess."[56]

Philby arranged a party at which he introduced Burgess and Wylie. Before they left they had made a date to meet again, an agreement that represented a further development in the Philby case. The effect of giving such authority to Burgess was like letting a stoat among mink. Philby used Burgess, when the need arose, not only as a messenger and go-between but as a seducer, available to mark down the vulnerable, compromise them, or encourage them to compromise themselves, and thereby place another private secretary or personal assistant — the testing posts for men of the future in Whitehall — in the Soviet power. This association was to have many consequences for British and American national security.

7

Lockhart and Haushofer

1934–1939

I N 1934, about the time of Philby's entry into the Soviet service, one of its senior officers arrived in London. Leiba Lazarevich Feldbin, alias Alexander Orlov, was born on August 21, 1895, in Moscow. Under Lenin and Stalin, he had risen to high rank, first as a lawyer and then as an intelligence officer; as part of a long career, he had taught intelligence and counterespionage at the Red Army Academy. At this time — a year after Hitler's emergence in Germany and at a period of growing Soviet concern at developments in the relationship between Britain and Germany — Orlov was asked to establish in Western Europe the anti-Nazi intelligence networks that became known as the Red Choir or Orchestra. But his main task in London was to supervise operations to penetrate, and thereby to control or disrupt, the British Secret Service. To the Soviet service the British service was the main enemy, even the main cause of Russia's woes since before the Crimean War. It was an old feud; the main issue was whether Russian or British imperial power should rule Asia.

An exceptionally disciplined and well-trained Bolshevik, Orlov formed a high regard for Philby's ability and loyalty to Soviet causes. He wrote to the Center how, after about a year in the Soviet service, Söhnchen had developed "strikingly in understanding his tasks." He "is a very dedicated person with a keen appetite for agent work and he will make a great and valuable worker in the future."[1] Philby thought equally highly of Orlov as a "prototypical NKVD man" who gave the impression of being "stern" and "hard" but "very polite and courageous."[2] It was Orlov who gave Philby his first order: to obtain a staff post with the British service, no matter how long it took.

Philby proceeded to his main task. According to Gennady X, a KGB colonel who became his liaison officer with the Soviet secret services between 1970 and 1980 and to whom Philby related something of his life, he began to undertake "very subtle measures to attract the attention of the British Secret Service, and those of his father's friends who might be useful to him in that work."[3] One of Philby's first known tasks was to cultivate St. John's good friend Sheikh Hafez Wahba, the Saudi political agent in London and a member of Ibn Saud's privy council. A graduate of al-Azhar University and the Moslem Jurisprudence College in Cairo, the sheikh was forty-five when Philby first came calling. He had been in the Persian Gulf buying and selling pearls when he first met Ibn Saud in 1913. In 1930 Ibn Saud appointed him as his political agent in London, a post he held for so long that he became the doyen of the diplomatic corps at the Court of St. James's. The Foreign Office judged him an envoy of importance and made him an honorary Knight Commander of the Royal Victorian Order, established in 1896 for Britons and foreigners who had rendered "extraordinary, important or personal services" to the British sovereign or the royal family.[4]

That Kim should have gained the confidence of Wahba as he did owes much to St. John's influence. Wahba's business in London was important. The old frictions between the Hashemite and the Saudi dynasties had remained a warlike factor in Middle East politics, as had the old British concerns about the Third Wahhabi Revival and the possibility that Ibn Saud might move against the British-controlled sheikhdoms on the Persian Gulf, the Indian Ocean, and the lower part of the Red Sea. Wahba saw to it that relations remained tranquil. Above all, perhaps, was the enduring question of the Caliphate of Islam and whether Ibn Saud would seek his patrimony. How much the younger Philby got out of Wahba will probably never be known, but Orlov thought the matter important enough to advise Moscow Center that contact existed. The caliph would have great power in the large Moslem states of the Soviet Union.

In the summer of 1935, Kim Philby's Saudi connection provided, as Orlov reported to Moscow Center, an opportunity "to bring Söhnchen into play at the highest level." In August 1934, Philby had begun to look for work as a cover in Fleet Street, London's newspaper quarter. St. John, a vigorous puller of strings with many to pull, instructed Dora to get in touch with Hugh Wortham, a friend at the

Athenaeum and an admirer who edited an important column in the *Daily Telegraph*, a main newspaper of the official and conservative classes. There could have been no better cover for Kim at this stage in his career as a Soviet spy bent on obtaining a connection to the British Secret Service. But, as St. John warned, he did not think that "Kim would fit into the DT at all." It was "much too respectable and my connection with them ceased years ago owing to *my* Communistic tendencies."[5] He was right. There was no room at the *Telegraph* for Kim. Nor was there room at any of the other leading houses in Fleet Street. His communist reputation continued to dog him. And so Kim found himself working for £4 a week — a pittance — as the assistant editor at the *Review of Reviews*, a small, struggling Liberal journal at Holborn, that medieval warren just off Fleet Street.

The following summer, Kim met up with a famous British secret agent of the era. A "Scot of the Scots," Robert Bruce Lockhart had been the British vice-consul in Moscow for several years before the Bolshevik Revolution. During the revolution he was deputed by Prime Minister David Lloyd George as chief in Moscow of a special mission to establish unofficial relations with the Bolsheviks, his main purpose to persuade the Bolshevik leaders to continue in the war against Germany. In 1918, after an attempt to assassinate Lenin, Lockhart was arrested as the man behind the gunwoman. He was alleged, too, to have been involved in a plot by another famous British secret agent, Sydney George Reilly, to overthrow the Bolshevik regime. Lockhart was deported in October 1918 and sentenced to death *in absentia* by the Bolshevik government.

A man with important connections to the British service and its masters in the Foreign Office, Lockhart was the editor of the London *Evening Standard*'s diary when he encountered Philby. The newspaper was owned by Lord Beaverbrook, a leading light in a political cabal of great power and influence, and Lockhart's social and political diary was regarded as the best informed of the period. How Philby met Lockhart is not known, but the two men did know each other. It is possible that St. John made the introductions, in the spirit that Kim would do much better for himself at the *Evening Standard* than was likely at the *Review*. It is also possible that one of Lockhart's writers, Malcolm Muggeridge, played a part, for he was close to Lockhart and recalled in a memoir that he met Philby early in 1935. Muggeridge and Philby became firm friends, and Lockhart, an approachable man who liked the company of young writers of promise, may well have found it useful to have a connection to Abdullah Philby. Wittingly or otherwise, Lockhart provided young Philby with an important service in his attempt to gain the attention of the British Secret Service.

According to Soviet records, in the summer of 1935 the Saudi crown prince, Saud, arrived in London. Orlov learned that he had made known to St. John his desire to recruit an English teacher and saw a chance to plant Kim in the British Secret Service. He proposed to Moscow Center that Söhnchen offer himself for the job. If Saud accepted him, as seemed likely, given his father's relationship with Ibn Saud, Kim would inform "ANNA (the well-known English intelligence officer who is known as Lockhart)" of his appointment and offer to act as a British spy at Ibn Saud's court.[6] Kim would work in Saudi Arabia "like a slave for about six months for the [British] intelligence service, that is write frequent reports about every movement in the palace, about every guest, depicting everything in interesting terms."[7] The object of all would be, Orlov advised the Center, "to get good references on his file with the British intelligence service."[8]

After six months, according to plan, Philby would fall ill because of the rigorous climate and return home.[9] After a decent interval he would resume his career as a journalist and travel to the Soviet Union on assignment. He would resume contact with Lockhart, and this would lead to an invitation from the British service to work in Russia as a free-lance spy. The Center would feed him information and thereby "we could get Söhnchen out into his large role," that of a British intelligence officer acting in the Soviet interest. And as Orlov wrote further, "His personal qualities would assist a plan like this. He is educated, clever, modest, taciturn when needed — and the main thing is that *he is one of us by his ideas.*" The only question in Orlov's mind was whether the British Secret Service would accept him. He thought it would.[10]

The Center approved of this witty play. One of its senior officers, a certain Slavatinski, noted with confidence, "I don't think his intelligence service will refuse the services of Söhnchen."[11] But the plan came to nothing when Prince Saud chose another tutor. It is not impossible that the Foreign Office advised against Kim's employment. However, that summer of 1935 a second such chance opened up when Philby was offered the post of a press officer with the Indian Civil Service in New Delhi. Orlov ordered Philby to accept the offer on the grounds that, as Orlov advised the Center, good work by Kim in New Delhi "will put an end to his past 'left-wing' reputation."[12] He would inevitably come into renewed contact with the British intelligence service. Did Moscow Center approve? Before it could respond, Orlov's career in London came to a quick end. The possibility arose that his cover — that of an American refrigerator salesman — had been blown, and he was forced to leave the country in October. Arnold Deutsch then resumed his control of Philby.

By late 1935, the Center had become ever more concerned about the relationship between Hitler's government and some members of the British ruling class. For its part, the British service became vigorous in its quest for men with the necessary ability to illuminate what was happening inside that most mysterious of all the world's major institutions, the Kremlin. Over the years Lockhart had remained on excellent terms with the wartime chief of the British Secret Service, Sir Mansfield Smith-Cumming, and his successor, the present chief, Admiral Sir Hugh Sinclair. Lockhart's diaries, which ran to about three million words and were eventually deposited for safekeeping in the House of Lords, show that he was frequently in touch with one of Sinclair's "venerable scoundrels,"[13] Commander R. T. H. Fletcher, who became Lord Winster, Governor-General of Cyprus. And as Lockhart recorded of a meeting with him in July 1929, about the time he took over the diary: "Dined with Fletcher at the St. James's Club. He gave me a lot of information about our Secret Service." Admiral Sinclair was "a terrific anti-Bolshevik" and "hard up for men for Russia."[14] By 1936 the British service had begun to expand its activities against both Berlin and Moscow.

Whether Philby was in contact with the British service by 1936 is nowhere clear. But that year Kim began to pursue a course in which ideological purity blurred his conduct of affairs when Hitler's government started to seek an alliance with Stanley Baldwin's government against the Soviet Union. As was evident in *Mein Kampf,* Hitler believed that Germany could become a world power again only through an alliance with Great Britain or fascist Italy or both.[15] The first step in his grand strategy was to eliminate France as a rival in order to free him from the threat of a two-front war and enable him to proceed to his main task, the destruction of Bolshevik Russia. He required that for two reasons: to eliminate an ideology that would destroy Germany if it was not itself destroyed, and to provide the German people with "living space" (*Lebensraum*). He intended to establish a German empire on Soviet territory up to the line of the Ural Mountains, the traditional line between Europe and Asia.

Hitler had begun to talk of a new order in Europe directed against Bolshevism. And it was these prospects that appealed to a large part of the ruling class of Britain. The reason for their interest was expressed in a special study on Bolshevism by the U.S. Department of State:

> The international revolutionary activities directed by Moscow and carried on in various parts of the world have been particularly objectionable to Great Britain. The internal organization of the United Kingdom and of the Empire is such as to render it extremely difficult for the British Government to cope with communist propaganda within the confines of the Empire, and the economic and political interests of Great Britain outside the borders of the Empire, particularly those in Asia, are especially vulnerable to Moscow's attacks. Successive British Governments, therefore, regardless of political complexion, have not been willing to condone or to ignore the anti-British activities of Moscow.[16]

These sentiments were strongly held throughout the government, especially in the Foreign and Colonial Offices and the secret services. In society they were held also in an organization called the Anglo-German Fellowship, a cabal of businessmen, society figures, and other persons of rank and wealth who, while not necessarily approving of all that went on in Germany, wished to maintain and improve commercial and social connections between the two countries. The Fellowship's counterpart in Germany was the Deutsch-Englische Gesellschaft, which had strong Nazi affiliations. The Fellowship aimed at the rich and powerful; among its membership, it claimed, were fifty members of both Houses of Parliament, three directors of the Bank of England, and "many generals, admirals, bishops and bankers." "It isn't numbers that matter," the secretary of the Fellowship declared in a press interview at the time. "We want 'Names,' otherwise how can we have any influence with the Government or the Foreign Office."[17] Among these "names" were some of the most blue-blooded British and German political, landed, and financial leaders of the two powers.

As part of the process to change his political coloration, Deutsch ordered Philby to join the Fellowship, but not as an English fascist. He was to represent himself as "an independent-thinking Englishman who perceives Hitlerite Germany as a fact of middle European life in the mid-1930s, and is trying to derive from it economic as well as cultural benefit for his own country."[18] Such a conversion would serve to banish Philby's reputation as a "leftie" for good. Perhaps through the good offices of Robert Bruce Lockhart, who may have been a member of the Fellowship, Philby joined the organization and began to attend its functions. Both Philby and Lockhart were present at the Dorchester Hotel in white tie and tails for the Fellowship's dinner in

July in honor of the Duke and Duchess of Brunswick, the most ardently pro-Nazi nobles in the Third Reich.

In due course, Philby presented his card to the German Embassy in London, he interviewed its press attaché, and he soon began to receive invitations to attend the embassy's functions. In 1936, he was among the guests at a garden party given by the new German ambassador, Joachim von Ribbentrop, who had been sent to England to further Hitler's attempt at rapprochement with England. Philby recorded that "suddenly I found myself whom I hated" but nonetheless "saw it as my duty to do what I was doing."[19] When it became known that he was the son of St. John Philby, the well-known anti-Zionist, he was invited to become the editor of the Fellowship's magazine, *Germany Today*. He resigned from the *Review;* as he remembered, "It seems to me that this consent of mine was the beginning of my actual work for the Soviet Union."[20]

He visited Berlin for a week each month in middle and late 1936. He called on Josef Goebbels, the Minister of Propaganda and Enlightenment, to get Nazi money for *Germany Today*. He interviewed the Duke of Saxe-Coburg-Gotha, a German aristocrat born in England and related by blood to the throne through his grandfather, Prince Albert. King George V was a relative of Tsar Nicholas II, who had been killed by the Bolsheviks in 1918, at the end of the Russian Revolution. And since George V feared that the Bolsheviks were plotting to do to him what they had done to the Romanovs, he was inclined toward an Anglo-German understanding. So was his heir, the Prince of Wales. Coburg had power and influence. He was a knight of the premier British order, the Most Noble Order of the Garter, which consisted of the sovereign and twenty-six knights, and he was president of the Deutsch-Englische Gesellschaft. So it was that as King George V lay dying, in March 1936, Anglo-German-Russian politics took another turn. Coburg appeared at Sandringham Castle, the king's residence, during the death watch to await an audience with the Prince of Wales as he prepared for his succession.

In a report, Coburg related how, in "carrying out the Führer's commission," he talked with the new king, Edward VIII, on the morning of his father's death. The talk took place "with pipe at fireside" for "a little more than half an hour." He claimed to have accompanied the king to Buckingham Palace, where he took tea with Queen Mary, George V's widow, and had a second conversation with the new king. Later that day, the duke claimed, there was a third conversation with Edward "between State dinner and reception at Buckingham Palace." Coburg reported that "the conversations took place in the same way as before in familiar frankness." As to the substance of the audiences, the duke reported:

> An alliance Germany-Britain is *for him* an urgent necessity and a guiding principle for British foreign policy. Not, of course, against France, but, of necessity, including her. In this way safeguarding a lasting European peace.[21]

The smart London social group in which the new king moved was, at this time, pro-Nazi. And as Harold Nicolson, the diarist and author, wrote of them: "They think Ribbentrop a fine man, and that we should let gallant little Germany glut her fill of the reds in the East and keep France quiet while she does so."[22]

David Lloyd George, the prime minister for much of World War I, called Hitler "the greatest German of the age." He talked about "the advantage to Europe of strong men being in office" because "a powerful statesman is in himself a guarantee of peace." He gave Hitler to understand that "public opinion in Great Britain was to an increasing degree showing more and more understanding for Hitler's position and the one anxiety of British public opinion today was to bring about the closest co-operation between the two countries."[23] And behind the Fellowship, but part of it, lay an ominous organization called the Link, whose chairman was a former director of naval intelligence, Admiral Sir Barry Domvile. Domvile had been aide-de-camp to King George V, he had commanded battleships and a cruiser squadron, and he had only lately been president of the Royal Naval College at Greenwich and was still in good standing at the Admiralty when he retired in 1936 as a full admiral. At the Link, Domvile controlled the British financial support of Philby and *Germany Today;* he had social connections with Heinrich Himmler, chief of the Nazi intelligence and security services, the Sicherheitdienst and the Gestapo. Domvile's deputy at the Link was the formidable geopolitician Professor Sir Charles Beazley, the geohistorian and vice president of the Royal Historical Society, a member of the council of the Royal Geographical Society and of the House of Laity of the Church Assembly. Such men — and the Fellowship and the Link were full of them — regarded themselves as the first line of defense against the barbarians, the Bolsheviks, who were so assiduously undermining the structure of the state.

Hundreds of leading Britons went to Berlin for the Olympics as guests of Hitler, Ribbentrop, and the deputy führer of the Reich, Rudolf Hess. Göring had six hundred foreign guests to dinner at his house. The British press was full of tributes to the German national spirit; British sportsmen claimed that only a power like Nazism could produce such Olympic winners; and many of them spoke of Hitler as "that remarkable man of vision who directs the destinies of Germany" and who has "done away with those class divisions which had corroded British life."[24] The Nuremberg Rally ensued, and the British ambassador wrote of the scene at a dinner given by Reichsführer Heinrich Himmler:

> The camp in the darkness, dimly lit by flares, with the black uniform of the SS in the silent background and the skull and crossbones on the drums and trumpets lent to the scene a sinister and menacing impress. I felt, indeed, as if I were back in the days of Wallenstein and the Thirty Years' War in the seventeenth century.[25]

It was the heyday of Anglo-Nazi entente. And it virtually ended when Edward VIII advised the government that he wished to marry Wallace Warfield Simpson, a divorcée from Baltimore, and make her the Queen of England. There were suspicions about Mrs. Simpson's relations with Ribbentrop, constitutional problems about Edward's desire to marry a divorcée who was also an American, and political problems about Edward's wish to become a political king. The British government sacked its king, but the German link remained. Guy Burgess was set the task of establishing a relationship with a member of Ribbentrop's political staff, Wolfgang zu Putlitz, from a family of Junkers, who became an informant on the great affairs inside Ribbentrop's cabinet.

Kim, too, made a move. He met the second woman in his life, Bunny Doble, an acquaintance from the 1930s tinsel world of Dora and St. John. Like Alice, she suited Kim's cover requirements exactly. The divorced wife of a baronet, St. Anthony Lindsay-Hogg, lately of the Grenadier Guards, in 1934 Bunny was thirty-five, Kim twenty-five. She was a daughter of a Montreal banker, Arthur Doble, and lived at 40 King's Road, Chelsea, a good bourgeois address. She had had one son by her marriage and had arrived on the London stage in the late 1920s or early 1930s. Her name glowed quite brightly; she was a star of light romances and melodramas, and she was seen often at country house weekends, after-theater dinners, and champagne parties. She had played the lead opposite Ivor Novello in *Sirocco*, a play by Noël Coward, *The Constant Nymph*, *The Chinese Bungalow*, and a lightweight movie, *Dark Red Roses*.

As interesting from Kim's aspect, she was on terms with the former King of Spain Alfonso XIII, who had "suspended" his reign in 1931 and gone into exile in London when it appeared that his continuing presence in Spain might cause a civil war. As Bunny Doble recorded, Alfonso had approached her at a party and this conversation ensued:

"Senora! May I join you."

He was carrying a bottle of champagne and two glasses. I curtsied and then we sat by the fire.

"I hear that you love my country and I should like to talk to you about it," he said.

A friendship grew up between us and our friends made a point of inviting us to the same parties. Sometimes he called on me at my flat. It was always a ceaseless chatter about Spain. What did I think of the bulls, of Spanish music, of painting? He was a tall man with a good figure, and a heavy-featured rather brutish face. I adored him.[26]

But she adored Kim more. They became lovers and remained so until 1939, although she still was friendly with Alfonso, who became of use to Philby.

When Ribbentrop became Hitler's ambassador to the Court of St. James's in 1936, Kim encountered an important figure in the upper middle rank of Nazi foreign policy. Albrecht Haushofer was a son of Professor General Karl Haushofer, some of whose ideas as a leading ideologist had found their way through Rudolf Hess into Hitler's *Mein Kampf.* Both Karl and Albrecht Haushofer shared the view that Britain could be Germany's main friend, that Bolshevik Russia was the main enemy. In recent years Albrecht had become Hess's liaison officer with the German foreign ministry, and when Ribbentrop went to London, Albrecht found it necessary to visit him as Hess's agent. He never became a member of the Nazi Party; he was a passionate German nationalist and was partly Jewish, a fact that Hess had concealed almost successfully — Ribbentrop knew and wished to have Albrecht removed and consigned to a concentration camp. But Hess's protection had proved more powerful so far.

During his London visits Haushofer began to develop associations with Britons of rank and influence. Among the most powerful of his connections was the Marquess of Clydesdale, the son and heir of the premier peer of Scotland, the Duke of Hamilton. Clydesdale was a prominent aviator who had made a great name for himself when, in 1933, he became the first man to fly over Mount Everest. It was this exploit — and Clydesdale's account of it, *The Pilot's Book of Everest* — which brought Clydesdale to the attention of Hess, who was himself an aviator of high ability. The scene was set, therefore, for one of the most remarkable conspiracies of the era: Hess's attempt through Albrecht Haushofer and Clydesdale to produce a political understanding between the Third Reich and Great Britain against the Soviet Union.

Haushofer himself was markedly but secretly pro-British, an attitude he shared with Hess. Philby entered the conspiracy through a periodical in Berlin, the *Journal for Geopolitics,* which Karl Haushofer had founded and edited some twenty years before. In 1936 he was still in charge of the journal's Asian section; Albrecht was the editor of its Anglo-American affairs. One basis for their association may well have been that both Kim and Albrecht were expert mapmakers. Another was undoubtedly that Haushofer was a secret enemy of Hitler.

Philby now used all these connections to obtain the journalistic credentials he required to go to Spain as a Soviet secret agent and report on the Civil War from General Franco's headquarters. General Oleg D. Kalugin, one of Philby's KGB chiefs in later years, would relate in his foreword to Philby's memoir, *My Silent War,* that Kim obtained the papers of "a staff member" of Haushofer's "geopolitical journal." Then, Kalugin related, "with the help of the well-known British intelligence officer Robert Bruce Lockhart," he obtained the "non-staff credentials" of the *Evening Standard* in London.[27] He obtained also a letter of introduction from the Duke of Alba, Franco's political agent in London, to his son Don Pablo Merry de Val, one of Franco's press officers in Spain. Last, about the time that Philby left London, one of his Soviet managers there advised Moscow Center on January 24, 1937, that Kim had received a letter of recommendation from "Hausehofer" [*sic*] of the German foreign ministry.

Philby's mission in the Soviet interest was his first operation in the field. His aim was to make himself and his work known to the British Secret Service, which was operating near Franco's headquarters. Another purpose was to provide intelligence on Spanish fascist conditions and help in the arrangements being made by the Soviet service to assassinate General Franco. This mission was to have very far-reaching consequences, for it led to his penetration of the Abwehr, the intelligence service of the German General Staff.

Philby set out for Spain early in February 1937 and arrived in Seville — an area he knew quite well from his visits to Major Fisher's estate on the Guadalquivir River — toward the end of the month. His credentials held up, at first. But he had great difficulty in locating Franco's headquarters, which were probably nearer Salamanca, and had failed to find them two weeks later, when he was arrested by Francoite security officers while on a weekend visit to Córdoba to watch a bullfight. By his own account, his arrest took place at his hotel in the middle of the night, and he was taken to police headquarters to be searched.

But he succeeded in swallowing his cipher, specially treated rice paper in the ticket pocket of his trousers, thus destroying evidence that he was indeed a spy. How he had attracted attention is nowhere explained. He himself mentioned a talk he had with Italian officers during his rail journey to Córdoba; and he may have asked one too many questions. The police may have been making a routine check of the aliens in the city; they were likely to do so all the time.

Philby was lucky again. But he had caught his first whiff of the firing squad. He also needed a new code; until he got one he could not work for the Soviets. But there was no word for *code* in the code he had been using, so he was forced to write to Guy Burgess in London that he needed "a new book" and money. But this took weeks to arrange, and it could hardly have failed to attract further attention of some sort: Philby and Burgess met at a hotel at Gibraltar, a British crown colony and a place where MI5, the British Security Service, was especially alert, given the gravity of the situation across the frontier in Spain. But the meeting did take place. Shortly afterward Philby was recalled to London to report on his first ninety days in Spain. On his arrival he saw Deutsch, who upbraided him on the dullness of his reports to Paris. This did not sit well with Philby, who invited Deutsch to try writing an interesting report in a code based on the need to write "something serious in every fifth word."[28]

Philby appeared to be very troubled in particular by the nature of his mission — the assassination of Franco. Teodor Maly, one of Deutsch's assistants in the management of the Cambridge Group, reported to the Center:

> The fact is that Söhnchen has come back in very low spirits. He has not even managed to get near to the "interesting objective." But I think or rather feel from my talks with him that, even if he had managed to make his way through to Salamanca, even if he had managed to get near to Franco, then — in spite of his intention — he would not have been able to do what was required of him. Though devoted and ready to sacrifice himself, he does not possess the physical courage and other qualities necessary for this attempt.[29]

New instructions were cut for Kim. He was to improve his credentials by obtaining a staff position with a major London newspaper, with one eye on improving his status in Spain and making himself more attractive to the officers of the British Secret Service in the Peninsula. This would have been impossible but for another stroke of great good fortune: his father had arrived in London for cricket and business.

Kim asked St. John to do something for him with his friends at *The Times,* and St. John proceeded to do so.

St. John had influence at *The Times.* He had been its occasional correspondent in Arabia since 1926, and his work was well regarded, particularly by the military correspondent, Basil Liddell Hart, a Trinity contemporary, the leading British exponent in the field of armored warfare, and a personal adviser to the war minister, Leslie Hore-Belisha. In May of 1937 St. John lunched with his Westminster schoolmate Robin Barrington-Ward, the deputy editor of *The Times.* But it was not St. John who proposed Kim for a staff position in Spain; it was Barrington-Ward. He had been impressed by an article Kim Philby had written for *The Times* in the vague hope of impressing the editors. Ward recorded in a diary note on May 20, 1937, that he proposed Kim as "our special correspondent with Franco's force in Spain." St. John "jumped at it" and Kim "duly came to see me. He looks good. We fixed him up."[30] Kim was in. He became a correspondent for the newspaper of the imperial ruling and upper middle class. The editorial rooms were then in Queen Victoria Street, and over the front door, carved in stone in the spandrel, was the royal coat of arms and the motto *Honi soit qui mal y pense,* "Evil to him who evil thinks."

On May 24, Kim passed under the arms and duly became *The Times*'s special correspondent with General Franco. The *Sunday Times,* which had no connection with the daily *Times,* later investigated the circumstances of Kim's appointment and recorded: "This was an important job by any reckoning. Philby returned to Spain, now wearing the full protective panoply of the British Establishment. It is hard to imagine any more perfect cover."[31] To make his triumph the sweeter, Philby claimed, he was formally appointed a full-fledged officer of the Soviet intelligence. This statement is not true, according to General Kalugin. Philby's status was never that of an "intelligence officer." He was, as he remained throughout his long career with the Soviet secret services, "a secret collaborator," a spy who worked through ideological conviction.

St. John now had a further service to render his son. He submitted Kim's name for membership in the Athenaeum Club, an august institution at the heart of the English establishment. Its membership rules specified that only persons *established* in their professions could belong, hence the term *Establishment.* The Athenaeum had been founded in 1824 by an illustrious Secretary of the Admiralty, J. W. Crocker, as an "association of individuals known for their scientific and literary attainments, artists of eminence in any class of the fine arts and noblemen and gentlemen distinguished as liberal patrons of science, literature or the arts." Its reputation was for "intellectuality, gravity, deep respectability and episcopacy," and the average age of its members was high. Membership was granted automatically to the Speaker of the House of Commons, cabinet ministers, bishops and archbishops, high court judges, ambassadors, high commissioners and governors general, and the presidents of the Royal Society, the Royal Society of Antiquaries, the Royal Academy, and the British Academy. Charles Graves thought it to be "*the* centre of backstage but top-level administrative manoeuvre, diplomacy and intrigue."[32] Its atmosphere was well described as that of "a cathedral between services." The leading civil servants belonged, as did the more distinguished scientists, politicians, lawyers, bishops, and a scattering of the highest officers in the armed services. A Soviet spy seeking a post in the British Secret Service could not wish for a better place from which to observe and eavesdrop on the establishment at play, to make connections. It reeked of distinction and conferred upon the member a special augustness.

St. John's suit on behalf of Kim did not at first prosper. He buttonholed two friends and members, St. C. T. Carr, counsel to the Speaker of the House of Commons, and Sir E. Denison Ross, Keeper of the Records of the Indian government and professor of Persian studies at the London School of Oriental Studies, to second Kim's nomination. Both were Trinity contemporaries, so St. John could expect that Kim's acceptance would be quick. But although both Carr and Ross agreed to second Kim's election, for reasons known only to themselves they did nothing, probably because they learned something of Kim's communism at Trinity from Sir Donald Robertson, Regius Professor of Greek at Cambridge, one of the two Robertsons who declined to give Kim a reference for the Foreign Service examination in 1934 and himself a member of the Athenaeum.

St. John spoke with another Trinity man and club member who was *The Times's* military correspondent, Captain Basil Liddell Hart; he agreed to speak for Kim and Kim was elected. In that moment his Soviet cover was proofed to sweet perfection; the hallmarks of the Establishment were his: St. Aldro, Westminster, Trinity, *The Times* — all served to obscure his communism. The scene was now set for Kim to complete his main task in the Soviet interest, to gain a place in the British Secret Service. Who was there to gainsay him now, for was it not then reckoned that if a man was good enough for the Athenaeum, surely he was good enough for everyone else?

After two weeks' familiarizing himself with the personalities and procedures at *The Times,* Kim returned to Spain in the late summer of 1936 as one of the bright young men of Geoffrey Dawson, the editor and

Prime Minister Neville Chamberlain's personal adviser on foreign policy. Kim was twenty-five, his salary and allowances came to £1,225 a year plus a car — good wages in hard times. He claimed not to have received pay from the Soviet service, a claim that is, strictly speaking, true. And his case officer in the absence of Deutsch, a Hungarian and former priest named Teodor Maly, felt able to advise the Center that "Söhnchen had achieved their objective," suggesting that Kim was approached by the Secret Service in London. This may have been so, for these were times when there was a closer connection between "acceptable" foreign correspondents and the Secret Service. Foreign editors in London encouraged such associations; they added luster to a correspondent's standing. If the Secret Service trusted a correspondent, it followed that so should everyone else in the official world. The correspondent received the official view of events, and this improved the balance of his dispatches. Further, he enjoyed that special dispensation that could be invaluable at times of disorder in foreign parts. Then his communications might be assured. As for the service, it received the correspondent's information and advice. The correspondent could travel where the official could not and ask questions of foreigners that might, if asked by the officer, prove dangerous for him.

Kim arrived back in Spain wearing what *The Sunday Times* would term "the full protective panoply of the British establishment." He himself expected to be approached by a man who would be "lean and bronzed, of course, with a clipped moustache, clipped accents and, most probably, a clipped mind. He would ask me to stick my neck out for my country and frown austerely if I mentioned pay."[33] Sure enough, he met his first British Secret Service officer almost on his arrival. Edward Cuthbert de Renzy-Martin was exactly the type Philby had expected to encounter. He was fifty-four, the son of a late Victorian general who had been made a knight commander of the Bath. In World War I de Renzy-Martin had served with a Ghurka regiment and the King's Own Yorkshire Light Infantry. He had been rewarded for his gallantry in action with the Distinguished Service Order and the Military Cross, and until lately he had served as the chief of the gendarmerie of King Zog of Albania. After that he had moved to the Secret Service, which he was now serving ostensibly as a passport officer in the British consulate at San Sebastián on the Franco-Spanish border. He was tall, slim, well tailored, and circumspect.

Perhaps as arranged, perhaps not, Philby called on de Renzy-Martin at the consulate to report his arrival in Spain and to leave his card, a wise precaution for a foreign correspondent entering a war zone. It is said that de Renzy-Martin asked Philby to bring him news and he agreed. He thereby became an "honorary correspondent," as the service called Britons who undertook to do work for the service, not for money, but for "the honor of the flag." This was an important moment in Philby's intrigue to obtain a post in the British Secret Service in the Russian interest. Philby had started the service file on de Renzy-Martin that Orlov deemed so important a first step in the maneuver. This did not necessarily mean that Philby had become a British spy, but it did mean that he had formed a connection with an agency of the Foreign Office.

Having moved on to Burgos, Franco's provisional capital in Old Castile, Philby presented his *Times* credentials to Franco's press officer, who was still Don Pablo Merry de Val, thereby establishing himself with Franco's military government. They were accepted — who in Spain would tangle with *The Times*'s accredited correspondent at el Caudillo's headquarters? — and Philby began to go about his business under the tight control of Franco's escorting officers. As his biographers would write, some of Kim's journalistic colleagues

> thought they detected a whiff of the intelligence agent about him. No one, of course, connected him with Russia. Rather, there was a strong suspicion that he was in British pay, as it was known, or at least believed, that the British Secret Service sometime employed correspondents of *The Times*. His strategic grasp of the campaigns on the different fronts, his sheer level of information, seemed to give substance to this view. For some of the pressmen, this supposed secret role made Kim's mild pro-Franco sympathies more palatable, although journalists reporting from the Republican side of the war regarded his cool, unmoved despatches as a betrayal of the democratic cause.[34]

Philby may well have had the benefit of de Renzy-Martin's information and wisdom. And he may well, also, have had the benefit of the wisdom and knowledge of the chief of German military intelligence in Spain, Major Ulrich von der Osten, alias Don Julio, who was also the chief agent in fascist Spain of Admiral Wilhelm Franz Canaris, the chief of the Abwehr, the espionage, counterespionage, and special operations service of the German General Staff. Canaris was to become a major figure in the Philby case, as he was soon to become a major figure in World War II.

As Philby would state when he lectured to the Soviet service in 1977 about his career, his encounter with von der Osten marked the point at which he began to become known to the British Secret Service as an expert on the German intelligence services, a reputation that served him well later on. Philby evidently thought highly of his association with von der Osten; he gave the German a third of a page in his memoir, *My Silent War,* more than any other foreign intelligence officer he met during his fifty-three years as a spy. It seems sure that Philby insinuated himself into von der Osten's confidence through the judicious use of such names as Goebbels, Ribbentrop, and Haushofer. He related how von der Osten "used to take me to Abwehr headquarters in the Convento de las Esclavas, in Burgos, and explain his large wall maps dotted with the usual coloured pins." This proved to be of essential importance in his career in the British Secret Service, for it gave him a picture of German methods, disposition of agents, and capabilities and intentions in the Iberian Peninsula that may have been unique, to a Briton at least, for von der Osten controlled espionage networks, not just on the Spanish front, but also on the Gibraltar Strait, which had more long-term interest — the British naval strategists considered the Pillars of Hercules as important in their affairs as the English Channel. More, probably. He also gained an insight into the relationship between the Abwehr and the Francoite intelligence and security services, which was close and remained so. It was said that Canaris controlled Spain through his Abwehr.

Philby recalled how von der Osten "dined and wined me in desultory fashion for a year or so, and it proved a useful contact as far as it went." But when Osten asked Philby for an introduction to Bunny Doble and was obliged, "he propositioned her forthwith, both espionage-wise and otherwise." Lady Lindsay-Hogg repulsed von der Osten and thereafter "his manner to me became distant."[35] That Philby so early in his career as a *Times* man could be on terms with the Soviet, the British, and the German intelligence services was testament indeed to his resourcefulness and his cool nerve. It owed much also to his rare gift, well developed even at an early age, of being able to control how much he wished to reveal about himself to men who had reason to study him. As his biographers remarked:

Kim's disguise as a fascist sympathizer was always skillful, never insistent: he adopted an air of neutrality [in the war], as behooved the representative of the mighty *El Times,* but let it appear, without actually saying so, that his personal attitudes were conservative and gentlemanly. Other journalists stormed at the censorship, some . . . were even expelled for what they wrote. But Kim was always on the most friendly terms with Nationalist officials, and in particular with Pablo Merry del Val . . . Avoiding blatant partiality, he always managed to give a flattering gloss to Nationalist Spain, making a point [in his dispatches] of mentioning the normality of life, the maintenance of

law and order, the high standing of Franco's credit abroad, his concern with the people's well-being.[36]

He spoke and behaved with such conviction that he even convinced
his father. As St. John wrote to Sir Reader Bullard, the minister at
Jidda, "He's not only reporting for the Franco side, but he seems to
think they're right." Yet at the same time Kim was engaging in espionage work against not only Franco, but also the Trotskyite agents who
worked for him — after Gorbachev appeared in Moscow, it would be
alleged that Philby provided the intelligence that led to the executions
of some eighty such agents in Spain in the latter half of the war. He
was playing an exceptionally dangerous game at Burgos, for as Arthur
Koestler, the author of *Darkness at Noon,* wrote when he was arrested
and jailed as a Soviet spy, at nights the prison was alive with the cries
for their *madres* of other young communist spies posing as journalists
as they were led out to face the firing squad.

Nor was the terror of life at Burgos confined to ideological strife.
In Russia itself, and indeed throughout the world, Stalin launched his
great purges to eliminate all from his administration who opposed
him or were ambiguous in their loyalties. Even within the Soviet clandestine services, the watchword of the period was the peremptory
"Arrest, try, shoot." The 1917 revolution began to drown in the blood
of revolutionaries. Most men caught up in the murderous lunacy of
the period, cultivated men such as Philby, would have escaped to safer
havens, as did Koestler. But Philby did not.

By 1937, Alexander Orlov, one of the men who had trained Philby,
had developed a deep admiration for his skill, courage, and nerve as
a spy close to Franco's inner councils. Their relationship took on
personal aspects. They met from time to time at one of the frontier
towns in France. At one such meeting Philby was dismayed when Orlov
appeared in garb that resembled a guerrilla leader, carrying a tommy
gun; Philby admonished him for having become involved in the violent side of secret service. They had other connections as well. The
wife of Orlov was one of his couriers; she was in contact with Alice
Friedman, another courier who carried Philby's intelligence between
Spain and Lisbon, where a certain Lukacevics, a Soviet case officer,
transmitted it to the Center. That Alice was in the network is regarded
as a sure indication that their separation was at the dictation of the
party — *the party comes first.* It was therefore a shock for Philby when
suddenly, in about June or July of 1938, Orlov vanished. Philby did
not know what had become of him until much later and believed that
he had become involved in the purges.

So began the first of the major security crises in the Philby case, for Orlov was under orders from Moscow to return "for consultations." However, something in his orders made him conclude that he was to be "liquidated," and instead he got on a ship to Canada with his wife and daughter, then deserted to the United States. There he wrote to Stalin and the chief of the Soviet service, a certain Yezhov, stating that if any harm befell his family or himself, his lawyer in the United States would reveal the identities of the sixty-six high-grade secret agents he had controlled in Western Europe. Orlov included the text of the letter deposited with his lawyer as well as the code names of the agents whom he would expose, including those of Philby (still Söhnchen) and Maclean (then Waise). He concluded his letter to Yezhov:

> Always remember that I am no traitor to my Party or my country. No one and nothing will ever make me betray the cause of the proletariat and of Soviet power. I did not want to leave my country any more than a fish wants to leave water, but the delinquent activity of criminal people has cast me up like a fish on ice. From my knowledge of other cases I know the identity of the forces which will have been committed to my physical liquidation. Put a stop to the misuse of our people. It suffices to say that they have caused me extreme misery by depriving me of the right to live and fight within the Party to enjoy the just rewards of long years of unselfish service.
>
> I have not been deprived of my mother country, but the right to live and breathe the same air as the Soviet people. If you leave me alone, I will never embark on anything harmful to the Party and our country. I solemnly swear, to the end of my days, not to utter a word which may harm the Party which brought me up or the country in which I grew up.[37]

This letter and its accompanying menaces had a profound effect on the activities of Philby and the rest of the Cambridge Group except, possibly, Burgess. In the belief that Orlov would, despite his assurance to the contrary, reveal the identities of the Soviet secret agents in Europe, Stalin directed the Soviet service to cease all further efforts to kill Orlov.* Also, Yezhov ordered the Soviet service to deactivate all the agents affected and to instruct them to lay low until they received other

---

* Such evidence as there is shows that from the time of his arrival in the United States, Orlov did not reveal the identities of his agents to any Western authority or individual. He was, he could have claimed, as good as his word. He lived underground with the knowledge and assistance of the U.S. government, including the FBI, until he died in 1973. He was examined at length throughout those years by the U.S. security and intelligence services, especially in 1954, and formed what appeared to be a close working relationship with the counterespionage departments of the CIA and the FBI. Whether he did in fact at least reveal Philby's name to them constitutes an important element in this volume, one that may be recalled by the reader when Philby's relationships with the CIA and the FBI are discussed.

orders. Thus from about the third quarter of 1937 until about the same time in 1939 Philby had no further contact with the Soviet service.

Through Orlov's desertion, Philby could never feel safe again, although his career, which was to lead him to the top in both the American and British secret services, had only just begun. For the next thirty years, he could never be sure that Orlov would not, in order to protect himself or to obtain some dispensation from the FBI, reveal his name. An entirely new dimension had entered into the Philby case and the affairs of the Cambridge Group in general. At a crucial time in world affairs, the group found itself without the means to pass its intelligence to Moscow.

The disappearance of Orlov proved to be but the first of three such crises to strike at Philby's self-assurance during that epochal year of 1938, the year of the Munich crises, in which Britain nearly found itself at war with Germany. In the second such crisis, the Security Service found in London the spoor of the man whom Philby called his "ersatz father," Arnold Deutsch. Deutsch placed the Cambridge network under the command of his deputy, Teodor Maly, then left the country. At great risk Deutsch returned once, briefly, early in 1938, then disappeared; Kim never saw him again. In fact, as it was learned later, he remained in Moscow with some responsibility for the management of the Cambridge Group, for it was emerging as the Center's most important source in the capital of the main adversary. Deutsch remained at the Center until 1942, when he was killed in South America while on a secret mission for the Center.

He was succeeded in his work with Philby's group by Maly, a former monk who came to Bolshevism while serving in the Austro-Hungarian army during World War I. Philby regarded him as "an inspirational figure, a true comrade and idealist." But Maly did not last long. In 1938, while Philby was on leave in London, Maly received the Center's order to return to Moscow "for consultations." Sensing that he was to be executed, he told Philby, "Kim, we will probably not meet again but whatever you hear about me continue on the true path!"[38] What Philby never knew was that on his arrival in Moscow, Maly was taken before the Military Collegium of the Supreme Court of the USSR and charged with having been a secret Trotskyite with connections to the British Secret Service. His sentence was handed down on September 20, 1938: he was taken to the execution chamber in the cellars of the Lubyanka and given the *Genickschluss,* the single bullet in the nape of the neck. Another of the "glorious lights" of the revolution had been extinguished through what Philby, in a lecture to the KGB in 1977, called a "unfortunate socialist illegality."

Now the Philby group was without a leader. A Soviet case officer, Gregory Grafpen, did arrive in London early in 1938 to replace Maly. A polished man who wore good suits, evidently an able officer, he seems not to have had direct contact with any of the group. In the case of Maclean, Grafpen worked through a comely Russian female agent, code-named Norma, who was brought in specially for the task. The record shows that they soon became lovers, which was quite contrary to Moscow rules. But by the end of the year Grafpen, too, had vanished, to take up special duties, it is believed, in the United States. Norma remained in charge.

Then came what proved to be the most dangerous of the three security crises of 1937–1938. In the summer of 1937 Walter Krivitsky, a senior Soviet intelligence officer at The Hague, was recalled to Moscow. Like Orlov, however, he became aware that he might be liquidated for "socialist illegality" and instead deserted to the United States. As reports in the American press began to show, he arrived in New York in December and was interviewed by Raymond E. Murphy, the head of a small Soviet intelligence research section at the State Department. Krivitsky testified before a House committee that had warned the U.S. government about the growing collaboration between Hitler and Stalin, of the intelligence collaboration between the two countries, and also the strong probability that Germany and Russia would make a pact against the Western powers.

These major revelations began to impinge directly on Philby. When Krivitsky mentioned that the Soviet service had in its employ a Briton who was a coding clerk in the Communications Department of the Foreign Office in London, he was turned over to Derek Hoyer-Millar, the official at the British Embassy responsible for intelligence and security affairs. The clerk was identified as Captain John Herbert King, who had been controlled by Maly, now purged and dead. Krivitsky's name was to return to haunt Philby in 1940, 1945, 1951, and 1963, for as he would discover in the Secret Service's file on Krivitsky, the Russian had revealed that there was another British spy in the Soviet service, "a journalist who had gone to Spain during the Spanish Civil War." For the moment, however, that fact was not known to Philby. Nonetheless, it lurked about him like the shadow of Nemesis. Somebody at the Security Service had only to inquire about Krivitsky's statement to be led to Philby in Burgos.

Then Philby was almost killed by a Soviet shell.

At the front near Tereul, in Aragón, on December 31, the eve of his birthday, a communist shell made in Russia hit the car in which Philby was riding with Karl Robson (*Daily Telegraph,* London), Richard Sheep-shanks (Reuters), Edward Neil (the Associated Press), and Bradish Johnson (*Newsweek*). Johnson was killed and Sheepshanks and Neil died soon afterward. Robson and Philby were injured, the latter more spectacularly than the former: a superficial but bloody scalp wound. He was able to dine that night with Bunny Doble at a restaurant in Saragossa; his head swaddled in a soiled bandage, Kim wore a woman's motheaten fur coat. His hands trembled with shock. But Bunny be-haved like a hero's consort, and Kim sent a cool message off to *The Times* that his companions had died in the incident but that "your correspondent who was in the same car escaped with light wounds and has recovered."

The next day, January 1, 1938, Kim's twenty-sixth birthday, found St. John and Dora in Alexandria, he on his way from London to Jidda, she for a holiday in the Valley of the Kings. When Dora heard the news on the BBC, she wanted to fly to Kim's side; perhaps she would have but for her unease that one of her husband's closer friends, Pamela Lovibond, a librarian at the Athenaeum, was due to go on a trip with St. John. A telegram arrived from Kim saying that he had been lucky: shrapnel had scratched his scalp and wrist but there was no need to worry; Bunny Doble was looking after him well. Dora decided that prudence dictated that she remain with St. John.

She thus missed an occasion that would have made her bosom swell with pride: Franco's award to Kim of the Red Ruby, the Order of Military Merit instituted by Queen Isabella II in 1864 and the seventh in seniority of the honors Franco could bestow on heroes of Spain. The investiture was, therefore, noteworthy in a man's career, in more ways than one. Recently Sir Robert Hodgson had arrived as the For-eign Office's agent near Franco. He could be accorded no higher rank, as his government had not recognized the legitimacy of the Franco government. A stately man of great experience, especially in Soviet affairs, and a member of the Athenaeum, Hodgson had held various diplomatic and consular posts in Russia between 1911 and 1927. Philby had reason to be careful about him, for he had studied the Soviet secret services, having been the object of many attempts to compromise him and the members of his mission when he was in Moscow. Hodgson's arrival at Burgos was a political event; when he was received by Franco, he gave the Nazi-fascist salute, as protocol specified. Philby sent a dispatch to Printing House Square, drawing attention to the salute; perhaps he was thinking of the uproar that had ensued when the Duke of Windsor similarly saluted Hitler when they met recently in Berlin for the first time.

In a world where a nuance, a nod, a wink, a whisper, could all be made to tell, Philby's report did cause trouble. The heyday of Nazi and fascist respectability had begun to pass with Edward VIII's abdication. Hodgson was greatly embarrassed; in a letter to the foreign secretary he felt compelled to explain that he had not given the full Hitler salute, only a halfhearted variant of it — a sort of wave. A *Times* man was expected to support a British political agent on a delicate mission, not attack him. The report cast doubt on whether Philby was as pro-fascist as he represented himself. This view of him might have gone further but for the incident of the Soviet shell.

Franco sent for Philby; publicly, with Hodgson present, he pinned the famous Red Ruby on Philby's lapel and kissed him on both cheeks, as was the custom. Hodgson went over to congratulate Philby on his escape and the medal. Other events connected with the medal also seemed to gloss over the incident of the Hitler salute. The Red Ruby marked the point at which Philby became acceptable on the right. As St. John wrote to his mother on March 8, "Wasn't it splendid Kim getting the Red Cross for Military Merit?! It must have pleased him especially getting it, I understand from General Franco himself. *The Times* will also be pleased & it will do him a lot of good all round."[39] The Red Ruby did just that. Kim found that, as he wrote, it helped both his journalistic and intelligence work no end. Until then, Franco's staff regarded the British in general as a "lot of communists because so many were fighting with the International Brigade. After I had been wounded, and decorated, I became known as 'the English-decorated-by-Franco' and all sorts of doors opened for me."

The only communist member in Parliament asked the Foreign Office why a Briton was allowed to wear a fascist award, a question that again served to strengthen Kim's cover story and the appearances of his cover personality. As *Hansard,* the official record of parliamentary business, recorded in what was the first (but not the last) mention of Philby in Parliament:

> On behalf of Mr. Gallagher (Fife W. Comm.), Mr. Kirkwood (Dumbarton, Lab.) asked the Prime Minister whether he was aware that Mr. H.A.R. Philpot [*sic*] had been authorised to accept this decoration.
>
> Mr. R. A. Butler (Parliamentary Private Secretary at the Foreign Office): I assume that the Hon. Member is referring to Mr. H.A.R. Philby, a newspaper correspondent serving with General Franco's forces. I have seen in the press a report of the award of a medal by the Spanish nationalist authorities to this gentleman. Mr. Philby has not sought and has not been given any official authority to accept the distinction in question.

When the Spanish loyalist ambassador in London accused *The Times* of printing right-wing "falsehood and propaganda" from its correspondent Philby, Printing House Square bridled and spoke for him: its correspondent was trustworthy but it was watching the work of all its correspondents in Spain for any sign of propaganda.

Such statements were rare and perhaps unprecedented, and they served to proof Philby's cover — then defined as "a status, bona fide or assumed, which serves to explain the place of an individual in a community" — further still. His personality as Deutsch's sensible man of the center who nonetheless believed that Hitler was Europe's destiny was accepted, sometimes contemptuously, even by the most experienced correspondents.

In August 1939, a month before the outbreak of World War II, Philby reported back to *The Times*. The Spanish Civil War had cost almost a million lives in battles, air raids, executions, and the special tribunals that now began to sit. His editors thought highly enough of him to offer him the post of chief military correspondent of *The Times* at the headquarters of the British Army, which would proceed to France if war with Germany broke out. That the newspaper's most important foreign post should have been offered to a man who had yet to reach his thirtieth birthday was again remarkable, so much so that it was almost as if someone in the British Secret Service was fostering his career. Philby accepted the post, was cleared by the security authorities, and went on leave. In another direction, however, it seemed that his career had advanced not at all. It had been five years and two months since Orlov had told him: "Give your consent to any work that you consider useful, but always keep in mind that your goal is the British intelligence service." Whatever his relationship with de Renzy-Martin, Philby remained outside the Secret Service, although perhaps connected to it as an "honorary correspondent."

In London there arose still another crisis to imperil his security and that of the Cambridge Group at a time of great anxiety and stress. Through the departures of Deutsch, Maly, and Grafpen, the group found itself without the administrative services, the couriers, the financial assistance, the political direction, and the tactical advice on which hitherto it had depended for its security and survival — and its success. The new crisis had its origins in the events that led to Deutsch's flight. Edith Tudor Hart, one of Deutsch's assistants and the group's "grandmother," had been visited by two officers of the Special Branch of Scotland Yard concerning a camera she had purchased in 1936; it was believed that Deutsch had used it to photograph the plans of a new fourteen-inch naval gun at Woolwich Arsenal. The attempt had been detected by the security authorities, and a number of Deutsch's agents had been arrested. Some had been tried and sent to prison for espionage. This incident led to Deutsch's partial exposure as a Soviet agent and his departure from England.

During Hart's interrogation, when the officers asked if she had bought such a camera, she prevaricated, saying that she was a professional photographer who bought many cameras. They produced an invoice for the camera made out to a Dr. Hart of 63 Acre Lane, London. Was this her name and address? She again prevaricated and the officers left. She had heard nothing more, but it was clear that she was suspect in some way in the Deutsch case. Also, the officers' sudden abandonment of their questioning seemed to indicate that their descent had been an attempt to disquiet Mrs. Hart and the people with whom she was associated, a common police stratagem; disquieted people with guilty consciences become careless. Philby was seriously disquieted, as will be seen. Mrs. Hart had seen much of his wife, Alice. Had she led the police to Alice, to Burgess and Maclean? It was a time therefore for cool heads, to tread warily, to go to ground, perhaps.

It was in these circumstances that Guy Burgess gave Philby cause for further concern. Bereft of the firm control and discipline of a case officer, Burgess had become dangerously impetuous as he went questing far and wide in attempts, largely unauthorized, to recruit more spies to the Cambridge Group. Such was the extent of his forays that he sent to the Center — he alone had contact at this time, by mail through a Soviet agent in Paris — a list of no fewer than two hundred prominent Britons as his friends and connections. Some were pro-Soviet persons of prominence in the great universities. Others were abroad in the leadership of the Hitler Youth and the SS. Still others were on the fringes of the British and French cabinets. The rest were in the financial, scientific, and social leadership of England. A few were in the intelligence and security services. Among them was Colonel Valentine Vivian, chief of the Secret Service's foreign counterespionage service, David Footman, the deputy chief of the service's Political Section, and Guy Liddell, chief of the home counterespionage branch of the Security Service.

To his consternation, Philby found that Burgess had entered into the service of both British secret services and also maintained ambiguous and secret relations with the German intelligence and security authorities at the German Embassy in London. The danger for Philby in such a situation is evident. It could only be a matter of time before Burgess, the most audacious homosexual in all London, gave SIS and MI5 cause to examine his record, and their findings would inevitably lead the investigators to Philby. What then? He had even gone so far as to meet with both Winston Churchill and his son Randolph. And Footman had arranged the introductions that led to Burgess's staff appointment late in 1938, when, in secret, a new section known only as D was formed within the service "to investigate every possibility of attacking potential enemies other than the operations of military forces." Burgess's work in D entailed political warfare, which gave him an insight into that most secret of all interests at the time: the nature of Chamberlain's intentions toward Germany. It was recorded that in December 1938, about a month after formally joining the Secret Service, Burgess reported to Moscow that the policy of Chamberlain's government "was directed more against the Soviet Union than the Third Reich" and that "the broad intention is to work with Germany wherever possible and ultimately against the USSR."[40]

In all, Philby did not find Burgess's situation desirable. How long would it be before Burgess committed some indiscretion and led some SIS or MI5 officer to inquire into his associations? It was to Philby's great relief, therefore, that early in 1939 the Center activated a secret agent already in London, A. V. Gorski, who set about curbing Burgess and restoring the Philby group's communications with Moscow. Gorski, then thirty-two, perhaps lacked the authority required to restore the discipline necessary if the Philby network was to survive. His rank was that of a second secretary at the Soviet Embassy. He had arrived in Britain, possibly as a cipher clerk, in 1936. According to his FBI file, he was 5 feet, 5 inches tall, 165 pounds, stocky, with brown hair and brown eyes with gold rimmed spectacles — although an NKVD file has the color of his eyes as blue. Who was Gorski therefore? This became an enduring conundrum in his case, for as his file developed between 1936 and 1953, it emerged that he had no fewer than thirty-eight aliases, many of them variations of his code name, A. V. Gorski, and his real name, Anatoli Borisovitch Gromov, by which he became widely known to the U.S. intelligence services.[41]

Philby found Gorski to be a bright little cracker but one who was liable to go off if pulled too hard. Otherwise Philby thought him "dry," and Anthony Blunt, the ultimate sophisticate, regarded him as "a flatfoot and unsympathetic." None of the Philby group accepted Gorski with the same affection they bestowed on his predecessors. He was an apparatus man, and a formidable one. But, again, Gorski did not remain long. In August 1939, so great were the dangers for a Soviet secret agent that he, too, vanished, not to reappear until late 1941. In all, during the years between the wars and since his recruitment in 1934, Philby had six controls: Ignace Reif, Arnold Deutsch, Alexander Orlov, Teodor Maly, Gregory Grafpen, and Gorski. This represented a change of control, on average, every seven months — no great credit to the Soviet service. Was something wrong in London? The Center thought so. Gorski's successors, and Gorski himself when he returned to London in 1941, concluded that they must never lose sight of the possibility that there was a traitor in the group, someone in contact with the Security Service. Burgess became the first suspect. The second was Philby himself, for, as one of the successors, Yuri Modin, concluded: "It seemed to me that he was so completely, psychologically and physically, the British intelligence officer that I could never quite accept that he was one of us, a Marxist in the clandestine service of the Soviet Union." The greatest danger of working for the Russian Center in the era after the purge had begun to emerge. This was what the CIA would term in a major study of the Soviet service before and during World War II "Stalin's deep distrust of the Western Powers," "a peculiar Soviet paranoia" that "permeated the Russian intelligence services as well."[42] The Soviet party, too, shared that distrust. British communists were "ideological shit."

When Kim Philby arrived at the London family house in Maida Vale, he found his father there on political business for Ibn Saud and for the cricket. Of late St. John had grown weary of life in Arabia and wondered whether he was not wasting his time there, whether the Saudi treasury would ever pay its large and long overdue debts for the machine guns, radio stations, and automobiles that it had bought on credit through Philby's trading company, Sharqieh. But St. John remained devoted to Ibn Saud.

St. John spent much of the first few weeks at the Palestine Round Table Conference, called by the British government in an attempt to settle the interminable quarrel between the Jews and Arabs over the proposed Jewish homeland in Palestine. This foundered on the rock of the opposition of the British military chiefs of staff: with a general war coming on and faced with the need to guard the Middle East against the growing German, Italian, and Japanese interest in the region, they wanted no political settlement that might raise the Moslem world against Britain. But it did enable St. John to arrange what he called "a secret lunch party" at his home for the Zionist leaders, Chaim

Weizmann and David Ben Gurion, and Ibn Saud's specialist in Palestinian problems, Fuad Hamza. As supple and ingenious as ever, St. John made the startling proposal that King Feisal of Iraq should be made King of Palestine, thereby tranquilizing the Arabs while permitting, as a quid pro quo, the immigration of fifty thousand Jews over the coming five years.

None present trusted Philby overmuch. He wrote to Dora about how he was "playing my part, though very much behind the scenes," which was where he was usually to be found in great affairs. The Philby plan, as he called his proposal, did not prosper. Nor could it. Fuad Hamza said not a word during the luncheon; he would have cooked his goose with the Moslem leadership if he had. So why was this queer little meeting held at all? It is possible that St. John wished to be seen as the Wahhab peacemaker at work, keeping the scales even between Jew and Arab at a desperate time in world affairs, just as he was to be seen keeping the balance among the Sikhs, the Jat, and the Dogra in the Punjab in the interest of the Raj before World War I. But what was his angle this time — for there was almost always an angle in everything he did politically. Was he working in Britain's interest, in the interest of the Whitehall officials he professed to detest so heartily and whom he had done so much to injure in the Middle East between the wars? Had he become an instrument of the chiefs' policy of preventing any political settlement between the Arabs and the Jews at the Round Table Conference? Maybe. As will be seen, he used these meetings in an attempt to get £20 million for Ibn Saud's exhausted treasury out of the Zionists.

Anything was possible with St. John Philby. It is perhaps unfair to mention his name in the context of what was plainly a maneuver to split the Zionist movement just now. For at precisely this same time, the diabolical Burgess was on his first mission on behalf of Section D of the Secret Service. (He had just joined the service as a staff officer under the cover of a position in the Department of Statistical Research at the War Office.) In a letter to the Center, he explained that he was to create opposition toward Zionism and Dr. Weizmann on behalf of the British Secret Service. To this end he would solicit the support of his Trinity friend Victor Rothschild — who had succeeded to the great Jewish banking baronetcy in 1937 — for the notion of "a Jewish community in an area between Lebanon and Egypt." The object of this strategy was "to isolate and neutralise" Weizmann "so that the British Government could strike a deal with the Arabs."[43] The eve of war was a weird period, pregnant with labyrinthine schemes intended to enable the Chamberlain government to hold what it held — oil and political hegemony — in the teeth of German and Italian adventures in Iraq, Iran, Kuwait, Bahrain, the Persian Gulf sheikhdoms, and Arabia. Again anything was possible during that last phase before war broke out.

But there was something in all this for St. John, a reward from Whitehall, even though he was in bad odor with the British government. For in 1936 the Colonial Office alleged, with good reason, that St. John led a party of thirty-six Saudi soldiers and invaded the Hadramaut, a desert territory along the South Arabian frontier with the British crown colony of Aden, one of the vital naval oiling and victualing stations between England, India, British Asia, and Australasia. It was a pinprick to test British resolve in the area, which had long been coveted by Ibn Saud. St. John's "invasion" caused a great protest. Then Philby had published some articles alleging that British bombers were using tear gas against unruly tribesmen in the Aden deserts, and the high commission in Egypt alleged that he had become an Italian fascist propaganda agent, an assertion that may have held a grain of truth. When Rome was captured and the Mussolini government archives were examined, it was found that the Italian propaganda ministry in 1927 and again in 1935 had listed St. John among a small group of Britons, perhaps a dozen, regarded as fascist sympathizers or agents. Plainly St. John had tricked the Italians; he was, as he stated repeatedly, "a Communist who reads *The Times*." The only question is why he wished to make the Italians at Jidda believe he was their man. He probably wished the Italians to supply Ibn Saud with arms on easy terms. This they did in about 1938. A boatload of Italian weapons and munitions — enough possibly to enable Ibn Saud to establish the Arab realm and caliphate as a Wahhab dominion — arrived secretly at Jidda. They were, the Italians claimed, never paid for.

Philby then made matters much worse when, lecturing at the Royal Central Asian Society on his adventures in South Arabia and Aden, he enraged the audience, which included some of his friends, by alleging that the British in Aden "wanted to shoot me." The uproar was such that Colonel Stewart Newcombe, Lawrence's sabotage engineer during the Arab Revolt, stood up and shouted "Nonsense!" There were cries of "Rubbish!" throughout the room, and some people walked out. Philby cared not at all, although as the *Times Literary Supplement* would state in a review of his biography in 1973, there was evidence that Philby had been right. In the event, nobody took a shot at Philby. Far from it.

Returning to England in 1939 for the cricket and the Round Table Conference, St. John renewed his desire to become a socialist member of Parliament. He put his name down for consideration and received an invitation to contest the Epping Division, where the conservative member was Winston Churchill, whom St. John considered an enemy. Realizing that he stood no chance, Philby withdrew his name and entered into a relationship with the Marquess of Tavistock, the heir to the dukedom of Bedford, who was found to be in secret communication with the pro-war German foreign minister, Ribbentrop, through the German Embassy in Dublin. St. John liked Tavistock's British People's Party and its quasi-fascist platform and agreed to run for it at Hythe, a Tory safe seat in Kent. The truth was that he ran on a pacifist ticket, although that sometimes sounded like fascism. There was no prospect that he would succeed; he had precious little money for such a campaign, and one can only wonder why he went ahead.

The campaign began. Dora went to church to show that "we are not Muslims," and Philby worked hard and spoke three times a day to the electorate, his theme being one that interested Kim. St. John begged people "to think carefully whether you are really keen on an alliance between this country and Bolshevik Russia [and] the blood-thirsty assassins of the Kremlin." He assured his listeners that an "honourable peace" could be secured with Germany because "Germany wants it. The Pope wants it. America wants it."[44] But the electorate did not, rejecting him with derision. In a poll of about twenty-two thousand votes, he won just under six hundred and lost his deposit. The campaign cost him more than £1,000, which he could not afford. St. John's reputation, however, suited Kim's cover, that of a man of the right. It also suited the view of St. John at the headquarters of the British Secret Service, and that may have provided him with a reason for entering his name in support of such a hopeless cause at all.

In August 1939 the government opened the War Book, and all departments began the countdown to general war, filling war establishment posts, opening new departments, calling specialists to the colors. Among those called was St. John. He was offered the post of chief of British counterespionage in the Middle East, an astonishing moment in the Philby case. Expressing the view that a man could be a patriot without agreeing with his government's policy, St. John offered his services to the government as an Arabist. He was fifty-four and fit when an associate at the Royal Central Asian Society, Colonel W. G. Elphinston, whom Philby had known since Lawrence's operations in 1917, mentioned that there might be a job for him. Although the Colonial Office had only recently expressed a desire to shoot him, another, the Secret Service, saw him as its counterweight to those famous German spies of World War I, Wassmuss, von Hentig, and Grobba, who had arrived recently in the region to restart the old Anglo-German spy war there.

Philby accepted a formal offer of the post on two conditions. Ibn Saud had cabled him, asking him to return "on the wings of speed" but that he must hold no military rank and that the king must be told what post he held. These conditions were accepted by the high authorities in London, and Philby began to mark time until October, when he expected to sail for Jidda to begin his new and secret work against the fascist enemies, whose causes he had so vigorously advocated in the Hythe by-election. Here, then, given Philby's long record of animus toward the government, was a curious appointment. At the Colonial, India, and Foreign Offices his name was anathema; by 1939 they had lost patience with St. John Philby and his anti-imperial ways. His unsuitability for such a post, which would have made him a power in wartime Middle Eastern politics, seems evident from his record:

1. His "red-hot radicalism" in India.
2. His rifling of Sir Percy Cox's files at the Political Office in Iraq during World War I.
3. His handling of the treasury funds at Amman.
4. His "unauthorised correspondence" with Ibn Saud while at Amman in 1924.
5. The Tamini case.
6. His connection with Hassim Hakimov Khan.
7. The depiction of him as a *persona ingrata* by the British consul at Jidda.
8. His duplicitous handling of the Saudi oil concession.
9. His connection with Nazi and Italian agents before the war.
10. His association with prominent English fascists during the Hythe by-election.

There was, it is true, an urgent need for a man of St. John's caliber at Jerusalem. None knew more than he about the Arab nationalist and Jewish secret societies, and none of his age and experience knew the Middle East's politics, personalities, geography, and communications better than he. To Britain, the Middle East represented the most important possession after the homeland itself. Sir Edward Grigg, who became Minister Resident in the Middle East, explained why:

As a funnel of communication between the western, eastern and southern peoples of the British Commonwealth, as their richest reservoir of lubricant and motive oil, and furthermore as an area in which, without desiring to commit ourselves, we cannot allow any other Power to dominate and must preserve for ourselves the maximum of friendship and goodwill, the Middle East is no less vital to Britain than Central and South America to the United States, or than the eastern and western glacis of the Russian landmass to the Soviet Union.[45]

The British Empire might stand or fall through the maintenance or the loss of British primacy there, and it was for this reason that the Chamberlain war cabinet sent Britain's first, and for a time its only, tank division to Egypt at the outbreak of war.

The immediate and tactical reasons that St. John was offered the post seem evident. The region seethed with all manner of intrigues as German, Italian, and Japanese secret agents began operations to undermine the British hegemony. At that moment, Grobba, von Hentig, and Wassmuss were at work in Damascus against the French and in Baghdad and Tehran against the British. They had offered arms and munitions to the Pan-Arabian nationalist leaders, including Ibn Saud. Consequently, the post was linked directly to the Secret and Security Services in London and to those responsible for the higher direction of the war. Indeed, there was no more secret work except that of a senior staff officer at the headquarters of the British Secret Service. The only explanations for the offer can be therefore that either those responsible for St. John's appointment were ignorant of his silent war against Britain since 1924 or that they believed that, for all his malefactions, Philby would prove loyal to British causes, even if he believed them to be wrong.

It was all very odd. Odder still were Kim's activities at this same time.

During this period, and largely through St. John's insistence, Kim began to see much of a family friend since St. John's days in Amman, between 1922 and 1924. Mrs. Flora Solomon lived in considerable comfort in Addison Road, Kensington. Born in Pinsk in the Pale of Settlement in 1895 (making her seventeen years older than Kim), she was a Benenson, from a family of leading bankers in imperial Russia. She gained the higher reaches of Anglo-Jewish society when she married Colonel Harold Solomon, an officer of the eighteenth Hussars and a member of the staff of Sir Herbert Samuel, the British high commissioner in Jerusalem in St. John's day. As Mrs. Solomon wrote later in a memoir, she had been fortified against life's hazards by "my personal trinity — Russian soil, Jewish heart, British passport."[46] She had some political and social influence and claimed to be one of those responsible for the establishment of the State of Israel.

When she and Kim met again in 1936 at a luncheon given by a Sassoon, Kim was a young married man. With him was Alice Philby, whom Flora knew to have been a communist activist in Vienna. He had grown up well. "The Kim Philby I now got to know was not a talkative man," she wrote. "He had a gentle charm, never drinking to excess at my house, and mingled easily with my other friends."[47]

At one time or another the socialist elite passed through Flora Solomon's drawing room in Addison Road; as she wrote in her memoirs, she used every opportunity to "preach the justice of the Jewish cause in Palestine." But, she recalled, "this never worked with Philby. He evinced not the slightest interest in the Palestine conflict." If she was photographed with famous persons such as Mrs. Franklin D. Roosevelt and Mrs. Winston Churchill, the reality of her politics and the nature of her association with the Soviet secret services in London were so ambiguous that Assistant Director Peter Wright of MI5 found her "a strange, rather untrustworthy woman, who never told the truth about her relations with people like Philby in the 1930's, although she clearly had a grudge against him." Flora Solomon "knew far more than she was saying [and] she had obviously been in the thick of things in the mid-1930's, part inspiration, part fellow accomplice, and part courier" between Philby and the Soviet service.[48] In 1938, Mrs. Solomon recalled, Philby declared to her that he was "in great danger," that he was "doing a very dangerous job for peace and that he needed help." Would she help him in his task? It would be a great thing if she would join the cause. Mrs. Solomon said she "refused to join the cause, but that he could always come to her if he was desperate."[49] The cause of Kim's fright is clear.

As Philby learned from John Cairncross, who had replaced Maclean as the Soviet's mole in the Foreign Office, a major security inquiry had developed in the Communications Department. The situation was "appalling," as the permanent head of the office, Cadogan, remarked in his diary. A Soviet official, A. A. Doschenko, had been arrested and was being interrogated for having been responsible for "activities that do not commend themselves to His Majesty's Government." The Soviet ambassador, Ivan Maisky, had called on Cadogan and delivered the strongest protest. Investigations had begun in all the most sensitive branches of the government to establish whether there had been other such penetrations; Krivitsky, the informant who had exposed John Herbert King, was to be brought to London — by submarine, it was said — to assist in that task. More ominous in Philby's mind, perhaps, was the government's statement that, to enable it to deal with the internal security crisis brought about by the German situation, the Habeus Corpus Act of 1679 — "the great writ of liberty" — would be suspended, as indeed it was shortly. Late in September 1939, King was brought before a secret tribunal and sent to prison for seventeen years. The fact of his trial would not be made public until June 7, 1956, when it was announced only that King, "who had worked in the Communications Department of the Foreign Office," had been sentenced under the Emergency Powers Regulations for "passing information to the Russian Government."[50]

Against that background, as the last days of peace ran out in August 1939, Kim Philby went to tea with Flora Solomon, and she introduced him to one of Marks and Spencer's floor detectives. Aileen Amanda Furse was exactly the type of woman Philby was looking for to replace his wife, Alice, and his mistress in Spain, the actress Lady Lindsay-Hogg. Born in British India in 1910, Aileen was judged by Mrs. Solomon as belonging to a class, "now out of fashion, called 'county.' She was typically English, slim and attractive, fiercely patriotic, but awkward in her gestures and unsure of herself in company." She knew little of politics, she was not well read, but she was intelligent, practical, and incapable of disloyalty, either personal or political.[51] The Furses were known favorably in society. The record at about this time shows that one was the master gunner of the British Army, another had been the private secretary to Winston Churchill as colonial minister and then head of recruitment for the Colonial Service; still another had been director of the Women's Royal Naval Service and then of the World Bureau of Girl Guides and Girl Scouts, and a fourth was a leading light at St. Albans Cathedral.

Aileen herself had association in the Somerset world of horses and point-to-points. She was just the mate for a progressive conservative, which was the political coloration Kim had assumed at *The Times* — but not convincingly enough for Aileen's mother, who disapproved of Kim on the grounds that she knew him to have been a communist.[52] How she had established that fact, and what she did with the knowledge, is not known. But to Mrs. Solomon's surprise and perhaps her dismay, Kim and Aileen became lovers. "I was," she wrote, "pleased for her."[53] The couple moved into an apartment together, and in due course Kim made it known to his circle that they had married. This was a lie, for they lived as a common-law couple until 1946. Aileen took Philby's name by deed poll, and she also kept up her association with Mrs. Solomon. But Flora never completely forgave Kim for the way he treated women — "like Arabs," she said — and she kept a close eye on Aileen, who was a sick woman.

Since the age of fourteen, Philby discovered too late, Aileen had a history of self-mutilation when she was depressed, even, it has been said, setting herself on fire and infecting herself with her own urine. At some stage before she met Kim, she had opened an appendix cut, and her mother, a wealthy woman, had placed her in the care of Lord Horder, one of the leading doctors in London. To complicate his personal life still further, and perhaps to assure himself of Aileen's complete loyalty to him should she discover anything untoward about his political life, as she did, Philby made Aileen pregnant more or less immediately, for a daughter was born to the couple in 1941. Then followed two sons, in 1942 and 1943. The question of Aileen's attitude toward Kim and her emotional instability became further factors in the Philby case.

Whitehall became ever more vigilant as the days of peace started to run out. As Lord Hankey, chairman of the Committee of Imperial Defence and a member of Chamberlain's Cabinet, warned the administration:

> We cannot be sure that, when the real emergency comes, the traitors within our gates, directed by some organisation which we may so far have been unable to detect, may not deal us a crippling blow. For this reason I trust that all concerned will give the fullest possible weight to any precautions which the Security Service may see fit to recommend. We simply cannot afford to take any risks, and any injustices to which such precautions may give rise are of minor importance compared with the safety of the State.[54]

Time ran out. When Hitler and Stalin made the pact to which Krivitsky had alluded in Washington and the German army invaded Poland, Britain declared war on Germany on September 3, 1939, as did France. The Hammer and Sickle of the Soviet Union flew alongside the Swastika of the Third Reich outside the Soviet foreign ministry in Moscow. Nazism and Bolshevism were now allied against the Anglo-French democracies. The Soviet Union became a hostile neutral. World War II had begun.

At that vast moment in human affairs, Philby seems to have realized that there could be no escape from the Soviet service, even if he wished for one. Since 1936, the Soviet service had constantly shown that its arm was long in dealing with defectors and traitors. The commitment Philby had made to Deutsch that spring morning in 1934 was for life. With the onset of general war, irreversibly he came under that "absolute control of an invisible, strictly secret, central body composed of intellectual leaders" of which Lenin had spoken at the time of the October Revolution.[55] In later life, he left some notes about this irrevocable moment in his life. Why, after the Nazi-Soviet Pact, did he stay the course when so many of his contemporaries quit the party in disgust at Stalin's compromise with Nazism? He wrote:

> It seemed to me, when it became clear that much was going badly wrong in the Soviet Union, that I had three possible courses of action. First, I could give up politics altogether. This I knew to be quite impossible. It is true that I have tastes and enthusiasms outside politics; but it is politics alone that give them meaning and coherence. Second, I could continue political activity on a totally different basis. But where was I to go? The politics of the Baldwin-Chamberlain era struck me then, as they strike me now, as much more than the politics of folly. The folly was evil.[56]

And the evil to him was plainly his belief that Chamberlain and Stanley Baldwin were bent on encouraging Hitler to strike at the Soviet Union, which remained for Philby the socialist motherland.

Philby continued, endowing the lie that he now lived with a noble, knightly gleam. He saw

> the road leading me into the political position of the querulous outcast, of the Koestler-Crankshaw-Muggeridge variety, railing at the movement that had let *me* down, at the God that had failed *me*. This seemed a ghastly fate, however lucrative it might have been.[57]

His third course was

> to stick it out, in the confident faith that the principles of the [Soviet] Revolution would outlive the aberration of individuals, however enormous. It was the course I chose, guided partly by reason, partly by instinct. Graham Greene, in a book appropriately called *The Confidential Agent,* imagines a scene in which the heroine asks the hero if his leaders are any better than the others. "No, of course not," he replies. "But I still prefer the people they lead — even if they lead them all wrong." [She responds,] "You choose your side once and for all — of course it may be the wrong side. Only history can tell that."[58]

8

War

1939–1940

S T. JOHN AND KIM were at the family home in Hampstead when Prime Minister Chamberlain declared war on Germany at eleven o'clock in the morning. The great ideological issue was at last joined to decide whether national socialist Germany was to dominate the world. It would be, Churchill remarked, "a very dangerous war." All the isms — British imperialism, American capitalism, Russian communism, Italian fascism, Japanese militarism, Spanish falangism, German Nazism — were now to be tested. The world had reached a point of no return. There were some thirteenth-hour attempts to avoid an immediate general war. Britain would loan Germany £1 billion and return some of the colonies the triumvirs had confiscated after World War I. There were intimations that the President of Prussia and commander in chief of the German air force, Herman Goering, would fly secretly to England and attempt to restore the modus vivendi with the British foreign secretary, Lord Halifax. A British secret agent, a certain David Boyle, flew to Berlin. His mission, whatever it was, failed. Two British secret agents in Holland were authorized to open secret conversations with emissaries, it was believed of Admiral Canaris, the German spymaster, and his masters in the German General Staff. In all the great capitals there was a fizz of diplomatic attempts aimed primarily at making the principal belligerents see that the main enemies were not themselves but the Soviet Union. But nothing prospered, and the powers opened their War Books, and smoothly and silently their armies, navies, air forces, and civil systems proceeded to mobilize and dispose themselves in readiness for total war.

At once both Philby's sprang to their various duties. St. John, fifty-four, received the first intimation that his name was under consideration as chief of British counterespionage in the Middle East. Kim, twenty-seven, prepared to accompany a headquarters of the British Army to France as *The Times*'s special correspondent — and as a Soviet spy. At this, a supreme moment in the history of great events in the twentieth century, there was an important administrative change in the Center. As he later claimed in his memoirs, the chief of the Administration for Special Tasks, Lieutenant General Pavel Anatolyevich Sudoplatov, sent an instruction to his agent at the Soviet Embassy in London, presumably A. V. Gorski, "to resume contact" with Philby and Donald Maclean, who was still at the British Embassy in Paris. This, it seems, had been broken at Stalin's order as a precaution arising from the desertion of Alexander Orlov to the United States and the possibility that he might have named the sixty-two Soviet spies in Europe, Kim Philby among them, to the U.S. government. And as Sudoplatov was to record, the order was placed in Maclean's file at the Center along with his signature on a document which estimated that Philby and Maclean were regarded as of 1939 as loyal and trustworthy secret agents.[1] Also, it is not improbable that at this same time Kim met or had business through intermediaries with the chief of military intelligence at General Headquarters in France, General Gerald Templer, a formidable figure. It paid to meet *The Times*'s correspondent at an early date, and Templer had many connections at Broadway, the headquarters of the British Secret Service.

For Kim Philby, the triangle within which he would operate at GHQ for the next nine months was complete. He left nothing of his relations with Templer, who had control of the correspondents at GHQ, but Philby's friend Malcolm Muggeridge did. He too served under Templer and found him to be "a dashing figure," wearing "superbly polished boots" and "a great-coat which almost swept the ground," a man with "a sallow, lean face, with a moustache so thin as to be barely perceptible," who "spoke in sharp, clipped words," "a d'Artagnan [out of] *Le Rouge et le Noir*."[2] In his work as a Soviet secret agent, Philby would have to watch out for Templer.

St. John's position in the secret circle was less certain. Shortly after the declaration of war the counterespionage position was proposed. But little happened immediately, during which time Philby busied himself with Chaim Weizmann, the Zionist leader, concerning his proposal for a settlement to the Arab-Jewish quarrel in Palestine. There was a luncheon at the Athenaeum, with Kim present, in which St. John proposed audaciously that the Zionists pay Ibn Saud £20 million for western Palestine as a national home. Weizmann distrusted Philby as an "adventurer and enemy," a "political dilettante."[3] But Weizmann did not reject the "Philby plan." He agreed to discuss it further with FDR and Churchill when he saw them shortly. Why St. John took Kim with him to this most delicate meeting is not known, but it does raise a perennial problem: Did St. John know that his son was a Soviet secret agent? There is no answer to this question. It seems impossible that he did not, but there was never any evidence anywhere in his vast writings that he did. When he wanted to, no one was better than St. John at keeping a confidence.

Late in October 1939, as Kim was making his way to join GHQ in Arras, in northeastern France, news came that St. John's appointment as chief of counterespionage was canceled without explanation. Worse still, a rival Arabist, Colonel Gerald de Gaury, had been appointed instead. Someone in Whitehall had taken the trouble to look at St. John's file, and doubtless politics intervened — de Gaury had accompanied Sir Andrew Ryan, the first minister to Jidda, and had been present during the oil negotiations, which St. John had so effectively torpedoed, between Anglo-Persian and Standard Oil of California. St. John left for Saudi Arabia in November 1939, angry and dangerously disappointed that his services had been rejected, and leaving behind a puzzle: Why had he been offered so important a post in the first place? He seemed genuinely sad to leave, for he had had hopes to the last moment that his Athenaeum friends might be able to change the War Office's mind. But they did not, and as St. John wrote to Dora woefully at Cairo, "I have the queer consolation of knowing that another King and Country not only need me but want me desperately." He reached Port Sudan on Christmas Day of 1939 and crossed the Red Sea to Jidda. There he wrote to Dora about his "lonely morning tea" and his sense of emptiness when he reached his mansion near the Mecca Gate.[4]

After a few days at Jidda and Mecca — attending to what he called his "very confidential" mail, which he kept locked in the right-hand drawer of his desk — he went on to Riyadh in his Ford to attend his first privy council in just under a year. He found the waiting room crowded with princes and foreign envoys; to his distress, he found de Gaury among them. Ibn Saud, still lithe, vigorous, and hawklike at fifty-one, greeted Philby with many salaams and nose kisses, as always. The council sat, and Philby found de Gaury sitting where he himself usually sat. He saw Ibn Saud wink at de Gaury, and that annoyed St.

John further. From that moment, he began to make war on the new-comer: de Gaury would make a formal statement on behalf of the British government, and Philby would contradict him or scoff.

St. John displayed his attitude toward the war for the first time when, at this meeting, the king asked what news he brought from London. Philby replied that the news for the English was not good. When Prince Saud, the crown prince, asked why, Philby replied that it was a matter of arithmetic: the Germans were sinking x tons of merchant shipping a week, the British merchant navy possessed y tons. Within eighteen months x would exceed y and the British would have to seek terms — a statement that produced exclamations among the council-ors. After the audience St. John told Ibn Saud privately that he had rejected the offer from the British Secret Service because the Foreign Office had refused his condition — that he would serve only if the Arabs were granted their independence immediately.

St. John began to pursue his defeatist themes with an obstinacy that aroused the wrath of the British and French ministers at Jidda. By February 1940 the Foreign Office became concerned when the British minister at Jidda, Sir H. Stonehewer-Bird, reported that Philby had been "openly indulging in disloyal and defeatist talk in both Allied and neutral company" and that among the remarks he had made was that this was "an unnecessary war"; that it was ruining Arabia and might ruin the world; that a British victory was impossible; that there would have to be "a patched-up peace" between Britain and Hitler; that the British still had no intention of implementing their promises about Arab independence made after World War I. He claimed that Ibn Saud had sent for him from England "because he wished to learn the truth which he felt he could not get from British representatives whose lips were officially sealed." These remarks, Stonehewer-Bird de-clared, constituted "a political menace."[5]

So they were, and Whitehall treated them as such. A comprehensive set of defense regulations had been introduced at the outbreak of war, and under one of these a false statement or report on the part of a British subject at home or abroad could lead to summary punishment. Given that Philby's conduct might lead to a disturbance in the flow of Persian Gulf oil to Britain, the authorities sent Philby's file to the head of the Eastern Department, Lacy Baggallay, who had been involved in the investigations into the Tamini papers earlier, and the phrase popped out that Philby had been dismissed as chief British representative at Amman "for taking certain unauthorized action of a highly important nature, which was entirely contrary to the policy of His Majesty's Gov-ernment. He has not since been employed in the Public Service." A proposal was made that Stonehewer-Bird talk to Philby in a friendly fashion, but this was rejected because, the official minuted, "he has known for years exactly what we think about him and his activities and is entirely unrepentant." Something must be done about him but not until Philby stepped on British territory; if anything was done against him in Saudi Arabia, he would be further embittered and might become a great thorn in the flesh if Ibn Saud was compelled to deport him.

As usual, St. John then went too far. In the presence of the French minister at Jidda, M. Ballereau, he declared that Hitler was "a fine man" and a mystic comparable with Christ and Mohammed. Ballereau complained to the French prime minister, Daladier, who felt the need to bring Philby's "scandalous conduct" to the attention of the British government. Thus the case was elevated to the level of the foreign secretary, Lord Halifax, and the secretary of state for India, Lord Zetland. One of Ibn Saud's intimates told Bird that "the King liked Philby but laughed at his opinions" and the only effect of Philby's "disloyalty to England was to arouse suspicion in the minds of his listeners that his anti-British talk was a cloak for pro-British activities." The intelligence authorities did not dismiss Philby's statements so lightly. Philby was placed on the Middle Eastern watch list as a man to be detained if encountered, and Colonel Cawthorn, chief of the Middle Eastern Intelligence Center at Jerusalem, warned all intelligence stations about him. But when St. John learned this, as he did, he remarked almost gaily in February 1940 to Stonehewer-Bird that "he was not afraid of finding himself in serious trouble" for "every Englishman has the right to tell the truth." Philby's point, Stonehewer-Bird reported to Whitehall and Simla, "is that he is really a better Englishman than any of us in that he has the courage, which we lack, to face the truth."

On March 30, 1940, correspondence between the Foreign and the Indian Offices mentioned the possibility that Philby's statements and actions might "be regarded as treason or giving aid and comfort to the King's enemies." Action was taken to ensure that, should Philby enter British-controlled territory, the British authorities would cancel his British passport and provide him with one that would allow him only to return to England. Furthermore, the view of Philby by the Chamberlain administration was given point when the chairman of the Joint Intelligence Committee, Victor Cavendish-Bentinck, noted pithily that "it would serve Mr. Philby damned well right if his pension [from the Indian Government] were cut off!"

By the first week of May, the month in which Hitler unleashed his blitzkrieg against Western Europe and France, the India Office, referring to Philby by his Arabic name, Haji Abdullah Philby, enclosed a report to the government of India from the resident at Bahrain that "this reptile [Philby] has long been a critic of British policy in the Near East" and that while he was merely a nuisance in peacetime, he had become "a menace in wartime." The emphatic nature of the India Office's attitude persuaded the Foreign Office to urge all to caution, in case, through the loss of his pension, "Mr Philby might thereby be encouraged to pursue his objectionable activities with greater malice." There the matter rested when, later in May, Churchill became prime minister. Philby listed Churchill among his enemies; moreover, Philby had alluded from time to time to the "corruptions" of the Conservative government in its dealings with the Zionists.

At the French surrender in June 1940, the Battle of Britain began and a state of siege was declared. To meet the internal threats that developed through this emergency, on May 22 Parliament passed an amendment to Defence Regulation 18b, under which the government could detain without trial any person who held sympathies with any "power with which his Majesty is at war." Among the hundred and fifty persons so detained were many members of the British Union of Fascists, the former Anglo-German Fellowship, and the British People's Party, organizations with which both St. John and Kim Philby had been associated. Among those arrested, too, were two cousins by marriage of Clementine Churchill, the prime minister's wife.

Against that legal background the Churchill administration dealt with St. John Philby. In a brief, the India Office asserted that Philby himself would "indignantly deny the charge of disloyalty" made against him and that he would claim that "he serves his country far more truly than those who represent it officially, because he tells the Arabs (as he claims) the truth, instead of giving it a twist on the side of what might be, on a short view, considered British interests; and, more generally, that he promotes British interests in the long view by endeavouring to ensure that his country deals justly with the Arabs." But "none of this alters the fact that his misguided ideas of what constitute truth and justice are a serious potential danger."

On July 12, with the Battle of Britain intensifying and the start of a powerful movement in the United States against American intervention on the side of Great Britain, the Foreign Office received a telegram from Stonehewer-Bird in Jidda:

> I received this morning a message from Ibn Saud informing me that Philby was leaving the country and asking me to facilitate his journey.

Philby was, the King thought, mentally deranged, he never ceased heaping curses and insults and scorn on the British Government. He had told Ibn Saud that he wished to travel to India and the United States of America for the purposes of conducting anti-British propaganda. Ibn Saud has given orders to the Saudi authorities to keep close watch on him pending his departure and to inform him that if he indulges in anti-British talk he will be imprisoned.

Ibn Saud had betrayed his grand vizier in the interests of his treasury. The Americans were abandoning the oil concession and making their way home in case the Germans, the Italians, or the Russians invaded the region. The pilgrimage revenues were drying up rapidly, and the king hoped that the British would again provide him with the gold he needed to maintain his throne and his kingdom.

To this message Stonehewer-Bird attached Philby's itinerary, obtained by the British consul at Jidda when Philby called to obtain a passport endorsement that would permit him to leave Arabia through Bahrain, a British-protected territory and, under wartime security regulations, the only point of exit and entry in Arabia. The security services were alerted to expect Philby, and they looked forward eagerly to arresting "this renegade." His itinerary showed that Philby intended to leave Jidda for Bahrain on July 17, Bahrain for Bombay on July 28, and Bombay for San Francisco on the S.S. *Adams*. His U.S. visa had been obtained through American oilmen known to support his views on the German war; they were also paying for his passage. Stonehewer-Bird telegraphed the Foreign Office his advice:

> I think you will agree that it is most undesirable to allow Philby to travel to the United States of America. A very close watch can doubtless be kept on his activities in India and I feel it is best that he should remain there under strict surveillance for the duration of the war and I trust the Government of India will be willing to receive him.

The Home Office agreed, for this was a a desperate time in British affairs. There were real reasons for supposing that the Germans would invade England. Stonehewer-Bird's telegram was read against a background in which prominent British fascists had made "secret plans by which, in the event of a German invasion, they would either join the enemy or attempt to seize power and make terms with him." Thirty-four fascists, including their leader, Sir Oswald Moseley, had been arrested. St. John's association with the Duke of Bedford and the Peace Pledge Union was not forgotten, although the duke had not been detained. (He would have been if the Germans had invaded.) The

British authorities in Bahrain were instructed to "facilitate" Philby's journey to Bombay. There, Philby would be arrested under the Defense of India Rules, which were the same as those adopted in England, and held in the Ranchi Mental Hospital until he could be sent to England. As Lacy Baggallay minuted with satisfaction on learning of the government's intention: "No doubt Mr. Philby will be extremely annoyed, but people are being detained right and left for far less reason and he must lump it."

St. John Philby was arrested when he landed at Bombay on July 29, 1940, despite his protests that he was the guest of the California Arabian Standard Oil Company. He claimed later that he was tricked by the Indian security authorities, who invited him on his arrival to a cocktail party in a British warship at Bombay, a party at which Philby's brother, Tom, nautical adviser to the Government of India, would be present. But when Philby went aboard he found only an arresting party awaiting him. On August 24, he was transferred to the British steamer *City of Venice*, bound for Liverpool via the Cape. The master had orders to prevent St. John's landing at any port during the voyage. Philby began his journey across the world under close arrest.

In November 1940, he arrived in Liverpool in the middle of a heavy German air attack. He was arrested on a warrant signed by the minister of national security, Herbert Morrison, who was a socialist, and then, as St. John put it, he was "thrown into the foullest jail in all England" — Liverpool Prison.[6] Dora was there to meet the ship, but she had to wait five days to see him, for the charges against him were grave: he had "engaged in activities prejudicial to the safety of the Realm." From Liverpool he was taken by police van to Walton Prison and, as prisoner 90644, found himself in a cell measuring eleven by six feet. Here, in a letter to Dora, he protested that his only crime had been criticism, not disloyalty, as had been alleged. "Obviously," he wrote, "if I had had a guilty conscience I would not of my own free will have left the security of neutral Arabia."

Later in November, the Home Office moved St. John to a camp at Ascot, the royal racecourse, which was now being used to house dissidents. This was closer to London and made it easier for Dora to visit. He spent some of his time attempting to better the world through a book he called *Philosophus in Carcere*, in which he presented his prescription for a socialist, rationalist welfare state. He wrote a book of poetry, *Quatrains from Quod*, which was noteworthy only for its terrible puns. He lectured on Arabia to his companions in suffering, men whom he called "priests, professors, peacemongers *et hoc genus omne*." He played in bridge tournaments; and he read Hitler's *Mein Kampf,* G. H. Hardy's *Mathematician's Apology,* Sir James Jeans's *Mysterious Universe,* Olaf Stapledon's *Philosophy and Living,* and other such works. He was allowed to receive visitors but only "within sight and hearing of an officer." One of these visitors from time to time was Kim. His thoughts about his father's incarceration can only be imagined.

When Kim Philby took up his post as *The Times*'s correspondent at the headquarters of the British Army at Arras in November 1939 — a post that implied official War Office confidence in him — he was not out of the woods over the defection to the United States in 1938 of Walter Krivitsky, the senior Soviet agent at The Hague. The *New York Times* took a close interest in him after he had prophesied accurately and in timely fashion that the Soviet Union and the Third Reich would make a pact, and he had sought shelter at *The Times*'s offices when he encountered a man he knew to be a Soviet assassination agent at Child's Restaurant in Times Square. In December 1939 it was reported that Krivitsky had left the port of Halifax in Nova Scotia for London, a fact that became known to Philby at some stage, as it became known to Donald Maclean. Over the next ten years the Krivitsky case haunted him time and again.

Krivitsky's business in London was with the British Security and Secret Services and the Foreign Office, which had taken a formal interest in him when he exposed John King. None of Krivitsky's revelations bore on Philby personally, it has been stated officially, although several authors have claimed knowledge that Krivitsky gave descriptions that might have led the spycatchers to both Philby and Maclean. But the official historians, in their one statement on the Cambridge Five, did not agree. In discussing the Krivitsky case, they stated only (without mentioning either name) that "the success of the Russian intelligence services in the 1930s in recruiting agents with no overt Communist associations, but with Communist sympathies and educational and social backgrounds which would be likely to ensure that they would in due course reach positions of responsibility, remained hidden until after the war."[7]

Krivitsky "insisted that the Russians would use the [British Communist Party] as a Fifth Column on a large scale in the event of war. He also claimed that former friendly contacts between the Russian and the German intelligence services would have been revived following the German-Soviet pact and they would be collaborating against the United Kingdom, the Soviet diplomatic bag being put at the disposal of

Germany for the despatch of espionage material. His opinions could not be lightly dismissed." With one eye perhaps on Burgess's activities around the cabinet office, the official historians acknowledged that "a strong case has been made for thinking that information which reached the German embassy in London in the summer of 1939 about the progress of the Anglo-French-Soviet negotiations was obtained from King by his Soviet controller and used selectively to move the German government toward a pact with Russia."[8]

Krivitsky's defection, then, was of great consequence in the early history of the war. Through an arrangement with the State Department, the British government brought Krivitsky to England, by submarine so it is said, in 1940. So important was he regarded that he was interviewed extensively by the Security Service's expert in Soviet clandestinity, Miss Jane Sissmore, and by Gladwyn Jebb, who was both private secretary to the permanent head of the Foreign Office, Sir Alexander Cadogan, and the liaison man between the Foreign Office and the secret services. Among much else, Krivitsky asserted that the Soviets had a second spy in the Foreign Office, one other than King. He was a "Scotsman of good family" who had been educated at Eton and Oxford and was an idealist who worked for the Russians without payment. He had had access to the documents of the Committee of Imperial Defence, and "he occasionally wore a cape and dabbled in artistic circles."

It would seem that Krivitsky had confused two spies here to the point where neither could be identified. John Cairncross was a Scotsman, he had been a Foreign Office man, and he was a communist idealist who worked without pay. But he was not "of good family" — his parents were of humble means, and his success in life was due entirely to the excellence of his brain — and he had not been to Eton and Oxford. He was a Cambridge man. But he was on detachment from the Foreign Office as private secretary to the chairman of the Committee of Imperial Defence, Lord Hankey, who was also a member of Chamberlain's cabinet. Hankey was the author of the War Book, the document that laid down the step-by-step basis by which the British administration made the transit from peace to war; he was also the man who had established the structure of the modern war administration.

In Cairncross, therefore, the Soviets had a spy of cardinal importance at the very center of great affairs in Whitehall. He has been described as the best brain of his generation in Whitehall and, moreover, during that winter of 1939–1940 his chief, Hankey, was engaged in a major inquiry commissioned by the prime minister, the foreign secretary, and the chiefs of staff into the effectiveness and internal security not only of the British Secret Service but also its associated services, the Government Code and Cipher School and the Security Service. These inquiries arose in part through the conviction that "the Soviet intelligence authorities" had been exploiting "Communist loyalties for espionage purposes" since the 1920s, and particularly during the 1930s; that conviction was founded, again in part at least, on the findings concerning Philby's immediate masters, Deutsch and Maly, and on Krivitsky's statements. Thus in Cairncross the Soviets had a spy who could not only inform them about the situation inside the secret services but also could warn and protect Philby as he made his various moves. This was consistent with Soviet policy, which was that it was necessary not only to penetrate but to advise and warn the penetrator during his maneuvers. This Cairncross did.

But that is not all. During his debriefings, which lasted for three weeks, Krivitsky listed a total of nearly a hundred Soviet agents working against the Whitehall administration in various parts of the world. Of these, sixty-one were "legal" operators, Soviet citizens working in official Soviet organizations, and twenty of them were "illegals" in Britain. Those, according to Krivitsky, were three Americans, three Germans, three Austrians, two Dutch, one Pole, and eight Russians. Nine gave themselves out to be businessmen, three as artists, one as a journalist, one a student, one an ice skater. The occupations of the others were not certain. This group provided the administrative service for the Soviet service in Britain — forgers, communicators, messengers, and so on. In all, that group consisted of thirty-five people working in the Soviet interest. Sixteen of these were Britons, the rest odds-and-sods from Eastern Europe and the empire. They included eight persons active in politics and the trade unions, six in the civil service, and two in journalism. Half the names offered by Krivitsky were new to the security services; the others were on watch lists.[9]

In April 1940, the Foreign Office did circulate a secret memorandum based on Krivitsky's disclosures, but it identified none in the Cambridge Five or in the Oxford University cells. By the end of May 1940 a state of siege existed in England in which British vigilance was directed toward the immediate enemy, German intelligence. With the fall of France, Donald Maclean, accompanied by his bride, the former Melinda Marling of New York City, was evacuated to England. There he learned how close he had come to being unmasked by Krivitsky's disclosures. One respected British writer with MI5 connections, Gordon Brook-Shepherd, has suggested that Maclean's "distress at having so nearly been identified led the NKVD (the KGB's predecessor, extant in the 1930s and 1940s) to redouble its efforts to dispose of [Krivitsky]," for his fate was certainly mysterious enough to warrant such speculation.

After returning to the United States, Krivitsky was summoned to testify about the NKVD before Congressman Martin Dies, chairman of the House Committee on Un-American Activities. On Wednesday, February 5, 1941, Krivitsky left his wife, Tanya, and his son, Alexander, aged seven, in New York, traveled to Washington and from there to Charlottesville, Virginia, to stay with a friend, Eitel Wolf Dobert, a German refugee who lived on a rented farm while awaiting his naturalization papers. There, Krivitsky visited a hardware store and, using the name Walter Paref, of Barboursville, Virginia, bought a .38 pistol and fifty dum-dum bullets. On Sunday, February 9, he returned to Washington to be on hand for his testimony on Monday morning; he registered at the Hotel Bellevue, near Grand Union Station, at about 6 P.M., again using the name Walter Paref. He was not seen again until the chambermaid tried to enter his room. Finding the door secured from the inside, she obtained a passkey and let herself in at about 10:20 A.M. to find his body on the bed. Near Krivitsky's right hand (but with whatever fingerprints there were obliterated by bloodstains) was the revolver he had bought. There were only two openings to the room, the door and a window, which was secured from the inside and gave out onto the sheer side of the building, with no fire escape and no ledge. There was no sign of a struggle in the room, there were three notes in his handwriting that suggested Krivitsky intended to kill himself, and the revolver had been discharged close to his right temple. Everything suggested suicide.

The body was identified by J. B. Matthews, an official of the Dies Committee, who declared that Krivitsky had told him, "If they ever try to prove that I took my own life, don't believe it." None of Krivitsky's family, friends, or associates believed his death to be anything other than an NKVD "liquidation," and such were the surrounding circumstances that, in issuing a death certificate, the coroner agreed to empanel a jury if more evidence developed. Krivitsky was cremated at Fresh Ponds Crematorium in New York after dark so that the identity of the mourners could be concealed. Afterward, Krivitsky's wife and son went into hiding at the Maryland farm of Whittaker Chambers, another Bolshevik turncoat. The night of the funeral, the office of Krivitsky's lawyer was burgled and his safe was opened and rifled, evidently as part of a search for papers Krivitsky had left.

The Krivitsky case was to return to trouble Philby when, in 1947,

Raymond Murphy of the State Department reopened it on the basis of captured German archives that tended to show that the executioner was a certain Stein, a German agent working in the Soviet interest.[10]

At Arras, Philby lodged with the rest of the press corps, which included a correspondent of the *New York Times,* at the Hôtel du Commerce on the rue Gambetta, just around the corner from the house where Robespierre was born and where he practiced law until he emerged as the leader of the Jacobins, who coined the jargon Lenin used to such profit later — the bourgeoisie, the proletariat, the communes, the 9 Thermidore, the 3 Brumaire, and so on. The shooting war between the German and the French armies had not yet broken out, and the first British soldier would not be killed in action until the end of December. Ten British divisions were assembling near the Franco-Belgian border, and the French were more or less fully mobilized along the wider front from the North Sea to the Swiss frontier. But over all there hung a sinister silence. This came to be known as "the Twilight War" or "the Bore War" in British circles and as "the Phony War" in the United States.

Philby had established contact in Paris with his controller, a certain Henri Robinsohn, who is described by the CIA as "probably a German Jew and identical with Henri Baumann, born 8 May 1897 in Frankfurt am Main, Germany. According to Gestapo files, Robinsohn was born in St. Gilles, Brussels. Among his aliases were Otto Wehrli, Albert Gottlieb Bucher, Alfred Merian, Harry Leon, Giacomo, Alfred Duyen, Harry Merian, André, Lucien, and Leo." Reportedly he could speak "fluent German, English, French, Italian and Russian. He was about 5 feet 8 inches tall with a dark complexion, black greying hair, a high forehead, deep-set eyes, a big curved nose, full lips, wore glasses and pince-nez, dressed well, had a quiet appearance, and frequently carried an umbrella and briefcase." The French intelligence service in later years uncovered indications that Robinsohn had been in London in 1939 in charge of a Soviet network that became known at a later date as Harry II. As to his ideological convictions, the CIA has recorded that the director of the Center in Moscow "had warned that Robinsohn had been in ideological conflict with the Kremlin, that he was politically untrustworthy, and that he was suspected of being an informant of the French Deuxième Bureau" — an assertion that may well have been the source of the French service's claim that he had had control of Philby in London in the period when he was without a leader immediately before the declaration of war.[11]

Again, like Krivitsky's, Robinsohn's name would return to haunt Philby, especially when, after the German invasion of Russia, Robinsohn was instructed to place himself and his networks, including Philby, under the control of the *grand chef* of Soviet intelligence in Western Europe, Leopold Trepper. How much these unending ideological suspicions affected Philby's disposition to work for these quarreling high priests of Stalinism we shall never know, but he may have had no choice, for, as he recorded in his memoirs, he visited Paris frequently "and not only for the purpose of philandering." He recorded something too of his attitude toward danger:

> I have often had occasion to reflect that the really risky operation is not usually the one which brings most danger, since real risks can be assessed in advance and precautions taken to obviate them. It is the almost meaningless incident . . . that often puts one to mortal hazard.[12]

Philby's first main task for the Soviet service was to establish the German Army's order of battle in the west, especially the location of its ten tank and nine motorized divisions, which would spearhead any major land campaign. This information was of concern to the Red Army General Staff: for the rest of 1939 a hundred and ten Anglo-French divisions stood motionless in France against twenty-three German divisions in Germany. The official Soviet history of the war would allege: "This passiveness, rare in the history of wars, was combined with intensive preparation by the British and French command for intervention against the USSR."[13] There was truth in this.

The Franco-British Supreme War Council at Versailles regarded Germany as the main enemy, the German Army the main threat to Western Europe. Nevertheless, Churchill, whom Chamberlain had brought into the War Cabinet as the First Lord of the Admiralty, planned large naval operations to turn the Baltic into a front against both Germany and Russia. As Russia transferred large quantities of oil and other such valuable materials of war, the British and the French air command planned large-scale operations, from air bases in Turkey, against the Soviet oil industry and transportation facilities at Baku. And the Kremlin's old bogey remained — that the British in particular might do a secret deal with the German General Staff, without Hitler, that would give the German Army a free hand to destroy Russia. There was evidence for this, too.

The main strength of the German Army remained in eastern Germany and Poland, indicating that Hitler was undecided about whether to strike in the east or the west. Beyond this was the attitude of the Chamberlain government. As it was discovered later, in October 1939 Sir Arthur Rucker, the prime minister's private secretary, remarked to a junior, Sir John Colville, who had a connection with John Cairncross, that "communism is now the great danger, greater even than that of Nazi Germany." It was thus "vital that we should play our hand very carefully with Russia, and not destroy the possibility of uniting, if necessary with a new German Government against the common danger." What was needed, said Rucker, was "a moderate conservative reaction in Germany: the overthrow of the present regime by the army chiefs."[14] British and German secret agents had connection with each in the Netherlands and also at the Vatican, through Pope Pius XII.

As Philby lolled about the Hôtel du Commerce in Arras that November 8, 1939, there was little to write about. The Bore War continued, with the censors examining every dispatch, even to *The Times*. All that Philby was permitted to transmit was such a color piece as this, sent to Printing House Square on November 9:

> Only a narrow vista meets the eye from the turf-banked blockhouses that form the British Front. A damp heavy atmosphere, foreboding copious rain, obscures the further horizons. Towns and villages, built of brick and set closely together amid the endless fields, are stained by persistent smoke to a monotonous reddish-grey. "La Belle France" seems far away. Comfortless skies follow one another in dreary procession . . . "Adolf" is the enemy, the infernal nuisance, the target of the private's wit and the goal of his endeavours. Adolf must go, cost what it may. Many express disappointment at the slow tempo of the overture to Armageddon. They expected danger and they have found damp.[15]

Philby is said to have been an idle man, more interested in dining with the general staff at headquarters than in roving about the front, looking for news. He had connections to the commander in chief, Field Marshal Lord Gort. Attentive to his cover as usual, and to improve his standing with the British and French high command, he acquired a fresh consort, Lady Margaret Vane-Tempest-Stewart, a name to conjure with. She was the daughter of the Marquess of Londonderry, a peer at the very heart of the English ruling generation, an anathema to socialists. Londonderry had six titles, five of the grandest residences, £4 million gold, and scores of thousands of acres in England, Scotland, and Ireland. He had been air minister, lord privy seal, and leader of the House of Lords; he had been a leading member of the Anglo-German Fellowship, and he had been on political terms with Hitler, Göring, Himmler, and Mussolini. Lady Margaret's mother was a daughter of the Duke of Sutherland — and this was still a day and age when to know a duke was to know enough. Philby spent most weekends in Paris, where the Duke of Windsor was installed as an intelligence officer with the British Military Mission to the French government. The military correspondent of *The Times*, Basil Liddell Hart, the man who had seconded Kim's membership at the Athenaeum, came calling with news from London and the higher councils of the war.

But, it seems, Kim had no doubt that there was a reason for the pause or that the reason was political. Something was occurring behind the scenes. It had become a time for watchfulness when the first tremor occurred in the intelligence underworld. On November 9, 1939, a bulletin from Berlin announced that an attempt had been made to murder Hitler in Munich, but, to the "profound gratitude of the German people to the Almighty for watching over the Führer's safety," the plot had failed. Large numbers of the Nazi faithful had been killed and injured when Hitler had been addressing the Old Guard on the anniversary of his attempt in 1923 to seize the power of the Bavarian state. The spokesman then declared:

> The instigators, the financial backers, the people who are capable of so infamous, so execrable an idea, are the same ones who have always employed assassination in politics! They are the agents of the [British] Secret Service! and behind them stand the British war agitators and their criminal satellites, the Jews![16]

Later that day the German spokesman again tried to fix responsibility for the attempt, again in equal measure on the secret service and on world Jewry, and called attention to the demand of an American Jew, Max Rosenberg, that the U.S. government should release fourteen gangsters from prison on the condition that they murder Hitler.[17]

On November 9 there was still another tremor, one of a different nature and this time from The Hague. The General Netherlands Press Agency reported that there had been "an unexplained incident on the German frontier" the previous afternoon. Shots had been fired by "people wearing civilian clothing." It appeared that "one person was shot whilst the others were taken across the frontier" into Germany. What had occurred, it emerged, was that on November 8 Hitler had arrived in Munich, where he had two engagements. The first was to visit the Honorable Unity Valkyrie Mitford, a daughter of Lord Redesdale, a member of the Anglo-German Fellowship. Reputed to have been Hitler's paramour, Miss Mitford was an ardent Nazi who was so distressed by the outbreak of war between England and Germany that, according to a U.S. diplomatic report, she had attempted suicide. She was now recovering from her attempt, and Hitler called on her to cheer her up. His second appointment that day was at the Munich beer hall where the assassination attempt took place.

Little if anything was announced officially in London; the censor's control was total. But the *New York Times,* which had a man in Berlin, did report the incident extensively and immediately as the German government, jubilant at the news it had to release, announced that the security services of the Reich had arrested two British secret agents stationed at The Hague, S. Payne Best and Richard H. Stevens, and a Dutch carpenter, a certain Elser, who had manufactured the bomb used in the incident. They were all to be tried publicly for murder and for having attempted to murder Hitler.

As Philby undoubtedly became aware, the affair on the Dutch-German border was but the latest stage in the series of events that began in 1936 with Hitler's attempts to establish an understanding with Prime Minister Stanley Baldwin of England that would free him for a military campaign against Bolshevik Russia. At the outbreak of the war, the British Secret Service's examination of the prospects of there being an alternative government to that of Hitler became "detailed." A senior British secret agent, S. Payne Best, a veteran of World War I with many contacts inside the Dutch and the North German aristocracies, began the task of feeling out and seeking meetings with "the German opposition to Hitler." In all, there were six such meetings.

Their relevance to the Philby case was that these meetings were evidence of a disposition on the part of the Chamberlain government "to dicker with the Germans," as Philby put it, after the outbreak of the war. They represented an interim stage between the earliest contacts with the German dissidents on the part of the British Secret Service and the Hess incident that would come in May 1941, episodes of cardinal importance in the early political history of World War II and the Soviet-British-German triangle.

Under these unpromising circumstances, the cabinet met to decide whether to confirm as chief of the secret service Colonel Stewart Graham Menzies, who had been in charge of the meetings and had close ties to Sir Alexander Cadogan, chief of Chamberlain's Foreign Office. The appointment was confirmed on November 28, 1939, and Menzies became the third chief of the service since its formation in 1909. He assumed the traditional code letter C. And since the new C was to be a figure of great importance in the Philby case, something must be known about him. He became Philby's chief and was the embodiment of the class enemy in the case — the Whitehall mandarin, the bourgeois. Angus Maclean Thürmer would state that the case was "deeply plugged into the character, personality, and the operating methods of C personally."

Born in 1890, a son of an amalgam of Edwardian capital — Scotch whiskey, London dry gin, and North Sea shipping and fisheries — C was the king's man and he wore the royal cloak. His credentials as a leading member of the ruling generation were long — Summerfields, Eton, Grenadier Guards, Second Life Guards, Military Cross in the First Battle of Ypres, Distinguished Service Order in the Second Battle of Ypres; at twenty-five, chief of counterespionage at the headquarters of the British commander in chief in France. He had made the secret service his career at the end of World War I. He was personal assistant to its founder, Sir Mansfield Smith-Cumming; under the second C, Admiral Sir Hugh Sinclair, Menzies became in turn chief of the Military Section, chief of the German Section, and then deputy chief of the service. He was High Tory, a country gentleman, a prominent member of White's in St. James's, a Regency institution, and he spent much time hunting foxes with another Regency institution, the Beaufort Hunt, of which the master was the Duke of Beaufort, the Master of the King's Horse. Menzies, too, was on terms with Buckingham Palace through his stepfather, Lieutenant Colonel Sir George Holford, commander of the Reserve Regiment of the Life Guards during the reigns of Edward VII and George V. He and his brothers and cousins were well known to the heir to the throne, the Prince of Wales, and his brother, who became king when Edward abdicated in 1936. The new queen, Elizabeth, was a Bowes-Lyons, a family who lived on the estate adjoining the Graham Menzies's family estate at Hallyburton, near Coupar Angus in Scotland. Accordingly, Menzies's chief asset was his network of like-minded persons throughout Whitehall and in the upper reaches of society.

Professionally, there were three opinions of Menzies. His enemies thought him a ruthless man; his rivals thought him devious; his friends thought him courtly. As a successor, Dick Goldsmith White, wrote in his entry in the *Dictionary of National Biography*, foreigners found him "the personal embodiment of an intelligence mystique they believed characteristically and historically British." This "contributed to his international influence and it was a potent factor in establishing the Anglo-American and other Allied intelligence alliances." During the interwar years he ran the *cordon sanitaire* against the Soviet Union.

During World War II "his service had a greater role to play than ever before." He surprised all who knew him through his stamina and toughness; he had been a long-distance runner as a boy, and as a man who lived hard he had kept himself in excellent condition through his hunting. And, so a senior colleague remarked, his cover was superb — "He posed as himself."

A man who lived only for his work — he defined intelligence as "high politics and a rough game to play" — he had a personal life that was not as satisfactory as it might have been. In 1920, when he was just thirty and embarking on his secret service career, he married Lady Avice Sackville, a daughter of the Earl de la Warr, a family that had served the crown for eight hundred years and had provided one governor for New York and another for the state of Delaware, which was named after the family. This marriage did not prosper, and Menzies sued his wife for divorce on the grounds of her adultery with Captain Frank Spicer of Spye Park, a friend and neighbor. At the beginning of the 1930s, when he was forty, he married Pamela, a daughter of the Honorable Rupert Beckett, the owner of the Yorkshire Penny Bank, the *Yorkshire Post,* and much else besides. The couple produced a daughter, Menzies's only child. But early in the marriage Pamela Menzies developed anorexia nervosa and bulimia, complaints for which there was then no cure and from which she died in 1953. For most of their marriage, therefore, she was little more than a wraith.

Menzies emerged eventually as one of the immortals of the war; but the main question about him, in the context of the Philby case, was whether he knew St. John and Dora. One of Menzies's colleagues in the Secret Service, Frederick W. Winterbotham, chief of the Air Section, would state that Menzies "knew Philby's mother and that was how Philby got into the secret service."[18] This statement is of such importance that the character of the man who made it must be examined as part of the process of reckoning its worth.

An able, distinguished man, Winterbotham was nonetheless given to petty jealousies. He had regarded Menzies with a determined dislike ever since an incident in 1936, when Menzies's hunt and Winterbotham's held a joint point-to-point meeting in which Winterbotham rode and Menzies was a steward. During the race Winterbotham was accused of rough riding — a serious offense among horsemen that implied an arrogant disregard for the safety of other riders — and was ordered off the field. He appealed to Menzies in the expectation that, since Winterbotham held there was no merit in the accusation and since they were members of the service, Menzies would find in his favor. But Menzies ruled against Winterbotham, who was "ridden off the field," an indignity not often forgotten by men of his station. Winterbotham felt so humiliated, he confessed, that he disliked and distrusted Menzies thereafter — a petty enough cause for vendetta. But that is not all. Winterbotham alleged that after World War II Menzies vetoed a proposal that he receive a knighthood for special services rendered and that Menzies then forced his retirement when otherwise he might have become chief of the service.[19]

Winterbotham's statement is not inherently improbable, although the charge was a grave one: it implied that Menzies had used his patronage, a practice that the Civil Service had been attempting to eradicate, and that through it a Soviet secret agent was enabled to enter the British service and effectively destroy it as an instrument of national security. As is usually the case when malice enters into such allegations, the accusation is more easily made, and more likely to stick, than it is to get at the facts. There are only probabilities by which to make a judgment. Menzies's station in life was much higher than Dora Philby's, but this did not mean that their paths could not have crossed.

The Bore War ended with an almighty bang when, on May 10, 1940, Hitler launched Case Yellow, his gigantic offensive in the west. The substance of the *casus belli* was that, in assisting the British Secret Service, the Dutch and the Belgians had breached their neutrality. The details appeared in the *Deutsches Polizei,* the journal of the German police, in which it was related by the Reichsführer SS, Heinrich Himmler, to the Nazi interior minister, Wilhelm Frick: "It is well known that collaboration between British intelligence, neutral Holland, and neutral Belgium has not been abandoned. Rather it has been enlarged, with the knowledge and approbation of official circles working efficiently under British orders." The work of "disaffection, corruption, sabotage, and blockade" carried on against Germany in World War I had been continued and even expanded by the British Secret Service, whose strongest supporter was the "homme de confiance" of the Queen of Holland, the police commissioner of Rotterdam, Visser van t'Sant, who accepted not only British money but also put the prince consort, whose confidant he was, in touch with the British. Payments from British intelligence funds financed the prince consort's extravagant way of life and were partly responsible for the smooth working of this service in Holland.[20]

The invasion of Holland and Belgium followed, urged on by the

Soviet Union. Foreign Minister Molotov assured the German ambassador, when he was brought news of Case Yellow, "that he understood that Germany had to protect herself against Anglo-French attack." Three German army groups began to march westward. Hitler unleashed the panzer divisions of the army group of General Gerd von Rundstedt through the Ardennes Forest toward Sedan. The French Ninth Army collapsed, and Rundstedt's tank divisions poured into the French interior in the direction of the Channel ports, the gateways to England.

At GHQ Arras and the Hôtel du Commerce there was rout on rout. Philby moved out with the British Army and reached Brussels that same day. He and the rest of the press party then moved to the Catholic university town of Louvain, which they found almost deserted; a German massacre had taken place there at the outbreak of World War I, and nobody was going to wait to see whether there would be another. By May 17, Rundstedt's tanks were behind the rear of the Anglo-French army in Belgium and Holland, and then Belgium surrendered, and with General Erwin Rommel's tank division nearing Arras and GHQ, Philby and his colleagues were ordered back from Louvain to Arras.

The great retreat had begun. Philby and his party made first for Bruges, the capital of West Flanders, where they arrived as the Chamberlain government fell and Churchill succeeded. In a café there, a distinguished-looking British officer, learning that Philby was *The Times*'s correspondent with the British Army, introduced himself and asked advice about where he should go and what he should do. It was His Royal Highness, Major General the Duke of Windsor, the former King Edward VIII. No one knew what he was doing so close to the German spearheads, for he should have been in Paris with the British military mission attached to the Supreme War Council at Versailles. Philby may have known — at this time he himself had no communication with *The Times* — that there was great anxiety in London about the duke's whereabouts. Lord Lloyd, the colonial secretary, declared in a telegram of advice — which he drafted for Churchill to send to the dominion's prime ministers —

> The activities of the Duke of Windsor on the Continent in recent months have caused H[is] M[ajesty] and myself grave uneasiness as his inclinations are well known to be pro-Nazi and he may become a centre of intrigue. We regard it as a real danger that he should move freely on the Continent. Even if he were willing to return to this country his presence here would be most embarrassing both to HM and the Government.[21]

There was similar anxiety about the Duchess of Windsor. As Eric Seal, Churchill's principal private secretary, would inform Sir Alexander Hardinge, private secretary to the king:

> As I told you once before this is not the first time that this lady has come under suspicion for her anti-British activities and as long as we never forget the power she can exert over [the duke] in her efforts to avenge herself on this country we shall be all right.[22]

The Foreign Office and its Secret Service were not unaware that Joachim von Ribbentrop, the Nazi foreign minister who had so carefully tried to cultivate both when he was ambassador in London, might have some scheme to capture the duke and duchess and restore them to the English throne as puppets should the German Army invade England.

Philby never recorded what, if anything, he communicated to *The Times* about this interesting encounter. He himself was in danger of capture, and he sped on back to Arras that same day. No sooner had the press party arrived at the Hôtel du Commerce than they were ordered to leave for Amiens. But it proved no haven. With Rommel's scouts at the outskirts of the city, at three o'clock in the morning the press party received an order to make for the Channel port of Boulogne, where Philby and his colleagues were evacuated to England. The panzer divisions had accomplished in forty days what the German Army had failed to do in the four years of World War I.

On May 15 they broke across the Meuse between Mezières and Namur as the Dutch Army surrendered. On May 27 the British, French, and Belgian armies were surrounded and Belgium capitulated. The next day the British began evacuating their army at Dunkirk. The Germans took Ypres in a flash and appeared on the English Channel. On June 5 the Battle of France began when the Germans forced the Somme. On June 9 the Norwegians surrendered. On June 10 Italy declared war on Britain and France and invaded the South of France. On June 14 the Germans entered Paris. The mood of Whitehall was captured by Cadogan, the head of the Foreign Office, who recorded in his private diary: "These days are dreadful and my knees are beginning to go! Gather French haven't fought at all — simply shattered by air-tank attack. Our staffs living in the days of the Zulu war . . . Never did I think one could endure such a nightmare."[23]

During that period the new C succeeded in exfiltrating King Haakon of Norway. He was considered essential to the British cause because he controlled the Norwegian gold reserve and the Norwegian mercantile marine of three million tons. Out came Queen Wilhelmina of the Netherlands and her government and its gold reserve. Despite a telephone call from C to the King of the Belgians, Leopold III, in which he reminded Leopold that he was an Etonian and had an important duty to render the alliance, Leopold elected to remain in his country. Charles de Gaulle, his wife, their children, and a small staff arrived from Bordeaux to establish the Free French Forces.

On June 11 Philby returned briefly to France with a smaller press party. Landing at Cherbourg, he and his friend "Potato" Gray, representing the London *Daily Mirror,* spent a day at an army canteen and got drunk. On June 13 they drove in glorious weather through winding country roads toward Le Mans, but they received orders to return to England and did so on June 15. On June 17 Marshal Pétain of France, the "hero of Verdun," became president and at once sought an armistice. Hitler presided personally over the negotiations. The surrender was signed on June 21, with the transfer of three fifths of French territory, including Paris, to German control. Vichy, a spa town in the Auvergne, became the new capital. *L'Humanité du soldat,* the French Communist Party's newspaper for the troops, rejoiced with a policy instruction: "The enemy, which in any imperialist war is within one's own country, is overthrown. The working class of France and the world must see this event as a victory and understand it means one enemy less." The day after the French surrendered, Foreign Minister Molotov of the Soviet Union invited the German ambassador in Moscow to express to Hitler "the warmest good wishes of the Soviet government on the Wehrmacht's brilliant success."[24] And at that moment all Eurasia between Calais on the English Channel and Vladivostok on the Sea of Japan seemed united against the British Empire.

9

"The Stupendous Double-cross"

1940–1942

PHILBY RETURNED TO LONDON to find that, in expectation that the German Army was about to invade England, Churchill had imposed a state of siege — the first since 1588, when Philip II of Spain had launched his fleet at England to overthrow Elizabeth I and establish himself on the English throne. Churchill appeared in Parliament and delivered his greatest speech, one calculated in the first instance to calm the population. To Britain and the empire, he gave "some indication of the solid practical grounds on which we based our inflexible resolve to continue the war," how Britain might win, but how

> in casting up this dread balance-sheet and contemplating our dangers with a disillusioned eye I see great reasons for vigilance and exertion, but none whatever for panic or fear . . . During the first four years of the last war the Allies experienced nothing but disaster and disappointment . . . We repeatedly asked ourselves the question "How are we going to win?" and no one was able to answer it with much precision, until the end, quite suddenly, quite unexpectedly, [when] our terrible foe collapsed before us, and we were so glutted with victory that in our folly we threw it away.
>
> However matters may go in France or with the French Government or other French Governments, we in this Island and in the British Empire will never lose our sense of comradeship with the French people . . . If final victory rewards our toils they shall share the gains — aye, and freedom shall be restored to all. We abate nothing of our

just demands, not one jot or title do we recede . . . Czechs, Poles,
Norwegians, Dutch, Belgians, have joined their causes to our own.
All these shall be restored.

And then with an eye on the United States, "the great neutral":

> The Battle of France is over. I expect that the Battle of Britain is about
> to begin. Upon this battle depends the survival of Christian civilisa-
> tion. Upon it depends out own British life, and the long continuity
> of our institutions and our Empire. The whole fury and might of the
> enemy must very soon be turned upon us. Hitler knows he will have
> to break us in this Island or lose the war. If we can stand up to him,
> all Europe may be free and the life of the world may move forward
> into broad, sunlit uplands. But if we fail, then the whole world, in-
> cluding the United States, including all that we have known and
> cared for will sink into the abyss of a new Dark Age, made more
> sinister, and perhaps more protracted, by the lights of perverted
> science. Let us therefore brace ourselves to our duties, and so bear
> ourselves that, if the British Empire and its Commonwealth last for
> a thousand years, men will still say: "This was their finest hour."[1]

It is not likely that Philby was much impressed by Churchill's oratory. He was, it is evident, much more interested in the Communist
Party of Great Britain's requirement, deriving from Communist International headquarters in Moscow, to pursue a course of "revolutionary
defeatism," the better to assist the Nazi-Soviet Pact. Philby was the
enemy, the secret agent reporting to the Soviet camp. Who knew what
became of the intelligence he provided the Soviet Union at this time
— the ability of the army to resist, its morale after the tremendous
defeat at Dunkirk, the solidarity of the working class, whether Churchill would endeavor to make a peace with Hitler or the German
General Staff directed against the Soviet Union, the world citadel of
socialism? Was it not being sent to Hitler under the intelligence-gath-
ering provisions of the Nazi-Soviet Pact?

In his position as a *Times* reporter not back in Printing House Square,
Philby was himself well positioned to inform himself about the Churchill government's policies, despite the government's extreme secrecy.
The Times was subject to all manner of official and informal guidance
and advice from Whitehall about what it should, and should not, publish during this period of grave emergency. These became available to
Philby, formally and informally. However, as good a place as *The Times*
was to spy from in the Soviet interest, it was not good enough for his
Soviet chiefs. His orders remained in place; he was to do all in his

power to obtain a post in the British Secret Service. But it was now
almost exactly six years since Deutsch had given him those orders, and
no appointment had eventuated. Was Philby still suspect as a communist? Or as a fascist? He remained a *Times* correspondent, but one now
with an uncertain future even though the Secret Service was virtually
press-ganging university men and was desperate for men with Philby's
experience and qualifications. Philby seemed to be irrevocably compromised, perhaps by his father's arrest in Arabia, for what amounted
to "revolutionary defeatism," perhaps by his record over the decades.
Perhaps there were traces against Philby in the Security Service's actions against Deutsch in 1937. In fact, there were no such traces,
although he did not know it at the time. That he was on the Secret
Service's list of university men to be called to the colors in the event
of a national emergency counted for something. But what? Was his
recruitment being held back against the time when some special task
suitable for him arose? All things were possible.

The task of a "straight penetration agent" was not a simple one.
Philby could not simply apply for a position in the British Secret Service. It did not exist either in law or on the table of organization of the
government. The whereabouts of its headquarters and its various out-
stations was a state secret. In its recruitment policy, invariably it chose
the men it wanted, not the other way round. Neither could he simply
walk up to one of the officers at the bar of a club and ask for a job.
Only one man had the power to make an appointment, and he was
C. And he was well aware, as will be seen, that communists were seeking to penetrate his organization. He was also well aware of the dangers of such a penetration. These dangers have been well defined by
an American intelligence officer, James McCargar, who worked with
Philby:

> A successful penetration of the opponent's secret operations organi-
> zation puts you at the very heart of his actions and intentions towards
> you. You share his mind and thinking to an intimate — and reliable
> — degree impossible in any other secret operation. This means that
> so far as intelligence is concerned, you know what he knows. You
> have therefore annulled, in one stroke, the value of his secret intel-
> ligence about you; you have neutralized the power of his secret know-
> ing. Even more importantly, through your knowledge of his intelli-
> gence interests and of his political operations, as revealed in his
> policy papers and instructions, you are in the possession of the most
> reliable possible indications of his intentions. Most importantly, you
> are in a position to control his actions, since you can, by tailoring

intelligence for him to your purposes, by influencing his evaluations, mislead him as to his decisions and consequent actions.[2]

But Philby did try. He obtained an interview with Frank Birch, a don at King's College, Cambridge, who was recruiting graduates for work at the Government Code and Cypher School (GC&CS), a branch of the Secret Service engaged in vital intelligence work against the codes and ciphers being used by the German government to protect the secrets of its signals traffic at all levels of its command structure — from Hitler himself and his Supreme Command down to the battalion in the field, the ships in its fleet, its squadrons of aircraft in the skies. When Philby approached Birch, there was a great need for staff. GC&CS had already made some important discoveries about these codes and ciphers, and these presaged other, greater successes at an early date. Some of the codes and ciphers of the German Air Force were already being read. The decrypts became known generally by the code name Ultra or the term MSS, Most Secret Source intelligence.

Philby had obviously heard something of the work. But if he believed that he could commence his penetration of the British Secret Service by becoming associated with it, he was disappointed. While the best brains were required for this work, Birch rejected Philby, he wrote, on "the infuriating ground that he could not offer me enough money to make it worth my while." Whether Birch's rejection stemmed from a continuing miasma of political doubt about him — the same doubt that had beclouded his attempt to enter the Foreign Service in 1934 and the Athenaeum in 1936 — we do not know. It is possible, even probable. But with this rejection it seemed inevitable that his call-up into the army was imminent. Then Guy Burgess acted.

Burgess, still with Section D of the Secret Service, arranged for Philby to have an interview with Miss Marjorie Maxse, an elderly lady whom Philby found likable. She was "in a position at least to recommend me for 'interesting' employment."[3] But she did not tell him what that employment might be or the department involved. She proposed a second meeting. Kim agreed. In the interval, she doubtless checked Kim's record with the Security Service, as the regulations required. His name was passed through the Security Index, the record run by the Security Service of "undesirables" since 1909, when it was established. When the name was inserted, back came only the advice "NRA," "Nothing Recorded Against." He was fitted for secret work. His communist activities at Cambridge, his work with the German communists when Hitler came to power, his marriage to Alice Friedman, his work in the Austrian underground, the adverse reports regarding his loyalty by the Cambridge dons, his connection with the Anglo-German Fellowship, his association with Haushofer and Goebbels in Germany and with Major von der Osten of the Abwehr in Spain, his connections to seven Soviet secret service officers and to Mrs. Tudor Hart — nothing, it seems, had caught the eye of any authority. The Security Service (MI5) and the Secret Service (MI6), both of which had been in close combat with the Soviet services since 1919, had not found a trace of his communism, even though it was still common knowledge in both Oxford and Cambridge.

This was indeed a surprising factor in the Philby case. It is now known that for much of September 1940 the mechanical data system of the Index was capable of finding very little. The Index and some of the records had been damaged, some say destroyed, by German air bombs in the third week of September. The Index had been only imperfectly copied on microfilm, so a further copy had to be made before the system worked again. Moreover, it was being prepared for evacuation from the fastness of Wormwood Scrubs Prison in London to Blenheim Park, the Churchill family's estate in the Oxfordshire countryside. The Security Service itself had "all but broken down" through what is officially described as "divided management, inadequate leadership and severe internal jealousies," and the weight of the work produced by the very large numbers of men and women being brought into confidential work.[4] There were many other such security tasks, not the least of which was the activity of the Communist Party, which had been ordered by Moscow "to remain ready to exploit any revolutionary situation."[5] It is also possible that, overwhelmed as it was by requests by other departments for security clearances, the service gave only cursory treatment to a request for a security reference on Philby, given his *Times* references. But whatever the case, Philby was cleared for secret work.

When Philby appeared for his second interview with Miss Maxse, therefore, she was unaware of any adverse information about him. She was accompanied by a second officer of Section D — Guy Burgess. As Philby recorded:

> I was put through my paces again. Encouraged by Guy's presence, I began to show off, name-dropping shamelessly, as one does at interviews. From time to time my interlocutors exchanged glances; Guy would nod gravely and approvingly. It turned out I was wasting my time, since a decision had already been taken. Before we parted, Miss

Maxse informed me that, if I agreed, I should sever my connection with *The Times* and report for duty to Guy Burgess at an address in Caxton Street, in the same block as the St. Ermin's Hotel.[6]

Philby left *The Times* in August 1940 "without fanfare," he related, "in a manner wholly appropriate to the new, secret and important career for which I imagined myself heading."[7] With Burgess guiding his pen, Philby completed his personnel forms. His salary would be £600 ($3,000) a year, paid monthly in cash, in new notes, and tax-free — new notes and no taxes left no traces. He reported for duty at an office in Caxton Street, the headquarters of Section D. He was given a small office, bare except for a table, chair, and telephone. He filled out his personal papers for the file. Philby might have been expected to be judicious about the facts he set forth, but he was not careful. He notified Section D on September 1, 1940, that he had married Aileen Amanda Furse, who was born in India on August 24, 1910 — though he was not in truth married to her. He made no mention of the existence of Alice Philby, to whom he would remain married until she obtained a divorce in 1946. Any inquiry on this point would have established that Philby was in fact still married to Alice, who was now in England and still a communist underground worker. But he was very cool, and he may have been much encouraged to find that the SIS administration was not as eagle-eyed as he had feared.

Philby now began to work. He thought himself "in" the Secret Service. But he was wrong. He was not "in" at all. He was out. As he wrote of that queer experience, "Sometimes, in the early weeks, I felt that perhaps I had not made the grade after all. It seemed that somewhere, lurking in deep shadow, there must be another service, really secret and really powerful, capable of backstairs machinations on such a scale as to justify the perennial suspicions of, say, the French."[8] Here Philby was correct. There was such a service elsewhere. But it was not Section D.

In recent days, in secrecy, Churchill had ordered Section D to be removed from the Secret Service and, in the interests of administrative tidiness, joined to two other such organizations doing the same work. Thereby he created the Special Operations Executive (SOE). Philby was transferred to the new organization along with everyone else in Section D. The task of the new department was "to set Europe ablaze." SOE would be the "Democratic International" — as opposed to the Communist International — and its task was to create, arm, train, and lead the Continental resistance movement, which was expected to emerge within Hitler's Fortress Europe.

Philby's recruitment was supported by Hugh Gaitskell, the leading socialist who had been present at Philby's marriage to Alice Friedman in Vienna in 1934. He was now personal assistant to St. John's friend Hugh Dalton, the chief of SOE, and he was aware that Philby had joined SOE. Gaitskell said nothing about Kim's marriage to Alice Friedman. All he did say when asked for his opinion of Philby's politics was that he thought Philby to be "a rather altruistic left-winger, mixed-up and Byronic in outlook, eager to assist the leftwing cause without leaning quite as far as communism."[9] As with Burgess, so with Philby: the SOE existed to use the parties of the left, among others, to fight the fascists. Yet if Philby's politics had suddenly become fashionable, Burgess did not remain in SOE for very long after his arrival. Hugh Dalton made Gladwyn Jebb, a leading light at the Foreign Office, SOE's first director. Jebb then sacked Burgess for being "quite exceptionally dissolute and indiscreet and certainly unfitted for any kind of confidential work."[10] Philby might easily have become embroiled in Burgess's mess, but he was required for a special task. SOE needed someone like Philby, someone with a knowledge of left-wing European politics who also understood something of the German forces of repression, someone who might have ideas about how to raise the left wing, the trade unions and the communists, the leading troublemakers in European politics, against their natural enemy, the Nazis and the extreme right wing. SOE's chief of operations, Brigadier Colin McV. Gubbins, the leading British exponent of unorthodox warfare, asked Philby to write a paper on what he thought SOE's political objectives should be if it was to carry out Churchill's order to "set Europe ablaze." A Hebridean islander by birth, a wearer of kilts, and a man whose first principle was, as he wrote in a field manual, to "kill informers immediately," Gubbins became a man of distinction by the end of the war. He called Philby to his headquarters in Baker Street, London, where Sherlock Holmes and Dr. Watson had their practice in fiction, and as Philby recalled of their meeting:

> The air of his office crackled with energy, and his speech was both friendly and mercifully brief. A friend of mine nicknamed him "Whirling Willie" after a character in a contemporary comic strip. It was rumoured that he could only find time for his girlfriends at breakfast. But he was man enough to keep them.

Gubbins began

> by asking me if I knew anything about political propaganda. Guessing that he would like a monosyllabic answer, I replied: Yes. He went on

to explain that the new training establishment was being planned on an ambitious scale. There would be a considerable number of technical schools for demolition, wireless communications, and the rest. In addition he was setting up a central school for general training in the techniques of sabotage and subversion. Underground propaganda was one of the techniques required, and he was looking for a suitable instructor. He wanted me to go away and produce a draft syllabus on the subject. He showed me to the door with the words: "Make it short."

Philby now took some steps that would place him in the inner circle of war diplomacy, that secret side of the Foreign Office that had always found a few good brains, mainly from Cambridge or Oxford, who were capable of what were known as "special means" — what Philby called "dirty tricks." In the sixteenth century such brains had seen to it that the Catholic plots against Elizabeth I by Mary Queen of Scots and Philip II of Spain were undone; in the seventeenth century they had undone royalist conspiracies against Oliver Cromwell from foreign parts; in the eighteenth, the younger Pitt helped undo some of the work of revolutionary France; in the nineteenth there had been the acquisition of Persian oil and the defeat of the Russian service in India, as told by Kipling in *Kim;* in the twentieth, the defeat of the kaiser's service throughout the world and the maintenance of the *cordon sanitaire* around the Soviet Union. Now they were at work against Hitler. Yet when Philby got down to his syllabus, he

realised that my knowledge of propaganda left much to be desired. I had no inside experience of modern advertising methods. My few years in journalism had taught me to report what was happening, often a fatal mistake in a propagandist whose task is to persuade people to do things . . . To be on the safe side, I took the trouble to consult a few friends of mine in the advertising world from whom I picked up some basic principles that could be padded out to fill quite a few lectures. I have found that advertising people can be relied on for two things. First, they will tell you on no account to go into advertising; second, they will expatiate at length on the dirtier tricks of their profession.[11]

Philby wrote his draft syllabus — a document Gubbins intended to be the basic political training for the thousands of SOE and Allied secret agents who went into Fortress Europe over the coming four years of war — on one and a half pages of foolscap paper. It was a bold document, for it reflected the views of a man of the extreme left. Philby wrote that the Foreign Office's objective through clandestine warfare was not compatible with the objectives of SOE itself, or with those of the European resistance. The Foreign Office "wanted a simple return to the status quo before Hitler, to a Europe comfortably dominated by Britain and France through the medium of reactionary governments just strong enough to keep their own people in order." But "setting Europe ablaze" could not be done

> by appealing to people to co-operate in restoring an unpopular and discredited old order. It could not even be done by working on the feelings of the moment; they would be conditioned largely by Hitler's uninterrupted sequence of victories. We could operate effectively only by anticipating the mood of Europe after a few more years of war and Nazi domination had steeled them to take the future into their own hands. This would, without doubt, be a revolutionary mood. It would sweep away the Europe of the Twenties and Thirties.[12]

To his surprise, his paper was accepted at a meeting with Gubbins, which included a staff drawn from the higher reaches of the banks, the commercial houses, and the universities. Gubbins declared, so Philby claimed, "Exactly what I wanted. *Exactly.*" He asked his staff what they thought of it and they agreed, according to Philby, that "it all sounded very sensible."[13] Gubbins then told him to expand the document into a series of lectures on the question of how SOE should promote revolutionary war in Europe. He intimated too that he might require Philby to teach the subject to the trainee agents. That concerned Philby because

> I knew that I would make a lousy lecturer. Since the age of four, I have had a stammer, sometimes under control, sometimes not. I also had qualms about the subject matter of my course. The prospect of talking about political subversion did not worry me. There were very few people in England at that time who knew anything about it, and I had had at least a little practical experience in that field. But I was disturbed by my rudimentary acquaintance with propaganda techniques. I had drafted leaflets before, but had never printed one.[14]

Philby therefore obtained permission to consult with the high authorities in political warfare techniques, who were at a place code-named SU. It was Woburn Abbey, one of the stately homes of England located forty-two miles from London in the charming, rolling countryside of Bedfordshire. SU, now in embryo, was an agency responsible for the fraud in Churchill's war policy of force and fraud. The chief was Sir Reginald Leeper, an assistant under secretary of state, one of the men who had worked against the Soviet Union after World War I, and his personnel consisted, broadly, of a combination of foreign political eminences and advertising executives. The latter possessed, Philby wrote, "just the sort of expertise I stood most in need of." Their main business was deception and other such acts of legerdemain, which was then a secret business — even the word *deception* was never used. It was known in the lexicon of the Churchill administration as "special means."

Among the luminaries he found there was Robert Bruce Lockhart, who was still under sentence of death in Russia for the part he had played, if the Russians were to be believed, in the attempted assassination of Lenin in 1918. The man who befriended Philby in Fleet Street, Lockhart was now responsible for special means in Central Europe with the Political Intelligence Department of the Foreign Office; before long he was to find himself the chief of the newest of Churchill's seven secret services, one that came to be called the Political Warfare Executive (PWE). He was still on close terms with the Soviet ambassador in London, Ivan Maisky, a Russian with Chinese blood who had begun life as a hand in the caviar industry of the Caspian Sea; and he was still known to the Soviet secret services in London as Anna. What Lockhart's relationship was with young Philby was anyone's guess. But Philby was not immediately welcomed at Woburn Abbey, despite his connection with one of its leading mandarins. He was, he wrote, received "with some reserve. Like all departments, especially new ones, Woburn was on the lookout for trespassers." But they soon realized "that my interest in getting to know them was sincere, and that I was more than ready to accept advice." The Special Operations Executive was one of the several arms of the Churchill administration that would do PWE's work for it worldwide and, Philby went on, "it was clear that secret agents in Europe would indulge in propaganda, whether we wanted it or not. That being the case, it was good policy for Woburn, as the authority for [political warfare], to get a foot in the door in the shape of a co-operative [SOE officer]."[15]

Accordingly, it was not long before Philby had his own foot in the door of PWE. As the agency for all forms of propaganda and political warfare to enemy and enemy-occupied territories, PWE did not carry out such operations until "they have been approved on strategical aspects by the Chiefs of Staff and on foreign policy by the Foreign Office." Nor were its operations undertaken without the approval of the Defence Committee, whose chairman was Prime Minister Churchill.

The ease with which Philby entered this secret world demonstrated a number of truths. As Deutsch, Philby's tutor in Soviet clandestinity, had remarked to him in 1934, "An avowed Communist can never get near the real truth, but somebody moving as real bourgeois among bourgeois could." Here was Philby's moment. The bourgeois secret agent was accepted by the bourgeoisie running the war diplomacy of a great power that was still in a state of near-war with the Soviet Union. Thereafter he began to visit Woburn Abbey as the need arose, especially during the period, which was now beginning, when it seemed certain that Hitler intended to invade Russia. What then would be the attitude of the war diplomats? Would they advocate that Britain join Germany. Or would Hitler remain the enemy?

Philby had risen in the world. But to his dismay, so highly did Gubbins regard his lectures that he ordered him detached from his headquarters to teach his subject at an SOE "finishing school" for secret agents at Beaulieu, a large estate in the New Forest of southern England eighty-six miles by road from London. There, he realized, he might be buried for months, perhaps years. Resignation crossed his mind:

> Such a distance would interfere horribly with my other pursuits. Sometimes it seemed that I would do better to throw my hand in, but I was deterred by two considerations. In the first place it was essential to keep my foot in the door of the secret world to which I had gained access. It would be stupid to resign until I had a clear prospect of other employment in that same world. In the second place, knowledge is seldom wasted, and I could not lose by finding out what was going on in the Special Operations' far-flung training establishments. I decided to stay on until something more rewarding turned up.[16]

Philby departed for Beaulieu, there to begin the "finishing training" of the first school of SOE secret agents, the men who were not only to ignite the forces of the underground resistance against Hitler in Europe but, in Philby's view, were to help reestablish the Foreign Office's status quo in Europe. He began his lectures in October 1940. Beaulieu had been commandeered by the government for the duration of the war, and when Philby arrived, it was already a bustling, purposeful place. The agents there had passed two training courses, about twelve weeks in such arts and crafts of clandestine work as living rough in hostile territory, "silent killing," "knife work," "rope work," "boat work," pistol and submachine gun training in British and enemy weapons. The lambs were separated from the lions, and the survivors took the advanced course, "the elements of clandestine behaviour: how to change identity (be thorough), how to follow a suspect (be inconspicuous), how to be interrogated (be silent), how to escape (be quick)."[17] And the purpose of all this was not only to cut German throats and blow up German installations on a dark night but "to help break Nazi power." To achieve that end, SOE would and did work with anyone. Its chiefs "did not favour or disfavour any other political creed at all. Notoriously, SOE supported monarchists against communists in Greece, and communists against monarchists in Yugoslavia, because that seemed to be the best way to defeat Hitler." SOE was ready to work with "any man or institution, Roman Catholic or masonic, Trotskyist or liberal, syndicalist or capitalist, rationalist or chauvinist, radical or conservative, Stalinist or anarchist, gentile or Jew, that would help it beat the Nazis down."[18]

Philby's role was to teach the agents an understanding of such agencies as the Gestapo and the Sicherheitspolizei. He had learned much about them at the knees of men like Orlov and Deutsch and Germans such as Major von der Osten at Franco's headquarters. He lived and taught at "the German House" at Beaulieu.[19] He taught, too, about the Nazi Party and political warfare — poison pen letters; rumor mongering; the big lie; the sib, a term derived from the Latin *sibillaire*, to whisper. Already trained in the Soviet craft of such warfare, he now added British expertise; he combined the skill of Lenin with the doctrine of perfidious Albion — a powerful, insidious combination. Of necessity he spoke the lingo of the left, for the left, not the right, promised to be the main instrument of rebellion against the Nazi state. None at Beaulieu, it seems, saw him as more than a somewhat critical and disgruntled upper-middle-class intellectual who read the *New Statesman & Nation*, a journal that reflected the line of the pale Marxists. The other tutors found him a good companion, and for the first time there is evidence of the saintliness and supercriminality in him. As Patrick Seale and Maureen McConville note of his colleagues' view of him: "He had something about him — an aura of lovable authority like some romantic platoon commander — which made people want to appear at their best in front of him. Even his senior officers recognized his qualities and deferred to him."[20] Certainly none at that remote place realized that Philby was using the offices, facilities, knowledge, money, and status of the crown in order to expand the power of the Soviet Union.

And not for many years did it become apparent, as a CIA expert would remark in a paper on the Philby case, that Philby's job at Beaulieu led to his becoming "inextricably interwoven" with four wartime Soviet institutions in the underground of Europe:

1. The German communist resistance movement, known as the Rote Kapelle (Red Orchestra).

2. Soviet point for operations inside Germany. The main Soviet network there was code-named the Rote Drei, the Red Three.
3. An unspecified component of the French resistance movement.
4. A German operation against the Dutch resistance movement, one code-named North Pole.[21]

It is with the North Pole connection that we are first concerned. It was a grave matter. There is some evidence — not good enough for a jury but enough to warrant the opening of an official inquiry to establish the facts — that Philby was, while at Beaulieu, able to strike at least one blow for the Kremlin against one of the Comintern's main enemies, the House of Orange, the Dutch monarchy. The Dutch crown had long been locked in underground warfare with the Comintern. The head of the Dutch communist underground, Gouwlooze, was a determined opponent of the royal family, and among his other objectives was to destroy Dutch imperial rule in the Dutch East Indies. Before the war he had participated in a failed plot to assassinate Queen Wilhelmina. She had been on her throne for almost exactly fifty years when, in May 1940, the German Army opened its campaign in Western Europe with the conquest of Holland and Belgium. Wilhelmina and her government and intelligence service were evacuated from the Hook of Holland to England by the British Secret Service in three British destroyers.

Almost immediately the Dutch government-in-exile began work on a plan known as the Return to Holland. This required the insertion of Dutch secret agents to open the way for the Return, and in November 1940 these agents came to Beaulieu to complete their training. Philby remembered them well; he wrote in his memoirs: "It is only with sadness that one can recall the party of Dutchmen who attended our first course. Too many of them, owing to an operational disaster, were soon to be sent to certain death."[22]

These first agents were Hubert Lauwers, a wireless operator, and his partner, Thijs Taconis, a saboteur. Their task was to establish themselves in German-occupied Holland and form a structure for the agents who would follow them. They arrived imbued with rare passion. As Lauwers recorded, they

had one thing in common — a deep love of their country and, in their duties, a blind trust in their superiors. The long-standing reputation of the British Secret Service throughout the world and the training which the agents received brought their trust in their service to the heights of an almost mystical belief. Without this confidence

not one of them could have been brought to undertake the dangerous tasks which lay before them.[23]

After leaving Beaulieu, the men were left on a Dutch beach by a
British motor torpedo boat in August 1941 — the month when Philby
left Beaulieu for another secret post — to begin their work. The chief
of German counterespionage in Holland, Helmuth J. Giskes, claimed
to have learned of their impending arrival, and he and his men observed their landing and their activities until March 1942. Then he
arrested them. Under the threat of execution, they sent wireless messages to England at Giskes's instruction. Lauwers did manage to insert
CAUGHT in his signals to London, but the warning was not detected.
In all, Giskes managed to arrest a total of fifty-five secret agents. They
were exploited for intelligence about Allied plans in Holland, and the
information enabled the German intelligence services to infiltrate both
the Dutch and the French resistance movements. This action had
grave consequences that were not detected until September 1943,
when two of the agents managed to escape to Switzerland and warn
the British Embassy that the Dutch underground had been penetrated
by German informants.

But that is not all. Almost all the captured agents were executed at
Mauthausen and Gross-Rosen concentration camps, with many — perhaps a hundred and fifty — of their collaborators. Lost, too, were the
crews of twelve Allied aircraft that went to Holland on supply missions,
trusting signals written by Giskes, and were ambushed by German Air
Force night fighters. Of the 144 Allied agents sent to Holland between
May 1940 and September 1944, only 28 survived. At the end of the
war, a Dutch Royal Commission investigated what Lauwers, who mi-
raculously survived, described as "a suspicion that there had been
treachery in London." But nothing was proven, and the commission
concluded that "there is not a shred of evidence that points to the
possibility of treason."

Louis de Jong, the foremost Dutch authority on the Dutch resistance
movements, disagreed and, in a final analysis of the disaster, he wrote
of his conviction that the missions "were tragically finished the moment they began." He suggested the possibility that "a Russian mole"
in England had been responsible, but Philby's role, or the possibility
that he had been responsible, was not advanced at the time.[24]

Only at a much later date, and only after it became known definitely
in 1963 that Philby had been a Soviet agent since 1934, was his name
mentioned in connection with the disaster. In 1988, a memoirist on

the Dutch resistance movement, Herman Friedhoff, related how the new prime minister–designate to the Dutch government-in-exile, Dr. Herman B. W. Beckman, was captured by Giskes's men as he waited late at night on the beach at Scheveningen for a British motor gunboat to convey him to England and his post with Queen Wilhelmina. A number of Beckman's associates in the Dutch underground were also captured. These had particular importance to C, the chief of the British Secret Service, because one of them had established a secret contact between C and his German counterpart, Admiral Canaris, the chief of the Abwehr. Canaris's object was to produce a *modus vivendi* between Britain and Germany should Canaris and the generals overthrow or kill Hitler.

Friedhoff noted that Philby "had a particular interest" in cutting the link between C and Canaris, since "it was not in the Russians' interest to promote a democratic Germany."[25] Then, in 1991, a newly retired CIA Soviet analyst, William E. Henhoeffer, looked more closely into Philby's "inextricable involvement" in the events of 1940–1941. He concluded that Philby, while at Beaulieu, had learned the identities, aliases, and missions of the Dutch pupils and passed this intelligence to his Soviet contact in London. His case officer in London passed the information to Moscow, which had long been interested in overthrowing the Dutch monarchy, and the Center sent Philby's intelligence to Berlin under the terms of the intelligence-sharing agreement established by the Nazi-Soviet Pact of August 1939.[26] The evidence before Henhoeffer was entirely circumstantial; its main merit was a possible answer to what had remained a mystery — and a suspicion that the Royal Commission had been prevented from reaching the conclusion that the disaster had been caused by treachery in Special Operations Executive.

Henhoeffer was not alone in his theory. The infection in the Dutch underground spread everywhere, except to the communists, who remained relatively unaffected and invulnerable to Giskes's operation, for reasons that will soon become evident. In northern France and Belgium, Resistance members were executed or vanished into prison camps. Rebecca West, who was particularly well informed about the Philby case, explored the mysteries left by the Royal Commission and wrote:

> We are left to consider the possibility that this was one of the cases where members of the resistance groups wished their movement to be wholly Communist, in order that it might become a revolutionary

force at the end of the war and take over the government of all countries . . . Some men in Holland and in England would wish the collaboration between Holland and the West to be broken, and all Dutch anti-Nazi passion to be diverted to the support of the Soviet Union. They would therefore wish to frustrate the Dutchmen who had gone to England to work with the Allies.[27]

Half of Holland believed this to have been the case; and that the Royal Commission had done no more than draw the shroud over the tragedy. The commission laid the main blame for the affair on SOE for its "lack of experience, utter inefficiency and the disregard of elementary security rules." And but for Philby's mention in his memoirs of his meeting with the original Dutch agents — mention intended to provoke the reopening of the case, with all the political embarrassment that would have caused — no one would have been aware of his involvement at all. His purpose was probably to create embarrassment for the Dutch government and its relationship with the British and German governments in NATO.

While still stationed at Beaulieu in late 1940, Philby had developed an important connection. There had developed a social group of younger Secret and Security Service officers in both intelligence and counterespionage whose work focused on Spain. They were known among themselves simply as the Group, and they met in a magnificent house at 6 Chesterfield Gardens, the home of one Tomas Harris. Harris's father was a leading dealer in Spanish art treasures, specializing in the work of El Greco, Velázquez, and Goya. Tomas had inherited much of his father's artistic talent, as he had inherited the house and his father's fortune. He won a major scholarship to the Slade School of Fine Art in London at the age of fifteen.

Philby had met Tomas Harris and his wife, Hilda, in his early days in the SOE. He spoke of Harris's "brilliantly intuitive mind" and Harris's conception of "one of the most creative intelligence operations of all time."[28] This was an operation by a Spaniard code-named Garbo, who has been described as the most important double agent of World War II.

The Group included Tomas Harris, Guy Burgess, Lord Victor Rothschild (who became the head of the House of Rothschild), David Liddell (who became an artist after the war), and Anthony Blunt (the Cambridge art historian and Apostle), of MI5. The MI6 officers included Richard Brooman-White (chief of the service's small but expanding counterespionage organization in Spain and Portugal), Kim Philby (still with SOE), Tim Milne (a nephew of A. A. Milne, begetter of Christopher Robin), and Peter Wilson (later chairman of the London auction house Sotheby's). Others in the two services drifted in and out. But not everything became known about the Group, largely because Tomas Harris suffered an untimely death in 1964, before he could be examined by the Security Service. His was one of several such deaths, the first being Krivitsky's in Washington early in 1941 after his return to the United States from making his statement to the Foreign Office and the secret services about the Soviet penetration of the British government.

One noteworthy characteristic of the Group was that its members arranged jobs for one another in the Security Service. Another was that they collaborated in the handling of enemy double agents, that most dubious species of the secret war, and the planning and execution of deception operations against the Abwehr. A third was that, in the view of the CIA, they constituted "a group of Young Turks"[29] who had decided that the services required revitalization and that they should be the inheritors. A fourth was that some of them were agents of the Soviet intelligence service, but not all. Some had connections to the Apostles in Cambridge, and some displayed great ability in their secret work. There was much speculation that some of them on the inside used their positions at the Security Service to prevent the uncovering of the Cambridge spies and also arranged for Philby's entry in the Secret Service. These speculations are not improbable, but the facts were obscured by Harris's sudden death.

The circumstances in which Philby began to make his move coincided with a major reorganization inside both secret services to execute Churchill's deception policies. In January 1941, while Philby was still at Beaulieu, the directors of intelligence established the W Board, which "reported to no one" in the government "and was responsible to no one." It needed for its efficient functioning "not only total secrecy, but the greatest possible measure of flexibility and informality in the conduct of its affairs." When the Prime Minister was informed of its establishment, he replied through intermediaries that "obviously there was a job to do" and that the board should "get on with it." Churchill made it known that "if there was ever a row," then it could rely on the Prime Minister's "unofficial approval."

The task of the W Board was to do what a member called "odd things." Among them were actions that "might lead to certain targets being attacked by the German Air Force in order to spare others," to encourage by deception the bombing of one town in order to spare another. The board's main task was to "give guidance" on the nature of the true and false intelligence to be passed to the enemy in order to facilitate the work of double agents under British control and to deceive the German intelligence services about British capabilities and intentions.[30] Its first measure was to create an entity called the XX Committee, the double *x*'s representing not the Roman numerals but a double-cross. This body came into existence shortly after the W Board was established, and this appears to have been its first "odd job." The XX Committee became a subcommittee of the W Board; its secretary was J. C. Masterman, then the provost of Worcester College, Oxford, and later the vice chancellor of Oxford University. It was not long before the XX Committee came to have seven clearly defined tasks:

1. To control the enemy system, or as much of it as we could get our hands on.
2. To catch fresh spies when they appeared.
3. To gain knowledge of the personalities and methods of the German Secret Service.
4. To obtain information about the code and cipher work of the German service.
5. To get evidence of enemy plans and intentions from the questions asked by them.
6. To influence enemy plans by the answers sent to the enemy.
7. To deceive the enemy about our own plans and intentions.[31]

Connected to it were a number of departments of the government, including the Secret and Security Services; and the object of all was to arrange the smooth but totally secret passage of "special intelligence" to the Germans, mainly in Spain and Portugal, through double agents under the control of a section of the Security Service known as B1A. The chief of this section was Lieutenant Colonel T. A. R. Robertson, an outstanding officer of MI5 — a fact of importance in this tale.

Whether Philby's involvement with the Group — some of whom, notably Tomas Harris, were connected to Robertson's section — came to the attention of the W Board and the XX Committee is not known. But it is known that, at least at a date later than January 1941, Philby became "intimately involved" in certain aspects of the work. Whether this involvement concerned that most mysterious event of World War II, the case of Rudolf Hess, the Deputy Führer of Germany, is the subject of this analysis.

After the fall of France, in June 1940, Hitler began to plan the invasion and destruction of the Soviet Union. He had, however, assured his general staff that he would not lead Germany into that most disastrous of military situations, a two-front war. Therefore he instructed Rudolf Hess to ascertain whether a truce could be arranged with Britain. Hess talked the matter over with Albrecht Haushofer, who had given Philby some of the credentials he had needed to work as a British reporter at Franco's headquarters. He was also the man who had succeeded in establishing a reasonably close connection with the Marquess of Clydesdale, who had recently succeeded his late father as the premier peer of Scotland in the title of the Duke of Hamilton.

In the course of a secret letter, dated September 19, 1940, Haushofer advised Hess that he was prepared to write a letter to the duke through an elderly British widow living in Lisbon, Mrs. Violet Roberts, who was on terms with the Haushofer family; her husband, Ainslie Roberts, had been an official of the British Embassy. Hess agreed, for as Haushofer advised in his letter, Hamilton was "the closest of my English friends" and he had "access at all times to all important persons in London, even to Churchill and the King."[32] Accordingly, on September 23, 1940, Haushofer wrote to the Duke of Hamilton through Mrs. Roberts, to arrange a meeting in Lisbon. The letter has survived.

B[erlin] Sept. 23rd

My Dear Douglo,

Even if there is only a slight chance that this letter should reach you in good time, there is a chance, and I am determined to make use of it.

First of all, to give you my personal greeting. I am sure you know that my attachment to you remains unaltered, whatever the circumstances may be. I have heard of your father's death. I do hope he did not suffer too much — after so long a life of permanent pain. I heard that your brother-in-law Northumberland lost his life near Dunkirk — even modern times must allow us to share grief across all boundaries.

But it is not only the story of death that should find its place in this letter. If you remember some of my last communications in July 1939, you and your friends in high places may find some significance in the fact that I am able to ask you whether you could find time to have a talk with me somewhere on the outskirts of Europe, perhaps in Portugal. I could reach Lisbon any time (and without any kind of difficulties) within a few days after receiving news from you. Of course I do not know whether you can make your authorities understand so much, that they give you leave.

But at least you may be able to answer my question. Letters will reach me (fairly quickly; they would take some four or five days from

Lisbon at the utmost) in the following way: double closed envelope: inside address: Dr. A.H. Nothing more! Outside address:
Minero Silricola Ltd.,
Rus do Cais de Santarem 32/1
Lisbon, Portugal.
  My father and mother added their wishes for your personal welfare to my own . . .

Yours ever,
A[33]

Within a short time this letter was forwarded and soon was in the hands of the Imperial Censor, a worldwide service established by the British at the outbreak of the war to intercept German mail. By November 22, it was being studied by the Secret and Security Services, and in due course "Dr. A.H." had been identified as Albrecht Haushofer, "Douglo" as the Duke of Hamilton. Between November 22 and February 16, 1941, the implications of the letter were being studied, and perhaps plans were laid, for on the latter date a senior air intelligence officer wrote to ask the duke whether he would be in London "in the near future, as he was anxious to have a chat with him on a certain matter."[34] The meeting took place in London on April 15, and the senior RAF officer handling the letter, a certain Stammers, told Hamilton that "the Intelligence authorities were of the opinion that Haushofer was a significant person who had close connections with the German Foreign Office. They also thought it might be of considerable value to make contact with him."[35]

Ten days later Hamilton was instructed to return to London, where he met two officers, one of them Major Robertson, chief of the XX Committee. As the duke's son, Lord James Douglas-Hamilton, recorded in a history of the Haushofer-Hess-Hamilton affair, Robertson and his colleague at the meeting

> were eager that Hamilton should volunteer to go to Portugal in order to acquire all information possible from Albrecht Haushofer. Hamilton said reluctantly that he would of course go if he was ordered, and he was told that for this type of job people volunteered and were not ordered. He would be given time to consider the proposition and the technical arrangements of getting him there and back could easily be laid on.[36]

There the matter of the letter rested until May 1941. But in February 1941 Philby was told that the British service required his services. Tomas Harris, in the XX Committee, discussed Philby's appointment with Richard Brooman-White, chief of the Spanish desk at Secret Service headquarters, who mentioned Philby's availability to Colonel Felix Cowgill, the new chief of Section V, the counterespionage branch of the Secret Service. Whether Philby had been present at a session of the Group when Haushofer's letter to Hamilton was discussed, whether he had identified Haushofer, whether he proposed Haushofer as a suitable candidate for a double agency — nothing of this will be known. But the entry of Colonel Robertson into the case suggests that the Haushofer letter reached the W Board and the XX Committee; subsequent developments in the Haushofer case suggest that it produced one of the board's "odd jobs." And as Philby himself would report to his Russian masters after the end of the Hess matter, there had been a plan by the Secret Service to use the Duke of Hamilton connection to lure Hess to England.

Thus the Philby case acquired an element beyond mundane espionage and commonplace conspiracy. Philby began to emerge as a prince of the darkness. When Hugh Trevor-Roper, Regius Professor of Modern History at Oxford, wrote an essay on Philby, he saw him not only as a spy but also as "the New Machiavel." As Niccolò Machiavelli wormed his way into the court of the Medicis in 1498, so Philby, after seven years of coat-trailing, arrived at a central place in the British war establishment, the court of C, to play power politics. It is noteworthy that Machiavelli was twenty-nine when he arrived to play the game, and so was Kim.

In February 1941, St. John Philby stirred himself to petition for his release from detention at Ascot. Among those to whom he pleaded was an acquaintance since World War I in Mesopotamia, Lord Lloyd, the colonial secretary, banker, former intelligence officer, and a high commissioner in Egypt at the time of the Tamini case and other such Philbian rampages along the Red Sea. In recent years Lloyd had come to know St. John still better through the Royal Central Asian Society, an institution dedicated to the advancement of Oriental learning. Its members were often retired intelligence or political officers, specialists in Oriental affairs; Philby had belonged since 1909. In 1925 it did him the honor of publishing his Sir Richard Burton Memorial Lecture, on his camel ride across Arabia in 1917–1918, and awarded him its Burton Medal for the same exploit; but from time to time its governing board had remonstrated with him for some of his more anti-British statements. As with several of these centers of imperial learning, the society had influence at the Foreign, the India, and the Colonial

Offices, the Committee for Imperial Defence, and the intelligence services.

Lloyd, who had plenty of pull in Whitehall, may have been the man behind the offer to Philby of the post of chief of counterespionage in Arabia, for he was on terms with the new chief of the British Secret Service, Colonel Menzies. Lloyd too was a mandarin. He had sat on a commission to examine the Secret Service for its efficiency at the outbreak of the war; and he enjoyed that special official regard in Whitehall for men of wealth who had been to Eton and Trinity and had served as "honorary correspondents" of the Secret Service for many years. He held a number of orders for services with Lawrence in the obscure corners of the world. Regarding St. John, Lloyd believed that he was one of those oddities who, while enjoying the security and warmth of the establishment, found few things more satisfying than to annoy, confound, and irritate it. And so early in 1941 Lloyd wrote to the minister for national security, Herbert Morrison, a socialist in Churchill's coalition government: "Philby, in all the years I have known him, has always been a bit of a *mauvais coucheur** and has a tendency to be 'agin' the government, but I shall never believe that he was really disloyal or anything like that."[37]

Accordingly, a star chamber sat to hear Philby's plea for release from detention. On February 4, 1941, Philby found himself before three knights of the realm, to whom he lectured for hours about the misdeeds of the British in the Middle East. They decided he was no more than a dotty fanatic and recommended his release, and he was let go in March, but his passport was withheld and he was restricted to the British Isles. He left Ascot to begin writing his latest book — he wrote thirty-eight, nineteen of which were published — and as he did so he received a note from a figure in his distant past. "General" Valentine (Veevee) Vivian, his colleague in the Raj's work against the Sikh seditionists at the outbreak of World War I. St. John was in error: Vivian was not a general, but he was the colonel in command of the Secret Service's counterespionage service, under the command of C, Menzies.[38]

Vivian did not say why he wanted to lunch with Philby. But from this moment forward the Philby case began to enter the infernal grove, that place where nothing is true and nothing is false and yet where everything has meaning. C in particular knew the truth, for he was in daily and nightly contact with Prime Minister Churchill, who was now engaged in an exceptionally devious war diplomacy, a combination of

---

*The French *mauvais coucheur* refers literally to a person who is difficult in bed; colloquially, it suggests a person who is difficult to deal with.

force and fraud that would, he trusted, leave his enemies not only defeated but also baffled. He wrote of "craft, foresight, deep comprehension of the verities, not only local but general; stratagems, devices, manoeuvres on the grand scale," not excluding "elements of legerdemain" and "sinister touches."[39] War had been joined with Germany, but powerful Chamberlainite elements still believed that the Soviet Union would prove to be the main enemy. Consequently, C preserved his German card, Canaris, while the chiefs of staff planned the destruction of the Baku oil fields, then a main source of Soviet motive power, in case Stalin entered the war on Hitler's side. Churchill's game, however, was still two-edged. There was still the prospect that artful diplomacy might wreck the Nazi-Soviet Pact and produce what Churchill called that "tremendous thing,"[40] an Eastern Front in which Hitler would relieve Britain of the menaces against the islands and the empire.

During the winter of 1940–1941, in great secrecy Hitler began to withdraw the German Army from France into Eastern and Central Europe. His generals received orders to plan for the invasion of Russia, and there is some evidence that Hitler and his deputy, Hess, "discussed the advantages of a peace with England at the cost of a free hand for Germany against Russia."[41] By March it had become more evident that Hitler was transferring his armies from west to east, which raised the hope in Whitehall that in the spring he would invade Russia, not England. But to maintain an appearance of interest in Britain, the German Air Force continued its intense night bombardment of British cities. This bombardment had begun on November 14 with a dusk-to-dawn raid on the industrial cathedral city of Coventry, resulting in a thousand casualties. On November 19 and again on November 23 Birmingham was heavily bombed; Southampton, Bristol, Liverpool, London, Liverpool again, London again, Cardiff, Swansea again and again and again, London again, Portsmouth, Bristol, London again, Plymouth again and again, Bristol again and again and again, Coventry again and again, Birmingham on two successive nights, Belfast, London, and Portsmouth again, London again, Plymouth again on two nights in succession and again a week later, Liverpool on seven successive nights, Belfast, Clydeside, the Humberside. Many scores of thousands of people were killed, many more scores of thousands were wounded, and hundreds of thousands of homes and other structures were destroyed. The political purpose of this bombardment was to demonstrate Hitler's might and to beat England into accepting terms.

Accordingly, Churchill began to contemplate a new policy with Stalin, one in which he would join forces with anyone to defeat Satan. The employment of communists had become more in vogue in the Secret Service than it had been. As in olden times Catholics had been used to treat with Jesuits, so in modern times British communists were used to talk with European and perhaps even Soviet communists. But at that time there were two sorts of communists: the "national communist," who owed no allegiance to Moscow or the world revolution of the proletariat (although the Communist Party of Great Britain took its policy line from the Communist International), and the "international communist," the man who accepted Moscow's orders and worked for the revolution. In the terms of the class war of the times, the former was regarded by the establishment as a traitor to his class and could therefore be employed in secret work. Many communists of this type were so employed. On the other hand, the international communist was regarded as a potential or actual traitor to his country, and such a man was considered unemployable by the government in any capacity, except in the lowliest of work.

How did C regard Philby when Vivian wrote to St. John? There is no more vital question in the entire case, for on it turns the question of how C intended to employ Kim Philby. As one of Churchill's "elements of legerdemain" against the Soviet Union? Or in some less intricate capacity? Such evidence as there is about Menzies's knowledge of Kim's communism is confined to a single sentence in a letter from C to one of his senior staff in 1968, twenty-seven years later: "one could not have thought him an out and out traitor."[42] This indicates, but does not wholly prove, that when Vivian wrote to St. John, C had believed Kim was a traitor only to his class. Certainly C did not know that Philby was already a Soviet secret agent.

It was against this background that, on his release from Ascot, St. John accepted Vivian's invitation, Kim came to town from Beaulieu, and they met for luncheon at the East India and Sports, the Raj's watering hole in London. In the lobby were two king-size elephant tusks and portraits of such imperial figures as Lord Roberts, Lord Kitchener, and General Sam Browne. Indian waiters served glowing curries, and the furniture was covered in hunting pink. St. John left no letter or note about this engagement, but Colonel Vivian did. In a letter, he remembered that when Kim left the table briefly Vivian asked St. John about his politics. "He was a bit of a Communist at Cambridge, wasn't he, I inquired." With this question Vivian showed that he knew Kim had been a communist at Trinity. And it was in his response that St. John's career-long campaign against the Establishment culminated. "Oh, that was all schoolboy nonsense. He's a reformed character now."

St. John passes his old friend a poison pill, perhaps wittingly, perhaps unwittingly.[43]

Plainly, Vivian's purpose at this meeting was not more than a survey of Kim's character and personality, conducted perhaps at the suggestion of Brooman-White and Tomas Harris of the Group. But what was surprising about it was that, as Professor Trevor-Roper later wrote, Vivian even considered Kim for most secret work unless "Philby had particular virtues" that made him indispensable.[44] Here Trevor-Roper touched on the reason for Vivian's interest. Kim did possess those virtues. He was indispensable alike to the anti-German and anti-Soviet policies now afoot at Secret Service headquarters. Vivian was not the fool of the piece; Guy Burgess, in a report to his Soviet masters when Vivian attempted to recruit him in 1938 as a secret agent against the Soviet Union, noted that Vivian had displayed an "encyclopaedic knowledge of Marxist theory and a grasp of Comintern politics" that had left him "overwhelmed."[45]

Rebecca West, too, touched on a reason for Vivian's desire to employ Kim Philby and for his attempt to recruit Guy Burgess in 1938. "The security organizations," she wrote on the basis of considerable inside knowledge, "have shown a disposition to believe that by skilful manipulation they can persuade Communists that Communism is not incompatible with patriotism, and they will be drawing the Soviet Union and the West closer together if they act as British agents."[46] As chief of counterespionage in the British Secret Service, Vivian was to provide his government with channels for passing deceptive information to the Soviet service, to identify Britons working for that service or who might work for the British service, and to find out what the Soviets intended toward Germany. The difference between Philby and Burgess was that Kim evidently won Vivian's confidence. He established himself, at the luncheon and the proceedings that followed, as a trustworthy man.

In fact, as events were to show, Vivian had made the worst misjudgment of his career.

There, for the time being, rested the question of Philby's entrance into the Secret Service. Their luncheon ended, the three men returned to their business. St. John went back to his cottage in the Welsh hills to resume work on *Arabian Days*. He remained there until the end of the war, with monthly expeditions to London, more often when the cricket was on at Lords. Kim went back to Beaulieu, confident perhaps that he was closer to the fulfillment of the mission set him in 1934 by Orlov and Deutsch. And Vivian went back to his headquarters in Broadway. But nothing more was heard from him, or at least nothing has been recorded. March, April, May — ninety days later, Philby was still to be found at the German House at Beaulieu.

But then occurred a matter of moment in the history of World War II. On May 10, 1941, a Saturday, Philby was in London during a gigantic air attack, one that caused great damage to Whitehall and Westminster, including Kim's school. As it took place, a single German fighter plane, a twin-engine Messerschmitt 110, entered Scottish air space and flew in spirals, as if the pilot was seeking a particular place below. Then a man parachuted to the ground. It was Rudolf Hess, who had flown more than a thousand miles from an airfield in Bavaria. He asked to speak with Hamilton, but the duke was on duty with his fighter squadron that night and he could not see Hess until the next morning, Sunday, May 11.

Why Hess had come, whom he represented, what his mission was — there was much obscurity on these points. But gradually it emerged that Hitler wished for terms and had sent Hess as his messenger. Hess intimated that if the British agreed, Hitler would guarantee the sovereignty of the British Empire. He made no mention at that time of Hitler's intention to invade the Soviet Union, although it came up a little later. Surprised by Hess's appearance, Hamilton telephoned the Foreign Office and reached one of Churchill's private secretaries, John Colville, who arranged for Hamilton to fly to Churchill's weekend retreat in Oxfordshire. That same evening Hamilton told his story to Churchill. "Do you mean to tell me," Churchill asked Hamilton, apparently surprised, "that the deputy führer of the German Reich is in our hands? Hamilton replied that that was so. Churchill then remarked, "Hess or no Hess, I'm going to see the Marx brothers"[47] and disappeared into the mansion's private cinema. But he reappeared later and began to question Hamilton closely. There was, it seems, no sign whatever that Churchill had any foreknowledge of Hess's mission.

Hess vanished as "a prisoner of the state" in the care of two of C's most senior officers; and although he lived for a further forty-seven years, he never again saw the light of day as a free man. He died, by his own hand, it is said, in 1987, still a prisoner. Churchill ordered complete secrecy on Hess's arrival, and knowledge of Hess's presence in the United Kingdom was confined that Monday morning to only a few persons. But Kim Philby was one of them.

In 1991, the KGB in Moscow released to the public a file of messages from Philby concerning Hess's arrival. Philby's code name was still

Söhnchen, and on May 14, a Wednesday, the Soviet Embassy in London sent this telegram from its intelligence chief to the Center in Moscow:

> Information received from SÖHNCHEN is that HESS arrived in England declaring he intended first to appeal to HAMILTON who he had become friendly with in connection with their common interest in aviation competitions in 1934. HAMILTON is a member of the so called CLIVEDEN set. HESS landed near the castle of HAMILTON. KIRKPATRICK the first person of the SAKULOK [code word for British Foreign Office] to identify HESS who tells him he has brought peace offers. We do not yet know the details of the peace proposals.[48]

The KGB went on to claim that Philby's source was Tom Dupree, deputy chief of the Press Department of the Foreign Office, whom, it stated, Philby had met in 1936 in Spain and regarded as a friend. In another signal received in Moscow, on May 18, the Soviet intelligence chief in London reported further word from Söhnchen that

> during his conversation with officers of British military intelligence Hess declared that he went to Britain to confirm a compromise peace which was to stop the deprivation of the two belligerents and preserve the British Empire as a stabilizing force [in world politics]. In his conversation with Kirkpatrick, HESS declared that the war between two Nordic nations was criminal and he believed that there was a powerful anti-Churchill party in England which wanted peace and would receive a powerful stimulus in the struggle for peace with his arrival.[49]

The anti-Churchill party was, of course, the Anglo-German Fellowship, centered around former King Edward VII and the Duke of Saxe-Coburg-Gotha, among others.

The signal went on to state that Philby had asked Dupree whether "a British-German Union against the U.S.S.R. was what Hess wanted," and Philby had advised that was "exactly what he wanted." Philby claimed knowledge that Hess had written a letter to Hamilton "before Hess's arrival" and that it was "surely intercepted by the British *counter-intelligence service*," which did not send it on to Hamilton for "some six weeks." Philby did reassure the Center that this "was not an appropriate time for peace negotiations" but that, in his opinion, "as the course of the war develops," Hess "could become the centre for intrigues for a compromise peace and would therefore be useful for the peace party and for England."[50]

Philby's claim to knowledge that Hess had been lured to England seems, in the light of history, to have been soundly based. For reasons unknown, he apparently had been well informed, especially concerning the activities of the "British counter-intelligence service." Philby usually called there when he was on weekend pass, as seems to have been the case on the weekend that Hess arrived. His claim to knowledge that Hess had come "in an attempt to sue for peace on behalf of Hitler, who was planning to attact the Soviet Union," has never been admitted by any British government, although the Russians believed it to have been true. The official Soviet news agency, Tass, announced at the time that it had evidence that, by luring Hess to England, the British Secret Service had "strengthened Nazi hopes of the possibility of concluding a peace treaty with Britain, thus inveigling Germany into a war with the Soviet Union."[51] Stalin was certain that "Britain was inciting Germany to attack the USSR, that secret negotiations were taking place in London based on Hess's proposals." Britain had remained "the chief enemy of the Soviet state," and "the old enemy of the Soviet regime, Winston Churchill, was behind it all as "an experienced and wily politician."[52] And as Churchill himself recorded when he met with Stalin,

> I had the feeling that he believed there had been some deep negotiation or plot for Germany and Britain to act together in the invasion of Russia which had miscarried. Remembering what a wise man he is, I was surprised to find him silly on this point. When the interpreter made it plain that he did not believe what I said, I replied through my interpreter, "When I make a statement of facts within my knowledge I expect it to be accepted." Stalin received this somewhat abrupt response with a genial grin. "There are lots of things that happen even here in Russia which our Secret Service do not necessarily tell me about." I let it go at that.[53]

The Hess case therefore remained, as it remains still, a mystery. At the time, it was the greatest political mystery of World War II, for as one historian said of it, Hess's arrival "astonished the British, bewildered the Americans, horrified the Germans, and struck fear into the Russians."

On June 22, at 3 A.M., 17 tank, 13 mechanized, and 110 German infantry divisions invaded the Soviet Union on three narrow fronts under covering fire from 7,100 guns, 2,770 aircraft, and 3,300 tanks. Operation Barbarossa was the largest military operation in history. Churchill spoke to Russia and the world over the BBC and declared that Britain would render all assistance in its power to the Soviet Union. "No one has been a more consistent opponent of communism than I have for the last twenty-five years," the prime minister declared, and "I will unsay no word that I have spoken about it." But the past "with its crimes, its follies, and its tragedies, flashes away." The "Russian danger" was "our danger, and the danger of the United States, just as the cause of any Russian fighting for his hearth and home is the cause of free men and free peoples in every quarter of the globe."

There was not complete agreement about Churchill's speech in either Washington or London. Senator Harry S. Truman spoke for many Americans when he said he hoped that Germany and Russia would claw each other to death; and a former ambassador to the Soviet Union, William C. Bullitt, spoke for many others when he publicly proclaimed that country's government "a godless tyranny, the sworn enemy of all free peoples of the earth."[54] President Roosevelt stressed America's inability, through prior commitments to Britain, to be of much help. Churchill's air production minister, J. T. A. Moore-Brabazon, expressed the same sentiments as Senator Truman and was reproved by Churchill for having done so.

But the Eastern Front, which Churchill had desired so intently, was created. On July 12, 1941, the Soviet government announced that the war, hitherto an "imperialist conflict," had become a "liberating and anti-fascist one." They renamed the conflict the Great Patriotic War, and both governments at once arranged an exchange of military missions "to work in assisting the mutual war effort against the common enemy." The Soviet mission arrived on July 7, 1941; yesterday's foe appeared to be today's friend.

As part of the enmeshment of war machines, His Majesty the King of Great Britain, Ireland, and the British Dominions Beyond the Seas, Emperor of India signed an agreement with the Presidium of the Supreme Council of the Union of Soviet Socialist Republics for "joint action in the war against Germany." Since the Russian Air Force had no aircraft with the necessary range, the Royal Air Force undertook highly dangerous missions from bases in the British Isles to parachute Soviet secret agents and wireless operators to the communist underground in Germany, the Rote Kapelle.

But such operations were no more than tokens of an alliance. The game went on between Britain and Russia as it had since the Crimean War. Philby's case officer, Anatoli Gorski, who had vanished at the outbreak of the war, reappeared on the distant horizon with his wife, Zinaida Mihailovna. To avoid German-occupied Europe, he took the long way around — Moscow, Siberia, Japan, New York, Lisbon — and arrived at the Soviet Embassy in London with the rank of first secretary in October 1941 to discover, doubtless with pleasure, that Philby had succeeded in his mission for the Soviet service: he had penetrated the British Secret Service. On the morning of the German invasion of Russia, Philby was still at Beaulieu tutoring secret agents.

> My batman woke me with a cup of tea and the words: "He's gone for Russia, sir." After giving two rather perfunctory lectures in propaganda technique, I joined the other instructors in the mess before lunch. My colleagues were clearly plagued by doubt in this perplexing situation. Which way should the stiff upper lip twitch when Satan warred on Lucifer? . . . Mr. Churchill would address the nation that evening. It was clearly wisest to wait until the Prime Minister had spoken.
>
> As usual, Churchill settled the question. By the time he had finished his speech, the Russians were our allies, my colleagues approved, and the upper lip clicked back into place . . . It was now more than ever necessary for me to get away from the rhododenrons of Beaulieu. I had to find a better hole with all speed.[55]

There are two versions about how Philby found his better hole. First there is his own.

In July 1941 he encountered Tomas Harris, the well-to-do art dealer who was now engaged in handling double agents. Would Kim be interested in a job with the Secret Service in charge of counterespionage operations in Spain and Portugal? It was explained to him that a high proportion of German intelligence operations were mounted from those countries. What he was really after was a post in the political section at headquarters, which would place him at the heart of the foreign affairs at the seat of government. The counterespionage section was nineteen miles from Whitehall, in St. Albans, a small country town in Hertfordshire. But a post in Section V, as the counterespionage department was listed on the Secret Service organization chart, would place him at the very center of the security system of Britain, the nature of which was officially defined as "the defence of national interests against hostile elements other than the armed forces of the enemy: in practise against espionage, sabotage and attempts to procure defeat by subversive political activity."[56]

At the Iberian section he would be in charge of "operations intended to negate, confuse, deceive, subvert, monitor or control the clandestine intelligence collection operations and/or agents of foreign governments or agencies."[57] For the successful execution of these duties he would be required to know, or at least to learn, about all the policies, overt and covert, and the secret operations of the government. This would afford him a view of the secret war at all levels that was altogether rare elsewhere in Churchill's administration and would give him operational control of the most important sector in the secret war with Germany. But it was not the area of main interest to the Soviet Union. On the other hand, he noted, "My new job would require personal contacts with the rest of SIS and with MI5. There was also a suggestion of a Foreign Office interest, not to mention the service departments." And by accident he "discovered that the archives of SIS were also located at St. Albans, next door to Section V."[58]

Philby gave Tomas Harris the green light, and before long he received a telephone call from the chief of Section V, Felix Henry Cowgill, asking to meet him at an inn at Markyate, a village on the Great North Road near St. Albans. As Philby recorded of that meeting:

> It is a measure of the informality of the times that I had not definitely applied for the job and that Cowgill could not have indicated his acceptance. Yet, in the course of a long evening, he told me exactly what my duties would be against a background of the structure of the SIS as a whole. As his discourse was of a highly secret nature, I took it as a formal statement of intention. In other words, I considered myself hired.[59]

Such was Philby's version of his recruitment. He glided into the secret circle as a spy and the avenger. But there is another, one that reflects more of the ruthlessness of the survival politics of the period, and especially those of "that tremendous thing" of Churchill's war strategy, the Eastern Front. Churchill had been profoundly affected personally and politically in World War I when, through Lenin's revolution in 1917, which had been assisted by the German intelligence service, the kaiser was able to transfer very large forces from the Russian to the French front for the purposes of an overwhelming offensive intended to produce a German victory in the spring of 1918. The first blow fell while Churchill was in the front line in France. The entire British Fifth Army was crushed, five other such offensives were launched, and so real was the prospect that the war might end in a German victory that it made what Churchill called a lasting imprint on British political history. As prime minister in World War II, he had no intention of permitting another separate peace, this time between Hitler and Stalin, as was always possible — not a year of the war passed without some indication that either Hitler or Stalin was seeking a Soviet-

German accommodation. If one of these matured, then America and Britain would find themselves facing the full brunt of the mightiest army in the world, with little prospect of victory.

With these politics in the background, Allen Dulles, a major figure in U.S. intelligence between 1942 and 1963 and late in his career a director of operations and then chief of the CIA, would relate how

> before entering [SIS] Philby made what was accepted as a clean breast of all his earlier Communist connections, including those of the Spanish Civil War . . . His particular task was to mastermind British double agents, to penetrate [German] intelligence and — ironically — *to feed false information to the Soviets.* He soon established a reputation for brilliance in the work . . . *Since one of his official duties was maintaining liaison with Soviet intelligence, his open and frequent contact with them was above suspicion,* and at the end of the war he received the Order of the British Empire.[60]

Here, indeed, is an interesting view of Philby's recruitment — that C, initially at least, recruited Philby as a deception agent for work against both the Soviet Union and the Third Reich. Dulles's high authority in world espionage, his trustworthy mien, lend his statement a rare credibility. Dulles was there; he knew about Philby. And it was a view to which Philby could never admit.

There is little if anything improbable in Dulles's story. It was not a new one, and its origins were respectable. In 1964 the *Saturday Evening Post* commissioned and published a major article about Philby by Edward R. F. Sheehan, a notable American writer who had known Philby well and was qualified to write it; during their association, Sheehan had acted as a press attaché at the U.S. Embassy in Beirut. According to Sheehan, his main source was another friend of Philby's in both Washington and Beirut, Miles Copeland, a former CIA officer who was now an oil company executive. Copeland told Sheehan that he obtained his knowledge from studying the CIA files on the Philby case and his information was not improbable; it had been obtained originally from the British Secret Service. Copeland was then well regarded as a reliable and informed man in U.S. intelligence matters, so Sheehan went ahead and wrote his story.

But again, according to Sheehan, the editors of the *Saturday Evening Post* challenged Copeland's statement, in particular that part of it dealing with the circumstances of Philby's recruitment. To be safe, they instructed Sheehan to see Copeland again and get him to agree to the accuracy of the text. This he did, and Copeland repeated his statements. In the meantime, an editor checked the manuscript with CIA sources in Washington. It is not known that the CIA confirmed Copeland's story, but it is assumed that the *Post* found both Sheehan's and the CIA's statements satisfactory, for the article was published. It was then reprinted in the *Reader's Digest*.[61] Dulles reprinted it as the editor of *Great True Spy Stories* four years later, ample time for the intelligence authorities to have intervened. There was no such intervention; the story was printed by Dulles as Sheehan had written it.

It is true that Philby himself was evidently stung by Sheehan's article, for he referred to it on the next to last page of his memoir, *My Silent War,* which appeared about the same time as Dulles's book. But he did not address the main question: the circumstances of his recruitment by the British Secret Service. Nor did he address the implication that Britain had double-crossed its wartime ally. He merely referred to the "bland invention" which had characterized "so much of current writing on secret service matters" and remarked, "The writer of an article in the *Saturday Evening Post* told a stirring story." He did not "know whether the writer had his tongue in his cheek; unless I misjudged him sadly, he is too intelligent to fall for such twaddle."[62] This was not a convincing repudiation of Sheehan's story. There were immense opportunities in Sheehan's article for Philby to make mischief, but he did not avail himself of them. He preferred silence.

There was, of course, some support when, after the fall of the Soviet Union and the liquidation of the KGB in October 1991, an opportunity arose to check Sheehan's statements against the special knowledge of the small group of KGB officers with whom Philby associated in Moscow. A guarded story emerged that C had formally introduced Philby as his liaison to General I. A. Chichayev, of the Soviet secret service. Chichayev arrived in London in September 1941, at about the same time that Philby was being recruited, as the official representative of the Russian secret services to those of Britain. With him was a staff of ten. Yet when the Russians examined Philby's record after the war to establish whether Philby was a British plant in Moscow, as the Center feared he might be, the finding was positive — the SIS had indeed employed Philby to operate *against* the Soviet Union.

Nor were these opinions without support from the British side. Malcolm Muggeridge described Philby's action as a "stupendous double-cross," suggesting that Philby had accepted the post of liaison between the British and Soviet services in order to fulfill the mission given him so many years before by the Soviets — to penetrate the British Secret Service.[63] At another time and place Muggeridge wrote, "At some point

Philby must have been functioning as a double agent with the approval of the Secret Service and KGB superiors alike." And who was there to gainsay Muggeridge, Philby's old friend and a man who had been on the inside of the secret circle himself?

There was even a modicum of support for Dulles's story that "since one of his official duties was maintaining liaison with Soviet intelligence, his open and frequent contact with them was above suspicion."[64] The British official historian of intelligence and strategy in World War II recorded that a "special section of British Military Intelligence [was] set up in August [1942] to liaise with the Soviet Mission." It was under the direct control of the Director of Military Intelligence at the War Office. However, this section "left no record of its activities."[65] Thus there is no record of what intelligence was given to the Soviet Union — an omission that illustrates the secrecy and the sensitivity of these transactions. And the reason for that sensitivity is clear: the need to protect at all costs the secret that the British had developed the capacity to read the wireless communications of the German Supreme Command and its intelligence services. There is no public record that Philby was involved with this liaison office, but it will be remembered that his appointment was secret and that he was protected by an anonymity guaranteed by law and usage. Philby became in truth a secret servant of the British state. Such a man did not leave traces of his activities.

No study of the circumstances and politics of Philby's recruitment can be complete without reference to the human relationship between C and his secret agent. In secret work, trust and circumspection are vital. C did not ordinarily spend much time with the younger members of his staff. As a colleague, James Easton, would state, Menzies adopted noblesse oblige and reserve in his dealings with them. But he did not do so with Philby. It will be seen that C came to regard Kim very highly and with considerable and genuine affection.

In this context, in June 1942 an opportunity arose that definitely required a liaison officer to the Soviet service. With Churchill's permission C, distrusting the security of the Russians' ciphers, stopped sending MSS intelligence — the Ultra decrypts, C's most vital source of intelligence — to Moscow in order to protect its source, cryptanalysis and code-breaking. But he remained aware of the need to maintain the Eastern Front, that "tremendous thing" in Churchill's strategy. C therefore resorted to expediency to induce the Soviet representatives in London and Moscow to accept his intelligence as true and valuable. The highest intelligence authority, Chairman Victor Cavendish-Bentinck of the Joint Intelligence Committee, approved an unorthodox operation. As his authorized biographer, Patrick Howarth, would record, "One of the methods adopted for conveying information of strategic importance to the Soviet Union was to leak it through SIS to known Soviet agents in neutral countries, particularly Switzerland. This served incidentally to enhance the credibility, and also the postwar reputations, of the Soviet agents involved."[66] This statement has been endorsed by Lord Bullock, a British historian who has written that "the British intelligence service had succeeded in infiltrating the Soviet spy ring in Switzerland, and by this means (without revealing their hand in the transaction) passed on to Moscow as early as April the date of mid-June for the German attack (subsequently corrected to June 22) and exact details of the German order of battle."[67] The CIA's *Review of Intelligence* asserted that the "lines and personalities of the Philby case [were] inextricably interwoven" with the Rote Drei (the Red Three), the Soviet intelligence system in Switzerland, which was controlled by C.[68]

On balance, therefore, there is good evidence that C passed intelligence to the Russians, and there is some evidence — Muggeridge's — that it was passed by Philby in order to give it the full flavor of authenticity; Stalin would believe no intelligence received from Britain unless it was obtained by an established Soviet agent who had passed it over the Soviet communications system. If Muggeridge is correct that this was done with the knowledge and assent of both C and the Center, then C knew at least that Philby was in contact with Soviet secret agents. Under such circumstances, disinformation could not have been passed. To have done so would have endangered that "tremendous thing," the Eastern Front.

But this is not quite all. There are two other matters to be mentioned briefly. The first is that, while Philby's loyalties were always uncertain and ambiguous, his record at the Center was such that he was completely trusted by all KGB officers except one, who had *direct* contact with him. Second, there is evidence that, with the onset of the Cold War at the end of World War II, Philby did betray C. And therein lay one of the great tragedies of the Philby case. The truth about Philby was that, as his close friend and colleague Nicholas Elliott would write at the end: "He was a schizophrenic with a supreme talent for deception."[69]

This was the second version of Philby's recruitment into the British Secret Service. As is so often the case in human affairs, the truth lies between the two, with more emphasis on the former. Only one question remains, and that concerns Churchill and his Eastern Front policy. Did that policy require that C resort to so dangerous an expedient as the employment of a known communist as a secret agent? There is some evidence that it did.

In 1979, the professional papers of William J. Donovan, the chief of the first U.S. secret intelligence, political warfare, and special operations agency, were made available quasi-officially in the United States for biographical purposes. In them was a peculiar document entitled "German Spring Offensive Against Russia." Subsequently a second copy of this same document was found in the records of the U.S. Joint Chiefs for its fourth meeting, in March 1942. At first reading, the document seemed as innocuous as the title. But at second reading it became evident that it bore on Churchill's policy of ensuring that the Eastern Front be maintained at all costs. In simple terms, the principle was that every German soldier killed in Russia constituted one less German for the French front when the time came for the Anglo-American powers to land there.

The circumstances in which this document was composed were that, four months after Philby's appointment, in February 1942, with America in the war but with Britain still facing invasion and defeat on every front, Stalin made a speech ostensibly to mark the twenty-fifth anniversary of the creation of the Red Army. In it he made no reference to any ally and thereby suggested that Russia was fighting by itself solely to free itself. This caused alarm at the Foreign Office, the more so because Stalin had made a conciliatory remark about the German people: "It would be ridiculous to identify Hitler's clique with the German people and the German state. History teaches that Hitlers come and go, but the German people and the German state remain."[70]

The effect of these statements in Whitehall was to revive the fear that Stalin might be seeking to make a separate peace with Germany. Consequently, it appears, the Foreign Office authorized a special operation to ensure that, whatever else happened, the Russians remained as combatants. The Political Warfare Executive (PWE), a secret service with origins in the Foreign Office, sent a proposal to Washington that both powers should undertake jointly an operation called German Spring Offensive Against Russia. A brief covering note explained the intention: "to commit the Germans to a spring offensive against Russia." How PWE intended to "commit" the German Army to such a move was nowhere discussed in the accompanying papers; in any case, it does seem that the means to be used were communicated only orally. A request for a written proposal was made to the PWE agent in Washington, but either it was not sent or it did not survive. But it can be assumed safely that secret means were to be used. The probability is that PWE intended to reveal through its underground apparatus — which included Philby's in Iberia, the main front in the secret war between Britain and Germany — that the Germans had a plan to capture certain regions and cities in Russia by a given date. These were well beyond the capacity of the German Army, so that when it did not capture these objectives, PWE would undertake a further campaign to show that the German Army had been defeated.

The proposal was before the Joint Chiefs by March 25, 1942, and they rejected it. Their secretary, Walter Bedell Smith, explained the decision to the PWE agent.

> a. If the Germans do undertake the offensive and are successful, our propaganda will have emphasized their victory.
> b. If the offensive is not undertaken in whole or in part and instead Germany attacks in the Middle East, both our propaganda and our intelligence will have been discredited at home and abroad.
> c. Russian propaganda has been attempting to force a United States–British offensive in Western Europe to relieve German pressure on Russia. The proposed propaganda plan would support the Russian contention and arouse public opinion to force a strategic commitment which may or may not be in accord with the strategic plans of the United States.

While it is true that the document in no way seems to show that it was intended to provoke a battle of annihilation between the Germans and the Russians, nevertheless Whitehall was well aware when the PWE agent presented it that (a) Hitler was already assembling his armies in order to destroy the Soviet Union that year and (b) Russia stood in what a paper on the subject called "very urgent need of help" if it was to survive. Why, therefore, was a plan such as this written at all if it was not intended to increase Russia's distress? That was the way Robert Bruce Lockhart, who took over PWE as the plan was making its way through the Allied command, read the paper. And he pointed to its dangers, writing: "Stalin is reading into our activities the most sinister intentions." Among them was that "Britain has an interest in bleeding Russia white." Further, Britain "still has up her sleeve the card of a compromise peace with the German generals and . . . this card will be played whenever there is a risk of Russia spreading westwards." Nothing, he added, "spreads quicker than the kind of rumor that Britain will fight to the last drop of Russian blood."[71]

In November 1941, Philby reported for duty, with the rank of major, at War Station XB at St. Albans, the headquarters of the British Secret

Service's counterespionage branch. He was a staff officer who would engage, when the need arose, in "special means," then the British term for deception and stratagem in accordance with Churchill's doctrine. His real mission was, of course, to use his British position in the Soviet interest. This he succeeded in doing for the next decade, without, perhaps, provoking any suspicion — a tour de force of nerve, brains, intuition, and knowledge of how the system could be made to work in his favor.

At some stage early in his duties he encountered C at Broadway, the SIS headquarters; his version of that encounter suggests that if C had known Dora Philby, he had not hitherto encountered Kim.

> Broadway was a dingy building, a warren of wooden partitions and frosted glass windows. It had eight floors served by an ancient lift. On one of my early visits I got into the lift with a colleague whom the liftman treated with obtrusive deference. The stranger gave me a swift glance and looked away. He was well-built and well-dressed, but what struck me most was his pallor: pale face, pale eyes, silvery blond hair thinning on top — the whole an impression of pepper-and-salt. When he got out at the fourth floor, I asked the liftman who he was. "Why, sir, that's the Chief," he answered in some surprise.
>
> At that stage, I knew precious little of the Chief. His name was Stewart Menzies, his rank Colonel. His office was on the fourth floor. His stationery was a vivid blue, his ink green. He wrote an execrable hand . . . His official symbol was CSS but in correspondence between Broadway and overseas stations he could be designated by any three successive letters of the alphabet, ABC, XYZ, etc. In government circles outside SIS he was always known as C . . . That was the sum total of my knowledge of the Chief at that time of our first encounter in the lift.

And as Philby added with great care, from the safety of his KGB flat in Moscow:

> As will be seen, I came to know him much better, and I hasten to say that I look back on him with both affection and respect, though not necessarily with respect for those qualities on which he would have prided himself.[72]

10

War Station XB

1941–1944

K IM PHILBY was twenty-nine when in early October 1941 he
arrived at War Station XB. The code governing political activities had remained as it was in his father's days with the Raj:

> An officer must be loyal to his service and to his country. He may
> hold whatever political opinions he likes but as long as he is serving
> he must not allow politics to affect his loyalty to his service or to the
> Government which is in power, even if he thinks that it is not the
> right form of Government.

He signed a document called the Official Secrets Act, which bound
him in perpetuity not to disclose without authority any matters pertaining to his government service; and as was then the custom he
signed a personal contract with C, the nature of which bound Philby
to C personally. An important part of this obligation was that he must
keep note of any contact with all persons outside the service, especially
with aliens. He was "requested and required" to seek the advice of
Colonel Vivian before making any appointments of an official nature
outside the service. The "consideration" for his services and the obligations to secrecy that he accepted was, in accordance with custom, a
goodly £600 a year, free of tax — SIS men did not pay personal taxes
because they left traces — paid weekly in new notes. The service paid
no pension, as this too left traces, but, if he wished, he could make a
pension provision out of his salary with a small, discreet company
associated with the small discreet bank used by the service, Drum-
mond's in Admiralty Arch.

The War Station was at Glenalmond, a large Victorian mansion in King Harry Lane on the edge of St. Albans. And the War Station's mission placed Philby at the heart of the service's most confidential affairs, for the section — the word *section* was itself code, for a section could be any size, from a battalion to two or three clerks scribbling away at some special job in a remote corner of the service — was responsible for all counterespionage outside the three-mile limit of the British Isles and all territories of the empire. Its responsibilities were therefore global. Counterespionage within the three-mile limit was the responsibility of the Imperial Security Service, known as MI5. Until 1937, Section V had devoted almost all its time to the study of international communism; after that date its mission was expanded to handle what has been officially termed "double-cross agents and deception, enemy espionage communications, Soviet espionage and Communism, the protection of the SIS itself against penetration." From the end of 1943 it was further extended to include operations against "German trans-Atlantic smuggling of strategic materials."[1]

In Europe, there were Section V staff members in Portugal, Spain, Turkey, and Sweden, and Philby was chief in both Portugal and Spain, the two most important sectors in the intelligence war with Germany. His area of operations was very large, extending as it did to the far corners of the Spanish and Portuguese empires and areas of influence in the Americas, Africa, the Atlantic islands, and their little outposts in the Indian Ocean, the Arabian Sea, and the Dutch East Indies. By the end of the war, there were sections in every capital of importance throughout the world, and it was noted by Malcolm Muggeridge, when he visited the Lisbon office in May 1942:

> These SIS corners of British Embassies, of which I got to know quite a number before the war was over, all had a character of their own. They were different from the other departments, like Chancery, or Trade, or Information; more free-and-easy — men in shirt sleeves, their feet up on the desks, a lot of coming and going, and strange visitors. The old Secret Service professionals, it is true, tended to look more like diplomats than diplomats did, and were given to spats and monocles long after they passed out of fashion among the regulars. The prevailing fashion among the war-time MI6 intake, on the other hand, was to aim at being as unlike the conventional idea of a diplomat as possible; slouching about in sweaters and grey flannel trousers, drinking in bars and cafés and low dives rather than at diplomatic cocktail parties and receptions, boasting of their underworld acquaintances and liaisons. Philby, in this sense, may be taken as the prototype of them all, and was, indeed, in the eyes of many of them, a model to be copied.[2]

Philby's chief, Lieutenant Colonel Felix Henry Cowgill, was forty-one, a son of the perpetual curate on the Duke of Portland's estate at Shireoaks, a mining colony in Northumberland, by repute a region that bred hardy and industrious men. He had gone to the local church school and then one for curates' sons, St. John's, Leatherhead. Here he received an excellent classical education, but not one to compare with that of Westminster and Trinity. At the age of twenty-two, he was accepted for service in the Indian Police. He had done well in the police and had entered the Special Branch, the political police, which existed to maintain the safety and dignity of the Raj against internal and external subversion.

Working with the chief of the Intelligence Bureau at New Delhi, Sir David Petrie, Cowgill had been mainly responsible for thwarting the Meerut conspiracy with the arrest of the thirty-two leading Comintern agents, men and women, British and Indian by birth, who were, as their indictment read, "conspiring to deprive the King Emperor of the sovereignty of British India [with] a view to the establishment of a Socialist State under the Dictatorship of the Proletariat and the supreme command of the Communist International." All but four were awarded sentences at their trial in March 1929. The government of India expressed its satisfaction with the work of Cowgill and his colleagues when the judges declared that "by this decision a conspiracy fraught with the gravest dangers to the well-being of India has been stopped at an early stage."[3]

Afterward, Cowgill and Petrie wrote the official history of the Meerut conspiracy, *Communism in India,* which became the standard work on communism in the empire. This was a book by a committee for a committee and its prose was the policeman's, a report of the facts, with attention to the detail and methods of communist conspiracy. Petrie became director general of the Security Service in London, MI5, the Secret Service's sister department; and it was Petrie who commended Cowgill as the man for chief of Section IX of the Secret Service in London. This was the service responsible for the study of Soviet espionage and international communism, and, with the Nazi-Soviet Pact, it became extremely active.

When Vivian was appointed by C as the deputy director of the Secret Service in charge of counterespionage and security, Cowgill succeeded Vivian as chief of War Station XB. There was often friction between the Secret and the Security services — where did the jurisdictions in international conspiracy cases begin and end? — and C hoped fervently that Petrie and Cowgill would work together as well in Whitehall as they had in Meerut. By this time Cowgill was almost forty and his persona had emerged. He proved to be a level-headed North Countryman, tough-minded, brisk, efficient, independent, and as apolitical as a policeman can be. He was not an anticommunist zealot, and, indeed, he seems not to have been a student of the theory and practice of communism.

But to a communist like Philby he was the class enemy, a man to be destroyed. First Kim worked to gain Cowgill's confidence, concealing his animus as he concealed his political opinions behind a mask of convention. When Philby and Aileen arrived — she had by now taken his name by deed poll — they established what seemed to be excellent relations with Cowgill and his wife, Mary, a daughter of a canon of Lahore. The Cowgills claimed to have known nothing of Philby's communism at Trinity, although there is some slight but good evidence that they did learn, probably from Vivian, that Philby had been a leftie during his university days. But this the Cowgills did not hold against him. To the contrary, Cowgill thought him the admirable type who "made a good cricket umpire" — a wise, calm man of good presence who made quick, sound decisions.[4] At no time, Cowgill claimed, did he ever suspect that Philby might have other responsibilities, that he might be C's authorized liaison officer with the Soviet intelligence Service, and he would have been surprised had Kim held such a delicate position without his knowledge. Their personal relations were always "good to excellent"; among the many services that Philby rendered for the Cowgills was to arrange for them to spend some of their leaves at St. John's cottage in the Welsh mountains. The Cowgills proved excellent guests, getting in firewood, mending the windows, plugging leaks in the roof, fixing the plumbing, planting vegetables, marigolds, and daffodils, and generally showing what decent folk they were. St. John sent a note to Dora after one of their visits:

> If ever you see the Cowgills, who were here, please bless them. They really did the cottage proud and must be very nice people. They put two beds in my room but moved one back to yours on leaving and left enough wood for weeks and I haven't sawed a single log yet. Also their window mending saved the cottage from the Friday deluge — not a drop came in.[5]

Aileen and Kim made a most pleasant impression. There were children by now. Josephine, the first, was thought to be her father's favorite, and she was born in 1941 while Philby was at Beaulieu. Next came

John, in 1942, and Dudley Thomas, in December 1943. Miranda and Harry George came later.

Philby made himself indispensable to Cowgill and became his deputy in charge of operational matters. At the same time, he won the respect and affection of the rest of the staff at the War Station. These then numbered twelve officers, mainly Oxford and Cambridge men of Philby's generation, with a further twelve deputies and perhaps thirty administrative staff. In time, the staff rose to sixty officers at home and sixty abroad; attached to it, by 1944, were another sixty American officers in London and sixty overseas. None, it seems, took the trouble to look into Kim's past, perhaps because there was a strong Liberal element in the staff, perhaps because Russia was an ally, and perhaps because of the monstrous demands of their main task, which was "the active pursuit and liquidation of the enemy intelligence services." Also of importance was Philby's personality. Testimony about that personality came from Sir Robert MacKenzie, who later played a part in Kim's exposure.

MacKenzie was "idle but far from stupid," as Philby acknowledged. He was six years older than Philby, a product of Eton and Trinity, Cambridge, and, at the War Station, chief of the Franco-Belgian section. As such, he had important responsibilities in the defense of the British Isles. MacKenzie recalled as one of Philby's most impressive attributes "the beautiful English of his reports," which he wrote "in neat, tiny writing." Philby never did a first draft, "yet the English was magnificent — never a word too many, never a statement open to two interpretations. And, of course, there was his attractive personality."

> [He had] inherited from his father that same sense of dedicated idealism in which the means did not matter as long as the end was a worthwhile one. Although he had a facade on other matters, this sense of dedication and purpose to whatever he was doing gleamed through and inspired men to follow him. He was just the sort of man who won worshippers. You didn't just like him, admire him, agree with him; you worshipped him."[6]

That air of personal excellence never left him, even after he became suspected of high treason involving his closest friends and colleagues and his wreckage of their careers. Even after it became known that he had much blood on his hands, even after it was known that he had worked throughout his career only in the interests of a dangerous tyranny, Kim remained everybody's darling.

There were of course almost as many opinions of him as there were men to make them. But one of those most qualified to make a judgment was Professor Hugh Trevor-Roper. In 1942, Philby and Trevor-Roper worked together on a major problem — Canaris. C had formed the impression, rightly, that the heart of his most important enemy, Admiral Canaris, was not in the war. He believed also that Canaris might be an opponent of Hitler who could be used to bring about a coup d'état in the Third Reich. Trevor-Roper, who knew that Philby had been a communist at Trinity, wrote many years later:

> I admit that Philby's appointment astonished me, for [an] old Oxford friend had told me, years before, that [Philby] was a communist. By now, of course, I assumed that he was an ex-communist; but even so I was surprised, for no one was more fanatically anti-communist, at that time, than the regular members of the two security services, MI6 and MI5. It was quite inconceivable, in ordinary circumstances, that MI6 would want to employ anyone who had ever been a communist, or that the department of MI5 which supplied the "trace" [the history of every new employee] would clear him for such employment . . . That these men should have suspended their deepest convictions in favour of the ex-communist Philby was indeed remarkable. Since it never occurred to me that they could be ignorant of the facts (which were widely known), I assumed that Philby had particular virtues which made him, in their eyes, indispensable.

Accordingly, Trevor-Roper regarded Philby's arrival with interest. As they talked and worked together, he did encounter Philby's intellectual remoteness. Philby was plainly an intellectual, but he never made an intellectual statement. Once only was there an intellectual engagement between them, and then "the conversation flared in a sudden and unpredictable manner, which seemed to provoke Philby. He blurted out: 'Of course, every attempt at historical analysis is nothing once you compare it to Marx's *Eighteenth Brumaire!*'" Some importance was attached to that remark later, for Trevor-Roper claimed to have experienced a "sharp, momentary impression that he was talking with Kim on a serious level, and that there were no defences between them." But it was very brief. Philby, "as though embarrassed at his own uncharacteristic vehemence, changed the subject and returned to his normal pose of amiable, disengaged worldliness."[7]

And then there was Philby's social appearance. In his bearing Philby appeared to be exactly what he was — a Scholar of Trinity who wore his father's military tunic when in the office and herringbone tweeds with patches at the elbow after hours. He had a slight port-wine accent. On the surface, Kim's relations with Cowgill were good, even excellent, and Cowgill never recovered when he learned that in Kim he had clasped a snake to his bosom. In private, however, if Philby's recollections are true, Kim was scornful and contemptuous of Cowgill:

> His intellectual endowment was slender. As an intelligence officer, he was inhibited by lack of imagination, inattention to detail and sheer ignorance of the world we were fighting in. His most conspicuous quality, apart from personal charm of an attractively simple variety, was a fiendish capacity for work. Every evening he took home bulging briefcases and worked far into the small hours. Friday nights, as a regular habit, he worked right round the clock. Mornings would find him, tired but driving, presiding over a conference of his sub-section heads and steadily knocking an array of pipes to wreckage . . . He stood by his own staff far beyond the call of loyalty, retaining many long after their idleness or incompetence had been proved. To the outer world, he presented a suspicious and bristling front, ever ready to see attempts to limit his field of action or diminish his authority.[8]

But neither Felix nor Mary detected this contempt, and such was the family atmosphere that Felix fostered at Glenalmond that when Aileen Philby was introduced to the other wives by Mary Cowgill, she found that she might easily have been transported back to India. Glenalmond gave out on to wide lawns on which there was a cricket pitch and pavilion. At the end of the property, uncovered just before Section V took up residence there, was a fine mosaic, put down, it was said, by Verulam, the Roman town major of Verulamium, the Roman name for St. Albans, in about A.D. 303. When the townspeople — St. Albans was only a small town, so everybody knew everybody else's business — sought an explanation for the presence of so many official-looking men, women, and cars in King Harry's Lane, it was put about that they were from the British Museum, there to survey the pavement and to excavate the Roman ruins.

Kim detested "all that green," as he called the pleasant countryside around Glenalmond, but, as was important to him, there were some good pubs, apart from the King Harry in King Harry's Lane. There was the Fighting Cocks Inn, which was close to the River Ver and the Abbey Gatehouse. There was the Red Lion, the Peahen for paydays, and in Barnet, about ten miles away, there was the Green Dragon for meetings of a special nature. There was cricket-and-curry on the lawns on Sundays, and almost every lunchtime the staff went to the cricket pavilion, which had been turned into a restaurant by a Mrs. Rennit, who served excellent plaice and chips on Fridays and such delicacies as steak and kidney pudding or veal and ham pie the rest of the week.

The novelist Graham Greene, then one of Philby's deputies, would write of the gatherings at the various pubs long after Philby had been exposed and in his introduction to his old chief's memoir, *My Silent War:*

> If this book required a sub-title I would suggest: The Spy as Crafts-man. No one could have been a better chief than Kim Philby when he was in charge of the Iberian section of V. He worked harder than anyone else and never gave the impression of labour. He was always relaxed, completely unflappable. He was in those days, of course, fighting the same war as his colleagues.

Only one element in his colleague disquieted Greene, and that was his drive for power, which caused Greene to resign from the service, as will be seen. Otherwise,

> I remember with pleasure those long Sunday lunches when the whole sub-section relaxed under his leadership for a few hours heavy drink-ing . . . If one made an error of judgement he was sure to minimise it and cover it up, without criticism, with a halting stammered witti-cism. He had all the small loyalties to his colleagues, and of course his big loyalty was unknown to us.[9]

These judgments on Philby's character and deportment were valid at the time. All, to an extent, withstood the passage of time. He seemed to those who had business with him to have been an exemplary man. Yet all reflected only the skill with which Philby concealed his real loyalty behind a mask of charm, calm, good judgment and manage-ment, sanity, and a political realism divorced from ideology that al-layed any suspicion of him. The thought was that if he had been a communist at Cambridge, he could not possibly be a communist now. But in the end, in the early 1990s, when it became possible to make a judgment based on some knowledge of his betrayal of Great Britain and the United States, Nicholas Elliott, a colleague in those days and a friend for many years, came at last to the opinion that he was "a schizophrenic with a supreme talent for deception." This cannot be faulted, although another close friend, E. J. Applewhite, who became the deputy inspector general of the CIA, held the view that Philby's services to the United States, the U.K., and the Soviet Union were "riddled with ambiguity." This sense of him was also shared by the Russians.

One of Philby's characteristics that remained for the twenty years he worked as a Soviet spy was his lucky star. Fortune was on Philby's side throughout his stay in XB, which lasted for the next four years of war and the ensuing two years of Cold War. But he was rarely luckier than during his first ninety days, when there occurred the modern version of a miracle. In it lay the origins of his power in the secret circle and beyond. In December 1942, C's code breakers at the Government Code and Cipher School (GC&CS) developed the ability to read the signals of the Abwehr, the intelligence and counterespionage service of the German General Staff. Such was the importance of the news that it went to the prime minister, and he made C responsible for the security of all Most Secret Source (MSS) intelligence, the term for all such decrypts. Of these there came to be many variants — the highest level German military, naval, air, police, political, diplomatic, economic, railroad — and all were known by the general code name Ultra.

The intelligence decrypts were called ISOS, which stood for Intelligence Service Oliver Strachey, the section of the code breakers responsible for attacking the communications of the enemy's intelligence services. Enemy signals transmitted by landline remained secure for the entire war. But the Abwehr stations abroad, particularly those in such key neutral capitals as Madrid, Lisbon, Stockholm, and Ankara, used radio, and these signals could be and were intercepted and decoded. The flow of ISOS to the War Station rose from thirty to seventy a day during 1941 to more than two hundred by December 1941. They were delivered from the code-breaking center at Bletchley with as little fuss as the milkman calling, and in much the same manner. Mrs. Diana Marchant, wife of one of the code breakers, arrived at Glenalmond in a little blue four-cylinder baker's van to deliver the pouch to Cowgill. When more than 280 intercepts began to arrive daily in May 1944, the month before the invasion of Europe, Mrs. Marchant came twice a day. In all, she delivered 268,000 such intercepts; these constituted what has been described as "a very large proportion of the total German traffic" of 78 German war stations at the end of 1941 and of 147 such stations by the end of 1942.

Hitherto, Cowgill had fought the secret war as a blinkered man. Now the European scene and, later, much of the world became illuminated, and the secret enemy and his works could be seen and heard. In the secret world such knowledge soon becomes political power, and the more Philby received of these intercepts, the greater was his power. Shortly, it became possible through the use of ISOS to — as an American paper on the subject put it — "affect the fundamental reasoning power of the enemy."[10] So important was this potential that just before Pearl Harbor, C sent Cowgill to the United States to open an office at

British Security Coordination (BSC), the secret service in the Americas, which was located in the International Building at Rockefeller Center in New York City. Then Cowgill went on to Washington, arriving on December 7, 1941, the day the Japanese fleet destroyed the American fleet at Pearl Harbor. The United States declared war on Japan, but not on Germany or Italy. A day or two later, in conformity with the Tripartite Pact, Germany and Italy declared war on the United States.

All this proved useful to Cowgill in his task, to wield ISOS — which was as effective in the countries of Latin America as it was in Spain and Portugal — as an instrumentality by which the United States might be drawn into the war. But within a week the United States and the British Empire had become allies in that war in fact and name, and Cowgill's task was narrowed to that of acquainting the chiefs of the U.S. intelligence and security services with the work of ISOS. All went well. The American chiefs now had urgent need of intelligence such as ISOS in North and South America. Cowgill arranged with the director of the FBI, J. Edgar Hoover, and Colonel William J. Donovan, chief of the intelligence agency that became, in June 1942, the Office of Strategic Services (OSS), to send U.S. officers for training at War Station XB. Many other such arrangements were made, and there grew an intimacy and trust between the two services. This came to form an important part of the "special relationship" between the British and American governments. It lasted until 1951 — when suspicion first arose that Philby was a Soviet agent.

Colonel Cowgill returned to St. Albans from his business in Washington on February 2, 1942, and resumed operational control from Philby, who thereupon returned to his Iberian section. Cowgill never knew that in his absence Philby had worked his way through the "source books," the most secret holdings of the Secret Service's Central Registry, which was located next door in a mansion called Prae Wood. As Cowgill explained later:

> The source books were volumes containing the personal files of all past and present British secret agents since, I understood, the formation of the service in 1909. There were a number of these volumes for each country where these agents operated, and the information included name, aliases, date and place of birth, moneys paid, work undertaken for us, and accounts of their character, ability and reliability. Philby had the right of access to the volumes concerning agents in Spain and Portugal, and their empires and areas of influence. There were two volumes for Russia and the Soviet Union. These he

had no right to see. All the source books were located at Prae Wood next door but they were not my responsibility. They were the responsibility of the head of Central Registry, a man called Woodfield.[11]

Philby himself recalled how this had happened. Woodfield had "a liking for pink gins, which I shared, and a prudish appreciation of dirty stories." They used to meet at the King Harry Arms, a nearby inn, to "discuss office politics, of which he had a long experience." This friendly connection "paid off, and I was usually in a position to get files rather more quickly and easily than many of my colleagues. Bill [Woodfield] was seriously understaffed, and the people he had were often ill-trained."[12]

> [It was] natural for me to want information on the agents operating in the Iberian peninsula, and my perusal of the source-books for Spain and Portugal whetted my appetite for more. I worked steadily through them, thus enlarging my knowledge of SIS activity as a whole. When I came to the source-book for the Soviet Union, I found that it consisted of two volumes. Having worked my way through them to my satisfaction, I returned them to the Registry in the normal way.

As Philby continued, there was trouble ahead:

> About a week later, Bill telephoned to ask me for the second volume of the Russian source-book. After consulting my secretary, I called back to say that, according to our books, it had been returned to Registry on such-and-such a date. After further fruitless search in Registry, Bill contested the accuracy of my records, and urged me to make a further investigation. I turned our office upside-down, with negative results. Bill and I met once or twice in the evening to discuss the mystery over a few pink gins. He told me that the normal procedure on loss of a source-book was for him to report immediately to the Chief. I managed to stall him for a few days, during which my alarm grew. I doubted whether the Chief would appreciate the excessive zeal which had led me to exhaustive study of source-books, especially as it had apparently resulted in the loss of one dealing with a country far outside the normal scope of my duty.

According to Cowgill, had Woodfield advised C, as the procedures required, there would have been a board of inquiry, and that would have led to Philby's suspension. If C was not the source of Philby's protection, as is sometimes assumed, then at the least his case would have been dealt with summarily. But nothing occurred. As Philby wrote:

> The lowering sky suddenly cleared. Bill telephoned me to offer a full, personal apology. It seemed that one of his secretaries handling the

source-books, wishing to save shelf-space, had amalgamated the two volumes into one. She had then come over queer, and gone home with a severe bout of flu. She had only just got back to the office and, on being tackled by Woodfield, had immediately remembered what she had done. I accepted the apology gracefully, and suggested meeting again that evening. We did so, and drowned the painful memory in another flood of pink gin.

Whether Philby's version was the truth, the organization of the British Secret Service throughout the world stood exposed to an enemy, the Soviet service. That office knew everything it needed to know to disrupt the British, whereas C knew little of the Soviet service — except that it was seeking to penetrate his. As Menzies stated at a meeting on the question of whether MI5 should attempt to collaborate with the Soviet services, such would be "a waste of effort and an embarrassment," since the Russians were "more interested in penetrating our intelligence than in helping."[13]

By mid-1942 the tumult of events changed Philby's junior status at War Station XB. Cowgill informed him that the decision had been made by the Anglo-American command to undertake Torch, the invasion of French North Africa, later in the year.

In this operation, nine hundred warships and transports would leave ports in Maine, Virginia, and Scotland, cross an ocean infested by large numbers of enemy submarines grouped in "wolf packs," and land 180,000 assault troops, with all their equipment and supplies, for ninety days of combat, at Casablanca, Oran, Algiers, and in Tunisia near the French naval base of Bizerte. Large-scale secret operations were to be undertaken to bring important French armed forces over to the Allies. Also, large-scale deception operations were to prevent all the foreign powers involved — Germany, Italy, Spain, and Portugal — from learning the key secrets of the operation, where and when the landings would take place, and the weight of the Allied forces involved.

To meet the requirements of this vast enterprise, Cowgill widened Philby's responsibilities from Spain and Portugal and their territories to include the French territories in the zone of operations. As D-Day neared, Cowgill extended Philby's responsibilities still further to include the command of counterespionage in Italy, Sardinia, Corsica, and the western and central Mediterranean islands. Later still Cowgill made it known officially that Philby was his deputy in charge of all the War Station's operations. And when the decision was taken to establish Special Counter-Intelligence Units (SCIU), a new service formed to supply the security and counterespionage elements in the invading armies with the ISOS intercepts, he was offered, and accepted, responsibility for their control. One SCIU would be attached to each major headquarters, with a staff recruited by Cowgill and subject to his direction at all times, and each SCIU would have its independent communications provided by Broadway. And the object of all was to ensure that the existence of the intercepts did not become known to the enemy services. Otherwise each SCIU represented a small intelligence service in itself, one that could, when the need arose, keep Philby advised, and thus his Russian masters, about those points of essential interest at the Center — the strength, morale, and fighting capabilities of the Allied armies ashore and the reaction of hostile powers to the operation.

In June of 1942 there occurred an event that was to have, as Philby recorded, "a profound effect on all subsequent development of British intelligence work."[14] The high officers of the new American Office of Strategic Services (OSS) arrived in London to establish their headquarters there. They were led by their chief, William J. Donovan, a leading lawyer, a close associate of Roosevelt's, and a Medal of Honor winner in World War I. He was, however, a beleaguered man. He and his new service were under severe and continual attack from the established U.S. intelligence agencies — the FBI, the Army and Navy intelligence chiefs, the Treasury, the State Department, and others. If he was to survive, Donovan needed successes. Any disaster affecting Torch might well cause his dismissal and the liquidation of the OSS. Philby set out to give Donovan the successes he needed. The man Donovan brought with him to become chief of the OSS's London station was David K. E. Bruce, another leading light in the American Establishment's legal, social, and political hierarchy. They visited War Station XB, and Bruce recorded in his private diary that they were received by "Colonel Cowgill and Major Philby."[15]

The entry of the new service produced many strains in the alliance. Donovan believed that the United States would never become a great power until it had established a great intelligence service, and he set out to create just such a service. The OSS was aggressive, ambitious, eager to learn from the British services but not prepared to subordinate itself to British policies. The keynote of its existence was independence for its operations.

In the highest reaches of intelligence in London, David Bruce began to experience C's early attempts to control the OSS as he controlled the intelligence services of all the governments-in-exile in London.

Bruce alerted Donovan to warn Anthony Eden, the Foreign Secretary, that if C continued to try to prevent the OSS from operating as an independent and sovereign intelligence, this "would, in the first place, attempt an infringement on our national rights" and it would also "influence the relationship between Britain and the United States."[16] After the war, Bruce would note of the relationship:

> Throughout the early history the attitude of SIS towards us was, on the whole, consistently friendly and cooperative. They gave us generously their intelligence during a period when we had little to offer in exchange. As we expanded and became more expert and more productive, they may have viewed our growth with some jealous forebodings, but there was never any rift between us. I am sure they feared the emergence of an American system which might compete globally with their own, but they bowed to what may have seemed to them inevitable.[17]

Only in the fields of counterespionage and special operations did Donovan permit any subordination of American interests to those of the British, and then only because C controlled ISOS. Since 1941, enemy agents entering Britain and the United States were routinely apprehended; thirty-three German agents were arrested by the FBI at the end of 1941. During that time, Philby's Abwehr patron on Franco's staff during the Civil War, Ulrich von der Osten, was killed in Times Square in New York City when a taxi ran over him twice. Osten was the chief of the Abwehr in New York. And while there is no evidence that Philby played a part in Osten's death, it is noteworthy that Osten's was the second of what became a line of untimely deaths involving some of those who knew him, the first being Walter Krivitsky.

In Britain, the arriving enemy agents were all arrested and either hanged or jailed. Those whose rank, personalities, and responsibilities made them seem useful as double agents were spared, but only if they agreed to undertake "special duties" under the control of the Security Service, with which Philby now began to work closely. The object of compelling these spies to work for the Allies was to expose more of the enemy intelligence services in the Torch zone of operations. All these operations constituted warfare on a small scale, involving individuals or small groups rather than hosts of men. But the consequences for the victor could be large, as indeed they proved to be. Such operations as these represented the first culmination of Churchill's policy of using "elements of legerdemain" that left the enemy "baffled and as well as beaten." It was through one such operation that Philby emerged as a man to be listened to in the Secret Service.

The very first intercepts had alluded to the existence of a secret Abwehr operation, being undertaken with Spanish collusion, called Bodden. With time Philby identified Bodden as a chain of fourteen stations, equipped with infrared devices, on both sides of the narrow Gibraltar Strait, through which two of the three Torch task forces would have to pass. They were linked by wireless to submarine packs lurking about the Atlantic and the Mediterranean entrances to the strait, and it became essential to neutralize them. But how?

Philby's account of the Bodden operation reflected his formidable understanding of the way secret intelligence could be used for military ends. For the first time on record he began to use the technical intelligence term "disruption of the enemy" — what C called "confounding the king's enemies" — in his memoir. He wrote, in a disquisition that reflected much about the acuity of his mind and perhaps the excellence of his British and Soviet training:

> One problem of intelligence is how to get it. Another, equally important and sometimes much more difficult, is how to exploit it. Picking up enemy agents as they reached British territory was all very well and good. But what about our painstaking analysis of the German establishment in the peninsula as a whole, and the organisation in Germany from which it emanated? It was borne in on me gradually that our comprehensive knowledge called for more imaginative action than had been contemplated in the past.[18]

It should "surely be possible to put our information to good use in disrupting, or at least seriously embarrassing, the enemy on his own chosen ground in Spain." The introduction by the Germans of Bodden showed him "that the time was ripe for a new suggestion designed to scare the daylights out of the Abwehr in Spain."

So he did. First he "considered, and discarded, the possibility of putting SOE on to the Germans in Spain." He doubted whether "anyone on our side would really welcome a free-for-all in Spain, where the authorities would have been against us. On reflection, it seemed that the diplomatic approach would be the best. We had a legitimate grievance against the Spanish Government for allowing the German intelligence a free hand on its territory, and a strong protest, based on detailed and cogent evidence, seemed quite in order." It was "a good assumption that Gustav Lenz, the head of the Abwehr in Spain, would be severely shaken if" the Spanish government itself was enabled to show that "his secrets were no secrets at all."

Cowgill remembered Philby's paper well. It was a model document, calculated to force the Spanish government to (a) close the Bodden stations, (b) restrict the collaboration between the Spanish and German intelligence services on all Spanish territory, and (c) embarrass and discredit Lenz, the Abwehr chief in Madrid, with the Spanish government by using terms that suggested that the highly detailed intelligence was derived from a traitor in the German service who was in communication with the British service, thus concealing the real source, ISOS.

"It was," Cowgill recalled, "a very clever document, and I was much impressed by it." So impressed was he that he sent it to C. So well camouflaged was the source of the intelligence that C elected to send it on to the Foreign Office for final approval. However, so detailed and extensive was the intelligence that the official declared himself to be "amazed" at the extent of Section V's knowledge of the enemy intelligence services in Iberia. He wondered whether that detail would not expose the source. Philby produced a summary of results that showed the intelligence had derived from human, not cryptanalytical, sources. The paper was then sent to the British ambassador at Madrid, Sir Samuel Hoare, along with an instruction to present the document personally to Franco. Accompanying the protest should be a "grand remonstrance" by Britain against Franco's toleration of all German intelligence activity on neutral Spain's territory.

There, for the moment, the Bodden operation rested. It took many weeks for the proposition to make its way through the systems, and in that time Philby and his five colleagues went to work on the flood of decrypts to expose the German espionage networks not only in Spain but also in the Americas and in Britain itself. In Britain, it was judged, all spies being operated by the German spies in Iberia were apprehended and, against the prospect of being hanged if they did not collaborate, were induced to work for their captors as Controlled Enemy Agents (CEAs). Some of them were placed in the hands of Philby's friend Tomas Harris; and in this association Philby may well have seen something of his own fate should he have been identified for what he was, a Soviet secret agent.

In all, 130 male and female enemy agents became CEAs. Most of them came from the Abwehr in Iberia, and most of those through warnings provided by Philby and his colleagues in the Iberian section of War Station XB. Most agreed to work for their captors, and they did so under the supervision of J. C. Masterman, the Oxford don whose title was Secretary of the XX Committee, the MI5 section responsible for handling double agents. Masterman's main premise in his war duties was that a live spy had utility, a dead one had none. Most were psychological cases, wrote Masterman with dainty menace.

> The high-souled fanatic may repudiate even the suggestion that he would be capable of giving way to pressure or acting as a double agent, but the majority of spies are not of this Spartan breed, and many, perhaps a majority, of them are ready and willing to commit treachery either under pressure or for some simple reasons of self-preservation. There are, too, certain persons who are genuinely anxious to serve the side against which circumstances have induced them to operate temporarily; there are others who have a natural predilection to live in that curious world of espionage and deceit, and who attach themselves with equal facility to one side or the other, so long as their craving for adventure of a rather macabre type is satisfied. Again there are some who are ready to play with both sides and who — whilst they feel no moral objection to deceiving both sides — yet appear to maintain a kind of professional pride which compels them to render reasonably good service to each; and finally there are cases in which the spy is caught, interrogated, and executed or imprisoned but in which messages purporting to come from him are still transmitted by his captors to their enemies. The spy "being dead, yet speaketh."[19]

In July 1942, the Bodden case was resumed when the Anglo-American diplomatic corps presented the documents to Franco in what was called "a grand remonstrance." Franco presented the document to Canaris, and Canaris complied. The infrared devices were removed, and Canaris suffered the first check to his activities in Spain. It was as neat and effective a stratagem as had occurred until now, and it was the one that brought Philby into personal contact with C. It was therefore important to Philby in his Soviet career. As Yuri Modin was to remark, it was Philby's acceptance in the highest reaches of a service that was otherwise quite impenetrable that made his case unique.

Menzies was now in his early fifties and since 1941 had been Prime Minister Churchill's principal adviser in intelligence. It was rare for him to see anyone who was not one of his senior officers. According to Sir James Easton, a senior member of Menzies's mandarinate at a later date, C's position made him unapproachable by any young officer except those on his personal staff.[20] The business between Menzies and Philby concerned another British service operating in the peninsula, one about which Easton knew little. It was directed by Captain Hillgarth, who worked as Menzies's spymaster in Spain from behind the post of naval attaché at the embassy in Madrid. He had come to Menzies from Churchill in 1940, and his sources concerning the Abwehr were excellent. Thirty senior officers of Franco's general staff were being bribed by Hillgarth to maintain Spain as a neutral from a fund of $10 million on deposit in New York City. And the object of all the activity was to prevent Franco from entering the war on the side of Germany and Italy.

As Philby recalled of his business with C:

One day, Cowgill asked me to make an appointment with the Chief to discuss an important communication from Armada. It was about the Germans in Spain . . . I was as shy in his presence as he was in mine, but I found him in a playful mood. He had been poaching on my preserves, he said; doing a spot of counter-espionage in Spain. He had given Armada authorisation to buy, "for a very large sum," details of the leading Abwehr officers in Spain. Those details had been received, and he handed me a telegram, a distressingly short one, containing about a dozen names and a few particulars about each. Gustav Lenz, head of the outfit; Nans Gude, in charge of Naval Intelligence, etc., etc. I remarked, somewhat tactlessly, that the information, so far as it went, was accurate. The Chief's eyebrows rose. How did I know it was accurate? Because we knew it already. How much more did I know? A very great deal. Why hadn't the Chief been informed? But we compiled regular monthly reports of the progress of our investigations, and a copy always went to the Chief. At this point he showed what an essentially nice man he was. "My dear Philby," he said with his characteristic quick smile, which had gone almost as soon as it came, "you don't expect me to read everything that's put on my desk!" We agreed that Armada should be asked for more, but of course nothing came of it. What incensed me was that I soon identified this precious source . . . and I knew that his price would have been very high indeed. And I had to fight to get an extra £5 a month for agents who produced regular, if less spectacular, intelligence![21]

Hugh Trevor-Roper, then attached to War Station XB, studying Canaris and the Abwehr in preparation for their destruction, had business with Philby at this time. He found in the phenomenon of Philby's treachery, the skill with which he bore himself, the failure of clever officers who were forever alert to the prospect of being betrayed by an ideological adversary, something of the clerical politics of the sixteenth century. Philby had become a communist fanatic. But such a man was not always a fanatic:

> Like the inquisitors and martyrs of the ages of the warring religions, he has often begun as a sensitive, intelligent, cultivated man. He may even have been a sceptic, wandering in the beguiling labyrinth of doubt. But conversion ends all that. For ideological conversion is often a form of intellectual cautery; the intensity of the experience burns out a part of the mind so that it can never be restored. So the culture, the urbanity, the sophistication of such men may remain untouched elsewhere; but where the faith is involved they are moral and mental automata. The sixteenth-century Jesuit, ex-humanist and new Machiavel, poet and assassin, equivocator and saint, has his successors in a new age of ideological strife. Such men may seem to us almost schizophrenic. They live in two worlds, operate at two levels at the same time. In fact, one life has overtaken another, devouring the heart while leaving untouched the habits of the mind.[22]

Gradually, therefore, Philby began to insinuate himself into the upper reaches of Broadway. The importance of this to his Soviet controller was great. If the Russians were only marginally interested in his Iberian work, they were vitally interested in his climb into the Secret Service hierarchy, in his developing knowledge of the inner politics of the service, particularly as it bore on Russia and its secret service. Their concern was in the real nature of the relationship between the British and American secret services and in what they regarded as the danger that both Britain and the United States might yet strike an alliance with Germany against Russia. Nowhere in Whitehall could Philby learn more about such matters than at Broadway. Moreover, he might destroy C and the service itself, for a secret service is only as good as its reputation. His own progress into the hierarchy might lead him into the inner circle of other services, and they might be in league with the British service in their Russian policies. He might himself become chief of the British Secret Service, which they regarded as their omniscient enemy. What then?

Certainly, Philby's earliest relationships within the service's inner circle during the period before Torch were all calculated to give him a solid base from which to advance himself. If his own account is true, his earliest friendships were with three of C's principal officers. David Boyle may have been the first, other than Colonel Vivian. One of C's two personal assistants, Boyle was a man whom C consulted in matters of policy. His task at Broadway was to waylay the diplomatic mail of foreign embassies in London and abroad, and especially the courier of the Spanish ambassador in London, the Duke of Alba. As Philby wrote of his association with Boyle from the safety of Moscow many years later:

> I was prepared to dislike him thoroughly, as I had heard appalling reports of him; his nickname was Creeping Jesus. My first impressions tended to confirm the awful reports I have been given. He had most of the qualities I dislike most; it would be no justice to describe him as a selfish and conceited snob. Yet he had a capacity to ingratiate himself with senior members of the Foreign Office, which, much to my surprise, I came to admire. Furthermore, I was increasingly drawn to him for his inability to assess the intelligence that passed through his hands. Although he was more than twice my age, he came to rely on my judgement. In my turn, I paid him all the outward signs of respect. Our personal association, despite its inherent absurdity, became quite a happy one. It was also of great value to me because, among the waffle and gossip that fills most diplomatic bags, there is sometimes a pearl of price.[23]

But a pearl of price to whom? The British? The Americans? The Russians? Or to himself alone? At that time Trevor-Roper thought Philby to be an exceptional and virtuous man, one who had devoted himself to the search for a new society. When he discovered the truth, he thought Philby's motivation to be "the exquisite relish of ruthless, treacherous, private power." How was it possible, Trevor-Roper asked himself, for

> such a man — favoured by society, liberally educated, regarded by all who knew him as intelligent, sensitive, and transparently "sincere" — to become not only a traitor but a traitor of a particularly despicable kind, lying, deceiving, breaking oaths, abusing confidence and destroying friends in the service not of a natural patriotism nor even of a consistent ideological doctrine but of a particularly revolting tyranny?

The answer, Philby always maintained, lay to some extent in the British Secret Service itself. He spoke of the actions of one officer, Colonel Dansey, who was at this time busily running the Rote Drei, the Soviet intelligence service, in Switzerland. Dansey's title was assistant chief of the Secret Service (A/CSS), which later was changed to vice chief of the Secret Service (V/CSS). Gruff, bearlike, and prickly, he was the subject of two views inside the service. "Claude Dansey was an utter shit; corrupt, incompetent, but with a certain low cunning," Trevor-Roper himself noted. The Russian expert Edward Crankshaw thought him to be "the sort of man who gives spying a bad name."[24]

Few doubted that he was, however, the ablest spymaster in Europe. And it was the rivalry between Vivian and Dansey that gave Broadway politics the peculiar flavor which Trevor-Roper had in mind when he wrote:

> Colonel Dansey and Colonel Vivian, *ACSS* (or was it VCSS?) and *DCSS* — what old frustrations they call to mind! All through the war these were the grandees of our Service, the Aaron and Hur who, from right and left (but with eyes steadily averted from each other), held up the labouring hands of our Moses, *CSS* or C, Sir Stewart Menzies. How we used to sympathise with Menzies![25]

Philby did see enough of Dansey to form an opinion of him:

> Dansey had the lowest opinion of the value of counter-espionage, as well as a reputation for unnecessary combativeness. I was therefore surprised by the courtesy he showed me. It proved to be always so. Dansey was a man who preferred to scatter his venom at long range, by telephone or on paper. The only way to deal with him was to beard him in his office; a personal confrontation lowered the temperature, and made it possible to talk common sense. As soon as I grasped this, I had little difficulty with him, except to keep a straight face when he started to make cracks about Vivian, my boss's boss. Happily, our paths did not cross often, as he was good enough to strike me off his list of pet bugbears.

Philby argued that he did what he did because Dansey had been merciless in his handling of agents. Through his actions many had perished in France at the hands of the German security services. He was guilty, too, of betraying Britain's allies, notably Russia and sometimes France. Dansey had to be destroyed, Philby contended, in the interests of the Allies and England. He was an evil man heading an evil service devoted to reaction.

Through Philby's acceptance in the secret circle, his involvement in Torch and its attendant deception and double-agent operations, he became a familiar at the headquarters of Broadway's sister service, MI5. And as he recorded of his ventures into that other lion's den:

> It was a short walk from Broadway Buildings across St. James's Park to the wartime headquarters of MI5 in St. James's Street. But the difference in style was considerable. Even the entrance compared favourably with the dingy hall at Broadway, and the first good impression was confirmed upstairs. The offices looked like offices; so far as I know, there were none of the makeshift rabbit hutches which disfigured so much of Broadway. The officers sat at desks uncluttered

by dog-eared paper. At most, half-a-dozen neat files, each nicely in-
dexed and cross-indexed, would be awaiting treatment. This had its
drawback. At Section V we used to complain of the inordinate detail which MI5 officers found time to pack into their long letters.
Some of it, at least, was unwarranted by the significance of its subject-
matter. Nevertheless, MI5 wore an air of professional competence
which Broadway never matched.[26]

His main operational interest lay in Guy Liddell, the chief of counterespionage in the Security Service. Philby's process of cultivation
and insinuation began with one great advantage. He knew the quarry.
Anthony Blunt was Liddell's personal assistant. Liddell, too, had Guy
Burgess for a friend. Moreover, Tomas Harris was now in MI5.

Philby was devoted to Secret Service politics. When the chief of the
Security Service, Sir David Petrie, Cowgill's associate in the Indian
Police, retired, Liddell's service would, in Philby's view, have "voted to
a man for Liddell to succeed." But Liddell did not succeed Petrie.
Another policeman did, and Liddell's disappointment was evident.
Philby explained:

> He, like most of the MI5 professionals, maintained that MI5 was an
> intelligence organisation, not a police outfit. The techniques for com-
> bating espionage were different from those adapted to crime. Since
> spies are backed by the great technical resources of governments,
> while criminals are not, there is clearly much to be said for that view.
> The government, however, took the view that the appointment of a
> senior policeman, trained to Whitehall procedures, would be safer.
> Liddell was awarded the doubtful dignity of Deputy Director, and he
> would have been inhuman if he had felt no resentment. I am sure
> that spies, had they but known it, would have rejoiced at Liddell's
> discomfiture. One did.[27]

By June 1942, Philby had become something of a familiar to all
these most secret personalities in their most secret departments. He
seems to have been suspect nowhere, and he enjoyed the respect and
affection of most and perhaps all of Menzies's officers, who themselves
constituted a group of power and influence throughout the secret
world.

For the moment, the greatest success was that of Torch, based in part
on the intelligence derived from the decrypts that Philby controlled.
On November 8, 1942, by night, twelve aircraft carriers, six battleships
and battle cruisers, fifteen cruisers, eighty-one destroyers, nine subma-

rines, eleven corvettes, five sloops, twenty-six minesweepers, fifty-six ships carrying the assault infantry, fifty-five with their equipment, twenty antisubmarine ships, seven tankers, eighteen motor launches, one seaplane tender, two cutters, five antiaircraft ships, one monitor, and a hundred and seventy transports bringing in the follow-up forces and supplies — all eluded the U-boats, most of them concentrated far from the Gibraltar Strait, pursuing a red herring, an empty British convoy, SL125, homeward bound by the Canaries from Sierra Leone. On the task force's arrival, one British liner, the S.S. *Scythia*, was torpedoed but managed to stay afloat. It was the only casualty.

No one man could claim the marvel of this triumph of planning, seamanship, and surprise. But if Bodden had been operational before the task forces passed through the strait, there would have been no surprise. Because there was, credit reflected to Philby. Donovan survived, and so did the OSS. As for Canaris and the Abwehr in the peninsula, their failure to warn the German supreme command of the timing, weight, and places of the landings marked the point at which Hitler lost some confidence in the Abwehr and its chief, Canaris. Worse, he began to regard it as defeatist, incompetent, probably treacherous, and undoubtedly corrupt. Writing in his memoir, Philby felt that he might now have a permanent career in the British Secret Service, that he was now "on the up and up." Yet even in his time of success, Philby caught his second whiff of the firing squad from the ISOS decrypts on his desk.

At Christmastime, just after the Torch landings, the German security services in France completed a hunt throughout Europe for Bolshevik spies with the capture of Henri Robinsohn, who had been Philby's case officer when he was in France in 1939–1940 as the *Times*'s senior correspondent. The Abwehr decrypts at War Station XB reported his capture by an Abwehr team at the Palais de Chaillot in Paris, the last stop on one of the Métro lines. They spoke too of having found Robinsohn's operational archives under the floorboards of his hideaway. These included his identity documents, reports, coding data, and his correspondence with the Center. Among what the CIA later called several hundred documents were the coded names of a number of persons, many of whom would not be positively identified. They may have included some reference to Philby. Within the Anglo-American services these became famous as "the Robinsohn papers." The British service recovered them at the Abwehr headquarters at Brussels in 1944. A note that they had been found was circulated through the Secret and Security Services. But as with Robinsohn himself, they vanished. When they were found twenty-two years later, it was discovered that they had been "misfiled."[28]

The investigations sparked by the inquiry into the activities of some of Robinsohn's spies in London reached everywhere, even War Station XB. A female assistant in the travel section was released from the service not because she was a communist but because her husband was. And after an internal investigation, Vivian warned C that his service had been penetrated by the Soviets. Accordingly, on August 23, 1943, C advised the head of the Foreign Office, Sir Alexander Cadogan, that, as Cadogan wrote in his diary, "I have Communists in my organisation."[29]

Philby's lucky star was still gleaming brightly when the first Americans arrived for service with the War Station. Norman Holmes Pearson, who had been a Rhodes Scholar and now taught English at Yale, was chief of X2, as the new U.S. foreign counterespionage service was called in the OSS table of organization. He would establish a "special relationship" with Cowgill and Philby. With Pearson came John McDonough, also a Rhodes Scholar; Hubert Will, a future federal judge in Chicago; Robert Blum, a professor of European history; and Dana Durand, another Rhodes Scholar.

The group arrived by air on April 13, 1943, Pearson's thirty-fourth birthday. None of the group had had any experience in official intelligence work except twelve weeks of training in elementary clandestinity at an OSS school near Washington. At St. Albans they were known as V48 — Section V plus the forty-eight states of America — and moved into a cottage, Abbotshay, in the nearby village of Ayot St. Lawrence. Pearson became Philby's X2 counterpart in counterespionage operations in Spain, Portugal, Spanish and French North Africa, Corsica, Sardinia, Sicily, and Italy for most of the rest of the war — the key corner of the intelligence war in the Atlantic at that time.

Pearson's intellectual qualifications for the work were excellent. He was three years older than Philby, a Yale honor student, editor of the *Yale Daily News,* and one of two editors of the two-volume *Oxford Anthology of American Literature,* which was considered to be among the best collections of American prose and poetry. He had studied at Magdalen College, Oxford, and the University of Berlin and had received his doctorate from Yale in 1941, with a dissertation on Hawthorne's *Italian Notebooks.* Politically, it is said, he had been vaguely pro-Nazi in Berlin but had switched to the left on his return to Yale and had put about some leftist antiwar ballads.[30] He had won two Guggenheim fellowships, a rarity.

He and the other officers took up posts that were the exact counterpart of the British structure within the War Station, and their responsibilities were very great. As the X2 War Diary shows, their task was to:

> a. Establish and operate throughout the world (exclusive of the Western Hemisphere) a secret counter-espionage organization. [It] will cover and operate in all theaters of war and in such other parts of the world as the national interests and the military operations of the United States warrant.
>
> b. Institute such measures as may be necessary to protect the operational security and to prevent the penetration of OSS espionage and other secret activities.

X2's other objectives were to:

> effect the security of the United States and allied Armed Forces and other national agencies from the espionage activities of the enemy and other unfriendly nations in cooperation and coordination with the Intelligence Services of the Army and the Navy.

To do so:

> X-2 will ascertain the identity, location, and activities of all espionage agents and organizations operated by the enemy and unfriendly countries, and those countries whose intentions are questionable. Upon the determination of this information, X-2 will take appropriate and coordinated actions with other agencies of the United States, friendly or allied nations cause the activities of these espionage systems to be neutralized, rendered ineffective, diverted to serve the purposes of the United States, or destroyed.

Furthermore, in carrying out its mission the group was authorized to exchange information with the "Military Intelligence Service, the Office of Naval Intelligence, British Intelligence, Federal Bureau of Investigation, State Department, Treasury Department, Office of Economic Warfare, Office Censorship, British Censorship, French [Intelligence Service]."[31]

Thus, through Pearson's relationship with Philby, on whom he was entirely dependent for some time in almost every professional respect, nearly the entire security system of the United States in theory, and also to some extent in practice, was penetrated from the outset, vulnerable to Soviet espionage. Philby's opportunities for espionage against the United States in the Soviet interest became greater when the decision had been to locate the operational headquarters of X2 in London, not Washington, for three reasons.

The first and main reason was that Section V possessed "sources of information which could not be transmitted to Washington." They were probably variants of ISOS, double-agent activities perhaps having to do with Admiral Canaris of the Abwehr. As the War Diary noted: "X2 was extremely fortunate in that it was able from the very beginning to gain the trust of the British to a greater extent than any other Allied CE organization." Such was the "delicacy" of this special intelligence that its transmission "dictated the location of the operational headquarters" of X2 "at a point where the British Central Registry could be immediately consulted" — the Central Registry being at Prae Wood, which Philby had so recently plundered in the Soviet interest. A second factor was the location in London of other Allied counterespionage organizations that X2 needed as sources. A third, "the fact that London would be the operational headquarters for any military operations on the Continent of Europe." Moreover, under the rules of association between the two agencies, X2 was obliged to check the names of all X2 agents and operations against the Central Registry. Under these circumstances of remarkable intimacy between XB and X2, the personal and professional relationship between Philby and Pearson became of importance.

Gradually the X2 section of the War Station expanded until its contingent equaled that of the British. The main work at the intermediate and lower levels was known as carding, transferring the data from the decrypts to a Security Index, which by D-Day held ninety thousand names of enemy intelligence officers and their agents and friends throughout Europe and the Middle East. It was routine but vital work in the task of preparing for "the active pursuit and liquidation of the German intelligence services." It was done cheerfully, the spirit of the War Station was good, and one of the American secretaries wrote a song about it. It was set to the music of "I'll Be Seeing You," a wartime hit:

> I'll be carding you,
> In all those old familiar places,
> Everywhere, our long arm chases
> All year through . . .
>
> In that queer café
> That dive across the way
> The well-known underground
> The neutral port
> The suspect town.

Cowgill called the spirit "the cheerful amorality of spycatching." And with the expansion, in January 1944, five months before D-Day, there arrived a person of importance in the history of the Philby case. James Jesus Angleton, age twenty-seven, had been a protégé of Norman Holmes Pearson's at Yale. A son of a man who had married a young Mexican girl while riding with General John J. Pershing's force after the Mexican bandit Pancho Villa just before World War I, Angleton, until he was fourteen, lived in Idaho, where his father was sales manager and then a director of the National Cash Register Company. In December 1933, the family moved to Italy when the father obtained the NCR franchise in Rome. He sent his son to an English public school, Malvern College, a place of beauty in Worcestershire. James Jesus — his mother was a devout Catholic and named him after the Savior — moved on to Yale and then to Harvard Law School. He was literarily inclined and kept company with the poet e. e. cummings, who is said to have remarked of Angleton's mind, "What a miracle of momentous complexity is the poet."[32] He was quite right. But if Angleton was ambitious when he met Philby, he had no vocation. It was Philby who provided him with a trade, counterespionage, and taught him its arts and crafts. Whether Philby hooked him in the interests of the Soviet Union would often be debated, but there is no doubt that Angleton fell under Philby's spell. It must be mentioned, however, that Angleton, while not mature politically when he encountered Philby, did appear to be a determined American patriot of Republican stripe. As with Philby, so with James Jesus: his record was riddled with ambiguity and inexplicable actions that resulted in the question asked by a high authority at the CIA: "Was Angleton the American Philby?"[33] This was not possible, but the thought did exist when Angleton eventually became chief of the CIA's foreign counter-espionage service and his conduct of office gave rise to investigations.

Part of Philby's work, until Pearson was sufficiently informed to do it himself, was to brief the arriving X2 personnel on the work of the War Station. It was Philby who taught Angleton the structure of the Secret Service — there were fifty-three officials whose missions Angleton needed to know about — and how the enemy's wireless and mail messages were intercepted; what to watch out for in the decrypts in regard to enemy sabotage operations; the use of double agents in South Africa and Canada; the nature of British Security Coordination, the all-in-one British Secret Service in the Americas, and of Security Intelligence Middle East; a study of the work at Bletchley Park, the code-breaking headquarters, probably the most secret establishment in England; the personalities and the administrative and security procedures of the British Secret Service. But above all there was the XX

Committee, the agency that handled the double agents, its method and its doctrine.

This doctrine, and the system for its implementation, made a great and lasting impression on Angleton, who possessed what has been called "the counterespionage mind," a combination of high intelligence, intuition, curiosity, the ability to put two and two together and make four, energy, connections, and a pleasing personality. He became fascinated with ISOS, over which he pored as if they contained the secret of the Trinity. He began to debate whether counterintelligence was a science, not an art, and he displayed the qualities of zealot and hermit that interested Philby. Angleton's associates felt him to be "a student of ambiguity," a man who advocated the principle in counterespionage that "everything begins — and ends — with the proper methodology."[34]

As chief of the Italian desk of counterespionage under Pearson's direction, Angleton was in closer contact with Philby than might otherwise have been the case. Like most of the other Americans, he came to admire Philby as the apprentice admired the sorcerer. And, as Philby would write of Angleton in his memoirs, he "earned my respect by openly rejecting the Anglomania that disfigured the young face of OSS"[35] — a reference to the intense admiration that Pearson and most of the staff of X2 exhibited for the British Secret Service, especially for Philby. Thus "the new Machiavel" had by the spring of 1943 developed a solid basis for the next stage of his conspiracy. This was to seize control of the War Station from Cowgill and operate it in the Soviet interest.

At this time St. John, too, emerged from the obscurity of North Wales to discover that, even though the British government continued to regard him as an anathema, the OSS was interested in him and his knowledge of Arabian affairs. In 1941, a friend of Norman Holmes Pearson's at Yale, Donald C. Downes, had undertaken a world tour for the U.S. Office of Naval Intelligence and the British Secret Service. His mission was to recruit spies for both. Having sailed across the Pacific and Indian oceans in a Dutch steamer that called at many ports, Downes arrived in Bahrain in the Persian Gulf. There, he claimed, he met St. John Philby; this was when Philby was making his journey by way of India to the United States. Downes wrote that he was "anxious to know how this thoroughly English scholar became so estranged from his homeland."[36] He had learned, he wrote, that St. John was "conspiring against Britain in her extremity." He could not understand how Philby had become so "embittered" and why his conduct was "irresponsible and hysterical." Downes tucked away the encounter in his recollections of his long journey.

After the battles of Stalingrad and El Alamein, Donovan of the OSS — who as a lawyer had defended Standard Oil and other oil companies against cartel charges — decided to establish a strong OSS presence in the Middle East. Whether Donovan's interest in St. John personally was spurred by a 1942 State Department report from London is nowhere evident, although the State Department was one of the OSS's sources. This report announced that the Foreign Office had given a "chilly reception" to Philby's application for an exit permit to give some lectures on Arabian conditions at the University of Chicago. The letter from the U.S. Embassy in London noted two aspects of Philby's politics:

> Mr. Philby apparently advocates a drastic solution for the Arab problem, giving most of what is now Palestine to the Jews, but granting to the Arabs all of the original MacMahon proposals of 1915. He does not, however, wish himself to be quoted to this effect.

The second matter concerned Philby's views on Indian political conditions.

Recently Churchill had been irritated by pressure from President Roosevelt to grant India full independence, and the Churchill administration therefore had no desire to enable St. John to lecture in the United States. The embassy letter also noted:

> As a former member of the Indian Civil Service his policy for India is no less sweeping in its conception, considering that he believes that the British must yield, point by point, wherever opposition is advanced by Indian Nationalist leaders.

Statements such as these made in foreign parts at the height of a great war were likely to land St. John back in jail, on more serious charges than last time. In consequence, Philby was advised by the Foreign Office:

> I am directed by Mr. Secretary Eden to inform you that no exit permits can be given for a visit to the United States of America unless the application is supported by a department of His Majesty's Government on the grounds that it would be in the national interest. I am to add that Mr. Eden would not feel justified in recommending your application.[37]

St. John returned to his rainswept hillside in North Wales to continue work on his autobiography, *Arabian Days*. It is indelicate to suggest that what then occurred was a bid by the OSS to establish an espionage relationship with Philby, but that is in effect what happened.

Donovan asked Downes in 1942 to provide him with a list of names of persons who could be depended on to work in the Middle East in the U.S. interest. In July, Downes submitted a paper which mentioned the utility of St. John Philby. King Ibn Saud's political adviser had turned "violently against his own country" while becoming "very pro-American." As well as being "Grand Vizier to His Majesty, and the exclusive Ford agent for the Arabian peninsula, [Philby] is trusted and even beloved by the tribes from Oman to the Shammar in the North and from Alkoweit to the Yemen." Downes added that any OSS agent going to Arabia could, "if he is at all careful, be able to get the cooperation of St. John Philby, whose history of Arabia cast a great deal of light on this extraordinary and magnificent part of the world."[38]

Then there was further movement. In August 1943 an OSS agent, Colonel Harold B. Hoskins, called on St. John in London to discuss a plan for a Palestinian settlement which Philby had dreamed up in 1939 in order to get £20 million — $100 million — from world Jewry for Ibn Saud's treasury. By now the plan had made its way up to the desks of Roosevelt and Churchill, and both had considered it a possible instrument through which Arab-Jewish quarreling might be ended and the Balfour Declaration, which was still on the table after thirty-five years, fulfilled. Hoskins was on his way to Arabia to try to get Ibn Saud to talk about Palestine with Chaim Weizmann of the Jewish Agency. Hoskins continued his journey to Arabia and was received by the king.

Hoskins's proposal — that Ibn Saud accept the Philby plan and the £20 million — produced an almighty explosion, much of it directed at Philby. The king handed Hoskins an aide-mémoire for the president explaining that his position on Palestine and the Jews had not changed and that all that he desired was that "the obvious rights of the Arabs, which are clear as the sun, may not be dimmed by historic fallacies or social or economic theories of the Zionists, which theories God has not ordained." Concerning the president's proposal that Ibn Saud meet with Dr. Weizmann, the king declared:

> I wish the President to know that we meet anyone who comes to us, whatever his religion, and we welcome him and do everything which his position requires in the matter of hospitality. But the Jews are a peculiar case and the President must know about the enmity which is between us in earlier and in recent times. This enmity is well known

and mentioned in our holy books and it is rooted from earliest times
and forever. From this it is clear that we cannot guard against the
treachery of the Jews and we cannot discuss anything with them nor
trust in their promises . . .

There is a great personal enmity between him and me owing to
the criminal affront which this person has committed against me by
choosing me from among all Arabs and Moslems to charge me with
a dastardly thing — that is that I should become a traitor against my
religion and my country. This affair increases my hatred against him
and all connected with him. This insult took place during the first
year of this war when he sent me a well-known European person
[Philby] who asked me to abandon the question of Palestine and the
support of Arab and Moslem rights in connection therewith against
a payment to me of £20 million, which amount would be guaranteed
by His Excellency President Roosevelt himself.[39]

The aide-mémoire seemed to put paid to Philby's career in Mecca, for
plainly the king held him wholly responsible and had disavowed him
as all confidential agents may be rejected when schemes go wrong. If
not, other matters were afoot that seemed likely to wreck Philby's
influence at the king's court.

Now, just as Pearson was picking Kim Philby's brains to learn the
business of counterespionage, so an official of another OSS branch in
London, the British Empire Section of the Research and Analysis Division, Joseph Charles, began to cultivate St. John. They had met in
London in late 1943 at the home of Colonel Newcombe, Lawrence's
sabotage adviser during the Arab Revolt. Thereafter Charles and St.
John Philby talked about once a month. Charles's interest lay in Britain's treaty powers with the Persian Gulf sheikhdoms, a matter in
which the Near East desk of the OSS was deeply interested. In a desire
to expand its knowledge, the section in Washington put out a letter
to all OSS outposts, asking for information about Philby. Charles replied to the chief of the division, William L. Langer, that he knew
Philby "fairly well" and that he thought him "one of the wisest men I
have ever met."[40] He

is still very interested in Near East politics and is very highly regarded
by the Near East people here, but I don't think he has any official
work. As you may know, he is very much out of favor with the Foreign
Office . . . Philby was acting as adviser to Ibn Saud when the question
of the American oil concessions first came up. He advised the King
to give the concessions to the Americans, even though the British
were offering more [because] with the Americans the matter was

purely a business arrangement. He thought [they] wouldn't try to extend their influence into that part of the world by means of the concessions. The British Foreign Office learned about Philby's advice to Ibn Saud, and it is, I think, the main thing that they have against him, although his whole point of view would be disturbing to them.

His only political activity these days was giving lectures to a new political party called Common Wealth, which suggested that Philby had abandoned fascist causes to return to pale Marxism; the Common Wealth Party stood for common ownership of great resources, "socialism for the middle classes," the retention of the multiparty system but with the abolition of the House of Lords and the substitution of merit for privilege as the basis for advancement.[41]

But, Charles warned, Philby was "very much worried about the future influence of America. He is afraid that we are about to go imperialist also . . . and is quite discouraged at the recent turn our politics have taken." From that moment forward Charles's communications about Philby were put in the OSS's XL list, which meant that his reports were of "an extra-sensitive nature" which would not be given "any foreign dissemination." The great game of Middle East oil politics had started afresh. Plainly, St. John had become "of intelligence interest" to the inner councils of the OSS.

St. John was very conscious of the new, wider U.S. interest in Saudi Arabia and the Middle East. With one eye on the great power rivalry, he wrote to Dora on June 6, 1944, that oil was now of much greater interest to the United States than the Zionist question, that the British government did not intend to relinquish its position in the Middle East to the United States, and to that end the British government had given Ibn Saud "£400,000 in 1940, £800,000 in 1941 and £2.5 million in 1942 & 1943 besides £500,000 in food." At the same time "the Americans are lease-lending as hard as they can." Ibn Saud was "making hay while the sun shines and his women are getting all the jewels, perfumes and silks they want. It is a great game and back of it is the oil." But he noted it was an ill wind that bore no one any good and reported that at long last the king had settled his debts with Philby's prewar company, Sharquieh — £80,000, or about a quarter of a million dollars at the going rate of exchange (and using U.S. Lend Lease–minted silver coins to do so) and that at last the Philbians could anticipate prosperity.[42]

Against that background, in those last crowded weeks before D-Day, the Philby family came more closely together than at any time in the past. Through ISOS Kim learned the highly secret knowledge that the Germans had placed large numbers of missiles in France, ready to bombard London when the invasion began. There was the V1, a jet-propelled cruise missile that was faster than any Allied fighter and carried a one-ton warhead. The other was the V2 rocket, launched into the stratosphere to descend on the 620 square miles of London. The existence of these weapons caused great anxiety in the Churchill administration, and Philby, gravely misusing his secret knowledge, warned his mother and sent Aileen and two of his children to stay with St. John at the cottage in North Wales. There they went shortly before D-Day, which was scheduled for any time after May 1, 1944. In the recent past, C had sacked a colleague and friend since schooldays for having evacuated his family to the country.

By now Aileen, at thirty-four a year older than Kim, had had three children and was pregnant again but keeping it secret. St. John liked what he had seen of Aileen and her growing family, but he knew very little about Kim's private life. He lived alone in the cottage, for he and Dora rarely cohabited during the four years he was in England in exile from Riyadh, although they wrote to each other almost daily in affectionate, even devoted, terms.

Aileen arrived on June 2, 1944, and soon St. John began writing about her to Dora and his mother, May, who were both sheltering from the V-bombs at May's home in Camberley, in Surrey. These showed Aileen in another light and may have reflected something of the truth about Kim's domestic life. They reflected, too, something of St. John's pettiness as the patriarch of the family, a character quite different from Abdullah, the Arabian statesman and explorer. St. John was approaching his sixtieth birthday and could be as bitchy as any of Trinity's old dons. In his first letter he told how he had found his daughter-in-law

really astonishingly feckless and always seems to depend on someone else for everything. Have you any matches, have you any envelopes, etc., etc. She would never take the trouble to use an old envelope or light her cigarette with a spill and then she will cheerfully leave a box of matches out in the rain or on the edge of the sink. Have you any stamps? is another cry, and have you any money? another. I suppose she had some money when she arrived but whatever she had didn't last long and she cheerfully goes to the Oakeley [a nearby inn] to run up a bill & asks me to pay it when I next go down, and while up here she has "borrowed" £5 or more but I don't think it worries her being without money provided there is someone else to pay the bills. And her extravagance! It is probably good for me to have such an experience but I can't say I admire the new way of the world and it would be a pity if the children (who are both charming) went that way.[43]

In another letter to "My own darling Mother," Abdullah, as he was now always known in the family circle, complained afresh:

I don't know what to make of Aileen at all — I don't think she has got any brain and certainly she never uses it for thinking — at any rate of other people. A. is completely selfish and she tries to be bossy, but that doesn't go down in this family! . . . So far we have avoided all quarrels for Kim's sake but things are distinctly trying and the atmosphere is not conducive to my sort of work. The children are alright but A is really intolerable!!

Aileen was still at the cottage on August 1, but as St. John wrote to his mother on that day she was "fed up with this quiet life and is longing to be in town with Kim to have a good time gadding about." But with the evacuations of mothers, children, and the aged going on from London into places like North Wales as the V2 added its fury to the V1 campaign, St. John was in despair at getting the peace and quiet he felt he needed. If Aileen left the cottage, he would not have her back again.

Mercifully for all, Aileen's mother arrived to take Aileen and the children with her to rejoin Kim. With their visitors gone, Philby and Dora began to clean the cottage, and as he wrote to his mother of that labor:

Well, all that is over. D and I feel as if a great load has been lifted from our shoulders and most of this morning we have been spring-cleaning! I took all the furniture out of the living room, carpet and all, and [the maid] is to sweep it clean and wash the floor with paraffin. You just couldn't imagine the mess! Then tomorrow the kitchen (which is almost worse) is to be spring-cleaned and next day my room which I gave to Aileen & which is just filthy. She had used the chamber-pot that night but had not troubled to empty it out!! In a few days we shall be quite ship-shape and we are already as happy as a pair of larks.

But St. John learned that Aileen was not returning to London at all. Kim had forbidden it because of the bombardment, which was making life dangerous and difficult. He told Aileen to get rooms near the cottage, so she found lodgings in the village of Maentwrog.

She remained there until September 1944 when Aileen's conduct took an almost imperceptible turn, but an important one. St. John wrote of the incident to his mother. His elder daughter, Helena, who now worked as a carder at the War Station, wrote that Aileen and Kim had invited her and Patricia, another of Kim's sisters, to meet them for "short drinks" at the Normandie Hotel in Knightsbridge. After a time Aileen "began to fidget about getting on and there was no suggestion of dinner being included." Finishing their drinks, Helena and Patricia went to an Italian restaurant in Brompton Road. As they finished their dinner, Kim and Aileen entered the restaurant with Guy Burgess and David Footman, by now chief of the Political Section of the Secret Service and a friend of Burgess's since 1937; it was Footman who had introduced Burgess into the Secret Service in 1938. Minor as it was, this incident showed first that all present were familiars, and, as the tenor of St. John's letter showed, all were known to him personally. If this was so — and it is a characteristic of counterespionage inquiries that everything, no matter how trivial, may have meaning — then it may be some evidence for the reason the FBI opened a file on St. John and the State Department asked the Foreign Office for a biographical statement on him. That request, too, had meaning in the official world as the war began to end and the State Department returned to the question of the oil interests in Saudi Arabia.

11

Overlord

1944–1945

A
FTER THE FALL of the Soviet Union, some of Philby's postwar professional papers for the KGB became available in Moscow. They were mainly proposals to the chieftains at the Center for the disruption of the CIA, the SIS, and the NATO intelligence services.[1] In these papers the word *disruption* is a constant theme, with other related professional intelligence terms like *deception* and *penetration*. But it is the use of *disruption* that is most striking. The word does not appear at all in *The International Dictionary of Intelligence,* which has its origins in the CIA's terminology. It does, of course, appear in the *Oxford English Dictionary* and is defined as "the action of rending or bursting asunder." In the political sense, it is associated with nihilism, a theory of revolution popular among Russian extremists that got its name from Ivan Turgenev's novel *Fathers and Sons* (1861) and was one of the forces that Lenin harnessed to overthrow Tsar Nicholas II in 1917. Nihilism advocated the destruction by any means of all existing structures if a bad world was to be made a better one. There was a strong streak of nihilism, of disruption, in both St. John and Kim Philby. St. John disrupted British policy whenever he got the chance, and displayed respect for some of the aspects of nihilism — the stern world of the hot desert, the physical severity of obeisance before the black stone of the Ka'aba, the cleansing of the spirit through the hot winds of the Empty Quarter. Kim Philby obtained nihilistic satisfaction in another direction: he felt that his ruthlessness made him the moral and intellectual superior of his colleagues and of the enemy. In the

view of Trevor-Roper, part of his mind had become cauterized, and from the time of his Viennese experience he began to seek not so much a new society "as the exquisite relish of ruthless, treacherous, private power." Trevor-Roper also saw the spirit of nihilism in him:

> All through his career this negative character is apparent. Philby touched nothing which he did not destroy — from within — while Russia, which alone he served, he did not touch; it remained a remote, unknown abstraction. While the policy which he served veered and shifted, his destructive zeal remained constant. Institutions, persons, friendships, marriage, all crumbled around him. His career illustrates yet another aspect of that intellectual nihilism which seems to be a feature of this century.[2]

There were many instances of his rejection of the institutions into which he was born; they began when, as a child, he proclaimed himself to his grandmother as having become "a godless little anti-imperialist"; and while many people regarded this as an admirable state of mind, he used the term in the sense of a desire not to improve the tranquillity of that little domestic world in which he found himself but to disrupt it — and to show his Russian masters that he was born a revolutionist. There were many such instances to show that, while he regarded his aspirations as noble, he was basically dishonest. His tutor Luce's warning letter to St. John is evidence of that. His corruption of the unfortunate Wylie at the War Office is more evidence of his inner amorality. Now, in the decisive year of 1944, that year when the fates changed horse and history changed its tune, there emerged another personality defect, corruption, while all the time Kim concealed himself in what Trevor-Roper called "his benign, distant irony."

With the arrival of the War Station in St. James's in preparation for D-Day, he came to be seen more and more at a curious, some would say sinister, establishment at 5 Bentinck Street, one of the more agreeable quarters of London. There, in an apartment under the offices of *The Practitioner,* a leading medical journal, he met with his friends. The apartment was owned or leased by Victor Rothschild, the heir to the Rothschild financial concern deeply rooted in the British and European financial system for three centuries, with close links then to the British Secret Service, which had a long tradition in political, financial, and economic intelligence.

Muggeridge went there once and discovered a cabal of what he called "displaced intellectuals." He met Burgess there for the first and only time, and he gave me a feeling, such as I have never had from someone else, of being morally afflicted in some way. His very physical presence was, to me, malodorous and sinister; as though he had some consuming illness — like the galloping consumption or leprosy . . . The impression fitted in well enough with his subsequent adventures; as did this millionaire's nest altogether, so well set up, providing, among other amenities, special rubber bones to bite on if the stress of the Blitz became too hard to bear. Sheltering so distinguished a company . . . all in a sense grouped around Burgess; Etonian mud-lark and sick toast of a sick society, as beloved along Foreign Office corridors, in the quads and the clubs, as in the pubs among the pimps and ponces and street pick-ups, with their high voices and peroxide hair. . . There was not so much a conspiracy grouped round him as decay and dissolution. It was the end of a class; something that would be written in history books, like Gibbon on Heliogabalus, with wonder and perhaps hilarity, but still tinged with sadness, as all endings are.[3]

In these moral and political circumstances, at the turn of the year 1943–1944, with the assent of his superiors in the Secret Service, Philby went to work on his first major act of disruption: to wreck the Abwehr, the intelligence service of the German General Staff, so that it would be unable to divine the central secrets of Overlord — the place, the date, the time, the means, and the weight of the armies to be landed. Admiral Canaris was still the chief, he was still plotting to kill Hitler, and he had failed consistently to supply the German supreme command with the intelligence it required if it was to deploy effectively its great power: the German Army, still the most powerful in the world. So powerful was it indeed that, as the Allied Supreme Command acknowledged, if for any reason the Russian front failed, the Allies would not be able to undertake Overlord at all. It would have to rely on aerial bombardment to force the Germans to surrender.

Through his failure to predict the time and place of the Torch invasion in late 1942, Canaris and his service had come under heavy criticism. That criticism had been sustained through his subsequent failures to predict accurately and in timely fashion the invasions of Sicily and Italy. The result was the fall of Italy as Hitler's main ally in Europe. The reports based on ISOS by Trevor-Roper and Philby had had much to do with Canaris's discomfiture. And as Trevor-Roper noted in a biographical statement on Canaris, his chief weakness was that he was not qualified by personality for the post of spymaster to the Reich. The chief of a secret service must be a bureaucrat, and as a bureaucrat Canaris was a failure. "He was unable to organise his office, unable to control those distant stations where subordinates of dubious loyalty yielded easily to profitable temptations," wrote Trevor-Roper.[4] He could not delegate responsibility, he alone could make decisions, and in the end, during the run up to Overlord, the burden of office became intolerable.

As Trevor-Roper recorded:

> While Canaris flew in feverish perpetual motion from capital to capital, or plunged into Spanish cathedrals to relieve his melancholy, the Abwehr lost all cohesion, all discipline. Among its own members it became notorious, a mere comfortable family concern, not to say a family racket — "The Canaris Family Ltd," as one captured Abwehr officer described it — and in the Nazi Party it was despised as incompetent long before it was suspect as disloyal.

Through Anglo-American diplomatic pressure, nourished by ISOS and Philby's use of it, at the beginning of 1944 Canaris lost his Franco friends. They, scenting an Allied victory, declined to receive him when he came calling, and this, again revealed through ISOS, "convinced those of us who could appreciate it at the time that the fall of Canaris would now no longer be delayed." For there was to be considered, too, the question of the loyalty to the regime of his service.

It was the Canaris matter that first brought Philby and Trevor-Roper together and also raised the first question in Trevor-Roper's mind about Philby. As Trevor-Roper remembered:

> Late in 1942 my office had come to certain conclusions — which time proved to be correct — about the struggle between the Nazi Party and the German General Staff, as it was being fought out in the field of secret intelligence. The German Secret Service . . . and its leader, Admiral Canaris, were suspected by the Party not only of inefficiency but also of disloyalty, and attempts were being made by Himmler to oust the Admiral and to take over his whole organisation. Admiral Canaris himself, at that time, was making repeated journeys to Spain and had indicated a willingness to treat with us: he would even welcome a meeting with his opposite number, C. These conclusions were duly formulated and the final document was submitted for security clearance to Philby. Philby absolutely forbade its circulation, insisting that it was "mere speculation."[5]

Later, Philby suppressed a second such study, one suggesting that Canaris and his associates were plotting to murder Hitler, a study that again was proven correct. Yet Philby again was unyielding: the report was not to be circulated, as it was "speculative" and "unreliable." Trevor-Roper recorded:

> At the time we were baffled by Philby's intransigence, which would yield to no argument and which no argument was used to defend. From some members of Section V, mere mindless blocking of intelligence was to be expected. But Philby, we said to ourselves, was an intelligent man: how could he behave thus in a matter so important? Had he too yielded to the genius of the place? In retrospect I can see that there may have been another reason. It was not to the Russian interest that the Western Allies should exploit the political division of Germany, or support the conservative enemies of Hitler, while the Red Army was still too far away to intervene.

Cowgill supported Philby, holding that if Trevor-Roper's report was circulated it would expose the existence of ISOS. But, as Cowgill related, Trevor-Roper was "a very difficult customer to handle" and decided on his own authority that his conclusions had such importance that they should receive the widest circulation at the highest level. He sent a copy to Lord Cherwell, an intimate of Churchill's and the prime minister's scientific adviser. Trevor-Roper was known to Cherwell, who had been a distinguished figure at Oxford between the wars, and hoped that Cherwell would forward the paper to Churchill. That he did. Churchill read it with interest and asked C about it. C knew nothing of the paper and expressed annoyance to Cowgill that Trevor-Roper had gone through back channels to get it to the prime minister.

The consequences were inevitable. Cowgill demanded that Trevor-Roper be court-martialed, a procedure that would certainly have ruined his career. The hearing took place at Broadway, with Vivian and Cowgill as prosecutors, Trevor-Roper as defendant, Patrick Reilly of the Foreign Office (and one of C's personal assistants) as defense counsel, and C as judge.[6] Cowgill laid evidence, not only of the circulation of the paper, but also that without authority Trevor-Roper had given decrypts to MI5 officers who Cowgill thought were not trustworthy. It was also charged that Trevor-Roper had had unauthorized contact with the enemy in Ireland — a grave offense in time of total war. Cowgill and Vivian both demanded that Trevor-Roper be dismissed from the service. It was then left to C to render the judgment of Solomon. That he did.

C recognized that the relationship between Cowgill and Trevor-Roper was such that Trevor-Roper could not remain with Section V. On the other hand, he did not wish to lose Trevor-Roper's services nor do anything that would reflect adversely on his record. C therefore removed Trevor-Roper from Cowgill's service and transferred him and his team to Section VIII, the Communications Branch, which was run by Richard Gambier-Parry, an old Etonian who was more used to independent characters such as Trevor-Roper. Thus, possibly through Philby's engineering skills, Trevor-Roper, Kim's only rival at War Station XB, vanished from the central scene, although he continued to work on the Canaris problem. What these skirmishes achieved, without anyone being fully aware of it, was to prepare the way for the fall of Cowgill and his replacement by his brilliant subordinate, Kim Philby.

By C's own statement, at this same time — March 1943 — Canaris managed to get word to C that he would like a meeting to find a way to end the war, based on the death of Hitler. The theory was that this was Hitler's war and it would last only as long as Hitler was alive. C was disposed to meet Canaris at a castle on the Portuguese-Spanish frontier through the good offices of Nicolas Franco, the Spanish ambassador to Portugal and a brother of Generalissimo Franco, but the necessary permission of the foreign secretary, Anthony Eden, was not forthcoming. The policy of unconditional surrender had only recently been announced, and any compromise of that declaration would serve only to incense Stalin. Thus C replied that he was not interested in meeting Canaris.[7]

However, the doctrine of unconditional surrender did not preclude meetings between Allied secret agents and German emissaries for the purposes of intelligence, a term that included deception, espionage, and counterespionage. ISOS showed that Canaris was traveling widely during the spring of 1943, especially in Iberia. These ISOS have survived in Donovan's papers and make it clear that Philby knew where Canaris would be on any date, the names of the hotels where he would stay, and his aliases. Philby therefore formed a plan to assassinate Canaris — an action that would have been much in the Soviet interest, for Russia had no desire for a rebellion in Germany while the Red Army was as far to the east as it was — and he communicated this to C. As Philby recorded:

In 1943, I received [a decrypt] revealing that Canaris was to visit Spain. He was going to drive from Madrid to Seville, stopping overnight at a town called Manzanares. I knew the town well from Spanish civil war days, and I knew that the only place Canaris could stay would be at the Parador.

So I sent Cowgill a memo suggesting that we let SOE know about it in case they wanted to mount an operation against Canaris. From what I knew about the Parador, it wouldn't have been difficult to have tossed a couple of grenades into his bedroom.

Cowgill approved and sent my memo on up to C. Cowgill showed me a reply a couple of days later. Menzies had written: "I want no action whatsoever taken against the Admiral."[8]

In Cowgill's view, C protected Canaris on the grounds that as long as the admiral was in office, C would not lose the intelligence war. And it was against this political background that, partly at least through Philby's actions in the case, Canaris was toppled from office in February 1944.

Only rarely in great wars do individuals count for much in high councils, but in this case they did. In February 1944 at Istanbul, Erich Vermehren and his wife, the former Elizabeth Countess von Plettenberg, were members of the Abwehr with a special interest in the British political position in the Near East. Neither Vermehren nor his wife was unknown to Section V, for early in 1943 they made an attempt to defect to the British at Lisbon. In November 1943, they offered to defect again but were instead recruited into the XX Committee, where Erich labored under the code name Junior. There was, consequently, much about them in the Section V personality indexes. These showed that there was a strong pro-British, anti-Nazi streak in the family, and there were also signs of instability in both Erich and the countess. Vermehren's father, Kurt, a lawyer born in about 1893, was a member of an old Lübeck family connected to the Hanseatic League, and through the ancient trade between England and the Baltic ports they had developed an admiration for England.[9]

Erich Vermehren was a brilliant student at the Gymnasium and he went on to the university. Twice he was awarded a Rhodes Scholarship but was prevented from accepting when the Nazi authorities confiscated his passport in 1938. Also, Vermehren was related by marriage to Dr. Franz von Papen, the former German chancellor and now, in 1944, the German ambassador at Turkey and therefore Vermehren's head of mission.

In February 1944, acting with the authority of London, Nicholas Elliott, Cowgill's representative at Istanbul, received yet another defection overture from Vermehren. While both C and Cowgill had much to gain from inducing a defection, they also had much to lose: the defector would almost certainly bring with him the German codes and ciphers as evidence of his goodwill and high rank, and these C was already reading, but the defector's colleagues would realize that the codes and ciphers were gone and would inform Berlin, which would change its code and cipher systems, including those being read by the British code breakers. For a time, perhaps, War Station XB would lose the ISOS decrypts that were illuminating the German secret political world, and the code breakers would have to try to break the new ciphers at a vital time — just before the invasion.

There were great dangers in encouraging these defections. But the question was whether a greater danger lay in the continuing existence of the Abwehr. Through Philby and Trevor-Roper, C knew already that the Abwehr and the Sicherheitsdienst were locked in a battle for primacy and that a serious run of defections could bring the Abwehr crashing down just as D-Day itself was culminating. Hitler would then be left without an effective intelligence service as the Western powers began the campaign in northwest Europe. On balance, it seems, C decided to risk the effects defections might have on the code-breaking and deception operations, and he authorized them.

In quick succession senior Abwehr personnel defected in the Argentine. Then came the Turkish desertions. Four of the agents went over to the OSS, the Vermehrens to Elliott. Like Philby's leakage of the names of the Abwehr's personnel in Spain over the Bodden operation in 1942, the defections were then leaked to the Associated Press in Istanbul on February 9, 1944. The bulletin concerning the Vermehrens' defection has survived in Donovan's papers:

> Istanbul, Feb. 9 (A.P.) — A German who deserted the Nazis and gave himself up to the British several days ago was officially identified by an Allied spokesman today as Erich Vermehren, clerk to the military attaché in the German embassy here and son of Petra Vermehren, German authoress.
>
> Vermehren's wife, the former Countess Elisabeth Vermehren, accompanied him. His mother is now in Lisbon.
>
> The 24-year-old attaché and his wife declared that they had deserted the Germans because they were disgusted with Nazi brutality. He is said to possess detailed information of greatest value. At the German embassy he served directly under Dr. Paul Leverkühn, the assistant military attaché.
>
> Vermehren said that he and his wife reached Allied controlled territory despite every effort by Germans in Turkey to apprehend him. Ambassador Franz von Papen interrupted a vacation in the Bursa mountains to go to Istanbul to direct an investigation into his disappearance.[10]

Vermehren, it was said in subsequent bulletins, had been involved in much of the Abwehr War Organization throughout the exceedingly sensitive region of the Balkan states. A special commission arrived from Berlin to investigate the security of the German Embassy's main ciphers, including those of the German diplomatic service, the Abwehr, and of the Sicherheitsdienst, the foreign intelligence service of the SS. The commission claimed to have obtained knowledge of links between the Vermehrens and a treasonable group of high rank in Berlin, including Count Helmuth von Moltke, a high-ranking figure of the German Supreme Command; Ludwig Gehre of Canaris's staff; and Otto Kiep, a former German consul general in New York City. All were considered to be especially dangerous because they were in contact through intermediaries with the Allied Supreme Command, von Moltke with the United States through Donovan of the OSS. Only recently he had given the OSS a long paper on the nature of the conspiracy against Hitler and proposals for an armistice should the plotters succeed. Von Moltke had been arrested for high treason on his return to Berlin and was in the Gestapo's prison, awaiting the guillotine. He was duly executed. On their arrival in London, the Vermehrens were, for a time, placed in Philby's charge, and while Philby's men interrogated them, they stayed at Dora Philby's apartment in Drayton Gardens.

As to the defections, the consequences for the German intelligence system were calamitous. For years Heinrich Himmler had been complaining to Hitler of the treason and defeatism of Canaris and the Abwehr. Hitler's reaction to the run of defections was to summon Canaris to his office to explain what was happening inside his service. When Canaris pointed out that the defections were no more than an indication of what was a fact — that Germany was losing the war — Hitler flew at him, knocking over the table between them in his anger. Canaris was dismissed as chief of the Abwehr, but no other action was taken against him. He was given what Trevor-Roper described as "a dignified sinecure" on the Economic Warfare Commission near Potsdam so that "none might deduce too disastrous consequences from his fall."[11]

Otherwise, on February 12, only four months before the invasion, Hitler signed an order combining the Abwehr and the Sicherheitsdienst into a single service under party control. A rump of the old Abwehr remained autonomous, under Wehrmacht control, for the special purposes of military espionage. But the rest of the Abwehr was carved up and divided between, mainly, the Sicherheitsdienst and the Gestapo. There followed a period of nearly six months in which the German intelligence bureaucracy was reorganized, at a time when Germany would have been better served if the secret services had been able to give their entire attention to the task for which they had been created — watching out for the invasion and guarding the Reich against both internal and external enemies. But no. The high-level administrative conferences began on February 20 and lasted until September 1, the entire duration of Neptune, the period when Overlord was prepared and executed.

These conferences were accompanied by considerable reshuffling of personnel, files, furniture, offices, telephones, communications, and procedures, and the installation of new filing equipment. The most intensive part of the reorganization took place in May, when the German services would otherwise have been entirely occupied with operations against Overlord; and in the end the higher degree of efficiency hoped for eluded Himmler. The German intelligence system emerged with the same personnel doing the same work but under different leadership. At the beginning of June, only a few days before the invasion was due to be launched, the reorganization was completed with the establishment of a new military intelligence service, the Militaerisches Amt (known as Amt Mil), as a branch of the Sicherheitsdienst but with an army chief, Colonel Georg Hansen, whose political views were the same as those of Canaris. A new Amt Mil-SD headquarters was created and placed under the control of Brigadeführer Walter Schellenberg, chief of the foreign espionage service of the Sicherheitsdienst. A party intellectual, aged thirty-four, Schellenberg was the son of a Saarland piano manufacturer and a lawyer by trade. He was gentle, persuasive, seductive, and known chiefly as a specialist in society intelligence and what Hitler called the Purple International, the European aristocracy and plutocracy. He was known, too, as an expert in certain types of special operations, notably the kidnapping of persons considered useful to the Reich. One of his coups had been the arrest in November 1939 of Payne Best and R. H. Stevens. He had been in Lisbon when the Duke and Duchess of Windsor arrived there in 1940; his purpose was to kidnap them and bring them to a place in the German sphere of influence where the duke would be made the puppet king of England. In this mission he failed because, he claimed after the war, he had been poisoned by the British Secret Service officers who guarded the duke and duchess.

In the defection of the Vermehren group, therefore, Cowgill and Philby had scored a remarkable victory, one in which Philby may well have been the leading light; the operation bore his signature. Canaris had been eliminated at a critical hour; the German intelligence system had been disrupted; and therefore the German Supreme Command was vulnerable to the vast deception schemes now under way to mislead Hitler about Overlord. As to the quality of Schellenberg's new

intelligence service, Chester Wilmot, the leading newspaper correspondent during the invasion, would write in his *Struggle for Europe:*

> In trying to estimate Allied intentions, the German High Command
> was working under a serious handicap, for its Foreign Intelligence
> Service, now under Himmler's sinister control, was producing infor-
> mation of the most doubtful character. Himmler's absorption of the
> Abwehr in March could not have come at a less opportune time.
> Inefficient though Canaris's organization was, it did exist, and Himmler
> had no adequate substitute. For the most part the Gestapo types
> whom he sent abroad were gauche thugs, ignorant and inept . . . and
> in the weeks immediately preceding the invasion Himmler's men
> were deliberately swamped with "secret information" which they had
> neither the time nor the wit to sift and appraise. The German intel-
> ligence machine became clogged, and the material sent in by the
> Abwehr who were still in the field was lost among the rubbish. After
> the war in the records of the German Admiralty the Allies found a
> dossier containing some 250 individual reports from agents dealing
> with the time and place of the invasion. Of these, only one, from a
> French colonel in Algiers, was correct, but this had been filed away
> unheeded with the dross. The majority opinion gave July as the month
> and the Pas de Calais as the place.[12]

Undeniably, Philby played a major role as an executor of the cover
and deception plans, Bodyguard and Fortitude, which affected, as the
deception doctrine provided, "the fundamental reasoning power" of
the German Supreme Command. Furthermore, he still controlled the
Abwehr and Sicherheitsdienst decrypts, which revealed so completely
the German reaction to the deceptions he was providing; he knew
what the Germans knew. And his superb handling of his part of the
operation to prevent the English Channel from "running red with
blood" became, doubtless, another reason that he came to enjoy the
personal admiration and confidence of C.

Philby was the born professional in the Allied secret services.

The British, American, and Canadian armies began landing on Normandy in the first hours of June 6, 1944, despite a series of crosses
and double-crosses in which Philby, having already helped to disrupt
the German intelligence services, himself played a principal role. The
object of all intelligence endeavors at that time and in the coming
weeks of heavy battle was Plan Fortitude, intended to mislead the
German commanders about the key elements in D-Day — the date,
the time, the place, and the weight of force to be landed. And in the

background there was Churchill, fearing Stalin's treachery. As he stated, Stalin "would have ample means of blackmail when the invasion began by refusing to advance beyond a certain point, or even tipping the wink to the Germans that they can move troops into the West. Although I have tried in every way to put myself in sympathy with these Communist leaders, I cannot feel the slightest trust or confidence in them."[13]

Three parachute divisions, the spearhead of the invasion, began landing in Normandy at about two o'clock on the morning of June 6, followed at daybreak by the First American and the Second British armies, the assault forces. Behind them waited three army groups. As part of Fortitude, the Allied counterintelligence and security services made an audacious move: they informed the enemy that the invasion had begun. Their purpose was to build up the credentials of a double agent called Garbo, who had been the chief German intelligence officer in the British Isles since his arrival in 1942. Philby and his section, with ISOS, had helped to identify him, and he agreed to work under the control of the XX Committee against his German control in Lisbon. Over the years Garbo had proved to be an ingenious and resourceful double agent; his controlling officer, Tomas Harris, one of Philby's close friends, proved to be as ingenious and resourceful. Garbo and Harris were now to play the key role in the operations over the coming hours, days, and weeks to confuse the German High Command about Allied intentions and capabilities.

Just after midnight of June 5–6, with Philby watching each ISOS decrypt for signs that the Germans had obtained foreknowledge of the invasion, and while the invasion fleets were approaching the Norman shore for the assault at daybreak, the High Command gave its assent to the boldest stratagem of the war — one that Sir Ronald Wingate, one of the deception planners, later noted reached into Hitler's headquarters in the Bavarian Alps. The circumstances were propitious for such a deception, for Hitler had retired early that night, had taken a sleeping pill, and had given orders that he was not to be awakened until his morning conference with his generals at ten o'clock. Expecting that the Allies would cancel the operation because of a severe spring storm, coming in fast from the western Atlantic, most of the German commanders were on leave or attending map-reading exercises at Rennes. They were therefore remote from their command posts. They were also confident that the Allies would have to postpone their operation until the July moon — by which time the V1 and V2 missiles would be ready to devastate the invasion forces in England.

But the Supreme Allied Commander, General Dwight D. Eisenhower, having been advised that there would be a break in the weather that would favor the invasion, decided to make the assault that night. The Garbo operation then followed. Just after midnight he went on the air by wireless to ask his controller in Madrid to keep that station open throughout the night, as he was expecting vital intelligence. The Madrid controller agreed. But when, at 2:30 A.M., Garbo called Madrid to report that the first phase of the invasion had begun — a leak calculated to ensure that Garbo would be listened to with great care over the coming days, weeks, and months — there was no reply. Garbo called again on several occasions before daybreak without getting a reply, and assumed the German operators were asleep. His inability to transmit the information required some rapid script rewriting, but Tomas Harris had prepared a fresh scenario for transmission to Madrid at daybreak, when the assault troops would be disembarking. Here, behind the few wireless messages, lay what Norman Holmes Pearson would call the "conscientious and clever men" who were "the ecologists of double agency," a game where "everything was interrelated" and where "everything must be kept in balance." For "in the end there was an enemy to be induced down the wrong path, wrong for them but right for us."[14]

In his first and second messages to Madrid on D-Day, Garbo did not mention that he had been unable to contact the Madrid operator throughout the preceding hours. But having transmitted a bulletin on the movement of Allied forces in England on June 6, Garbo found an occasion to work into his report this bit of self-congratulation: "Fortunately this first operation has been robbed of the surprise which the enemy wanted to achieve with it, thanks to information I was able to pass to you on the night of the invasion."[15] When Garbo's controller in Madrid asked what he meant, advising that he had had no such message, Garbo exploded with contrived but convincing fury: "Were it not for my faith in the Führer and the vital importance of his mission to save Europe from the twin tyrannies of Bolshevism and Anglo-American plutocracy, I would this very day give up my work, conscious as I am of my failure."

Mortified at the prospect of losing the confidence of his most valued spy, the German controller sent Garbo a long signal emphasizing Germany's appreciation for "your splendid and valued work." He added: "I wish to stress that your work over the last few weeks has made it possible for our command to be completely forewarned and prepared ... I beg of you to continue with us in the supreme and decisive hours of the struggle for the future of Europe." Only very reluctantly did Garbo agree to continue in the German service. The scene was set for what was to prove the decisive deception of Overlord.

At 7:30 P.M. on June 8, 1944, when it became evident that Hitler had ordered the mobile divisions of the 15th Army in the Calais area to go to the assistance of the 7th Army in Normandy, a strength sufficient to overwhelm the two Allied field armies now landing, Garbo was given a prefatory message to send to his controller at Madrid to ensure that a misleading signal was read personally by the chief of the German service there: "Have had a very busy and anxious day. Hope to give you what I consider to be my most important report to date. Trust you will be standing by at 22 hours GMT."

Then, in the first minutes of June 9, Garbo's wireless operator, a British signals sergeant, began to transmit a message that took 129 minutes. Its object was to force Hitler to cancel the order to the 15th Army to reinforce the 7th. On Omaha Beach, the Americans were in trouble overcoming German resistance. If Omaha went, the entire front might collapse. In the message, Garbo warned Berlin that the Normandy operation was a trap and that the main operation was about to take place near Calais. He concluded with the imprecation:

> I trust you will submit my reports for urgent consideration by our High Command. Moments may be decisive at the present time. Before they take a false step through lack of full knowledge of the facts they ought to have at their disposal all the present information. I transmit this report with the conviction that the present assault is a trap set with the purpose of making us move all our reserves in a rushed strategic re-disposition which we would later regret.

All these reports were written by Tomas Harris with the approval of the G2 at Eisenhower, and Montgomery, headquarters.

On its receipt in Madrid, Garbo's report was sent to the Sicherheitsdienst in Berlin for comment and transmission to Hitler's headquarters at Berchtesgaden. When the warning arrived, an SD analyst wrote on it:

> The dispatch is believable. The reports received in the last week from the [Garbo] enterprise have been confirmed almost without exception and are to be described as especially valuable. The main line of enquiry must now be concentrated on the enemy group of forces in eastern and southeastern England.

As Cowgill was to recall, Philby's work reminded him of an X-ray being taken of a giraffe as it consumed buns. Through ISOS, Philby could establish every movement of the buns — Garbo's deceptive messages — and the effect they were having on the giraffe, that is, the German intelligence service. It was a homely simile but an accurate one. Through ISOS the War Station was able to follow each development in the Garbo saga.

Later that same afternoon — the afternoon of June 9 — Hitler read the warning from Garbo. Partly because it was from the Pas de Calais that he was about to launch his missile bombardment of London, and believing that the Allies would wish to liquidate the threat in their earliest military operation, and partly because Hitler was inclined to believe that the enemy would follow the strategy that was now unfolding, he now acted to maintain his strength in the Pas de Calais sector. He ordered that the movement of the 15th Army tank and infantry reinforcements to Normandy be suspended until the situation in France was clarified. At about 7:30 A.M. on Saturday, June 10, Field Marshal Keitel, chief of the German Supreme Command, telephoned the German commander in the West, Field Marshal Gerd von Rundstedt, to order that the movement of the strong armored and infantry units from the Pas de Calais be stopped.

Rundstedt obeyed; the 15th Army's orders were canceled and the divisions involved remained under 15th Army command. Further, Hitler ordered reinforcements to the Calais area. On D-Day, the 15th Army had three tank and nineteen infantry and parachute divisions. A month later, twenty-two infantry and two tank divisions were still there waiting expectantly for an army group that had never existed in the first place. The German command on the Normandy front was deprived of the reinforcements that might otherwise have repulsed the Allied armies now digging in at Normandy. Yet the German ring around the bridgeheads remained strong, despite the surprise and uncertainty that Fortitude had wrought. Garbo remained, and his large band of nonexistent agents was in play until the last day of the war. He celebrated the third anniversary of his service as the German's main agent in Britain with a vast letter to his controlling officer in Madrid, Carlos. In his usual flowery style, it was written in secret ink with Garbo's help by Tomas Harris, and it concluded:

> On approaching the completion of the third year of my stay here I now, more than ever, feel pride in my work and desire to prove myself worthy of all the evidence of friendship which you have expressed on me. I feel more than ever a sensation of hatred, more than death, for our enemy, and an ever increasing irresistible urge to destroy his entire existence. The arrogance of this rabble can only be conceived when you live among them.

In the course of the letter he thanked Carlos for all his assistance —
which included the £33,000 Carlos had sent him by safe hand over
the years — and noted that

> one could not say to an English Lord what one may say to a National
> Socialist Comrade. The former would consider himself ridiculous if
> he had to accept an observation from a subordinate. We accept,
> within the discipline of hierarchy, that advice of subordinates. Thus,
> the Great Germany has become what it is. Thus, it has been able to
> deposit such great confidence in the man who governs it, knowing
> that he is not a democratic despot but a man of low birth who had
> only followed an ideal. The Fatherland! Humanity! Justice and Com-
> radeship!

Garbo ended the letter: "Receive a cordial embrace from your comrade and servant. JUAN."

Yet for all the surprise and uncertainty caused by Garbo within the
German command on the Far Shore, the German ring around the
bridgeheads remained. The Allied command therefore needed to play
another card to disrupt the enemy. This may be called the Canaris
card, for, simultaneously with Montgomery's operations to break out
into Belgium and France, Hitler's enemies in the German General
Staff attempted to kill the Führer. It is not known whether the encouragement to the generals to kill Hitler and overthrow the Third Reich
represented official Allied policy conveyed by Philby. This will be known
only when the archives of the Political Warfare Executive are opened
to the public in A.D. 2025.

Facing bitter resistance from the German Army on the Norman front,
the field commander of the Allied armies, General Sir Bernard Montgomery — St. John Philby's best man at his marriage to Dora all those
years before — prepared his breakout operations, Cobra on the American front, Goodwood on the British. At the same time, the Germans
began the bombardment by missile of, mainly, London, a bombardment that, before it was ended, caused thousands of casualties and
damaged more than a million buildings in and around London, including Philby's home in Acol Road, Maida Vale. It was rendered
uninhabitable and was later demolished. Philby's mother, Dora, and
two sisters were in the house when the missile fell close by, but they
were unharmed although badly bruised and cut by flying glass, bricks,
and slates. It was against this background that a German secret agent,

Otto John, reappeared in Madrid to report to one of Kim Philby's agents, a certain Graham Maingott.

Otto John had been known to Philby and to Trevor-Roper since 1942 as a corporation lawyer with Lufthansa, the German civil airline. As such he was able to fly between Berlin and Madrid; behind him was the German intelligence master, Admiral Canaris, and certain important German generals; in May 1942 he had arrived in Madrid with a letter from Prince Louis Ferdinand, a relative of the old kaiser, Wilhelm II. Prince Louis had it in mind to overthrow Hitler and reestablish the old Hohenzollern monarchy at the head of "the new Germany." John contacted Juan Terraza, the deputy secretary in the Spanish Foreign Office and very pro-British, and asked him to arrange a meeting with a British and an American official in the peninsula. His purpose was to lay the groundwork for peace negotiations between the Western powers and the leaders of the German resistance movement. His mission failed, blocked perhaps, even probably, by Philby.

But in July 1943, according to the notes of an interrogation of Otto John, almost certainly in the hand of Trevor-Roper, who was still at work on "the Canaris problem" and the loyalty of the Abwehr, Otto John advised one of Philby's officers in the peninsula, Miss Rita Winsor, that the main center of Hitler's missile program was at Peenemünde, a town on the German Baltic. That information, it is stated in Trevor-Roper's notes, led to the attack on Peenemünde by 597 heavy bombers of the Royal Air Force on August 7, 1943. There is, moreover, further testimony that revealed the Peenemünde information in the diaries of Robert Bruce Lockhart, director-general of the Foreign Office's Political Warfare Executive, who had a close interest in John's movements and activities.

Plainly, therefore, John was a member of a determined conspiracy in Berlin to bring about an end to the war at all costs, a fact that could not have been lost on Philby, whose Iberian section was handling his case. Four months later, in December 1943, John reappeared in the peninsula, this time representing himself as the agent of a powerful anti-Hitler group of generals, industrialists, and labor and religious leaders led by Field Marshal Fritz Erich von Manstein, a tank warfare specialist regarded by many in the German General Staff as the leading strategist in the German Army. Manstein had recently been dismissed from his command by Hitler for the failure of the great German counteroffensive at Kursk in July 1943 — a failure caused, in part at least, by Ultra intelligence conveyed to his Soviet case officer by a member of the Cambridge Five, John Cairncross, who worked with

Ultra at Bletchley as, by now, an officer of the Secret Service.[16] Again, it seems, John's mission was blocked by Philby. But this time Otto John, acting throughout at great risk to his life, had devised an alternate route to communicate with the Allied governments: he tried to approach General Eisenhower through the French Red Cross delegate at the Gaulliste embassy in Madrid.[17]

Two months later, in February 1944, John was again in Madrid, and again in April. Afterward he wrote in a paper for Philby, called "Some Facts and Aspects of the 20th July Plot Against Hitler," how he met one of Philby's agents in Iberia, a man he named as Graham Maingott. There was an agent of that name in Iberia working for Philby's Section V. John revealed the composition of what he called "a shadow government with military support" to overthrow Hitler. During his discussion with Maingott, the Briton, in John's view, "meant to urge me to press for the carrying out of the proposed coup d'état." Whether Maingott communicated anything else — for example, the Western governments' attitudes toward the conspiracy if it succeeded — is not clear from the evidence. But John flew back to Berlin to inform his principals, Klaus Schenck, Colonel Count von Stauffenberg, an aristocrat in a high position on the German General Staff who had personal access to Hitler, and Colonel Georg Hansen, who had succeeded Canaris as chief of military intelligence in the Nazi Party's intelligence service, the Sicherheitsdienst, when the Abwehr was liquidated by Hitler in February 1944. In Berlin, John claimed, he told Hansen that it had "already struck twelve and that imminent developments which we desired could only be achieved by action and a fait accompli, if at all."[18]

John returned to Madrid on May 15, sixteen days before D-Day, and spoke again to one of Philby's agents, either Miss Winsor or Maingott, for this statement appears in Trevor-Roper's notes concerning John: "Army planning coup but no hurry — Italian campaign being so slow." He remained in Madrid until July 19, when he flew suddenly to Berlin at the order of Hansen, which had been sent over the Lufthansa wires and received by John in Madrid on July 15. The text said something to the effect that, as Trevor-Roper recorded in his notes, "Opposition Group now ready for action and needing his help." On arriving in Berlin, John made contact with his brother, who was also in the plot, and was told that "the thing" was about "to go off," probably on July 20. It did. That it did so constitutes one of the most interesting political and intelligence events of World War II.

The fact that an attempt was to be made on Hitler's life had been known by the Anglo-American secret circle at the highest levels in both

Washington and London. But, through Philby's interference in the free flow of John's reports, the OSS knew more about the plot than did the SIS. Of the highest importance to the Goodwood and Cobra breakout operations were Dulles's messages from Switzerland dated July 13 and 14 from his contact with the conspirators. At a time when the official British political guidance to the Supreme Command was that "these people . . . won't act without our backing, which, if given, might gravely embarrass us later," Dulles advised the OSS that "an attempt to assassinate Hitler might take place at any time."[19] While Dulles was skeptical that Hitler would be attacked — there had been so many such reports since late 1942 that he was not prepared to give this latest one much credit — nonetheless he reported, too, that the German government was aware of "impending revolt in high military circles" and was "preparing to place the military establishment under Nazi control."

That this intelligence reached the highest allied military authority seems evident, for in his diary entry of July 21, Field Marshal Sir Alan Brooke, chief of the British General Staff, recorded: "This morning when I turned on the 8 A.M. news I was astounded to hear of the attempt on Hitler's life, although this was exactly what I had been expecting for some time."[20] General George C. Marshall, the leading American soldier, expressed the same expectation and the same surprise; and there is in the papers of General Donovan of the OSS a file code-named Breakers, which contained the plotters' reports at each stage of the plot to Allen Dulles at OSS headquarters in Switzerland. But equally, as Trevor-Roper states, Philby, who still had charge of the Iberian section of Section V at this time, did not communicate his knowledge within the Secret Service.

This seems to have been the case, for immediately after a bomb exploded in Hitler's headquarters, C felt compelled to ask David Bruce, the OSS chief in London, for his file on the plot. The Breakers file was sent to C at once, but his request on such a weighty matter did not go unnoticed by Bruce. As he wrote in his diary eight days later: "The truth is that, on the positive intelligence side, Broadway is lamentably weak — especially as regards Germany — and most of the reports they send us are duplicates of those already received by us from foreign intelligence services."[21] How could it be that C, who had followed the anti-Hitler movement since 1936, was so ignorant of what had occurred on July 20 that he had to ask a rival — and none too friendly — service for its file? Where was his own? C himself must have been surprised by the amount of knowledge acquired by Dulles and by the contents of a proposal on May 13, 1944, that the conspirators stood "ready to help our armed units get into Germany under the condition that we agree to allow them to hold the Eastern Front."[22] The proposal went on to state in detail that German forces loyal to the conspiracy would assist:

1. Three allied parachute divisions to land in the Berlin region, with the assistance of local army commanders.
2. Amphibian landing operations of major proportions either at or near Bremen and Hamburg along the German coast.
3. The isolation of Hitler and high Nazi officials by trustworthy German units posted in the Munich region.

The German commanders in the West would "cease resistance and aid Allied landings, once the Nazis had been ousted."[23] The conspirators were willing to act if they could deal "directly with the West Allies alone after overthrowing the Nazi regime." They would cooperate with any leftist elements except the communists, "as the group feared the political and ideological sway over Central Europe by Bolshevism." The file also contained Dulles's advice that he thought little of any of this as he doubted whether the generals would have the "political courage" to act. The group's activities might therefore be "useful to undermine the morale of the top echelon in the German Army."

But no such proposals were acceptable to Philby. The Soviet interest that he served so ardently would not be furthered by any understanding, formal or informal, with the German General Staff and its intelligence service. In the event, the conspiracy, brave as it might be, was used to undermine the military leadership of the German Army.

What had occurred on July 20 was that early in the morning, Stauffenberg flew to Hitler's headquarters at Rastenberg in East Prussia to report on the preparations by the Home Army to meet the advancing Russians; the floodgates on the Eastern Front had burst open and the Red Army was advancing rapidly into Eastern and Central Europe. In East Prussia the Soviet leading elements were only fifty miles from Rastenberg. At the meeting with Hitler, Stauffenberg took a two-pound British-made bomb (captured stores, so it was claimed) from his briefcase and placed it close to Hitler and under the map table at which he and his high commanders were working. Stauffenberg then left the room and watched from a knoll nearby. The bomb exploded with such tremendous force that he estimated that Hitler must have been killed. He then flew back to Berlin to implement Valkyrie, a plan by which the General Staff intended to seize Germany and all Europe from the Nazis' control.

But Stauffenberg was mistaken. By the devil's luck the blast went in another direction, killing and wounding everyone in its path, and Hitler escaped with what seemed at the time to be superficial wounds. Later the blast did prove to have affected him much more seriously, but, having survived, Hitler took action against Valkyrie, and it failed everywhere except in France. There the German General Staff arrested the Nazi leadership in Paris and prepared to send envoys to Eisenhower with an offer (along with much else besides) to stop the missile bombardment of England. But Valkyrie did not prosper. Hitler launched a counteraction, and the SS was just able to maintain his power of command over the German Army. His staff canceled the Valkyrie directive to all commands at the very moment of its transmission from the communications center at Home Army headquarters.

Immediately a blood purge began throughout the Greater German Reich. The leadership of the conspiracy was either executed that same night or arrested for high treason and then executed. On the French front both the new commander in chief, Field Marshal Günther von Kluge, and the army group commander, Field Marshal Erwin Rommel, were implicated in the plot, and both committed suicide. Many other important officers were similarly implicated, and the military command structure in the West collapsed at the very moment Montgomery launched Goodwood and Cobra, on July 25. The breakout was completed by August 13. By August 25 Paris had been liberated, and by September 14 the Allied armies were closing in on the German frontier. In the East between July 10 and December the Red Army drove Finland out of the war, liberated the Crimea, drove to the environs of Warsaw, conquered Rumania, caused the defection of Bulgaria, drove through to Latvia on the Baltic, invested Budapest, took Belgrade. By September it seemed that the Grand Alliance had won the war, that the scene was set for the unconditional surrender of the Third Reich. That this did not occur, and that the war would last a further eight months, owed much to Philby's blocking of John's reports. As a result, the Joint Intelligence Committee, generally disposed in the past to undervalue the German resistance movement for reasons of Russian policy, again underrated its importance at the very time when there was a sudden and marked interest by the other high intelligence authorities.

But it was all over now for the German opposition, which represented the remnants of the intellectual and social elite of Germany.

Some seven thousand people were liquidated by the Gestapo. Otto John escaped back to Madrid on July 24, four days after the attempt on Hitler's life. Under dangerous circumstances, for the Gestapo was after him, the British Secret Service exfiltrated him to Lisbon and thence to London. John was one of the few to escape. Stauffenberg and his immediate circle, John's brother among them, were executed by firing squad the night of July 30. Many thousands of others were arrested, including the families of all the key conspirators. Canaris, too, was arrested and executed.

Philby left a trace of his thoughts about this carnage. In 1988 he admitted having played a part in the obliteration of the German General Staff and its intelligence service. "One of the reasons I acted as I did was," he stated, "because the total defeat of Germany was almost a personal matter for me. I had strong feelings about the war." There was, too, his statement, again made in the context of the July plot but without actually associating himself with it, that he had been "directly responsible for the deaths of a considerable number of Germans, thus doing my modest bit towards winning the war."[24] When Erich and Elisabeth Vermehren arrived in London from the prolonged debriefing that followed their defection at Istanbul, they stayed with Philby at his new home in Carlyle Square, an elegant and fashionable part of London. Devout Catholics and members of the German Catholic underground movement, they are said to have provided Philby with a list of leading Catholic activists whom the Anglo-American powers would find useful in establishing an anticommunist government in Germany after the war. When, later, the Allies tried to contact these people, most of them were found to be dead.

After this triumph of deception and disruption on the grand scale, Philby suddenly and quietly disappeared from the War Station to take up a new and major post in the Secret Service, whence he could act in the Soviet interest with the greatest possible effect at a time when the forces of the world revolution emerged to seize power in France, Belgium, the Netherlands, Norway, northern Italy, and all Central Europe and the Balkans from Stettin on the Baltic to Trieste on the Adriatic.

In September 1944 there came a sharp change in policy. Churchill looked across the world scene and decided, "The Soviet menace, to my eyes, had already replaced the Nazi foe."[25] The Cold War had begun. The prime minister instructed C to revive R5, his anti-Soviet service, to handle the large new problem of Red Russia triumphant. By the autumn, the Red Army's summer offensive, launched to support

D-Day, stood two thirds of the way from the old Soviet frontier to the English Channel.

The German card was being played anew, just as it had after World War I when Churchill sent an agent to Munich to see the old enemy on the Western Front, General Erich Ludendorff. Ludendorff had proposed an Anglo-German army to march on Moscow: "Tell Churchill this. We are standing at the crossroads, and a decision has to be come to. Either the world is going down under Bolshevism or the world is going to kill it."[26] It was exactly the same twenty-five years on. The world was going down under Bolshevism, and Philby had been selected to lead the department responsible for killing it — and also to keep an eye on Donovan and the OSS. They, too, had become ambitious and dangerous; in the first days of 1945, at a conference between Donovan and his chiefs in Europe, the decision was taken that

> OSS should proceed on the basis that the comparable Russian and British Services would seek to penetrate the U.S. Sector and that OSS should not limit its secret activities to the U.S. Sector. Such arrangements should be exclusive of such open arrangements as might be made between OSS and [the Soviet Secret Service, NKVD] for exchange of information and missions.[27]

The world had begun to turn anew as, with Europe in ruins and with conditions for the world revolution extant, the hot war began to turn into the Cold War — the final war between capitalism and communism. It was under these circumstances that Philby began to make his move to secure control of Section IX, the anti-Soviet branch of Section V. C's decision to reestablish Section IX followed the discovery that the Soviet secret services were still bent on penetrating SIS. He made his decision in March 1944, and an interim chief and a staff of three were appointed to resume the study of international communism and Soviet espionage.

Philby, realizing the political importance of this development, consulted his Soviet chief in London. Philby knew that after the defeat of Germany, which was now in the wind, there would be an economy drive; the two counterespionage sections would be combined and Cowgill would become its chief. His Soviet chief consulted with the Center in Moscow, and as Philby remembered in his memoir, he received instructions that:

> I must do everything, but *everything*, to ensure that I became head of Section IX . . . They fully realised that this meant that Cowgill must go. I made an attempt to demur, pointing out that my access to many

obscure places in the service had been gained through my refusal to engage in office intrigue. But the argument failed to convince. The importance of the post was well worth a temporary loss of reputation. Besides, my friend pointed out, quite rightly, that within a few months Cowgill, and the manner of his going, would be forgotten. There was truth in this, but I faced it with qualms. I liked and respected Cowgill, and had much to thank him for. But he was a prickly obstacle in the course laid down for me, so he had to go.[28]

He went. But not as quickly as the Soviet service wished. A drumbeat of complaint began to develop at MI5, where the Soviet interest was powerfully represented in the person of Anthony Blunt, the art expert who was also the personal assistant to the director of counterespionage, Guy Liddell. Cowgill was withholding ISOS from MI5 because (as Cowgill himself admitted in later years) "I did not like the look of the people to whom it was going."[29] He was not wrong, but to make such allegations — to his close friend and first lieutenant, Philby — was grave enough to warrant a tribunal. Cowgill, of course, never knew until too late that Philby passed his assertions to Burgess, who passed them to Blunt. In short order, Cowgill's goose was cooked. But before it was, intervention appeared from an unlikely source — Graham Greene, the chief of the Portuguese desk under Philby.

Greene must have known about the recreation of Section IX, and he certainly knew of Philby's communist past. When Philby began moving the pawns around at the War Station, Greene became aware that Philby was placing himself on the board to take over the post that would become Cowgill's. Tim Milne, Philby's deputy, also became aware. That winter, 1943–1944, Philby gave a dinner for Greene and Milne at the Café Royal in Regent's Street. With its decor of red, gold, and purple cascades of seraphim and cherubim playing flutes, the place still had the naughty air of the 1890s and Oscar Wilde's seduction of Lord Alfred Douglas.

Greene knew a good deal about his chief, and Philby knew that he knew. A Balliol man who had been a *Times* reporter just before Kim's appointment, Greene may have had Philby in mind when, in six weeks in 1938, he wrote *The Confidential Agent*. Philby had read and analyzed it. It concerned a secret agent, D, who was a communist without a party card, who was not trusted by the Communist Party, and who realized that the party was right not to trust him. As Greene said, writing about the circumstances in which *The Confidential Agent* was written, as a Catholic he could not help having a certain sympathy for anyone who believed sincerely in his faith, whatever that faith might be.

Greene saw that he and Milne had parts to play in Philby's plot against Cowgill, and he suddenly resigned from the service on June 2, 1944, four days before D-Day, that supreme moment in the intelligence history of the war. It seemed impossible that a senior officer could resign at such a time. The sense that the world stood on the brink of a mighty endeavor was palpable throughout Britain; no Briton engaged in vital war work, it may be thought, would quit his post at such a time or be let go by his seniors. But Greene did quit, going off to the Political Intelligence Department of the Foreign Office. Then he left crown service altogether and became a director of Eyre and Spottiswoode, the London publisher. As Greene explained later in his writings, he had spotted Philby's conspiracy against Cowgill, and "I resigned rather than accept the promotion which was a tiny cog in the machinery of his intrigue." He "attributed it then to a personal drive for power, the only characteristic in Philby which I thought disagreeable."[30]

Philby's conspiracy against Cowgill culminated in September 1944. With Vivian's knowledge and approval, he brought to Cowgill's attention the sorry state of counterintelligence in Italy, a secondary but still major front in the land war. When Philby suggested that he go there and straighten things out, Cowgill made a mistake: he presented Philby's suggestion to Vivian, who was still at headquarters as chief of counterespionage and security. Vivian felt that the matter required a more senior man than Philby, one who had good relations with the OSS. Cowgill flew off on what was to prove to be a month's absence, and during that time Vivian made his proposal that Philby be made chief of the new anti-Soviet section. As Vivian advised C, relations with the Security Service had gone from bad to worse over Cowgill's restrictive handling of the Most Secret Source decrypts, the pure gold of the secret war with Germany.

C had heard a great deal about the intrigues in the counterespionage service and about Philby's personal desire for advancement. Menzies therefore asked his acting personnel chief, Commander Kenneth Cohen, to obtain the opinion of the counterespionage staff about Cowgill and Philby. Inevitably Cohen asked Muggeridge for his candid opinion of Philby, remarking that anyone as able and energetic as Philby would almost certainly be offered a permanent post. Muggeridge answered the question with his usual sharp tongue. "You can't be serious, Kenneth. I like the man as well as you do, but I wouldn't give him house room." Why not? Cohen asked. "For one good reason," Muggeridge replied. "Kim simply can't be trusted. He happens to be one of nature's *farouches,* a wild man capable of turning the place upside down for his own ends." Muggeridge remarked later: "If Kenneth Cohen had believed me, and forced his superiors to listen, the secret service would have saved itself and Britain an awful lot of trouble."[31]

But there was no such intervention. With more speed than was usual at headquarters, the deed was done. Philby, who had been kept completely informed by Vivian, recorded of that supreme moment in his career so far:

> It was by no means the first time I had visited the *arcana.* But on this occasion, Miss Pettigrew and Miss Jones, the Chief's secretaries, seemed especially affable as I waited in their room for the green light to go on. The green light flashed, and I went in. For the first time, the Chief addressed me as "Kim," so I knew that no last-minute hitch had occurred . . . He told me that he had decided to act on Vivian's proposal and offer me the immediate succession . . . Had I anything to say? I had. Using the sort of I-hope-I-am-not-speaking-out-of-turn-Sir approach, I said that the appointment had been offered to me presumably because of the well-known incompatibility between Cowgill and his opposite numbers in MI5. I hoped that I would be able to avoid such quarrels in future. But who could make predictions? I would be much happier in the job if I knew for certain that MI5, the people with whom I would be dealing daily, had no objection to my appointment. It would make me just that much more confident. Besides, MI5 approval, officially given, would effectively protect the service against criticism from that quarter.

C quickly got the point "with evident appreciation," and as Philby recounted:

> Before long, he was throwing my own arguments back at me with force and conviction. He dismissed me with great warmth, saying that he would write to Sir David Petrie [chief of MI5] without delay. I left him in the hope that he would claim, and perhaps more than half believe, that the whole credit for the idea was his own. In due course, Petrie returned a very friendly reply. The Chief was delighted with it. So was I.

Within a few days, Philby began the move from Ryder Street to the seventh floor of Broadway, C's headquarters. He then went to see Menzies again, for as he related:

> I suggested to the Chief that, to regularize the position of the new Section IX, I should draft myself a charter for his signature. I cannot remember its exact wording. But it gave me responsibility, under the

Chief, for the collection and interpretation of information concerning Soviet and Communist espionage and subversion in all parts of
the world outside British territory. It also enjoined me to maintain
the closest liaison for the reciprocal exchange of intelligence on
these subjects with MI5. The Chief added a final clause. I was on no
account to have any dealings with any of the United States services.
The war was not yet over, and the Soviet Union was our ally. There
was no question of risking a leakage. The leakage which the Chief
had in mind was a leakage from the United States services to the
Russians. It was a piquant situation.[32]

Piquant it remained. Cowgill returned to London from his Italian
tour and only then did he learn that C had appointed Philby. He went
to C to challenge the decision on the grounds that he had been brought
from India in 1939 to head Section IX and that there had been agreement that he would return when the German war was over. C proved
apologetic but adamant, and Cowgill resigned with effect on January
1, 1945, well aware that he was the victim of an administrative intrigue
against him by Philby and Vivian. But this was not the end of his crown
service. Vivian was appointed town major of München-Gladbach, a city
in western Germany, after its capture. In 1947 C sent an officer to ask
Cowgill to take over Vivian's foreign counterintelligence service, but
Cowgill declined. "It was," he said, "a soul-rotting business and I had
had enough."[33]

What Philby intended by his intrigue was, of course, to make the
counterespionage branch of SIS into the unwitting intelligence arm
of the Soviet government. Toward that end, he prepared another paper and sent it to Menzies's Foreign Office representative, Robert
Cecil. According to Cecil, Philby's proposal included "a substantial
number of overseas stations to be held by officers under diplomatic
cover, who would be directly responsible to the Head of IX." With
hindsight, it is easy to see why "Philby pitched his demands so high
and why he aimed to create his own empire within SIS." Quite apart
from "his covert aims, it is also clear that he foresaw more plainly than
I the onset of the Cold War, bringing with it more menacing surveillance and making necessary more permanent use of diplomatic
cover. My vision of the future was at once more opaque and more
optimistic." Cecil rejected Philby's paper, or he tried to. He sent the
document back to Philby, suggesting that he scale down his demands.
Within hours Vivian and Philby had descended on Cecil, "upholding
their requirements and insisting that these be transmitted to the FO."
Aware that he was to be transferred in April 1945 to Washington, Cecil
gave way.[34]

More or less immediately Philby began to recruit men of high quality who, while entirely loyal to the British government, also held Philby
in high regard. Equipped with personal ciphers that enabled them to
communicate with Philby privately and directly, they began to leave
London and to situate themselves at every important British diplomatic outpost on foreign territory; their mission was to keep Philby
informed about Soviet, American, British, and French intelligence
activity in their areas of operations and to establish working relations
with the local foreign counterespionage and security systems where
they existed. Philby thereby created a worldwide empire consisting of
a headquarters staff of sixty officers, with another sixty officers overseas. In addition, he received all the dispatches from the British security and counterespionage authorities in the United States, Canada,
the Middle East, Southeast and East Asia, the African colonies, and
Australia. Since the target of all Western counterespionage agencies
had begun to swing against the Soviet services from the successful
conclusion of the invasion phase of Overlord onward, Philby became
perhaps the best-informed intelligence officer in the Western alliance.
And as Trevor-Roper would write in retrospect of this moment in
Philby's career:

> So he established himself at the very centre of the Service on the eve
> of the new struggle which was already threatening to break out: the
> Cold War. In secret, how he must have relished that triumph! . . . His
> Russian masters, too, must have smirked, a complacent, Machiavel-
> lian smirk, as they saw their chosen agent moving into this central post.[35]

As each Western European country was liberated, Philby went to its
capital to restore the old prewar counterespionage alliance that had
formed the basis of the *cordon sanitaire* against the Soviet Union. The
first and the most important of the new liaisons was with General
Charles de Gaulle's Services Spéciaux in Paris. First he sent Malcolm
Muggeridge to represent him and then he himself arrived soon afterward. Intelligence officers often were, and are, the harbingers of important political developments, and such was the Soviet menace that
urgent military talks had become a necessity.

Philby stayed with Colonel the Lord Rothschild at the Rothschild,
his famous mansion on the Avenue Marigny with its electrically operated bronze gates. Muggeridge accompanied his new chief on a visit
to Jacques Soustelle and André Dewavrin, de Gaulle's spymasters, at
their offices on the Boulevard Suchet, where Muggeridge found that
the French service was under "heavy attack" as a crypto-fascist organ.
If it came out that Soustelle's service was "supplying anti-Soviet mate-

rial to Allied Intelligence agencies, these suspicions would seem to be confirmed." At the same time, "I knew quite well that in the reconstructed French counterespionage services, Soviet activities were by no means being overlooked." Philby's earliest questions were: Where were the headquarters of the French Communist Party? Who was its effective boss? In retrospect, the irony of Philby's inquiries did not pass unnoticed with Muggeridge. Nor did the fact that Philby seemed to be on the best terms with the British ambassador, the august Sir Duff Cooper.

Muggeridge and Philby dined together. This proved to be "a very strange, though by no means unhappy, evening; certainly, it is one that I can never forget." For once "we felt at ease with one another." Philby spoke of Aileen "in the style of an affectionate father and husband." There was much laughter when Muggeridge imitated Vivian's account of how one of his agents, about to be executed by the Turks, managed to send a message: "Tell the Colonel I kept the faith." When they left the restaurant "the evening seemed very mild and agreeable, the lights very bright, the people strolling about and sitting in the cafés, very delightful." They strolled by the Seine. Then

> quite suddenly Kim said: "Let's go to the Rue de Grenelle." I didn't know then (though I should have) that this was where the Soviet Embassy was situated, and supposed he might have in mind some favorite café or night spot. Anyway, I was in a mood to go anywhere, so we set off. Kim now began at last to talk about his new responsibilities [as head of the anti-Soviet section], and I realized, at the time without any particular amazement, that we were making for the Soviet Embassy. How are we going to get in there? Kim kept saying, and went on to expatiate upon the special difficulties of penetrating a Soviet Embassy as compared with others . . . No chance of planting a servant when all the staff, down to the lowest maids and porters and chauffeurs, are imported from the USSR, and sometimes, in reality, hold quite senior positions in the Intelligence apparat. Tremendous obstacles, too, in the way of bugging the place; they never let foreign electricians or builders, or anyone like that, into the Embassy . . . Look at it! — by this time we were in the Rue de Grenelle — every blind drawn, every door locked, every window with its iron grating, the very fire escape contained in steel netting; even so, behind the doors and windows, round-the-clock guards, burglar alarms, every imaginable and unimaginable security precaution.[36]

Philby carried on like this, Muggeridge went on, "in an almost demented way; not exactly shaking his fists, but gesticulating and shouting at the hermetically sealed Embassy, standing so insulated and isolated in a Paris street, as though it had been just dropped there out of the sky, to be removed intact, when its purpose had been served."

In the end the only explanation for Philby's behavior that Muggeridge could provide was that "it arose of the seeing double which is inescapable in the role Kim had taken on." What happens, Muggeridge later offered in yet another version of his own experience in double agency, was that when one plays the double agent game, "the magnetic field of one's mind gets dispersed, with the particles flying here, there and everywhere. Instead of straining after an integral self, one becomes first two, then maybe several selves, functioning independently. Which of them happens to be uppermost at a particular moment depends on circumstances."

Such was Philby's position as World War II drew to an end in Europe. As it did, there occurred an episode in great affairs that demonstrated the sensitivity of the matters of state to which he was now privy on the eighth floor of Broadway. These concerned, in the first instance, that most powerful source of intelligence of the war — Ultra, the decrypts of the German Supreme Command's radio traffic.

When Philby was in Paris with Rothschild and Muggeridge, Rothschild startled Muggeridge by raising the matter of C's policy of withholding Most Secret Source intelligence — Ultra — from the Russians on the grounds of their poor cipher security. The British and the Russians were supposed to be fighting on the same side, so to deny them such vital information was worse than an unfriendly act. Muggeridge contradicted him: "Such caution was legitimate in view of the way the Russians had passed on to the Germans everything they knew about us and our intentions during the period of the Nazi-Soviet Pact. Another similar occasion for treachery might arise, and we were right to guard against it." For once Philby weighed in, as Muggeridge remembered: "He spluttered and shouted that we were in duty bound to do everything within our power, whatever it might be, to support the Red Army, including risking — if there was a risk — the security of [Ultra]."[37] Muggeridge had never seen Philby so angry. The sequel occurred when Roosevelt, Churchill, and Stalin met at Yalta in February 1945 to decide the fate of Europe and Asia, to complete the defeat of Germany and Japan, and to lay a firm foundation for a lasting peace. The conference appeared to have been a great success, and it was marked by a blaze of amity that seemed to assure the future.

But the accord did not last. The war ended as it had begun — with an outburst of suspicion from Stalin, his fear of doctored British intelligence, and his worry about the Anglo-German card. By now Philby knew much about those connections. In December 1944, the German General Staff began new attempts to surrender in the west and south while maintaining the war against Russia. With the Red Army on the River Oder, forty miles from Berlin, it became evident that the German military wanted an armistice with the Western powers while, at the same time, the Nazi foreign intelligence service was at work to provoke a war between the Anglo-Americans and the Russians, in which the Germans would join forces with the West. Here was another of those moments when Philby was required to exercise maximum vigilance over British secret intelligence in the interest of his Soviet masters.

The first major German approach was received the day after Christmas of 1944. Alexander von Neurath, the German consul in Lugano, presented indications that Field Marshal Albert Kesselring, the commander in chief of German forces in Italy, and Wilhelm Harster, the SD chief in Italy, were prepared to surrender to the Western powers but not to Russia.[38] Strong rumors spread everywhere that the American and British armies were about to join the German forces, which, with eleven million men still under arms, remained formidable. United, they would drive the Red Army back to its own frontiers.

The deputy chief of the OSS in Washington, Ned Buxton, reported to the Joint Chiefs on December 28, 1944, that Dulles at OSS Switzerland had commented that "this whole project appears rather fantastic to him. He believes, however, that the British know more about the whole matter than they are telling him." Fantastic or not, Dulles was close to the truth. A German secret agent, Karl Marcus, appeared in Paris in November and made contact with C's representative at Allied supreme headquarters. Then he was sent to London and into the custody of the British Secret Service. C advised the OSS of his presence, but this did not prevent an outburst of suspicion in both Moscow and Washington that resembled the one that followed the Hess affair in 1941.[39] Then, simultaneously, Dulles in Berne received a personal approach from Dom Emmanuelle Caronti, Abbot General of the Benedictines, who was undoubtedly acting under the behest of the Sicherheitsdienst. Dom Caronti brought the message that:

> In the sixth year of war, Germany finds herself alone in the fight against Bolshevist Russia. In the interests of saving mankind, Germany now looks to the highest ecclesiastical authority to intervene with the Anglo-Americans and guarantee absolute secrecy to any negotiations with the Vatican.[40]

As Philby himself remarked to a London journalist, Phillip Knightley, he was able to frustrate this "dickering with Germans," even if it resulted in a prolongation of the war in Europe by five months. Then, after Dom Caronti's intercession, there came what was known as the Alapka incident, Alapka being the code name for military conversations that accompanied the political aspects of the Yalta Conference. This was to prove the *fons et origo* of the fresh and intense suspicions that marked relations at the end of the war between Churchill and Stalin.

At the Yalta Conference on February 6, 1945, the chief of staff of the Red Army, General Alexsei I. Antonov, asked General George C. Marshall, his American counterpart, whether he had information concerning the whereabouts of the Sixth SS Panzer Army, the still very powerful tank army that had spearheaded the German attack against Eisenhower in the Ardennes. It had then vanished eastward.

Marshall replied that "he had received a message on the previous day which gave definite information of the moves of certain divisions of the Sixth Panzer Army from the Western Front" and he promised to get "an exact statement on this matter and give it to General Antonov."[41] Marshall asked Sir Alan Brooke, the chief of the British general staff, to do what he could to satisfy Antonov's request. Neither Brooke nor Marshall, however, controlled Ultra. C did, and his permission had to be obtained before Ultra could be given to the Russians. Consequently, it was not until February 9 that the British chiefs of staff agreed to ask C to send the Russians what Brooke termed "intelligence of a certain character"[42] — an unfortunate phrase, for it was also used to describe intelligence that was intended to deceive an enemy. That ambiguity in the term was to have grave consequences, for which, perhaps, Philby was responsible.

In response to Antonov's request, the Ultra managers in London and Washington sent similar intelligence. C informed Antonov that there were two German groupings to watch out for: (1) in the area of Torun, in the most northern part of the Russian front, and (2) a southern grouping, one including part of the SS Sixth Panzer division, around Vienna. This may have had importance, for Churchill was planning to send the British Eighth Army, one of his best, over the Alps to grab Vienna and establish a major British military presence there before Stalin did.

By his own statement, made later, Antonov made important fresh dispositions of the Red Army to meet the attack on the basis of the Allied intelligence. He sent his best fighting elements to the Torun area. But as he complained when the SS Sixth Panzer Army struck on March 5–6 in Vienna and the southern region — the exact opposite of the Anglo-American intelligence forecasts — he found that the intelligence was inaccurate. The attack on the Vienna front was one of the heaviest of the war. But the Red Army on the Vienna front recovered, counterattacked, and took Vienna before the British expedition could reach the Austrian capital. Antonov was courteous enough about the erroneous intelligence when first he wrote to General Marshall on March 30, 1945:

> A possibility is not excluded that some of the sources of this information aimed to disorientate the Anglo-American Command as well as the Soviet Command and to divert the attention of the Soviet Command from the region where the principal offensive operation of the Germans was being prepared on the Eastern Front . . . I consider it my duty to inform General Marshall regarding the above with the only purpose that he could make certain conclusions regarding the source of this information.[43]

In other words, Antonov thought Marshall had been tricked. But by whom? In closing, Antonov hastened to add that he hoped Marshall would "continue to inform us regarding available data about the enemy" — another indication that the Russians did not themselves possess Ultra. Antonov ended his letter by stating that he wished General Marshall to accept "my respect and gratitude."[44]

Intelligence continued to flow to the Russians except in one important aspect of the war — the secret negotiations that had been going on throughout the Yalta Conference between the German and Allied agents, Stalin believed, to arrange a German surrender on the Western Front. On or about February 27, 1945, Eisenhower felt sufficiently sure of his information to advise the Combined Chiefs of Staff in Washington:

> I have received word via OSS channels of a possible approach by one or more senior German officers with the proposal of facilitating an Allied victory in the West in order to end the war promptly. I understand that OSS has reported the fact in detail to Washington with a copy to London.
>
> I have reported to my informant that, as these reports have gone to my governments, any action on political levels will obviously be taken at their direction, and that so far as any purely military approach is concerned, the channels should be those which are recog-

nized by the customs and usage of war. However, I have no intention of choking off this channel of possible communication with me.[45]

That signal provoked an unusual reaction. An unnamed officer at Broadway — perhaps Philby or a representative — telephoned his counterpart at Eisenhower's headquarters to inquire whether there was any truth in reports that Eisenhower was considering German terms for a cease-fire. The message, which survived in Donovan's papers as evidence that there had been a serious leak, conveys something of the anxiety of the caller. As Commander Lester Armour, the OSS agent at Supreme Headquarters, reported to Donovan personally: "British SIS are pressing us for confirmation of report from British Chiefs of Staff that Eisenhower has received through OSS a peace feeler from German generals." The "pressure from SIS is such that I am making available copy of Bern telegram."[46]

But whoever made the call, it was followed by a troubling message from Soviet Foreign Minister Molotov. By that date mass German surrenders had already begun when, in the afternoon of March 23, Churchill left London to observe Montgomery's operations to cross the Rhine. While still there on March 24, Churchill received a copy of a telegram sent by Molotov to the British foreign secretary and the U.S. secretary of state alleging that

> for two weeks behind the back of the Soviet Union which is bearing the brunt of the war against Germany, negotiations have been going on between representatives of German Military Command on the one hand and representatives English and American on the other.[47]

Using expressions that indicated that he was being kept informed by a spy or spies somewhere in the Allied High Command, Stalin entered the telegraphic correspondence with the statement to Roosevelt:

> You insist that there have been no negotiations yet. It may be assumed that you have not yet been fully informed. As regards my military colleagues, they, on the basis of data which they have on hand, do not have doubts that the negotiations have taken place and that they have ended in an agreement with the Germans, on the basis of which the German commander on the western front . . . has agreed to open the front and permit the Anglo-American troops to advance to the east, and the Anglo-Americans have promised to ease for the Germans the peace terms.[48]

The Soviet leader insinuated that the British were behind these negotiations, an insinuation that again may have come from intelligence supplied by Philby, for he was on the list of SIS officers who were entitled to read all communications relating to German peace overtures.

Against that background, and with the presence of Hess and Marcus in London, Stalin now went on to make the gravest allegation against the Western powers:

> As a result of this at the present moment the Germans on the Western Front in fact have ceased the war against England and the United States. At the same time the Germans continue the war with Russia, the Ally of England and the United States.

President Roosevelt replied that he had received Stalin's messages "with astonishment." He reminded Stalin that he had sent a full explanation concerning such talks as there had been and expressed the opinion that Stalin's information "must have come from German sources which have made persistent efforts to create dissension between us in order to escape in some measure for responsibility for their war crimes." He ended his reply by stating:

> With a confidence in your belief in my personal reliability and in my determination to bring about together with you an unconditional surrender of the Nazis, it is astonishing that a belief seems to have reached the Soviet Government that I have entered into an agreement with the enemy without first obtaining your full agreement . . . Frankly, I cannot avoid a feeling of bitter resentment toward your informers, whoever they are, for such vile misrepresentations of my actions or those of my trusted subordinates.

Churchill was so astounded that he sent a telegram to Stalin denying the Soviet allegations and denying also that the Germans had stopped fighting in the West. As Churchill advised (being sure to remind Stalin of Anglo-American air and land might), the Germans had

> in fact fought with great obstinacy and inflicted upon us and the American Armies since the opening of our February offensive up to March 28 upwards of 87,000 casualties. However being outnumbered on the ground and literally overwhelmed in the air by the vastly superior Anglo-American Air Forces, which in the month of March alone dropped over 200,000 tons of bombs on Germany, the German Armies in the West have been decisively broken. The fact that they were outnumbered on the ground in the West is due to the magnificent attacks and weight of the Soviet Armies.

But neither FDR's nor Churchill's protests produced a retraction from the Soviet leader. Stalin insisted that

> it is hard to agree that the absence of German resistance on the Western Front is due solely to the fact that they have been beaten. The Germans have 147 divisions on the Eastern Front. They could safely withdraw from 15 to 20 divisions from the Eastern Front to aid their forces on the Western Front. Yet they have not done so, nor are they doing so. [They were] fighting desperately against the Russians for Zemlenice, an obscure station in Czechoslovakia, which they need just as much as a dead man needs a poultice, but they surrender without any resistance such important towns in the heart of Germany as Osnabrück, Mannheim and Kassel. You will admit that this behavior on the part of the Germans is more than strange and unaccountable.

As to the reliability of his spies, Stalin declared, in terms that could again be taken to indicate Philby and the rest of the Cambridge Five,

> I can assure you that they are honest and unassuming people who carry out their duties conscientiously and who have no intention of affronting anybody. They have been tested in action on numerous occasions.

And at that point the signal took a more sinister turn. Stalin returned to the question of the intelligence sent to General Antonov by Brooke and Marshall in February and did so in terms that suggested he believed that an attempt had been made by the Anglo-American staffs to trick him in order to keep the Red Army out of Vienna. As Stalin declared, the attack came not where the American and British generals had said but near Vienna:

> The Germans, as we now know, had concentrated 35 divisions in the area, 11 of them armoured. This, with its greatest concentration of armour, was one of the heaviest blows of the war. Marshal Tolbukhin succeeded first in warding off disaster and then in smashing the Germans, and was able to do so also because my informants had disclosed — true, with some delay — the plan for the main German blow and immediately apprised Marshal Tolbukhin. Thus I had yet another opportunity to satisfy myself as to the reliability and soundness of my sources of information.

To that statement, Stalin appended another note on the subject by Antonov. Antonov retraced the history of the intelligence and carefully noted that "I am very much obliged and grateful to General Marshall for the information, designed to further our common aims, which he so kindly made available to us." But nonetheless it was "my duty to inform General Marshall that the military operations on the Eastern Front in March did not bear out the information furnished by him." It may well be, General Antonov went on, that "certain sources of this information wanted to bluff both Anglo-American and Soviet Headquarters and divert the attention of the Soviet High Command from the area where the Germans were mounting their main offensive." Yet "despite the foregoing, I would ask General Marshall, if possible, to keep me posted with information about the enemy. I consider it my duty to convey this information to General Marshall, solely for the purpose of enabling him to draw the proper conclusions in relation to the source of the information." Churchill wired Roosevelt that this exchange indicated a deep change of Soviet policy to the Western allies and expressed the view that

> all this makes it the more important that we should join hands with the Russian Armies as far to the East as possible and if circumstances allow, enter Berlin . . . I believe this is the best chance of saving the future. If they are ever convinced that we are afraid of them and can be bullied into submission, then indeed I should despair of our future relations with them and much else.

Roosevelt replied on April 6 with a telegram that foreshadowed, perhaps, as deep a change in FDR's attitude toward Russia as in Stalin's toward the West. Roosevelt stated that he was "in general agreement" with Churchill's suggestion that the Allies meet the Russian armies as far to the east as possible and, again if possible, take Berlin. He added, too, a message that made a powerful impression on the British inner circle. "Our armies will in a very few days be in a position," the president declared, "that will permit us to become 'tougher' than has heretofore appeared advantageous to the war effort."[49] Here, then, was the first indication of what might have become Roosevelt's policy had he lived. But he died suddenly on April 12, the crisis with Stalin still unresolved, to be succeeded by the vice president, Harry S. Truman.

In the wake of FDR's death and the bitter exchange with Stalin, Truman accepted Churchill's advice and ordered Donovan of the OSS to break his contact with German representatives. But at that moment the German Army in the West collapsed, and the war in western Germany entered its last phase. German forces began a series of surrenders everywhere except on the Russian front, where the German Army continued to fight. Rumor again swept Germany that Britain and the United States were about to join the German armies on the Russian

front, fueled doubtless by Churchill's issuance of some veiled direc-
tives. Among them was, it is claimed, a secret order to Montgomery
to stack all the captured German arms "so that they could easily be
re-issued to the German Armies with who we should have to work with
if the Soviet advance [into Denmark and the North Sea] continued."

The Cold War between Britain and Russia had begun. Philby, who
had been at the center of great events for four years, remained there
as chief of the R5 anti-Soviet intelligence service when the last trumpets sounded. And Trevor-Roper, about to go to Berlin to establish
whether Hitler was alive or dead, watched Philby across a crowded
room and remembered, in enigmatic fashion:

> Who could possibly compete with Philby, trusted by all, favoured by
> his superiors, experienced in both war and peace, in counter-espio-
> nage against both Germany and Russia, tested in both the office and
> the field, strong in his contact with the American secret service? I
> looked around the world I had left, at the part-time stockbrokers and
> retired Indian policemen, the agreeable epicureans from the bars of
> White's and Boodle's, the jolly, conventional ex-naval officers and the
> robust adventurers from the bucket-shop; and then I looked at Philby.
> I was reminded of Tiresias among the ghosts of Hades. He alone was
> real: they flitted like shadows in their crowded coulisses.[50]

12

Suspicion

1944–1947

PHILBY FOUND HIMSELF in his thirty-fourth year when the German war ended and the Cold War with Russia began. "The German foe lies prostrate before us," Prime Minister Churchill proclaimed at the Palace of Westminster. "Advance Britannia!" C had just reached the mandatory retirement age of fifty-five in 1945 and wished to retire — to hunt, shoot, garden, race his horses, ride to hounds with the Beaufort. He had had enough spying. It was forty years almost to the day since he had begun his career in counterespionage at Haig's headquarters in France. His reputation in the trade, and that of his service, was tremendous. Had the SIS not penetrated and then disrupted and destroyed the German Secret Services? He was, the mandarins said of him, the world master at the game. Churchill asked C to remain, and he agreed. When Clement Attlee succeeded a few months later and he, too, asked Menzies to stay on, again he agreed and remained for the next seven years. Philby remained at his side, and headquarters remained at Broadway Buildings, that large office in the crooked street of that name where Milton wrote *Paradise Lost*.

To prepare the service for the Cold War, which would be fought with all the intensity of the medieval wars of religion during the next forty years, in September 1945 C established "the committee for the postwar reorganisation" and made Philby a member. Now the senior counterespionage officer in the service, he made a study of the structure on which the reformed service should rest. Should it be reformed along vertical lines? Or horizontal? And as he wrote, "If the vertical solution were adopted, work against the Soviet Union and Communism generally would be divided regionally. No single person could cover the whole field." Some committee men preferred the vertical solution, others the horizontal. Plainly, from the point of view of the security of the service, the vertical solution was the more desirable course. But from his point of view as a Soviet secret agent, Philby threw his weight behind the horizontal solution, "in the hopes of keeping, for the time being at least, the whole field of anti-Soviet and anti-Communist work under my own direct supervision."[1]

Working as he did by indirection through others, one member, David Footman, chief of the Political Section and the officer who had recruited Guy Burgess into the service, became a strong ally. Philby recorded: "In fact, it was he, in his dry and incisive way, who made most of the running, with myself in support where necessary." Of those who favored the vertical structure, much turned on the view of a single member, and Philby saw to it that he was removed from the committee. In due course, the horizontal structure was accepted. The committee then turned to the system. There was, Philby recalled, some "arduous donkey work" in which five directories of equal status were established: (1) Finance and Administration, (2) Intelligence Production, (3) Intelligence Requirements, (4) Training and Development, being "concerned with the development of technical devices in support of espionage," and (5) War Planning. When the donkey work was over and the committee's "bulky report" was ready for presentation to C, "we felt we had produced the design of something like a service, with enough serious inducements to tempt able young men to regard the service as a career for life." And as Philby recorded of C's reception of the plan:

> The Chief did not accept all our recommendations. There was still a certain amount of dead wood which found no place in our plan but which he could not bring himself to cut out. But, by and large, the pattern sketched above was adopted as the basic pattern of the service. For all its faults, it was a formidable improvement on anything that had gone before. As for myself, I had no cause for dissatisfaction.

No cause for dissatisfaction. True. He had engineered a considerable victory for the Soviets. If a secret service is to be effective, its personalities, policies, and structure must be secret. The structure adopted should have been the vertical one, not the horizontal. But with the adoption of the horizontal, all the service's activities were exposed to

Philby's gaze and thus to that of the main enemy, the Soviet service. Philby's penetration of the Secret Service was now complete; as James McCargar, a CIA official who worked with Philby, would observe of the implications:

> A successful penetration of the opponent's secret operations organization puts you at the very heart of his actions and intentions towards you. You share his mind and thinking to an intimate — and reliable — degree impossible in any other secret operation. This means that so far as intelligence is concerned, you know what he knows. You have therefore annulled, in one stroke, the value of his secret intelligence about you; you have neutralized the power of his secret knowing. Even more importantly, through your knowledge of his intelligence interests and of his political operations, as revealed in his policy papers and instructions, you are in the possession of the most reliable possible indications of his intentions. Most importantly, you are in a position to control his actions, since you can, by tailoring intelligence for him to your purposes, by influencing his evaluations, mislead him as to his decisions and consequent actions.[2]

Section V of wartime glory was abolished and in its place came R5, a foreign counterespionage service operating globally with Russia as the main adversary and directed by Philby.

At that moment in the modern history of the Whitehall bureaucracy, Philby reached the top of his profession, for the time being, in both the British and Russian services. He had been in the Soviet service for eleven years, the British for, as far as we know, five years. He began to recruit his staff and officers from, mainly, the best and the brightest of the four hundred and fifty officers who had passed through War Station XB during the war. Also, the service closed ranks. It withdrew from almost all its wartime links with the Whitehall administration, in particular from MI5, the Security Service, with which the wartime squabbles had remained so intense as to make observers wonder who the real enemy was. As for the Americans, the wartime semi-intimacy was replaced on both sides by liaison officers whose function was to maintain a friendly relationship while letting the other side know as little as possible. The Secret Service resumed its prewar status, that of the secret citadel of imperial intelligence at the heart of but detached from Whitehall.

In his personal life Philby displayed many of the signs of the successful bourgeois. He had acquired a fine house in Carlyle Square in the Chelsea of high fashion, he was still a member of the Athenaeum, and he had joined the Authors' Club, a snug place in Whitehall Court for the use of "gentlemen concerned with literature or of the learned professions." He wore tweeds, suede shoes, sometimes a cravat. He acquired a Homburg, that symbol of the Whitehall mandarin, from Lock & Co. of St. James's, "of black felt with ribbon to crown and ribbon binding to gently upturned brim, size $7\frac{3}{8}$ inches." In January 1946 *The Times* announced in the New Year's Honours List that Philby had been admitted to the Most Excellent Order of the British Empire in the rank of Member, the motto of which was "to encourage all valorous hearts and show them honourable example." It was, it is thought, the only such order to have been made to a wartime entrant into the Secret Service. This was still a day and age when men killed to obtain such preferment, and it entitled Philby to wear a pink ribbon edged with gray on his lapel when in black tie, a silver cross patonce with pink and gray silk collar when in white. He thereby became a man of the hour and of the future; it was the first step toward a knighthood.

As it was to emerge shortly, those outward and visible signs of his success gave his Soviet case officer, ever vigilant for signs that his principal spy in Whitehall might be becoming a bourgeois in reality as well as appearance, cause for concern that he might have outgrown the Marxist passions of his youth. There was at this time a saying that a man who has not been a communist by the time he is twenty has no heart, and one who remains a communist after he is thirty has no brains. Was this happening to Kim? Was C not corrupting his Soviet allegiances? The only sure way of testing his fidelity to Marxism was the quality of his work for the Soviet Union. Was he maintaining the high order of intelligence that had marked the early phase of his career? We shall return to this question, for it was a main task of the bureaucrats at the Center to test the intelligence provided by an agent against the reports on him from his case officer in order to establish whether he had begun to work for the bourgeoisie against the proletariat. Much could be deduced about this from his home life. And much was.

Malcolm Muggeridge, who had left the Secret Service but retained his connection to it, found Philby at Carlyle Square with his family. They

> made a most pleasant impression; she was pretty, sensible, a good but not doting mother, intelligent rather than intellectual — just the kind of girl I like. She and Philby seemed very happy together; he was quite at his best with his children and the sunshine of domesticity . . . she and Philby gave me no sense of strife or strain; all that was

nicest and simplest and gayest in Philby came out, it seemed to me, when they were together with their children.[3]

But Muggeridge remained uneasy about his old chief without saying why. Now the deputy editor of the *Daily Telegraph,* a newspaper then second only to *The Times* in its conservative influence, he wrote in his diary after a party in November 1945 how he had

> spent a miserably jovial evening with [his wife] Kitty and Kim Philby and his wife Eileen [sic]. Drank too much, and mixed drinks badly. Wondered afterwards why it was so miserable, and reached the conclusion that it was due to the falsity of my relations with Kim, the disproportion between form and substance.[4]

Form and substance, those twin key elements in any counterespionage inquiry, as in philosophy. Muggeridge had known Philby fairly intimately since 1936 and their days together in Fleet Street journalism, through Philby's transformation from a communist activist to a vaguely right-wing functionary of the Anglo-German Fellowship, *The Times,* and the British Secret Service. During the war Philby had given him the task of studying the files of double agents in an attempt to establish where their loyalties really lay. Muggeridge learned something about the intensity of Philby's passions when Kim spoke of the justice of Russia's war in Paris early in 1945 and the need to supply the Russians with Ultra in order to maintain them in the war. At the time of his appointment to the anti-Soviet section, Muggeridge had spoken to Commander Kenneth Cohen, a power in the Broadway mandarinate. "Kim simply can't be trusted," he is said to have advised. "He happens to be one of nature's *farouches,* a wild man capable of turning the place upside down for his own ends."[5] Plainly, in his anguished diary note about form and substance, Muggeridge believed that there was another personality maneuvering behind the engaging, charming, able Philby. He may even have deduced that the other man was a Soviet agent. But if he did he said nothing in his million-word diaries. Indeed, he never mentioned Philby again in those diaries.

But Muggeridge did talk with Patrick Seale and Maureen McConville for the purposes of their biographical statement about Philby, as did Colonel Vivian, who was still Philby's department chief in the Secret Service from 1945 to 1947. From these talks, Seale and McConville felt able to make certain other important statements about Philby's state of mind during this period. Philby's real task as a Soviet spy may be said to have begun only in 1945. Philby chose "Stalin's murderously repressive Russia to Attlee's humane Britain."[6] But to what extent did he have a real choice but to continue in the Soviet secret services? Had he not committed himself in his youth to serve not for a weekend, or a month, or even a year, but for life?

> Could he not have gone back to *The Times*, where his reputation as a correspondent was high, just as so many of his colleagues returned to their civilian careers? Could he even have made a clean breast of his Soviet attachments to the SIS? The damage he had so far done might well have been forgiven him had he agreed to be "turned" and played back against the Russians. In his methodical way he must surely have explored where these paths would lead him. Fidelity to the Marxist ideals of the 1930s can at this point have counted for little in the careful calculations of this bureaucrat of espionage.[7]

That is exactly what troubled his Soviet case officer, especially in 1947, when the benign but dangerous Yuri Modin appeared in London to take charge of his case. Philby appeared to Modin to have become so completely the typical bourgeois English Secret Service officer that it was impossible to believe wholly that he continued to accept Marxism. Had he indeed been turned? This question also troubled the Center in Moscow. The Russians "can have left him in no doubt that they would tolerate no defection: Philby knew too much. His contact with the Russian service had been too extensive. To get out would have been a sentence of death."[8] There was a further facet of his character which, Seale and McConville recorded, "militated with perhaps equal force against withdrawal from the Soviet service." He had his measure of human frailty. "Although he may have enjoyed physical excitement and there can be no doubt of his courage, he was physically squeamish, hating pain and violence. He was not "the steely secret agent of popular fiction, but an averagely sensitive, averagely vulnerable human being." Beyond this was

> the intellectual and moral arrogance inherited from his strong-willed father. "You've got to live with yourself," the old man would say, "and be true to your own moral inclinations." [And so] almost independently of his will, the choice was taken, a course of continued treachery made inevitable by a combination of fear, egotism and guts. From the start it was a double life which entailed formidable risks. It is not surprising that it resulted in heavy drinking and a high state of neurosis. The strains were relieved only by a greedy grasping for the everyday pleasures of life, what he called "living life to the full." [His became] the attitude of a soldier on leave, a man permanently at war.[9]

It was almost fifty years, in 1994, before it became known what some of his Russian masters thought of their most remarkable spy in the British camp. The Russians could never bring themselves wholly to trust those bourgeois Marxist spies, Philby, Burgess, and Maclean, and their co-conspirators, for much the same reason that they could never bring themselves to trust the Labour Party or the European socialist movement in general. They were, the ultra-Marxists of the Center declared, untrustworthy, "ideological shit."[10] The first known active distrust of Philby arose late in 1946, not from anything he did or said, but from what Maclean was reporting from the British Embassy in Washington about the Marshall Plan, the U.S. plan to rebuild war-dev-astated Europe.

According to General Sudoplatov, of the Administration of Special Tasks at the Center and the authority who gave the Cambridge Group their war orders in 1939, when word of the Marshall Plan first began to circulate in Moscow, Stalin's first reaction was that the Soviet gov-ernment would "cooperate with the Western allies in the implemen-tation of the [plan, giving] special attention to restoring the devastated industrial facilities in the Ukraine, Byelorussia, and Leningrad."[11] But then there was a sudden change of policy, and Sudoplatov was sum-moned to meet with the Soviet deputy foreign minister, Andrei Vyshin-sky. Vyshinsky explained that they had received a signal from an agent code-named Orphan, who was Maclean, the acting head of chancery at the British Embassy in Washington and as such a man with access to "all of the embassy's classified traffic." Maclean had stated that the goal of the Marshall Plan "was to ensure American economic domina-tion of Europe" and that the "new international economic organiza-tion to restore European productivity would be under the control of American financial capital. The source for Maclean's report was Brit-ish foreign secretary Ernest Bevin."

Vyshinsky "knew he must immediately report this message to Stalin." However, first he wanted to check the credibility of Maclean and the others in his group, Philby, Burgess, Cairncross, and Blunt. Vyshinsky was concerned that Alexander Orlov, the Soviet chief of intelligence in Western Europe until his defection to the United States in 1937, "had been in contact with these agents and might have compromised them." To what extent, Vyshinsky wished to know, might Philby, Maclean, and Burgess be engaged in a double game? As Sudoplatov wrote:

I was the one responsible for giving orders to resume contacts with Philby and Maclean in 1939 after Orlov's defection. Since my signature was on the formal order registered in Maclean's file, Vyshinsky created an awkward moment when he asked if I was still confident of Maclean's reliability. I told him that I was responsible for the orders I signed, but that I was aware of Maclean's work only until 1939 and it had not been reported to me since 1942. At the same time I added, "Every important source of information should be subjected to regular checks and evaluation, with no exceptions for Philby, Burgess, and Maclean."[12]

Vyshinsky was "clearly distressed" by Sudoplatov's report and directed that the Cambridge Group's records be examined for any sign that they had been purveying "tainted" information.

In 1994 Nicholas Elliott, a retired senior SIS officer who was closely involved in the Philby case, stated that he had learned that "a very senior and experienced" female officer at the Center, Zoya Nikolayevna Ryskina, investigated the reliability of the Cambridge Group's intelligence and concluded that Philby, Burgess, and Maclean "were all under [SIS] control and suggested that they should be assassinated."[13]

In a real sense the Philby case became a contest for professional and intellectual primacy between Philby and Angleton, who was destined to become chief of foreign counterespionage operations in the United States for twenty of the forty years of the Cold War — and therefore one of the key men in the system created to defend the United States against the secret services of the Soviet Union. Their relationship, formed at War Station XB in the last phase of the hot war with Germany and the first of the Cold War with Russia, was of importance, the more so when, in September 1945, President Truman suddenly liquidated the OSS amid a press furor that OSS IS BRANDED BRITISH AGENCY TO LEGISLATORS and BRITISH CONTROL OF OSS BARED ON CONGRESS PROBE. The OSS's main departments were divided among the FBI, the State Department, and the Pentagon. Its espionage and counterespionage elements were folded into a holding agency known as the Strategic Services Unit (SSU). But most of the senior staff returned to civilian life, leaving SSU little more than a shadow of the OSS's strength, wealth, and power. As the Cold War broke out in Europe, as before Pearl Harbor, the United States found itself with no more than a fragmented intelligence service — a state of affairs that sat well with Philby and his Soviet masters.

A few OSS men decided to make secret intelligence their career in SSU, and one of these was Angleton. As Philby had emerged as the leading counterespionage expert in the British camp, Angleton filled that role for the Americans. His citation for the Legion of Merit asserted that between October 28, 1944, and December 4, 1945, while chief of an X2 unit in Italy, he captured "over one thousand enemy intelligence agents." It spoke of his "dissemination of clear, concise, and comprehensive descriptions in a form originated by him." The working relationship between the two men undoubtedly owed much to the ISOS decrypts that Philby sent to Angleton, backed by the rich intelligence on the personalities of the German and fascist intelligence services from the SIS and MI5 central registries. Some of their colleagues would speak of a rather close personal friendship developing between the two, and there was some truth in this. But the reality was that Angleton, an ambitious man, became heavily dependent on Philby for the continuation of his professional success, a state of affairs which remained for some years into the future.

It is not clear that Angleton appreciated this situation. Politically he was a vigorous Republican patriot interested in learning what he could from the British and then establishing U.S. primacy over Britain in the field of secret intelligence. Philby had few illusions about friendship, and so each used the other to further his ambitions. Philby's operational intention was to ensure that the left emerged stronger than the right in European politics in general, and in particular in Italy, where the communists were extremely powerful. As it was to turn out, Angleton's was exactly the reverse. Against that personal background there occurred a number of counterespionage cases which, Angleton claimed in later years, gave him an insight into Philby's personality. The first of these was a lurid and tangled affair involving a Florentine princess, Maria Pignatelli.

In April 1944, Angleton learned through a decrypt that Princess Pig (as she was generally known) had crossed the front lines between the German and American armies in Italy in a Red Cross vehicle, using the false papers of an Allied Military Government official. There, according to the decrypt, she visited prominent German intelligence officials in Rome, which was then in German hands, and explained that she had come to them on behalf of her husband, Lieutenant-Colonel Antonio Pignatelli, who had organized a fascist political intelligence network in southern Italy and therefore behind the Allied lines. She had revealed information, which she claimed had been obtained by members of her husband's organization, about the impending Allied operations to take Rome.

When this information was checked against the Security Indexes, it emerged that the princess was on the OSS's books as an American spy.

She was therefore a double agent and therefore liable to the firing squad. It was then established that she had been put across the lines by another OSS agent, Lieutenant Paolo Poletti, one of whose relatives was Charles Poletti, the deputy governor of New York State and, at present, the military governor of Naples, where the Allied Supreme Headquarters was located in the royal palace at nearby Caserta. A leading figure at Supreme Headquarters, Harold Macmillan, Churchill's minister of state, knew him well. Charles Poletti was, Macmillan recorded in his diary, "pure Sicilian, pure American, and pure Tammany Hall . . . a 'hundred-per-center.'"[14]

Through his U.S. political power and the force of his charm, Poletti enjoyed access to the inner circle at Supreme Headquarters. Through Paolo Poletti's influence with Charles, Princess Pig (as she was known to OSS X2) had been introduced into the highest OSS circles at headquarters in Naples and even into Supreme Headquarters. She had become the mistress of an important American officer, and she herself was recruited as an OSS spy because her family had been closely connected with Mussolini, who now ruled northern Italy through the Fascist Grand Council. Also, she had been a client of General Donovan's law firm before the war. Princess Pignatelli's credentials seemed good, therefore, for she had offered her apartment in Rome as an OSS safe house, and it was used by an OSS officer controlling important networks in Rome, Peter Tompkins, who knew the princess personally and also employed her son Emmanuele as one of his spies.

Now Princess Pignatelli had been shown to be an Italian fascist spy working for the Germans. It was to emerge that she had probably betrayed Peter Tompkins to the Germans and fascists in Rome, an act that had caused much bloodshed and cost the OSS one of its major intelligence networks in Italy. Angleton warned OSS Naples, but he was too late. The British Field Security Service arrested Paolo Poletti and another of the princess's associates in the OSS, an Italian identified only as Morris, as German or Italian fascist spies. When Poletti, an American, tried to escape, his British guards shot him dead, an incident that caused much indignation at OSS Italy, which was already concerned by the British domination in the theater, while the British Security Services in Italy regarded the OSS as green, dangerous, antagonistic, uncooperative, and corrupt.

As the case evolved, however, the British appeared to have acted with justification. Poletti had himself come through the lines only a few months before and, since he was an American, had been employed by the OSS to put agents over the front line. He carried out his work in an American uniform and had, according to the X2 London War Diary, "been given carte blanche in his selection of recruits."[15] Some proved to have been associates of Colonel Pignatelli's fascist intelligence service, which reported to Mussolini in northern Italy. Still more then emerged about this alarming situation at OSS headquarters, all of which became known to Philby and Angleton at Ryder Street.

A German signal intercept on May 14, 1944, from the German ambassador in Rome, Dr. Rudolf Rahn, to Foreign Minister Ribbentrop showed that Rahn had reported that "the Italian princess, Maria Pignatelli, fled from her home in Naples to Rome, in the disguise of a midwife with Allied military papers she had bought."[16] In Rome, Rahn continued, Princess Pignatelli had seen the German commander in chief, Field Marshal Albert Kesselring, and had then gone on to fascist headquarters at Fasano, where she had seen Mussolini. She had talked with both Kesselring and Mussolini about the "secret Fascist and military organization which has been organized by her husband in southern Italy" and about German intelligence plans to use her as a "transmitter of sabotage data." Meantime, the message continued, the princess had "probably made her way back to Naples, through the lines from Rome."[17] This intelligence proved timely, and she was arrested by toughs from the Field Security Police as she passed through the front lines for the third time — an impressive achievement for a lady of rank who had passed her fiftieth year. Under interrogation she maintained she knew nothing of a fascist sabotage organization in the Allied rear and said she had gone to Rome only to help her son, who was now destitute and in danger through her own betrayal of the OSS network. In other words, Princess Pig had betrayed her own son, although perhaps unwittingly.

No one believed her, and there was a suspicion that, apart from all else, she might have betrayed another team of OSS spies behind enemy lines, the Sweeney-Moscatelli mission. That OSS Naples was prepared to arrest and incarcerate one of their own agents, the princess, did not placate Philby. He made the strongest protest, that the princess had not been put up for trial, to the Allied Supreme Commander, General Sir Henry Maitland Wilson, and since the British ran this theater, so did Philby's Section V. The OSS was *ordered* to cease all secret intelligence operations for a month until it became clear what, if anything, the princess had known and could have given to the Germans. At the end of the month, the OSS was again not allowed to resume operations, for a group of Italian assassination agents was arrested. It was established that their mission was to kill the army group commander, General Sir Harold Alexander, the commander of the

U.S. Fifth Army, General Mark W. Clark, and General Lucian K. Truscott, a senior U.S. Army officer involved in the march on Rome. It was feared that the assassination squad was acting on intelligence provided by the princess.

The Pignatelli case had many repercussions, and these were important in that Philby's good offices had to be obtained by X2 officers if they wished, as was frequently necessary, to check the loyalties and affiliations of their agents against the holdings in the SIS's records. This widened Philby's knowledge of OSS activities and his authority throughout the theater of operations. It also earned Philby the gratitude of several important OSS officers who, being anxious to avoid another Pignatelli case, took the precaution of double-checking their findings in the American files against those of the British. But it was in the aftermath of the Pignatelli case that there arose the most important development in the relationship between Angleton and Philby.

For reasons that are not evident, no proceedings were taken against the princess or her husband. Both were released from jail at the end of the war, probably at Angleton's intervention, for he wished to recruit Colonel Pignatelli as an SSU agent. By that time Angleton's tasks were beginning to change direction; the powerful communist underground in Italy had begun to emerge and to threaten the stability of the coalition government of Alcide de Gasperi, a Christian Democrat who enjoyed the support of the U.S. government. In the tasks with which Angleton was charged — to encourage the Italian intelligence services to suppress the left while nourishing the forces of the right — he saw that, for all his iniquities during the war, Pignatelli might become a force to be reckoned with in southern Italy, where he had had his political intelligence service. By now chief of Z, the SSU counterespionage organization in Rome, Angleton decided to recruit Pignatelli as an SSU agent. But Philby, as chief of R5 in London, had no interest in fostering this intention, and Angleton's attempt was foiled by Philby's R5 agent in Rome. When Angleton discovered this, he "developed a grudge against British counter-espionage and against Kim in particular."[18]

There is no reason to doubt these statements, for there is other, good evidence — Angleton's own "eyes only" communications to Donovan — that something of a local quarrel had already broken out between R5 and Z in Rome through a case code-named Dusty which began late in 1944 and concluded early in 1945. At the beginning of that period, Angleton started to report that Dusty was an intelligence source inside the Vatican itself, at that time a society almost as closed as that of the Kremlin, impenetrable and suspicious, a mysterious group headed by the remote and enigmatic Pope Pius XII. The intelligence appeared to be the dispatches from the apostolic delegate at Tokyo to the Vatican's foreign office, the Department of Extraordinary Ecclesiastical Affairs. The material reaching Angleton through intermediaries between himself and Dusty seemed to consist of papal documents, aides-mémoire, transcriptions of highest-level conferences, agendum, apostolic telegrams, and minutes. The intelligence appeared to Angleton to be relevant to the war against Japan, and, since the war with Germany was ending, this increased its importance at OSS Washington. It was accepted as gospel at OSS headquarters.

Everything about the material — its content, its noble turns of phrase, its theological dignity, its beautiful dialogue — all was impressive to the OSS. Such was Angleton's confidence in his intelligence, and Donovan's confidence in Angleton, that Donovan began to send Dusty's intelligence to President Roosevelt. Roosevelt read it attentively, aware that if his armies were compelled to invade Japan they might suffer a million casualties. Among other matters conveyed by Dusty in January 1945 were Japan's minimum demands for a negotiated peace, apparently obtained by the apostolic delegate from the Japanese government.

But later that month, having minutely examined the Dusty file, Angleton began to question whether Dusty was a master spy, a faker of documents of majestic ability, or an extremely clever German deception agent attempting to cause the United States to overcommit military strength to the Pacific at the expense of the European front. All were possible. It says much for the quality of his mind, and the courage with which Angleton approached his task of looking into his source, for the entire OSS hierarchy had accepted the Dusty reports; they had vouched for their authenticity, and they had been passed for presidential eyes. Careers and reputations were at stake, and so was the future of the OSS, for this was the time that Roosevelt was finally making up his mind whether to establish the OSS as the permanent postwar U.S. intelligence service, which he was disposed to do.

Angleton's inquiries showed that Dusty's reports were tainted meat, as Angleton wired to his chiefs in Washington, "a mixture of the obvious, the unimportant if true, and plants."[19] Donovan now had the difficult task of stopping the flow of these reports to the president while Angleton determined who Dusty was. He proved to be Virgilio Scattolini, a short, fat journalist and failed writer whose principal claim to fame, until now, was that before World War I he had written two scorching pornographic books, one entitled *Such Women*, about the experiences of a Roman prostitute, the other, *Amazons of the Bidet,* a novel that became a bestseller. By birth a Florentine, he had not remained a pornographer. Undergoing a religious conversion, Scattolini began to study the works of Saint Thomas Aquinas and became a minor lay officer in the Franciscan order. In that capacity he attained some new fame with a set of verses called "The Poem of Holy Rome," a work in praise of the papacy.

Through this poem, Scattolini gained a post writing film reviews for the *Osservatore Romano,* the Vatican's semiofficial daily newspaper. However, in 1939 the editor discovered that he was none other than the author of a pornographic bestseller and sacked him. To earn his living, Scattolini turned first to freelance reporting, which earned him only small wages. But with the Allied occupation of Rome in June 1944, he began to invent secret intelligence reports. In this he prospered greatly, for there were many espionage services at work in Rome.

Having discovered all this about Scattolini, Angleton now had the appalling task of advising OSS headquarters. This he did, despite his youth — he was twenty-eight — while he kept Scattolini under watch to discover who, if anyone, was behind this audacious figure. As Angleton declared, the persons behind the journalist were members of the British counterespionage service in Rome, whose chief was Philby. But, he also declared, he never discovered the purpose of the plant, except that in his view it had been part of a British plot to discredit Donovan, who by then had become unpopular and unwelcome at Broadway. As Angleton was recovering from his surprise that his mentor in counterespionage, Philby, might have been responsible for endangering his career, a further case arose in Italy. This was another curious affair, which Angleton code-named Dagger.[20]

By his own account in a number of personal communications that he sent directly to 109 — Donovan's security designation — Angleton learned through informants that Marshal Rudolf Graziani, the fascist defense minister of Italy, had hidden much treasure and many documents in and around the church of St. Agnese on the Via Nomentana in the Vatican quarter of Rome. He had placed them in the charge of his son-in-law, Count Sergio Gualandi, and the head priest at St. Agnese, Don Marchi, before escaping to rejoin Mussolini's rump government in northern Italy, which was controlled by Germany.[21]

In all, Angleton found nineteen large wooden cases stored in the church tower and in the catacombs around the church. These contained the coronation regalia and other treasures of the Emperor of Ethiopia, Haile Selassie, which Graziani had looted when he commanded the Italian Army in the Ethiopian campaign in 1936. The

The Philbys with Feisal, the future
king of Saudi Arabia, on the steps of
St. Aldro, Kim's boarding school at
Eastbourne. St. John is the second
from the right in the back row, Dora
stands below him, and Kim stands
at her right shoulder.
St. Antony's College, Oxford

Kim Philby, about age five
Kim Philby Collection, Moscow

After becoming a Moslem at Mecca and taking the name Abdullah, Slave of God, St. John joined King Ibn Saud and his court at Riyadh.
St. Antony's College, Oxford

St. John's first home in Jidda,
the Bait Baghdadi, had been the
residence of the Turkish ruler,
the Wali. St. John tied a team of
baboons at the front door to keep
Moslem pilgrims from intruding.
St. Antony's College, Oxford

St. John in Jidda with the American
lawyer Lloyd N. Hamilton, a signa-
tory to the Saudi oil concession —
"the richest commercial prize in
the history of the planet." A bitter
foe of the British government,
St. John used his influence with
the Saudi king to ensure that an
American company, not a British
one, obtained the concession.
Middle East Institute,
Washington, D.C.

St. John's Arab wife, Rozy, and their sons, Khalid and Faris.
Kim Philby Collection, Moscow

Kim Philby with his mother, Dora, a memsahib from a leading military
family in the British Empire. *Kim Philby Collection, Moscow*

Alice Friedman, the Viennese underground communist whom Kim married in 1934. Sunday Times, *London*

Aileen Furse, the daughter of a prominent "county" family, took the name Philby by deed poll and bore Kim three of their five children before he divorced Alice and married her in 1946. *Times Newspapers Ltd., London*

Sir Stewart Menzies, Churchill's spymaster, recruited Kim for secret work against the Germans during World War II and appointed him chief of the secret counterespionage group against the Soviet Union in 1944. *Author's collection*

James Jesus Angleton, who worked for the U.S. counterespionage service in wartime London, later served as the head of the CIA's counter-espionage service. Kim Philby was his friend and mentor in both London and Washington and is said to have helped destroy Angleton's service during the Cold War. *Estate of James J. Angleton*

Philby with one of his daughters in the early 1950s. Ordered back to London from Washington within days of the defections of Maclean and Burgess, he was suspected of warning Maclean of his impending arrest on treason charges. Philby was dismissed by the Secret Service and eventually appeared before a tribunal that sought to establish that he was a long-term Soviet spy. *Kim Philby Collection, Moscow*

After being exonerated in Parliament by Foreign Secretary Harold Macmillan in 1955, Philby gave a masterful performance at a press conference, declaring that he had not knowingly talked to a Communist since 1934. *Jane Bown/Camera Press*

Kim Philby in Riyadh with his father and his Saudi half-brothers. Reemployed by the British Secret Service in 1956, he had been sent to Beirut as a journalist to spy on American diplomatic and intelligence activities in the Middle East. The Observer, *London*

In January 1963, three years after St. John's death in Beirut,
Philby was confronted by a colleague in the British Secret
Service with "definite evidence" that he had been and was
still a Soviet secret agent. He confessed and then vanished.
This revealing portrait was taken by the KGB on his
arrival in Moscow. *Kim Philby Collection, Moscow*

Down and out in Moscow, after being abandoned by the KGB.
Kim Philby Collection, Moscow

On the up and up in East Germany, with Markus Wolff, the chief of the
Stasi, the secret intelligence service. *Kim Philby Collection, Moscow*

Philby and his fourth wife, Ruffina, a Russian introduced to him by his KGB case officer. In 1973 the KGB evacuated the couple to Yerevan, in Soviet Central Asia, after reports that the British Secret Service would try to assassinate Philby in Moscow. *Kim Philby Collection, Moscow*

Philby with the novelist Graham Greene, his friend and colleague. Philby's letters to Greene found their way to Maurice Oldfield, chief of the British Secret Service under Margaret Thatcher. *Kim Philby Collection, Moscow*

Philby's official KGB portrait, taken when he was admitted to the Order of Lenin, the highest award he received from the Soviet government. *Kim Philby Collection, Moscow*

СОВЕТСКИЙ РАЗВЕДЧИК

11·1990

КИМ ФИЛБИ
1912—1988

5 к ПОЧТА СССР 1990

Philby's portrait on a postage stamp issued by the Soviet government shortly before its collapse. *Author's collection*

James Angleton in 1975. His stewardship of the CIA's foreign counterintelligence department is still being investigated. When asked near the end of his life whether the time had come for him to talk about his relationship with Philby, Angleton replied, "There are some matters that I shall have to take to the grave with me, and Kim is one of them." *UPI/Bettmann Archive*

Ruffina Philby grieving at Philby's state funeral in Moscow, in May 1988. He is buried among members of the Muscovite ruling class at Kuntsevo cemetery. *Reuters/Bettmann Archive*

treasure was returned to the emperor by the State Department later in 1945. But it was the documents that interested Angleton the most. They consisted of seventy-seven files, which he took into his possession because, he reported to Donovan, "the subject matter" included "materials of interest to other Allies," and therefore "great secrecy was employed to protect the actions of this Unit." The files contained "a large amount of intercept cable material dealing with Allied ciphers [and] considerable information on personalities of interest to" the United States. And as Angleton further advised Donovan on February 6, there was much Italian intelligence material concerning Graziani's Ethiopian campaign. Among the documents mentioned were what Angleton called "memoranda and letters" by or involving Patrick Roberts, the British minister in Abyssinia, F. H. Stonehewer-Bird, the British consul general in Addis Ababa, and W. L. Bond, whom Angleton's memo described as being "attached to British Consul General at Addis Ababa" — a description sometimes appended to persons who were in fact British Secret Service officers.

The subject of much of file 73 concerned G. M. Mohammedally and Company, a large trading concern in the Abyssinian capital, Addis Ababa, with branches throughout the Red Sea and East African areas. As Angleton reported, the Italians believed that Mohammedally and Company was "the agency through which the [British] 'Intelligence Service' for Italian Africa operated," and it had been liquidated by Graziani when he captured the capital. Angleton's report did not go beyond this except to state that the files contained important "personality intelligence." Angleton's memo did not reveal whom this intelligence concerned, and it was not to be found in any files publicly available. There were, however, in the FBI files five documents entitled "H. St. John Philby: Philby, Burgess and Maclean." But these were closed indefinitely under Section 1b of the U.S. National Security Act "under criteria established by Executive Order to be kept secret in the interest of national defense or foreign policy."

In 1983, however, Angleton stated that among the personalities discussed in file 73 was St. John Philby. Although he declined to say what these references were, he did state that "they were not favorable to the subject in the case." Since by that time Angleton had made a number of statements that he had had cause to believe that Kim Philby was a communist since about the end of World War II, he was asked a further question: Did anything known to him at that time, 1945, lead him to believe that Philby was or was not a communist? "That," Angleton replied enigmatically, "was at that time a question involving a number of nuances not unlike those which arise when you ask yourself whether

a man is high or low church." Did that mean that Angleton knew that
Philby was a left social democrat but that he had had cause to turn
over in his mind whether Philby might be a communist? Angleton
replied only that "such matters are a question of faith." There, for the
moment, the question of what Angleton knew concluded.[22] There was,
in the entire history of the Philby case, no more important a question.
For on the answer rested a matter of consequence regarding the national security of the United States and its foreign policy.

Late in 1945, however, an incident occurred that did throw further
light on the question of who knew what about Philby's politics. At the
transformation of the OSS into the SSU, a new U.S. chief, Winston
Scott, arrived in London to take up his position as liaison officer to
the British Secret Services. Scott had had extensive wartime FBI and
X2 counterespionage experience under J. Edgar Hoover and was, therefore, by no means a novice. As he settled in, a problem arose from the
period that Philby was at the war station in charge of (with much more
besides) Iberia, Italy, and the western and central Mediterranean. A
large OSS espionage operation in Spain was found to have fallen into
the hands of a Spanish Marxist revolutionary, a certain Sicklar, a cor-
poral in the OSS who had become an American citizen. In March 1942
the Spanish government had complained to the American ambassador
in Madrid, who in turn complained at a high level in the State Department, that it had been established that the OSS network, which was
code-named Banana, was being operated in the interest of Moscow.
The Francoites had arrested some two hundred OSS subagents and
had executed twenty-five of them.

This report caused consternation at OSS X2 in London, and an
investigation was begun to establish how such an astonishing state of
affairs had arisen. How could it have been that X2 London, hitherto
so completely informed about intelligence in Iberia, was ignorant of
the fact that one of the OSS's most important networks anywhere was
(a) being attacked by the Spanish and (b) was operating under Moscow's control? Norman Holmes Pearson, the chief of the X2 desk at
the time, flew to Madrid to look into the matter on the spot. But
neither investigation, in London or in Madrid, was complete when X2
was liquidated along with the rest of the OSS.

Some attempt was made to talk to Philby about this, for the OSS
uncovered through a source operating independently of the Iberian
intercepts — Allen Dulles in Switzerland — that the German Sicherheitsdienst in Madrid had transmitted at least one signal, and probably
more, advising Berlin in considerable detail how the Spanish government had discovered that an American intelligence network in Spain

had been taken over to serve clandestine communism in the peninsula. In the event, Philby could not be found, for he had recently taken over the anti-Soviet section and he was under C's orders to have nothing to do with the OSS. Not until the OSS was liquidated did he surface, and then it was too late, for all the principals in Iberian matters, except Angleton, had returned to the United States to be demobilized. Nonetheless, the Banana case continued to rankle with all who knew about it. As the X2 London war diarist noted in his final report on the case: "There are many aspects of the case which have never been clarified to the satisfaction of all concerned."[23] How much had Philby known about this large matter, one that Kermit Roosevelt, the official historian of the OSS, called "the largest intelligence blunder of the war"? If he had read the Sicherheitsdienst signal, why had he not informed his allies in the OSS?

Winston Scott arrived at a time when a new phenomenon had begun to appear in British political life, that of the "fellow traveler," a supporter of the Soviet Union who had not gone so far as to embrace communism but who was generally anti-American. Scott took up his post in the belief that he was among socialists and must therefore be vigilant. He was. Early in his stay, having learned that Philby had become chief of R5, Scott attended a private party at which there were present a number of British Secret Service officers. He found himself talking with a British woman whom he did not know and, according to Cleveland Cram, who learned of the incident verbally and in writing from Scott, she showed herself, in Scott's view, to be "vigorously anti-American and pro-Russian."[24] Scott inquired about her and found that she was a member of Philby's family and that she had worked with Kim at War Station XB. This encounter may have been the point at which, in the American secret circle, doubts began to form about Philby's own politics, that Philby, too, was a fellow traveler. And it was possibly the origin of what Cram called "the first black mark" against Philby. The executive officer of the OSS, E. J. Putzell, remembered such a "warning" circulating among the OSS executive, that it mentioned "one other officer" of the British service, who was named in it, and that the report had originated with the chief of X2 in London, James R. Murphy.[25]

Such, then, was the state of affairs in the Philby case toward the end of 1945 when there occurred another matter, the Volkov affair, to interest Angleton about Philby. Seale and McConville noted shrewdly and accurately Philby's predicament at this juncture in his career:

> However careful one may be — and Philby was very careful — it is virtually impossible as a secret agent to avoid brief moments of ex-

posure, tiny inconsistencies, the scattering of microscopic clues which one day, perhaps years later, a counter-espionage officer will piece together into an incriminating pattern. Above all, one cannot be proof against the unpredictability of others, against slips, defections and betrayals in one's own camp. In the agonized calculations of every spy must be the near certainty that such hidden time-bombs are ticking away and will one day blow him into the open. The nice and dangerous judgment he must make is how long he can work in the shadow of this threat before he must jump clear. Philby, a C-E specialist himself, knew more exactly than most agents the nature of the risks he was running, and that somewhere, sometime, a C-E man would be waiting for him. He also knew better than most how far he could push his luck.[26]

So far there had been many such tiny inconsistencies. There had been his tutor Luce's warning to St. John that Kim was by way of becoming a liar. In Vienna in 1934, it was common knowledge that he married a communist activist and that he himself had become a communist underground worker. At Cambridge, the Robertsons had refused to give him the references he required to enter the Foreign Office on the grounds that he might prove disloyal to the British government. In Fleet Street, Muggeridge had concluded that he might be a secret communist. Then Philby had suddenly changed his political direction from right to left. He terminated his marriage to the Austrian communist Alice Friedman. He began to exhibit signs of fascism and to meet with leading Nazis in London and Berlin. He went to Franco's headquarters early in the Spanish Civil War as a stringer for British and German journals. Who had financed that expedition? He had objected publicly when the British political agent at Franco's headquarters gave Franco the fascist salute. He was an associate of Guy Burgess, a known Marxist-turned-fascist. He was also an associate of Colonel von der Osten, the German intelligence agent at Franco's headquarters. He had indicated that he was prepared to work for Colonel de Renzy-Martin, an SIS officer at the British agency on the Franco-Spanish border.

In applying to the British Secret Service in 1940, he had uttered false personal papers with the intention of concealing his marriage to Alice Friedman. His father had admitted to Colonel Vivian that he had been "a bit of a communist at Cambridge." In Section V, he suppressed the circulation of two papers by Trevor-Roper concerning the German opposition to Hitler and reports from Otto John pointing to the imminence of an attempt to assassinate Hitler. He may have been employed by the SIS in order to pass intelligence to the Russians. He had been outspoken in his criticism of C's decision to stop supplying Ultra to the Russians, whose cause was the "only just cause in the war." And what about Banana and Dusty? The "misfiling" of the captured papers of Henri Robinsohn, the Soviet intelligence officer who had been his case officer in France in 1939–1940 and had then been captured by the Germans on Christmas 1942? And Krivitsky's warning in 1939 that the Soviet service had sent a young Briton to Franco's headquarters in 1936–1937 posing as a newspaperman? What of the Pignatelli case and his determined attempt to prevent Angleton's recruiting him as an SSU spy?

There were undoubtedly more of these fragments. In all, except for the Robertsons' actions and his marriage, none constituted more than ambiguities suggesting, and not proving, that Philby was a secret communist who owed his allegiances to Moscow. None in itself could have illuminated the fact that he was a Soviet secret agent being employed as a "straight penetration agent" against the SIS. But they did constitute grounds for suspicion if (a) all or some of them were concentrated in a single file and (b) in the event that something occurred to give them meaning. That event now occurred. It came to be known as the Volkov case. And after Volkov, Philby could never feel safe again.

In September 1945, C called Philby to his office and handed him a file. A Soviet vice-consul at Istanbul, Volkov, had contacted a British consul, John Reed, and proposed to defect in return for £27,500 and political asylum. In return, he would provide intelligence that included the names of all Soviet secret agents in the Middle East. And he produced a selection of his wares for mailing to London. But Volkov insisted that his proposal should not be sent by signal because there were two Soviet agents operating in the Foreign Office and "one in counterespionage." Volkov did not provide the names, but clearly the persons he had in mind were Donald Maclean and Guy Burgess in the Foreign Office and Philby in R5. He wished that a handwritten communication be sent only by pouch to a high official and demanded an answer within three weeks, at which time he would produce the names of the spies working at the Foreign Office and "in counterespionage."[27]

Reed, who could speak Russian, reported at once to the ambassador, Sir Maurice Peterson. Peterson agreed to sign a covering letter to the Foreign Office but emphasized that his embassy would act only as a post office; SIS must handle the business itself. Reed wrote a memo on Volkov's disclosures and sent it in the diplomatic pouch to the

Foreign Office, where it went to Cadogan, who was still the permanent head and still the official responsible for liaison with C.

Cadogan sent Reed's letter to C, who sent for Philby as the head of the Soviet section. When Kim entered C's office, he related afterward, C "pushed across at me a sheaf of papers and asked me to look them through." Philby did so, concealing his severe fright with remarkable self-control. They discussed the case for a short time and Kim "told the Chief that I thought we were on to something of the greatest importance and that I would like a little time to dig into the background and, in the light of any further information on the subject, to make appropriate recommendations for action." The chief "acquiesced, instructing me to report first thing next morning and, in the meanwhile, to keep the papers strictly to myself."

That same evening the MI5 organization responsible for watching diplomatic wireless traffic in London noted a period of heavy traffic on the Soviet service's radio circuit between London and Moscow and, shortly afterward, traffic of identical length between Moscow and Istanbul. There was little doubt that the Soviet service in London had sent an important message to Moscow, which had repeated it to Istanbul. That information was recorded in the MI5 logs, where it remained until other information emerged that enabled MI5 to associate this wireless traffic with the meeting that day between Kim and C.[28]

As Philby himself was to state in another context, "There is often a good reason for eccentric behaviour in the secret service," and he was himself vigilant for any sign that C or his associates thought Philby himself might be the head of counterespionage in Britain referred to by Volkov. But as far as he could detect, there was no such suspicion. Kim then recommended that "somebody" should fly to Istanbul. After several twists and turns, C agreed that Philby should handle the case personally; and as Philby lumbered east he reflected on all aspects of the Volkov case. As he wrote, "I tossed around in my mind a problem which baffled me then and baffles me to this day." This was the "oddness of the reaction, shared by the Embassy in Turkey, the Foreign Office [C], and Sir David Petrie [chief of MI5], to Volkov's terror of communication by telegraph." As Philby wrote further:

> The oddness of their reaction consisted in the fact that they eschewed telegrams mentioning Volkov, and *only* telegrams mentioning Volkov. Telegraphic correspondence on every other subject under the sun, including many that must have been Top Secret, went on gaily as before. If we believed Volkov's warning we should have concluded that all telegraphy was dangerous . . . Not being an expert on codes

and cyphers, I concluded that it was no business of mine to draw attention to the gross inconsistency of our conduct.

Plainly, Philby felt uneasy. Was Volkov a trap set for him personally?

By the time Philby arrived and tried to make contact with Volkov — on the day Volkov's deadline expired — Volkov had disappeared. Inquiry showed that he was probably the man who, unconscious and swaddled in bandages, had been placed aboard a Soviet aircraft at Istanbul at about the time of Philby's arrival. As Kim then reported to C:

> The Russians had ample chances of getting on to him. Doubtless both his office and his living quarters were bugged. Both he and his wife were reported to be nervous. Perhaps his manner had given him away; perhaps he had got drunk and talked too much; perhaps even he had changed his mind and confessed to his colleagues. Of course, I admitted, this was all speculation; the truth might never be known. Another theory — that the Russians had been tipped off about Volkov's approach to the British — had no solid evidence to support it. It was not worth including in my report.

Philby returned to London. But he broke his journey home at Rome to talk with the chief of U.S. counterespionage in Italy, James Jesus Angleton, who had remained with the SSU when the OSS was liquidated. Kim's motive for stopping had little to do with friendship; he wanted to test the waters after the failure of his Volkov mission. Angleton was curious at Kim's unannounced arrival. Noting Kim's drinking, he put up with his visitor for two days and three nights while Kim described his version of the Volkov affair. Having heard him out, Angleton made a few consoling remarks, agreed to look him up when he came to London on leave shortly, and then put Philby on the plane for London, worse for wear of the considerable amount of alcohol they had consumed.[29]

Angleton claimed in later years that he found Kim's story unsatisfactory. It seemed to him that had Philby really wanted to interview Volkov, he would have reached Istanbul in twenty-one hours, not twenty-one days. Angleton may or may not have officially recorded his dissatisfaction, but John Reed, the Istanbul consul, did. He expressed disquiet about Philby's unhurried handling of the Volkov affair and his casual reaction when he learned that the Soviet ambulance aircraft had taken away a figure swaddled in bandages. Reed assumed that Volkov had been betrayed, and he communicated his belief to an SSU officer in Istanbul, asking, If he had not been betrayed by Philby, then who did?[30] Reed made formal mention of his concern over the way the Volkov case had been handled.

Those inquiring into the Volkov affair accepted Philby's view, supported as it was by the Foreign Office official at Istanbul who had been involved in the case, that the leakage had occurred as the result of Volkov's telephonic communications with the British Embassy. But as Hugh Trevor-Roper wrote, Philby's "combination of deliberate personal responsibility and almost criminal *insouciance*" when he was questioned about his handling of the case "long rankled with those who had hoped, through it, to make a notable contribution to counter-espionage."[31] But the quality of the evidence he gave was good, and his word was accepted by almost all who were present. But it was not accepted by the Young Turks inside MI5. A certain David Martin, an expert in the study of wireless communications, the same man who noted the surge in the pattern of Soviet wireless communications during the period of Philby's briefings concerning his Volkov mission, began to make some cautious inquiries about Philby's background.

As he did, the Philby case took another of its serpentine changes of course. A second Soviet officer, Igor Gouzenko, a cipher clerk at the Soviet Embassy in Ottawa, defected to the Canadian government at about the same time as Volkov, and his case was taken over by the chief of the British Secret Service in the Americas, William S. Stephenson, to whom Gouzenko made two major assertions: (1) That a chief of counterespionage in London was a Soviet spy whose code name was Elli. (2) That a distinguished British physicist, Allan Nunn May, who had worked in Canada on the Manhattan Project, was also a Soviet spy. His code name was Alek.[32]

Yet again, if any disquiet arose about Philby at Broadway there is no sign. To the contrary, as chief of R5 he became involved in the investigation into the Nunn May case with two senior British counterespionage officers, Leonard Burt of the Special Branch, the security service of the Metropolitan Police, and Roger Hollis, a senior official of MI5, the Security Service — the two officers who would have been immediately involved had the suspicion against Philby in the Volkov case gone beyond Martin. Plainly there was no evidence or even suspicion whatever against Philby in the Volkov case; it was not likely that either Burt or Hollis would have allowed Philby to continue on the case had there been anything against him. Conducting himself with his customary nervelessness and audacity, Philby remained with the case until the end, and was sitting in the Number 1 Criminal Court at the Old Bailey with Burt and Hollis when the jury found Nunn May guilty and the judge sentenced him to ten years' penal servitude at hard labor.

The identity of Elli remained a mystery for the next thirteen years until, at last, when it was too late to matter, it became clear that the only possible candidate was Philby himself.

In 1946, C appointed a new assistant director, Sir James Easton, who had organized the clandestine flight program to Europe during the war. At first acquaintance, Philby recorded in his memoirs, Easton "gave the impression of burbling and bumbling."[33] But this proved "dangerously deceptive. His strength was a brain of conspicuous clarity, yet capable of deeply subtle twists." The occasional glimpse of "Easton's rapier made my stomach flop over. I was fated to have a great deal to do with him." Almost at their first meeting Easton did cause Philby's stomach to flop.

According to Easton himself, by chance one day in 1946 he happened to learn that Aileen was again pregnant, for the fourth time. When he congratulated Philby, Kim made an unforgettable remark: "Thank you, sir. I can think of nothing more rewarding in life than the sight of a row of descending heads at the breakfast table." Being a gentleman of the old school, Easton, who did not then know Kim well, thought: "What a very nice thing to say. What a very nice chap Kim must be!"[34] He was to remember this minor courtesy with clarity, for at some stage Easton discovered that Philby and Aileen had not been married — as he thought and as Philby himself had indicated.

After that exchange, and perhaps because of it, Philby realized that he had to act quickly and do something, first about Alice Friedman, his wife, whom he had never divorced, and then about Aileen, the mother of his children. He had stated on his SIS documentation on joining the service in September 1940 that he had "married" Aileen, having "divorced" Alice. Calculating that candor was the best policy, Kim saw his patron, Colonel Vivian, now chief of SIS security. He explained that as a young Cambridge graduate he had fallen in love with a Viennese girl who had proved to be a communist activist. He continued, with his agreeable candor mixed up with his amphibiology, that Alice had been in peril of arrest or worse, for she was Jewish, and he had married her to give her the protection of his passport and had then brought her to England. There he had tried to talk Alice out of her communist ways but failed; the marriage had collapsed through the great differences in their views; and they had parted in 1936. Alice had gone to Paris because she disliked England, and they saw each other again only once, in 1939.

Kim explained that divorce was impossible because he thought Alice had been overrun in the German occupation of Paris in 1940. Consequently, when Kim met and fell in love with Aileen, they decided to live together as a married couple, Aileen taking Kim's surname by deed poll. In all, Kim concluded, they had had a normal and happy relationship and had produced three children with a fourth on the way. Vivian was won over and gave him permission to go to Paris to see Alice and get her to petition for divorce on the grounds of his adultery; the decree became absolute on September 17, 1946. Kim married Aileen on September 25, 1946, in the Chelsea registrar's office. The witnesses were Tim Milne, Philby's closest colleague and perennial deputy, and Mrs. Solomon, the lady who had introduced Kim to Aileen on the day the war broke out — and whom Philby had attempted to recruit into the Soviet service.

St. John had known all along that Kim and Aileen had not married and had even lied for them at his lunch with Vivian in 1941. He sent a telegram of congratulations and good wishes, and soon sent a second telegram of congratulations, this time on the occasion of the birth of Kim and Aileen's child. He also sent a check, as was his custom at the arrival of a new grandchild, for £100.

There the Philby case rested in London, Washington, and Moscow at Christmas 1946, when there occurred yet another twist. C, Stewart Menzies, whose conduct of office was noteworthy for its deviousness, relieved Philby of command of the anti-Soviet branch of SIS and sent him back to Istanbul as the station chief in Turkey. This was still a major appointment, where the main work was to keep an eye on Turko-Russian tensions and also on the Americans, who were, it turned out, just about to take an important interest there. But the post was by no means as sensitive as that of chief of R5. Philby found this sudden posting away from the executive at Broadway curious.

He wrote to his Soviet masters, in an effort perhaps to explain away statements that he was effectively demoted from R5 and that he had been sent to Turkey as a high-level double agent:

> One aspect of SIS from the counter-intelligence point of view is that it conducts offensive as well as defensive operations. After the war, a major reorganisation of the service was effected. One of the principles adopted may be called the principle of non-specialisation. Thus, after a number of years in the service, officers are expected to have familiarised themselves with a wide variety of offensive and defensive techniques, so that they can be posted anywhere at any time, to do any job.[35]

This policy, he went on to explain, might limit the value of a future Soviet recruitment of an officer, for it was unlikely that any officer will be posted to R5 for a long period. The usual term of service would be for two to three years. An officer with a flair for counter-intelligence might be posted to R5 two or three times in the course of his career. Even so, he would not spend more than a quarter of his career in that section.

Nonetheless, C had relegated Philby to a lesser task when the Cold War was coming on, when the service was under attack from the Soviet secret services, and despite his outstanding record. Why? The thought that there should be exceptions to the new policy certainly crossed Philby's mind, for as he himself noted in his memoir:

> The three senior officers of the service, the Chief, Vice-Chief and Assistant Chief, had no experience of counter-espionage and no practical knowledge of work in the field. But I was not senior enough to benefit from any such dispensation. As all my work for SIS had been concerned with counter-espionage at headquarters, I was obviously due for an early change of scene.[36]

At face value, therefore, Philby's appointment appears to have been routine. But there are inconsistencies about it that made it far from routine. There was as much trouble as ever between C and the Security Service over its attempts to "meddle" in the Volkov case. This was the time therefore to get Philby out of London and into a position where MI5's writ did not run — SIS operated only on foreign territory, MI5 only in Britain and the empire. Philby's replacement as chief of R5, Brigadier Douglas Roberts, was chief of the Middle East Intelligence Center and knew about the Volkov case, which still rankled with MI5. But C showed some regard for Philby when, with others, he authorized Philby "to trail his coat" and pose as a disaffected officer who wished to be of service to the Soviet Union — exactly what Philby was already. Two other R5 officers were involved in this dangerous game.

There was one other reason why C may have seen an advantage in having Philby as chief of the British Secret Service in Turkey. St. John Philby had returned to Mecca and resumed his place on Ibn Saud's privy council. At that time Britain had major political and commercial interests in Saudi Arabia and — most important of all — the king had become a notable figure in the maneuvers to create the State of Israel. The service knew of no more valuable an informant on Arabian politics than St. John Philby.

In May 1945, St. John learned privately, possibly from the Saudi diplomatic agent in London, that King Ibn Saud wished him to return to his court. All had been forgiven in regard to Philby's proposal in 1939 that Ibn Saud would be paid £20 million to use his offices to enable the Jews to establish a national home in western Palestine. By 1945, the king again felt the need for the services of his adviser in foreign affairs. His wartime grants-in-aid from the British government and from the U.S. Lend-Lease program were being terminated, and his royalties from Standard Oil were insufficient. The position was further complicated by a quarrel between the United States and Great Britain over oil in the entire region and by the prospect that the United States would back the establishment of Israel. Ibn Saud was alarmed. Would Philby return on the wings of speed? The Foreign Office, perhaps seeing an opportunity in Philby to counter the rising influence of the United States in Arabia, returned his passport to him and arranged for his official transportation.

By the end of June 1945 St. John was in a first-class cabin on the troopship *Carnarvon Castle,* bound for Alexandria with a load of Zulu and Basuto infantry. Rarely had a British government moved so quickly. St. John felt pleased with himself; his trading company, Sharquieh, still existed at Jidda. The OSS still existed and it had an interest in Philby's arrival at Alexandria, as did the British security authorities. As he disembarked, St. John remarked in a letter home, he felt like "a marked man and lots of people seem to know a good deal about me." Perhaps this was so. Roosevelt had recently appointed Colonel William A. Eddy, another of Donovan's officers, as consul general in Saudi Arabia, and he was already on his way there with $7 million to establish his ministry.

Eddy's departure for Jidda was accompanied by a marked change in Arab policy at OSS headquarters in Washington, one that boded no good for St. John, despite his services to the OSS. In June 1944, Major Carleton Coon, a Harvard anthropologist and an OSS secret agent, wrote a paper for Donovan called "Intelligence Work in Arab Countries." In tasking Coon, as the paper shows, Donovan had said that "he would like to have some very much under cover intelligence done in Saudi Arabia."[37] Although there is no evidence that St. John was aware of this change in policy or the existence of the paper, nevertheless he knew Coon's name — in 1934 Coon had entered Saudi Arabia without a visa to study some Ikhwan skulls, and he and Philby had fought almost to the death at Jidda, culminating in Coon's deportation, an indignity that the professor never forgot nor forgave. The opportunity to even the score came in September 1944, when Coon presented his paper.

Coon's case was that since Mecca was in Saudi Arabia and every Moslem endeavored to reach the holy places at least once, all Moslems between Morocco and the Philippines regarded King Ibn Saud as "the great leader of the free and holy motherland of true believers." Coon advocated the establishment of a special Moslem Department of the OSS to operate in Saudi Arabia and elsewhere in Arabia on three main grounds "(a) Oil (b) Airbases (c) Future markets." He argued that the enhancement of American interests in the Moslem world depended on the survival of the Saud dynasty. But first, Coon stated, the OSS needed to erase St. John Philby's influence at the Saudi court. As Coon advised Donovan, St. John was

> an extremely jealous man. He considers Arabia his private preserve as far as all scientific work is concerned . . . Any archeologist, anthropologist, geographer, geologist, etc., who comes to Saudi Arabia to work will have to reckon with Philby, and if Philby cannot wreck an expedition politically, he will do it by other and less agreeable means. It must be remembered that Philby can get any number of Arabs to do any dirty work he desires for him, and that he is an insanely jealous man. Only exceedingly well-trained men can hope to handle the Philby problem.

When the *Carnarvon Castle* arrived in Alexandria at daybreak on July 9, 1945, St. John was allowed to enter Egypt for the first time since his "kidnapping" in 1940. He made his way to the Heliopolis Palace Hotel, where, he was delighted to record, "even the waiter recognised me."[38] The next day Ibn Saud's private plane, a DC3 that was a present from FDR, took Philby to Jidda. He landed there on July 26, the day the Labour Party swept the Churchill government from power. There was no suggestion in his letters, however, that he cared at all. His mind was set on Ibn Saud and profit. There were riches now to be made in Araby.

Arriving at the Green Palace, he found everything just as it had been. He told Dora how Mustafa Nadhir, his head servant, was at the door, and his Sudanese cook, Muhammad, had not forgotten a jot of his old routine:

> iced lemonade for me and Mustafa after we got in, and Mustafa had a curry prepared at his house and sent it over for lunch, and the rest to do for dinner though Muhammad said that I would never eat curry at dinner! Grapes and my first fresh dates for five years were the pudding and the only thing I had to ask for was those little beaded nets of yours to keep the flies off the fruit.

Good times were back again.

The next morning he went by car to Riyadh, where he found "all the same people and the same doings." Nothing had changed except the cost of living and the princes' new habit of traveling not by camel or car but plane. He dropped into the routine of saying his prayers, attending three court sessions daily, arguing with the king, listening to the evening readings from the Koran. His association little impaired by war, politics, or absence, St. John resumed his position of grand vizier. During the next eight years, he wrote home to Dora, May, or Kim each week, sometimes twice a week. These letters constituted a unique correspondence concerning the king's affairs and politics at a time of tempest in the region — oil, Israel, Islam, imperialism, communism, the entry of the Americans, the gradual withdrawal of the English. No diplomat, no spy, no oil man, no reporter, could convey the rich opulence of Ibn Saud's political world as well. St. John alone could capture it, for he was the only Occidental to sit with the king, although Eddy buzzed about the court precincts on behalf of Standard Oil's interests and installations on the Persian Gulf coast of Arabia.

If the intention of the Foreign Office in allowing St. John to return to Arabia was to intercept his correspondence, the risk would have been repaid amply. Oil was the prize, and from time to time the Americans risked losing it through the unending royalty quarrels between Eddy and his successors and the Saudi administration. And the British oil companies waited in the wings to recapture the concession. The correspondence began the moment St. John arrived at the king's palace. "The Americans are all out to dominate everything here and at present they are having it all their own way as they can supply the goods and don't seem to worry too much about payment for them." He was "beginning to think that the Arabs really did not want independence," for with "all the money etc. which is being thrown at them they are quite content." Ibn Saud remarked to him at the privy council, "'I wish somebody would give me £10 millions.' To which I replied: 'What good would that do you? You would give it all away in a day or two!' So he would — he is silly in money if you like, but the gold, etc., seems to keep pouring in." As to the world situation as seen from Mecca,

> The state of affairs in Europe, and indeed of the rest of the world looks pretty gloomy, and there seem to be quite a lot of folk trying to egg the countries on to another war; but personally I don't think that there is any real danger of a war in the near future though it might start from some spark in Palestine if the Great Powers don't take care. I certainly don't think Russia wants a war at all, as Communism is much more likely to pervade the world under peace conditions. But there are certainly people in other countries including England who want a war with Russia while we have the monopoly of the atomic bomb in the right hands.

Then he added, "Anyway if there is to be another war I shall stay in safe Arabia, as I have no desire to be in jail as a Communist in one war, having been there as a Fascist in another!" These attitudes were to cause him much trouble yet again, this time with the Americans in Arabia.

St. John began to send tidbits of intelligence from the privy council for "Kim's delectation." In 1945 the British government had begun a manhunt for the grand Mufti of Jerusalem, a leading Moslem holy man who was wanted for trial for having started a violent rebellion against the British forces in Iraq in 1941, at the behest of the German intelligence services. The rebellion had been suppressed, but the grand mufti had escaped to Germany and was given asylum by Hitler. There he remained until the end of the war, when he again escaped and vanished. Writing from Hawiya Camp near Taif in Saudi Arabia, St. John revealed that the grand mufti was in hiding in Saudi Arabia under a grant of protection by Ibn Saud from the British, who still wanted to hang him.

As to that all-important question in Arabian politics, Ibn Saud's health:

> I am afraid our old man is now feeling the effects of anno domini and doesn't seem to have any spunk in him, perhaps because of his knee which seems to get steadily worse. It was rather pathetic seeing him limp to his place at the banquet the other day, as he thought it infra dig to be wheeled to it in his chair, which he uses freely whenever he is among his own folk to save his knees. Tell Mother he wouldn't dream of walking upstairs though he can't be more than 68! However I hope he will last another two years to celebrate his golden jubilee.

St. John returned to the question of Ibn Saud's vigor and virility again on November 7, 1948. "I fear he is steadily losing a lot of vitality," wrote Philby, adding that the king was now "very somnolent and inclined to be morose." The Arabs were "disgracing themselves," he declared, adding that there was nothing to stop the Jews from "conquering the whole of Palestine." It was "very difficult to explain the collapse of the Arabs," he went on, but "there is no doubt that it is the fault of their leaders including the great man here." All they think of "is making money and many of them are making lots of that." Also, Philby asserted, using terms reminiscent of those of 1940 that had landed him in jail, most at court hoped for

> another world war, in which case they can make lots more money without doing any fighting as in the case of the two last wars. But they

don't stop to think that perhaps Russia will occupy their oilfields! Anyway I take much pleasure in telling them that there is not likely to be another war in time to be of any use to them.

Yet, as Philby felt compelled to acknowledge in a letter only a few days later, he was not doing so badly himself. After being on or near the breadline for most of his life since 1925 and his resignation from government, he earned £1,200 in the first year after the war and now was receiving £11,500 — not a fortune, perhaps, but enough to enable Dora to live in genteel comfort. In December, revealing much in the area of matters of the highest interest to both the American and the British governments, the state of the king's health and general news about the dynasty, he was writing in a further outburst of indiscretion:

> Life is astonishingly dull here nowadays, with the King always som-
> nolent and all the high-ups concerned only with feathering their own
> nests. No wonder that Palestine has gone west with all the incompe-
> tence and graft that is ruining the Arab countries! And they don't
> like being criticised, though I am afraid I do a good deal of that,
> whether they like it or not.

As a precaution against sudden deportation he had removed all his books and papers from Jidda, placing them partly at Mecca and partly at Riyadh. In December he announced that he had secured a deal with the Saudi government worth £65,000 to build oil tanks at Jidda, but no prospect of riches stilled his tongue. Writing to Dora on December 16, 1948: "The king is all het up over the prospect of [the Jordanian king] Abdullah becoming King of Palestine" and that excited him "much more than the idea of the Jews getting what they want." He "wouldn't be at all surprised if some day with Jewish arms and help" Abdullah "were to stage a come-back against the Hijaz! He would not have much difficulty in taking Mecca as "the Saudi Arabian Government is in a bad way with corruption widespread in the highest circles and inefficiency evident at every turn." Philby ended, "I am afraid we must conclude that our Ibn Saud has seen his best days and lost the power of initiative which once made him great." Interesting stuff to C and the Foreign Office.

St. John returned to his favorite themes early in 1949, writing to Dora from Riyadh on February 25 that "the Arabs have made a mess of their affairs, an appalling mess, and the Jews are right on top of the tide, as they deserve to be as they are at least intelligent and know what they want and how to get it." The Arabs were quite unready and unfit for action and were "thinking of nothing but oiling their palms while the going is good." And he added: "Actually I think the Jews are the only people for whom I have any admiration in the world as it is today, and of course the Communists!!" Pro-Jewish or not, on January 31, 1949, Philby received a rude reminder that prudence might pay: his name appeared in the Egyptian press among a list of those to be killed by Hasanah, the Zionist intelligence service, or so he said in a letter to Dora.

He kept on and on, and on April 10 he returned to the inner matters of the privy council. It was "very dull these days" as Ibn Saud was "definitely getting old-mannish and is also . . . very annoyed that we are not going to fight the Russians just yet for his amusement." He also went back to his concern over corruption at the palace. But St. John personally grew prosperous as the middleman at Ibn Saud's court. In 1949 he won a contract for his principals to build a metaled road from Jedda to Medina. In 1950 he won the contract worth £400,000 to build a palace at Riyadh for the Amir Abdullah ibn Abdul Rahman. He also secured the contracts to build oil tanks at Mecca and discussed schemes for a radio telephone system, water pipelines, a quarantine station for pilgrims, and the provision of jet fighters and trainers for the Royal Saudi Air Force.

He was not becoming rich but he did remain prosperous, and he continued to use his position at court to attack the extravagance of Ibn Saud's sons, who had come to number some forty or fifty, all of them royal princes. Ibn Saud was an indulgent father, although, as he exclaimed, "A man's possessions and his children are his enemies."

By 1951, Ibn Saud's life had begun to ebb. When in September he tried to make the pilgrimage, he collapsed on the first day. He remained alert, but Philby was aware he could not last much longer. St. John remained at Ibn Saud's side. The king, too, remained loyal to his old friend, proclaiming on one occasion when prescribed a blood transfusion, "Give me some of Feelbee's. He's never ill." And at the outbreak of the Korean War in 1950, Philby wrote to Kim,

> The news from Korea is rather disturbing, but I don't imagine it means very much yet; just another little bite by the Communists, who seem to be meeting with little serious opposition except American talk at the Security Council! Surely they must have known that Russia was arming and training the northern folk for some venture of the kind . . . I can't help feeling that America is doing too much talking and boasting, while the Russians are going quietly about their business with every intention of dominating the East.

Shortly, Kim received a further letter from his father:

I can quite understand the Americans going all hysterical and squealing for help [in Korea]. After all they talked themselves into war, and thought they were on an easy thing; but they have found out their mistake, and what ever happens afterwards, it looks as if they will be pushed out of Korean before long. And they won't like that. It looks to me as if they are trying to divert attention from the mess they have made in Korea by talking of defending Europe, etc. If they go on talking like that much longer, they may find themselves involved in a real war, and they won't like that either, with the reds making all the running while they get ready and try to ginger up their unwilling allies to do some of the fighting. I must say the hesitation which all the United Nations are showing in actually coming forward to fight is making the whole thing a bit of a farce.

Through this and a tidal wave of other such letters, St. John's days at court were, by 1953, numbered.

But there was one matter he did not discuss in his correspondence, and that was his private life. In November 1945 the king paid all his debts to Sharquieh, of which St. John was still resident director. Ibn Saud also sent St. John two personal presents. The first was four thousand rials. The second was a new consort, a girl so slim and pretty that, though unseen by strangers, all Riyadh knew about her. When the driver called to deliver the child, he remarked that there was "an eight-cylinder girl" inside. Chosen by one of the king's wives — by Eddy's count, Ibn Saud had had a hundred and twenty-five — Rozy al Abdul Aziz had been one of the girls in the royal household. There was belief indeed that she was one of Ibn Saud's daughters. As usual, St. John kept Rozy a secret from all his English family, except Kim, but he confided to his diary that her real name must be Firuza, that she might be Baluch but more probably Persian, and that she was four-foot-eight, shy, and about sixteen. When she produced a son, Fahad, in 1947, the king directed that her status be changed to that of Umm Fahad. St. John was proud of his fatherhood rather late in life — he was sixty-one when Fahad emerged. In May 1947, while Philby was in India on the king's business, Fahad died, just five months old.

It was not long before Rozy was pregnant again and, while Philby was in England on leave, she presented him with another boy, Sultan. On Philby's return the king gave him a mansion at Riyadh, worth a princely £15,000, as a present for life and indicated that he wanted Philby "to spend the rest of my life here," which was "more or less my idea too." Philby took huge pleasure in Sultan's every activity, recording the boy's prowess in his diary. Philby, Rozy, and Sultan spent ten months shuttling between Mecca and Riyadh in his Land Rover. St. John and Rozy also took Sultan to Mecca to kiss the Ka'aba at Mecca and become a Moslem. But disaster afflicted the household of the faithful as inexorably as if Philby was no believer.

In July 1949, Sultan got whooping cough and severe diarrhea. And as Elizabeth Monroe recorded, by August his heartbeat was weak. Philby, racked with anxiety, drove first for a doctor, then for drugs and medicines. But in vain. On his return from the last of these errands the boy was dead. "Poor Firuza," he wrote in his diary, and bought her a lamb to be sacrificed to feed the poor. Philby's distress was patent when, a week later, he went to Jidda; an American newcomer, Bill Peyton, who had asked to meet him, was told that the dinner would be a quiet one because of his sorrow.[39]

In January 1947 Kim left London for Istanbul, traveling via Cairo. There he sent a telegram to his father at Mecca, and Ibn Saud ordered that a royal plane be sent to bring Kim to Saudi Arabia. As Kim recorded, he was "a happy man when I felt the warm breath of the desert and Cairo airport under my feet" — he had not had more than ten days' leave in the six years since joining SIS and felt in need of fresh sights. At Jidda, Kim was welcomed by his adoring father. It was, as Kim explained, his first acquaintance with the country to which his father had devoted the greater part of his life. But

> neither then nor thereafter did I feel the slightest temptation to follow his example. The limitless space, the clear night skies and the rest of the gobbledygook are all right in small doses. But I would find a lifetime in a landscape with majesty but no charm, among a people with neither majesty nor charm, quite unacceptable. Ignorance and arrogance make a bad combination, and the Saudi Arabians have both in generous measure. When an outward show of austerity is thrown in as well, the mixture is intolerable.[40]

Philby was not well received by Ibn Saud, who was tired and disgruntled. For his part, Kim "could not hide at least from his father how unimpressed, even bored, he was by the Saudi court and its petty indulgence." As for St. John's precious Arabia, Kim found it "alien, bleak, unbeautiful." St. John, however, was beside himself with joy that at last he and his son were together there. As St. John wrote to Dora from Jidda on paper bearing the Saudi coat of arms, the palm, salver, and scimitar, he felt ecstatic at the courtesies extended to Kim by the crown and court. In all, Kim spent five nights and six days at Riyadh, sharing a room with his father in the palace guesthouse and messing with the privy council. All from the king downward knew that Kim was to be the new station commander of SIS in Turkey, and appeared greatly impressed at the youth of a man to hold such an appointment.

On the last night but one, the king gave a banquet in the palace for Kim and another visitor, the Egyptian minister, at which there was the "usual long row of whole sheep on platters." The Amir Abdullah, the king's brother, placed Kim at his right hand and after the banquet gave Kim an elementary book on Arabic to study, "saying he really must learn the language now that he is to be so near and will have a chance of visiting the country again." At the end of the visit, the king presented Kim with a white headdress and gown woven with gold thread and £30 in gold, which Kim, surprisingly, accepted. He and his father then engaged in a complicated arrangement whereby Dora received the money as a gift without having to pay tax on it.

The royal aircraft took St. John and Kim to Taif, the mountain resort outside Jidda, where they spent thirty-six hours at the headquarters of the brigadier commanding the British military mission in Saudi Arabia. Then Kim left for Istanbul, where he formally took up his appointment in the middle of January. He was disguised as a first secretary at the British Embassy; his staff consisted of five men and his headquarters were at the consul general's offices in Istanbul, which SIS preferred to the embassy in Ankara. Thus he had begun learning his trade as a spy when, suddenly, the United States abandoned the quasi-isolationism into which it had retreated at the end of the war and became an active participant in the Cold War everywhere, but particularly in Turkey. Twice in just over a century Russia had invaded Turkey. Now it appeared, or at least it was feared, that it might try to do so again. In August 1946 President Truman had approved a joint paper by the State, War, and Navy departments which concluded that the Russians intended the breakup of the British Empire, starting with a bid to dominate the eastern Mediterranean. This would separate Britain from its empire in the Middle East, in Africa, and in southeastern Asia. "This is a blatantly crude plan," Walter Lippmann, the most influential columnist in the United States, wrote of the Soviet moves, "to transform the Mediterranean from a British into a Russian lake."[41] This was not in accord with Truman's policy.

Philby, so often a lucky spy, was lucky again. He arrived in Istanbul as station commander on January 26, 1947, just when Truman signed the National Security Act, which established such bodies as the National Security Council and the Central Intelligence Agency. It legalized the existence of the Joint Chiefs of Staff and empowered that body to prepare strategic plans and to provide for the strategic direction of the military forces. With its warrior population of more than sixteen million lying under the stomach of Russia, Turkey represented an important ally to the United States in the power equations of the Orient. It represented, too, an ally stronger still if Greece, with its six million men, made an alliance with Turkey against Russia.

Confronted with the threat of Russian expansion into the eastern Mediterranean and the Middle East, on March 12, 1947, about eight weeks after Philby reached Istanbul, Truman announced his doctrine. If Greece should fall to the communist element in the civil war that racked the country, the effect on Turkey, its neighbor, would be immediate and serious. Free institutions everywhere would collapse, including in the Middle East, with its oil so needed by Western industry. Congress allocated $225 million in military assistance to the Graeco-Turkish armed forces, and Turkey became a hot Russian intelligence target. Thus vanished Kim's prospects of a paid holiday beside the Bosphorus at the expense of the British government.

During that early period, Aileen parked her four children with Dora for a few weeks and followed Kim to Istanbul, where they leased a Turkish villa at Beylerbeyi, on the Asiatic side of the Bosphorus. In the distance to the left were the minarets of the Sophia mosque, and to the right the great bulwarks of the Hisari fortress. About half a mile downstream was the station from which Kim caught the ferry across the strait to Istanbul. All was ready therefore when the liner brought the children to Istanbul in February: Josephine, six; John, five; Dudley Thomas, three, and Miranda, who was born seven weeks after Kim's marriage to Aileen in September 1945.

The children and Aileen, at least at first, adored the house and its views, the cool breezes and the quiet after the heat, dust, and hubbub of Istanbul. Kim explained that he had chosen the villa because it was out of the diplomatic round, which he found a bore. He also thought that the diplomatic round might be dangerous, for his relations with Aileen were not as good as they had been and he did not wish to become the subject of gossip. All he wanted to do was to reestablish the reputation he had enjoyed at St. Albans: a man of great ability doing secret work for the government who was well and happily married with a brood of charming children. From the point of view of espionage, too, it was well placed; since anyone who wished to visit him had to come by water, it was simple to see who was approaching and to prepare.

In these idyllic circumstances, Kim and Aileen approached middle age, he the personification of a senior member of the official class *en poste* and vaguely *en fête* — he affected Palm Beach suits, bow ties or cravats, suede shoes. His charm was catlike. And there was always that slight stammer behind which he could hide when he wished. She was dark, slim, fairly tall, with good bones, long legs, a silvery laugh, and, in public at least, fun. Trevor-Roper, still keeping his eyes and ears open, received word about Kim from a friend at Istanbul. Philby seemed

> to have acquired completely the protective colouring of the office. That air of weary cynicism, that pose of the unhurried, sophisticated, worldly politician *Who sees through all things with his half-closed eyes* had become, as it seemed, entirely natural to him, as if he, too, had drunk from the drugged chalice of that secret church . . . Kim, I was told, had now become entirely corrupted. He lived an agreeable, self-indulgent life, in a pleasant villa on the Bosphorus, with a private lobster harbour, in lotus-eating ease. All passion, it seemed, was spent. He had become a *routinier* and a voluptuary — but still an efficient *routinier* and an agreeable voluptuary. He would ensure professional standards; but he would not disturb the ancient habits of the professionals. He was both efficient and safe.[42]

The private persons were very different. Aileen knew something of Kim's real work, although Kim rarely discussed his business with her. She knew at once too much but not enough for peace of mind. And here was the root cause of the trouble between them. There was a woman in Istanbul who knew almost everything that Kim did. She was a young, pretty, able SIS girl named Edith Whitfield, who worked as Kim's confidential secretary throughout the rest of Kim's career in the British Secret Service. Miss Whitfield, of course, knew nothing about Kim's work in the Soviet service, although at a later date she was interrogated about it by both the British and the Americans. Work soon beckoned, and it may have been that the Soviet service, to further its ends and his, fed him one or two castaways. We cannot be sure and neither can anyone else be. But the Akhmedov case caused some interest at a later date.

In 1942, Lieutenant Colonel Ismail Akhmedov, of the Soviet Army Military Intelligence Service at Ankara, had decided he wished to desert. A Tatar Moslem who had graduated from the General Staff War Academy, he had worked in Berlin on intelligence duties connected with the Nazi-Soviet Pact; on the German invasion of Russia, he had been arrested by the Gestapo as an enemy alien. When it was established that he had not been circumcised, the operation was performed, and he was then sent to a concentration camp and performed latrine duties.[43] A week later, however, Akhmedov and his companions were sent to Turkey in exchange for an equal number of Germans who had been trapped in the Soviet Union when war was declared. The exchange had already taken place when Akhmedov received an order from the Center to remain in Turkey as a Tass News Agency correspondent, which was to be his cover as a recruiter of French, Polish, Czech, Yugoslav, and other agents who wished to be trained in underground operations and then smuggled back into Europe to fight the Germans.

A good Moslem and a proud Tatar, he was content with life in the Moslem world of Turkey, although he was instinctively anti-Russian. By May 1942, suspected and disliked by his Russian colleagues, he was ordered to return to Moscow under Soviet escort, but he made contact first with the British and then with the Turkish intelligence services and was given Turkish asylum. He then became a Turkish citizen. Philby had known of Akhmedov's defection from the Turks, who had an intelligence alliance with the British service during World War II; and shortly after his arrival in Turkey, Philby received an instruction from his successor as chief of R5, Brigadier Douglas Roberts, the chief of the Security Service in the Middle East during the war (the job that St. John would have had but for his troublous record). Roberts wanted Philby to submit Akhmedov to "deep interrogation" as part of R5's work to obtain a full picture of the KGB.

Philby began the interrogation, under the auspices of the Turkish Secret Service, in June 1947. Akhmedov recalled:

> Philby was all smiles and courtesy: the impeccable English gentleman full of attention. For starters we had a drink and then got down to business, business which was going to last four weeks — each day from nine to five, with short interruptions for lunch, which was served in the same room. Oh, my God. If only I had known that this smiling courteous Englishman named Philby was the man who had tipped the KGB about [Volkov] and had sent him to certain death! If only I had known that here in this most luxurious apartment I was actually sitting in a KGB den and was being interviewed by a KGB agent![44]

But Philby was a thoroughgoing professional and Akhmedov had no reason to suspect him. He did note, however, a special thrust in Philby's interrogation:

> While neglecting my background, Philby showed an intense interest in my reasons for defecting, in the circumstances surrounding it, in how I was handled by the Turks, and finally in the attempts, if any,

of the KGB to whisk me out of Turkey or to liquidate me. He was
obsessed with learning the smallest details of the Turkish handling
of my protection . . .

He was extremely interested to find out how much I knew about
Soviet espionage activities in England. Here he tried his best to grill
me. Of course I did my best to tell him everything I knew of all those
matters, because I wanted to expose the scale of Soviet worldwide
espionage activities conducted through all channels. Also, I was hoping, as a result of our long association during these meetings, that
he might help me settle in England.

As Akhmedov also recorded, the interviews were taken down in
shorthand by Philby's secretary and were also tape-recorded. And from
time to time Philby asked questions that seem to have concerned him
personally. "How do the Soviets treat their double agents?" he inquired
at one stage. And at another, "Please, tell me again . . . how the Soviet
intelligence treats foreigners who work for them." None of his questioning conformed to standard practice; what Philby was after conformed to what the Russians wished to know — how much Akhmedov
had passed on regarding the Soviet high command, the general staff,
its military schools and academies, its research organizations, its leading personalities, and so on. Philby showed only delight when Akhmedov described his Turkish interrogation, which had not dwelt on these
subjects at all.

There were other such operations, more delicate, more dangerous,
more nocturnal. As the London *Sunday Times* Insight Team recorded
when they investigated the Philby case in 1968:

> Clearly, throughout his Turkish period, he was closely in touch with
> the Soviet intelligence network and equally clearly his superiors in
> London knew this. The vital question is how far the superiors had
> given him permission to venture into this moral twilight. The authors
> have had confirmation that Philby had been given permission to play
> the full double game with the Russians — to pretend to them that
> he was a British agent willing to work with them: which, unknown to
> London, was exactly what he was. This is the only way to explain the
> passionate defence of Philby by his colleagues of the SIS when the
> security officers of MI5 were convinced that he was a traitor. It was
> to be some time yet before things did go wrong for Philby but when
> the day came the SIS stood by him with an extraordinary, apparently
> inexplicable determination.[45]

Philby and his agents undertook several such adventures against the
Abwehr in Iberia during World War II, notably with Otto John and

with the German high command through the double agent Garbo. Tremendous dividends had been obtained through such dangerous connections, including the disruption of the Abwehr during the D-Day period and the success of the Fortitude deception plan. If such contact had worked against the Germans in a hot war, why should it not work in the Cold War with the Russians?

There is some evidence to support the *Sunday Times's* story. A retired senior SIS officer described in 1991 how he and one of Philby's officer's in R5, who was also senior, trailed their coats in the period 1947–1948 in the hope that the Russians would bite. The object: to obtain some knowledge of the Russians' capabilities and intentions and to obtain foreknowledge if the Russians uttered war orders. The possibilities through a successful penetration were immense. John le Carré, in a biographical statement on Philby's career, mentioned just such a stratagem: "He has been playing a damned difficult game flushing out Russians" in which his actions were "misinterpreted by a lot of outsiders, including those lower class buffoons in [MI5]."[46] His activities seem also to have generated Russian suspicions of him other than those begun when Andrei Vyshinsky, the Soviet deputy foreign minister, asked Sudoplatov to check the loyalties of Philby, Burgess, and Maclean over their reporting on the Marshall Plan in 1947. As Michael Lyubimov, a senior officer of the KGB who had much to do with Philby, would state, in about 1948 Stalin's chief of foreign secret services began again to investigate Philby. Was he London's man? Moscow's? Both? As Lyubimov stated:

When I read Kim's files to prepare myself for work as the deputy chief of the British Section I found a big document, about twenty-five typewritten pages, dated about 1948, signed by the head of the British Department, Madame MODRJRKSKAJ [sic]. Later she left the service to study Marxist-Leninism at the Academy of Sciences in Marxist-Leninism. This document was an analysis which proves that you can prove anything. Richelieu said, "Give me a pen and paper and I will hang a man." In an obstinate and tendentious way Madame MODRJRKSKAJ analyzed the work of Philby, Maclean, and Burgess. And she came to the conclusion that Kim was a plant of the MI6 working very actively and in a very subtle British way. This document went up into the hierarchy. It went still higher, as I recall, for at that time they wanted cases. A campaign had begun, you will recall, against cosmopolitanism. There was a fear of foreigners. The Party tune was that all foreigners were enemies of the people, and the NKVD wanted to play to that tune. The deputy chief of SMERSH, General Leonid Reichman, a friend of mine and of my father, told me only four years ago: "I am sure that [Philby, Burgess, and Maclean] were British spies. This shows I think that somewhere in the upper echelons was the feeling about "these subtle British spies." The idea was not therefore confined to Madame MODRJRKSKAJ. It was a stubborn suspicion within Beria's hierarchy.[47]

The effect on Aileen of the long journeys Kim took with Miss Whitfield, and his nocturnal disappearances, may be imagined. What could explain such behavior unless Kim was having an affair with his secretary? Gradually Aileen became sure that Miss Whitfield was destroying their marriage and she again began to display signs of a chronic neurosis: a combination of self-injury, self-humiliation, and pyromania. About ten months after Aileen had arrived in Istanbul, Kim advised his mother in case it became necessary to hospitalize Aileen and send the children home. Kim placed Aileen in the care of a leading Turkish psychologist to determine whether to send her home; at the clinic, she set fire to herself and, it was suspected, sought to inject her arms with her own urine, an attempt that produced serious boils.

Kim's letter to his mother resulted in the appearance of Dora at Beylerbeyi in late September or early October of 1948. Dora satisfied herself that Kim was not having an affair, but beyond that she achieved little. Aileen brightened up at the sight of her sensible, hard-drinking, burly, red-headed mother-in-law but remained acutely depressed. Dora wrote to St. John at Mecca and he replied with the advice that "it will be a long time before [Aileen] is really well again" and the best thing would be "for Aileen to go to England to rest and recuperate without the children, as Nanny is capable of looking after them." Poor Kim, St. John exclaimed. "He must be having a rotten time as he can't leave his work, and all the time must be worrying like hell."

Having been sent to one hospital and two clinics, Aileen seemed to pull herself together. But the real crisis came with the appearance at Beylerbeyi of Guy Burgess, whose arrival from London Kim announced with the words: "I've got sitting in my Jeep outside one of the most disreputable members of the British Foreign Office Service."[48] He in no way exaggerated. Now private secretary to Hector MacNeil, the socialist MP and minister of state at the Foreign Office, Burgess was still as plainly homosexual as he had been before he entered high office. He was still also a Soviet spy.

Guy's appearance in the home of Kim was bound to attract attention and cause gossip. It did. Guy drank ferociously — when the time came for Kim and Guy to settle the bill at the exclusive Moda Yacht Club, it was found they had drunk fifty-two brandies — and "behaved in a shamelessly disorderly fashion" reminiscent of an episode in the famous Dean's Bar, at Tangier. It was reported to the British consulate that Burgess had been heard to sing an obscene song:

> Little boys are cheap today
> Cheaper than yesterday . . .

Aileen could not bring herself to believe Kim's statement that Guy had come to Istanbul to see Edith Whitfield, who had been described as Burgess's girlfriend, an explanation he used again. Instead, Aileen saw the worst in the relationship. It is quite possible that Aileen knew that Guy's and Kim's ties included Soviet espionage, and she may well have deduced that Kim was still a Soviet spy; they had, after all, been living together for more than a decade. In any case, when Guy returned to London and Kim went off to the Russo-Turkish frontier for some secret reconnaissance near Mount Ararat, Aileen's affliction reappeared. Then, early in 1949, Kim was ordered back to London for what St. John's letter to Dora described as "a course lasting two or three weeks."

Philby left for London in March 1949, stopping briefly in Athens to see the SIS chief there, Pat Whinnie. The two men did not know each other except by repute, and Whinnie, one of the best men in the service, saw what Philby rarely if ever exhibited to his colleagues — the unpleasant side of his character:

> Maria and I had to go out. We left him with dinner, and the whisky decanter, all of which he drank. He was so sure of himself, so sure he was right. He would not warm to you unless you were prepared to flatter him, which I was not, or to match him quip for quip, which I was not prepared to do because I knew he'd beat me. He was . . . caustic and sarcastic, full of intellectual arrogance.[49]

While Kim was still in London, Aileen, without warning, suddenly arrived from Istanbul with the nurse and the children on March 14 and descended on her mother-in-law at "an unearthly hour." She was distraught, and Philby arranged for her to be hospitalized for observation while Dora took charge of the children. Aileen remained there for several weeks until she appeared to have recovered her composure, then returned to Istanbul, but it was not long before more trouble emerged. She had, she said, been attacked by a Turk near the villa. She was certainly bruised and injured, but no one could make sense of her story. Philby therefore asked his friend and colleague Nicholas Elliott, the SIS station chief at Geneva, whether he knew of a specialist in female fantasies. Elliott found one, and Philby flew with Aileen to Switzerland. Aileen entered a clinic for observation but once again she tried to set her room on fire and to inject herself with her urine. Except in general ways, the doctor was not able to discover the basis of her desire to harm herself. Aileen then recovered her better senses and the couple flew back to Istanbul, leaving Elliott with the belief that their relationship could not be the same again, that Aileen had deceived him in not telling him about her childhood mental illness. Nor did the marriage really recover.

Such was Aileen's medical condition when she learned that Kim had been offered, and had accepted, that most important appointment: chief of the British intelligence and security services in the Americas, with headquarters in Washington. Given the suspicion that had developed over the Volkov case, questions arose about why he should have been chosen for such a delicate post, why the Americans accepted him, and why MI5 cleared him for the appointment. Philby would be chief liaison officer with the CIA, the FBI, the NSA, the Royal Canadian Mounted Police; he would handle certain types of prime ministerial correspondence with President Truman; he would receive special intelligence about the Soviet service deriving from an early, successful, and major attack on the Soviet ciphers used to protect their cables between Washington, New York, and Moscow, and much else besides. It emerged authoritatively that the officer in charge of Anglo-American relations, which had become as important at the outbreak of the Cold War as they were at the outbreak of World War II, was Sir James Easton. As assistant chief of the Secret Service, he was third in the line of succession to the post of chief, and he had been promised that he would succeed chronologically when he joined the service. Accordingly, C went to special lengths to keep Easton informed about policy and operations.

Easton, in a series of interviews in 1986, related how C had written to the chief of the new CIA, proposing Kim Philby as the liaison officer between SIS and the CIA. But Philby's was not the only name proposed. Two other SIS names were offered in the same letter. It was the CIA that selected Philby's name. In the view of Dr. Ray Cline, an assistant director of the CIA during the Philby case and a noted historian of the CIA, it was James Jesus Angleton who selected Philby's name.

Two explanations have been offered by a senior retired CIA officer who had official reason to interest himself in Angleton and the conduct of his office. The first was that Angleton continued to regard Philby highly even after the Volkov affair; the second was, he saw that in Philby there might be a way to communicate to the Kremlin information designed to affect its "fundamental strategic planning," as had been done during the war. If this was so, it supposes that Angleton knew something of Philby's politics but that he did not communicate his knowledge either to the FBI or to the British authorities. It follows therefore that Angleton had a particular reason for selecting Philby, notwithstanding the concern about his handling of Volkov. What was that particular reason? We shall never know for certain unless the CIA makes public its secret study of Angleton, but as the author of that study remarked, "By this time Angleton had made deception his game and whenever it was about in the CIA you can be sure he was behind it."[50] But it must not be forgotten that Philby himself possessed what Nicholas Elliott called "a supreme talent for deception."[51]

As Philby wrote, it took him "all of half an hour to decide to accept the offer." He would be taken "right back into the middle of intelligence policy-making and it would give me a close-up view of the American intelligence organisations [which] I was beginning to suspect were already of greater importance from my point of view than their British opposite numbers." Not bothering to wait for "confirmation from my Soviet colleagues," he left Istanbul early in September 1949. It was a desperate time.[52]

War with Russia seemed imminent because of the Red Army's siege of Berlin, which it had begun in June 1948 in an attempt to force the Western powers to abandon Berlin, and continued when Philby returned in September 1949. The headquarters was in "a preparatory state for war," as Easton put it, as Philby spent most of September being briefed for what he called "the unlimited possibilities of my new assignment in the Lion's Den." He spent much time with Easton, from whom he received most of his instructions. He wrote enigmatically: "I appreciated, not without misgiving, his command of the elusive patterns of Anglo-American cooperation." What he meant is anyone's guess, but it at least suggests that Philby was alert to all the possibilities inherent in his appointment, among them that a plan might be afoot to use him as he had used the German intelligence service during Bodyguard, the deception plan for D-Day. By his own account, he also spent time with his Soviet controller in London, Yuri Modin, but, Modin remembered, "we spent not a second more than necessary in each other's company." Where did they meet? "On the South Bank of the Thames by County Hall at lunchtime when there were crowds of people who all looked like us, gray officials, clerks eating sandwiches."[53]

Easton had considerable knowledge of the personality, politics, and operational intentions of the CIA and FBI, having visited the American capital frequently on air intelligence matters — an area in which the intelligence relationship was particularly close, now and for a long time in the future as England became the forward air base of the United States against Russia. Philby's task was to further this Anglo-American relationship. Easton warned Philby about the perils of adopting what had been the general attitude of many British officials in Washington during the war, that the United States might have gained the raw power, but the British had retained the experience and the wisdom in great affairs. The Truman administration, of which Easton had had experience, was considered at the British Embassy to be narrow, sensitive, inexperienced, and quick to take offense. But there remained the "special relationship" between the two countries, although this was not admitted for fear that the Soviet Union would conclude that there was a plot afoot. Above all, Easton warned Philby, a special political attitude awaited British intelligence officers in Washington.

From Easton, Philby proceeded to other important briefings. One was with "the formidable" Maurice Oldfield, now chief of R5. Philby had not been aware that both Washington and London had developed the capability to read some Soviet ciphers from September 1945 onward on the New York–London and New York–Washington circuits. But now he did learn about it, and the discovery gave him still another reason for anxious thought. There must be code names in the Russian traffic. Was his name there? Kim wrote of that briefing:

> My briefing on the counter-espionage side also aroused grave anxiety in my mind . . . and included a communication of the first importance. Joint Anglo-American investigation of Soviet intelligence activity in the United States had yielded a strong suggestion that there had been a leakage from the British Embassy in Washington during the years 1944–45, and another from the atomic energy establishment at Los Alamos. I had no ideas about Los Alamos. But a swift check of the relevant Foreign Office list left me in little doubt about the source of the British Embassy. My anxiety was tempered by relief, since I had been nagged for some months by a question put to me by my Soviet contact in Istanbul. He had asked me if I had any means of discovering what the British were doing in a case under investigation by the FBI — a case involving the British Embassy in Washington. At the time of asking, there was nothing that I could have done. But

it seemed, after my talk with Oldfield, that I had stumbled into the heart of the problem. Within a few days, this was confirmed by my Russian friend in London. After checking with headquarters, he was left in no doubt that information from the FBI and my own referred to one and the same case.[54]

The Los Alamos spy proved to be Klaus Fuchs, a German physicist who had acquired British nationality when he fled Germany and joined the British atomic bomb program. The second suspect proved to be Donald Duart Maclean, one of Philby's coconspirators, who recently had left the embassy in Washington to become, first, the counsellor at the British Embassy in Cairo and then head of the American desk at the Foreign Office. When the cloud burst over Maclean, as it did, it did little to enhance Philby's standing at the FBI, an office that was, through its links to MI5 in London, the center of reserve about Philby in the American capital. Maclean's code name in the Soviet service was Homer.

By September 1949, the time had come for Philby to leave London for Washington. The world situation was grave, as Churchill himself had stated only recently in a speech to the Massachusetts Institute of Technology. The "thirteen men in the Kremlin have their hierarchy and a church of Communist adepts, whose missionaries are in every country as a fifth column, obscure people, but awaiting the day when they hope to be the absolute masters of their fellow countrymen."[55] It was "certain that Europe would have been Communized, like Czechoslovakia, and London under bombardment some time ago but for the deterrent of the atomic bomb in the hands of the United States."

As Philby wrote of that final period:

> My last call in London was at the Chief's office. He was in the best of form, and amused me with malicious accounts of the stickier passages in Anglo-American intelligence relations during the war. This turned out to be more than just pointless reminiscence. He told me that the news of my appointment to the United States appeared to have upset Hoover [who] suspected that my appointment might herald unwanted SIS activity in the United States. To allay his fear, the Chief had sent him a personal telegram, assuring him that there was no intention of a change of policy; my duties would be purely liaison.

The reason for J. Edgar Hoover's reserve about having Philby in the United States has never been made clear. It may have been no more than his usual reaction toward the presence of a foreign spy in the capital. It is on record that he objected repeatedly to the presence of

William S. Stephenson, the wartime British intelligence chief in the United States and that he tried to declare Stephenson persona non grata. But there may have been another reason.

On June 16, 1945, Air Marshal Sir John Slessor, a major figure in operations during World War II and a future chief of the air staff, wrote a paper for the highest levels in Whitehall in which he advocated a continuation of the "close cooperation" with the United States in both scientific development and intelligence. But Slessor also noted:

> If this proves impractical — and for commercial reasons the Americans make it so, though I believe we have both of us more to gain commercially from cooperation than from competition — then our secret scientific intelligence organization should be extended to cover the U.S. The Americans are insecure people and I do not believe we should have any serious difficulty in finding out all they are doing if we were prepared to spend the money to do so. Conversely their secret intelligence is amateur to a degree and I do not think we should have much to fear from them.[56]

Slessor's advocacy received much support in Whitehall; and there was a good deal of interest and concern about U.S. activities in a number of directions, including war planning and the growing demand all along the political spectrum for a preventive war by the United States against the Soviet Union.

Philby hinted that he received some private instructions when he concluded in his account of his meeting with C: "The Chief showed me the telegram, then gave me a hard stare. 'That,' he said, 'is an official communication from myself to Hoover.' There was a pause, then he continued: 'Unofficially . . . let's discuss it over lunch at White's.'"[57]

Thus Philby departed for the United States under that best of covers for a Soviet secret agent, that of the senior British secret agent in the Americas.

13

Washington

1949–1951

PHILBY REPORTED for duty at the British Embassy, which resembled an English manor of the Queen Anne period, on October 10, 1949. The note to Secretary of State Dean Acheson from the ambassador, Sir Oliver Franks, was entirely formal and revealed nothing of Philby's appointment in the British Secret Service, the peacetime existence of which was never acknowledged by any British government. The note said:

Sir,
    I have the honour to inform that Mr. H.A.R. Philby has been appointed to be First Secretary at H.M. Embassy for the United Kingdom as of 10 October 1949. I would be grateful if his name might therefore be included in the Diplomatic List.
    Mr. Philby is married and his address is 5228 Nebraska Avenue, Washington, D.C., telephone Emerson 4117.

The note then gave a brief outline of Philby's career, stating that he was educated at Westminster but, curiously, not mentioning Trinity College. He had been a *Times* war correspondent, 1936–1940; "Civilian assistant at War Office 1940–1941" (his SOE cover); "attached to a Department of the Foreign Office, 1941–1947" (SIS cover); "1st Secretary H.M. Embassy Turkey, 1947–1949" (SIS).[1]

    That was all. He was thirty-seven and he had been in the British Secret Service for nine years and the Soviet's for sixteen, and the American service had known of him, or had worked with him, for seven years. The embassy was the largest in Washington, the most important in the British foreign service; it was a combined diplomatic and military establishment, for it housed the British Joint Staff Mission to the Department of Defense at the Pentagon. The chief of the British staff was Marshal of the Royal Air Force Lord Tedder, who had been deputy supreme commander to General Eisenhower before and during the campaign in Europe. It is said that Philby's communications with London were regarded as the most secure available to the embassy and that his office handled all political and military communications of top secret and higher classifications between the two governments. This included communications relating to Soviet and Anglo-American atomic bomb matters, then the most secret of all.

The ambassador was one of Britain's ablest, the Right Honourable Sir Oliver Franks, Privy Councillor, Knight Commander of the Bath, Knight Commander of the Order of the British Empire, sometime Praelector in Moral Philosophy at Glasgow University. The key elements in Franks's policy were (1) to maintain and strengthen the wartime special relationship with the United States; (2) to increase British world prestige; and (3) to help counter Soviet expansion diplomatically.

Philby's main tasks were to establish and maintain good working relations with the CIA, the FBI, the National Security Agency (NSA), and the Canadian secret services. None of these tasks except the last was likely to be simple. U.S. civil servants were not uniformly friendly toward official Britons. Their own history, the U.S. tradition of anti-colonialism, the latent xenophobics of sections of the official classes, the spirit that America alone had won World War II, press hostility, the Palestinian and Irish problems, the distaste for the London social-ist government— all combined to require that British civil servants such as Philby conduct their business in as diplomatic a manner as possible. As Captain H. R. M. Laird, a senior British operational naval intelligence officer in the U.S. capital had warned of his long experi-ence there:

> As regards the future, I should like to restate what I know has been reported on verbally and otherwise by all officers who have been to the United States, that is, the importance of the careful selection of all officers who are sent over the Atlantic. Access achieved in obtain-ing information depends to a very large extent — almost unbeliev-ably so to those without firsthand experience — on the personality of the officers concerned and their ability to hit it off with their

American opposite numbers. It should be made certain that the officers selected "enjoy" their life in the States and are prepared to like Americans and appreciate the American way of life.

It must be realized that, pleasant as any appointment in Washington is, all British officers and their families are under continual criticism by Americans of all classes and types and if an officer is to be successful he must be prepared for this and able to cope with it in the natural course of his public and private life. Many of us have felt very strongly that this is not sufficiently appreciated in the United States.[2]

A Russian view of Philby's attitude toward the United States, that of Mikhail Lyubimov, reflected how difficult he was likely to find his two years in Washington — and how well he concealed his inner attitudes. As Lyubimov stated:

He was very British here. He felt as do so many Britons that the Americans were only two hundred years old, and that they were a crude civilization. You know, the typical British attitude towards America — condescending, they appeared only two centuries ago through a war with Britain. They have no culture. Oh! The Americans have no style, that sort of thing.

But there were other reasons for his dislike — the complete commercialization, the complete subordination of the cult of the yellow devil, as we call the dollar — a statement deriving from Maxim Gorki when he wrote about New York being "the city of the yellow devil," meaning gold. Kim thought that the Americans were imperialist. He shared the view that Nagasaki and Hiroshima and the war in Vietnam and other matters were crimes. In all this his views were much more emphatic when he was talking about the United States than he was about Great Britain. He deplored the loss of British independence to the United States. American culture was not his cup of tea. He thought the Americans were dangerous people, in the thermonuclear sense, and he could conceive an American surprise attack upon the Soviet Union.[3]

James Angleton became Philby's control, his point of contact at the CIA. Angleton was now reaching his best, physically, mentally, and politically. He was tall, lanky in the much admired Marlboro cowboy style, tailored by Brooks Brothers, and wore a gold fob watch, New and Lingwood shirts, and the official Homburg. His mode of transport was less grand: his official vehicle was a battered Studebaker. His hair was going steely gray already, his facial bones were good, and his skin was light brown velvet. But he was not quite a WASP. He was different.

Apart from all else, he was Anglo-Mexican in origin. That was then a rare blend. He had never really been accepted at Yale, except by the literati; and he was not quite accepted as a WASP at the CIA. But he was a handsome man who was eyed by the women in the long corridors of L block, the temporary wartime buildings by the Reflecting Pool near the Lincoln Memorial, then the CIA headquarters. The great temple of intelligence at Turkey Run on the George Washington Parkway was not built until 1954, the year in which Angleton became chief of the new CIA counterintelligence service.

He was exceptionally secretive, even to the point of using a spy name when moving about headquarters; and for many years the gnomes of the agency thought that he was a crack Soviet counterespionage analyst called Lothar Metzl, a Viennese café pianist before the war. In the exquisite higher reaches of Georgetown where he moved socially, he was known as James Jesus Angleton, although he always objected to the use of his second Christian name. But no one knew his job description at the agency. He proved to be an exceptional manipulator of men, his colleagues, and even the agency itself. But he did not have the highly disciplined classical mind of Philby; and that was why Philby was able to make mincemeat of him, even on his home ground. Angleton did, however, fancy himself as the Machiavel of the new agency and was regarded as such. Philby acknowledged his special abilities. Whereas, he wrote to Sir James Easton, most of the men he met in the Truman administration were "one step removed from the plough," Angleton needed watching.

If Angleton had doubts about Philby (as his statements concerning the Dusty and Dagger cases in Italy and Banana in Spain and Putzell's and Winston Scott's statements just after the war suggested), then, as will be seen, Angleton concealed them effectively. As Philby remarked years later, had there been any suspicion of him, he would never have been sent to Washington by C, and the Americans would never have accepted him. Yet he may have been in error here. Of all the many statements about Angleton's knowledge of Philby's loyalties, the most telling and authoritative is that of Sir Patrick Reilly, chairman of the Foreign Office's Joint Intelligence Committee, the highest British intelligence authority, when he declared that "Angleton had suspicions about Philby" but "that he never took any action to warn us, the close allies of the United States. Nor did he inform the FBI."[4] This statement suggests that Angleton had a purpose in accepting Philby into such a confidential and important position; that there was a purpose seems clear from a statement by Sir James Easton, C's deputy in charge of relations with the CIA: When the CIA proposed that the SIS establish a liaison officer, C submitted the names of three officers whom he believed the CIA would find acceptable, one of them being Philby.[5] In the view of a retired CIA officer with special knowledge, if this was so, then it was Angleton who advised the CIA management to accept Philby.[6]

And what could his purpose have been? It may have been that Angleton wished to establish whether Philby was really as reliable as his reputation suggested. It may have been that he wished to establish whether Philby was spying against the interests of the United States. But it may also have been that he wanted to recruit Philby for a deception against the Soviet Union. Such tasks were part of Angleton's work. It was very dangerous work, requiring much agility of mind and skill. Whether Angleton possessed the skill required to match wits with Philby was a matter that would be debated later. For in the light of what occurred during Philby's two years in Washington, the degree of acceptance that he came to enjoy at the CIA, and the near-war situation that existed throughout that period between the United States and the Soviet Union, it seems that by facilitating Philby's entry into the United States, Angleton unwittingly endangered the U.S. national security for some unknown purpose of his own. It was on this point that Angleton would himself be investigated by the CIA to establish, among other things, whether he was or was not a Soviet secret agent. For much about Philby's Soviet mission in Washington can be deduced from a paper he wrote for his KGB masters much later in his career, which plainly reflected what he intended to accomplish in Washington — the penetration and disruption of the U.S. intelligence system — just as he had penetrated and disrupted the Germans during World War II.

As Philby wrote to a high-ranking KGB officer after his Washington service, the best way of penetrating the U.S. secret circle was through the British secret circle.[7] He emphasized the merit of attacking the United States through, in particular, the British Security Service in London because, while MI5 "offers a narrower field for counter-intelligence purposes, since its sphere of action is confined to British territory," nonetheless, "its files contain a much wider range of information than might be supposed." In the

> extensive exchange of intelligence with R5, SIS's foreign counter-intelligence service, on the principle of the indivisibility of counter-intelligence, MI5 had always maintained its legitimate interest in the headquarters, branches, personnel, methods, etc. of enemy intelli-

gence services. [Furthermore,] there is close liaison, and voluminous exchange of intelligence with the FBI, and even, though on a much lesser scale, with CIA. At least some CIA information, which is not passed direct to MI5, reaches it indirectly through SIS channels. It may also be added that MI5 intelligence is generally more easily accessible than that of SIS, owing to its immeasurably superior filing system.

The greater advantage of penetrating MI5 was that "virtually all its activity is of interest to us [the KGB]. Its chief function is to protect Britain from our intelligence services and those of our allies." As a very important sideline,

> by collaboration with the FBI, it also helps to protect the USA . . . The main disadvantage of MI5 [as an agency through which to penetrate the security services of the United States and the rest of the English-speaking world] is that it plays no part in offensive operations except in respect of embassies and consulates on British soil. It is likely to know nothing at all about British or U.S. attempts to obtain political, military or economic information from the Soviet Union or its allies. Nevertheless, in spite of these drawbacks, it remains a highly important target for penetration.

The range of interests of the Government Communications Headquarters (GCHQ) in Britain "is a still narrower, though still vitally important, field for penetration." Although it is concerned solely with cipher-breaking,

> the information which it yields is probably more important than that of all the SIS and MI5 agents put together. Yet direct penetration may not give appreciable results, as the work is highly specialised and highly compartmentalised. For instance, any agent infiltrated into [GCHQ] might well find himself detailed to study codes of only secondary interest to us.

It would be therefore "more profitable to penetrate [GCHQ] through either SIS or MI5." The SIS

> receives virtually the whole of the [GCHQ] product while MI5 receives anything of counter-intelligence interest. Thus, an enterprising SIS officer of standing in the service should be able to find out which codes have been broken, though he probably would not know how they had been broken. Similarly an MI5 officer of standing should know what foreign intelligence service codes had been broken.

Philby then turned to the U.S. intelligence services. Much the same considerations applied to the

> FBI, CIA and the National Security Agency, but with a difference. The FBI is a far more self-contained organisation than MI5. It has been deliberately kept so by Hoover. The cleavage between the FBI and the CIA goes far beyond the normal inter-departmental rivalry. The organisations have totally different mystiques. The average FBI officer is a "midwestern" type, aggressively American; CIA is largely drawn from the eastern seaboard, and has a strong cosmopolitan streak. For these reasons, among others, exchange of information between the two organisations is deliberately kept to a minimum. Both the FBI and CIA receive more information from the British than from one another. When I was in Washington, I often received intelligence from the FBI which I was not on any account to pass to the CIA, and vice versa. Thus, in the USA, it is not so easy to penetrate one organisation from a foothold gained in the other as it is in Britain.

It followed that

> an agent in the FBI would be valuable for the protection of our operations in the Western hemisphere but might well be useless in respect of American attempts to penetrate the Soviet Union or its Allies. Similarly an agent in the CIA should be able to uncover plenty about American penetration without ever knowing much about counter-measures against our activities in the Western hemisphere.

Through his experience and knowledge of the U.S. intelligence circle, Philby advised the KGB that an American penetration had to be

> considered a very long-term operation. It would be unreasonable to expect a new recruit to gain access to a wide range of intelligence; his duties would be severely limited. Only after perhaps five or ten years would he be given extended responsibilities and thereby access to a wider field. The first years should therefore be devoted to nursing him and building up his personal standing in the organisation.

As to the most penetrable U.S. service, he concluded, the FBI, "curiously enough, is less security-minded than the CIA." It began

> as a police organisation and, although its security division is now perhaps the most important of its divisions, its techniques still bear the stamp of a police organisation. It relies on blanket methods, using huge human and technical resources, but it is rare to find subtlety or deviousness in its activity. Thus it forms a strong contrast to MI5,

where the relative poverty of resources puts a corresponding premium on sheer brain power.

As to the NSA, his knowledge was "strictly limited to the section which worked on Soviet intelligence material in 1949–51." Philby "imagined" that what he had said about GCHQ applied also to the NSA and advised that

> if any agent is infiltrated into either cypher-breaking organisation, he should preferably be a Russian-speaker; in which case there is a strong likelihood that he would be posted to one of the sections dealing with Soviet wireless activity.

Philby's inner and secret attitude toward the CIA, defined at a much later date, reflected the attitude of the Soviet service: the CIA was becoming a main adversary in the Cold War, or as Philby put it: "OSS was a product of the hot war, CIA of the Cold War." The question before him, therefore, was how the CIA "turned into the raving beast." Its staff consisted of "a lot of very sensible chaps, but a lot of maniacs were allowed to go off every-which-way and do more or less what they liked." The "dirty tricks multiplied of their own momentum. Naturally, if you think in terms of global struggle, dirty tricks are inevitable; but without control and purpose, they become incredibly wasteful and too often counterproductive."[8]

His inner attitudes, combined with his exceptional ability as an intelligence officer, therefore made Philby a very dangerous friend, especially with a man such as Angleton, an original and determined Cold War warrior not very far from being a McCarthyite. Angleton's main responsibility was to ensure that Philby learned nothing about the CIA — its personalities, its policies, its operations — except what the CIA wanted him to know. In addition, Angleton was to pass to Philby such secret intelligence as the CIA felt he should have as part of the Anglo-American intelligence-sharing agreements. For his part, Philby was expected to do what a CIA officer with a large experience of liaison work would call "legalized espionage, that is to say to learn as much as he could about the CIA without getting himself *png'd*."[9]

As chief of the Secret Service in the Americas, Philby had his offices in the most secure area of the chancery, which were known in the embassy as the Rogues' Gallery. On the garden level facing Massachusetts Avenue, the gallery consisted of a number of individual offices with steel-grille doors and combination locks along sixty feet of corridor. His personal staff comprised an assistant, Geraldine Dack, a Canadian woman of ability and undoubted loyalty, and Edith Whitfield, Philby's secretary from his days in Istanbul. Also in the gallery was Geoffrey Paterson, representing the Security Service, MI5, and Sir Robert MacKenzie, the Foreign Office's security officer in the Americas. Later, Guy Burgess joined the group. A further member of the gallery was Dr. Wilfred Basil Mann, of the SIS's scientific intelligence service and an expert in intelligence relating to the Soviet atomic bomb. Later, it would be alleged against Mann that, having been the fifth man in Philby's group, he deserted the ring and became Angleton's man inside the Rogues' Gallery.

Born in 1908, Mann was a British citizen by birth, an outstanding scientist, a product of the Imperial College of Science and Technology in London and a series of imperial scholarships that had enabled him to study in Denmark and at the radiation laboratory at Berkeley, California. He became attached to the Establishment that grew up in the formative days of wartime nuclear physics and the early British work on the atomic bomb. In 1943, when the United States and Britain fused their research and development on the bomb into the Manhattan Project, Mann joined an organization that was, under another name, the British scientific intelligence service — the service to which Air Marshal Slessor referred in his paper on the need to engage in scientific espionage against the United States in 1945.

Mann was posted to Washington in 1943 and remained there with some gaps while engaged in atomic matters in Canada and the U.K., until 1951. Between 1948 and 1951 he held the rank of attaché at the British Embassy, and during the Philby period, from 1949 until 1951, he occupied a specially equipped office almost next to Philby's in the Rogues' Gallery. As Mann himself related, it was here that he kept his files of British decrypts of Soviet signals traffic relating to their atomic bomb experiments. These were produced in Britain and sent to him for passage to a most secret committee of the CIA, one responsible for studying intelligence relating to the Soviet atomic bomb. Despite the McMahon Act, which terminated the exchange of atomic information with the London government, Mann's association with the CIA atomic group continued illegally, largely because Mann had the Soviet decrypts and the CIA did not. As he remarked, the CIA was "voraciously eager to receive British raw and processed intelligence," and "this great asset was the only thing that made my job tenable."[10]

When Philby arrived in October 1949, he became Mann's chief of station and, as such, under long-standing rules, he handled for transmission Mann's top-secret communications with London. These were put into one-time-pad ciphers — the one virtually uncrackable code — and sent over Western Union's wires to Mann's headquarters in London, in Shell Mex House in The Strand. There they were read only by Commander Eric Welsh, the chief of C's scientific intelligence service, a man with a tremendous reputation for his work during the war. This traffic may have been secure from the attentions of Philby, unless he had access to the texts before they were encoded — a matter about which there is no clarity. Still less sure was the fate of the messages initiated by Mann that bore a still higher classification than top secret. These were sent by Philby in his own cipher to C in London. The contents of this particular series of telegrams were considered by the standards of the times to be "astronomically sensitive," according to Mann.[11] But as he wrote of that second class of telegrams when Philby deserted to Russia in 1963, he felt that "all the work I did during the eighteen months that we were together in Washington had been almost a complete waste of time."[12]

Against this background, the Philby case took one of its most peculiar turns. Mann and his wife formed a friendship with Angleton and his wife, one that lasted many years. There were many insinuations concerning this association, but the gravest of them was that Angleton learned from an Israeli intelligence officer in 1948

the name of the British nuclear scientist whom they had unearthed as an important Soviet agent. For various reasons . . . Angleton decided not to share this knowledge with his British colleagues. He arranged for "Basil" to be "turned." "Basil" agreed to change sides as directed, gratefully accepting guarantees of protection and the promise of American citizenship when his work was done.[13]

Basil was Mann, and one of his tasks was to "keep a vigilant eye on Philby." The worth of this story, as told by Andrew Boyle, is impossible to estimate. It is not improbable, for with the advent of the atomic and thermonuclear bombs there grew up apace an entire industry devoted to espionage, counterespionage, and deception. Angleton was part of that world, a sort of thermonuclear Hades where the object of all was, again, as Norman Holmes Pearson wrote, "to lead the enemy down the wrong path, wrong for him, right for us."[14] So was Mann. It is not likely that Mann betrayed the SIS in these various arrangements, for he remained persona grata in Britain for the rest of his life.

As to Mann's personal assessment of Philby, "In public he was always suave, self-possessed, gracious, charming and erudite. Only later did we realize what powers of instant dissimulation he possessed."[15] Of his own involvement in this serpentine case, Mann said that it was "a story of how an ordinary scientist was caught up in a web of suspicion" and that "we must accept that in the process of safe-guarding national security *and* our freedom, the innocent cannot always be protected from harassment."[16] Thus the Mann aspect of the Philby case concluded, not with a resounding libel action against Boyle, which Mann would have won if he had been able to get Angleton's testimony, but a suspicion that there was some truth in Boyle's allegations that could never be proven or disproven. Mann had become caught in the webs of the secret circle, and Angleton himself made Mann's predicament the greater when he leaked the substance of a statement of Colonel William R. Corson, a U.S. intelligence officer, in a history of the Washington intelligence community, *The Armies of Ignorance*. Corson described how, through his connection with the Israeli intelligence service, there was produced "some remarkable results and intelligence coups." One in particular was worth mentioning briefly, for

it involved the identification and subsequent manipulation of three British intelligence officials who were Soviet spies. The three were [Donald] Maclean, who was in charge of the chancery at the British embassy in Washington between 1944–48; Guy Burgess, who was posted to Washington in 1950 as the second secretary in the British embassy; and Harold Adrian Russell Philby, known commonly as Kim Philby, who served as England's anti-Soviet intelligence chief and who in 1949 was the British SIS representative in Washington, working in liaison with the CIA and the FBI.

As a result of the American-Israeli secret intelligence connection, each of these three spies was identified, Maclean's identification leading to Burgess' and thence to Philby's. By itself the mere act of identifying these three Soviet spies is noteworthy; but the subsequent manipulation, which included providing them with intelligence disinformation to mislead the Soviets, makes the overall operation a classic one. In the course of manipulating them — playing on their personal, physical and moral weakness and vanities — the CIA's small band of secret intelligence professionals were able to discover the identities of other Soviet agents in place in the United States and elsewhere, and to use that information to thwart Soviet subversive initiatives in a wide variety of government, business, and scientific endeavors.[17]

As to the worth of the recurrent theme of deception in this phase of the Angleton-Philby relationship, a single statement merits attention. This statement was made by Major General Edwin L. Sibert, who in the war in Europe had been chief of intelligence to General Omar L. Bradley, commanding general of the U.S. twelfth Army Group, and then to General Eisenhower. Sibert was therefore a member of the U.S. military establishment when he joined the CIA, a civilian agency. He became an assistant director of the CIA with zone responsibility in strategic deception. It was in that capacity, he claimed, that he learned that Philby was used as a conduit of disinformation about the effectiveness of the Strategic Air Command (SAC) and the size of the U.S. atomic arsenal "at the time of the Korean War"[18] — a statement that raised majestic possibilities in the Philby case in Washington.

According to Sibert, there was considerable doubt in Washington between 1948 and 1950 that the SAC would be capable of carrying out its mission, which was, in the event of war, to strike Russia instantly with a single, war-winning blow. Under this plan, then called Trojan, Moscow and Leningrad were to be destroyed by D plus nine days with 18 other first-priority cities. The first attacks would require 133 atomic bombs, of which 8 would be dropped on Moscow and 7 on Leningrad. The second phase consisted of 70 cities and 292 atomic bombs. The offensive would be conducted by B-29 and B-50 medium bombers flying mainly from England, Cairo-Suez (then under British control), and Okinawa, with B-36 bombers flying from the United States. The findings of the Pentagon were that the first phase of Trojan might succeed but not the second, owing to it was feared, loss of bases through Soviet reaction, losses of aircraft, weapons and fuel stockpiles, and transport aircraft, and, in particular, the unserviceability of the surviving strike aircraft after the first phase.

This estimate was widely accepted within the U.S. Air Force, and it was assumed that the Soviets were aware of the SAC's inadequacies. Moreover, there was a political question affecting the credibility of the SAC. In December 1948, the secretary of defense, James Forrestal, visited Europe and called on Churchill, General Clarence Huebner, the senior American general in Europe, and General Lucius Clay, the U.S. military governor of Germany. All had spoken of Stalin's success in deprecating the power of the American atomic response while, at the same time, emphasizing the tremendous power of the Red Army in Europe. On his return to the States, Forrestal brought these points to the attention of President Truman and suggested a program to counter the underestimation of the power of the bomb at the Kremlin.[19] Stalin's campaign to suggest that the atomic bomb was a weapon "to frighten children" and Chairman Mao's that the SAC was "a paper tiger" had begun.

In these circumstances, it became vital to the national interest, to the balance of power itself, that Stalin be induced to accept that the SAC and the atomic arsenal were capable of dealing the Soviet Union the "single war-winning blow," that the great U.S. deterrent existed and could be employed at any moment. As always with Stalin, he would read only the reports of tried and tested agents whose information had reached him over the tried and tested lines of the Soviet intelligence service. Philby was surely a candidate, and a very good one, for such a stratagem. Thus the SAC became the center of a web of stratagem to make it seem not just powerful but more powerful than the Red Army and, in fact, the most powerful destructive force in the world.

That such a conception existed over the SAC and its war plans seems sure: it was standard operational procedure to write the actual war plan in concert with a cover plan. Yet if comprehensive knowledge of the real war plan came into existence, it is significant that *no* knowledge of the false one has ever been found, thus demonstrating the axiom of deception: that it is, as Dulles himself wrote, the most secret of all secret operations. That Philby would have been involved in Trojan is also evident. In the interests of secrecy, and through long-standing communications arrangements, much of the highest-level consultation concerning the Anglo-American aspects of Trojan passed through Philby's office in Washington to C in London. C acted as the agent in such communications for Prime Minister Attlee. And the U.S. government was required by agreement to consult with Britain in the military use of atomic weapons from bases on British soil. For one thing, the range of the B-50 and B-29 bombers was so limited that they were required to stage through British bases on their way to the Russian targets; for another, Britain was becoming the principal base for the storage of the nonnuclear assemblies, which consisted of the bomb casing, the electrical and mechanical components, and the explosive charge used to detonate the nuclear component. The nuclear cores were held in the United States, mainly at an air base in Maine, to be flown to England or the other main forward base, Okinawa. In the period before 1952, President Truman authorized the positioning of 664 such assemblies overseas, 220 of them in Britain.

Philby was well received at the CIA. His record had preceded him with both the Americans and the Britons. William Harding Jackson, the deputy director, had been deputy chief of intelligence at General Omar Bradley's command in Europe, the twelfth Army Group, and at the end of the war he had inspected Broadway to see whether any parts of the SIS could usefully be incorporated into the CIA when it became law. His report had had a small but influential circulation in Washington. It had spoken of the SIS's close association with the Foreign Office, which Jackson felt had led to the "undue conservatism" he had encountered in Broadway. But he thought that quality also provided the SIS with its "great homogeneity of organization and purpose," and that "aids greatly in preserving the security of its operations." Finding that the SIS had rendered "extremely valuable services" during the war, Jackson also observed that "the informal and seemingly casual organization and methods of British intelligence" might not flourish in the United States; nonetheless, "few competent observers would deny that, on the whole, the British intelligence system has worked satisfactorily under the severe stress of war."[20] The entire relationship between the British and the Americans was founded on mutual trust and discretion.

One of the first officers to work with Philby was James McCargar, a member of a prominent San Francisco family who was educated at Stanford University and had served during the war as a vice-consul in Irkutsk in Soviet central Asia and at Vladivostok in Siberia. They were about the same age. McCargar had married into the Cooper-Keys, a political family with large interests in Associated Newspapers, a leading London newspaper house, and he and Philby worked together for eight months on an operation proposed to the State Department by the Russia Committee of the Foreign Office. They intended to use royalist Albanians recruited and trained by the CIA and SIS to overthrow the Stalinist government in Albania.

McCargar regarded Philby as something of an odd man out at the embassy. He wore suede shoes, cravats, and crumpled suits when the rest of the senior staff subscribed to a strict dress code. At the time, Washington was the most conservative city in the United States, and this informality caused some surprise. But he was very highly regarded at the CIA because, as McCargar wrote,

> for one thing, he came to us with a very high reputation. Americans are admirers of "Young Turks." And Philby was of course a certified Young Turk, having been the ringleader of a sort of revolt of younger officers in MI6, who then showed his mettle by consigning to oblivion the man who had given him his chance in that organization. For another, the CIA generally, having worked closely with the British during the Second World War, was devoid of the anti-British sentiment afflicting some parts of the American Government and population . . . and the British SIS was held in high regard by those who had had close association with it.[21]

Then there was his agreeable personality. McCargar found him to be "devoid of pretension. He was courteous, and not lacking in engaging warmth." He was witty. "His smile, suggestive of complicity in a private joke, conveyed an unspoken understanding of the underlying ironies of our work. He was capable. Behind the modest, slightly crumpled exterior, there was no mistaking a quick mind and a tenacious will." His house was sparsely furnished, and his entertaining usually consisted of a pitcher of martinis, some ice, and some glasses. McCargar also noticed that Philby was not above the tricks of his trade. As he related:

> Philby and I were engaged in jointly conducting an operation abroad, reports of which reached us separately from the American and British agents in the field. In those days, American communications left much to be desired. The British worldwide communications network, on the other hand, was one of two invaluable assets which the British War Cabinet had retained at all cost during the wartime liquidation of British overseas holdings. (The other was the reinsurance business.) On three successive occasions, Kim came into my office with urgent reports which I had not yet received through our channels. The third time, when I again had to confess ignorance, Philby, with an air of anxious helpfulness which had just the right degree of opacity, asked, "Well, look, wouldn't you like us to handle your communications for you?" The offer of the poisoned apple was adroit. (I of course had no idea that it was doubly poisoned.) In declining it, I laughed. The charm part was that so did he.[22]

Philby's relations with the FBI were not as agreeable. For the rest of his life Philby entertained a special detestation for the director, J. Edgar Hoover, telling Phillip Knightley at a meeting in Moscow how "Hoover hated and distrusted just about everybody — Slavs, Jews, Catholics, homosexuals, liberals, 'niggers,' and the rest. They blinded him to his real job, luckily."[23] Hoover had opposed Philby's appointment in a signal to C, and he believed all liaison officers such as Philby were no more than spies. It was well remembered that Hoover had sought to arrange the deportation of one of Philby's famous predecessors in the United States, Willie Wiseman, whom Hoover suspected of fabricating the Zimmermann telegram, which had brought the United States into World War I. Similarly, he had accused Wiseman's successor in World War II, William S. Stephenson, code-named Intrepid, of conspiring to compromise the neutrality of the United States in the war with Germany, of fabricating intelligence calculated to show that a German-Mexican army had assembled south of the border to invade Texas, and of conspiring with Donovan to establish the OSS as a British control in the United States. There had been several indignant meetings at the embassy between the wartime British ambassador, Lord Halifax, the U.S. attorney general, and Hoover at which Hoover had demanded Stephenson's removal as chief of the Secret Service in the Americas. Hoover failed. Similarly, as Philby later alleged from the safety of Moscow, his home and even his office were likely to be bugged, his private mail intercepted, his personal movements watched. Hoover, he asserted, had been determined to wreck his relationships at the CIA. As Philby related in his memoir:

> My first house in Washington was off Connecticut Avenue, almost directly opposite that of [Mickey Ladd] the Assistant Director of the FBI in charge of security. It seemed a good idea to camp at the mouth of the lion's den for a short spell — but only for a short spell. The house was a small one, and I was soon arguing the need for moving to larger quarters at a safer distance, eventually settling on a place about half a mile up Nebraska Avenue. [Ladd] was my principal contact with the FBI and I saw him several times a week, either at his office or at home. He was one of Hoover's original gunmen in Chicago — "the guy who always went in first" when there was shooting to be done — and he looked the part. He was short and immensely stocky, and must have been as hard as nails before he developed a paunch and the complexion that suggests a stroke in the offing. He had no intellectual interests whatever. His favourite amusement was to play filthy records to women visiting his home for the first time. He had other childish streaks, including the tough, direct ruthlessness of a child. By any objective standard, he was a dreadful man, but I could not help growing very fond of him.[24]

But Philby could not avoid the FBI, where he and his office were known by the code name Stott. He had serious business to transact there with Ladd and Robert J. Lamphere, the FBI Soviet Section's chief analyst. That business concerned Homer, the Soviet spy and senior British official who had been detected at work inside the British embassy, but not yet identified, between 1944 and 1945. Philby was obliged to see much of Lamphere, and as the American would write later of their first encounter, at the FBI the British Secret Service "had the reputation of being a bunch of skilled horsetraders with whom you trafficked at your peril."[25] Lamphere was a busy man, for the FBI's cryptographers had broken into one of the KGB ciphers used on the New York–Moscow and the London-Moscow signals circuits between 1944 and 1945, and, as he described his position at that time, he was "immersed in dozens of other investigations that were coming out of the deciphered KGB messages."[26] In all, the decrypts were to reveal forty-nine major cases of Soviet espionage directed mainly against the U.S. atomic bomb program, among them the Homer case. Kim handled MI5's signals for them and so was kept fully acquainted with all the twists and turns in the case and, indeed, even recommended lines of inquiry. It was Homer who eventually brought about the first dénouement in Philby's case.

When Philby came in, Lamphere removed some files from his chairs, brushed some imaginary dust away, shook hands, sat his visitor down, and then made conversation. Kim was excellent at small talk and usually hooked his victim with a witticism and his modest stutter there and then. But Lamphere was not engaged immediately, although he was exactly the type Kim had in mind when he described his American colleagues as "one generation removed from the plough." Lamphere's father was a miner; his son was born in 1918 in the Coeur d'Alene mining district of Idaho. Philby was dismissive of Lamphere and described him as "a nice puddingy native of Ohio [sic] who was responsible for the detailed analysis on the American side"[27] of the investigation into the identity of Homer. But Lamphere was much more formidable.

Lamphere was a plump man who wore roomy suits and two-tone shoes; Philby wrote later that "I could hardly believe that this unimpressive man was being spoken of as a future chief of MI6, in line for a knighthood." Most disturbing "was his lack of friendliness; he seemed to have little interest in the conversation. Perhaps, I thought, his sterling qualities were hidden, and he'd be warmer when I got to know him better." At that time, of course, there was "no way I could conceive of the depth of treachery reached by the seedy-looking man next to me."[28] Nor could he have realized that Philby knew from his Soviet case officer in London that Homer was in fact Donald Maclean, who was now rising toward the position of head of the American desk at the Foreign Office, where he would be able to make a comprehensive sounding on a daily basis of the American political position in relation to Russia. Nor could Lamphere have known that he and Philby were headed toward an intense national crisis that profoundly affected the morale and safety of the United States itself. A second grave Anglo-American case was breaking, one that bore directly on the absolute American monopoly of what had become the weapon of deterrence in the situation between the United States and the Soviet Union, those "two scorpions in a bottle," as the leading U.S. atomic scientist, J. Robert Oppenheimer, termed the adversaries.

In mid-September 1949, shortly before Philby's arrival, Lamphere had found in the 1944 Soviet decrypts questions concerning the gaseous diffusion process, one of the main processes by which the American scientists had obtained the type of uranium required for the atomic bomb. When he read the message, "it became immediately obvious to me that the Russians had indeed stolen crucial research from us."[29] On September 23, President Truman announced that the Russians had carried out their first atomic explosion. Until that moment Truman had been confident that the Russians would not, as he had said to Oppenheimer, be able to build their own bomb. The main intelligence estimates, those of the Joint Chiefs of Staff, were that they might develop a small limited atomic capability, and the main war plan of the period, Trojan, reflected that belief. But now all war planning and foreign policy estimates had to be revised against the possibility that the Soviet Union would possess thirty such weapons by mid-1950, and, with their copying of the B-29 Superfortress, the means to carry them to their targets in the United States, if only by one-way suicide missions. Also, the Truman administration had to accept that the Soviet Union might be developing the thermonuclear bomb, a weapon with a special menace to the United States.

By December, attention had fastened upon Klaus Fuchs, a German physicist of high ability who had been given British citizenship early in the war and had then been employed on first the British and then the Anglo-American atomic bomb program. Fuchs was arrested and began to confess to an MI5 interrogator. He admitted having passed to the Russians all the data relating to implosion and the thermonuclear weapon theory on which he had worked at the Kellex Corporation and the Manhattan District, the two organizations responsible for the research and development of atomic weapons. As a special White House committee met to decide whether, in response to the Soviet atomic explosion, to recommend that the United States proceed to develop a thermonuclear weapon, the counselor at the British Embassy, Sir Derek Hoyer-Millar, appeared at the State Department to report that Fuchs had that day confessed to spying for the Soviet Union and that his espionage covered American work "on thermonuclear phenomena through the summer of 1946."*[30] Fuchs admitted that he had given the Russians the Teller studies that the Manhattan District had made in 1945 and 1946. These had intimated that

*On February 2, 1950, Fuchs was charged with violations of the Official Secrets Act, and on March 1 he was sentenced to the maximum imprisonment permitted in law, fourteen years.

the thermonuclear weapon would prove to be a feasible weapon of war. This intelligence had reached Moscow by late 1947 at the latest, and consequently the Soviets knew what the Americans knew by that date.

The news struck the administration and the electorate with great force. As a special assistant on national security at the Truman White House would record of the emotions and fears released through Fuchs's confession:

> By the time of Truman's decision the cold war was raging. The Soviet menace was everywhere; the dream of a cooperative postwar world was long dead; the iron curtain was solid; the Berlin blockade was a recent and instructive memory; the captive nations were not a slogan but a vivid reality. Soviet hostility and duplicity were taken for granted. China had "fallen" [to communism], and "Who lost China?" was the question of the hour. Alger Hiss had been convicted of perjury early in January, and Klaus Fuchs confessed his treason just four days before Truman's final decision.[31]

His confession came too late to influence Truman's action, but "it would have had a quite different weight if the president had been leaning the other way." As it was, the president took six minutes to decide that there must be a crash program to build the H-bomb.

As a result of the Fuchs confession, the Anglo-American atomic research and development program established by Churchill and FDR at Quebec in 1943 was irreparably damaged. Fuchs's treachery served to reinforce the American "sense of betrayal by a recent ally," Russia, who had "now become a minatory foe."[32] The intelligence exchange between Britain and the United States was seriously damaged for a time. Because the McMahon Act already forbade U.S. agencies to pass atomic intelligence to any foreign agents, contact ceased between the highly secret CIA committee for atomic energy intelligence and the British. Mann, the British scientific intelligence service's representative, found himself excluded for some months from the committee's meetings, at least until it discovered that he had decrypts from his office in London relating to the Soviet atomic bomb program. Then the CIA, in Mann's words, "voraciously eager"[33] to see this raw data and the finished intelligence arising from it, resumed contact and allowed Mann to attend its meetings, despite the McMahon Act. The exchange became lawful only when the Blair House agreements were signed. The Fuchs affair also produced a serious quarrel between Philby and Hoover that had several important implications.

As Philby recorded:

> Hoover, who had contributed nothing to [Fuchs's] capture, was determined to extract maximum political capital from the affair for himself. To that end he needed to show that he had material of his own, and such material could only be obtained through the interrogation of the prisoner by one of his own men. He announced his intention of sending [Lish Whitson, a senior FBI agent] to London to question Fuchs in his cell. Paterson [the MI5 representative in Philby's office] and I both received instructions to tell him that such a course was quite out of the question. Fuchs was in custody awaiting trial, and it was just impossible to arrange for his interrogation by anyone, let alone by the agent of a foreign power. I found Hoover in a state of high excitement, and in no mood to be impressed by the majesty of British law. He refused to budge. [Whitson] was sent to London, with peremptory instructions to see Fuchs, or else. The answer was "or else."[34]

A foreign agent, Attorney General Sir Hartley Shawcross decided, could not be allowed to interrogate a prisoner facing trial on the gravest charges. Whitson returned to Washington empty-handed to face an irate Hoover and found himself banished from the executive to the junior offices, which as well as ended his career.

The worsted Hoover suspended all FBI-British exchanges concerning the Soviet decrypts, known by the code name Venona-Bride, a suspension that lasted from February until May 1950. From this period forward Philby began to limit his visits to the FBI to about one a month, leaving the question of the Homer decrypts and British interest in the Venona-Bride decrypts to Paterson, MI5's man in the Rogues' Gallery. Paterson adopted the practice of calling on Lamphere once a week. Philby's reasons were clear. With Hoover on the rampage over Britain's refusal to let a senior FBI officer see Fuchs on a matter that affected the safety and dignity of the United States, a situation had arisen that might, through the Homer inquiry, prove dangerous to Philby personally in his Soviet duties. What these duties may have included at that time, Lamphere concluded later, was to reveal to his Russian masters the existence of Venona-Bride, the only major Anglo-American intelligence source available with a bearing on current Soviet intelligence operations in the United States. Also, Philby intended to reveal the identities known to him through his knowledge of the forty-nine Soviet spies mentioned in the intercepts, including Homer.

Philby's remarkable game with the American intelligence and security services began. In May 1950, Lamphere noted, evidence was obtained that someone who knew of the existence of the Venona-Bride decrypts and the identities of the forty-nine Russian spies had passed his information to the Soviet intelligence service in the United States. Some of the suspects fled. Some of them, including the Rosenbergs, the principal figures in the Soviet atomic spy ring, did not. As Philby himself notes in his paper to the Russians, they were caught indirectly through evidence provided from the decrypts. On receiving news of the flight, Lamphere concluded that there was a traitor somewhere in the secret circle. To his great personal cost he did not conclude that it might be Philby. He simply observed that in not calling on the FBI as frequently as in the past, Philby was now engaged in his main work in Washington, liaison with James Jesus Angleton at the CIA.

Yet it should be observed that, while Philby saw an opportunity to penetrate and disrupt the FBI in its social composition and operating methods, he misjudged it. By its very discipline and special nationalism, its reserve about foreigners and its intimate knowledge of the magnitude of the Soviet's penetration of the U.S. government, the FBI proved impenetrable to any important degree. At the FBI Philby failed.

The same could not be said about the CIA.

In his memoir, Philby made much of the social aspects of his relationship with Angleton. They lunched weekly at Harvey's, noted for its lobsters. Their "close association was, I am sure, inspired by genuine friendliness on both sides," he remembered, "but we both had ulterior motives." By "cultivating me to the full, he could keep me better under wraps. For my part, I was more than content to string him along. The greater the trust between us overtly, the less he would suspect covert action. Who gained the most from this complex game I cannot say." But "I had one big advantage. I knew what he was doing for CIA and he knew what I was doing for SIS. But the real nature of my interest was something he did not know."[35]

That there was a contest between the two men is evident. But Philby's version of their interaction says its object was administrative, to transfer the intelligence exchanges and thus the power from Philby's office in Washington to the CIA's office in London. This may have been so, but there is no evidence of such a maneuver at the CIA. To the contrary, a senior official there, James Critchfield, would state that all Angleton's meetings with Philby were "one-on-one meetings, and none but they knew what had transpired."[36] Nor did anyone ever learn what had transpired at these sessions. Angleton is known to have written a memorandum for the record after each of them, and it was known that there were thirty-two such memoranda. But they did not survive. When the time came to investigate Angleton, it was found that all the memoranda had disappeared.

As Philby noted in one of his memoranda to the KGB, the CIA was much more cosmopolitan than the FBI, much less insular. Either by Angleton's design or his own skill in insinuation, Philby was able to visit CIA headquarters more or less at will, although not without Angleton's knowledge and permission. For a time early in the Korean War he had entry into the offices of Frank Wisner, the chief of the major CIA branch running operations against the Russians worldwide, and he is described as having been "particularly close" to one Gerry Miller, the senior CIA man running operations in Western and Central Europe.[37]

But there was another aspect of Philby's acceptance inside the operating sections of CIA, and that was very long-term in its implications. The CIA had begun a policy of recruiting what were known as CTs, career trainees, who were the best and the brightest of young Americans. They had been carefully selected and trained so that they would some day take over and run the CIA. They probably did not number more than fifty officers at one time, but in the twenty months he was in Washington, Philby met most, perhaps all, of the CTs of his time. It is said that he even lectured them in clandestine doctrine and technique and, through his ready admittance in Georgetown society, met many of them socially.[38] It will be recalled that in Philby's earliest days in the Soviet service, Arnold Deutsch, his first case officer, encouraged Philby to write potted biographies of all intelligence persons of potential importance. "'You will produce a lot of rubbish,' Deutsch told me, 'but one useful page will be worth lots of waste paper.'" Philby had his father's sharp eye for men's weaknesses. He was also like his father in that he was extremely disciplined. All his observations about the CTs went into the biographies he wrote and thus provided the Soviet service with a vast store of personal intelligence that was used when the time came for the KGB to match wits with the CIA. Of course, the CTs knew nothing about their adversary. This proved to be a source of infection in the security system of the CIA that was never cured and that provided a weakness in the CIA that lasted throughout the 1950s, the 1960s, the 1970s, and perhaps even into the 1980s.

In June 1950, the Korean War broke out, producing the sharpest crisis in Washington since Pearl Harbor. The evidence suggests that the relationship between Angleton and Philby, and between Philby and the CIA management, was still close and, indeed, under the prospect that Korea might well be but the first shot in a global war, it became still closer. Philby himself recorded that his work load became monstrous: 95 percent of it concerned the Soviet Union, and 95 percent of that concerned war planning. There are two views about the nature of this planning:

> That Philby's collaboration was confined to preparing for the clandestine war that would develop in the event of general war with Russia — the establishment of cadres and infrastructure throughout western and central Europe for espionage, sabotage, political warfare, rebellion, similar to that developed by the Churchill government in World War II. But that he was not involved in that other aspect of general war with Russia, military and especially air operations against the Soviet Union, except in the handling of certain grades of the secret signals traffic between the embassy and the London government.
>
> The second view is that he was not only involved in the planning of the clandestine war but also air operations involving the movement of bombers and atomic munitions to British bases in Britain and the Empire, and particularly to the complex of British air bases in the Cairo-Suez area.[39]

There is also a third view, that by the very nature of his work Philby obtained a *complete overview* of all Anglo-American operations in both the clandestine and air operations.

At the outbreak of the Korean War, this knowledge became of the highest importance to the Soviet Union, for as the war developed and the belief grew within the U.S. administration that it foreshadowed World War III, the Truman government took the preliminary steps provided for under the war plan of the period, Trojan.

To prepare for the atomic offensive, a very large movement of "nonnuclear components" — the atomic bomb minus its nuclear core, which was held in the United States — began to SAC bases in England. There the assembled bombs would be used (a) to blunt the enemy's atomic delivery capability, (b) to disrupt the USSR's warmaking capacity, and (c) to disrupt the Red Army's advance.[40] The policy was laid out in the new National Security Council directive, NSC/68, which was to become the Cold War doctrine for the next forty years. In a nutshell, NSC/68 undertook:

> a. To reduce the power and influence of the USSR to limits that no longer constitute a threat to the peace, independence, and stability of the world family of nations.
>
> b. To bring about a basic change in the conduct of international relations by the government in power in Russia, to conform with the purposes and principles set forth in the UN Charter.

In pursuing these objectives, due care must be taken to avoid permanently impairing our economies and the fundamental values and institutions inherent in our way of life.

c. In the event of war with the USSR, we should endeavor by successful military and other operations to create conditions that would permit the satisfactory accomplishment of Allied objectives without a predetermined requirement of unconditional surrender.

d. To eliminate Soviet Russian domination in areas outside the borders of any Russian state allowed to exist after the war.

e. Assure that if any Bolshevik regime is left in any part of the Soviet Union, it does not control enough of the military-industrial potential of the Soviet Union to enable it to wage war on comparable terms with any other regime or regimes that may exist on traditional Russian territory.

f. To prevent the development of power relationships dangerous to the security of the Allies and international peace.

In his work for the Soviet intelligence service, Philby was required to be alert to whether the Americans would launch the type of war that Stalin feared the most — "preventive war," a sudden atomic attack by the SAC without warning against Russia. In July 1950, evidence that elements at the Pentagon might be planning just such an attack began to emerge. At a time when it was not hard to believe that war might only be days away, what was described in the National Security Council as "tangential evidence" emerged that Secretary of Defense Louis Johnson had begun to advocate preventive war. On July 6 a memorandum written· or inspired by Johnson and addressed to President Truman recommended that United Nations agreement be obtained "for use of the atomic bomb" in the "name of law and order and for the establishment of peace." Johnson argued that "the potentialities of the present crisis make it imperative that we . . . be fully prepared to take any measures necessary to preserve the days of world freedom, which but for the strength of U.S. resolve may well be numbered."[41] The world had entered a period of nightmare.

On August 17, the secretaries of the army, navy, and air force sent Secretary Johnson a memorandum proposing "that the Secretary of Defense indicate to Ambassador Spofford [the U.S. member of the NATO Council of Deputies] that the United States was prepared to undertake an aggressive war for peace, that psychologically the people of the United States are demanding an all-out effort to win such a war."[42] Speaking at the Boston Naval Shipyard on August 25, Secretary of the Navy Francis P. Matthews argued that the United States should bear any burden to achieve world peace, "even the price of instituting a war to compel cooperation for peace." In the opinion of Hanson W. Baldwin, the *New York Times*'s military correspondent, this statement was "clearly a trial balloon; the method of launching it was a favorite one of . . . Louis Johnson . . . who had been selling the same doctrine of preventive war in private conversations around Washington." President Truman repudiated any thought of such a war and rebuked the secretary of the navy.[43] Also, Truman accepted the resignation of Mr. Johnson. The nightmare period ended; Truman would not countenance preventive war.

By this time the Philbys had moved to a large frame house at 4100 Nebraska Avenue, and it was there, almost coincidentally with the outbreak of the war, that Aileen bore her fifth and last child. St. John was beside himself with excitement and sent Aileen the usual handsome present of £100, which he made to all his daughters and daughters-in-law upon production of a grandchild. He thought the boy should be called George Washington Philby, in honor of Kim's hosts. But, exhibiting the deftness with which Philby dealt with matters concerning his cover in both his personal and professional lives, he did not think this was appropriate and instead named the child Harry George, a compliment to St. John or President Truman, or both, and to George Washington.[44]

In the midst of the turmoil created by the war, Harry George developed severe convulsions that, it seemed from time to time, might prove fatal. Aileen and Philby took turns sitting up with the child, which brought them close to yet another of their periodic crises. His work in connection with the war overwhelmed him; he fell ill with pneumonia or bronchitis and the summer heat sapped his vitality. It was against that background that Philby received a letter from Guy Burgess in London in July. "I have a shock for you," Burgess announced. "I have just been posted to Washington," and he asked whether Philby could lodge him "for a few days" while he looked for an apartment.[45]

Philby's reaction was to weigh the pros and the cons of his own intricate position in Washington and the danger to him of associating with Burgess. He concluded:

> In normal circumstances, it would have been quite wrong for two secret operatives to occupy the same premises. But the circumstances were not normal. From the earliest days, our careers had intertwined. He had collected money for me at Cambridge after the revolt of the

Austrian Schützbund in February, 1934. I had put forward his name as a possible recruit for the Soviet service, a debt which he later repaid by smoothing my entry into the British secret service. In between, he had acted as courier for me in Spain. In 1940, we had worked closely together in SIS, and he had paid me a professional visit in Turkey in 1948. Our association was therefore well-known, and it was already certain that any serious investigation of either of us would reveal these past links. It seemed that there could be no real professional objection to him staying with me.[46]

There was, moreover,

> another consideration which inclined me towards agreeing with Burgess's suggestion. I knew from the files that his record was quite clean, in the sense that there was nothing recorded against him politically. But he was very apt to get into personal scrapes of a spectacular nature. A colleague in the Foreign Office, now an Ambassador, had pushed him down the steps of the Gargoyle Club, injuring his skull. There had been trouble in Dublin and in Tangier. It occurred to me that he was much less likely to make himself conspicuous in my household than in a bachelor flat where every evening would find him footloose.[47]

Philby had scarcely finished replying to Burgess when the embassy security officer, Sir Robert MacKenzie, who had been in Section V with Philby, showed him a letter from G. A. Carey-Foster, chief of security at the Foreign Office in London. It contained a summary of Guy's homosexual, drinking, and social escapades and advised that the decision to send Burgess to Washington had been made because his "eccentricities would be more easily overlooked in a large embassy than in a small one." But he might make worse trouble in Washington; as MacKenzie muttered: "'What does he mean *worse?* Goats?'" Kim then told MacKenzie, "I knew Guy well, that he would be staying with me, and that I would keep an eye on him." MacKenzie "seemed happy that there was someone else ready to share the responsibility."[48] Yet as Philby was to admit:

> In the light of what was to come, my decision to fall in with Burgess's suggestion looks like a bad mistake. I have indeed given it much thought . . . It will not do to plead that the twist events were to take a few months later were utterly unforeseeable; security precautions are designed to give protection from the unforeseeable. But, on reflection, I think that my decision to accommodate Burgess *speeded by a few weeks at most the focussing of the spotlight on me.*[49]

He added that Burgess's arrival "may even have been lucky" in that *"suspicion fell upon me prematurely, in the sense that it crystallised before the evidence was strong enough to bring me to court."*

Philby never explained what he meant, but it is evident that what he feared was that Homer would be exposed as Donald Maclean, whom Philby had recruited with Guy Burgess as an ideological spy in 1934. He believed that the exposure of Maclean might lead to the exposure of himself and Burgess — as, indeed, proved to be the case. His one advantage as the FBI and MI5 probed the Venona-Bride intercepts was that he controlled the communications relating to the case between London and Washington. But there is no doubt of his concern about the way the Homer case was unfolding. As he wrote:

> The development of the affair was giving me deep anxiety. It was beset by imponderables, the assessment of which could be little better than guesswork. We had received some dozen reports referring to the source, who appeared in the [decrypts] under the code-name Homer, but little progress had been made towards identifying him.[50]

Philby added that the inquiries were becoming very intensive because "we were dealing with a man of stature" who had "dealt with political problems of some complexity." On more than one occasion "Homer was spoken of with respect."[51]

Meanwhile, Burgess prepared to leave London. How and why such a man was being sent would always remain mysterious, with the possibility that someone else higher in the Whitehall structure who was also a Soviet agent had arranged his posting in order to provide Philby with support in the event that Homer was exposed and the Soviets evacuated him to Moscow. This is not impossible. Burgess had remained popular and acceptable in a certain circle of London society, so his farewell party at a flat in Lower Bond Street was attended by a constellation of Foreign Office, intelligence, and security luminaries. Among them was Hector MacNeil, now in the Cabinet as secretary of state for Scotland; his successor as minister of state at the Foreign Office, Kenneth Younger; David Footman, still chief of the political section of the SIS; Professor Goronwy Rees, a Welsh writer and fellow of All Souls whom Burgess had tried to recruit as a Soviet spy before the war; Guy Liddell, deputy chief of the Security Service; Anthony Blunt, of the Cambridge Five; and so on. As Rees recalled of the party: "There were two women who seemed to be even more out of place than anyone else." There was Jimmy, Guy's batman, lover, and protector; "there were two very tough working-class young men who had very obviously been picked up off the streets." And throughout "the drink flowed faster," and one of the young men hit another over the head with a bottle while another "left with a distinguished writer."[52] As Footman left, he claimed to have heard MacNeil lecturing Burgess on the "three basic don'ts to bear particularly in mind when you're dealing with Americans. The first is Communism, the second is homosexuality, and the third is the colour bar. Do please memorise them, won't you?" Burgess "smiled his seraphic smile" and replied instantly: "I've got it, Hector, so, there, don't worry. What you are trying to say in your nice, long-winded way is — 'Guy, for God's sake don't make a pass at Paul Robeson.'"[53]

To the end, Guy begged Younger to let him stay in London, but in what were his final words in wishing Guy every success, Younger warned Burgess that he either behave himself in Washington or it was the sack. Burgess was propelled by his colleagues and friends onto the *Queen Mary*. He took up his post as second secretary at the embassy on August 4, 1950, and moved into Philby's home on Nebraska Avenue. This made the house crowded, for living there by now were Kim and Aileen, their five children, and Edith Whitfield. Burgess was installed in the basement apartment, much to the distress of Aileen, who continued to detest him, fearing the hold he seemed to have over Kim. Burgess began work at the embassy's Far Eastern Department, one with vital responsibilities throughout the Korean War, and on August 7 he was appointed an alternate member of the United Kingdom's delegation to the Far Eastern Commission, which had ceased to have much use but which might, through the Korean War, regain its former importance.

Here he was responsible for such matters as Japanese reparations to the Western powers; the payment of the cost of the occupation forces; financial and monetary problems; economic affairs; the "strengthening of democratic tendencies" in Japan; war criminals; and the Aliens in Japan subcommittee, which met most frequently. The lady representing the State Department told the FBI later that Burgess "seemed to believe firmly in cooperation between the British and Americans" and that he "had a good attitude with respect to the work of the committee." On a few occasions, however, she had "noted the odor of liquor on Burgess's breath." But as a man he seemed to be "intelligent, well educated, and very clever," though he "presented a very poor personal appearance in contrast to the usual type of person associated with the British Embassy."[54]

Burgess did not stay with the commission long. The head of the Far Eastern Department, Hubert Graves, refused to keep him on his staff, so he was transferred to the Middle Eastern staff of Denis Greenhill. This proved, too, a disheartening experience. As Greenhill remembered, "Burgess's conversation was always entertaining and sometimes of arresting interest. He was at his most congenial on someone else's sofa, drinking someone else's whisky, telling tales to discredit the famous. The more luxurious the surroundings and the more distinguished the company, the happier he was. I have never heard a name-dropper in the same class."[55]

Burgess was then transferred to the Rogues' Gallery, where, as Mann recalled, his presence diagonally across the corridor seemed a surprise, for he was "a pretty uncouth character who sported a battered duffel coat, and who was always more or less the worse for wear owing to the combined effects of alcohol and diabetes."[56] Burgess was assigned what seemed to Mann a minor task — reading newspaper clippings. Otherwise, his work gave him much free time. Philby introduced him to Angleton as "the most outstanding historian of his time at Cambridge," a statement that had some truth. There were few restaurants in central Washington in that period, and the circle tended to gather at the same one or two each day, Harvey's or the Occidental on Pennsylvania Avenue.[57] Several days a week, Wisner, Angleton, Philby, and their group were to be found lunching together while J. Edgar Hoover and Clyde Tolson munched lobster in another corner with William C. Sullivan, the assistant director in charge of domestic operations at the FBI against the Soviet secret services. Burgess, who was present from time to time, was bound to attract Hoover's attention, for as Lord Annan wrote of him: "He had the appearance of a man who had just stepped off the Golden Arrow after a night in the Rue de Lappe."[58]

Burgess found himself alone in Washington for much of August while Philby went to London with Wisner and Robert Joyce of the State Department to meet with the Russia Committee of the Foreign Office. Its objective was to "promote civil discontent, internal confusion and possible strife in the satellite countries. The orbit countries would thus become a source of weakness, internal confusion and possible strife." There were to be two main items of business:

> 1. To coordinate with the British operations to overthrow the pro-Soviet or Soviet governments of Albania, Latvia, and the Ukraine.
> 2. To reach a consensus with the London intelligence community on the probable date that the Russians would start World War III.[59]

At these meetings, Philby kept the British minutes while Joyce kept those of the United States. Wisner announced that the CIA would take an active part in the Albanian operations, its first landings to take place in November.

Another officer there was Michael Burke, then with the CIA in Frankfurt organizing the planting of American agents behind the Iron Curtain. He went to Wheeler's Oyster Bar with Kim for dinner and left a rare picture of him on active service:

> When I first met Philby in London I was aware that he was legitimately privy to my assignment; what surprised me was his easy familiarity with operational matters. Frankly, too, I was pleasantly surprised and flattered that a man of his rank would invite me to dine with him privately . . . His considerable charm was disarming, his slight stutter sympathetic, his face almost handsome in a neglected way. He gave the appearance of wasting no more time shaving or combing his hair than he did with his clothes, which were unfashionable and unpressed. Entirely likeable and very much at home in and on top of his profession, Philby's surface persona seemed to go right to his core . . . and the degree of self-control, of self-discipline demanded of Philby to sustain his enormous deception over so long a period of time is immeasurable.[60]

Philby returned to Washington on or about September 18, 1950, to find that Burgess was still at the house on Nebraska Avenue, playing trains in the basement with Kim's children. Philby became uneasy again when he found both Guy and Aileen parading their "utter contempt" for America and Americans. Burgess had escorted the foreign secretary, Anthony Eden, during an official visit to Washington, a service for which Eden presented him with a bottle of Kentucky Gentlemen, "Anthony Eden's favourite bourbon," Guy announced in the Gallery. His theme that day was that there was no such thing as an American intellectual. He had appeared at the National Press Club bar from time to time, loudly denouncing U.S. policy in Asia. He had appeared at Angleton's luncheon table at the Occidental and had asked for drink. Such conduct did not sit well then in official Washington.

Comment was already being made about the association between Philby and Burgess when an important incident occurred in the history of the Philby case. In September 1950, Teddy Kollek, an Israeli intelligence officer and later "the perpetual mayor of Jerusalem," visited Angleton at CIA headquarters in Washington. Leaving Angleton's office, historians of Mossad would write, "he happened to bump into a Briton he knew named Harold (Kim) Philby. Quite amazed, he hurried back to Angleton's office and asked him, 'What is Philby doing here?'" He had been present, he said, at the marriage of Kim Philby and Alice Friedman in Vienna in 1934. Angleton replied, "Kim is a good friend of ours and is the British MI6 representative in liaison with the CIA." The historians Dan Ravin and Yossi Melman recorded of this encounter: "Angleton noted what his new Israeli friend said, but took no action."[61]

Cleveland Cram, who wrote the official history of Angleton's twenty years as chief of counterespionage, thought this encounter to be "absolutely a key point" in "Jim's curious relationship with Philby." In a note he asked, "Why didn't Jim tell Allen Dulles [deputy director for intelligence at the CIA] or the FBI what he'd heard from Kollek? I found no memo about it in the files," but "that was par for the course with JJA." Angleton was "the sort who tucked information away in his hip pocket for future use. Not telling anyone. Not putting it in the file." Angleton's failure to report Kollek's warning became a point at which Angleton himself became suspect. When the file was examined by Clare Edward Petty, a senior CIA Soviet analyst, a man with a "wonderfully clear mind," Petty found evidence that Kollek and Philby had known each other operationally in Istanbul in 1947. Petty asked himself why, and he felt that Angleton was protecting Philby. What hold did Philby have over Angleton? In an investigation at a later date, Petty concluded that Angleton was "the American Philby." Petty's conclusion went to the Director of Central Intelligence, where it festered until subsequent events caused a major investigation into the Angleton-Philby relationship.[62]

Meanwhile, in October 1950, the first seaborne infiltration into Albania was ambushed by the Albanian security authorities. A little later another such operation, undertaken solely by CIA, was also ambushed. There were casualties, and, Tirana radio had announced, there would be a public trial. Reports reached the CIA and SIS from the few survivors. Since there had been other such misadventures to both American and British operations in Latvia, Estonia, the Ukraine, and Byelorussia, a report was made to Angleton's chief, William K. Harvey, the portly and perceptive head of counterespionage and the man responsible for the security of CIA operations. It was established that only four people knew the time and place of these operations. They were the members of the Special Policy Committee, which had been established to control the clandestine operations being undertaken throughout Eastern Europe: Robert Joyce, a Balkans expert at the State Department; Lord Jellicoe, of the Foreign Office; Frank Lindsay of the CIA; and Philby of the SIS.

On reading the reports from the field, the chief of the CIA department responsible for the operations, Frank Wisner, told Joyce that he believed that there was a traitor in the committee and that the only man capable of such treachery was Philby.[63] Whether Wisner communicated his fears elsewhere is nowhere evident. If he followed correct procedure, he should have informed, among others, William K. Harvey. This Wisner may have done, for three senior CIA officials later claimed that Harvey had known or suspected that Philby was a traitor. Hugh Montgomery, at the time Harvey's personal assistant, was "morally certain"[64] that Harvey developed suspicions as a result of the Albanian and other misadventures. In the course of his career, Montgomery became a U.S. ambassador at the United Nations and then, in 1989, a member of the CIA's collegium, a sort of board of supervisors.

When Admiral Stansfield Turner became director of the CIA in March 1977, his task "to clean up the CIA," he learned of the existence of "the Black Files," a collection of supersensitive case files, tied in black ribbon, that went back to the earliest days of the CIA. Fearing that they contained "time bombs" that could embarrass his administration, Turner instructed the Reports Division to examine the files. The task went to John Mapother, a charter member of the CIA, and he and a group of reports officers found the file on Philby that included profiles of and reports about Kim, "all very professionally written." Some were signed by Harvey, who believed that Philby was suspect at the time he arrived in Washington in 1949. A third CIA officer, Constantine (Deekas) Broutsas, the CIA's former station chief in West Germany, Austria, and Switzerland, remarked that "the only mystery left in the Philby case was when did Harvey come to suspect Philby?"[65]

In a world where a man could be sacked immediately on suspicion alone, these statements suggest that Philby should have been declared persona non grata then and there, especially because of the Korean War. But he was not sent home. As far as can be established, nothing untoward ensued. He proceeded about his business as usual, although, as we have seen, he himself felt that a cloud had formed around his head. His relations with the FBI in the still highly secret matter of Homer continued as before.

In the gallery, Philby continued to handle Dr. Mann's communications with the scientific intelligence service in London, which included intelligence from the CIA committee examining Soviet atomic capabilities. Philby's office continued its practice of putting this material into one-time-pad ciphers — the one virtually uncrackable code — for transmission by Western Union to Mann's headquarters in London.

Philby continued to send and receive his station's most secret traffic with London, which contained highly sensitive discussions about American requests to expand the number of airfields available to the Strategic Air Command from three to seven. There was more discussion regarding the SAC's further need of bases on Cyprus, a British colony, and an extension to the existing SAC facilities in Libya, a British mandate. There were, doubtless, myriad tasks affecting the British Embassy and its government involved in the positioning of the SAC air fleet on British home and colonial territory: signals, ground support of every description, meteorological and intelligence assistance, the air defense of the region in which the SAC bases were located, fuel supplies for the bombers and the air transportation fleet involved in their support. Under Trojan, 75 "nonnuclear assemblies" were being positioned in England in readiness for war. Later, the Pentagon decided that 220 such assemblies would be required, and this required much formal discussion between the American and British governments.[67]

Philby's relations with the CIA and the FBI again seem not to have been affected by Wisner's suspicion. And Philby's personal relations with Angleton seem, too, to have remained as agreeable as ever. In November 1950, it was noted, Philby and his family were the Angletons' guests for Thanksgiving. Also there was Dr. Mann and his family, as well as William F. Colby, director of security at the Atomic Energy Commission.

Late in November, Philby found that the CIA had a new director, whose personality and career became a central issue in the first dénouement in the Philby case. General Walter Bedell Smith had served with General George C. Marshall, and in 1942 General Eisenhower chose him as his chief of staff in Europe. Smith therefore was fully acquainted with the Bodyguard and Fortitude deception plans, which produced such a majestic victory on the far shore of Normandy. After the war he had remained with Eisenhower, as chief of staff to the U.S. Army in Germany, and from 1946 to 1949 was the U.S. ambassador to Moscow. As a CIA official involved in the Philby case would observe of Smith's appointment:

> He came in for a purpose. The first reason that comes to mind is that the CIA needed a firm hand. He supplied that. But it should not be forgotten that he kept Eisenhower's files on Bodyguard and Fortitude. He knew all about it and was witness to its brilliant success. It would have been quite natural for him to say: "We did it in World War II so why should we not do it again when the Korean War broke

out as, so it seemed, the opening blow of World War III." It was a
large enough crisis to demand such a measure. It might even be
argued that Bedell Smith would have been delinquent had he not
undertaken such a measure. The CIA had a deception capability in
place. These things were then ordered by the National Security Council with the knowledge of the president, the objectives were laid down
by them, and the CIA's liaison officer with NSC in deception matters
was a Marine with us, Peter Holcomb, who had served with X2 at War
Station XB during World War II and knew Philby quite well. He dealt
with Allen W. Dulles, then Bedell Smith's deputy director for intelligence. The NSC had no executive capacity in such matters. That was
left to CIA and its Staff "C," the counter-espionage branch under
William King Harvey. Whether there was such a deception is not
known to me. But I would not be surprised to find, given the immensity of the Korean crisis, that there was one.[68]

If the CIA was indeed seeking to misinform Philby, it seems to have
been a *coup manqué*, for George Kennedy Young, a senior SIS officer
during Philby's time, called Angleton "a gullible soul who saw himself
as a Machiavelli and fell completely under Philby's spell. Kim made
mincemeat of him."[69] As Sir James Easton would remark of Philby's
capacity for detecting disinformation, "Anybody who tried that with
him was a fool, for Kim had a quite remarkable sixth sense at detecting
the lie in a report."[70]

With the arrival of Smith, it was not long before Philby found himself in the director's office, discussing what he described as aspects of
the war plans. He found Smith to have

> a cold, fishy eye and a precision-tool brain. At my first meeting with
> him, I had taken a document of twenty-one paragraphs on Anglo-
> American war plans for his scrutiny and comment. He had flipped
> over the pages casually and tossed it aside, then engaged me in close
> discussion of the subjects involved, referring from memory to the
> numbered paragraphs. I kept pace only because I had spent the
> whole morning learning the document by heart. Bedell-Smith [sic],
> I had an uneasy feeling, would be apt to think that two and two made
> four rather than five.[71]

Philby's business with Smith had just begun when the Truman administration was plunged into its darkest crisis. On November 24,
1950, General Douglas MacArthur launched a great offensive to end
the Korean War by Christmas, attempting to push the communist forces
from North Korea. This advance met with a stunning surprise: the

sudden appearance of a large, well-trained, and determined Red Chinese Army, which had crossed the Yalu River in secrecy and began to force the United States, South Korea, and United Nations armies into a retreat.

The effect of that sudden reversal of the fortunes of war was as unnerving in Washington as in the field. President Truman recorded in his diary: "I have worked for peace for five years and six months and it looks like World War III is near." On December 15, 1950, the president proclaimed a national emergency and told the American people that "our homes, our nation, all the things we believe in, are in great danger." Over the political scene there spread the notion that there was "some occult conspiracy" at work, that Korea was but "one link in a series of American defeats that stretched back at least to Yalta." In this conspiracy, Manchuria, China, Eastern Europe, the Baltic states, the Balkans, Berlin — all had been lost. McCarthyism started to flourish in Washington. Senator William Jenner declared to massive applause from the public gallery that

> this country today is in the hands of a secret inner coterie which is directed by agents of the Soviet Union. We must cut this whole cancerous conspiracy out of our Government at once. Our only recourse is to impeach President Truman and find out who is the secret invisible government which has so cleverly led our country down the road to destruction.[72]

Truman himself added greatly to the anxiety when, at a press conference on November 30, he seemed to be considering the use of the atomic bomb against the Chinese. He said he intended to take whatever steps were necessary to meet the military situation, and to the question "Does that include the A-bomb?," he replied that it included "every weapon that we have." Other questions, not connected with the atomic bomb, produced the answer that the use of particular weapons was for the theater commander to decide. Within minutes, Truman's words had begun to hurtle around the world: the president was considering using the atomic bomb, and the decision to do so would be left to the discretion of General MacArthur.

Prime Minister Attlee flew to Washington to consult with the president, and as he did, Truman authorized the Joint Chiefs to place the U.S. commands in the Atlantic, Pacific, Mediterranean, and Indian Ocean theaters on full alert, with the authority to put current emergency war plans into effect in case of attack but "without creating an atmosphere of alarm." At the meetings between Truman and Attlee, momentous steps were taken. The post of supreme commander in Europe was recreated and General Eisenhower was reappointed to it. Truman and Attlee agreed to support the formation of what became the North Atlantic Treaty Organization (NATO).

In all these matters Philby was in a position to keep himself well informed. Under long-standing arrangements between C and the prime minister's office, Philby's office was responsible for handling Attlee's special traffic with London. It has to be considered certain that all these communications reached Soviet hands. Furthermore, according to St. John's correspondence, Philby entertained some of the prime minister's officials at his home.

It was at this point that the Philby affair began to assume some of its gravest aspects. The United States and its principal ally, Great Britain, had become involved in a terrible little war that might become World War III. Yet if Angleton or C in London had any suspicions about Philby, neither did anything to remove him. To the contrary, Sir Patrick Reilly, chairman of the Joint Intelligence Committee, the apparatus that controlled all the intelligence departments, met with C and his deputy, Sir John Sinclair, and others, as Reilly recalled, late in 1950 or very early in 1951, to examine the question of a successor to C, who was then due to retire.[73] C joined Sinclair in a recommendation that, upon the expiration of his two years in Washington, in October 1951, Philby should be brought back to London and given a high post. C would be succeeded by Sinclair; Easton would move up as deputy chief; and Philby would be assistant director and therefore number three in the management. It seemed, therefore, that Philby was close to his goal — a goal in which he, a Soviet secret agent, would become C in about 1960, provided he kept his nose clean in Washington.

This, unhappily for him, Philby failed to do. And it all began with a social event.

There were various reasons for Kim to give the big party. One was to say farewell to Michael Burke, who was going to Europe as a CIA station chief; the guests were all of high rank "in the business" and included the luminaries of counterespionage in Washington and their spouses: the Ladds, the Lampheres, and the Greggs of the FBI; the Wisners and Angletons of the CIA; the Patersons of MI5; and Mac-Kenzie, the security officer at the British Embassy. The guests of honor were William K. Harvey, chief of counterespionage at the CIA, and his wife, Libby. Dr. Mann and his wife, Miriam, were also guests, and, Mann recorded, the dinner was a pleasant and orderly affair until Guy

Burgess arrived in "his usual aggressive mood" as coffee was being served about 9:30 P.M. Philby introduced him to the guests, and immediately afterward Burgess remarked to Libby Harvey that "it was strange to see the face he had been doodling all his life suddenly appear before him." Burgess was a talented cartoonist, and Libby Harvey asked him to draw her. This he did; and his work, swiftly done, caused an uproar.

One version is that Burgess's depiction of Mrs. Harvey suggested what the poets called "Her Vale of Pleasure." When she saw it she gave it to her husband, a small and fat man, and he lunged at Burgess. The party broke out in tumult. But there is another version, that of Mann. As he wrote in his memoirs, Libby Harvey was a "pleasant woman but her jaw was a little prominent; Guy caricatured her . . . so that it looked like the prow of a dreadnaught with its underwater battering ram." Libby Harvey rose and took her husband by the arm, saying, "I've never been so insulted in all my life; take me home." The Harveys left immediately. This ended Philby's party and, as Mann remembered, "after a few minutes' embarrassment everything became very calm," and he and Angleton went outside and sat on a low wall for about thirty minutes. When they went back into the house, "Kim Philby was in tears on a small settee" in a "state of extreme dejection." Aileen Philby had disappeared.

Then came the sequel.

The next morning between nine and ten, Mann returned to Philby's house to collect his car and met Aileen Philby at her housework. All she remarked was, "The boys are upstairs. Why don't you go up to see them?" Following the sound of voices, he entered a room and found Philby and Burgess in a double bed. They were propped up on pillows, wearing pajamas and perhaps also dressing gowns and drinking champagne. They invited Mann to join them. He did, although "the situation made me feel puzzled and uncomfortable. Aileen had treated the whole matter lightly and almost flippantly," but he "did *not* get the impression that the situation was homosexual in the sense that the two of them had spent the night together." Mann added: "I should emphasize that in that age of innocence" neither he nor "most people of my generation appreciated that a married man with a large family could also be a practising homosexual." He did not report the incident to MacKenzie, the security officer, on the grounds that "it was distasteful and embarrassing to bring to [his] notice an incident which had no obvious security implications." But Mann did report it to Commander Walsh, his chief in London. Walsh appeared uninterested in

Mann's doubts about the strange behavior of a senior officer of MI6. On the other hand, Mann claimed, he related the encounter to no one in Washington, not even Angleton, until early in 1952. Mann was always to regret that he never pressed his story in the quarters that counted, especially when events reflected more light on the relationship between Philby and Burgess.

For all the embarrassment occasioned at the party, business continued; after all, it was Burgess who had offended and a CIA officer who was affronted, not anyone at the FBI. And Philby's main business over the ensuing weeks was to deflect the search for Homer, the Soviet spy at the British Embassy. By April 1951, all other candidates had been eliminated and the finger pointed unmistakably at Donald Duart Maclean, one of the Cambridge Five. He was now thirty-seven, chief of the American desk at the Foreign Office, and on his way to a knighthood and an ambassadorship. His most important service to the Soviet Union, perhaps, was the information from Washington he had supplied to Russia between 1944, when he first arrived in the U.S. capital, and late 1947.

For some of that time he was head of the department that controlled the ciphers being used between the embassy and London. In January 1947 he was appointed the British secretary — there was also an American secretary — of the Atomic Trust, as the U.S.–U.K. Combined Policy and Development Committee was called. This body was responsible for many aspects of the development of the atomic bomb, in particular to locate the world's resources of uranium and thorium, the ores used in the atomic and the thermonuclear bomb later, and also to secure the deposits politically and mine them for export to the United States and Britain. Through this knowledge Maclean was able to provide data from which the Russians could deduce, but only roughly, how many atomic bombs could be built and therefore how many bombs there were in the U.S. atomic arsenal. Now, from his position as head of the American Department at the Foreign Office, Maclean could watch over the political aspects of Trojan and the peace treaties that might lead to the remilitarization of Germany and Japan.

Then, late in 1950, signals passing over Philby's desk indicated that Maclean's number was up. When Philby passed that information to his "friends at meetings outside Washington," two main points emerged. It was essential to the Russian interest that he not be arrested. Second, it was desirable that Maclean stay at his post as long as possible. To gain time, Philby wrote a note to Vivian at Broadway recalling the statements of Krivitsky, the Soviet intelligence officer who had deserted to the West before World War II and was interrogated in London late in 1940. Philby drew Vivian's attention to Krivitsky's assertion that the Soviet service in the middle 1930s had recruited "a young man who had gone into the Foreign Office," who was "of good family," had been "educated at Eton and Oxford," and who had been "an idealist, working without payment." Aware that there were enough inaccuracies in this statement to start hares and that the chase after them might give Maclean all the time the Soviets needed, he proposed that this statement be matched against the records of diplomats stationed in Washington during the period of the intercepts of Soviet secret service cable traffic between 1944 and 1945.

Philby learned later that this search yielded a list of about six names, four of them leading figures in British diplomacy: Sir Roger Makins, Paul Gore-Booth, Michael Wright, and Donald Maclean. It was not before April that the Foreign Office focused on Maclean. By that time Philby's escape plan had begun to unfold. Part of it required that Burgess commit some disgraceful act that would result in his being sent home by the ambassador. There he would warn Maclean of the dangers he was in. The incident involving Mrs. Harvey was fresh in the official mind when, accompanied by a homosexual with a police record, Burgess drove his gray 1941 Lincoln convertible into the narrow roads of the Virginia countryside. Three times that day he was stopped by state troopers for speeding. On two occasions his diplomatic immunity produced no more than cautions. But the third resulted in his arrest.

Burgess and his friend found themselves before a judge who, while recognizing Burgess's diplomatic immunity, instructed that the arresting officer place a formal complaint before the governor of Virginia. The complaint went to the Protocol Division of the State Department, which complained to the embassy. Concerned as he was always with the prestige of his embassy and its good order and discipline, Ambassador Franks dismissed Burgess and ordered him home. Burgess did not leave at once but dawdled for a while on an estate in South Carolina, which gave Maclean still more time. By March, however, Burgess was back in Washington. As Philby recorded of their final meeting, they

> dined together his last evening in a Chinese restaurant where each booth had "personalised music" which helped to drown our voices. We went over the plan step by step. He was to meet a Soviet contact on arrival in London, and give him a full briefing. He was then to

call on Maclean at his office armed with a sheet of paper giving the time and place of rendez-vous which he would slip across the desk. He would then meet Maclean and put him fully in the picture. From then on, the matter was out of my hands. Burgess did not look too happy, and I must have had an inkling of what was on his mind. When I drove him to the station next morning, my last words, spoken only half-jocularly, were: "Don't you go too."[74]

But he did. On his arrival in London off the *Queen Mary* boat train, Burgess received notice to appear before a Foreign Office disciplinary committee. That meant the end of his career. But he did meet with Maclean along the lines proposed by Philby. He met also with the Soviet case officer. Shortly afterward, Home Secretary Herbert Morrison agreed that the interrogation of Maclean should begin on Monday, May 28. Yuri Modin handled the escape simply, he claimed, by consulting *Bradshaw's,* the railway guide. How Modin learned that Maclean's interrogation was imminent he would not say except that he "acted from information received." This individual was probably the Fifth Man, whom the KGB never identified but who was thought to be alive in 1992.[75]

Maclean and Burgess were last seen at Southampton docks in the white car Burgess had rented in London on Friday, May 25. They abandoned the car alongside the cross-Channel steamer *Falaise* in such haste that one of the dockers shouted as they rushed up the gangplank that they had left one of the car doors open. Burgess cried over his shoulder, "Back on Monday!" But he never came back on Monday, or any other day, except as cremated ashes. The disappearance of Maclean was first noticed on Monday morning, when he did not appear for work at the Foreign Office. His wife, Melinda, advised that he had left home in the middle evening of Friday, a birthday party notwithstanding, and that he was in the company of a man who gave his name as Roger Stiles — Guy Burgess. The Foreign Office damage control apparatus went to work immediately and effectively while all foreign service and intelligence posts received instructions to apprehend the two "at all costs and by all means." Geoffrey McDermott, at the embassy in Switzerland, remembered the phrase "at all costs" and, sure that the fugitives would call on him if they passed through, prepared a decanter of poisoned Scotch. The Continental police and the American counterintelligence corps were similarly alerted throughout Europe. The silence of the press was maintained until June 6, when the news was leaked by the Paris police to the correspondent of the *Daily Express* in Paris, Larry Solon, whose publisher, Lord Beaverbrook, had been gunning for the Foreign Office for years.

There were many reasons for the uproar that ensued in every capital. Most of them had to do with prestige. For a century or more, the British diplomats had been regarded by foreigners with, one might say, awe. Now two of them, tenured servants of the crown, had vanished like felons somewhere in Europe. The news became a symbol of England's enfeeblement. The king was seriously ill with cancer, and there was some hope that the new reign might bring with it what was being called the New Elizabethans, a glorious restoration of the spirit of England during the reign of Elizabeth I. The Attlee government was giving way to the second ministry of Churchill. Was this new dawn to be wrecked by the actions of two — possibly more — traitors inside the Establishment itself? As Henry Fairlie, a leading political commentator, noted: "No one whose job it was to be interested in the Burgess-Maclean affair from the very beginning will forget the subtle but powerful pressures which were brought to bear by those who belonged to the same stratum as the two missing men."[76]

Something had gone horribly wrong. Philby remembered the sense of consternation he experienced when:

> One morning, at a horribly early hour, Geoffrey Paterson [the Security Service's representative at the British Embassy in Washington] called me by telephone. He explained that he had just received an enormously long Most Immediate telegram from London. It would take him all day to decypher without help, and he had just sent his secretary on a week's leave. Could he borrow mine? I made the necessary arrangements and sat back to compose myself. This was almost certainly it. Was Maclean in the bag? Had Maclean got away? I was itching to rush round to the Embassy and lend a third hand to the telegram. But it was clearly wiser to stick to my usual routine as if nothing had happened. When I reached the Embassy, I went straight to Paterson's office. He looked grey. "Kim," he said in a half-whisper, "the bird has flown." I registered dawning horror (I hope). "What bird? Not Maclean?" "Yes," he answered. "But there's worse than that . . . *Guy Burgess* has gone with him." At that, my consternation was no pretence.[77]

Philby was now in great personal peril: the FBI might arrest him at any moment. Thunderstruck, he sent a telegram to C expressing astonishment at the news of Burgess's departure — even as he himself gave thought to his own flight. As he related, if his escape plan was to work, it required some knowledge of what was happening at FBI headquarters in the wake of the disappearance of Burgess and Maclean. He saw the two officials who might have the task of arranging his own arrest, Mickey Ladd, chief of Domestic Intelligence, and Lamphere. Accompanied by the chief of MI5 at the embassy, Geoffrey Paterson, Philby formally reported the disappearance of the two diplomats and noted that Ladd made no more than a remark or two, "not without pleasure," that "the bloody British had made a mess of it."[78] Lamphere, who had been working on the arrest of Maclean since 1948, said little. But in his memoirs he recorded how "in a number of telephone calls back and forth between those of us in the FBI and the CIA" who had been at the "now-infamous Philby cocktail party, we speculated on the link between Burgess and Maclean, and worried about the more sinister implications of Burgess's having lived in Philby's home in Washington." What went through Lamphere's mind was: "Had Philby deliberately, or even inadvertently, tipped off Burgess about our inquiry into the embassy spy? Was it possible that Philby was a spy?" His reaction to that possibility was:

> I must admit that I initially doubted that Philby was an active Soviet spy. I reasoned that a real Soviet agent would have worked harder at establishing closer relations with me and with the other key people; I understood that Philby had concentrated on the CIA, which was certainly a KGB target, but why hadn't he taken the opportunity to penetrate the FBI as well? Since Philby hadn't spent much time on us, I temporarily concluded that he must not have been an active spy.[79]

But Ladd and Lamphere concluded that in some way he was involved in the matter.

Philby and Paterson returned to the embassy to send their reports on the FBI-CIA reaction. Philby gave further thought to the question of his own escape. Aware that the FBI might place him under close watch at any time and that there were suspicions developing about him with one or two of the embassy staff, he decided against making an immediate flight. As Philby wrote: "I was guided by the consideration that unless my chances of survival were minimal my clear duty was to fight it out." There might yet be "an opportunity for further service."[80]

At C's office the thought was developing that it was essential that Philby be brought back to London without further delay in case Hoover decided to detain him for interrogation. During the early evening of June 5, an opportunity arose for C to extricate Philby quietly and without fuss. As one of C's deputies, James Easton, who was present

in Menzies's office that evening, would record, C met in his office at
Broadway with John Alexander Drew, chief of the deception agency
in Whitehall, who was flying to Washington that night. After their
meeting, C asked Easton to write a letter to Philby instructing him in
friendly terms that he was to expect a telegram ordering him back to
London. It was late in the evening and Easton's secretary had left for
the day, so Easton went to his room and wrote a letter on an ordinary
airgram and gave it to Drew to hand to Philby on his arrival in Washington the next day.[81]

On June 6, 1951, Drew arrived in Washington and called at the
embassy annex to find great consternation. The news of the disappearance of Burgess and Maclean had been suppressed successfully until
now, but during the evening of June 5 it had become clear that the
Daily Express had learned of it and intended to publish it on June 6,
which they did. Drew encountered Philby, who told him how the ambassador had been up all night and the embassy in turmoil over the
imminent publication. Philby then asked Drew what news he brought
from London, and Drew handed him Easton's letter. Philby was to
record of that letter and what he believed to have been its purpose:

> The one I was expecting was a Most Immediate, personal, decypher-
> yourself telegram from the Chief, summoning me home. At last the
> summons came, but it took a most curious, thought-provoking form.
> An intelligence official specialising in the fabrication of deception
> material flew into Washington on routine business. He paid me a
> courtesy call during which he handed me a letter from Jack Easton.
> The letter was in Easton's own handwriting, and informed me that I
> would shortly be receiving a telegram recalling me to London in
> connection with the Burgess-Maclean case. It was very important that
> I should obey the call promptly. While the sense of the communica-
> tion was clear enough, its form baffled me. Why should Easton warn
> me of the impending summons and why in his own handwriting if
> the order was to reach me through the normal telegraphic channels
> anyway? There is often a good reason for eccentric behaviour in the
> secret service, and there may have been one in this case. My reflec-
> tion at the time was that, if I had not already rejected the idea of
> escape, Easton's letter would have given me the signal to get moving
> with all deliberate speed.[82]

In reality, the reason Philby's recall went out in such an informal
manner had nothing to do with any desire to force Philby into flight
and thereby to control the damage being done by the Burgess and
Maclean disappearance. When the two men vanished, Arthur Martin,

the young Security Service officer who had been burrowing away at
Philby's record ever since suspicion began to develop over the Volkov
case and Philby's handling of it in 1945, had discovered certain evidence about Philby in the Central Registry, evidence that had been
there for a long time. It had to do with his marriage to Alice Friedman
in Vienna in 1934. With clerkly diligence, Martin had also discovered
that Philby had made a false declaration about his marital status when
he joined Section D on or about September 1, 1940. Then he had
claimed that he was married to Aileen Amanda Furse, born in India
on August 24, 1910. Martin noticed that he had made no mention of
Alice Philby. A check into her background showed evidence of her
underground communist connections; and when Martin related this
mare's nest to the Volkov case and that of Burgess, it became evident
to him that there were now reasonable grounds for regarding Philby
as a Soviet spy and "the third man," the individual who had warned
Maclean through Burgess that he would be arrested on the Monday
when he arrived at the Foreign Office.

Martin advised the director-general of the Security Service, Sir Percy
Sillitoe, who was intending to fly to Washington on or about June 12,
1951, to talk to J. Edgar Hoover about the Burgess and Maclean disappearance and, as Easton added, "any possible connection of Philby
with it." According to Easton, Sillitoe "had let C know that he would
like Philby away from Washington during his visit," for "obviously if
Philby was still in Washington during that time, he might reasonably
expect to accompany Sillitoe on his rounds of visits, if he was quite
clear of any suspicions. Therefore the main purpose of [the letter]
was to get Philby back to London before Sillitoe reached Washington."

The letter was designed also to warn him of C's intention to recall
him and thereby to allow him to lose no time in putting his personal
affairs in order so that he would be able to return to London promptly
when so ordered. Easton asserted that his letter advised Philby that he
would get the recall signal in about four days. Another reason existed
for the letter: the thought that once he had left Washington, Philby
would not return, and that a "Most Immediate–Decypher Yourself
signal" would in itself precipitate his immediate departure. The letter
"*avoided any air of panic action*" that might lead the American authorities to conclude that Philby was indeed a Soviet agent. They were told
officially only that "Philby had been guilty of gross *indiscretion* in having
Burgess as his lodger." Otherwise, "the fact that John Drew," a deception agent, "carried the letter was because his visit to 'C' that evening
fortuitously gave us a quick safe channel for the letter which would be

in Philby's hands by the next morning. Drew had access to Broadway and 'C' and was familiar with secret activities & there was no good reason not to ask him to deliver the letter." That Philby saw the letter as an escape warning was, said Easton, "a sign of his own guilty conscience and also of his state of severe fright." Easton's estimate was probably correct, for Philby had received a severe fright. It had been nothing less than yet another whiff of the firing squad.[83]

As Philby himself concluded, "It was an ugly picture," in which he was "faced with the inescapable conclusion that I could not hope to prove my innocence." Nonetheless, he decided against bolting to Moscow because "a strong presumption of my guilt might be good enough for an intelligence officer," but "it would not be enough for a lawyer."[84] There, in Washington, as the FBI stirred and tapped his phone, Philby waited in suspension. At a garden party at the embassy, Lady Franks gave him a very scornful glance as she received him in the waiting line.

Leaving Aileen to settle their affairs, Philby left Washington on June 11, 1951, as Sillitoe and Martin left London. On their arrival they presented Hoover with a long paper on the escape of Burgess and Maclean and Philby's involvement. Lamphere asked Martin, "Where does Philby fit in? Burgess was living with him." Martin replied ominously, "Most of what I have to tell you relates to Philby. We now have the gravest suspicions about him." Lamphere was appalled. It is interesting to speculate what might have happened if Philby had still been in the city. Martin handed Lamphere a second, shorter memorandum consisting of MI5's evidence and suspicions that pointed to Philby's being a Soviet agent:

1. Philby, Burgess and Maclean had all been Communists or left-wing Socialists at Cambridge.
2. After graduating, Philby had switched to being pro-German; this was regarded as the sort of action taken when building a cover story.
3. Philby had married [Alice] Friedman, an Austrian Communist and a known Soviet agent.
4. Krivitsky had pointed to a British journalist serving with the Franco forces as a KGB agent.
5. The Volkov affair.
6. Philby was suspected of playing a part in the disappearance of Burgess and Maclean.

His immediate thought was that

I would have liked to interrogate Philby about all these matters, and more, but he'd been recalled to England. In the United States, he would have had diplomatic immunity anyway. But from the moment I learned the details of his life and how they intertwined with the lives of Burgess and Maclean, I had little doubt left in my mind that Philby had been a KGB man for many years.[85]

Lamphere now "began to hate Philby." But for him, he concluded, the FBI would have gone on and on, uncovering and rolling up KGB networks in the United States.[86] And what had happened in Korea, where sixty thousand Americans had been killed and countless wounded? In every direction he looked, he saw disasters wrought upon the United States by the hands of Philby, Burgess, and Maclean, and, doubtless, others. The whole story was

> incredible to me. All three men had acted so wildly, and on so many occasions, that it was difficult for me to comprehend how any competent intelligence service could overlook the danger they posed to their country's security. But for many years they had been promoted through the ranks until they reached high positions, and no one seemed to have been worried about them.[87]

The American sense of dismay and shock was great when Philby arrived in London on June 12, the day Sillitoe and Martin arrived in Washington. The last person Philby saw at the CIA was Angleton, who gave him a letter to deliver to a CIA officer in London. Otherwise, just before that the director of Central Intelligence, Smith, asked Angleton and William K. Harvey, and perhaps others, for their views on the association between Philby and Burgess. Harvey, whose wife Burgess had insulted so resoundingly, is said to have had a brainwave while stuck in traffic on his way to the office. This he put on paper to General Smith, pointing out that not only had Philby been a close friend of Burgess's for many years but that he had known the details of the Albanian operations and the Homer case, and he was also the officer who had gone out to Istanbul to interview the Soviet defector Volkov. Angleton's memo, on the other hand, discussed only Burgess and his conduct in Washington and barely mentioned his own relationship with Philby. All he did say was that Philby had introduced Burgess "as the most brilliant historian of his generation."[88] And as Philby himself recalled of that final meeting with Angleton, they passed "a pleasant hour in a bar" and Angleton "did not seem to appreciate the gravity of my personal situation."

As Harvey and Angleton prepared their papers, Sillitoe and Martin were meeting with Hoover and giving out the papers they had prepared as well as information about Philby's marriage to Alice Friedman. This evidence provided the basis for a letter from Hoover to Admiral Sidney W. Souers, the chairman of the National Security Council, for President Truman. The immediate effect of Sillitoe's communication was that Hoover advised General Smith. Further, he decided not to write to C personally but to send the letter to Sillitoe with Angleton's and Harvey's papers on Philby and Burgess. The main comment of the hour was made by Allen Dulles, who was about to become director of the CIA. He said, "Philby got the crown jewels all right. What we don't know is which governments got them."[89]

14

London

1951–1955

WHEN PHILBY ARRIVED in London on June 12, 1951, he went first to his mother's flat in Drayton Gardens, Kensington, lunched, and then telephoned James Easton at the headquarters of the Secret Service at Broadway. Easton asked Philby to come immediately to headquarters, which he did, but as Easton remembered,

> There was no case against him at this time, except that he might have committed a gross indiscretion by his association with Guy Burgess. There was nothing in his file that reflected in any way on his character and ability. Nor was there anything that showed that at any time he had been involved in deception work against the Russians.

Colonel Vivian was now in charge of the security of the service, and as Easton wrote:

> My conviction is that C may have been informed by Vivian at the time of Philby's entrance into The Firm of Philby's left-wing associations at Cambridge, but I feel sure that Vivian must have convinced C that like so many other University men in the early 30's Philby had dabbled in Marxism & had become disillusioned. St. John Philby had assured Vivian to that effect & I am convinced that the issue of Philby's security virtually became a closed book to Vivian, who could be very naive.[1]

But if C had retained confidence in his man, that confidence was not shared by the Security Service. There Arthur Martin's search into

Philby's record was fraught with political danger. Relations between the two sister services were never so good that C would tolerate MI5's investigation of one of his most senior officers on the gravest of matters without his approval; and that had neither been sought nor given. The evidence against Philby had not been enough, until now, to raise any question about his loyalties. C personally was inclined to believe that communists were, as he once stated, "traitors to their class," and he had accepted the MI5 view that espionage on behalf of the Soviet Union had become "a very present menace." But when he permitted Philby to attend a meeting with MI5, he did so because the Security Service was investigating the disappearance of Burgess and Maclean, not Philby personally.

A further element in the inquiry into the "gross indiscretion" was that, since the war, Whitehall had become anti-American and therefore disposed to give Philby the benefit of the doubt. And as Seale and McConville noted of Philby's personal situation during that first phase in London after his recall:

> Kim's ten years' service in the SIS had won him a fine reputation. It was not so much his talent as an intelligence officer that had impressed his colleagues, but rather that he appeared the personification of integrity. He seemed to embody the very British virtues of low-keyed, understated moral excellence, and this image, noteworthy in a world of men whose profession was cynicism, now did him sterling service. There were other factors working for him. To many people he appeared a casualty of the McCarthyite hysteria which was then sweeping Washington and which in Britain seemed exaggerated and despicable.[2]

But Dick Goldsmith White, the senior MI5 officer who interviewed Philby that day, was not in the mold of the old mandarins such as Menzies. Nor was he in the same mold as the old MI5 establishment, men who tended, as one of Churchill's aides had remarked, "to see dangerous men too freely" and lacked a "knowledge of the world and sense of perspective."[3] White was a more cosmopolitan figure and he knew Philby well from the wartime days, when White was a recipient of ISOS. They were rivals for preeminence in the secret circle. Easton was present at the "interview" at MI5 headquarters in Curzon Street, Mayfair. White knew what Arthur Martin knew about Philby; and Philby recorded the opening moves of what proved to be a remarkable and protracted intellectual engagement:

> This was to be the first of many interrogations, although an attempt was made, at this early stage, to conceal that ugly fact . . . It may be

imagined that there was some apprehension on my side, some embarrassment on theirs. I could not claim White as a close friend; but our personal and official relations had always been excellent, and he had undoubtedly been pleased when I superseded Cowgill. He was bad at dissembling, but did his best to put talk on a friendly footing. He wanted my help, he said, in clearing up this appalling Burgess-Maclean affair. I gave him a lot of information about Burgess's past and impressions of his personality, taking the line that it was almost inconceivable that anyone like Burgess, who courted the limelight instead of avoiding it and was generally notorious for indiscretion, could have been a secret agent, let alone a Soviet agent from whom strictest security standards would be required. I did not expect this line to be in any way convincing as to the facts of the case; but I hoped it would give the impression that I was implicitly defending myself against the unspoken charge that I, a trained counter-espionage officer, had been completely fooled by Burgess.[4]

As for Maclean, Philby felt he could not put a face to him, which was almost true.

Philby's first meeting with White appears to have been merely a reconnaissance in which White revealed little of anything that he knew about Philby. But at a second meeting, White began to show more interest in Philby. Plainly acting upon the basis of the long-ago information from Walter Krivitsky and other sources, White focused on Philby's *first* journey to Franco's headquarters, the one undertaken almost informally before he was appointed *The Times*'s correspondent and which ended with Philby's interrogation by the Spanish security police as a possible Soviet spy. White wanted to know who had paid for this journey. He suspected that the Soviet service had paid for it, which was the truth. As Philby recognized, with that question "all but the tip of the cat's tail was now out of the bag." As he wrote later,

> It was a nasty little question because the enterprise had been suggested to me and financed by the Soviet service, just as Krivitsky had said, and a glance at my bank balance for the period would have shown that I had no means for gallivanting around Spain. Embedded in this episode was also the dangerous little fact that Burgess had been used to replenish my funds. My explanation was that the Spanish journey had been an attempt to break into the world of high-grade journalism on which I had staked everything, selling all my effects (mostly books and gramophone records) to pay for the trip. It was reasonably plausible and quite impossible to disprove.[5]

It was also impossible for White to accept Philby's explanation. But the quarry bore himself well, and White was not able to shake him.

From that moment forward there began the cat-and-mouse game between MI5 and Philby that was to last for the next five years. Philby survived it, although only just. So subtly did he play on the notion C and his officers were disposed to believe — that he had become a victim of the McCarthyism and war hysteria sweeping Washington — that his closest colleagues in the service gave him much important moral support during the period of the MI5 "inquisition." Nor had the CIA or the FBI produced any evidence to support the allegation that he was a Soviet spy.

C decided to send Easton to Washington to convey the official view of Philby and to test the waters at both the CIA and the Royal Canadian Mounted Police's security service in Ottawa. He authorized Easton to tell Walter Bedell Smith only that "the present view of Broadway is that Philby is guilty of nothing worse than gross indiscretion in having Burgess in his house, but that an inquiry was being instituted into all aspects concerning him."[6] If anything more serious than gross indiscretion became known, then that information would be communicated to the CIA. Moreover, C did not instruct Easton to get to Washington by the fastest means, as would have been the case had there been a real emergency. To the contrary, Easton was sent on the *Queen Mary*, which suggests that C was not as alarmed as those around him.

Easton met with General Smith at CIA headquarters on July 13 and found him "frosty and angry," but no allegations were made against Philby. Smith merely asked Easton for the British view about him, and the meeting was "relatively short," probably because Easton had so little to impart. Smith did ask Easton to remain in Washington long enough to enable his officers to "confer" with him, and although Easton had received no instructions from C as to what he might say, he agreed, and a series of meetings was held at the Shoreham Hotel each day for the rest of the working week. Easton claimed that the meetings were cordial, and on no occasion was he able to conclude that CIA had any evidence that Philby was a Soviet spy, although it was clear that this was what they suspected. Indeed, such was the attitude he encountered that he sent a signal to C, asking him not to sack Philby until his return.

In all, therefore, the most remarkable thing about the Washington meetings was that they were unremarkable. But almost immediately on his return to London, Easton received a report on Philby. He never learned where the information came from, but he felt sure that it had existed *before* he left for Washington. Some of the information contained in the paper dated from as early as January 1940. As Easton recalled,

Early in the paper I encountered a document that showed that Philby had lied in September 1940 when he said in his *cv* that he had married Aileen Furse. In fact he was still married to [Lizzy] Friedman, and remained so until 1946, and that therefore four of Kim's five children were illegitimate.[7]

Easton recalled distinctly Kim's response to his congratulations on the birth of the fourth young Philby: Kim could think of nothing more rewarding than two rows of descending heads at the dining room table. As he looked at the paper now, the more certain he became of Philby's treachery. He realized, too, that "this man was a practised liar and was therefore capable of anything." In all, the paper consisted of ten points against Philby.

1. His lie about his marriage to Aileen Furse.
2. His marriage to Alice Friedman, a known communist.
3. His close association with Burgess, a known communist and now a defector to Russia.
4. The suspicious source of his finances during his first journey to Spain and while traveling generally in Europe between 1933 and his appointment to *The Times* in February 1937.
5. His communism at Cambridge and his sudden right-wing conversion after his director of studies refused to vouch for him politically in order that he might sit for the entrance examination for the Foreign Office.
6. The contents of his memo written from Washington about the identity of Homer that drew a red herring across the entire investigation.
7. The upsurge in Soviet wireless traffic from London to Moscow and Istanbul two days after C had briefed him regarding Volkov.
8. His handling of the Volkov affair.
9. His known association with other suspected communists during World War II at Burgess's flat in 5 Bentinck Street.
10. The jump in NKVD traffic between London and Moscow after the briefing about Homer.

After reading the paper, Easton went to see the deputy chief of the Secret Service, then C himself, to protest that his statements to the CIA would have been very different had he seen this paper before he went to Washington. As Easton stated:

As I recall, C said that the information had not existed before I went, that it had been compiled while I was away. But that really did not mean very much, for some of the information was old and the dates on most of it showed that the information was known at Broadway *before* I went to Washington.

Easton was never certain in his own mind whether C had known of these facts. He was, Easton remembered, so "sphinx-like and cunning that it was impossible to deduce anything." C, as cool as ever, asked Easton to have a talk with Philby. Accordingly, Easton called Philby to his office. Of that meeting, Easton recalled,

> I told Philby of the existence of the paper and went over each point with him. I spoke to him about his lie concerning his marriage, his various journeys while impoverished, Alice Friedman's associations with a Soviet agent in Germany, that she herself had been a Soviet spy in England in 1943, and drew Philby's attention to the fact that Burgess had visited Philby at Istanbul in 1948. I then pointed out that there was other evidence against him but that I felt he was "making no real effort to defend himself." I asked him why this was. Why did he have no answer to the statements being made against him? Philby attempted to answer each point, but he did so too cleverly. He looked and behaved like a rat in a trap. I let him go. But his attitude was such that he left me with the conviction that everything being said against him was true and that there was now a strong presumption of guilt against him.

Easton then put the entire matter up to Menzies. At their meeting C gave no indication of how he felt or what he was going to do. But at the end of July or the beginning of August, he acted. As Philby was to record, he received a summons from C, who "told me, with obvious distress, that he would have to ask for my resignation. He would be generous: £4,000 in lieu of pension." The accounts of others reflected no such distress. Further, as Philby himself related:

> My unease was increased shortly afterwards when C told me that he had decided against paying me the whole sum at once. I would get £2,000 down and the rest in half-yearly instalments of £500. The ostensible reason for the deferred payments was the fear that I might dissipate all in wild speculation, but, as I had never speculated in my life, it looked a bit thin. A more likely reason was the desire to hedge against the possibility of my being sent to gaol within three years.

Thus, at the age of thirty-nine, Philby found himself unemployable, bereft of the protection of C, soon to be deprived of his passport, and under the deepest suspicion for the gravest of crimes in the British statute book. There was a prolonged period of inaction during which the case against him was being prepared.

During that time, St. John had something to say about the affair to a friend from his Amman days in 1924, Elizabeth Riefenstahl, now an Egyptologist at the Brooklyn Museum. In the course of a long and revealing letter dated October 7, 1951, St. John declared what had become the family's official version of Kim's resignation and the reasons for it:

> My son, after a couple of years in the British Embassy in Washington in close contact with the American outlook on foreign affairs, has decided that he has seen enough of the seamy side of world politics, and has resigned from the British Foreign Service, as I myself did at exactly the same age for the same reasons. He was quite happy working in the secret service, mostly in London, during the war, and in Turkey for some years thereafter; but Washington introduced him to a new aspect of international politics, in which I fancy he was never comfortable, though he never complained and never said very much about it. He was actually nearing the end of his tour of duty in America, and was looking forward to a transfer back to the Middle East or India, when the Burgess-Maclean incident occurred. I fancy that he disapproved of the witch-hunt that ensued, and the pettifogging inquiry into the political orthodoxy of Government servants. So he decided to quit while the going was good and his own record unblemished and, for his age, quite distinguished; and he has now retired on very favourable terms. He is now looking for other work, though he is not very keen to return to journalism, in which he started his career and in which he could readily start again as a *Times* correspondent, probably in India.[8]

The Burgess and Maclean affair was not, however, to be dismissed as easily as St. John wished. After some months in the cold, drinking heavily, awaiting the crack of doom while living in a gatekeeper's cottage in the charming and silent Hertfordshire countryside, Philby was summoned by C in November 1951. C explained that a judicial inquiry had been opened into "the circumstances of the Burgess-Maclean escape" and that Philby was required to give evidence. The inquiry was to be conducted by Helenus J. P. (Buster) Milmo, King's Counsel, at MI5 headquarters. Of that ordeal Philby recorded:

> The mention of Milmo indicated that a crisis was at hand. I knew him and of him. He was a skilled interrogator; he was the man whom MI5 usually brought in for the kill. As I drove with the Chief across St. James's Park . . . I braced myself for a sticky ordeal. I was still

confident that I could survive an examination, however robust, on the basis of the evidence known to me. But I could not be sure that new evidence had not come to hand for Milmo to shoot at me.[9]

At headquarters, Milmo asked Philby to refrain from smoking, as this was an official body. The inquiry began. Philby sought to appear as a cooperative ex-SIS officer, but his real objective was to deny Milmo "the confession which he required as a lawyer." Philby wrote in his memoirs:

I was too closely involved in Milmo's interrogation to form an objective opinion on its merits. Much of the ground that he covered was familiar and my answers, excogitated long before, left him little to do but shout. Early in the interview, he betrayed the weakness of his position by accusing me of entrusting to "Burgess intimate personal papers." The charge was so obviously nonsensical that I did not even have to feign bewilderment. It appeared that my Cambridge degree had been found in Burgess's flat during the search which followed his departure. Years before, I had folded that useless document and put it in a book. Burgess, as anyone would have told Milmo, was an inveterate borrower of books with and without the permission of their owners. The aim of the accusation was to show that I had deliberately underplayed the degree of my intimacy with Burgess. It was flimsy stuff and went far to strengthen my confidence in the outcome.

But Milmo produced "at least two rabbits out of the bag which I had not foreseen, and which showed that the chain of circumstantial evidence against me was even longer than I had feared." Milmo raised the matter of the increases in NKVD communication after the Volkov and Homer affairs. "Taken in conjunction with the other evidence, these two items were pretty damning. But to me, sitting in the interrogation chair, they posed no problem. When asked in Milmo's most thunderous tones to account for these occurrences, I replied quite simply that I could not." Philby continued:

I was beginning to tire when suddenly Milmo gave up. [Arthur] Martin asked me to stay put for a few minutes. When I was invited into the next room, Milmo had disappeared and the MI5 legal officer was in charge. He asked me to surrender my passport, saying that they would get it anyway but that voluntary action on my part would obviate publicity. I readily agreed as my escape plan certainly did not envisage the use of my own identity papers. My offer to send the document that night by registered post was rejected because it was "too risky." William Skardon [an MI5 interrogator] was detailed to accompany me back to my home and receive it from me . . . I was

too relieved to listen, though my relief was tempered by the knowledge that I was not yet out of the wood — not by a long chalk.[10]

Philby was correct. He was not out of the woods. Neither the Foreign
Office nor MI5 had any doubt that Philby had been and still was a
Soviet agent. With the entry of Skardon, the character of the case
changed unmistakably. Skardon, a clerkly, humble, underpaid man in
appearance, had developed a doctrine of his own through his many
interrogations of men in the higher grades of the Civil Service who
were suspected of disloyalty. He was too insignificant a man to threaten
a suspect from the superior classes. He knew his Marxism and insinuated himself into the persona of his quarry, unnerving his man by
persistence. Since he was endowed with the full authority of the state,
there was no escape from him.

As Philby knew, Skardon had direct connections with the Security
Service and the FBI/CIA counterintelligence chiefs in London, for
they had their offices in the same building, above a bedding and
mattress shop just off Grosvenor Square. And very gradually, under
Skardon's questions, the weakness brought about by his heavy solitary
drinking, the strangers seen in the locality, the thought that his telephone had been tapped and that his mail, particularly with his father
in Saudi Arabia, was being intercepted, that letters written by him were
not being received in Mecca, Philby began to show signs of wear.
Relations with Aileen were all but collapsed, and she made matters
worse by threatening to go to the Foreign Office and denounce him
as "the third man." As Kim recalled of Skardon's visits:

> He was scrupulously courteous, his manner verging on the exquisite;
> nothing could have been more flattering than the cosy warmth of his
> interest in my views and actions. He was far more dangerous than
> the ineffective [Goldsmith] White or the blustering Milmo. I was
> helped to resist his polite advances by the knowledge that it was
> Skardon who had wormed his way into [the atomic spy Klaus] Fuchs's
> confidence with such disastrous results. During our first long conver-
> sation, I detected and evaded two little traps which he laid for me
> with deftness and precision. But I had scarcely begun congratulating
> myself when the thought struck me that he may have laid others
> which I had not detected.

By February 1952 he felt that he might be succeeding against Skardon, but he wrote to warn his father that his association with Burgess
was, as St. John expressed it, "still under investigation with extremely
little hope, though, of any final solution of the mystery and that,

naturally enough, his close association with B militates against his efforts to get important work of anything like a political nature."[11]

The Age of the New Elizabethans had just begun with the accession of Queen Elizabeth II to the throne. Churchill was back as prime minister. And C did not intend that his beloved service, the service that had saved England at its bleakest hour in 1940–1941, should enter the age on a note of high scandal. The pressures on Philby began to diminish as the pro-Philbyites worked to prevent a terrible scandal from breaking out in the press. Until now, all that had been published was that Burgess and Maclean were believed to be in Moscow; Philby's part in their disappearance was unknown except to a small group of insiders in the secret circle. And that was the way it would remain for three years, until 1955. The press nibbled but got nowhere. The CIA appeared briefly on Philby's horizon at some stage in 1952, when James McCargar, Philby's CIA colleague in the Albanian operations, met Angleton at the Hôtel Crillon in Paris.

They talked about the Philby case, and Angleton expressed the belief that Philby would recover from his present predicament and would yet become chief of the British Secret Service. At that remark, which McCargar presumed derived from a meeting between Angleton and C or some other high official at Broadway, McCargar suggested that, since he had been a friend and colleague of Philby's in Washington, he might call on Philby when he was next in London, which would be soon, and have a talk with him. Did Angleton agree? Yes, he said; that might prove desirable and necessary. So McCargar made contact with Philby and they met at a flat available to the American in Lowndes Square. Philby showed considerable strain at the official pressure to which he was being subjected, but he was more distressed at Aileen's condition. She had, he declared, become "insane" and had tried to kill him. In consequence, he said, he had moved out of the house and had taken to living and sleeping in a tent on the lawn. Accordingly, McCargar formed the impression that Philby's main threat lay not with Skardon but with Aileen Philby, who knew something about Philby's loyalties.

Otherwise, McCargar reported, Philby's status with MI5 at the end of 1952 was "guilt unproven but suspicion remaining."[12]

C finally announced his retirement in a signal to all stations on June 30, 1952, about a year after he had cast Philby into the wilderness. He was covered with honors, which he deserved richly. Menzies's nominee, Sir John Sinclair, a stately man of six foot three, succeeded as

C, with Easton as deputy chief. Easton stated of Menzies's retire-ment: "Stewart slid out. He knew that a great scandal was about, and he did not want to be involved." But his power remained and he exercised it through Sinclair. There now followed a series of retire-ment ceremonies that did not indicate that C was leaving in disgrace or as a defeated man, as his many enemies and critics imagined. To the contrary, the tenor of all the celebration was that the state had lost a servant of unsurpassed competence. The Joint Intelligence Com-mittee met on July 3, 1952, and the chairman, Sir Patrick Reilly, spoke of the "vitally important post" that C had held for thirteen years and how his work had been "distinguished by an extraordinary devotion to duty."[13] C had made "an immense personal contribution to the country which was clearly recognized despite ill-informed criticism." He said nothing of the cause of the criticism, only that it had existed. The state had "lost a great public servant." Goldsmith White, by now director general of MI5, associated himself with Reilly's statement, stating that "it had been his privilege to serve under Sir Stewart Menzies during the war."

The news soon traveled through the world intelligence community. On July 10, J. Edgar Hoover wrote in terms that scarcely suggested that C's conduct of his affairs had resulted in a transatlantic disaster:

> Dear Sir Stewart,
> It is with profound regret that I learn of your resignation as Direc-tor General, British Secret Intelligence Service.
> Your career has been a splendid example of unselfish and un-stinted loyalty in the finest tradition and I feel that your retirement is England's loss.
> The splendid cooperation you have extended to my representatives in London is very much appreciated and you have my best wishes for every future happiness.
>
> > Sincerely,
> > J.E.H.[14]

The next day came this message from Allen Dulles, who was now in the process of taking over the CIA from Smith. Although Dulles was no admirer of either C or SIS and was a leader of those who believed that the CIA should take the mantle of British intelligence ascendancy, his signal did not suggest either defeat or animus, at least insofar as the United States was concerned:

> Please express to Sir Stewart my warmest personal regards and my admiration of his career of accomplishment for his country and the cause.

I look back with the greatest satisfaction at our collaboration together, both during the war years and in working on the post-war problems facing us today. We shall all need his wise counsel in the future.

On August 1, a message came from Smith through his representative in London, D. Debardeleben: "I deeply regret your retirement no matter how much you have earned a rest. I urge your acceptance of our previous invitation to visit U.S."[15] But Menzies accepted no invitation to visit Washington.

There were several ceremonies at the Foreign Office. On July 22, 1952, the higher executive gathered in the permanent head's room when a pair of Georgian decanters and a set of matching glasses were presented, with a letter from Foreign Secretary Anthony Eden:

My Dear Menzies,

On the occasion of your retirement I am writing to express to you the thanks of Her Majesty's Government for the outstanding services which you have rendered to the State.

Before entering the Service from which you have just retired, you had a gallant and distinguished record in the First World War. For 20 years you have played a leading part in the valuable work which your Service then undertook with very limited resources. You succeeded to its highest post shortly after the outbreak of war had vastly increased its tasks. For nearly six years, with selfless devotion, you carried a personal burden of responsibility such as fell upon few of your colleagues in the whole great machine for the conduct of the war. Since 1945 you have had little respite. You have had to pursue the reconstruction of your Service, on a scale never before contemplated in peace, amid the insistent demands of a new and unprecedented world-wide conflict. You leave it full of promise for the future.

By its nature your work can receive no public tributes. For this reason I am all the more anxious that you should know how highly Her Majesty's Government have valued your services. By your retirement they have lost a devoted public servant.

In conclusion, may I say that I hope that you will enjoy for many years the leisure that you have so well earned.

Yours Very Sincerely,
Anthony Eden.[16]

After thirty-eight years in the political underworld, Stewart Menzies ended an epic career in the secret circle, although he remained an adviser in clandestine affairs for the next five years or so and was often asked to attend meetings concerning Philby. He was perhaps the only man who knew the inner story of the Philby case and remained an asset as long as Philby remained silent. C's great fear was the press.

For the next two years, from 1952 to 1954, the contest continued between Skardon and Philby. Skardon called from time to time to settle what he called "minor but oustanding matters of detail," and this unnerved Aileen as, no doubt, Skardon intended. She did in fact warn the Foreign Office that Kim was about to join MacLean and Burgess in Moscow, and her action — which she repeated in a letter to St. John in Riyadh and which he dismissed as "pure tosh!"[17] — became Philby's standard explanation for the difficulties he encountered in getting suitable work. All his efforts — with *The Times,* the *Daily Telegraph, The Observer,* with the Shell Oil Company — foundered on the rock of the Foreign Office's refusal to give him adequate references. A scheme to write a history of the Spanish Civil War, for which he received a £600 advance against royalties from a London publisher, evaporated when the publisher was told that it was unlawful for a former officer of the Secret Service to write such a book. The £600 had to be repaid, and this was done by Philby's Anglo-Spanish friend from the days of the Garbo operation, Tomas Harris, the Mayfair art dealer. Whenever he applied for a job he was required to explain why he had left "the Foreign Office" — the cover term for the British Secret Service — and since he could not do so, his applications withered on the vine. None of his colleagues in the service could or would speak for or against him.

He began to run into severe financial trouble. He could not pay his children's school fees, and he had a general want for money. St. John, who had a number of trusts squirreled away, sent Kim a good deal of money between 1952 and 1954. There was talk of Kim's joining his father's agency at Jidda in 1953.

But Kim remained at home, in real danger of being forced onto the dole, or some such other humiliation. He began to consider an escape plan:

> The plan, originally designed for American conditions, required only minor modifications to adapt it to European circumstances. Indeed, in some ways it would be easier from London than from Washington. But each time I considered the project, the emergency appeared to be less than extreme. Finally, an event occurred which put it right out of my head. I received, through the most ingenious of routes, a message from my Soviet friends, conjuring me to be of good cheer and presaging an early resumption of relations. It changed drastically the whole complexion of the case. I was no longer alone.[18]

Throughout this time of trial, Philby had had no contact with his Soviet masters, nor they with him. With the Security Services' interest in him, any such meeting might have provided the British with the proof they needed against him. It might also have resulted in the loss and capture of a senior Soviet secret agent. But in late 1952 or early 1953, the Soviet Secret Service became concerned or curious about Philby. There had been no mention of him in the press, and accordingly its reigning British expert, Yuri Modin, was instructed to make contact with the master spy.

Modin had no address for Philby, and it took him several months to reach him. This he did through Anthony Blunt, who by now had become Queen Elizabeth II's picture master at Buckingham Palace, a traditional post of considerable social importance. Modin attended a lecture given by Blunt at the Courtauld Institute, of which he was also the director. Modin managed to talk with Blunt without being observed, and they arranged to meet after dark in the place Modin favored as safe for clandestine conversations, an ill-lit street in Ruislip, a lower-middle-class wilderness of semidetached houses not far from the airport.[19]

When Modin reached the street at the appointed time, he became conscious that he was being followed. It was Blunt, who caught up with him and said that he had brought Philby with him, that he was in serious trouble, and that Modin must talk with him. A personal meeting with Philby was quite against Moscow's orders, for he was "far too hot." But Modin agreed. Blunt moved on, leaving Philby to catch up with the sauntering Modin. They talked as they strolled together for two or three minutes. Philby stated that he might yet have to use his escape plan, but he had no money left. He had severe trouble with Aileen, and he felt that he could be arrested at any time. Modin agreed to transmit £5,000 to him through, it is presumed, Blunt. Then they separated, vanishing in a moment in an area of London where nobody seemed much interested in strangers on the streets after eight o'clock in the evening.[20]

Yet if Philby was encouraged by the meeting with Modin, Skardon's visits continued, and Dora wrote to St. John in Riyadh to warn him that Kim had begun to show signs of losing confidence in himself. And as Skardon told the CIA's counterespionage chief, Cleveland Cram — each had an office in the same building — he was close to breaking Philby and getting the confession the state wanted. But then, oddly, Skardon came no more. In the official world the case seemed to enter a period of suspension. The press continued to nibble at the case of

Burgess and Maclean, but Whitehall's damage control worked to frustrate further penetrations. Certainly a good deal of apprehension remained after George Wigg, a socialist member, rose in Parliament and asked, "Would the Foreign Secretary institute inquiries into the suggestion made in a Sunday newspaper that there is widespread sexual perversion in the Foreign Office?" The foreign secretary responded, "I can only say that perhaps I have not been long enough at the Foreign Office to express an opinion."

By 1955, Whitehall believed that it had succeeded in burying what might have become a very great scandal. As an American observer of British politics, Edward Shils, noted, the British ruling class is "unequalled in secretiveness and taciturnity." No ruling class in the Western world, certainly no ruling class in any democratic society, "is as close-mouthed as the British ruling class. No ruling class "discloses as little of its confidential proceedings as does the British."

Philby knew this and exploited it. He now felt he could defeat any charge of treason against him, his confidence reinforced by an iron conviction that communism represented the only truth in an age dominated by the capitalism and the thermonuclear politics of the Pax Americana. He might be in the power of a state interrogator, but it was the ruling class that would find itself on trial if anything happened to him. "The last thing I wanted when I was director of central intelligence," William E. Colby remarked of his predicament over the CIA traitor Philip Agee, "was that Agee should be killed in a street accident or something."[21] So it was with the British ruling class in 1955. They wanted Philby alive, not dead, for none on the left would believe that they had not had a hand in his death. The Whitehall establishment would gladly have had him killed in order to remove a dangerous embarrassment to the Anglo-American connection, and there was concern that some rash American official might do the job for Whitehall if it did not act, as the official phrase put it, "to resolve Philby's status." But Whitehall was concerned that Philby might become a hero to the left, the individual around whom all the left-wing discontent in Britain might coalesce.

When, in 1954, Vladimir M. Petrov, the chief of the Soviet Secret Service in Australia, deserted to the Australian Security Intelligence Organization (ASIO), he took with him the first information about the whereabouts of Burgess and Maclean since their disappearance in May 1951. They were in Moscow. Petrov stated also that they were not homosexuals on the run, or malcontents, as was generally supposed, but since 1934 they had been trained Soviet secret agents. In the course of his interrogation by the Australians, Petrov stated that a colleague and friend at the Soviet Embassy in Canberra, Philip Kislytsin, had been at the Soviet Embassy in London between 1945 and 1948. There, Kislytsin had been responsible for transmitting to Moscow photographs of the Foreign Office documents that Burgess had passed to his Soviet contact in London. When he returned to Moscow in 1948, Kislytsin, according to Petrov, interested himself in the Burgess case, and was put in charge of the desk at Moscow Center responsible for handling Burgess's material.

In Sydney, meanwhile, the Petrov case had leaked to the press, thwarting Foreign Office attempts to hush news of the Maclean and Burgess defection. On September 18, 1955, *The People* splashed the Petrov story across page one. It proved to be a bombshell in which Petrov related what Kislytsin had told him — that Burgess and Maclean had been Soviet agents since their youth at Cambridge and had been spying for the enemy ever since. They had fled to escape arrest. The Foreign Office could stonewall no longer; it confirmed Petrov's statement and promised a full statement, which was published in the form of a White Paper on September 23. This document gave very little away, and nothing at all about Philby, whose name was being whispered about Whitehall but had been protected so far. Parliament was in recess, so there could be no debate, although one was promised.

By the time the House reassembled on October 25, the Labour member for Brixton, Colonel Marcus Lipton, had emerged as the government's main gadfly in "the case of the missing diplomats." He was certain that Burgess and Maclean could not have acted alone; there had been a serious conspiracy at the heart of the government. In the House he dropped this bombshell:

> Has the Prime Minister [Anthony Eden] made up his mind to cover up at all costs the dubious third man activities of Mr. Harold Philby who was First Secretary at the Washington Embassy a little time ago, and is he determined to stifle all discussion on the very great matters which were evaded in the wretched White Paper, which is an insult to the intelligence of the country?[22]

At the time of the disappearance of Maclean and Burgess, "'the right people' moved into action" and "no one whose job it was to be interested in the Burgess-Maclean affair from the very beginning will forget the subtle but powerful pressures which were brought to bear by those who belonged to the same stratum as the two missing men." Among them was Harold Macmillan, now the foreign secretary, who had ministerial responsibility for the British Secret Service. His attitude toward

Philby was: Don't try him, use him. He resisted any public inquiry in the Philby, Burgess, and Maclean hearings; as he told the Cabinet in a paper on October 20, 1955, "Nothing could be worse than a lot of muckraking and innuendo. It would be like one of the immense divorce cases which there used to be when I was young, going on for days and days, every detail reported in the press." He was "concerned that there was nothing to be said for holding an inquest into the past. This would give currency to a stream of false and misleading statements which could never be overtaken and corrected in the public mind."[23]

Macmillan prevailed. He established a committee of inquiry into the Philby case under the chairmanship of John A. Thomson, a rising young Foreign Office official. Thomson's committee examined all the evidence there was against Philby. Their finding was that the evidence against him was insufficient to withhold exoneration. The committee did recommend that Philby be reexamined formally but not by the Security Service, which remained convinced that he was a Soviet agent. The examination would be conducted by the Secret Service, which had the most to hide, with the Security Service supplying the technical means for recording the interrogation. The interrogation was held at a Secret Service safe house near Sloane Square. Two Security Service experts, Hugh Winterborn and Peter Wright, were in charge of its technical aspects, and Wright left an account of it, brimming with MI5's conviction that Philby was indeed a traitor and reflecting the class tensions of the period between the Secret and the Security services.

The room the Secret Service had chosen for the interrogation was, Wright wrote, "sparsely furnished — just a sofa and chairs surrounding a small table." Along one wall was an ancient sideboard with a telephone. "As it was important to get as high a quality of recording as possible, we decided to use a high-quality BBC microphone . . . We lifted a floorboard alongside the fireplace on the side on which Philby would sit and inserted the microphone beneath it. We arranged an amplifier to feed the microphone signal to a telephone pair with which the Post Office had arranged to feed the signal back to [MI5 headquarters in Mayfair]." Later, Winterborn and Wright sat down in a special room at headquarters to wait for the interrogation to begin. Wright wrote:

> In fact, to call it an interrogation would be a travesty. It was an in-house MI6 interview. Philby entered and was greeted in a friendly

way by three former colleagues who knew him well. They took him gently over familiar ground. First his Communist past, then his MI6 career and his friendship with Guy Burgess. Philby stuttered and stammered, and protested his innocence. But listening to the disembodied voices, the lies seemed so clear. Whenever Philby floundered, one or another of the questioners guided him to an acceptable answer. "Well, I suppose such and such could be an explanation." Philby would gratefully agree and the interview would move on. Winterborn fetched Cumming [the deputy director of MI5], who strode into the office with a face like thunder. He listened for a few moments, slapping his thigh. "The buggers are going to clear him!" he muttered. Cumming promptly sent a minute to Graham Mitchell, the head of MI5 counter-espionage, giving an uncharacteristically blunt assessment of the MI6 whitewash. But it did no good . . . I realized for the first time that I had joined the Looking-Glass world, where simple but unpalatable truths were wished away.[24]

Wright's statement may have had little worth as evidence of the proceedings, but it did convey something of the indignation of those in the Security Service who were convinced of Philby's guilt.

The House was advised that there would be a debate on the Philby question on November 7, 1955; and the FBI's representative in London, who took a very close interest in the case, wired that Whitehall remained "gravely concerned" over the case and had described it "confidentially" as "the gravest problem they have had for a number of years, as a public inquiry (which is being demanded) would undoubtedly affect a number of organizations." The "organizations" were the Secret and the Security services and their appendages. The FBI man added a note of urgency: "Bureau will be immediately informed of any further developments . . . the lid is about to blow off the entire affair." The FBI agent underestimated the Establishment's continuing capacity for damage control.[25]

What the Eden government faced was, with much else besides, a public inquiry into the activities of the Secret Service going back at least until 1941 and Philby's recruitment. The Secret Service had prepared for, and then fought, a world war. Afterward, the Cold War erupted. The service had conducted many actions that Churchill's government and its successors regarded as disavowable. For years the Soviet government had claimed knowledge that the Secret Service had, on behalf of another department, attempted to cause a battle of annihilation between Germany and Russia in 1942. There was the Hess affair, the manipulations over the activities of the European resistance movements, the disruption of the Abwehr and the German General Staff. Philby had been involved in all of these operations, and more. Were they to be investigated and made public at a time of continuing Cold War with Russia and when Britain was seeking to obtain admittance into the European Common Market? How would the survivors of the German services react to such an exposure, at a time that the new German Army provided NATO with important staff components, to say nothing of commanders for armies, divisions, and regiments? Did Britain really want to stir up all those old pools? Good relations with Germany, France, and the United States were essential. This was no time for an unholy scandal that would certainly damage the reputation of Britain for actions committed long ago and almost forgotten. Philby knew far too much about inner British policy, and Macmillan, representing the interests of the British Secret Service in Parliament, proved always to be a practitioner of the old political craft of least said, soonest mended. It was in the national interest that the fire flickering in Parliament and the press be put out.

In the House of Commons on November 7, Macmillan, the foxiest of foreign secretaries, rose to speak. He would prove to be the last of Churchill's men, the last of the *ancien régime,* an aristocrat undone by the Philby case and the central government figure involved in it. A man with the airs and graces of an Edwardian country gentleman, Macmillan was a type of politician peculiar to England — elegant, an Etonian, a classicist. He opened his statement:

> It can rarely have happened in our long parliamentary history that the political head of a Department should have had to unfold to the House of Commons so painful a story as that which it is our duty to consider today. To understand — though not, of course, to excuse — this story, it is necessary to cast our minds back to the 1930s and to recall the kind of background against which the two principal characters grew up.

That Macmillan now did, describing the political lives of Burgess and Maclean. He then defended the handling of the case by the socialist and conservative governments and reminded the House that

> action against employees, whether of the State or anybody else, arising from suspicion and not from proof, may begin with good motives, and it may avert serious inconveniences and even disasters, but judging from what has happened in some other countries [alluding to McCarthyism] such a practise soon degenerates into the satisfaction

of personal vendettas or a general system of tyranny, all in the name of public safety.

Macmillan then sought to remind the House of the circumstances in which these phenomenal events had occurred:

> Between May 1951 and April 1954, the first thought of those responsible had to be not how much they could tell the public but what they could do to minimise the harm that had been done. The Security [Service] still had extensive enquiries to make, not merely to reconstruct the story but to improve the Service.

But with the defection of Petrov in Australia, Macmillan continued, "a whole new vista on the case was opened up." Petrov had made a statement before a Royal Commission, and the possibility that Burgess and Maclean had been tipped off by someone within the government had now to be seriously considered, and "searching and protracted investigations into this possibility have been undertaken and are proceeding even at the present time." Macmillan went on:

> In this connection the name of one man has been mentioned in the House of Commons, but not outside. I feel that all Honourable Members would expect me to mention him by name and to explain the position. He is Mr. H. A. R. Philby, who was a temporary First Secretary at the British Embassy in Washington from October 1949 to June 1951 and had been privy to much of the investigation into the leakage. Mr. Philby had been a friend of Burgess from the time when they were fellow undergraduates at Trinity College, Cambridge. Burgess had been accommodated with Philby and his family at the latter's home in Washington from August 1950 to April 1951; and, of course, it will be realised that at no time before he fled was Burgess under suspicion. It is now known that Mr. Philby had Communist associations during and after his university days. In view of the circumstances, he was asked in July 1951 to resign from the Foreign Service. No evidence has been found to show that he was responsible for warning Burgess or Maclean. While in Government service he carried out his duties ably and conscientiously. I have no reason to conclude that Mr. Philby has at any time betrayed the interests of this country, or to identify him with the so-called Third Man, if indeed there was one.

At that point, Philby was formally exonerated of the charges against him of treachery, and Marcus Lipton withdrew his allegation against him:

> My evidence was insubstantial. Although I knew the name of the security officer who had pointed Philby out in the street, I could not

produce him [in the House]. It would have ruined the man's career. Members of MI5 had strict orders not to make contact with politicians. So when it came to a showdown my legal advisers counselled me to retract. Moreover I was shouted down in the House. Within the Labour Party, many members considered Philby a progressive left-wing influence in the Foreign Office, as he was clearly not part of the old guard. Their instinct was to protect him.

But was Philby's reputation restored? The MI5 file on him remained open. Suspicion of him remained in the CIA, the FBI, MI5, the Special Branch, even in some quarters in the Secret Service. According to James Easton, he and the new C, Sinclair, were not consulted before Macmillan cleared Philby's name. Had they been asked, they would, Easton stated, have advised that their verdict remained: "Guilt unproven but suspicion remains."

In the aftermath of Macmillan's statement, Philby held a press conference at his mother's apartment. Smiling and confident, freshly shaved and barbered, neat and trim in a blue pinstripe suit, his usual hesitations and stutter absent, he conducted himself ably as he made his statement. He had refrained from speaking earlier, he explained, because he was bound by the Official Secrets Act not to disclose information derived from his official position. He had no means of knowing whether words of his might not prejudice the government in its conduct of international affairs. The "efficiency of our security services can only be reduced by publicity given to their organization, personnel and techniques."[26] Very skillfully he emerged as the young, model, prudent government official.

> If there was a third man, were you in fact the third man? *No, I was not.* Do you think there was one? *No comment.* Mr Philby, you yourself were asked to resign from the Foreign Office a few months after Burgess and Maclean disappeared. The Foreign Secretary said in the past you had had Communist associations. That is why you were asked to resign? *I was asked to resign because of an imprudent association.* That is your association with Burgess? *Correct.* What about the alleged Communist associations? Can you say anything about them? *The last time I spoke to a Communist, knowing him to be a Communist, was some time in 1934.* That implies that you have also spoken to Communists unknowingly and now know about it. *Well, I spoke to Burgess last in April or May, 1951.* He gave you no idea that he was a Communist at all? *Never.*[27]

The whole affair was, one eminent reporter recorded, "wonderfully insolent."

Philby handled himself at the press conference with all the skill and cool of a statesman wriggling out of an affair of *la grande politique*. This was the more remarkable since it was known beforehand that he was not far from cracking up and, indeed, under Skardon's pressures, was about to flee to the Soviet Union. Aileen, fearing that he might take their children with him, had written to St. John in Saudi Arabia to ask him to prevent that from happening. He exclaimed in a letter to Dora: "Aileen's letter to me seems to have been pretty fair tosh, and it seems pretty clear that she is not in command of her senses." She was, it seems, threatening to ask the courts to give her custody of the children. "Surely no court would ever entrust the children to her in such circumstances."[28]

St. John, too, was satisifed, for as he wrote to Elizabeth Riefenstahl at the Brooklyn Museum:

It was a very good thing that the whole of that Burgess Maclean affair was thrashed out in public at long last. Kim's trouble was that he was never allowed to defend himself owing to the secret nature of the matters under investigation. And I certainly think he acquitted himself with dignity and restraint as soon as it became possible for him to do so . . . It is obvious that Kim, then in Washington, could not possibly have got any message to B or M. Secondly, it might have been mentioned that, when he had to be sacrificed to McCarthyism, the FO treated him with all possible generosity in the matter of compensation (£5000) [sic]. It might also have been mentioned that although B had been living in his house for some months, Kim had asked him to leave owing to his stupid behaviour. However, the whole thing is over now, and even B's mother telephoned to tell him how sorry she was that he got involved in her son's trouble.[29]

But if St. John thought the matter closed, he was wrong. It continued to reverberate for thirty-three years. In Washington, there remained a serious rupture and loss of confidence in the Anglo-American intelligence relationship — some say the relationship was terminated, although a high CIA officer thought in retrospect that "it was not quite as grave as that, although I never understood how all the broken pieces were put together again, or if indeed they ever were. Philby had shattered British prestige." In the wider reaches of the Eisenhower administration, the relationship continued to be plagued by General MacArthur's assertions that Philby as well as Burgess and Maclean had betrayed the plans and the order of battle of the U.S. 8th Army in Korea to the communist intelligence services, and that thirty thousand men had been killed, wounded, or captured through that betrayal.

That aspect of the case remained, therefore, in suspension. But in December 1955 another element reappeared.

Otto John, Canaris's contact with Philby during the attempt on the life of Hitler, had vanished while visiting West Berlin in July 1954 to attend the annual commemoration service for the victims of Hitler's blood purge after the assassination attempt in July 1944. At the nomination of the British Secret Services, John had been made chief of the West German Security Service, the BFV, created to replace the Gestapo by the first postwar German chancellor, Konrad Adenauer. As head of R5, Philby had had much business with John, and his reports on John had played their part in Menzies's approval of him as a liberal German with no Nazi or communist affiliations.

When John reappeared in West Berlin, on December 12, 1955, seventeen months after he had vanished, he told his interrogators that he had been kidnapped by the KGB and taken to Russia solely to determine whether Philby was "a double agent betraying the Russians to the British." Here then was another powerful asseveration against Philby, one that might have reopened the Philby case; but the worth of John's statement was diluted when John was accused of having been a traitor and was sent to prison for seven years.

But, oddly, Philby seems not to have been questioned concerning John's statement, perhaps because in January 1956 he left his London haunts and went to Ireland. There he remained for the next six months, helping to write a history of a company that was owned by a friend. While there, on February 11, the KGB produced Burgess and Maclean as evidence that they were still alive. They declared that they had never been communist spies and that they had come to the Soviet Union not to escape retribution but to

> work for a better understanding between the Soviet Union and the West, having both of us become convinced from official knowledge in our possession that neither the British nor, still more, the American government was at that time seriously working for this aim. We had in the positions we occupied every reason to believe that such an understanding was essential if peace was to be safe. We had every reason to conclude that such an understanding was the aim of Soviet policy. We had had every opportunity and grounds for fearing the plans and outlook of the few but powerful people who opposed this understanding.[30]

Then they vanished again. Philby continued with his working holiday amidst the soft and gentle Irish hills, tuning himself for further arduous work in the Soviet or British interests. For, incredibly, it was intended that he should rejoin the British Secret Service almost from the moment Macmillan cleared him in the House.

A main reason for this decision was the situation in the Middle East. A severe local quarrel had broken out between the British administration, which in 1954 still ruled the region and the CIA. Lord Hankey, a creator of the modern empire in the Middle East, the modern British Establishment and now the British government's agent on the board of the Suez Canal Company, had presented to Churchill what he called "reliable but sinister evidence" concerning the U.S. government's real attitude toward British power in the Middle East. In Hankey's opinion, and that of the powerful group around him, the United States was an "unreliable ally, and always ready to attack European 'imperialism' whilst exhibiting sublime insouciance regarding the same phenomenon in her own case."[31]

As Hankey related, even as the British administration was seeking to make the monarchy of King Farouk work, a group of CIA officers under the leadership of Kermit Roosevelt, a grandson of President Theodore Roosevelt, was directing a cabal of Egyptian military officers to overthrow the Egyptian monarchy. Late in 1954 the revolution succeeded; King Farouk was forced into exile at Monaco. In due course, after a period under General Muhammad Naguib, the power of the Egyptian state was ceded to Gamal Abdul Nasser, who, as president of Egypt, began a major campaign to eject Franco-British power from the Middle East. It came as a severe shock to the British government to discover that the CIA was working against it. As John Ranelagh, a British historian of the CIA, noticed, the Burgess and Maclean affair had played a part. Allen Dulles, by now the director of the CIA,

> saw the traitors as symbolic of what was happening to Britain. They represented the moral and political decline of a country living beyond its means and cracking apart. They were left-wing, homosexual, alcoholic, and none of them could be dismissed as unrepresentative radicals embittered by struggle. They were people in conflict who could not resolve their relationship to authority and therefore undertook self-destructive antisocial activity. Men such as Dulles felt there was an inbred quality to British life and were not taken in by the charm of British clubland.[32]

Dulles believed the worm was in the British apple, but not in his. They regarded themselves, Ranelagh wrote, as "the storm troopers of the cold war." Unlike the British Intelligence and Security services, they were in no danger of cracking. They were well financed. They had the complete support of President Eisenhower; and when this, too, was discovered by the British leadership, it added to the sense of shock it had experienced over the CIA intrigues over Farouk. The British had made Eisenhower, a man who had never commanded even a battalion of troops in action, when in 1942 they agreed to put their armies under his command. They had given him their highest honors and at the end of the war a Scots castle so that he would always have a home in the United Kingdom and water of his own to fish.

The CIA's support for Nasser did not last long when it was discovered that he had begun to purchase Russian arms. But while it did, it caused great alarm in Whitehall. "If Nasser 'gets away with it,' we are done for," Harold Macmillan recorded in his private diary. "It may well be the end of British influence and strength for ever. So, in the last resort, we must use force and defy opinion, here and overseas." Anthony Eden demanded that Nasser "be destroyed, not removed, destroyed." With these declarations came Musketeer, a major military expedition that in the event, came to include the armies of France and Israel. Its purpose was to restore Franco-British authority in the region. As the crisis developed, the Eden government prepared and implemented a deception plan that, Macmillan's official biographer recorded, was intended to mislead the United States about Anglo-French-Israeli intentions toward Nasser "in much the same way as the Anglo-American intelligence had fooled Hitler with their deception schemes preceding D-Day" in Normandy in June 1944.[33]

Thus the Kim Philby case entered a fresh realm of complexity. And the reason for the decision to rehire Philby was his father, St. John. In April 1955 St John had been forced into exile after a series of episodes in which he offended the Saudi royal family, headed by King Saud since the death of Ibn Saud in November 1953, and that formidable instrument of American power in the Middle East, the Arabian American Oil Company. As the Nasser crisis blew up, St. John had gone to live in Lebanon, where he had written a number of important articles laying part of the responsibility for the corruption at the Saudi court, by implication, on the Americans. Something of the great affection between St. John and Kim Philby was known, as was St. John's reputation for being the greatest living British expert on Middle Eastern politics. Since Kim Philby had been cleared in Parliament of the charges against him, which were largely American in inspiration, and since St. John had fallen foul of the Americans in Saudi Arabia, could not Kim, sent out to Beirut as a spy, rely on his father as his most valuable informant?

As Seale and McConville recorded of the circumstances in which the decision was taken to reemploy Philby:

> Even before Kim left County Waterford plans had been made for his future. With different degrees of secrecy both the British and the Russians had already made contact with him again, both judging at much the same moment that their man was sufficiently recovered to go back to work. Like a recidivist returning to his old habits, Kim was sucked back into the intelligence world, the world he knew best. But however real his recovery, he entered the system at a more lowly, more hazardous level. Previously he had been a commander, an initiator of operations, an inside man, a senior SIS officer under KGB control, trusted by both sides. Now he was an outsider not fully in the confidence of either service, but useful to both inhabiting the shadowy frontier area between them. Previously he had run agents, now he was an agent being run, one of those lonely figures used by rival services to maintain hostile contact with each other. Such a position puts great pressure on a man because he provides the battlefield in this subtle war, never certain whether he is using others or being used. Kim's next six years were not tranquil.[34]

In July 1956, on his return from Ireland, Philby was approached by two senior SIS officers, neither of whom believed that he was a Russian spy, and offered the prospect of work as the correspondent of two leading London journals, *The Observer* and *The Economist*, in the Middle East. Did he wish for such a position? His emoluments would total some £3,000 a year plus traveling expenses — good pay at the time. He accepted, and arrangements were made.

15

Beirut

1956–1963

Kim philby arrived in Beirut by jet on September 6, 1956. St. John was there to meet him as he hobbled off the aircraft in bedroom slippers; he had stubbed an ingrown toenail in London and had required surgery. St. John invested the event with a touch of desert mysticism, noting in a letter to Dora that Kim's arrival had coincided with the approach of Mars toward Earth, in Islam a sign of approaching war. The symbolism was not misplaced. The armies of Britain, France, and Israel were assembling to overthrow the revolutionary government of President Nasser of Egypt, restore the Suez Canal to international ownership, reestablish European prestige in the Middle East, and install a government more congenial to Whitehall and the Quai d'Orsay. Even as he stepped off the aircraft, the great crisis had begun.

Kim was now forty-four. He had been a Soviet agent for twenty-two years and a British agent for fifteen; he had been a suspected traitor working in the Soviet interest in certain quarters of the secret circle for eleven years, ever since the Volkov and Gouzenko desertion cases of 1945. By now it was forty-one years since St. John had arrived in the region from India; he remained on good terms with all the leading figures except the most sturdy Anglophiles, who nowadays were few and far between. If St. John had been banished from Saudi Arabia, his influence in Lebanon had not diminished. He remained the English seer.

In reflecting on Kim's activities in Beirut during those tumultuous and explosive years between 1956 and 1963, a CIA analyst would conclude that Kim's success owed much to the "enviable entrée"[1] into the centers of policy and power that St. John began to display from the moment his son set foot on the tarmac of Beirut airport. Their first call was on the president of Lebanon, Camille Chamoun, even though the *Beirut Daily Star* announced that "the third man" was in the city. This made no difference. Very few people knew who the third man was, and fewer cared. Chamoun and the Philbys talked for an hour or more, arrangements were made for future meetings, and the Philbys went on to an important luncheon at the Hotel Bristol. There, Kim was introduced to the leading Arabist, Professor Phillip K. Hitti, the Syrian-born American who had retired recently from teaching Oriental languages and Semitic literature at Columbia and Princeton. What Hitti did not know about Syrian politics, and especially revolutionary anti-French, anti-Western politics, hardly mattered; and Syria was now becoming the crucible of Soviet and Arab socialist power in the Middle East, a group through which Philby, again in the view of the CIA, became "one of the guiding lights of KGB, if not Soviet, policy in the Middle East."[2] Kim and his father also spent an afternoon at the villa of Uweini, the richest man in Beirut; and as they said of him in Beirut, he who knew Uweini knew enough.

After three days in Beirut, the father and son drove to the mountains and St. John's villa at Ajaltun, a white-painted structure with a red tile roof, surrounded by apple and peach orchards. Kim's rooms opened out directly onto the orchards. This time of the year was the worst in Beirut — hot, humid, dusty — and the best for places like Ajaltun. There, the air was crisp and clear; there was a grand view of the narrow coastal strip and the sparkling blue sea far below. It seemed for a few days that Kim might have found a haven. But the Philby ménage was not quite paradise. The noise made by Kim's Saudi half-brothers, Khalid and Faris, irritated him, as did Rozy, St. John's wife, whom his father described only as "the mother of my children." St. John and Rozy shouted at each other a good deal, and the uproar preyed on Kim's nerves, which were in a bad way.

In the five years since 1951, he had never known when he might be forced to flee to Moscow, or whether he would be arrested for treason at dawn. Aileen, too, continued to worry him and, as he confessed to his father and as St. John reported to Dora, "he had been having a series of nightmares, all roughly the same: Aileen committing suicide and all the children in tears and shrieking the house down."[3] Aileen was in and out of the mental hospital, and she had been reduced to a tragic figure, incoherent most of the time. She now lived with their five children at a house in Sussex that her mother had leased for her, and her mother also made her an allowance, but it was not enough and Aileen worked as a cook in a great house in Eaton Square, London, to make ends meet. Kim claimed he was supporting her financially, but Aileen contradicted him in a letter to Dora. When Dora wrote to Kim at Ajaltun about this, he replied irately that Aileen's claim was "hooey" and "that I had made a clear arrangement with her (duplicate in my possession here) that she should pay the household bills and forward me the receipts, whereupon I would refund her." So far, Kim wrote, he had not had a single receipt. "So, no receipts, no money." If Aileen could afford "the luxuries of risking her neck at point-to-points, she can damn well send me the receipts." He was "fed up with her idleness."[4]

To make the situation in England still more unhappy, Dora too was deeply depressed. Seventy and arthritic, it was not until recently that she discovered that St. John had produced an Arab family. What was she to tell their daughters? Why had he not told her earlier? St. John pressed her to join "his contentment" at Ajaltun, or at least shuttle between Beirut and their daughters in London. "I think we might all put our heads together and plan a migration en masse to Lebanon," he wrote. Then "there would be about a dozen of us to lay the foundation of a Philby colony in one of the nicest countries in the world."[5] But Dora felt St. John was not serious and that, in any case, she could not share a house with her husband's Arab wife and children. And so she remained in London, a burly redhead brooding interminably in an armchair with a tumbler on one side and a bottle of Gordon's gin on the other.

For his part, St. John filled his days writing more memoirs. *Forty Years in the Wilderness,* his nineteenth book, was published in 1957. In it he ascribed to himself something of the grandeur of the ancients. "I have lived in a setting which until quite recently was the very stage on which the greats of the past, like Abraham and Moses, played their part, as I have played mine," he wrote with satisfaction. He had now openly come to Soviet communism. His lectures at the American University at Beirut were, his biographer recorded, a "hymn of praise to the Soviet Union" and "a lunge at imperialist interference."[6]

As to the city to which Kim Philby had been sent, Beirut was a Frenchified place set in a wide bay and closely ringed by mountains, some of them tipped with snow the year round. Its population of seven hundred thousand was teeming, noisy, feverish, insomniac, neurotic, erotic. Since April 1955, when he arrived from Riyadh, St. John had become one of its darlings, hailed as he strode about the seafront in his white linen suits and heavy black beard. Appearing at his father's side from time to time, Kim too became a celebrity. He had stuck it to those bandits, the Americans and the British, and they had not caught him.

Every power maintained a large embassy in the city; every tremor was felt there, and the great game of the times came to be known as "the Game of Nations." It was defined by the vice-president of Egypt, Zakaria Mohieddin, as one in which "every player wants not so much to win as to avoid loss," "where all players have no objective except to keep the game going," and in which "the alternative to the game is war."[7] Accordingly, the city quivered and shook as the Cold War and Arab nationalism drove its several races and religions — mainly those old foes, the Christians and the Moslems — toward the civil war that eventually destroyed it.

In October 1956, King Saud called St. John back to Riyadh and his place on the privy council. His Arab family went with him, so Kim found an apartment in the Moslem quarter of Beirut. This, the CIA claimed to have discovered, was owned by "a SMOTH asset,"[8] Smoth being the CIA's code name for the British Secret Service. He was in place therefore when the British, French, and Israeli armies invaded Egypt to overthrow Nasser and retrieve the Suez Canal — an operation that almost succeeded when the U.S. Sixth Fleet disrupted the landing and air operations in a demonstration of President Eisenhower's displeasure.

The Baghdad Pact to prevent the Russians from entering the Middle East collapsed; British and French influence in the Middle East "went down the drain"; Eisenhower announced that the United States must fill the "power vacuum"; the Eisenhower doctrine, conceived with an eye to Franco-British participation, was ruined when John Foster Dulles blurted out that he did not want to collaborate with either France or Britain because "if I were an American boy, I'd rather not have a French and British soldier beside me, one on my right and one on my left."[9]

The grand alliance was dead, and Philby could only have rejoiced. In the wake of Suez, Whitehall began what was called "the orderly management of decline," withdrawal from the empire. One by one the British clerks, consuls, political agents, withdrew from the courts of the sheikhs, sultans, and emirs to retire in places like Tunbridge Wells, there to reflect on their belief that the empire had been "the greatest example of organized freedom the world had ever seen."[10] Pax Britannica was replaced by Pax Americana and Pax Sovieticus, the SIS by the CIA and the KGB.

St. John rejoiced at the discomfiture of the "old gang," the old imperialists. He came in from Arabia in April 1957, the last of the Raj.[11] "I think I must be quite the only person who has ever left the country with no share of the spoil," he wrote to Dora. He had fallen foul of King Saud and the new American grand viziers yet again, and he recognized without regret that his political life was at an end. Unlike almost all of his generation of advisers and administrators, however, he had salvaged something of the past: as long as he kept silent on politics, he could keep his house in Riyadh and return when he wished. He lashed out once more about his old rival, Glubb Pasha, the founder and commanding officer of the Arab Legion, the best Arab army in the Middle East. When the boy-king, Hussein of Jordan, a product of Harrow and the Royal Military Academy at Sandhurst, sacked Glubb, St. John wrote to Glubb with satisfaction:

> The line that divides me from you and your ilk is your conviction that the best interests of these Arab countries can only be served in some form of subordination to British imperial policy sweetened by lavish British financial aid, whereas I am equally convinced that only in unity *inter se* can the Arabs ever realise their destiny. Perhaps you will agree with me that your cause is lost beyond recall.[12]

It was. The British had become unfashionable, the Americans fashionable. A *Time* man became Hussein's public affairs adviser, a CIA officer his adviser on foreign political affairs. So it was everywhere. The end of empire happened very rapidly.

St. John reached Damascus on June 27, 1957, and he sent Dora a telegram announcing that he was "well on my way home." He reached the Hotel Normandy in Beirut the next day to be met by Kim, who had sad news. Dora had died in her sleep two nights before. His reaction to the news is not recorded, except that he spent the rest of that day alone. Then, in the evening, he went up to Ajaltun with Kim for a reunion with Rozy and the boys.[13] There came a letter from Dora written in her last days. St. John had advised her that he intended again to take up residence in Riyadh. This irritated Dora, as "it always makes me feel mad when I've seen for years people picking your brains for nothing."[14] Dora's letters to St. John since 1910 did survive, and St. John took them when he flew to England to attend to Dora's estate. They vanished much later, along with Kim's correspondence with his father. Gillian Grant, an archivist at St. Antony's College, Oxford, who read Dora's letters, remembered "a sad account of neglect, illness, loneliness and despair over many years." Dora's last note to St.

John survived: "No mourning. No garden of remembrance, no in memoriams."[15]

In the world of the SIS secret brotherhood, there were many ties between Kim Philby and John Nicholas Rede Elliott. They were both in the same web of connections in English society that went back to that minute elite, the Raj, when it was at the height of its power between the middle and the end of the nineteenth century. Elliott's father, Claude, was a son of the lieutenant governor of Bengal, Kim Philby's maternal grandfather and the commanding general at Bombay. Nicholas was born at Simla, the summer capital of the Indian Empire, three years after Kim's birth at Ambala in the Punjab in 1912. Claude Elliott and St. John were at Trinity together; so, almost, were Nicholas and Kim. Claude Elliott became one of England's most illustrious schoolmasters, becoming first headmaster and then provost of Eton College; St. John became Ibn Saud's grand vizier. Both were therefore candidates for membership in the power elite from which the British recruited its leaders.

For Nicholas, that process commenced when he was sent to the British Embassy as The Hague as an honorary attaché, a post created by the Foreign Office to give the sons of illustrious fathers a sense of the world into which they had been born and to prepare them for government. In 1939, Elliott was recruited into the SIS, his first task to handle double agents. When Kim joined Section V, Elliott became one of his officers, and he was one of those, as Sir Robert Mackenzie observed, who worshiped Kim and admired the style of his reports and the skill he exhibited in his office. Nicholas went out first to Cairo and then to Istanbul, where he handled the Vermehren defections that so disrupted the Abwehr. When Philby became chief of R5, Elliott went to Berne as chief of station; and there in 1948 he arranged Aileen's hospitalization when she arrived from Istanbul with Kim after her latest episode of self-mutilation.

After Philby's near-exposure in 1951, Elliott became one of Philby's three main supporters in SIS, believing that Kim had been a victim of McCarthyism in the United States and of the unending vendetta between MI5 and the SIS. When MI5 began its campaign to prove that Philby was a traitor, Elliott encouraged him to fight back with the counsel: "If I was accused of spying, I would go to the Prime Minister and complain."[16] During Philby's years out in the cold, it was Elliott who, through his father, arranged for Philby's children to enter exclusive schools. It was Elliott who sought to arrange Philby's rehabilitation into the service on the grounds that the country could ill afford to be without Philby's abilities. And when Harold Macmillan publicly cleared Philby, it was Elliott who arranged his employment in Beirut with *The Observer* and *The Economist.*

Elliott was a Praetorian, a defender of the established order. He was a close friend of the old C, Stewart Menzies, and when C died he was the only SIS officer to be allowed to attend the funeral. Philby, like Elliott, had been one of C's golden lads. Their friendship and their personal abilities had been established through the severe tests of war. And Elliott was rising into the highest ranks of the service, the code of which might well have been: "In adversity, loyalty. In trial, truth. In triumph, modesty. In all things, discretion." His wartime service apart, Elliott had already been chief of station at Berne (1945–1953), Vienna (1953–1956), London (1956-1960), and, after Beirut, he would become chief of the SIS in Africa and, later still during the 1960s, chief of the European and Soviet Division. By 1969, at the age of fifty-two, he was third in command as director of requirements, in which post he was responsible for the quality and relevance of the intelligence produced for the benefit of other government departments. But for his preference for operations, not administration, he might well have been appointed C. Instead, at a crucial time, he went on to become Prime Minister Margaret Thatcher's personal intelligence adviser.

In his bearing, dress, and manner he was an undoubted member of the upper-class Establishment. Philby used his stutter when confronted with a difficult situation, so Elliott resorted to his enormous fund of risqué stories. Such tactics might endear him in Belgravia and with like-minded men such as C and Philby, but they were not always well received by Americans. Nonetheless, Elliott became accepted as a member of the CIA-SIS transatlantic Establishment brotherhood and remained one for life.

In 1956, Elliott was in charge of an operation by a frogman to survey the undersides of the modern Soviet cruiser *Ordzhonikidze,* which had brought the new Soviet leaders, Bulganin and Khrushchev, to England on a state visit at the invitation of Prime Minister Anthony Eden. It was the period of the post-Stalin thaw in political relations between the Soviet Union and the Western powers, and Eden had high hopes that through the visit he might further reduce East-West tensions, not least in the Middle East, where the Russians were taking an active interest in local politics. In order to ensure that nothing untoward occurred, Eden instructed the SIS not to undertake any operation that might embarrass his guests or the British government. The chief of the SIS, General Sinclair, gave his assurance that his service would leave the Russian warships alone, unaware apparently of Elliott's mission, being undertaken for the Admiralty, against the *Ordzhonikidze*. The mission went ahead on April 19, 1956, at the very time that Elliott was negotiating Philby's employment by *The Observer* and *The Economist*. The frogman was spotted from the cruiser, he vanished, and his headless corpse was not found for many weeks. On April 29, word of the misadventure reached the press, and a large scandal developed. Eden formally apologized to the Russian leaders, and there the matter might have rested, but the opposition initiated a debate in the House, which Eden survived by a comfortable majority, 87 votes. Nonetheless, he was profoundly embarrassed by the incident and acted accordingly.

Sinclair was obliged to retire and (to the intense chagrin of the old guard at the SIS, which had fought any encroachment by MI5 into the SIS for decades) Dick Goldsmith White, now chief of MI5, succeeded him. Only then did White discover the SIS's secret, that Philby had been brought back into the service, largely through Macmillan's clearance of him in the House and Elliott's efforts to obtain his reemployment. This did not bode well for Elliott, who had not only engineered Philby's appointment but was also responsible for the operation against the *Ordzhonikidze*. It is said that White had remembered Philby's last statement to him: "You have won the first round; I shall win the last." Men with his power — White was the first and only man to be appointed both director-general of the Security Service and, after it, of the Secret Service — do not forget or forgive such menaces. Nor did he.

A mild-mannered man, a bureaucrat rather than a spy, a former schoolmaster turned spycatcher in the 1930s — he had something to do with Arnold Deutsch's rapid departure from London in 1937 — White elected not to order that the SIS cease contact with Philby. The connection was to proceed normally without, of course, endangering Britain's system of secret agents in the Middle East. But according to Phillip Knightley, a student of the Philby case, White did have a plan "to bring the case to a conclusion."[17] As Knightley related:

> The idea was to force Philby out into the field, to give him the profile of an active and industrious intelligence officer and thus force the Russians to use him again. Philby would be taken into Elliott's confidence; he would be made a part of SIS operations; he would learn information so important that he would have to pass it to his Soviet control. But although some of that information would be genuine, some of it would be a plant and Western counter-intelligence would be waiting to see where it surfaced. If it could be traced back to Philby,

and only to Philby, then the British authorities would at last have proof of his treachery.

It was a tricky game with many imponderables. Philby might suspect what was happening, but he could not refuse to play because that could be seen as a tacit confession. He could not go only part of the way — agree to his more active role for SIS but not pass anything to the Russians — because that would make his Soviet control begin to doubt Philby's loyalty.[18]

He would have to play the game "because it was Nicholas Elliott, his old friend, his most ardent defender in SIS, who was giving him this chance to work his way back into the club." There is no reason to doubt Knightley's version of the stratagem that White prepared to catch Philby. Nor is there any reason to doubt that Philby became aware of White's game. As Knightley wrote: "He must have known that sooner or later something like this would happen because he tried to take as many precautions as he could. He told me in Moscow: 'From 1951 on I began to prepare for the ultimate crisis, knowing it could come at any moment.'"

In Beirut, therefore, his connection with the Secret Service evolved quite naturally. The station commander, Godfrey M. H. Paulson, met regularly with Philby at the Normandy Hotel, a Third World place with beaded curtains known also as "the Sweet Home," where St. John had been a regular for many years. Paulson's officers doubtless played the game as the requirement arose. They were an agreeable quartet. Donald Prater was a scholar who spent his leisure hours translating A. A. Milne's *Winnie the Pooh* into Latin and writing a biography of Émile Zola. Michael Whittalls had been on Philby's staff at Istanbul in 1947–1949 and was writing some family reminiscences for private publication, "The Whittalls of Turkey." Merrick Beebee was a Beethoven man and *bon vivant;* and John H. Farmer had had an important career as a guerrilla leader against the Germans during the war in the Auvergne region of France and was now with C's Special Political Action Group. It was with Farmer, it seems, that the game began.

In 1956, at the personal instruction of Prime Minister Anthony Eden, the SIS undertook an operation not just to neutralize Nasser politically but to kill him.[19] This operation was afoot when Philby arrived in the city. It was being conducted not by Paulson but by a group of officers acting independently of the station. Farmer was one of these officers. And it is noteworthy that Farmer had had some previous connection of a private nature with Philby. Not only had Farmer been a member of his staff when Philby was chief of R5, but Farmer's wife was the daughter of Major Remy Fisher, St. John's backer in the Red

Sea trading post, Sharquieh, between the wars. "Francee" Farmer had grown up with Kim when she went to live at the Philby family home at Acol Road in the 1920s.[20] Her marriage to a certain Ducat, a peacetime Left Bank artist who had been on General de Gaulle's staff in London as an intelligence officer, had ended; she and Farmer had met when he was in St. Jean de Luz, on the Franco-Spanish border, "hunting Martin Bormann or something," and they decided to marry. But the Secret Service regulations provided that officers could marry only women whose parents were British on both sides; Francee's origins were far too exotic for the old C, Menzies. Major Fisher was of Hungarian-Jewish origins long resident in Egypt but naturalized English; his wife was of French Catholic stock long resident on the Nile and a devotee of the Third Order of Benedictines. Francee had been married to a Frenchman in the intelligence service of a French general who was regarded as no ally of England. There was accordingly only silence from C when he received their application for his permission to marry. Farmer and Francee bumped into Philby in the street near headquarters and explained their predicament to him; he intervened, successfully, with C. The Farmers had then married with Philby as a witness.

John Farmer was born in 1917 and educated at Beaumont, the English Catholic public school. He now became involved in an assassination conspiracy. In 1991, Farmer related how, at Rome in 1954, just after the Naguib-Nasser group had seized power in Cairo, he met with a Yugoslav secret agent from Egypt. The agent was associated with two powerful Egyptians. One was Prince Abdul Monheim, a son of the Khedive of Egypt, a former rector of the al-Azhar University; the other was Ahmed Mortada al-Maraghi, a leading Egyptian theologian and former interior minister, the official responsible for law and order in Egypt.[21] Behind these two lay a group of anti-Nasser army Establishment figures who intended that al-Maraghi should become prime minister in a post-Nasserite government. As the matter developed, Farmer took al-Maraghi to the British foreign secretary, Selwyn Lloyd, who assured him that Farmer had full powers to act on behalf of the British government and that that government would give the al-Maraghi group its full political and financial support. From this connection there developed Unfasten, an SIS operation to kill Nasser and thereby rid Eden of his gadfly.

Farmer's role in the plot was to keep contact with the conspirators' secret agent, Squadron Leader Isameddine Mahmoud Khalil, whose position in the Nasser administration as the deputy chief of the Egyptian air force's intelligence service required him to visit Beirut. And it was from Khalil that Farmer established the means by which Nasser was to be killed. The Egyptian leader had a very heavy beard, which, for appearance's sake, he shaved frequently. He kept an electric razor in his office for that purpose, but it was old. Farmer's plan was therefore to buy a new Remington Rand, have its empty internal spaces filled with the violent and malleable *plastique* explosive, and give it to Khalil to take to Nasser; when Nasser switched on the razor, the electricity would detonate the explosive and thereby, it was hoped fervently, kill him. The al-Maraghi group would then seize the power of the state and establish a new government. The razor was in fact given by Farmer to Khalil for delivery to Nasser, along with tranches of Egyptian money to the value of £166,000, in the region of half a million dollars; and a major radio propaganda campaign was launched from a British station on the island of Cyprus to prepare Egypt for political murder and a sudden change of power. The CIA, too, was made privy to the operation when, on instructions from his headquarters, Farmer briefed Kermit Roosevelt, the chief of the Near Eastern Division, who was visiting London.

Roosevelt appears to have thought little of the plan. Farmer was not keen on it, either. While the operation proceeded purposefully enough, he began to feel that there was an illusory element in Unfasten. It did not seem to him that it was as determined an operation as he had thought. The full power of the service was not engaged in it. He had received no directive concerning what he should do if Nasser were killed, especially in regard to the formation of the al-Maraghi government. Farmer's reserve about Unfasten proved to be well grounded. As the British historian Anthony Verrier would record, the "elaborate assassination plot" was "carefully arranged to fail."[22] Although Farmer was never advised at any stage that Unfasten had been terminated, his suspicions about its real purpose increased when an incident occurred that involved Philby. Until now the Farmers and Philby had had no contact in Beirut, although Farmer was one of those officers, like Elliott, who thought it inconceivable that an officer as important and as admired as Philby could possibly be a traitor. But at some stage early in 1957 Farmer left Beirut for Athens, he believed to attend a planning meeting concerning Nasser's murder. While in Athens (where he met with two other SIS officers from the Special Political Action Group), something strange occurred in Beirut. Francee Farmer ran into Merrick Beebee, one of Paulson's officers, and he invited her to come to dinner at his apartment, where, he told her, "she would meet an old friend." She accepted and, to her great surprise, she found "the old friend" to be Philby. As she related:

We spent a very enjoyable evening at Beebee's and during it Philby asked me why Johnny had not come. It was worth more than my life to tell him that he was in Athens planning the murder of President Nasser, and I told him that he was at the embassy attending to some administrative matters. Whether he believed me I shall not know. Nor did Merrick Beebee say very much to deflect him from Johnny. It was all very agreeable and civilised and we spent the evening playing Merrick's Beethoven sonatas, which Kim said he thought was the only worthwhile music.

Prime Minister Eden's order to proceed with the assassination was given on or about November 23, 1956, the day on which the Anglo-French-Israeli invasion of Egypt failed through Russo-American intervention. It was Eden's last act before he flew to Jamaica to recuperate from an illness at the home of Ian Fleming, the creator of James Bond. And as Verrier records, "The Prime Minister's order was disobeyed. SIS was not living in a James Bond world."[23] Four months later Nasser himself exploded Unfasten in a statement to the world in which he declared that the British Secret Service had plotted his assassination, that it had financed the undertaking to the tune of £166,000, that the money had been paid to Squadron Leader Isameddine Mahmoud Khalil, of the Egyptian Air Force, who had been loyal to Nasser all along, and that the money had been handed over to the mayor of Port Said to help in the relief of those Egyptians whose property had been damaged by the British naval bombardment of the city during the invasion.

Immediately after the announcement, Farmer, Francee, and their daughter, Denise, returned to England. It appears that the razor bomb was never delivered to its intended victim, and as Verrier noted, White, in working against his own operation, "could well have echoed the remarked of one embittered member of Eden's Cabinet: 'Even if Nasser goes, whom could we put in his place? We have run out of stooges.'" Whether White did indeed recycle Unfasten as a ruse to trap Philby we cannot know. It is possible, for he was a thrifty man with public money. But it seems more likely that the operation was betrayed not only by Philby but also by Squadron Leader Khalil. But the attempt to entrap Kim continued.

In September 1956, a gold DeSoto convertible with white upholstery drew up at the St. George Hotel in Beirut, an early sign of the new order in the Middle East, which was to become known as the Eisenhower doctrine — a joint resolution authorizing the president to spend up to $200 million in military and economic assistance in the Middle

East and to send U.S. troops to any nation requesting American assistance
to repel "armed aggression" from "any country controlled by international communism." From the convertible emerged Wilbur Crane Eveland, an agent who reported to Allen Dulles, now director of the CIA.
Life in Beirut was crowded with improbable men and lurid events, and
Eveland was one of them — a new carpetbagger. James R. Critchfield
would describe him as "a wheeler-dealer who took the grandest suites
at the grandest hotels, ran up huge bills, and got himself into a good
deal of trouble through his overly close association with Philby."[24]

Born in 1918 in Spokane, Washington, the son of humble parents
and a grandson of the local sheriff, Eveland was a brilliant autodidact
who had come up through the U.S. counterespionage ranks in World
War II. His record suggests that he was a member of "the Pond," a
strange service established by General George C. Marshall, the chief
of staff of the U.S. Army during World War II, with State Department
collaboration, largely to keep an eye on the OSS. He became a familiar
in the inner circle of the intelligence and defense communities in
Washington and claimed that he had the status if not the rank of
lieutenant general. Plainly he was highly placed in the Eisenhower
administration and held high security clearances. These he retained,
although it was found that his claim to a Harvard degree proved to
be false, based only on his having attended summer school there. He
claimed, too, to be a member of the family of Charles R. Crane, the
U.S. philanthropist with whom St. John had had connections in 1934.
But this, too, proved to be false.[25]

Eveland became an important CIA player in Beirut and the Middle
East between 1957 and 1960. He played some part in the CIA's operations to promote Nasser. On missions abroad, he frequently wore
the formal attire of a European diplomat, morning dress; and when
he arrived in Beirut, he did so as the particular agent of Allen Dulles.
He had, too, some relationship with the National Security Council,
the State Department, and the Pentagon. His calling cards showed
him to be a "special assistant" to the NSC chairman. He intimated that
he had a similar personal connection with Secretary of State John
Foster Dulles.

Throughout his tenure as Allen Dulles's personal agent in Lebanon,
which lasted from 1956 to 1960, Eveland worked independently of
the CIA station chief, although his main task in 1956 was to act as
paymaster for CIA operations to overthrow the Soviet-sponsored government in Syria. His other important task in Beirut was to establish
relations with the president, Camille Chamoun, and maintain the status
quo in that lovely but benighted country. When Eveland was in Beirut,

he used the apartment of the *New York Times*'s correspondent, Sam Pope Brewer, as his "second home," a place where "I was always welcome for a drink, a meal, or just chat to let off steam."[26]

It was the Brewer connection that facilitated Philby's entry into the special world of Pax Americana. Philby had had no more entry into the inner keep of the small but swelling U.S. community in Beirut than any other Briton, except that he was St. John's son, and it was St. John who had arranged matters at court so that the Americans obtained and kept their oil concessions in Saudi Arabia. As Eveland related in his memoirs, on September 12, 1956, Brewer was due to lunch with St. John and Kim at the St. George Hotel, to introduce them to his wife, Eleanor, who had recently arrived. She was a tall, slender, loose-limbed, attractive, and artistically inclined woman who was by all accounts apolitical and also out of love with Brewer. She too was born in Washington State, and this made for a friendship with Eveland.

But at the last moment Brewer was called away on assignment, and Kim asked Eveland to go to lunch instead. Eveland recalled Kim at their meeting as "quiet, polite, and physically unprepossessing." From then on, according to Eveland, Philby "took to frequenting the Brewers' home, where I saw him often. A heavy drinker, he spoke with a stammer, which seemed to abate as liquor relaxed him. By then I'd read some of Kim's articles and found him to be a talented writer." Brewer "told me that he suspected Philby was still with British intelligence. This, I assumed, might have accounted for Kim's frequent travels to Egypt and Syria." In Washington on business, he told Allen Dulles "what I knew about Philby and then explained that Kim had once, figuratively speaking, had the keys to the CIA's safes. The question was whether he'd ever used them and, if so, who'd received the information."[27]

Between September 1956 and May 1960 Eveland developed a close connection with Philby. Philby encouraged the relationship, for this was the "Eveland era in Middle East politics," according to Miles Copeland, a former CIA officer who represented James Angleton's interests in Beirut.[28] Nor was Eveland's secret business confined to Lebanon and Syria. He was present at various conferences whose purpose was to maintain the Saud dynasty at Riyadh; he was familiar with the CIA's policy and operations and with the principal personalities of the CIA and the State Department in Washington. He also had access to the CIA station in Beirut, which he visited, sometimes daily, to read the incoming intelligence. He came to admire Philby while regarding him as a dissident SIS man, one whose brain was there to be picked.

Eveland attempted to use Philby as an informant; and in that respect

Eveland had a great deal to offer. He spent an enormous amount of time during those years flying all over the region as well as to Washington and London. He had an excellent mind. But he found himself the odd man out in the WASP world of the CIA management. To Philby, therefore, he represented a first-class source. No CIA operation of any consequence succeeded during this period; and as Eleanor Brewer is said to have told the CIA of the association between Philby and Eveland, Philby had remarked to her "that all he had to do was to have one evening with Bill Eveland in Beirut and before it was over he would know of all his operations."[29] Certainly Eveland's masters at the CIA, the men in charge of the clandestine aspects of his operations to further the Eisenhower doctrine in the Middle East, came to believe that Eveland was Philby's most important source as a British and as a Soviet spy. Eveland was to pay dearly for this imprudence, for no institution was as savage as the CIA when it found that one of its key men had been bested by Philby.

In these circumstances of intimacy, there occurred that disastrous event of 1958, American military intervention in Lebanon, an event that, at the time, appeared to be the opening stages of a regional war and perhaps even World War III. One of the contributing factors to this calamity was the fragility of Lebanese politics. Lebanon was an Arab state, but a small majority of the population were Christians — they were Maronites. Under the Lebanese constitution, the president, the foreign minister, and the army commander were all Maronites; the prime minister and the speaker of the legislature were Moslem. This relationship had been effective for a generation or more, but it was known that any adjustment was likely to produce an explosion. In 1958 it did.

The balance between the Christians and the Moslems in Lebanon had already been affected by the arrival of Arab refugees from Palestine in 1956. President Eisenhower, concerned about the foothold Russia had gained in the Middle East, wished to preserve Lebanon as a base of Western influence should regional or world war break out and threaten the American oil interests in the region. Because Chamoun alone among the Middle Eastern leaders accepted the Eisenhower doctrine, Eisenhower was inclined to support Chamoun in his ambitions for a second term of office, though that would have entailed amending the constitution. But few other politicians supported his candidacy, and violence broke out between the Maronites and the Druze, an ancient hill people who appeared to lean toward Islam.

Dangerous complexities such as these were the stuff of life to Kim Philby, who was by nature and training a clandestine politician of considerable stature. By 1958 he had become one of the best informed of all Occidentals in Beirut in the theological and political complexities of the region; this probably accounted for the eagerness with which he was sought out. St. John was even better informed, for he was accepted and trusted by the Arab secret societies, whose members he had known and worked with since his days with Lawrence. If there was some fine point, there was always St. John to advise Kim, to introduce him to a mullah or a sheikh for talk in some far corner of the hill country. In 1958, these connections became of inestimable value in strengthening Kim's hand with the SIS and the CIA — and the KGB.

There was a local conflict raging when Armageddon began, or so it seemed, for all politics in the Middle East at that time had about them the quality of a desert mirage. And it began at Riyadh. In March 1958, King Saud of Saudi Arabia, Eisenhower's candidate to replace Nasser as leader of the Arab world, was swept off his throne by his brother, Crown Prince Feisal — the prince whom Kim received in 1920 at St. Aldro and who gave Kim a diamond as a keepsake of their meeting. The two Philbys were in Riyadh when Saud was deposed, and St. John left it to Kim to report the events that led to Feisal's assumption of his brother's powers. "King Saud hands over,"[30] the younger Philby reported to *The Economist.*

Both Philbys were back in Beirut when, early on the morning of July 14, 1958, the British lost Iraq to revolutionary army officers who murdered the twenty-three-year-old king, Feisal, the regent, Prince Abdullilah, and the prime minister, Nuri-es-Said. The British Embassy was torched. One arm of the Hashemites was at last swept away, after nearly forty years of, at least, order. That other arm of the Hashemites, King Hussein of Jordan, Feisal's cousin and schoolmate at Harrow, was also endangered. A civil war sputtered in Beirut between the Moslems and Christians. President Chamoun, still intriguing with Eveland to get the second term he desired so ardently, invoked the Eisenhower doctrine, and Eisenhower, believing that Lebanon was menaced by Russian and Nasserite intrigues, ordered his armed forces into the Mediterranean. He was probably correct to have done so, for the West was losing control of events throughout the region.

The Strategic Air Command and the U.S. Sixth Fleet stood to arms, and powerful forces of American marines landed across the beaches of Beirut to maintain the Chamoun regime while a light brigade of British paratroopers landed in Amman to maintain the throne of King Hussein. The Macmillan government recommended joint large-scale military operations — an Anglo-American crusade — to restore the West's position throughout the Middle East. The British would launch a counterrevolution in Iraq, the Turks in Syria; the Americans would intervene should the Iraqi army of the new regime march on Kuwait; Israel was to be unleashed against Nasserite Egypt. Atomic cannon were landed with the marines at Beirut, and General Nathan Twining, the chairman of the Joint Chiefs, was instructed by Eisenhower to "be prepared to employ, subject to [Eisenhower's] approval, *whatever* means might be necessary to prevent any unfriendly forces from moving into Kuwait"[31] — the emphasis on *whatever* being Eisenhower's. Khrushchev maneuvered twenty-four Red Army divisions on the Turkish frontier, and in all the region resembled the powder keg of the Balkans before 1914 and the outbreak of World War I.

But the crisis proved to be no more than yet another mirage. When the marines stormed ashore on the beach under the terrace of the St. George Hotel, they encountered only vendors selling 7-Up and eggs and bread. The correspondents who went ashore with the marines walked around to the St. George to find Philby, his eyes hidden by shades, drinking his usual noontime vodka and V-8. Eveland was in Istanbul, on his way back to Beirut after meeting with Allen and John Foster Dulles in Washington, and by nightfall he was back on the terrace of the St. George with his friends Philby and Eleanor Brewer.

Yet for all the Western alarm, the comings and goings of fleets, armies, special envoys, Philby's position as the leading correspondent in Beirut remained as it had been — love, laughter, and politics in the sun. The British appeared to be well satisfied with his work for them, and so, it seems, were the Russians. Yuri Modin, who was still involved with the Philby case in 1958, agreed with the CIA's estimate of Philby — that he was the "guiding light" of KGB policy in the Middle East — but with qualifications.

[He] was by no means our only asset in the Middle East, and the KGB had its own experts here in Moscow and in the capitals, highly trained Arabists all. But I can say that Philby sent us excellent reports that attracted much attention at the top, although occasionally there was criticism of him concerning his tendency to send us hard news wrapped up in beautifully-written political evaluations. We did not need this because we had our own people to make evaluations. What we needed from Philby was not his views but his news. But in all he served us well.[32]

As to Eleanor Brewer, she recorded of her interest in Kim,

What touched me first about Kim was his loneliness. A certain old-fashioned reserve set him apart from the easy familiarity of the other journalists. He was then forty-four, of medium height, very lean, with a handsome heavily-lined face. His eyes were an intense blue . . . He had a gift for creating an atmosphere of such intimacy that I found myself talking freely to him. I was very impressed by his beautiful manners. We took him under our wing. [Kim] soon became one of our closest friends.

Within perhaps only two weeks they became lovers, meeting secretly at little cafés, in the mountains, at the beaches, anywhere they would not be seen by other Occidentals. He showered her with little love notes written on paper from cigarette packages. In cold print they are embarrassing: "Deeper in love than ever, my darling, xxx from your Kim," and later the same day, "Deeper and deeper, my darling xxx from your Kim."[33] There is, however, good reason to believe that Eleanor had been asked by Brewer or Eveland or both to report on Philby's statements and attitudes — Brewer had long since ceased to concern himself with his wife's fidelity and kept the marriage in place only for the sake of their daughter, Annie. At first, Eleanor agreed. In Istanbul she had had her share of intrigue, and, as did so many OSS women after the war, she wanted more. Certain letters show Eveland advising a CIA officer about the relationship, suggesting that she was his controlled informant in the Philby case. But politically she was neither very bright nor very subtle.

Certainly she was no match for Philby, who was aware from the first that she might be in contact with the CIA. A strange situation arose, consequently, in which Philby and Eleanor sought to use each other but ended up in love with each other. Otherwise, of course, Eleanor suited his purpose, as had all his women. This time she was American, and as such she provided Philby with an entry into the American world in Beirut, which could be as exclusive as that of the British. Through their love talk he could establish what the CIA thought of him and also pass tidbits to Eveland knowing that it would not be long before they reached the CIA station chief. Also, through her, Brewer, and Eveland, Philby became accepted in the U.S. community in Beirut — the official, newspaper, and big oil professionals. He became what James Critchfield, a chief of the Near East division at the CIA, called "the darling of a certain type of American in the Near East."[34]

As Eleanor explained further in a book, "Like his beautiful manners, Kim's skill in writing letters was a reminder of a civilized way of living, particularly appealing to an American." These "drew me into his daily life by the little incidents he described so wittily and gracefully." In his notes to her Philby was at his worst. "You are one of the easiest, soothing presences I have ever met," he wrote to her early in their association when she had complained of his drinking. "If circumstances had made it impossible for me to become your lover, I would still have wished to be a very close friend. For a week or two, in fact, I thought I was just that."[35]

Rather quickly, Eleanor and Kim decided they wished to marry and made it known to Sam Pope Brewer on the terrace of the St. George. Sayed Abu Ris, a Palestinian stringer for Western newspapers, claimed to have witnessed the scene:

> Brewer was standing at the bar by himself when, much to his surprise, Eleanor and Kim entered together and occupied a table on the terrace, just outside. Brewer reluctantly consented to join them only after Eleanor's fourth or fifth invitation. Eleanor then turned to Kim and said, "Darling, tell him." This, too, she repeated several times and then, despairing, she said, "Kim and I . . ." She was interrupted by Kim, who stuttered, "We, we, we would like to get married." Sam hesitated before responding, "I hope I am not in the way." He returned to the bar and bought everybody a drink, but days later he went into a deep funk; friends said he realized that his only daughter Anne would have to live with the Philbys, and his CIA friends told him that Kim was still suspected of being a Russian agent.[36]

Otherwise Brewer placed no obstacle in the way. During their courtship, a further obstacle was cleared away. Aileen died.

With the children at school, the house at Crowborough was frequently empty, and when winter began to close in, a deep depression again seized her. This time it killed her. On December 15, 1957, Aileen was found dead in bed by her eldest daughter. The police were called, and a suspicion that Aileen had committed suicide through an overdose of some drug was investigated but dismissed; the coroner found that the cause of death was "congestive heart failure, myocardial degeneration, respiratory infection, and pulmonary tuberculosis." She was forty-seven. When he heard she was dead, Philby complained to a friend, "She can't even die in an uncomplicated way, it has to be all crumbed up with problems."

Eleanor left Beirut to seek a Mexican divorce, but it took a year, much longer than either had expected, and most of that period they spent apart. Then Kim and Eleanor were reunited at Beirut and set up home together, and the union was made legal on January 24, 1959, when they were married in London at Holborn Register Office. Philby was forty-seven; Eleanor, forty-five. "This is love with a capital L," he wrote to a colleague. "We shall take a house in the mountains: she will paint; I will write; peace and stability at last." After the marriage, according to Eveland, Eleanor asked if she and Kim might use Eveland's home in Rome. Eveland agreed, and as he acknowledged later: "The man who later surfaced as one of Russia's most damaging spies and his wife took their belated honeymoon in a CIA-subsidized apartment."[37]

Late in 1958, as part of the hundredfold reinforcement of the CIA that followed the near-destruction of the entire Western position in the Middle East, a new station chief arrived in Beirut in the spirit of Christ come to cleanse the temple. Edgar J. Applewhite was a WASP with a sting. Born in 1919 at Newport News, a major in the history of arts and letters at Yale, he had volunteered as an ordinary seaman in the U.S. Navy during World War II; he became a lieutenant commander, and he was in the aircraft carrier *Belleau Wood* when it was struck by two Japanese kamikazes, an incident in which the ship was awarded a presidential citation for the Navy Cross. After Beirut he became the CIA's deputy inspector-general, a man responsible for good order and discipline in the service. He was also a man with an interesting turn of mind. After his CIA service, he wrote books with R. Buckminster Fuller, the American architect and engineer who invented the "4-D house" and the Dymaxion auto. Applewhite wrote the best guidebook to the capital in modern times, *Washington Itself.*

He was something, therefore, of an intellectual whiz kid, bright, slight, and sharp in summer suits by, so it seemed, Louis and Thomas Saltz, the Establishment tailor of Washington, D.C. His black eyes glittered when visitors made a statement that Applewhite believed offensive to the safety and dignity of the United States, giving the impression that he might be dangerous. He might be indeed: he once declared that he was interested absolutely in the world primacy of the CIA and the United States. He was inclined to be an Anglophile, and later in life he accepted, when it suited him, the usual invitation by which the British Secret Service maintained its contact with "reliable" and influential CIA men even when they had retired — a week or more in England seeing old friends and familiar places, staying as the guest of the Secretary of the Royal Commonwealth Club in London.

Applewhite claimed to be concerned only with the strategic implementation of CIA policy in the Middle East, not the tactics of it. He lived in great style overlooking the Bay of Beirut in a large penthouse, the wide windows of which he had modified to keep out the gray brassy glare of the ocean. The embassy in which he was a senior official was a huge establishment of seven hundred persons, including sixty officials of the Federal Aviation Administration. The latter kept an eye on the utility of airfields throughout the Arab lands, should their use become necessary to defend the countries in which they were located against creeping Sovietization. And when the ambassador and his deputy were absent, Applewhite became, through his rank, what he called "de facto chargé." By now the institutional position between the American and British secret services had become, after the Philby disasters of 1951 and 1956, one of friendly but separate sovereign institutions in which the CIA was the dominant partner. Applewhite represented the U.S. national interest, Godfrey Paulson, the British national interest: "What we have left we hold."

Applewhite knew what the CIA knew about Philby, which was that there was no evidence that Philby was a Soviet agent, only suspicion — and suspicion, too, that he was now acting as a British secret agent in the Middle East. Accordingly, Applewhite took a personal interest in Philby, for he had once squired a sister of Melinda Maclean, Donald Maclean's wife. She was a WAVE and had what Applewhite described as "the best legs on Fifth Avenue."[38] But Philby was a question to which he did not receive an answer. Whenever the opportunity required, Applewhite requested information from Paulson about Philby's "unresolved status." Paulson declined to discuss Philby officially or unofficially, indicating that the matter was none of the CIA's business. Applewhite therefore decided that his interests would best be served if he cultivated Philby rather than hunt him; apart from all else, Philby represented to Applewhite the way to quiet chats with St. John.

In due course, Applewhite and Philby met and became friends. Their wives met socially and their sons went to school and played together; Applewhite noted the poor condition of Harry George's teeth and deduced that, with an eye on Philby's cover — that of the correspondent of modest means — the Soviets were keeping Philby on a tight financial leash. This observation caused Applewhite to admire the Soviet attention to detail and to wonder about who his Soviet case officer might be. Much later, when it was too late to matter, Applewhite discovered that the case officer's safe house, the place where he met with Philby, was just down the street from his own residence. Applewhite and Philby visited each other's apartments, stopped for conversation when they met in the street, greeted each other at parties. Applewhite cast flies over Philby when they were alone. Was he a right social democrat? A left social democrat? A Bolshevik? A nihilist? An anarchist? A syndicalist? A state socialist? A social aberrant? A *Narodnik* — a secret revolutionary — perhaps? Or nothing at all. All these possibilities were mentioned in the CIA files. Applewhite never lost sight of the fact that Philby might be a KGB agent. But he never found out what Philby was. He encountered only that "amiable, disengaged worldliness" of Trevor-Roper's recollection. Applewhite was "in touch with" Eveland and Copeland in the Philby case. Both had security clearances that entitled them to visit Applewhite's station and read his intelligence file. He consulted also with men whose judgment he trusted in the area and who, too, knew Philby: Justin O'Donnell, the CIA chief in Turkey; Larry Collins, the *Newsweek* man in Beirut; Robert R. Temple, the deputy chief of the British station; Rawle Knox, *The Observer*'s correspondent in New Delhi who, in times of crisis, came to Beirut to help Philby; Frank Stokes, "a suspected Smoth collaborator" known as such at the CIA; John M. Snodgrass, a press officer at the British Embassy in Beirut; John Brinton, an American living in Beirut and the son of a judge at the French courts in Egypt; and Michael Adams, the Middle East correspondent of the *Guardian* and a leading expert on the Palestinians.

What was expected of Applewhite in his association with Philby was that he should not be taken by surprise by any move that Kim made. After each session with him, Applewhite made a memo for the record, and this went to the Philby file in Washington. And in the end he concluded, wrongly, that Philby had "no flair for an absolute political philosophy" and seemed to be "much too sophisticated to give his allegiance to such a doctrinaire business as Marxism." And with the passage of time Applewhite formed the impression that both Eveland and Copeland were "scoundrels" and forbade them to enter his station. Situations such as these in hot climates and troubled times did not make for the best in the CIA's coverage of Philby, for both Eveland and Copeland used the hunted Philby to make brownie points in Washington, the former with Dulles, the latter with Angleton. Thus Philby continued to give everyone the slip. At no time, it seems, did Applewhite seek to recruit Philby as a CIA agent or otherwise to corrupt or entrap him, as Applewhite felt that Philby would "make mincemeat of me."[39]

Applewhite was not a trained counterespionage man but a bureaucrat in charge of a very large mission with many responsibilities. He tended, therefore, to leave "the tactics" of the Philby case to one of Angleton's men in Beirut, Miles Copeland. In a game where intellectual abilities counted for much, his were of interest. Born in Alabama, he was another whiz kid whose school was Erskine Ramsay Technical High in Birmingham, where he distinguished himself as a trumpet

player with an all-black radio band, J. Heathcliffe Jones and His Society
Orchestra, which broadcast "courtesy of the Violet Dream Perfume
and Toilet Water Company." His trumpet won him a place at the
University of Alabama, where he studied advanced mathematics. But
he did not, it appears, graduate. Instead he joined Benny Goodman's
band in 1940 and Glenn Miller's later that year.

At Pearl Harbor, Copeland enlisted in the National Guard's Rain-
bow Cavalry, and at the formation of the OSS he began a career with
U.S. intelligence and counterespionage which lasted from 1941 until
1952. He played his trumpet to the top and claimed to have been one
of the two hundred founders of the CIA. But he had not fit into the
Ivy League world of the CIA management, which considered him "the
Manhattan advertising type." In 1952 he became one of Allen Dulles's
bright young autodidacts, men who could be repudiated if they got
themselves or the Company into trouble. He arrived in Beirut in July
1957 as a partner in an industrial consultancy and public relations
firm, Copeland and Eichleberger, his partner being a former State
Department officer who had been involved with him in CIA operations
for — and against — Nasser. They opened flashy offices next to those
of the Trans-Arabian Pipeline Company, which ran the oil pipeline
between Dhahran in Saudi Arabia and Sidon in Lebanon. Copeland
began to entertain on a grand scale, and it was assumed that he was able
to do so through his connection with the Gulf Oil Corporation of
Pittsburgh, which owned a half-share in the Kuwait Oil Company. Gulf
Oil had assets of $3.5 billion. It bought Kuwaiti oil at ten cents a barrel
and sold it at $1.85, and it was seeking, according to Copeland, to up-
stage British Petroleum, which owned the other half of the Kuwait
Oil Company.

But the reality was that he was financed in part, at least, by Angleton
to watch Philby. Copeland claimed to have the credentials for the task.
Having been trained by Philby in counterespionage in London before
D-Day in 1944, he had "known and liked" him when he was in Washington between 1949 and 1951. Copeland further claimed to have
served on an Anglo-American committee which had cleared Philby of
the allegations that he had been a Soviet agent; he claimed also that
he knew Philby "better than anyone else, excepting two or three British intelligence officers."[40] Angleton had told Copeland that "if I would
keep an eye on Philby" in Beirut, "he'd pay all the costs — costs being
in the form of entertainment expenses, since it was under the cover
of social contact that I was to do my counter-espionage work."[41] Also,
the FBI in Washington and MI5 in London asked him "to report signs
that [Philby] might be spying for the Soviets."[42]

Thus a third shark began to circle Philby, and soon there was a fourth, James Barracks, of Urbana, Illinois, who worked in the city behind the front of an import-export merchant in pharmaceuticals. It was said that Barracks's role on Angleton's behalf was to conduct a late-night telephone campaign by "drunken American ladies" against Philby, not only at his residence but wherever he was. The purpose was to unnerve Philby and thereby soften him up against the time something would happen. Then the Lebanese Sûreté chief, Farid Chehab, would pull him in for deep and prolonged interrogation. Applewhite denied all knowledge of Barracks's activities, stating emphatically that Barracks worked not through CIA Beirut but directly for Angleton through Copeland.

As for Copeland, for the next five years, until January 1963, he would "throw a buffet dinner for forty people on a night when we were sure Philby was free to be one of them, and send the bill to Jim Angleton."[43] Philby and Copeland became good friends and Copeland claimed to have employed the Lebanese Sûreté to use its "street eyes" — teams of streetwise Arabs — to watch Philby. This was not difficult; Philby had never learned to drive and used taxis or hired cars, usually the same vehicle driven by the same man. For five years Philby and Copeland engaged in political and doctrinal gossip, talking about regional politics and the ambitions of the great powers there, including Russia, and in general Copeland felt that

> I earned what [Angleton] paid me. For example, I arranged for a senior official of the Lebanese Sûreté, whom I cultivated for general intelligence purposes, to subject Philby to the occasional "spot" surveillance and to report back to me anything of interest, and what he gave me indicated that Philby was still practising his old tradecraft. As a matter of habit, he invariably shook off his tail. Also from time to time Sûreté agents spotted him in some awfully strange parts of Beirut, such as the Armenian Quarter at the beginning of the road to Damascus, where we subsequently learned that he kept a top-storey flat from which to send "black light" messages to the KGB code clerk who saw them from one of the thousands of windows in his line of sight.[44]

However this may have been, Copeland, like Applewhite, obtained not the slightest evidence that Philby was anything more than what he appeared to be: an aging and amiable but able reporter who, through a famous father, was exceptionally well connected with the world that concerned Copeland vitally — Arab politics. Philby trod so carefully that when he vanished that night in January 1963, Copeland was dumbfounded at the supposition that he had gone to Moscow. If he was a communist, Copeland told a colleague, then "he was the best actor in the world." That was "unbelievable," for he would have had "to construct a fantastic intellectual framework and stick to it moment by moment" throughout their association. And that would also have been too fantastic to contemplate.

Months later, Copeland's wife, Lorraine, wrote a letter protesting that it was "painful to think that during the years we all loved Kim and had him constantly in our homes, he was all the while laughing at us." This reproach reached Philby and he replied, revealing something of the spirit that moved him:

> My dear Lorraine:
>   I hope you never have to learn, as I have, that one lives one's life in several planes, and when there is conflict between the plane of one's ideals and that of one's friends it is, believe me, no laughing matter. Please accept, for whatever they are worth, my assurances that I will always have only the fondest thoughts for you and my other friends in Beirut.[45]

By then yet another shark had appeared on Beirut's main drag, which ran along the waterfront for a mile or more between the U.S. Embassy, the British Embassy, Dmitri's White Russian restaurant, the Palm Beach Hotel, the Excelsior Hotel pool, the St. George Hotel, the Lucullus restaurant, and the British Club, that conservative Old World place where the aging sahibs and memsahibs of another age munched sausage and mash and Jesus fish on Fridays. This individual was Ernest Keiser, a New York German who developed a large reputation as a bounty hunter; later he played a major role in the capture of Edwin P. Wilson, a CIA renegade who made a real fortune in supplying arms to Muamar Qaddafi.

The American author Joseph C. Goulden claimed that Keiser was born in 1918, that he was a freelance correspondent for NBC News in Egypt and elsewhere during the 1950s "and thereafter a private businessman." Actually, Goulden wrote,

> he was an intelligence office [sic], first with the G2 section of the old War Department, then as a contract employee of CIA when the Agency was formed in 1947. Over the next decades Keiser (by his own count) was to work for more than 20 Western intelligence agencies, always as a contract employee, and usually with a cover job. Much of this time he lived in the Middle East, ostensibly a correspondent for the Hearst newspaper organization, then with NBC News. In Beirut he

was a neighbor, sometime drinking crony of H.A.R. "Kim" Philby, the Soviet mole.[46]

Again according to Goulden, Keiser's business at this time included bringing persons in the Soviet Union and Eastern Europe out to the West. How far this association between Philby and Keiser went is hardly worth pursuing. Applewhite had no knowledge of the man and no other principal player had either. But Keiser was big-time: among his later associates were Robert Vesco, the financier and swindler, and Jimmy Hoffa, the deposed Teamster president. The possibility exists that Keiser had his eye on Philby against the day when Angleton might require his exfiltration to the United States. But there is no proof.

Otherwise, the most interesting character on the main drag was old St. John. He had become one of its darlings, one of its boulevardiers, a potbellied, almost satanic figure in his white linen suits and heavy black beard waddling off to emcee the dances and dinners and judge beauty contests and other such functions at the casino on the northern headland, which was where, after dark, the main part of the great game was played. For Kim, so it seems in retrospect, there was no suggestion that the avenger, Nemesis, waited in the wings until Trevor-Roper and Philby encountered each other again in Baghdad during Development Week.

By now Trevor-Roper had done well in life. A bustling, sharp-faced, peering, bespectacled figure, he had made a great name for himself through his investigation at the end of World War II into what was a conundrum of the time: Was Hitler really dead? He had conducted this investigation under the direction of White, and it resulted not only in the final eradication of Nazism but also in the capture of Ernst Kaltenbrunner, the chief of the Sicherheitsdienst, the Nazi intelligence service, who was hanged as a major war criminal. During this operation, Trevor-Roper located Hitler's personal will and his final political testament. Then he returned to civilian life and Christ Church, Oxford. He wrote *The Last Days of Hitler,* a leading work about World War II, and he married a daughter of Field Marshal Earl Haig, the commander in chief of the British armies in France in World War I. He became one of Harold Macmillan's authors, a group that liked to regard itself as the cream of the crop. When Macmillan became prime minister, he saw to it that Trevor-Roper became the Regius Professor of Modern History at Oxford. In turn, Trevor-Roper would propose Macmillan as chancellor of Oxford. As to Trevor-Roper's and Macmillan's association with White, now the chief of the British Secret Service, each admired the other, forming thereby a power elite consisting of the prime minister and chancellor of Oxford, the Regius Professor, and the chief of the British Secret Service — a formidable triangle of power in the Establishment.

Trevor-Roper, who had so brilliantly unraveled the twists and turns in the life of Archbishop Laud before the war and Admiral Canaris during it, now applied himself to Philby's mind at their meeting beside the Tigris. As the professor recorded of that encounter, he

> found that a small party of journalists was about to travel round the country for "Development Week," and I applied to join them. On this expedition, I found myself constantly in company with my old friend, the new correspondent of the *Observer*. I was by now satisfied that he had been a Russian spy for over twenty years; but he did not know that I knew this, and I thought it wrong to give any indication of my knowledge. So we mixed again on old terms; and although I inwardly shrank from him as a traitor, I must admit that I found his company as attractive as ever, his conversation as disengaged, and yet as enjoyable . . . In our conversation I naturally made no reference to recent history, but I listened carefully for any allusion that he might make. In due course he made it. He wished to date some minor episode, and he chose to date in an oddly irrelevant way. "It was about the time," he said, "of all that absurd fuss about the 'Third Man' . . ." I made no comment; but I thought that he did protest a little too much.[47]

Elliott arrived in Beirut early in 1960 to succeed the incumbent station commander, Godfrey Paulson. Paulson was retiring to one of those marvelous sinecures available to SIS officers who had served the crown well and faithfully — the consulate-generalship at Nice, on the French Riviera — and Goldsmith White had decided that it was time that Elliott had his spell in the Middle East. Elliott himself would relate that his first encounter with Philby was quite accidental: on the very day he landed, he and his wife went for luncheon to a restaurant on the waterfront, the Lucullus, and found the Philbys lunching at a table nearby. Their encounter, according to Eleanor Philby, marked the opening of a "fresh and seemingly carefree chapter" in the official and personal relationship between Elliott and Philby. As she noted, Elliott at once said to her husband: "Fill me in, old boy," and leaned on Kim as his unofficial adviser — and perhaps an official one — on the riddle-me-ree of Beirut politics. Eleanor recorded that thereafter "they used to meet once or twice a week, vanishing into another room, and leaving me to gossip with his wife."[48] And in pondering on this devotion between the hunter and the hunted, Andrew Boyle wrote tellingly in his *Anatomy of Treason:*

> As for Kim, he seemed to relish the confidence reposed in him by a man he had always liked. Philby's Russian masters must therefore have anxiously asked themselves which side this double agent, whom they jealously thought of as "ours," was really serving, and when the strange confusion of his loyalties would cease.[49]

The troubled years since 1951 and the CIA charges that he was a traitor had left their mark on Philby, but is anything, as is often the case with men passing through middle age, he was still more attractive now than he had been. Patrick Seale of *The Observer,* a colleague who visited Beirut at about this time, found him to have become a

> rather washed-up, somewhat old-fashioned Englishman, hampered by a stammer, drinking more than was good for him and yet compelling a certain respect. The heavily marked face, the literary prose style, the humane, rather pessimistic judgements pointed to a mind shaped in the Europe of the 1930s, strikingly out of place in the Middle East. He was not one of those Englishmen who fall in love with Arabs. The call of the desert and the freedom of bedouin life which had so attracted his father left him quite unmoved. He saw only ignorance, corruption and the boredom of a denuded landscape, while the warm, showy life of Beirut seemed to have no greater appeal for him. Most foreigners in his position quickly get hooked on the daily drama of politics; Kim did not. He knew what was going on but quite simply did not care much about it. Perhaps for the first time in his life he was a spectator — and a minor one at that — rather than an active participant in the political situation around him. In this Arab context what marked him out from others was not any achievement of his own but the fact that he was St. John Philby's son.[50]

It was always this fact — that he was St. John's son — that made a valuable connection to Elliott. What made him still more valuable was that he had remained what he had been, a highly trained counterespionage officer of good bearing and manners — a rarity in that trade. Consequently, perhaps as part of White's plan to catch him, his career with Elliott as his case officer entered a new and very active period. Hitherto, Philby's travels had been confined to Syria, Lebanon, and occasionally Saudi Arabia. Now they widened greatly as the Cold War reverberated throughout the Middle East, the Persian Gulf, and Southwest Asia. His colleagues in Beirut met Philby everywhere. He became perhaps the leading British reporter in the Middle East and was, consequently, acceptable at every embassy, consulate, and mission. He was regarded as an assiduous, careful, dutiful reporter. In those days before commercial credit cards, such reporters traveled on the International Air Transport Association (IATA) card. His card number was known to the SIS so that his movements could be checked against the records of IATA headquarters in Montreal.

His work for Elliott was mainly political and personality reporting, but it is thought that there was another aspect to his travels, that of "the barium meal," which has been described as SIS jargon for "a bait or lure of ostensibly important intelligence to entrap or ascertain the identity of an opposition agent. Commonly used in provocation or deception. Barium meal, of course, is the term used in Roentgenology for the opaque liquid fed to the patient in the upper gastrointestinal series to detect the presence of stomach or duodenal ulcers or cancers."[51] In this context, *provocation* has been defined as "activity designed to induce an individual, organization, intelligence service, or government to take self-damaging action." It has further been defined as "the act of a provocateur intended to surface or expose an opposition service by causing it to react in taking countermeasures." If Philby did undertake such measures, then his game for Elliott — and perhaps also for Goldsmith White — was the same as it had been for Menzies at Istanbul in 1947–1949. In any case, as will be seen soon, Philby was plainly a master at the quick-witted craft of the sentence that, while seeming to be innocuous and even courteous, can devastate an individual, a service, and in the Middle East of this time, even a government. Certainly it was a most useful tactic in the process of destroying reputations, a tactic in which Philby was also a specialist.

Elliott's personal regard for Philby seemed to contain elements of admiration and compassion. There was certainly no evidence that Elliott was colluding with White to trap his old friend. Their relationship seemed unchanged — that of two old friends in crown service on the frontiers. When Elliott published his memoirs thirty years on, he wrote that he had found Philby to be "one of those people who were instinctively liked but more rarely understood." He had "an impressive clarity of mind and also, despite his stammer, of speech." His writing was "a model of economy and lucidity." He "very rarely discussed politics and his conversation on all serious topics appeared singularly devoid of emotion." Indeed, "he did not strike me as a political animal. I can hardly see him as a lecturer on dialectical materialism." To the contrary, "he was much more a man of practice than of theory. He did not bore and he did not pontificate." He enjoyed discussing the English batting averages and, on home leave, he spent many long hours watching the cricket from the Mound Stand at Lord's.[52]

Nor, it seems certain, did Philby care overly about how the British Establishment figures in Beirut regarded him. Like his father, he could be outrageous in the presence of such figures. As Elliott remembered, soon after his arrival he gave a cocktail party for forty people, including the ambassador, Sir Moore Crosthwaithe. This was one of the rare occasions that Philby met Crosthwaithe, an official and peremptory man, and Philby "caused a chain reaction of offence unparalleled in my experience." There was a pause in the babble of conversation when Philby was heard to remark, perhaps to Crosthwaithe, "Don't you think 'Anne' has the finest breasts in Beirut?" "Anne" was the wife of one of the senior officers in the embassy, who was standing next to Crosthwaithe. She was also the daughter of the governor of Rhodesia, which was then a British colony. Elliott described the incident:

> Moore was undoubtedly annoyed because, quite reasonably, he thought that the breasts of the wife of a member of his staff were not an appropriate subject of conversation for a cocktail party. "Anne," while doubtless justifiably proud of that part of her anatomy, was annoyed at having it discussed in public and in particular with the Ambassador. Her husband was annoyed as he, equally justifiably, agreed with the Ambassador that his wife's breasts were an off-target subject for cocktail party gossip. "Jane" (the wife of another member of the Embassy staff) was annoyed because she thought she had better breasts than "Anne." "Jane's" husband was annoyed, possibly because he felt his wife had been slighted. Eleanor Philby was more than just annoyed because she was not particularly well endowed in that respect and comparisons are odious. And, finally, [Elliott's wife, Elizabeth] was annoyed because she felt the whole party was getting out of hand. In fact the only person who thought the whole episode was a huge joke was Kim Philby himself.[53]

This may have been an attempt by Philby to show that he could not possibly be a Russian spy, for no such individual would draw attention to himself by acting in that fashion before the senior staff of the embassies in Beirut. It is possible to see in this incident that Philby had acquired something resembling immunity through his special work in Beirut. His connections were as useful to the British state and perhaps to the United States as they were to the Soviet Union.

But time and events pressed relentlessly on Philby.

First he lost his friend Eveland, whose activities could be tolerated no longer by Applewhite. Late in 1959, his discretion in doubt with Applewhite and the CIA station chief in Turkey, Justin O'Donnell, Eveland left Beirut for consultations with the CIA in Washington and did not return. He was sent to Africa as Allen Dulles's personal representative, with his base in Rome. There he was notified that he was considered a security risk. He had, he was told, "compromised" his "affiliation" with the "CIA during the period I'd served them in the Middle East." According to Eveland's obituarist and literary executrix, Mary Barrett, the CIA held the view that he passed "secrets to his old friend, double agent and Soviet defector Kim Philby." Eveland challenged this opinion when he appeared before a CIA security tribunal but, Barrett wrote, "Eveland was never able to get the government either to charge him with espionage or to pay him his pension."[54]

Eveland was a ruined man. He persisted in attempting to contact Philby after his own extrusion from the Middle East; he ran up one huge hotel bill too many at Singapore and went to jail there for hotel fraud, and after that wrote a book in which he exposed the CIA's policy and personnel in the Middle East, naming all the main players of his time along with a number of important deep-cover agents. He lost whatever claim he had to a CIA pension, he became unemployable, and he died a pauper in Massachusetts.

In these circumstances, the Philby case began to move toward its dénouement. First there were the consequences of St. John's sudden and unexpected death in Beirut.

In 1960, St. John entered his seventy-sixth year. He had, he declared, retired from politics, and if he was his son's best source, that state of affairs could not last much longer. St. John never compromised about the Saudi princes' extravagance. "The present regime has given us nothing but palaces," he declared in a newspaper article, careless whether he would be exiled again. He spent most of his time in Riyadh, living in an old-style house made of red mud and rejecting the suggestion that he move to a modern, concrete house. He spent his days hammering away on his old typewriter in a room lit by a naked bulb, writing a long book on his experiences in Jordan in 1924 (it never found a publisher) and then *Arabian Oil Ventures,* a semi-official history of the Anglo-American oil business, which was published by the Middle East Institute in Washington. He revised all the articles he had written on Arabia and the Saudi kingdom for the *Encyclopaedia Britannica* and wrote others on the new oil towns such as Dhahran and Ras Tanura. He spent his seventy-fifth birthday at the hill resort of Taif, "watching the bulldozers knock down half of my property for a new road through the town."

St. John arrived in Beirut in September 1960 for the last time. He had been in London for the cricket and in Moscow for an Orientalists' conference, a suspect body in the eyes of Western intelligence authorities. Philby and his father spent two days drinking at Joe's Bar and watching the belly dancers at the Kit-Kat. St. John lunched with Elliott and his wife; they were, Elliott recalled, "among the few English people to whom St. John was prepared to be civil." When Elliott asked his house guest, Sir Humphrey Trevelyan, a senior and formidable mandarin, whom he would like to meet, Trevelyan proposed Philby — which demonstrated the Establishment's capacity for interesting itself in its foes. The luncheon was memorable. Trevelyan had been the ambassador at Baghdad when Philby's old anathema, the Iraqi Hashemite royal family, was murdered, and he still held that post. Having recounted his eyewitness account of the revolution, Trevelyan drew St. John out on his relationship with Ibn Saud. It was almost St. John's last public performance and, as usual, his talk enthralled.

According to Elliott, St. John "left at tea time, had a nap, made a pass at the wife of the Embassy staff in a night club."[55] Later that evening he and Kim went to a large cocktail and supper party at the home of John Fistere, the former *Time* man who had replaced Glubb Pasha as the Westerner at Hussein of Jordan's court. It was a large, noisy, lively party, and at some stage St. John went out to the balcony, with its glorious view of nighttime Beirut and the Mediterranean. A young American teacher in Beirut, Richard Storm, was talking with St. John when the old man began to look "cardiacky" and collapsed on the balcony. As in life so in extremis: there was an uproar and then stunned silence. Kim was in a corner somewhere, quite drunk. It was well known that a heart attack is most damaging and dangerous in its earliest stages, but it does not seem that anyone called Kim immediately. Nor did anyone call a doctor or an ambulance. The hostess screeched, "God! I've poisoned him!"[56] Thus did the legend that St. John had been poisoned ricochet about Beirut.

Kim appeared soon afterward and took his father to the Normandy Hotel, where they were staying. A doctor pronounced that St. John had indeed suffered a cardiac arrest. But still nobody took him to the hospital until after daybreak, when, it appears, he suffered a second attack. Only then did Kim send him to the hospital. There, St. John woke only once and announced emphatically: "God. I'm bored." In his account, Kim recorded only that his father had said "I'm bored," omitting the word *God*.[57]

Those were his last words. St. John Philby died late in the afternoon of September 30, 1960. The sheikh of the Bashoura mosque buried

him under his Moslem name, Haji Abdullah, almost immediately afterward, as required by his religion, in the Moslem cemetery in the
Basta quarter of Beirut. The Fatiha, the committal of St. John's soul
to Paradise, was uttered over the grave: "In the name of God, the
Compassionate, the Merciful." The grave was closed, and later Kim
had his father's tombstone inscribed: "Greatest of all Arabian Explorers." John Slade-Baker, attending as a mourner, left this account of the
obsequies:

> No one from the Saudi Arabian or British Embassies came to the
> graveside or put in any appearance at all, the grave had been dug a
> long way from the gate, but we got there at last. It was a dreadful
> little ceremony, I thought. The coffin was opened and poor St. John
> was lifted out wrapped in some material and lowered into the grave
> by the grave diggers. They laid him pointing to Meccah and after
> throwing some earth on the body they proceeded to place enormous
> stones on it while a local *Imam* said prayers for the dead. An American
> by the name of Bruce-Conde, who has also embraced Islam, stood by
> the side of the grave repeating the prayers, with his cupped hands
> held out in front of him.
>   At last it was finished and we walked out of the cemetery and drove
> back to the Normandy. Anwar, the Barman, who is a great friend
> of Kim's and had been of [St. John's], came to the service at the
> graveside, which I thought charming of him. The proprietor of the
> hotel came too, and apparently insisted on paying the burial fees.
> The whole ceremony was simple and very quick almost as though
> they were burying a peasant instead of one of the leading Orientalists
> in the world.[58]

St. John Philby was not to remain long in Lebanon's soil. When,
through the very forces that he helped to unleash, the Bashoura cemetery became a battlefield between the Moslems and the Christians, his
grave was torn up and his remains scattered to the Beiruti wind. The
grave was then used to bury a warrior of the Palestine Liberation
Organization. To the Saud dynasty he became an instant unperson, as
he did with his sons Khalid and Faris. They abandoned the name
Philby, and when Lowell Thomas's cameraman, James Morrison, encountered them in Riyadh in later years, both were at pains to stress
that neither had British blood.

The Times devoted three quarters of a column to Philby's obituary,
but it carefully confined itself to St. John's achievements, not his politics. That judgment was left to his biographer, Elizabeth Monroe:

> Philby is often bracketed with Lawrence because they both worked
> in the Arab world, but they were opposites in their handling of its

arbiters. Where Lawrence rightly judged the tempo that suited the men in power, and was able to cajole them into doing as he advised, Philby, hectoring, intemperate and opinionated, provoked their wrath and lost his case. All through his life, he saw himself as acting from the highest motives, and with a right, in a free country, to think what he liked and say what he thought about broken British promises, or his conscientious objection to war. The flaw in him was not the creeds he preached but his immoderation in expounding them.

Sure of his worth, yet unable to make Englishmen see it, he sought abroad the name that he reckoned he deserved. When in Arabia, he practised its faith and way of life. Yet he remained sturdily British, with his pipe, his *Times*, . . . his five o'clock tea, his study of cricket scores and the Honours List, his relish of the Athenaeum, his concern that Kim should follow him into Westminster, Trinity and the Civil Service.[59]

As to his relationship with his son, Kim himself would write of it: "If he had lived a little longer to learn the truth, he would have been thunderstruck, but by no means disapproving." The fact was that St. John had committed treason by English standards in spirit, and perhaps in law, but he was never accused by any court; and in the end the wisdom that told for him was that which had governed the Treason Statutes since James I:

> Treason doth never prosper:
> what's the reason?
> Why if it prosper,
> none dare call it treason.

At the death of St. John, the Philby case began to reach one of its culminations. The Old Protector was no more and Kim was devastated. His carousals became self-destructive, perhaps through a combination of the strain of playing double and even treble games and his failure to react promptly to his father's original collapse. He may well have thought privately that had he been sober enough to call for a doctor or an ambulance immediately, his father would have survived. Eleanor Philby wrote that Kim became "intoxicated — vertically intoxicated, horizontally intoxicated, cracking his head in his own bathroom when intoxicated, and being removed from an Embassy party when intoxicated."

Philby's breakdown, for breakdown it was, lasted from late January until about late October of 1960. But by November he was fit enough to go to Riyadh to settle his father's estate. There was another consideration: the Saudi religious police, at Crown Prince Feisal's order, had seized St. John's library, his files, and his correspondence, including the papers he had shipped to Riyadh from England when Dora died. By all accounts, the collections, of great value, had been disordered by the police, and much of it might have been lost forever unless Kim obtained the support of ARAMCO. He wrote to George Rentz, the chief of ARAMCO's Research Department — its private intelligence service — and Rentz and his deputy retrieved the library and the papers. They were now all in a shed at Dhahran, ARAMCO's main base in Saudi Arabia.

In a further letter to Rentz, Philby announced that he would visit Dhahran shortly; he invited ARAMCO to purchase the library, which constituted perhaps the modern world's leading private collection of Arabian incunabula, for $10,000. The sum was to be settled on his Arab half-brothers, Khalid and Faris. Philby flew to Riyadh in November 1960, but was not well received by the Saudi administration, which saw him as the white son of the white wife who had come to the country of the brown wife and her sons.

As soon as his business would allow, Kim went to ARAMCO headquarters at Dhahran and stayed with Robert W. Headley, of the Department of Research. As Headley told it, the Saud princes had suspected St. John of espionage in the interests of foreign powers and, at his death, had seized his papers. Finding the bulk of the papers too great and, in any case, mainly in English, they turned them over to ARAMCO, and Headley had the task of sorting them and "flattening out the pages to get them back into files." In the process, Headley found a "bunch of letters" from Kim to his father. He recalled one long letter telling St. John how he had gone to "baby sit" in the Black Country. Apparently Kim looked after children while the parents were out working, foraging on the slag heaps for coal to sell for food. Kim said he was appalled by the poverty he had found. The tone of the letter indicated that this was the start of his interest in communism.

Another letter concerned Alice, Kim's first wife, telling St. John that to get her out of Vienna they were going to marry so that she would have British citizenship. The tone of the letters was "rebellious, philosophical." Kim showed no interest in them. Their business done, Headley took Philby to his home for drinks and dinner. That evening their talk drifted to Philby's troubles in Washington. Headley was aware that Kim was "not quite lily-white" at the CIA and listened with care. When the talk turned to J. Edgar Hoover of the FBI, Philby, according to Headley, "suddenly exploded" and, as Headley reported to the CIA, exclaimed, "If J. Edgar Hoover had spent less time worrying me in

Washington he would have found that there really was a mole at CIA"
— pointing to the existence of a Soviet spy at a high level of the
agency's management. That possibility had already begun to emerge,
and Philby, by making his remark, may have been attempting to fan
the suspicion, furthering its destructive effect on the effectiveness of
the CIA branches fighting the Cold War with the KGB. But he said no
more. He changed subjects, leaving Headley to report the remark.

Philby returned to Riyadh to catch the plane to Beirut. This required him to stay overnight in Riyadh, and he spent the evening with
the ARAMCO political agent, Ronald Metz, and his wife, who formed
the impression that Kim was in poor health. His hands shook as badly
as if he had palsy, he was nervous and uneasy, and this, the Metzes
thought, might have been due to the Saudis' disapproval of him in
the country.

The Metzes could not provide him with alcohol, as this was forbidden to Westerners in Riyadh. Instead, he had a soft drink and a supper
prepared for him by Mrs. Metz. Throughout, he showed that he was
"terribly worried about something," although neither Metz nor his
wife discovered what it was. They had not heard the rumors of Kim's
connection with the KGB, and both believed, as they had with St. John,
that he was with the British Secret Service. They were cautious, therefore, when Philby raised a very sensitive subject for Metz's opinion.
Would Feisal's regime survive in a society so rent with corruption, and,
if it failed, what would ARAMCO and the State Department do to
ensure that the royal family not be replaced by a regime favorably
disposed to Russia? A discreet man, Metz did not permit Philby's probe
to prosper. The talk then proceeded to the subject of Metz's faith,
Catholicism, of which Philby showed considerable knowledge, and
Metz wondered whether he were not a failed churchman seeking to
find his way back.

In all this, thought Metz, Kim "may have been being polite or cunning," but when he rose to leave Metz put his arm around his trem-
bling guest and "sensed a deep and genuine warmth." The reason
Philby may have begun to concern himself with the purpose of life is
not hard to fathom. He felt the loss of St. John deeply and genuinely.
But further, there was the aggravation of telephone calls late at night
from people he did not know. There was a pattern to these calls. It
seemed that they were intended to unnerve him, to indicate that someone was watching him.[60]

Toward the end of 1962, a new tremor struck the secret circle in
London and Beirut. There was another important Russian spy in the

British Secret Service. Goldsmith White's shock may be imagined when through an internal investigation, his attention fastened on a British officer studying Arabic at the Foreign Office's Middle East College for Arabic Studies (MECAS) at Shemlan, an old Maronite monastery in the hills outside Beirut. There the British government trained its foreign service and intelligence officers and certain individuals in commercial life and the oil industry before they took up their posts in the Middle East. Some fifty such men attended MECAS each semester, and Whitehall regarded it as one of the most important institutions in the process of safeguarding and expanding the British presence in the Middle East. But the Lebanese government regarded MECAS as "a school for spies," and, with the spread of Arab nationalism, there was growing demand that Britain remove the establishment from Lebanese territory. This had been successfully resisted by diplomatic means, but recently fighting had broken out around Shemlan between guerrilla bands taking part in the incipient civil war in Lebanon as a whole.

It was with much anxiety, therefore, that the Foreign Office learned that the spy was George Blake, a naturalized Briton of Egyptian-Jewish-Dutch origin who had joined the British Secret Service in 1947. He had come to be highly regarded, having played an important part in the direction of the spy war against the Russians in Berlin and in establishing and running the Berlin Tunnel, an Anglo-American operation to tap the telephone and teleprinter communications between the headquarters of the Red Army General Staff at Karlshorst, Berlin, and the Red Army Supreme Command in Moscow. If Blake was a Russian spy, it meant that the tunnel, which had cost some $48 million and was the Anglo-American secret circle's main source of intelligence about Russian intentions in Europe, had been a KGB control from the outset.

In March 1961 Nicholas Elliott was instructed to ask Blake at ME-CAS "to return to London for consultations regarding a possible promotion." Elliott went out to Shemlan to pass the message and, to allay any suspicions that Blake might develop, suggested that there was no hurry about his departure. If he had made plans for Easter, he could stay until after the holidays. Suspecting nothing, Blake remained for the Easter holiday and flew back to London on Easter Monday, April 3. But when he arrived at SIS headquarters and was confronted by White, he confessed to espionage in the interests of the Soviet Union. He was arrested and charged under the treason statutes, and in due course he was sentenced to forty-two years' imprisonment, the heaviest sentence imposed by a British court for more than a hundred and fifty years. Based on fourteen years on each of three charges, the sentence represented, so it was said, a year for each of the forty-two British secret agents whom Blake had betrayed to the KGB.

During the period in which Blake was awaiting trial, the security authorities went to great lengths to prevent any connection between Blake and MECAS becoming known in order not to give the Lebanese government the justification it had been seeking to close the school. But when the news eventually leaked into the press, the Druze hill tribes around Shemlan threatened to storm MECAS and burn it down. John Slade-Baker, the resident correspondent of the *Sunday Times* in Beirut and a friend of Philby's and Elliott's, went to see Elliott at the embassy to seek guidance about what could and could not be published in the Blake case. The conversation, which Slade-Baker later wrote up in his diary, reflected Elliott's capacity for dissimulation in state matters. As he recorded:

> The whole thing has been a piece of the greatest bad luck. Blake, who, I gathered from N[icholas] is not a permanent member of "the firm" [the SIS], was genuinely sent out here by the Foreign Office to learn Arabic and had been at Shemlan for about eight months.
>
> He was not sent here to get him out of the way while evidence was collected against him, and his posting was perfectly genuine in every respect. The Ambassador was most upset by it all and said he prayed that nothing more will be published about Blake or M.E.C.A.S. He thinks that if no more is heard on the subject it may be possible [to get the government and the Druze leaders] to forget about it and keep quiet.[61]

He then added:

> I forgot to say that N[icholas] told me this morning that he thinks that the Russians are about to launch an all-out campaign against our Intelligence Service out here, in fact all over the Middle East. He also said that what has upset him about the [*Telegraph*'s] dispatch is that it will alarm his agents all over the area, lest their names have been divulged [to the Russians] by Blake, which, in fact, he can not possibly have done, as he was not in a position to do so.[62]

By way of a little spice, Elliott then confided in Slade-Baker the information that Blake had been

> an excellent student and he had made such progress in his Arabic studies that he had been recommended for the Advanced Course. He was a good-looking fellow, tall and with excellent manners and universally popular. He was definitely not escorted to England but was arrested on arrival either in the Foreign Office or at Scotland Yard, and his wife [also in the SIS] who was expecting a baby at any

moment was spirited away to England unobserved. Poor woman! What a smash for them all![63]

Smash it was, indeed, for everybody, including Philby. In Lebanon, the Druze leaders demanded that MECAS be removed from Lebanese territory; it was reestablished in Cyprus. Kim saw his own fate in Blake's sentence; again his nerve failed him and again he took to the bottle ever more vigorously. That was dangerous, for in 1962 the CIA and MI5 obtained more proof that he was a traitor. To add to his growing sense of isolation, both Applewhite and Elliott were replaced, although not as a consequence of the Blake case. Their departure coincided with the development of new and more severe pressure from the CIA to "resolve Philby's status" and with the sudden arrival in Beirut of Philby's former Soviet case officer, Yuri Modin. Whom Modin saw, where he went, why he had come, he never said. But the fact that he had come from Pakistan raised the question that Philby was considering flight at this time. In London in 1951, and again in Beirut in 1956, he had raised the question with Pakistani officials of obtaining a Pakistani passport on the grounds that he was born at Ambala in the Punjab, which had become part of Pakistan when India was partitioned in 1947. It is evident that Modin brought Philby a warning, which was passed on to him through intermediaries, that his position was becoming increasingly endangered through an intensification of the Security Service's inquiries about him.

What had occurred to make Modin undertake his dangerous journey was that, after Elliott's return to London, fresh evidence had been obtained against Philby. In August 1962, Lord Rothschild, the merchant banker and wartime MI5 officer who still maintained close contact with that service and was familiar with the Philby case, went to Israel for a meeting at the Chaim Weizmann Institute. There he met Flora Solomon, the Jewish society woman and a Philby family friend whom Philby had first met in the 1920s and then again in the late 1930s, when she introduced him to Aileen. According to Peter Wright, an associate of Rothschild's in MI5 and the author of *Spycatcher* and the Security Service officer who dealt with her, at their meeting in 1962 Mrs. Solomon told Rothschild that she was very indignant about Philby's reports from Beirut in *The Observer,* which were pro-Nasser, pro-Arab, and anti-Israel. She then confided that she knew Philby to have been a Soviet secret agent in the 1930s. At once Rothschild saw the importance of her statement; she was a citizen of some standing who could testify against Philby in a court of law.

On his return to London, Rothschild reported Mrs. Solomon's assertion to Peter Wright. At the request of Arthur Martin, the Security Service expert in the Philby case, Rothschild persuaded Mrs. Solomon, with difficulty, to make a sworn statement that she knew Philby to have been a Russian secret agent in the 1930s and that he had attempted to recruit her personally. Interviewed in Lord Rothschild's flat in London, Flora Solomon was, as Wright remembered, "a strange, rather untrustworthy woman, who never told the truth about her relations with people like Philby in the 1930s, although she clearly had a grudge against him."[64] She related how she had known Kim Philby very well before the war and had been fond of him. When he worked for *The Times,* he had taken her out to lunch on one of his trips back to London from the Spanish Civil War. During the meal he told her he was doing "a dangerous job for peace and needed help." Would she assist him in his great task? He was working for the Communist International and it would be a great thing if she would join in too. But that, Mrs. Solomon had explained, she had refused to do, although she did admit to telling Kim that he could always come to her if he felt himself to be in danger.

She declared in her interview that she would never testify against him publicly because there would be too much risk for her and her family if she did so — she cited the recent sudden and somewhat mysterious death of Tomas Harris in a car crash in Spain as evidence of that danger. She expected, evidently, that the KGB would attempt to silence her if it knew she was making a statement against Philby. She changed her mind only when it was put to her that Philby unhorsed represented a continuing threat to the common cause, including that of Israel. But, it seems, the allegation that Philby was, and had been for a very long time, a Soviet secret agent, rested on more substantial grounds than those provided by Mrs. Solomon. For as Flora was making her deposition, a strange and sinister KGB deserter appeared on the distant horizon under Angleton's management, and warned the British government that Philby was a Russian super spy. The name of the deserter was Anatoli Golitsin, and his name will recur.

The process by which the decision was taken to confront Philby with the new evidence was heavily influenced by the personality of Prime Minister Harold Macmillan, an aristocrat of the old school with hooded eyes. By now, he had been personally embarrassed by a number of grave security cases, and he may have intentionally pointed to the way in which Dick White and Roger Hollis should handle the Philby confrontation when, in September 1962, Hollis called on him to announce, as he did with high satisfaction, that he had caught a homosexual Russian spy, a certain Vassall, who had worked in a confidential position at the Admiralty. When Hollis asked Macmillan why he looked so glum at the news, Macmillan replied:

> I'm not at all pleased. When my gamekeeper shoots a fox, he doesn't go and hang it up outside the Master of Foxhounds' drawing room; he buries it out of sight. But you just can't shoot a spy as you did in the war. You have to try him . . . better to discover him, and then control him, but never catch him.[65]

Now, Macmillan went on, there would have to be "a great public trial in which the Security Services would not be praised for how efficient they are but blamed for how hopeless they are." The government would have to hold an inquiry, there would be "a terrible row in the press" and a debate in the House of Commons. The "Government will probably fall." He turned on Hollis and asked, "Why the devil did you 'catch' him?"[66]

Plainly Macmillan expected White to handle the Philby case with extreme circumspection. Not only was American confidence in British intelligence and security again threatened, but so was the national prestige. The British Secret Services were becoming the world's laughingstock. How would the press react if it discovered that the case against Philby, whom Macmillan had personally exonerated in the House from the charge that he was the third man in the Burgess and Maclean defection, had been reopened and that he was in England being interrogated? And what would happen if the government found itself compelled to put Philby on trial? If these were the concerns before White, then it is possible to see why the Philby dénouement took the course it did; that his interrogation and trial in England was never a political option for White; that the only choice open to him was to unload this perennial hot potato onto his Russian masters.

An able man, Martin was not in the same league as Philby. A detective at heart, a slight man of medium build, sandy-haired, shy, quiet, ascetic, and reserved, Martin is said to have believed that the Robber Barons, as the upper-class senior officers of the Secret Service were known, had protected Philby all along and would do so again. Determined as he was to "catch" Philby, White may not have seen Martin as the right man for what he had in mind for Philby.

The second factor facing White was that a decision had been taken with Hollis to send Martin, who had made his career in the Security Service on his investigation of the Philby case, to confront Philby. The reason for this was that Martin disliked Philby personally and wished only to catch him, an attitude that had caused trouble for Hollis when he met with Macmillan in the Vassall case. Macmillan did not want traitors caught; he wanted them discovered and controlled.[67] Could Martin be depended on to deal with Philby as silently and finally as the political need in London required? Would Philby give him the chance?

Martin of MI5 was replaced by Nicholas Elliott of the SIS. Elliott persuaded White to send him on the grounds that he had been betrayed *personally* by his old friend, not once, but several times. Elliott claimed that he told White that "I was his greatest supporter in 1951 and that my anger at having been betrayed would suggest that we had more proof than he realized."[68] White's orders to Elliott have never been revealed. But it is evident that he thought that Elliott would do the job as dexterously as was required. He was a Robber Baron, so Philby would see him and listen. He could not afford to do otherwise. If Elliott maneuvered behind a combination of risqué and dirty stories and buffoonery, nevertheless he was regarded by White as a proficient, clever, and determined officer who would stop at nothing if the interest of the crown required, as it did in the Philby case. It was well known that behind his sometimes absurd facade, as his father had remarked, "the really nasty Etonian is nastier than the product of any other public school."[69] But how was Elliott to rid the government of its gadfly? The answer would remain a British state secret but, it is evident, one that contained some of the elements of Macmillan's advice to Hollis.

White's decision to send Elliott sat badly on the group at MI5. The possibility that Philby might be rendering the SIS important services in Beirut seems not to have been known to the group or considered by them. As Assistant Director Wright, another MI5 official determined to produce Philby's arrest and trial, wrote in his memoir:

> We in MI5 had never doubted Philby's guilt from the beginning, and now at last we had the evidence we needed to corner him. Philby's friends in MI6, Elliott chief among them, had continually protested his innocence. Now, when the proof was inescapable, they wanted to keep it in-house. The choice of Elliott rankled strongly as well. He was the son of the former headmaster of Eton and had a languid upper-class manner.[70]

Elliott's mission to Beirut was very secret. White was the only other person who knew the intentions and the details, although Hollis was made aware that the operation was being undertaken. Elliott flew to Beirut on January 10, 1963, and telephoned Kim from a safe house.

Responding to Elliott's order to come to the apartment immediately, when Philby arrived he greeted his old friend with a remark that was to have appalling consequences for MI5 and the SIS. According to Elliott, Philby uttered the words: "I rather thought it would be you."[71] These seven words indicated to Elliott that another Soviet spy in the British secret circle in London had warned Philby about Elliott's mission. Who was the traitor? That question began a molehunt throughout the British Secret Services that would last a quarter of a century.

Philby was not physically fit when the confrontation began. Drinking heavily the previous evening, he had fallen and hit his head on a radiator, so his head was swathed in bandages. And he gave the impression that he was not competent to deal with this great crisis in his career. But those who knew him believe this to have been more camouflage to enable him to outwit Elliott. Again according to Elliott, it took him five minutes to lay Flora Solomon's statement before his quarry. When this was done Philby, the first principle of whose modus operandi was "Never confess," denied the accusations against him and rose as if to leave. Elliott then became vehement and claimed to have declared in what became "a white-knuckle discussion": "You had to choose between Marxism and your family and you chose Marxism. I once looked up to you. My God, how I despise you now. I hope you've got enough left to understand why." Philby remained impassive. Elliott then delivered what he believed might prove to be a decisive threat, for it was well known that Philby was a gentle man who feared violence, menace, and jail. His life in the West would be destroyed if he did not confess. Elliott announced, "I'm offering you a lifeline, Kim. Immunity from prosecution if you co-operate. You have 24 hours. Be back here at precisely 4 P.M. tomorrow."[72]

Philby left the apartment, assuring Elliott that he would return as directed. It is probable that Elliott had arranged that Emir Chehab, the director of the Lebanese security service, an SIS asset in Beirut, kept Philby surrounded by "street eyes," although Elliott reported to White that he thought Philby would keep the appointment, that he might confess, but warned that he might commit suicide. Consequently Elliott counted the next twenty-four hours as being among the most anxious of his career, for he felt sure that Philby would make an emergency signal to his KGB controller in the city. What then? Would he vanish, and if he did, would Chehab's street eyes keep up with him?

At 4 P.M. the next day Philby returned to the apartment with two typewritten pages of confession. In the course of the next three days they met again and, Elliott claimed, Philby provided more information about his work for the Soviet Union. According to Eleanor Philby, who was present, Elliott and Kim dined together, and they both tried "to appear as if nothing had intervened to destroy an old and treasured friendship." Elliott then returned to London, presented the confession to White, and then left for Brazzaville, in the Congo, to take up his new appointment as SIS chief in Africa. This was a very strange and suspicious movement that White would have sanctioned only if he was sure that Philby would *not* come to London for his interrogation.

During the next thirty years, until 1993, Philby's confession remained a British state secret. But either it or a version of it was shown by White to a high CIA officer. The officer recalled that it was "a very bland document in which Philby admitted only that he had spied for the Communist International. It did not mention the Soviet intelligence services, and he admitted that his work for the Communist International had taken place only *before* World War II" — that is, before he joined the British Secret Service. As to Elliott's use of the words *destroyed* and *lifeline,* were they intended to mean ruin, prison, or even death if Philby did not comply? To the former CIA officer, their use sounded more like menaces intended to make Philby flee to Moscow rather than return to England to make his detailed confession. As the CIA officer further remarked, "Right from the start, right from the time Philby was recruited by the old C in 1941, the Philby case has baffled me. Was it an incredible series of botches, or was it an incredible series of operations to plant Philby in Moscow?"[73] We shall not know, for the Philby case was one in which the secret services of all three countries involved — Britain, the Soviet Union, and the United States — found it necessary and convenient to keep silent. No individual told the whole truth about what lay behind the affair, least of all Philby, for everything he wrote was done under the control of the KGB.

One of his main reactions was to Elliott's offer of immunity. This was, he asserted,

> no deal at all. It was contingent on my telling all I knew about the KGB and naming names in Britain. Elliott mentioned some names to me, several of which alarmed me. It became clear that my immunity could be withdrawn at any time unless I named names. So for me this deal was not on.
>
> My view, and that of my superiors in Moscow, is that confrontation in Beirut, rather than in London, and the offer of a deal that was patently unacceptable, was deliberately staged so as to push me into escaping.[74]

Then there was the question of the tape recording that Elliott made of the proceedings and took to London with him. It proved useless for any purpose, because, as Wright remembered, "the sound quality was so poor." The technicians in Beirut had used "a single low-grade phone" that collected not only the voices in the room but all the street sounds that flooded in through the open windows. But enough of it was readable to show to Wright, he wrote, that "the whole confession, including Philby's signed statement, looked carefully prepared to blend fact and fiction in a way which would mislead us" at MI5. Wright had heard such recordings twice before. In the first, he remembered Philby's "boyish charm, the stutter." In the second, Philby was interrogated by the SIS as a preliminary to Macmillan's clearance of him. Then Philby "ducked and weaved around his MI6 interrogators, finessing a victory from a steadily losing hand." And now there was Elliott, "trying his manful best to corner a man for whom deception had been a second skin for thirty years," but "it was no contest. By the end, they sounded like two rather tipsy radio announcers, their warm classical public school accents discussing the greatest treachery of the twentieth century."[75]

Philby now prepared to vanish. He was helped by the fact that he had brought two of his children out to Beirut for their Yuletide holidays. Their presence in the apartment led those who kept watch on him to conclude, with dismay, that a man so devoted to his children would never decamp to the Soviet Union while they were still in Beirut. The SIS station chief in the city, Peter Lunn, sent for Philby to establish his state of mind. Philby avoided the meeting by instructing Eleanor to tell Lunn that he was ill. Glen Balfour-Paul, a high political officer at the British Embassy, invited both Kim and Eleanor to dinner at his home on January 23. Kim accepted "with pleasure." During this same period, he succeeded at last in making contact with his KGB control in Beirut. His control was appalled that Philby had uttered even a part confession and, concerned that the SIS's men in Beirut might yet arrest him and spirit him back to Britain, placed him under KGB orders to prepare for evacuation to the Soviet Union. The reason why is clear: for more than thirty years Philby had been a key figure in the Soviet espionage networks in Britain, Europe, and to some extent in the United States. They could not allow him to remain at liberty, for he knew too much about them.

Philby recorded of his actions after Elliott's departure:

The truth is that I have been prepared for 12 years for the ultimate crisis because I knew that it might come at any moment. So when the day did come, what then? It's been said that I hesitated before going.

But no. Just a little stalling; just a little drinking to show that nothing untoward was afoot, just a little time to make certain the escape route was doubly sure. Then away and gone. How could they have stopped me? I had friends as well as enemies in Beirut.[76]

According to the Palestinian reporter Sayed Abu Ris, who claimed to have been in the bar of the St. George Hotel that late afternoon of the twenty-third, Philby appeared and had several drinks alone. He left just before nightfall as a violent storm battered Beirut. He telephoned Eleanor to say that he was on his way to the Central Telegraph Office to send a cable to London, that he would be a little later for the dinner party at the Balfour-Pauls, and that she should go on ahead of him. He would catch up with her a little later. According to Gennady X, one of his KGB liaison officers for many years, Philby told him that Lunn, a world-class skiing champion, left the city that afternoon to ski on the fresh falls of snow in the mountains, thus leaving Beirut open to Kim's disappearance — a story that is almost certainly another of Philby's black valentines, spoken this time to show that Lunn had absented himself from his duty on this vital day.

During the evening of January 23, 1963, Philby vanished in the streets of Beirut after dark. That same night a Soviet steamer, the *Dolmatova,* on passage from Alexandria to Odessa, entered Beirut Harbor briefly during the gale and then, according to General Kalugin, one of Philby's KGB chiefs, Philby went aboard.

Whether the operation was, or was not, White's attempt to plant Philby on Moscow, to unload this perennial irritant on the KGB, that was the effect of Elliott's confrontation. Philby spent the rest of his life in exile in Moscow, a fate that most other Britons would have regarded as worse than prison. Yet the operation left the permanent suspicion that by his conduct, Elliott had given his friend one more chance at life and that therefore he was complicit in Philby's treachery and escape, a suspicion that had a particular sequel when Elliott died.

Between 1963 and 1994, it was evident to those who knew Elliott well that he had become "obsessed" by Philby. It seemed to those who knew Elliott that his trouble was a matter of conscience — that he had been complicit in Philby's escape. But Elliott himself never explained what his anxieties were. On the contrary, he made three different statements concerning the confrontation and Philby's escape. This served only to obscure further, in the public and the official mind, what had really occurred in that room in Beirut. Nevertheless, the matter weighed so heavily on Elliott's mind that, so it is said, just before

his death Elliott asked his priest to be "shriven," to take the Anglican
sacrament in which the penitent is confessed or absolved of his sins.
This was denied by the priest concerned, Canon Peter Pilkington —
although Pilkington did admit to seeing Elliott before his death and
to having discussed "briefly Philby and other matters." Shortly afterward a curious document containing information about the shrive
circulated in Washington. In it a prominent but anonymous man in
London is said to have given what he thought were the terms of Elliott's confession, that

> in that final climactic confrontation with Philby in Beirut, the dictates
> of patriotism and duty were strained to the breaking point by bonds
> of friendship and class loyalty to Philby, and that in the event it was
> Elliott's great lapse that he had tipped Philby off and had "permitted
> him to fly the coop." That was what was weighing on the Elliott
> conscience.[77]

Thus the first phase of the Philby case concluded. It had lasted from
1934 to 1963, and it ended as it had begun, in the realm of ambiguity.
The second phase now began. It lasted from 1963 until 1988, and it
commenced in the suspicious miasma created by Philby's seven words
of greeting to Elliott — his black valentine to Whitehall — "I rather
thought it would be you." The first consequence of that remark was
to raise the awful possibility that, if there was another Soviet spy in
Whitehall's secret circle, it was either Sir Roger Hollis, director of the
Security Service, or his deputy, Graham Mitchell. That possibility sent
a severe tremor through Whitehall, which played its part in wrecking
the Macmillan government.

16

The Bullfrogs' Chorus

1963–1964

PHILBY ARRIVED IN MOSCOW on January 28, 1963, five days
after his escape from Beirut. He was well received personally by
Vladimir Yefimovich Semichastny, chairman of the KGB, in the
reception rooms of a mansion near the Lubyanka. There is a photograph of Philby taken at this extreme moment in his life. He had lost
perhaps forty pounds; recently he had had a crude haircut; he had
begun to grow a mustache for camouflage; he was rigid; his suit required pressing; he needed a fresh shirt and tie. For all the world he
looked just like his father when, all those years before, he had been
photographed on the steps of St. Aldro's with Prince Feisal. But the
time and the occasion were very different. Philby had at last crossed
the great divide from the West to the East. There could be no return.
By his own action and decision he had branded himself a traitor.

Semichastny, the brightest of the new generation of Soviet intelligence masters, advised him that he had been recommended to the
Central Executive Committee of the USSR as a candidate for the Order of Lenin "in recognition of special services to socialism." There
was tea with lemon and cakes. There was a pretty speech by the chief
of the First Chief Directorate. Then Philby was led away to begin that
long process known as debriefing. He had been in the secret service
of the KGB for twenty-nine years. Of some importance in the initial
phase of that process was the first principle of interrogation. Philby
was to be made aware that he was wholly cut off from the outside
world, that he could not escape. If he was to be accepted into the

normal life of the Soviet Union, he must satisfy his interrogators on his *bona fides*. Until these were established, he would remain suspect as a Briton operating in the Soviet service but in the interests of the British service. Yuri Modin, who had had contact with him since 1944, explained why:

> Moscow Rules stipulated that I was not to meet him at all. He was too important and too well known. The one meeting I had with him in five years was in the dark, in a district and a street of London where it was not probable that he was known, and which he had not visited himself before. The meeting was by lamplight so to speak. It lasted less than a minute. We were forbidden to eat with him, or drink with him, or sit in armchairs together over the pipe. You cannot take the measure of a man under these circumstances. You can judge such a spy only by his performance. His intelligence was consistently high-level, important, the sort that the opposition was not likely to want out, the sort that we could not get by other means. We concluded that he was *nash* — ours — but we all realised that this did not mean that he was so. Only Deutsch's early estimates of him spoke of his ideological loyalty. But men change, especially with men such as Philby, who before 1951 and his partial exposure could have had anything he wanted out of his life. He was psychologically the complete British Secret Service officer. He looked like one. We thought he could never be anything else.[1]

The times themselves made him suspect. Nikita Khrushchev was in power. Russia was raising the Third World — the old British Empire — in support of socialism. The United States had become "the main adversary"; the United Kingdom "the main ally of the main adversary"; and the KGB's main task was the disruption of the CIA and the SIS, what James Jesus Angleton was calling "the monster plot." Was Philby not a friend and professional colleague of Angleton's of many years' standing? It was a peculiarity of the KGB, as Philby discovered, that it was much more concerned with the present than the past. The men now in charge of him really knew little about him except that he was a British communist, and therefore liable to be what they called "ideological shit."

The loyalty investigation of Philby begun in 1948 by General F. N. Fitin, Stalin's chief of the foreign intelligence and security services, had remained in his file. The woman who made the accusations against him, Modrjrkskaj, had left the KGB to study Marxist-Leninism at the Academy of Sciences, but she was still available to the KGB. Many officers of the Old Guard were prepared to believe her thesis that

Philby, Maclean, Burgess, and the others had been British controls operating against the Russians in the interests of Anglo-American goals.

Philby's interrogation opened in accordance with the principles of Soviet investigation: courtesy, patience, thoroughness, the absence of dialectic. Throughout the long ordeal, Philby conducted himself with his usual skill and poise. His interrogators doubtless felt confident about him. However, some reserve remained, especially in regard to the depth of his acceptance of Marxism. Did he not reflect some of the tendencies of the despised social democrats? His record as a secret collaborator spoke well enough, but some of the interrogators had never been outside the Soviet Union, and they regarded British communists as people who did not necessarily believe in the violent overthrow of the bourgeois states but more in the acquisition of power by parliamentary means. This reserve remained with Philby at the KGB for the rest of his time in Russia.

By his own account to Graham Greene, the English novelist, he spent the first three or four months in a KGB safe house consisting of two rooms and a bathroom. In writing *The Human Factor,* the novel about a British Secret Service executive, Castle, who works for the Soviet service for ideological reasons, Greene consulted Philby about his first quarters in Moscow. What were they like? How did he occupy his hours alone? How were they furnished?

Greene wrote in the novel:

> It had belonged, both rooms of it with a kitchen and a private shower, to a comrade recently dead who had nearly succeeded before his death in furnishing it completely. An empty apartment as a rule contained only a radiator — everything else even to the toilet had to be bought. That was not easy and wasted a great deal of time and energy. Castle wondered sometimes if that was why the comrade had died, worn out by the long hunt for the green wicker armchair, the brown sofa hard as a board, without cushions, the table which looked as though it had been stained a nearly even color by the application of gravy. The television set, the latest black and white model, was a gift of the government . . . The most valuable object in the apartment seemed to be the telephone. It was covered with dust and disconnected, but all the same it had symbolic value.[2]

Between the long sessions of the debriefing, Philby and his inquisitors took long walks through the slush to inspect the monuments of socialism. During this time Philby acquired a guidebook from his minder, although it was forbidden. It was still on Philby's shelves, small, well printed and illustrated, but with no information about metro stations, bus stations, cab ranks — nothing that would enable a man on the run to get to the British Embassy. The introduction is marked with a pencil:

> The sun has been rising over Moscow for more than 800 years now. The city is built on seven hills, one of which is encircled by a crenel-lated red wall. The Kremlin stands atop this hill. Its walls curve slightly, and their outline resembles a human heart. Everything here speaks of the nation's glorious past, and everything testifies to the strength and vitality of its people today.[3]

Philby embraced his new capital in this spirit. But when he learned that there was to be no post for him at the KGB, that spirit withered soon enough. He was to become a pensioner with a tax-free monthly salary of eight hundred rubles a month. The reason for his rejection was the same as SIS's or the CIA's would have been had a Russian asked for a staff position at headquarters: he had to be Russian born and bred in all four quarters of his antecedents. So he found himself instead in what a KGB officer called "a golden cage." These were again dangerous times; nuclear war had been only just averted over the Cuban missile crisis the previous October, and the KGB was locked in battles for primacy in every part of the world.

Under Semichastny, the KGB officer responsible for Philby was a certain Budanov, whom a senior KGB officer, Oleg Gordievsky, would remember as "one of the most sinister KGB officers he ever met."[4] Budanov was concerned mainly with the security of the First Main Direc-torate in Russia and in foreign parts; he had day-to-day control of Philby's life and freedom. Under Budanov and his successors, Philby's status remained that of a spy — what the KGB classified as "a secret collaborator" — not as a Soviet intelligence officer, as Philby always thought of himself. And in this matter of rank lay a source of Philby's disaffection with the Soviet system. He had been tricked by his earliest case officer, Arnold Deutsch, into believing that he was an *officer* of the Soviet government, not an agent, which offended his pride of rank.

Gradually the debriefing came to an end, and Philby and his minder began to seek a permanent residence for him. He was offered a num-ber of apartments and houses appropriate to his new station in life, but these he rejected for a four-room apartment on a narrow lane in a hauntingly attractive part of Old Moscow near Pushkin Square, one of the livelier areas of the Russian capital. This was important, for as a KGB officer who became a friend, Mikhail Lyubimov, pointed out, there were many areas where, if you lived there, "you would commit suicide — you know, dark, no people, no bars."[5] His flat was on the eighth floor of the old building in Patriarch's Pond, and it could be reached only by the elevator or the stairs. The area had changed little since the time of Tsar Nicholas II, when it was a quiet and fashionable upper-middle-class area twenty minutes from the Kremlin. Now, forty-four years after Lenin's revolution, it had become decrepit, although it was exceedingly pretty under a fresh snow and charming in the spring, when the trees were out and the flowers were in bloom. From Pushkin Square, the building was approached by a warren of narrow and barely lit streets; an alley separated it from an oratory set behind a low wall surrounded by a lawn and the lovely Muscovy plane trees.

Not more than two people could walk along the alley abreast without bumping into those coming the other way; to enter the building, a visitor went down a narrow flight of brick stairs, pushed through a wooden door and felt along bare concrete walls to a push-button elevator. This stopped seven and a half floors up, and the caller then walked perhaps fifteen steps to Philby's padded-leather door. There was a rear service passage, but the building was not easily approached by an unwanted visitor, and it was impossible for Philby to come or go if the place was being watched. If the watchers had a radio, Philby would not have been able to get twenty yards without being stopped. His Russian female servant was a KGB informant. His telephone was tapped, and there were street eyes to watch him everywhere he went, day and night, for the next decade. As Lyubimov, one of the eight or nine KGB officers later allowed to associate with Philby, asserted, at this time there was not a minute of the day when he was not watched or heard. The only reason he was accepted at all was that "Kim had things to offer. Was he not a friend of Angleton of the CIA? Was he not a tremendous propaganda prize — a Scholar of Trinity, an English gentleman, a senior officer of the British Secret Service. A man of Westminster who had come voluntarily to Patriarch's Pond to continue the work of Marx!"[6]

From the day of his arrival, his status in Muscovy society was that of a member of the *nomenklatura,* the elite of the official class, comparable to an Old Bolshevik, a general, a personage at the Central Committee, a member of the upper managerial class. The *nomenklatura,* it has been explained,

> is another planet. It's Mars. It's not simply a matter of good cars or apartments. It's the continuous satisfaction of your own whims. Your every wish is fulfilled. You can go to a theater on a whim. No, you

don't own a yacht or spend your vacations on the Côte d'Azure, but you are at the Black Sea, and that really is something.[7]

The KGB builders were sent in to make an English fireplace in the sitting room so that Philby might feel "at home." The KGB plasterers, painters, and carpenters arrived. Instructions were sent to the Soviet Embassy in Beirut to ship his furniture and his books and gramophone records. While settling in at Patriarch's Pond, Philby had a reminder of Tomas Harris and his wonderful parties during the war. A year almost to the day after Philby's arrival and three months before Anthony Blunt, the queen's picture master, was offered immunity from prosecution, Harris was killed while driving his new, powerful Citroën toward his villa in Majorca. An investigation showed that his death was entirely accidental. But Tomas and Philby had quarreled badly not long before Philby's disappearance, and as an observer of intelligence history noted:

> Of the very few Allied intelligence officers who were allowed to learn Garbo's full story, it is extraordinary that at least two, Kim Philby and Anthony Blunt, should have turned out to be very senior Russian spies. The fact that Tommy Harris, the genius who masterminded the operation, should have been killed in such circumstances and at such a time is remarkable.[8]

It brought to mind Krivitsky's warning to his friends that there was a saying at the KGB: "Any fool can commit a murder, but it takes an artist to commit a natural death." To the end of his days, Philby's chief personal wish was that he could have made his peace with Harris before his death.

At Patriarch's Pond, the carpet was laid, the lighting and the linen arrived. A KGB engineer appeared with the telephone; the apartment was bugged throughout; bookshelves were built in the hall and the study and pictures were hung — a portrait of Lenin, of his father in full Arabian robes, and, later, of Che Guevara, Fidel Castro's first lieutenant. Lyubimov thought Philby chose this humble but quite charming apartment because it "more suited, one might say, his standards of how the intelligentsia of Russia should live." Philby himself liked the apartment. As he wrote to a family member in London in a letter that was intercepted by the CIA, he had "a comfortable four-room flat with all mod. con. (washing machine, bread slicer, huge television believe it or not! etc.)" It was not Albany. As to his pension, Lyubimov thought it to be "that of a tsarist prince."

Here Philby remained for the next twenty-five years, the rest of his life. He had few friends outside the intelligence business, which was really the only one that interested him. He was "a rather refined, a rather spiritual man, who did not like the world of the *nomenklatura*, with its unending boredom, large wardrobes, the coffee sessions, the large armchairs, the uniform furniture — places that had no flavor of an individual [other] than the uniformity of the party functionary."[9] Over his table was a picture of the Tower of London as seen from the river — the scene of Traitors' Gate.

But he was still alone, desperately alone. He could not leave the apartment without first calling his control. Once he tried to get a haircut at the Marco Polo around the corner. He was arrested by the two thugs who forever lurked in the shadows near the oratory. He could travel where he wished in the Soviet empire, but only with an escort after the arrangements had been made by the KGB travel office. The KGB arranged his visits to restaurants, the theater, the cinema. He acquired a furnished country cottage for weekends but always denied that he had one, believing that a dacha was bourgeois. When he wished for the cure, he was whisked off in a KGB limousine with curtains to the Semenskoya clinic, just outside Moscow. Here he was given four rooms with a TV, a colonel's suite. The clinic had a swimming pool, a large dining room with a special table for him, a medical staff that checked his heart and lungs. The kitchen provided a special diet when ordered. It had a dairy, and the food came from the state farm — milk fresh from the cow, and chicken killed in the morning and served in the evening. There was the balalaika in the evening. But his loneliness remained unendurable.

Philby undoubtedly lived well, much better than a pensioner with the British Secret Service. The only thing he could not be given was the freedom to do what he wished at any hour of the day or night. Above all, there was no *Times*. He may or may not have wished to see Guy Burgess, whom he often referred to as "that bloody man Burgess." Philby never forgave Burgess for defecting with Maclean despite Kim's orders not to do so. But Burgess had done so, thereby exposing Kim and wrecking his career. Burgess had developed angina and lived on nitroglycerine. He had liver trouble, hardening of the arteries, collapses through diabetes, and a general sense that life in Russia was not worth living. Now known as Jim Andreyvitch Eliot — Jim after the miner's son he had loved at Trinity, Andreyvitch after the character in *War and Peace,* and Eliot after the great novelist whose *Middlemarch* had remained a favorite — he lived with a Soviet lover provided by the KGB, a plumber by trade. He was greatly distrusted by the KGB, whose officers had been warned to have nothing to do with him. "He behaved so badly," his old controller, Yuri Modin, remembered wearily.[10] He wished only to return to St. James's, and sent a telegram to Harold Macmillan, asking to be allowed to do so, when the prime minister came calling on Khrushchev in February 1959. The attorney general advised that there were no grounds on which Burgess could be prosecuted, should he choose to return, but the government did not want him back, and Macmillan was advised to delay his reply until the last moment. Then he should say that neither the government nor the Conservative Party had the means to grant him the safe conduct for which he had asked. In that way "we may succeed in creating in his mind such doubt about the possible consequences of returning to this country that he will decide to stay where he is. This would be the most satisfactory outcome."[11] So it proved to be. There was another menacing fizz in the press, but it passed.

Burgess died in Botkin Hospital in Moscow on August 19, 1963. He is said to have denounced Philby to the KGB as still being a British secret agent. Nonetheless, in his will Burgess left much of his library, some furnishings, and £2,000 of his £6,000 capital to Philby. Philby accepted these bequests and sent the money to help provide for his five children. In the will Burgess also expressed the desire that his ashes be interred at the grave of his parents, in West Meon, Hampshire. This wish was duly carried out.

As to Philby's legal status — the Supreme Soviet granted Philby citizenship under Article 129 of the Constitution and Fundamental Law of the Union of Soviet Socialist Republics: "The USSR affords the right of asylum to foreign citizens persecuted for defending the interests of the working people, or for their scientific activities, or for their struggle for national liberation." He now enjoyed the right to work, annual vacations with full pay, free medical service, an old-age pension, equality of rights "in all spheres of economic, state, cultural, social and political life," a guarantee of the "inviolability of the person, the home, and correspondence." He accepted the obligation "to observe the laws, to maintain labor discipline, honestly to perform public duties, and to respect the rules of socialist intercourse."

In his work for the KGB as an adviser on Western affairs, Philby was available to the heads of all KGB branches, subject to the assent of Budanov, but his main "customers" were the counterespionage services and the Active Measures, or political warfare department. This last was run by a famous character, an Armenian Bolshevik called Ivan Ivanovich Agayants. He was in his late thirties and spoke English,

French, and Persian; his colleagues regarded him as "a prince, kind, cultured, courteous, charming."[12] Philby rarely if ever saw the chiefs of these departments personally; he acted through a liaison officer whom he usually met at Philby's flat. He was not allowed to visit any KGB installation without invitation, which was not forthcoming for many years. Colonel Gennady X, who served as the Active Measures liaison officer with Philby for a decade and became one of his closest KGB associates, defined Active Measures as:

> an intelligence means directed at influencing the foreign policy of target states, and carrying out the foreign policy goals of the Soviet Union. These were intended to strengthen peaceful coexistence between the Soviet Union and foreign powers; strengthening the national liberation struggles around the world as well as strengthening the influence of democratic power around the world.[13]

And as Mikhail Lyubimov would write in 1990 of Philby's professional life: "To the end of his days he remained an indispensable advisor and expert, his intellect and knowledge were highly prized, in the service he was respected, and we went as far as possible to give him a more or less comfortable life."[14] But there was, Lyubimov added, "always that other side of his head, his political thoughts, and these were not always understood by the KGB management. These served to increase the suspicions of him as a foreign communist and made his life unendurable at times."[15]

Very gradually the KGB made out of him a political icon, and the process served to fireproof him against ordinary wear. The only desire that remained unfulfilled was for a woman in his life. Again, the KGB management accommodated him. Arrangements were made for him to be reunited with Eleanor, and his children would be allowed to visit him. Given the immensity of the KGB's campaign against the West, and Philby's part in it, it is surprising that Budanov, a hard case, sanctioned this, for Eleanor may have had connections with the enemy intelligence services. But perhaps he had no choice if he was to keep his most famous agent content. Thus Eleanor became a witness to Philby's work, the comings and goings of KGB officers at Patriarch's Pond.

To return to that fateful night in Beirut, when Philby did not appear at the Balfour-Pauls' dinner party, Eleanor's first reaction was to fear that he had been drinking at the St. George and that, since the waterfront had been badly damaged by the storm, he had fallen and been washed out to sea. But there was also the possibility that he had left

Beirut in the pursuit of a scoop. Miles Copeland, who helped her in her search, did consider the possibility that Kim had fled. Accordingly he warned the chiefs of the CIA and SIS stations. Telegrams were sent to Washington and London and Sir Dick White, at the SIS, was informed of Philby's disappearance during the night of January 23–24, 1963. A bulletin went out to the secret intelligence and security authorities everywhere, including the CIA. Angleton was so incapacitated by the news that he sent his wife to the Maryland home of Dr. Mann. Mrs. Angleton told him that her husband had had "a terrible shock"; indeed, it seems one from which he did not recover.[16]

The warning that Philby was missing was waiting for the CIA staff when they came on duty early on the morning of January 24. A signal from SIS announced that Philby had disappeared and might have gone to Kenya, where, so SIS reported, the Philby family owned a coffee plantation. Would the CIA kindly assist in the search for him? A task force was formed by Gordon Torrie, the chief of the Arab States and Israel desk, to examine all telegrams that might have a bearing on Philby's disappearance. Torrie worked on the case for six weeks but found not a trace of Philby's whereabouts — a testament to the effectiveness of the Soviet escape and evasion system. The incoming reports, Torrie remembered, resembled those of the French at the time of the Scarlet Pimpernel: "I see him here, I see him there, I see him everywhere, that damned elusive Pimpernel!"[17]

In London, Macmillan's damage control apparatus was again deployed to keep the news out of the press for as long as possible. A British correspondent who had been at the Balfour-Pauls' dinner party and was aware of Philby's disappearance sent a dispatch to her newspaper in London, but it did not appear. The *Beirut Daily Star* reported the fact of Philby's disappearance. Some correspondents did send dispatches to London and New York based on that report, or partly so, but they were not printed, perhaps because no one knew where he had gone, or indeed that he had gone anywhere. It was possible that he was dead, murdered perhaps, that he was in Cairo, in Damascus, in Riyadh, in Baghdad, in Istanbul.

The British secret circle knew well enough that he might have gone to Moscow, but Nicholas Elliott returned to Beirut to interview Eleanor and put the British press on notice that, in the national interest, they keep their knowledge to themselves. In this he succeeded. Torrie concluded that the SIS had aided and abetted Philby's escape and had pointed the CIA in the direction of Kenya to set it in the opposite direction. Torrie suspected, accurately, as it turned out, that Philby had left Beirut aboard a Soviet ship. Eleanor Philby continued with

Miles Copeland to comb Beirut. Friends and police searched the night-club and hotel district. One couple drove out to an Armenian shanty-town to the north to call at a restaurant Kim frequented. But neither the police nor Philby's friends found any trace of him.

Among the searchers was James Russell Barracks, the CIA agent who had been watching Philby to ensure that he did not do what he had just done — escape. He interrogated some of the regulars and the staff at the St. George and, according to one of them, "exhaled a deep sigh of frustration" and asked, "How the hell did he do it? How did he get away?"[18] Not long afterward, Barracks himself left Beirut and reap-peared as a chicken farmer in Kaduna, in Nigeria, where on Christmas Day of 1964, about twenty-two months after Philby vanished, he died of, it was stated officially, penicillin poisoning. Said abu Ris, a Pales-tinian journalist who hung out at the St. George, claimed that Barracks was murdered, the implication being that he had been killed by the KGB at Philby's request.

There is no evidence that this was so. His body was examined after death and was shipped to Urbana, Illinois, his home town, accompa-nied by an official who said he represented the State Department. The funeral director thought at the time, and afterward, that "there was something obscure about the cause of Barracks's untimely death — he was only forty-one."[19]

Barracks had never married, and his only survivors were his parents. They paid the funeral expenses, although the air shipment of the body from Nigeria appeared from records to have been arranged by the State Department. Someone placed a brief death notice in the local paper and at the library, but otherwise Barracks's death attracted no attention. The speculation about the cause of death soon died down, although the thought that he had been murdered persisted in the town and was still to be heard as late as 1993. The thought is permis-sible that Kim, to settle an old score over the telephone campaign against him, arranged Barracks's death with the KGB on his arrival in Moscow. He was vindictive enough by nature. In a letter to Eleanor, he referred to the "inhuman livestock" in Beirut. But we shall never know the truth. A secret agent was dead, and he took with him much infor-mation about Philby that might otherwise have reached the public.

Eleanor Philby received the first intimation that her husband was still alive three days after he vanished, when she received a letter posted in Cairo without a stamp on the day of his disappearance. It was in Philby's handwriting and was undated. It said only: "I will be in touch with you soon and everything will be all right. Keep smiling and go to your sculpture classes at the American University like a good

girl. Tell my colleagues I'm on a long tour of the area."[20] He then told
Eleanor to look in a Bible on his shelves and to find the key to his
strongbox in the top drawer of his desk. There was nothing in the
Bible, but in Richard Burton's *Arabian Nights*, next to it, were $300
worth of Lebanese banknotes, the rent. This he had paid quarterly,
and it was now just past due. The strongbox held personal documents
relating to the family, but nothing of interest to Eleanor, nor was there
anything in his desk. However, when she looked at Philby's cable file,
Eleanor found a "fat little package" containing more money, a gold
bracelet, and a typed message: "For the sari, my adored beloved."
Philby had bought her a length of silk in Aden, and the money was
for her dressmaker to make it into a dress.

These discoveries were followed by a long period of silence in which
the wildest rumors about the disappearance flew about Beirut. But the
escape had been very carefully planned and executed, and — on the
chance Eleanor was in the hands of the British and American intelligence services — Kim went to lengths in his letters to indicate that he
was still in the Middle East at work on a major story.

Then on February 4, a further letter reached Eleanor. It bore no
address or date.

> My darling beloved,
>
> I should have written you sooner, and am feeling very contrite —
> especially as I see in the Beirut press some nonsense about my "dis-
> appearance." As you see, I am very much all here, haunted only by
> the suspicion that I'm putting on weight and thereby becoming less
> desirable in your eyes. Anyway, I can assure you that I have no inten-
> tion of "disappearing" from your life for many years yet!!
>
> I am kicking myself for having left so suddenly. I have managed to
> replace most of the essentials — comb, toothbrush, etc. The only
> bother is the lack of reading-glasses, which is trifling and temporary.
> (I hope you can read this better than I can!) I shall let you know my
> plans in fuller detail very soon. So chins up, and keep a pretty smile
> on your face.
>
> Give all my girl friends a kiss and lots of love to the other livestock,
> human and inhuman. Have yourself a nice time and do your lessons
> properly at school!
>
> Do you remember the first cable I ever sent you: "Constant thoughts,
> deepest love." They are still with you, more constant and deeper
> than ever.
>
> Happiness, darling, from your
> Kim[21]

Another letter arrived in mid-February, this one bearing a Syrian post-mark. Kim wrote that he was "trying to hurry up with my work as quickly as possible to cut short the period of separation from you," but that there was "no point in skimping matters at this stage." It would be "wonderful when it is all over and done with." He tried also to make it seem that their separation was due to journalism, for he ended this letter: "By the way, I would like my scoop to be really exclusive, so please don't let any of my colleagues know where this letter comes from. In fact, there is no real point in them knowing anything at all about it, is there? All love again, K."[22]

Prime Minister Macmillan was first informed on or about February 19, 1963, twenty-seven days after Philby's disappearance. He referred to it in his diary as "almost historic" and added:

> We think we have at last solved the mystery of who "tipped" off Burgess and Maclean. It was a man, much suspected at the time, but against whom nothing could be proved — one Philby. He was dis-missed in 1951 from the service and has lived since in the Middle East, chiefly in the the Lebanon, where he writes for the *Observer* and the *Economist!* In a drunken fit, he confessed everything to one of our men, so the whole thing is now clear. Maclean and Burgess were worse than mere *defectors* — they were spies, paid by the Russians, over quite a number of years. This man Philby seduced them and recruited them to the Russian service. He has now disappeared from Beirut, leaving £2,200 in cash for his wife. Whether he will appear in Russia or not, we do not know. Anyway, it means more trouble.[23]

Macmillan was wrong in the detail but right in the fact that there would be "more trouble" — trouble that helped to wreck his ministry and led him to "wonder whether all this game of espionage or counter-espionage is worth the candle." The reference to "this game" suggests that Philby was part of it. Having spoken confidentially to Nicholas Elliot, Patrick Seale of *The Observer* wrote when he arrived in Beirut to replace the missing Philby:

> Both East and West have built him up as the man who made monkeys of the British not once but twice, penetrated to the heart of their secret service, lived a double life for three decades — only to escape in the nick of time to comfortable retirement in Moscow. This sum-mary needs as much correction as the popular estimate of his char-acter. There are some grounds for believing that Philby was pawn as well as player, exploited as well as exploiter in his silent war, and that in the end he was allowed to "escape" to Russia — a poisoned gift sent by Britain to the KGB in an eleventh-hour attempt to limit the

damage of his long betrayal. The question of who won and who lost in any intelligence operation is always a ticklish one, and not less so in drawing up the balance sheet in the Philby dossier.[24]

On March 2, Eleanor received a telegram in which Philby used words reserved for the cables he sent each year to Eleanor on their wedding anniversary. It had been handed in at a Cairo post office at 3:38 A.M. on March 1, the signature was "H. Philby," and his address was given as the Continental Hotel, Cairo, where he usually stayed when he was in the Egyptian capital — and where, only shortly before his disappearance, his leather briefcase, still embossed with the letters H.M.G., was found. The briefcase was empty except for his airline credit card from the International Air Transport Association (IATA) at Montreal. A check there rendered the hunters with the hunted's entire itinerary in the Middle East since the card was issued in 1956.

The telegram had been handed in by a street Arab who told how a stranger had approached him and asked him to take it to the post office and had given him two shillings. The signature was not in Kim's hand, but the sentiments and words were his: FONDEST LOVE DEEPEST THOUGHTS HAPPY ANNIVERSARY ARRANGEMENTS FOR REUNION PROCEEDING.

By then Philby's bank accounts had been frozen, by whom it is not clear, and Eleanor found herself without money. She was forced to go to the U.S. Embassy as a "distressed American citizen." She found cold comfort at the hands of the U.S. ambassador, Amin Meyer, who supported her from embassy funds but threatened to terminate that help unless she "came clean" about Philby and his disappearance. Her distress was, however, of limited duration, for, by her own account, she recalled Kim's mention of a strongbox of his in the care of the British consul in Beirut. There she went, and sure enough, there was such a box, containing "a cache of dollar bills, hidden in the base of the box." Eleanor was therefore now well funded and no longer felt the need for the ambassador's subvention.

Here the case rested until in mid-April an untidy man appeared at Eleanor's door, thrust a large envelope into her hand, and made off down the stairs. Eleanor took the package into the bathroom and locked the door to read what she called Kim's "long, three-page letter, typewritten and composed in his characteristic, elegantly modulated style." Philby asked Eleanor to memorize the letter and then burn it in the bathroom water heater, carefully stirring up the ashes. It instructed her to go to the Czech Airlines office in Beirut and book a seat on a plane to Prague. Then she was to go to an alley near the apartment and write in chalk high up on a wall the date and time of the flight departure. If she encountered difficulties of any kind, she was to chalk the letter X up on the same wall. The chalk *must* be white and she *must* choose the date at least ten days before departure. Kim also warned, according to Eleanor,

> that a very dear and close friend of his would call on her shortly. He was a very able man. He had great powers at his command. He could do anything for me. I was to trust him completely. Kim suggested that I might recognize this man, but that, in any event, he would bring with him as a means of identification a book token which I had given Kim as a birthday present three weeks earlier.[25]

Throughout this period, with Nicholas Elliott still in the city, Eleanor decided against visiting Czech Airlines, as she felt that she was under surveillance by all manner of people, including the press. This made obedience to Philby's instructions difficult and dangerous. But the major obstacle to any plans — whether she would fly west or east — was that Harry George, Kim's youngest son, had been born in Washington, D.C., his father in India, his grandfather in Ceylon, and his great-grandfather in Burma. What was the boy's nationality? Harry George had been traveling on Philby's passport, but now that was impossible. The British passport officials at Beirut seemed determined to allow Eleanor to take the children only directly to London, with no stops anywhere.

At length, Eleanor accepted this; she crept down to the alley at three o'clock in the morning and put a white X on the wall to indicate that she was in trouble. About a week before her departure with the children for London, some sixteen weeks after Kim's disappearance, Eleanor's doorbell was rung at about 7:30 A.M.; the children had left for school and the maid had not yet arrived. "I'm from Kim," the stranger whispered. He had come to see Kim "a few years earlier" and had then introduced himself as the Far Eastern correspondent of a German news agency. He was tall, with a thick neck and blue eyes. "Kim's just fine," he said. "He sends his love. He wants you to join him. I'm here to help you." Eleanor told him that she could not go to Prague, for she would not get within a hundred yards of the Czech Airlines offices. The man insisted that she at least go with him to get some money, but she refused. He shrugged his shoulders and disappeared down the stairs.

On May 31, Eleanor and the two children left Beirut for London aboard a British Airways propjet, a large, comfortable, and comforting aircraft, where she and the children had a first-class compartment to themselves. They arrived in London on the hottest day of the year — 104 degrees — and stayed with Kim's sister Patricia. Soon Eleanor met with C, Goldsmith White. When she started to defend her man and argue that Kim had been kidnapped, White responded in a kindly but terse fashion that "we have definitely known for the last seven years that Kim has been working for the Russians without pay."[26] That meant C had known that Philby had been a Soviet agent at least since 1956, the year Philby was allowed to leave Britain and go out to Beirut as a correspondent and at least a part-time spy for the British service. C declined to offer any further information about what the British services had known of Kim before that date, but by the end of their talk, Eleanor had no doubt that Kim had been a Soviet secret agent for a long time. Despite that knowledge, she took steps to go to Philby in Moscow.

On September 25, 1963, Eleanor went to the Soviet consul in London, gave her calling card to a doorman, and was immediately ushered into a room where a man behind a desk

> rose courteously and said that he was very pleased to see me. He said he knew all about me. "We have heard that you want to go to Russia." I said, "Yes." "When would you like to go?" he then asked. I told him in three or four days as I had some shopping to do, and one or two other things to attend to. He said: "We should like you to be ready the day after tomorrow." I was rather taken aback and asked whether such speed was necessary. He said it was.
>
> I was to be at London Airport on September 27th at exactly eleven o'clock. There would be somebody there to meet me who would take care of everything. I should worry about nothing. Then he opened a drawer of his desk, took out an envelope and handed it to me. "Go buy yourself some very warm clothes."
>
> In the envelope I found £500 in notes. I went immediately to Harrods.

Just before nightfall on September 27, Eleanor Philby arrived in Moscow aboard an Aeroflot jet and disembarked in a remote part of the airport. As she stood on the tarmac, she heard a familiar voice call, "Eleanor, is that you?"[27]

The political and social consequences of Philby's disappearance were serious and became more so as the government's damage control broke down. For six months there was only rumor and speculation in the press, but the case broke at a most embarrassing time for Macmillan — on July 1, 1963, almost immediately after President John F. Kennedy had visited him informally in an effort to patch up the damage to the Anglo-American alliance caused by the Suez incident and by CIA and FBI concerns about the possibility that the KGB had effected other very high-level penetrations in Whitehall. Kennedy and Macmillan reached an important degree of renewed confidence when — bang! — the official newspaper of the Soviet government, *Izvestia*, ran an article entitled "Hello, Mr Philby!" It was a sketch of Philby in Pushkin Square and of the admiring welcome of him into Soviet society. In the middle of the month the Soviet government announced it had granted citizenship to H.A.R. Philby, although the legal papers were in Philby's spy name in Moscow, Andrew Marpunc. These statements served as the match placed to the tinder.

The Foreign Office then made its first announcement. Philby — the Foreign Office official whom Macmillan had cleared in Parliament eight years before of a grave charge that he was a Russian secret agent — was now known to have been a Soviet agent since 1946. He had become a citizen of the Soviet Union. To head off an outcry, the Lord Privy Seal, a stately office whose functions were known only vaguely, if at all, to the electorate, made a meaningless statement, evidently to quiet those who knew, or guessed, that Philby had been taken back into the Secret Service. The Lord Privy Seal's statement was to the effect that Philby had not had access to secret papers of state for many years.

A little later, Philby himself surfaced in Moscow and made a queer statement regarding his treason to a London newspaper correspondent:

> I regard myself as wholly and irreversibly English and England as having been perhaps the most fertile patch of earth in the whole history of human ideas.

His conspiracy, he said, had been against "certain temporary phenomena" that had prevented England from being herself. What those phenomena were, Philby did not say, but by implication he seemed to point at imperialism and capitalism, especially in the United States.

Somewhat later, in a statement to the *Sunday Times*, he repudiated this statement. To betray, a man must belong. He had not belonged to England or the empire. If he had belonged anywhere, it was to India, where he was born, or the Middle East, where his father had spent most of his life. Philby agreed that his conduct had appeared treacherous to those brought up under the canons of Queen Victoria and Edward VII, but, he argued, these were not his canons. The canons of his life had been, as they were still, "the fight against fascism and the fight against imperialism. Both are, fundamentally, the same fight."[28] Philby now went silent, more or less completely, for more than a decade. The same could not be said for the London press, indeed the world press.

There was a new generation of editors in Fleet Street, and they were avid to nail someone in the government, someone with a title, a double-barreled name, or a member of the Establishment. They were after the government, a dying aristocracy. The Lord Privy Seal's statement produced a new and vigorous storm in the press — what the Foreign Office called a bullfrogs' chorus: "one croaks, all croak." It was known widely that Philby had been the correspondent of the *The Observer* and *The Economist* between his exoneration and his disappearance; some knew or suspected that he had been admitted back into the British Secret Service and had been in its service when he vanished. Macmillan had a difficult time in the Commons and in his own Cabinet, and he wrote in his diary on July 11: "A very long Cabinet 10.30–1.30. The 'Philby' Case has been very difficult, chiefly because of the problem of answering the questions asked by the Press and Public without injuring and even hamstringing the work of the Secret Service" — a statement that clearly indicated there had been some tricky business in the Philby case. There was, too, a "deeply shocked public" which "do not know and cannot be told that he belonged to MI6, an organization which does not theoretically exist."[29]

In the hope that the principle "least said, soonest mended" might yet apply and save himself from yet another uproar in the House, the prime minister took aside the leader of the opposition, Harold Wilson and, he wrote in his diary, "tried to explain to him how the so-called Security Services really worked. [It] seemed to me right to do so." After the debate in the House, the prime minister wrote of "Wilson's high sense of responsibility" at a period "when I was very hard-pressed." Wilson continued to press matters, cornered Macmillan, and forced him to make a move that he would not otherwise have made in the Philby case. Macmillan invited Wilson to a confidential meeting with C, Dick White. Wilson was awestruck at being made, he believed, an "intelligence insider," and he was still awestruck thirteen years later when he wrote in his memoirs:

> I asked to see Macmillan [about the Philby case]. He was accompanied by the head of [the Secret Service] whom the Prime Minister

asked to tell me the whole facts. While what was public knowledge could not have justified the manifest failure of the Secret Service to keep Philby under control, one simple fact I was given made sense of the story. I was satisfied and felt it my duty to say so in the House without giving any reason, and to ask my Hon[orable] Friends to let it go. (I was promptly criticised in the press for gagging my backbenchers.)[30]

What White told Wilson has never been revealed, if indeed he told him anything of importance other than that the country was under a severe intelligence attack by the Russians. Wilson's text indicates that an attempt had been made to use Philby as a spy against the Soviet Union. Macmillan then went before the House again and stated only: "I hope the House will accept that it would not be in the national interest for Hon. Members to inquire any further into the past history of the case."

But one member was not to be diverted: Niall MacDermot, one of the backbenchers whom Wilson had "reined in" and who had found the experience uncongenial. A lawyer with a Secret Service background, MacDermot had met Philby during World War II in the company of White, then a high officer of the wartime Security Service. What MacDermot had to say cast doubt on the objectivity of White: "Dick White was thrilled by Philby and thought he was wonderful. He introduced me to him . . . he told me how brilliant he was and what a pity he wasn't the head of section, he was so able. Philby, I remember, had a very strong personality. He was intelligent, charming."[31]

MacDermot alleged that "the most serious aspect of the matter [is] the position then held by [Philby]." Aware that the root matter of the case might now be exposed, Macmillan asked the House to support his view "that we should not discuss some of these aspects of our national functions." Wilson then rose and said that in two meetings with Macmillan he had been given "a very full and frank account of this case which raises a number of issues which frankly cannot be discussed across the floor of this House." The case should "now be left where it is." This statement was printed in the press and in *Hansard*, the official record of parliamentary proceedings.

The case was not left where it was. There was great disquiet as it emerged, very slowly and over a long period, that Whitehall harbored many spies in high places. Macmillan had found it necessary to state in Parliament on November 14, 1962, that "I feel it right to warn the House hostile intrigue and espionage are being relentlessly maintained on a very large scale." Nothing had occurred to show that the situation had been changed for the better. Bit by bit, so it appeared at the time, and so it may have been, the Russians leaked a name or some facts in order to stimulate the press into more hysteria. The Pickwickian Mikhail Lyubimov of the KGB saw the bullfrogs' chorus from the inside, for he was at that time the Russian Embassy's eyes and ears in the Conservative Party, where, curiously, he claimed, he found himself quite a popular figure — until cheekily he tried to suborn the chief British code-breaker, Sir Clive Loehnis, in a London pub. It was a trap, and Lyubimov, who until then believed that the British Secret Services were staffed by English gentlemen, encountered another type, burly hearties of the Watchers' Service of MI5.

Lyubimov was declared persona non grata, but for reasons known only to the Foreign Office he was allowed to remain in England for a further six months before he was eventually escorted to the airport and deportation. He therefore saw the mist procession that so disquieted Macmillan, the Edwardian who viewed foreign spies with distaste. There was Vassall, the epicene Admiralty clerk; Lonsdale, a mysterious Russian who was found because he showed himself to have been circumcised when the prepuce of the man he said he was had never been removed; Peter and Helen Kroger, the friends of the Rosenbergs, who had been executed for espionage in a U.S. electric chair; the tragic Miss Fell, who had lost her heart to a Yugoslav communist spy; the implication of two junior ministers of the crown, one of whom "had suffered a socially pressing and plausible junior colleague a trifle too gladly," the colleague being Vassall. The litany goes on: Sir Anthony Blunt, the Queen's Picturemaster, a member of the Cambridge Five, who confessed all and was granted immunity and retained both his title and his place at Buckingham Palace; the mysterious "Peters," the deputy chief of the Security Service, who had been spotted, according to Macmillan's diary, "wandering around the loos in the park, passing things, probably opium or something"; when the case against "Peters" came apart, suspicion fell on the chief of the Security Service, Sir Roger Hollis, who was, a writer observed, "James Bond's chief, for God's sake." Then there was the secretary of state for war, John Profumo, and his relationship with Christine Keeler during a naked frolic at Lord Astor's swimming pool at Cliveden; Stephen Ward, Miss Keeler's "manager"; Captain Evgeny Ivanov, the Soviet naval attaché in London, and his frolics with Miss Keeler; Mandy Rice-Davies, the beautiful strumpet, and her relationship with everyone; the trial of Johnny Edgecombe, Miss Keeler's West Indian lover and a marijuana pusher by trade; "Lucky" Gordon, another West Indian lover, and his wounding of Miss Keeler in the street; Profumo's lie to the prime minister *and* Parliament that he was not in any way involved with Miss Keeler.

Macmillan said in his statement to Parliament that "all these people move in a raffish, theatrical bohemian society, where no one really knows anyone and everyone is 'darling'"; he described Ward as a "pimp" and then a suicide.

London society, once so elegant, was rent with scandal, and 1963 became the juiciest year for sex and spies. Sir William Haley, the editor of *The Times,* "the newspaper for top people," declared that "eleven years of Conservative rule have brought the nation psychologically and spiritually to a low ebb"; in a debate in the House, Wilson spoke of matters "without precedent in the annals of the House"; Ambassador David Bruce, of the United States, advised the Kennedy government that "the Macmillan government was mortally wounded"; Macmillan wrote to Queen Elizabeth of the existence of "a strange underworld" in which John Profumo, the keeper of the atomic bombs, had allowed himself to become "entrapped" in sexual scandal. He said in the same letter that he had seen "something in the nature of a plot to destroy the established system." Macmillan, failing fast, made a speech: every man in government was required by the code to "behave like an officer and a gentleman."

The new inquisitor emerged, Peter Wright of MI5, to defend the established order. Cleveland Cram, the CIA counterintelligence officer in London, found him to be "a top line man," with a large, Old Testament, patriarchal red face that was "generally rather flushed." He spoke with "a combination of stammer and lisp" and possessed a "very disciplined mind." He began to root out those in the secret circle who had been close to Philby. One was Andrew Ivan King, who had played a part with Philby in providing, with the authority of Sir Stewart Menzies, the old C, a Soviet espionage network in Switzerland with ISOS, the counterespionage decrypts of German intelligence signals about communist underground operations throughout Europe during World War II. Another was Tim Milne, Philby's friend at Westminster and companion on his motorcycle trips to meet the European proletariat, who had been the deputy for much of Philby's career in counterespionage, except for the Beirut phase. Milne was withdrawn as chief of station in Hong Kong and retired from the service with a sinecure, clerk to the House of Lords. He had been a main defender of Philby during the troubles of 1951 to 1963 and part of the anti-CIA school in SIS, "but a nice, well-mannered man. It was a tragic end to Milne's career." Christopher Robin himself had failed to defend the established order against foreign orders, and so, it is said, he was betrayed by Philby to the Security Service directly from Patriarch's Pond.

The investigations, the discoveries, the scandals, went on and on and on, and they had still not entirely died out thirty years after their outbreak in 1963. These events, combined with the still-sputtering menace of the Philby case and the implications of others, left Macmillan exhausted. He had only recently been directly and deeply involved with President Kennedy in the Cuban missile crisis, and recalled in his memoirs:

> I had been engaged in facing what seemed the opening phase of a Third World War, involving not merely the intellectual strain of constant talks with President Kennedy, but the physical disadvantage of scarcely sleeping more than one or two hours each night. Yet, so strangely is the human brain constituted, this terrible danger seemed to distress me less than the personal and human anxieties.
>
> I do not remember a more worrying time — and so wasteful of effort. I would have done better to have had a Judicial Enquiry of some kind at the start. Had I known all this mud would be thrown about, I would have done so. But we cannot have a tribunal every time we catch a spy. Now that the net is closing, we shall probably have some more cases. The public does not regard the catching of a spy as a success, but as a failure.[32]

Macmillan further recorded: "By an extraordinary combination of circumstances or an exceptional run of ill-luck, Parliament and the public were being continually stimulated into a sense almost of hysteria."[33] Only rarely does a politician leave such testimony to the special strains created by spy cases and the resultant press clamor.

Was Philby in his flat at Patriarch's Pond responsible for these stimulations, this steady drip of poison into the body politic of Britain, "the main ally of the main adversary," the United States? Many suspected him, then and later, of being the mastermind behind what became known as the KGB's "grand scheme," "the monster plot" to disrupt and destroy the "special relationship" between Whitehall and the White House. After all, political warfare had been his game against the Establishment ever since 1934. He had been trained in the black art by the Establishment itself. And now it was evident that he had placed his skills at the service of the world revolution.

Late in 1963, Macmillan resigned when he discovered that he had serious prostate trouble. "*E finita la commedia*," he wrote in his diary with relief. "One of the advantages of being dead (politically) is that I no longer read the papers." Glance at the headlines, he advised. "I feel a wonderful gain from not having to wallow through all that gossip and dirt — and the time saved allows one to read books."[34] The Philby affair and the accompanying security scandals had already weakened him physically and politically. Then "we heard the stunning news — overpowering, incredible — of President Kennedy's assassination in Dallas, Texas." Between them, Kennedy and Macmillan had restored the special relationship between America and Britain after the foreign policy debacle at Suez in 1956. The Russian game of divide and rule had itself begun to founder through the revived relationship. But he doubted that it would survive under the new president, Lyndon B. Johnson.

The comedy was not over by a long chalk. As for the CIA's view of events in London during that "strangely hysterical year" of Macmillan's recollection, Dr. Ray Cline was there working on joint estimates of Soviet capabilities and intentions — when and where World War III would develop — and he remarked to John Ranelagh, a Briton working on a history of the CIA:

> There was no other major service in the world with which to collaborate [other than the British]. The Germans were penetrated more badly [by the KGB]. The Israelis had a limited service of high quality. If we were to have any serious collaboration, we had to have it with the British. We had early on split the world with the Brits on code-breaking and monitoring. It would cost us millions to pick up the load on just monitoring open broadcasts. We had a lot of benefits from the [joint] operation and I would argue it was well worth taking the risks we took.
>
> Now there was at that time a feeling that they were stuffy, British old boy stuff, that they were careless. But then they argued that we could go and operate our machines and so on, but that they with their smaller service did about as well. And they did. I thought so, though a lot of my colleagues did not.
>
> The people who criticized had only one major argument in their favor: the unique case of the Cambridge cell — Blunt, Philby, Burgess, Maclean. It could happen in America too: feelings of utopianism, alienation, depression in the 1930s. It was an historical accident. When we didn't have an intelligence system, our problems were in government. We had Hiss — not as bad as the Philby case, but there. Take out the Philby case and what have you got? . . . I don't think our system worked any better except for the one damning thing of the Cambridge cell.[35]

At the airport when Eleanor landed, on September 27, Philby seemed gaunt and worn and in disguise — he wore a small mustache and a dark blue felt halt she had not seen before. She met Kim's "technical officer," Sergei, and as she wrote of him later:

> He is probably the only person in the world who has a complete knowledge of Kim's work (at least on the Russian side). I knew him merely as Sergei, but I soon learned that he was Kim's chief contact and colleague in the complex machine of Russian intelligence. He had apparently spent many years of his life in handling the Moscow end of Kim's activities. He often came to see us to help with all our problems, trying to assist us in adjusting to the unfamiliar Russian world in which we found ourselves. He was very charming, fortyish, with kind, twinkling brown eyes, and an excellent sense of humor. His English was fluent with only a slight trace of accent. I grew to like him very much indeed, and he always treated me with a grave, rather old-fashioned courtesy. He sometimes brought me flowers which cost the earth in winter. It was an unexpected human touch which I found appealing. He had a big car and a chauffeur, and was clearly a big shot in their Service.[36]

Eleanor's own interrogation began. Where had she been and whom had she seen since Kim's disappearance on January 23? She and Kim went over her experiences with the American and British intelligence services during those nine months. Kim was the interrogator, and what began as a conversation between the two soon became what Eleanor called a "grilling with Kim getting me to repeat the same things over and over again." This went on "for several days and I was becoming extremely bored with it. Kim was patient, but unusually stubborn and insistent."[37] After several days Kim's needle came to rest when Eleanor said that she had had to take into her confidence Nicholas Elliott, the SIS officer to whom Philby "confessed" at Beirut just before he vanished, and other British officers. She had been shown photographs of Soviet secret agents by Sir Dick White, and she had identified Kim's mysterious Russian friend who called on her that early May morning in Beirut. This was, she thought, perhaps her biggest mistake, for she felt that Kim was angry because "thanks to me, his wife, the Russians had lost a valuable agent." She quoted Kim as exclaiming, "What a pity! He was one of my greatest friends and our best man in the area. His career is finished."[38]

The other matter to which Kim paid the closest attention was the statement to Eleanor by Sir Dick White that "he had definitely known for seven years that Kim was working without pay for the Russians." Kim made Eleanor repeat her conversation with White several times, "looking very serious and reflective." Eleanor wrote, "This seemed to disturb him deeply, perhaps because it cast an entirely new light on his relations with the British." The apparition that he was C's plant on the KGB had reappeared, for as Eleanor realized:

> If the British — or some of them — had known about his Russian connections all along, he was the one who had been fooled. He thought he was spying on them, but they were keeping an eye on him — trying to use him against the Russians without his knowing it. If this were true, much of what he passed on to Soviet intelligence would be valueless.[39]

The truth was that Philby may well have been used by the SIS and the CIA, but he was not fooled. He played the game to build his worth inside the Anglo-American services while keeping his Soviet masters informed about the objectives of the game.

From that early date, therefore, Eleanor Philby's marriage was doomed as surely as the marriages of Alice and Aileen before her. With Kim engaged in what appeared to be most secret work, the KGB wanted no American woman peering over his shoulder. Philby must get rid of Eleanor if he wished to work. She became "an operational embarrassment" at a crucial time in Philby's career. To General Oleg Kalugin, the acting chief of station at the KGB mission in Washington and soon to be chief of the KGB's foreign counterespionage service in Moscow, Philby was a key player in the monster plot, the purpose of which was to disrupt and destroy the Western secret services operating against the Soviet Union. As Kalugin stated in March 1993 on a Canadian television program: "We always considered it our duty to fan discord among the allies of the United States, among the citizens and the structures of government, among those who were our enemies at the time."[40]

The stratagem by which Philby rid himself of Eleanor involved Donald Maclean or, more accurately, Melinda Maclean. After a little over a week, Kim told Eleanor that he had been in contact with Donald and Melinda Maclean and their two sons and daughter. The elder boy was twenty and attended Moscow University, the next was eighteen and studied at a technical institute, and the daughter, twelve, spoke Russian like a native. The Maclean family lived in large, modern apartment building overlooking the Moscow River, and they had asked the Philbys to dinner. Eleanor was delighted, for Melinda was also an American and had been in Moscow since she joined her husband with their children in 1953, two years after Burgess and Maclean disappeared.

This dinner took place within two or three days, and it established a relationship between the two families. Twice or three times a week they would dine, play bridge, gossip. And as Eleanor recorded of Donald, he

> was an enormous man, almost six foot six, in his middle fifties, undoubtedly intelligent, but with an unappealing conceit. From our first meeting I did not feel we would ever become close friends. His wife was short, plumpish, brunette, not unattractive, extremely nervous and highly-strung, with an annoying habit of repeating herself. On that first evening it was quite obvious that no love was lost between them. She was amusing in her way and someone new to talk to. We left their house late that evening feeling quite sorry for her.[41]

But whatever Eleanor felt about Maclean, so rigidly controlled was Kim that the Macleans were the only foreigners in Moscow that he was allowed to see socially; of all the Cambridge Five, Maclean alone was the most trusted ideologically. Kim seems to have enjoyed the Macleans and spent hours preparing specialties such as veal à la moutarde when it was the Philbys' turn to dine the Macleans. Also, the Macleans had a dacha in the woods outside western Moscow, and Kim and Eleanor spent many weekends there, not far from Molotov's dacha; they almost collided with him while gathering mushrooms in the forest. At first the main subject was the "good old days," when they were active in the cause of the world revolution. Eleanor said they sat around exchanging what she called "stale anecdotes about their past and laughing at how they had fooled everyone." Donald Maclean remarked to Eleanor, "If they hadn't caught up with Kim, you'd be Lady Philby by now." The group talked of the "good times they would have in Italy and Paris 'when the revolution comes.'" But beyond the Macleans, Eleanor had no other associates except for Philby's KGB case officer, Sergei, Viktor, a German, and the Soviet maid.

As for Kim's work, Eleanor found that he spent several hours of each day in his study, behind closed doors. Eleanor would hear a murmur of voices or the pit-a-pat of a typewriter. The usual visitor was Sergei, although there were other official-looking callers whom Kim never named. He never discussed his work with Eleanor, but he was well paid for it. Eleanor related that he earned £6,400 a year; about £2,400 of it was for his personal expenditures in Russia, the rest for the upkeep and education of his children in England. Kim's rent was no more than £240, and all personal services such as doctors and dental care were provided by the KGB. Kim ranked therefore very much as an upper-middle-class *apparatchik*. His only extravagance was the maid, and her salary was negligible. As for Kim's relationship with the KGB officers who called on him, Philby seemed

> pathetically pleased by the approbation of the Russians. Every pat on the back was like a medal or a bouquet of flowers. The Russians understood his psychological need for reassurance. Far from throwing him on the scrap heap now that his main work was over, they treated him with great deference. To them he must have been an extraordinary phenomenon, a model of ideological dedication. For thirty years he had served them devotedly, but now he was in their hands. He wanted recognition and got it . . . Kim's excitement at any word of praise seemed disproportionate. To me it seemed out of character, and he went down in my estimation.[42]

Philby's decision to rid himself of Eleanor took another step in November, when Eleanor learned she needed minor surgery. Almost the first thing the KGB did when Eleanor arrived was to provide "a complete physical check-up at a special KGB clinic"; she claimed that it was more thorough than any she had experienced before. The KGB confirmed Eleanor's need, previously recommended by an SIS doctor in London, for surgery to strengthen a sphincter weakened when Eleanor gave birth to her daughter. Her doctor arranged for a KGB nurse to treat her at home until she entered the hospital. Once she was hospitalized, Kim came twice each day, and she was still there on November 23. As Eleanor recorded afterward, she spent the day lying in bed trying to understand what the three other Russian women in her room were saying. All she understood was the name John Fitzgerald and that all three women were upset. When Kim arrived, Eleanor

> learned the terrible news that President Kennedy had been assassinated in Dallas on the previous day. The effect on the hospital was shattering. Doctors, nurses and patients wept openly. As most of them knew I was an American I was offered the most tender condolences. Whatever the political cynicism of the Russian leaders, the Russian people were profoundly attached to peace. They lost millions of men in the war. In spite of giant reconstruction, bullet scars are still to be seen in the cities of Western Russia. No one can live in Russia and witness the first signs of affluence, after the depredations of war and the rigours of its aftermath, without coming to believe in the sincerity of the Russians' longing for peace. To them Kennedy was a man of peace, and they mourned his death. Kim, who talked a great deal

about American politics, was also profoundly moved and depressed by the tragedy.

The "high points" of each week were the couple's trips to the central post office to get their foreign mail. Their chief relaxation was music, and Kim had already established what was to become a large collection of Red Army marching songs and Russian opera. They seldom missed a performance at the Bolshoi. Life was reasonably pleasant, except the discipline. As Eleanor was to write of that aspect of their lives:

> Several months had passed before I was fully aware of the strict control to which we were subject. The Russians were taking no chances. Just what they feared I could not fathom, until Kim hinted that they thought the British, perhaps even the the CIA, might try to assassinate him if they could find him.

In May of 1964, Eleanor reminded Kim of her promise to Annie, her daughter, that they would meet in New York on June 10, 1964. Could he obtain the exit visa she required to leave the Soviet Union? When Sergei opposed her departure — there was great suspicion in the United States that the KGB had trained President Kennedy's assassin, Lee Harvey Oswald — Philby warned Sergei that Eleanor was determined to go and that if she was stopped she would complain to the U.S. Embassy that she was being held in Moscow against her will. Go she did. Sergei obtained Eleanor's ticket and her exit visa and prepared her for the interrogation to which she would inevitably be subjected by the FBI. At length, it was decided that Eleanor knew so little of Kim's work that if she withheld his address, telephone number, and his work name, it would not matter what she said. If she did give them away, it would only complicate life; Kim would have to move. Kim felt sure that Eleanor would encounter trouble with the FBI or the Immigration and Naturalization Service, and he gave her four specimen cables to send: ARRIVED SAFELY ALL LOVE would mean that she had encountered no difficulty on entering the United States; ARRIVED SMOOTHLY ALL LOVE would indicate that there was trouble with the FBI; LANDED SAFELY ALL LOVE would indicate passport difficulties; GOOD FLIGHT ALL LOVE would mean that Eleanor was in trouble with both the FBI and the INS.

At the beginning of July, Eleanor was seen off at Moscow Airport by Kim and Sergei. She flew to Copenhagen by Aeroflot and then on to New York by SAS. There, her passport was confiscated, and in return she received a letter from Secretary of State Dean Rusk, informing her, she wrote, that "in view of my marriage to H.A.R. Philby and my activities in the Soviet Union which were against the interest of the U.S.

government, my passport was withdrawn until further notice." Eleanor
sent the appropriate telegram and remained in the United States for
the next five months. During that time a sequence of letters from
Philby to Eleanor was intercepted by Angleton's letter-intercept service
at the CIA. These were declassified in 1989. All reflected something
of this odd affair and something too of the clerkly aspects of Philby's
mind, his relationships with women, and his life in Moscow during the
period immediately after he had settled down at Patriarch's Pond.

Each letter was numbered and, in keeping with Secret Service usage,
dated by the month and the day but not the year. Letter seven was the
first, and it dealt with Dean Rusk's withdrawal of Eleanor's passport.
Philby had by that time begun to cuckold Donald Maclean. Melinda
Maclean revealed to Philby that Donald was impotent, and had been
so for more than fifteen years, and that this created difficulties between them that made it impossible to continue their marriage. Philby
may have been deft at concealing his relationships and thoughts about
people close to him, but he failed with Eleanor. Later in the correspondence, he began to make overly frequent references to Melinda,
which gave Eleanor serious pause about her future with Philby. But he
began with Eleanor's troubles in mind:

> My darlingest beloved,
>   I have been pondering over your first letter — not the most lucid
> of documents! — and it seems to me that the action of the State
> Department is based on a complete misapprehension. You say that
> the withdrawal of your passport was "based on your activities in the
> Soviet Union in conjunction with your husband who is believed, etc.
> etc." Surely it is up to them to say *what* activities they have in mind.
> You are, after all, nothing but a housewife, and to equate the duties
> of a housewife with "activities in conjunction with your husband"
> seems far-fetched in the extreme. It is clearly absurd to suppose that
> you would have returned to the US if you had in fact been working
> against its interests. Of course, the State Department has to play it
> safe, and one can understand their viewpoint. But, once they have
> convinced themselves that you are in fact a housewife and nothing
> else, I am sure that they will reverse their stand. Your lawyer will
> doubtless be taking up the matter with the official concerned, and
> please keep me closely informed of everything that happens. By the
> way, if you foresee heavy legal expenses, please let me know in good
> time, if necessary by cable, and let me know how much you will
> need.[43]

This intercept may have played its part in the restoration of Eleanor's
passport, but that did not occur for five months. During that time

Eleanor lived at a hotel and traveled extensively, and Philby sent her money in dollars through an arrangement with Melinda Maclean, who had a U.S. dollar account (and Philby did not). He sent a little cheerful domestic news in that letter:

> Guess what! I got back from downtown yesterday to find Anna [Sergeyevna, his housekeeper, who was also a KGB spy] in near-hysterics, and really thought she had suffered a heart attack. When she calmed down she told me that, on coming back from the market, she had gone into the living room and seen a parakeet on top of the [cages in which Philby kept some birds of his own]. Thinking that one of the little ones had escaped, she grabbed it, and popped it in with the parents. She then went to the little ones, and counted — five! All present and correct! Obviously, the bird had escaped from a cage nearby and, hearing the racket coming from our flat, had flown in to pay a social call. So now we have eight. It is a perfect little bird, green like Mom, and seems to get on quite well with the old ones. Another mouth to feed![44]

Eleanor was less cheerful in New York, where the weather was sweltering and matters became increasingly intricate. Her first husband, Sam Pope Brewer, was now the *New York Times*'s correspondent at the United Nations, and he was in touch with the CIA through an officer of the Near East Desk, Albert L. Hennig, who had been a senior officer at Baghdad and Karachi. Hennig traveled from Washington to New York every month to see Brewer and keep himself informed about what Brewer knew about Eleanor's relationship with Philby, her status, if any, with the KGB, and whether she intended to return to Moscow. "He was in poor shape and, most of the time, useless owing to the amount of drink he took on," Hennig remembered.[45]

The number of lives ruined in the Philby case now increased by one — Brewer's. With the hubbub in the press over the questions of Eleanor's passport and the custody suit brought by Brewer against Eleanor over their daughter, Harrison Salisbury, an assistant managing editor at the *New York Times* and a foreign correspondent of distinction, became concerned about the nature of the relationship between Brewer and Philby in Beirut, between Brewer and the CIA, and between the CIA and other *Times* correspondents. Salisbury felt that the relationship that had grown up over the years between the CIA and the *Times* was not desirable, that "there was always the danger that men who did maintain such special connections would find themselves involved in matters that were not the *Times*'s business." Brewer was a case in point.

Salisbury regarded Brewer as "a mediocre reporter" at the UN; plainly, he had been an informant of Philby's. As a correspondent with access to what Salisbury described as "semiprecious" information, he had even maintained the Philby connection *after* Philby made it known that he and Eleanor were lovers and wished to marry — and despite informal advice from the *Times* to break the connection. "Like so many others," Salisbury remembered, "Brewer had fallen under Philby's spell." The question was whether he had been a witting or an unwitting informant. In what was an informal investigation lasting two years and conducted with the knowledge and approval of such *Times* eminences as Cyrus Sulzberger and Clifton Daniel, Salisbury probed Brewer, his background, his politics. He read Brewer's cable files and correspondence and interviewed Brewer unsuccessfully. Brewer proved reluctant to discuss Philby; and when he was given further opportunities to do so and declined, according to Salisbury, "we had to let him go." Nothing that suggested Brewer had been a spy or a CIA secret agent was discovered but "the record was not satisfactory to us, and neither was his work." That was that. Brewer found himself in the cold.[46]

Meanwhile, Eleanor was interviewed by FBI agents about her relationship with Philby and his relationship with the KGB. As Philby wrote to her in letter eight on July 20, he was pleased

> to hear that the FBI boys turned out to be nice types. They are obviously entitled to ask you questions, and, as I told you before you left, I hope you will cooperate fully with them. I don't think they will be disappointed at your lack of knowledge. As it was always understood that you would return to the States whenever you wanted to, it is clear that would not be burdened by knowledge which, rightly or wrongly, might put you in a false position as an American citizen. So chin up, old girl![47]

He had, he said, spent "a very nice peaceful weekend" at the Macleans' dacha, and he intended to return to celebrate Melinda's birthday on July 25. He intended "getting her that kitchen unit — fish-slice, scoop, ladle, etc., which she is always sighing about and never getting round to buy. At least, it will stop her telling me for the hundredth time how much she wants one. As a matter of fact, she seems to be very much better the last few days." Philby related how Anna, the new housekeeper — Maria Sergeyevna had gone, probably because of his complaint about her prying in the flat — complained that "I don't eat enough. What she is really griping about is that I can't eat half a loaf of bread with every meal. As it is, I am being fed like a Strasbourg goose, and my green corduroy trousers are telling me that I am still putting on weight." He had, too, some advice to give concerning [Annie's] athlete's foot: "I recommend either Whitfield's Ointment (an English preparation) or Mycil (ointment or powder). I have used both to good effect in the past." He ended the letter with an expression of his love for Annie and "keep heaps for yourself. Pretty smile, please, for your Kim." There was a postscript: "Remember to tell me if you need $$!!"

Eleanor did. Sam Pope Brewer, in his custody fight for Annie, so Eleanor claimed, had leaked word that she intended to kidnap Annie and take her to Russia, a story that increased Eleanor's difficulties with the U.S. government. Philby wrote: "I see that the press row has broken out, thanks to Sam. He is clearly behaving like a hysterical old woman, but that is normal form with him and might have been foreseen." Eleanor went into hiding with friends in San Francisco to escape the clamor. "Oh God! Oh Montreal!" Philby exclaimed, adding: "Do please write a little more often; you can imagine how I long for news." As to Melinda's birthday party,

> the weekend passed pleasantly, in spite of worry [at Eleanor's predicament in San Francisco], and Melinda appreciated her birthday present. The breakfast fried eggs were presented unbroken. I also took down [to the Macleans' dacha] a capercailzie (a large variety of grouse) which I found in a game shop at Sretenka . . . It was terribly good, and provided six large portions, with a bit left over. We must certainly try it, as I am sure you would enjoy it. There were other goodies, too; a large seven-layer birthday cake from the Budapest, raspberry summer pudding, etc.[48]

He ended letter ten: "Well, my love, I will nip out and post this now, and settle down to another fish dinner and an evening's reading. All my love sweetie, and do be good about writing!" He appended a line of twenty-six typewritten "x's" — kisses.

While Eleanor was absent, political developments had occurred in Moscow that affected Philby vitally: Nikita Khrushchev was removed from office and replaced by Leonid Brezhnev. Of that momentous transfer of power Philby said nothing to Eleanor. But he had much to say about a weekend with the Macleans at Novgorod, the ancient Soviet city in northwestern Russia on the Volkov River at the point where it leaves Lake Limen. He wrote rapturously about the Cathedral of Saint Sophia — founded in 1054, destroyed by the Germans in World War II, and restored by the Soviets after the war. After that weekend, the tone of Philby's letters to Eleanor were very different. His letter at the beginning of August 1964 was almost cold and formal to a degree.

He had heard nothing from Eleanor for three weeks. She was still "My darling beloved" and "It was wonderful to hear from you again," he wrote. "But you haven't numbered your letters up to now," he chided, "so please start doing so right away; it will make it that much easier to sort things out" in regard to her passport at the State Department and to the custody fight over Annie, in connection with which she had visited Washington. Whom did she see there and with what result? He had had no news except the telegram C. BIZ. OK. What on earth did that mean? Did C stand for *custody* or *California*? If, as he suspected, she meant custody, he did not "see how you can possibly describe it as OK." She might have to sue the State Department, an action that might take three months. He had been reading up on the U.S. passport regulations. "The removal of your passport was an administrative action, not a legal one," he advised her, "and could possibly be reversed by administrative decision." As to the custody of Annie, her chances of winning in court were slender, and "the only thing to do is to hope that time will do its work and induce a more reasonable frame of mind in SPB."[49] His letter rambled on. "Now, Melinda (in case you have forgotten) wants some mint seeds, bobby pins, a garlic crusher, and also a set of rules for playing Scrabble." Their visits to Novgorod and Pskov, had been wonderful and he enclosed a photograph of "my favorite church in Novgorod, St. Theodore Stratilates." He advised that his favorite daughter, Miranda, had won her college diploma and "starts next week as secretary to the Bursar at Pembroke College, Oxford, at £8 per week with five weeks paid holiday. Horrid little beast — to think I began at £2 per week — with a Cambridge degree, three languages, and a sound general knowledge of politics!" Also, he would like Eleanor to get for him Nabokov's translation of Pushkin's *Eugen Onegin, Biffen's Millions* by P. G. Woodhouse, and the *Spy Who Came In from the Rain* [sic] by John le Carré. He gave up worrying on August 23, when he wrote letter twenty-one and ended it: "So all my love, darling. Missing you dreadfully, and have you constantly in my thoughts."[50]

They were reunited in Moscow on November 28, when Eleanor landed at the airport at Vnukovo. She thought that someone on the aircraft was following her, and this caused anxiety for the KGB, which had not yet finished its three-year debriefing of Philby. The thought that either the CIA or SIS might try to kill Philby was always present during those years and, indeed, for much longer. As Eleanor related in her memoir, when she boarded the almost empty Aeroflot aircraft at Copenhagen, "I did not wholly reject the idea that someone was following me." On her arrival at Moscow the captain of the aircraft took her passport, which was unusual, and then Sergei came bounding into the plane from the main airport terminal. But Kim was not with him. He had remained in a large black car drawn up some distance away.

When Eleanor approached the car, Kim did not get out to greet her, and when she got into the car beside him, he simply said, during a brief embrace, "So you've really come back." He then motioned her to silence as if he did not wish Sergei to know what they were saying. The car took a roundabout route back to their home, during which time Eleanor felt they were being followed by another car. As a consequence, the Russians in Kim's car "were worried that the British or the CIA might tail us home." Eleanor tried to "cheer Kim up" by relating that she had bought two bottles of whiskey at Copenhagen. This news produced more unease. Sergei

> wanted to know exactly where I had bought the bottles. Could they have been tampered with? Evidently, the Russians were still concerned that someone might try to murder Kim. I had not come all that way just to poison my husband. Kim, too, examined the bottles with interest, questioning me closely about the shop where I had bought them at the airport. But the idea of someone slipping a poisoned pill into a bottle of whiskey in Denmark seemed so ridiculous that I laughed at him. The minute we got home he broke open one of the bottles and got just about as drunk as he possibly could. I had a feeling that it was deliberate.[51]

It is evident that Eleanor's days in Moscow were numbered. She had been in Washington, she had been interviewed by the FBI, she may have communicated with the CIA. She had. She had had contact with both Applewhite and Evenland. These were abnormal times; the Warren Commission was investigating the possibility that the KGB was behind Kennedy's murder. Was it not possible that the U.S. government had restored her passport so that she could act as a witting or unwitting informant? All aspects of her visit to the United States had to be considered, despite her apparent lack of interest in politics. Had she not herself been connected with the OSS and OWI in Istanbul?

After her arrival at Patriarch's Pond, she found that Philby no longer worked there; he now had an office and secretary elsewhere in Moscow, probably at the Novosti news agency on Pushkin Square, for what he called "an unexpected and exciting new job." It emerged that he had had severe trouble with Donald Maclean. When Eleanor announced she had brought presents — the mint seeds, the Scrabble instructions, bobby pins, and the like — for the Macleans and asked whether she might telephone Donald, Philby asked her not to do so, his face darkening. He explained that they had had "a filthy row" at the *dacha,* and later, when Eleanor asked what had caused it, Kim replied that Donald had accused him of still being in the British Secret Service, as Burgess had been just before his death. Eleanor did not see Donald again. As she wrote of her own marriage:

> I have never experienced such a painful Christmas as in 1964. I was witnessing, in effect, the collapse of my relationship with Kim. He was lost to me in a haze of alcohol. Indeed, the whole of the holiday period was one great champagne binge, and even in his conscious moments his mind seemed elsewhere. I was again reminded of our last months in Beirut. Naively I believed that the source of his troubles was in his work.[52]

Eleanor was quite correct. Kim did have trouble in his work. With the arrival of Brezhnev, the KGB management had changed. Semichastny, Kim's patron, remained, but his future became more uncertain. The KGB management adjusted to the attitudes of the new regime; Philby had to tread carefully.

The KGB could judge Philby only by the man they saw, and many on the staff did not like what they saw. They were, by ideology and training, oddly Victorian in sexual matters and personal deportment. And because of events now to occur with Eleanor, only the few cosmopolitans in the KGB tended to see him as anything but a dissolute, corrupt, broken-down Englishman — the very type that made a double or treble agent. This tendency became more apparent through Eleanor's contact with the FBI while she was in the United States and the probability that she had remained an American patriot with connections to the CIA. All that saved Kim from complete isolation was that his debriefing was incomplete after twenty-one months; until it was finished, Philby remained of value to the KGB.

The view of him at the KGB could not have improved when it became clear, soon after Eleanor's return, that Philby expected his wife to live as part of a ménage à trois, with Melinda Maclean as the third person. He explained to her: "Melinda is so unhappy. Donald is impotent. She's had a miserable time for fifteen years."[53] Melinda moved into the spare room at Philby's home in January 1965. It was just behind the kitchen and across the passage from the master bedroom, and the tensions that arose may be imagined. It was not to be expected that Eleanor would have anything good to say about her guest, even though they were both Americans by birth. Philby drank heavily; the

KGB visited two or three times a week to continue his debriefing, and everyone in the apartment was required to watch what he or she said — the place was thoroughly bugged. All the members of the entourage were watched by "street eyes" from the time they left the building until they returned.

By April 1964, Philby appeared again to be close to nervous and alcoholic collapse. Just before May Day he complained of severe pains in his chest and was admitted to a KGB clinic. He smoked heavily, and the pain may have been the first sign of arrhythmia of the heart. On the other hand his complaint may have been a ruse to obtain relief from the tensions at home. As he was placed into the ambulance, Melinda noted that his eyes were closed and he looked serene. There was a faint smile on his face. "His troubles for the moment were over. Sergei had arranged for him to have a private room with his own toilet, a great privilege in the Soviet Union."[54]

Philby remained in the hospital much longer than anyone expected. As Eleanor recorded, "The Russians very much wanted to keep him alive. He was presumably still valuable to them, or it may have been their way of paying tribute to the long service he had rendered them. They kept him there for over a month, taking no chances." His interlocutors had reason to keep him alive, and to raise his spirits they brought news that he was being made a member of the Order of the Red Banner, an important honor awarded as "recognition of conspicuous bravery or self-sacrifice in time of war, special capacity for leadership, or the performance of some action contributing decisively to the success of Soviet arms." The badge is a laurel wreath, the upper part of which is covered by the Red flag bearing the words "Workers of All Countries Unite!" But the order really meant little. Kim had yet to face his fate when, sucked dry of his rich knowledge by the KGB, he would have to negotiate his future. What he wanted was the post as chief of the British section of the foreign intelligence of the KGB.

The end for Eleanor was close. Each day she struggled to the hospital on the bus, "taking him books, newspapers and mail." But it was an ordeal. "We had nothing much to say to each other." She waited until Kim was out of danger, then told him she was leaving him and Moscow. She wrote:

> We talked listlessly about what I should do next. I told him I always wanted to go to Ireland. And he said, "Ireland is lovely. I think that's an excellent idea. There is no extradition treaty between Britain and Ireland, so perhaps I could come and see you." (But they passed a

bill the following summer so that was just a dream.) Why, I wondered, did he suppose I should want to see him again when he would obviously be living with Melinda? It was a very strange thing to say.

After a while I had to go, but he kept saying, "Do stay a little longer." He handed me a letter and said, "Don't read it until you get home." Then we both started to cry. We gave each other a long embrace, and then I walked out of the hospital, down the long path to the gate, waving to him as he stood at the window of his room. As a parting present he gave me his old Westminster School scarf which he had worn constantly and which I knew he loved.[55]

With Melinda still at Patriarch's Pond, Eleanor left Moscow on May 18, 1964. She read Kim's note on the plane.

My darling beloved,
   I wanted to write you a proper "au revoir" letter, but the conditions are not very favorable! So I will content myself with a brief preface, to be followed by a long letter when I get back to the typewriter.
   From now on, darling, I shall be thinking hard of our happy days together, of your sweetness and goodness. I can never, never forget them. Please try also to remember the nice things. Write to me often — as I shall to you — and tell me all your thoughts.
   So to you — the best friend I ever had or ever will have — all the best and every possible lucky break.

> Au revoir, darling,
> Your sincerely devoted
> Kim[56]

Broken, Eleanor Philby went into hiding at Dun Laoghaire, just outside Dublin. During her journey, she claimed, she received an offer of £42,000 — about $100,000 — from the London *Sunday Express* for the story of her life with Philby. She refused because, although she was penniless, she said there was no story to tell. At this stage, in the official view, she was still loyal to Philby. This was confirmed in an interview with a U.S. government official at Dun Laoghaire, which lasted many hours. She had gone to considerable trouble to hide herself from the press; she had reassumed her maiden name, Kearns, and she had cut all her ties with her past except for her friends Isobel and John Fistere, on whose Beirut balcony St. John had collapsed in 1960. Fistere, too, had connections to the U.S. secret circle, and it was not long before a member of that circle found her living in a small apartment in an old Georgian house with a view of the sea. She appeared to him to be "a lonely and despondent creature with waning resources and with little sense of purpose." She had developed a bad case of arthritis, and her closest companion was a Siamese cat she called Sinjun, after St. John Philby. She allowed some students from Trinity College, Dublin, to use her rooms to watch television.

She spoke in a stream-of-consciousness torrent about her fortunes and misfortunes since her Beirut days; "she evinced complete sympathy for Philby, but she revealed no trace of doubts about her loyalty to the U.S.A." She did reveal the general whereabouts of the flat she called her home in Moscow, but not in terms that would enable an intelligence service to find him, a thought that may have crossed her mind. All she said was that it was a "little Lubyanka," a protected compound inhabited by "Western intellectuals" in Moscow. She spoke of Philby's great pride when the Soviet government awarded her husband its second highest honor, the Order of Lenin. She said, too, that Philby had warned the KGB that they would be wasting their time if they tried to get Eleanor to do anything contrary to her loyalty to the United States. She described Philby's work as "very important."

Philby's attitude toward her personally changed markedly to one of "cruelty and contempt" when he told her that, even before they met, his first loyalty was to the Communist Party. The official wrote in his report: "It was revealed to her that her husband's customary charm and expressions of sympathy and affection were a sham and a pretense. She had realised that she had been to him no more than cover."

Eleanor Philby died of cancer in California three years later, loyal to Philby despite her distress at her dismissal. Her successor, Melinda, remained at Patriarch's Pond for over a year, then returned to Maclean for about eighteen months of uneasy cohabitation. Greatly disillusioned by life and love in Moscow, she finally returned to Boston in 1970. Her legacy remained at Patriarch's Pond in the form of a novel that was still there in 1992. Philby had inscribed it: "An orgasm a day keeps the doctor away. Your ever loving Kim."

17

The Monster Plot

1963–1975

ELEANOR PHILBY LEFT one statement of political significance, and this had some bearing on the most intricate of all Philby's activities in his first months in Moscow — his degree of involvement in the monster plot against Angleton and the CIA, which had begun in 1959 and reached its full flowering in the summer of 1963. Only rarely, Eleanor wrote in a ghosted series of articles about her life with Philby and published in London in 1967, did Philby go out to work:

> Most of the work was done at home. He did quite a lot of typing in the study and talked at length with his Russian visitors. After years in British intelligence, Kim knew a great deal about its methods, operations and men. I realised that rival Intelligence agencies spend much of their time attacking each other, seeking to penetrate each other's organisations and "turn" each other's agents. It may be assumed that Kim is advising the Russians along these lines. He must be enormously useful with his prodigious memory. For the Russians he must be like a reference book, as valuable, say, as a Baedeker to a traveller in Europe.[1]

Many people at the CIA and SIS agreed with Eleanor Philby, and Angleton was chief among them.

Angleton always maintained that the KGB had launched a major attack against the CIA and that the KGB's "whole plan is being masterminded by Kim Philby in Moscow." Its object "is to destroy me and

550 TREASON IN THE BLOOD

the agency."[2] The main question is: if Philby was masterminding the KGB attack in Moscow, who was masterminding it in Washington?

The obvious candidate was Oleg Kalugin, the chief of counterintelligence at the Soviet Embassy in Washington. Kalugin was Angleton's main opponent there from about 1964 until about 1968, and such were the services he rendered that, when at the end of his tour of duty he returned to Moscow, he became the youngest general in the history of the KGB. He was also made first a deputy and then the chief of counterespionage in the KGB's foreign intelligence service, the First Main Directorate. For an officer who was only in his mid-thirties, these positions were remarkable testimony to his personal ability, his loyalty to the KGB, and his achievements in Washington. Nothing less than major successes would have led to such promotions, and one would have been a successful attack on the CIA's counterintelligence service, which controlled the main intelligence operations against the Soviet Union. By his own statement, Kalugin recruited and controlled the Walker brothers' espionage activities, by which for sixteen years the ciphers of the U.S. Navy were exposed to the Red Navy; and he also claimed to have penetrated Morton-Thiokol, the U.S. manufacturers of the solid-state missile boosters.[3]

Born in the mid-1930s into the old Bolshevik *nomenklatura*, Kalugin had received his higher education at Leningrad University's philology department as an English language specialist. After graduation he became one of the KGB men specially trained for the penetration of the CIA. On the wave of the post-Khrushchev thaw in American-Soviet relations, in 1959 he was sent to Columbia University in New York City, accompanied by two others of importance in the Philby case, Gennady X, who was Philby's liaison with the political warfare branch of the KGB, and Aleksander Yakovlev, who became an important figure in the Soviet Union's Central Committee and served for ten years as Soviet ambassador in Canada.

Kalugin returned to Moscow in the early 1960s and was trained as a radio reporter, the cover for his work in the United States. Presumably Philby gave Kalugin his views on CIA conditions, for Kalugin returned to New York to begin active service as a spy while working as a radio reporter. As he said, "For four years, I believe, I successfully combined journalistic and intelligence activity."[4]

In 1964 he was recalled to Moscow in order to develop a new cover, "something more reliable" than that of a radio reporter. In 1965 he went to Washington with a diplomatic passport and became, he claimed, "Soviet intelligence deputy resident in the USA and, when the resident left, I performed his duties for quite a long time."[5]

The term "monster plot" was CIA in origin and scornful in meaning, and at the center of it was Angleton, who had acquired a large reputation and even larger power. No overseas appointment could be made without his approval; no operations could be undertaken without his assent, and he alone, except for the CIA's signal master, saw all the agency's messages. One reason was that only Angleton had the means and the knowledge to verify the character of the appointee, to assess the security situation surrounding the operations, and to gauge the worth of the intelligence being received. Moreover, it was necessary for him in the daily exercise of his work to know what all the other chiefs of the agency were doing. The Counterintelligence Division became subject to his direction alone, and few if any directors of Central Intelligence interfered with it, largely because few understood his craft or had the time to study the endlessly complex games in which he was involved. He was completely trusted by his chiefs; few if any of his colleagues or subordinates dared question his work. Angleton became a law unto himself between 1963 and 1971, the main years of the monster plot.

But if he was a brilliant man, he possessed serious intellectual weaknesses. Cleveland Cram, a Harvard Ph.D. and a senior CIA officer for thirty years, was called back to the CIA from retirement in 1977 and spent four years researching and writing the official but internal history of Angleton's career on the basis of unrestricted access to the CIA's files. When done, the history consisted of eleven volumes on legal-size paper. Cram had dealt with British affairs for much of his CIA career and served as deputy chief of mission in London during the main period of the monster plot. A man of calm, measured judgment, and much respected in his trade, during his investigation of Angleton and his conduct of office Cram formed the view that Angleton was "obsessively theoretical, obsessively ambitious, and obsessed about Philby." When Philby defected, Angleton suffered "severe psychic damage." And as Cram also remarked, "If Philby had achieved nothing else in the Soviet service he would have earned his keep by the peculiar thralldom he obtained over Angleton's thinking."[6] Cram's judgment is shared by Angleton's wife. Cicely Angleton told how Philby's disappearance affected her husband "terribly, deeply — it was a bitter blow he never forgot."[7]

It will be recalled that when Philby was recruited into the Soviet service in 1934, he was required by his case officer, Arnold Deutsch, a psychologist, to write appreciations of all significant persons he met. "You will produce a lot of rubbish," Deutsch told him, "but one useful page will be worth lots of waste paper." By now, the early 1960s, these notes had become, as Philby recorded, "a thick bundle of papers" that included "every detail, however trivial," about each significant person he had met. He had concentrated over the decades "on those who might be useful as sources or dangerous as enemies" and it was, he wrote from the safety of Patriarch's Pond, "awesome to think of the libel actions that would lie against me if the Moscow archives ever saw the light of day."[8] We may assume that Angleton became one of Philby's subjects when they met in 1944; if this was so, it would account for the events that began in December 1961 when a KGB officer, Anatoli M. Golitsin, defected to the CIA in Helsinki and, with his wife and daughter, was sent to Washington for that intricate process known as debriefing.

A squat, powerfully built Ukrainian of peasant stock, Golitsin was a highly educated, trained, exceptionally crafty man. From the start of his interrogation, he proved to be a difficult subject. He made so many demands that he was, in October 1963, transferred from the Soviet Division, which was responsible for the debriefing, to the Counterintelligence Division of Angleton without the answer having been established to a most important question: Was he a "true" defector or a "false" one, a KGB agent ordered to defect with the task of penetrating the CIA. His debriefers did not altogether form a good impression of him, because his education and training had been largely without field experience. From the start and throughout his long career with the CIA, it was never established to the satisfaction of all that Golitsin had not been sent to the CIA for a special purpose.

But also from the start of his personal association with Angleton he displayed a remarkable ability to engage the spycatcher's mind. Angleton formed an unusually high opinion of Golitsin, as he declared in testimony to the U.S. Senate:

> Golitsin possesses an unusual gift for the analytical. His mind without question is one of the finest of an analytical bent . . . and he is a trained historian by background. It is most difficult to dispute with him an historical date or event, whether it pertains to the Mamelukes or Byzantine or whatever it may be. He is a true scholar. Therefore, he is very precise in terms of what he states to be fact, and he separates the fact from speculation although he indulges in many avenues and so on.[9]

But his fine mind was not all that interested Angleton. Golitsin knew something of Soviet deception strategy, and it was at this point that the lines created by Angleton's interest in Philby and Golitsin began to cross.

Angleton had seen during World War II how great careers had been made through the successful execution of grand deception; Bodyguard and Fortitude, created to mislead the German supreme command about the place, the date, and the weight of armies to be used on D-Day in Europe, were cases in point. This had been the basis for the association between Angleton and Philby. Now in Golitsin's claim to knowledge of Soviet deception strategy lay the basis for the relationship that developed between Angleton and his Soviet charge. In hindsight, it seems possible that Golitsin began to behave as a "false" defector, one sent to insinuate himself into Angleton's mind.

What Golitsin told Angleton was that in May 1959 he had been one of two thousand Soviet intelligence officers at a conference in Moscow held by the new chairman of the KGB, Alexander Shelepin, one of Nikita Khrushchev's protégés. The conference was intended to enable Shelepin to present the KGB staff with a plan to "affect the fundamental reasoning power of the enemy," the U.S. government. As evidence that such a grand plan was already in effect, that the monster plot had begun, Golitsin stated that the split between Russia and China was a fake, meant in part to cause the United States to miscalculate militarily and politically. The alliance between Russia and China, he insisted, still existed. In due course, he revealed more: to effect Shelepin's grand scheme, the KGB had placed a mole inside the Soviet Division of the CIA — an assertion that touched upon Angleton's greatest nightmare, that there was a Philby in the CIA. Moreover, KGB moles were inside all the governments and the intelligence services of the principal powers in NATO, including the United States.

The essential point about Golitsin's statement was that, given the near-war politics between Russia and the Atlantic powers and the security situation in Whitehall, it could not be dismissed. Angleton accordingly took Golitsin to see the director, John A. McCone, and he ordered a special CIA committee to investigate the worth of Golitsin's statement concerning the Sino-Soviet split. This came to be known as the Flat Earth Committee; it took time to test Golitsin's claims, and if it found that the split between Russia and China was real, who was there to say that the committee was correct? Angleton did not, and could not, accept the finding of the committee. In Soviet matters, Golitsin became Angleton's principal adviser. And as Walter Elder, a special assistant to McCone, found of that relationship:

The uncovering of Philby as a mole was, without doubt, one of *the* most important events in Jim's [Angleton's] professional life. The Philby affair had a deep and profound effect on Jim. He just couldn't let the Philby thing go. Philby was eventually to fit neatly into Jim's perception of a Soviet "master plan" to deceive the entire West. Long after Philby's defection in 1963, Jim just continued to think that Philby was a key actor in the KGB grand plan. Philby remained very prominent in Jim's philosophy about how the KGB orchestrated the "master plan" scenario. To Jim, Philby was a leader of the orchestra.[10]

In these circumstances, the evolution of the monster plot entered its most grievous phase. Golitsin warned Angleton that the KGB would send a real "false" defector to discredit him and the information he had provided to the CIA.

Against that background, the assassination of President John F. Kennedy took place at Dallas on November 22, 1963. It was established that his assassin was Lee Harvey Oswald, a young former Marine sharpshooter who had had Marxist associations, who had sought and obtained political asylum in Russia, who had married there, and who had had some contact with the KGB there and in Mexico City. The Warren Commission had been established to investigate the president's murder, and one of the most dangerous issues was the need to establish whether the KGB had been involved — which seemed possible and even probable. If the Warren Commission found that the KGB had sent Oswald, would that not become a *casus belli* for war with Russia?

With the CIA and the FBI, and especially Angleton's service, fully engaged in the Warren Commission's inquiries, in January 1964 another KGB defector, Yuri I. Nosenko, deserted his post as the chief security officer for the Soviet delegation to the American-Soviet disarmament talks in Geneva. Nosenko became the subject of intense interest in Angleton's department, the more so when he made certain statements about Lee Harvey Oswald and Golitsin.

As Nosenko related under interrogation, when Oswald shot Kennedy, panic had broken out in Moscow and he was put in charge of a KGB investigation into its relationship with Oswald. He denied that the KGB had had any connection with Oswald and offered to testify before the Warren Commission. As Richard Helms, then the CIA's deputy director of plans and the officer in charge of the CIA's investigation into Kennedy's murder, was to state:

Since Nosenko was in the agency's hands this became one of the most difficult issues to face that the agency had ever faced. Here a President of the United States had been murdered and a man had come from the Soviet Union, an acknowledged Soviet intelligence officer, and said his service had never been in touch with [Oswald] and knew nothing about him. This strained credulity at the time. It strains it to this day.[11]

Angleton and, indeed, almost all the senior officers involved in the Nosenko case formed the view that Nosenko was a "false" defector. Golitsin denounced him as being the false agent of whom he had spoken to Angleton. An attempt was made to break Nosenko, to make him tell "the truth" about the KGB's involvement with Lee Harvey Oswald, to force him to tell what he knew about the monster plot; he became the subject of the harshest "hostile" interrogation. He was held in solitary confinement from April 4, 1964, until October 27, 1967. Everything was done to break him. But he never changed his story that he was a "true" defector and that, extraordinary as it might appear, he had been involved in the KGB's investigation of its relationship with Oswald. At length, Nosenko was released from incarceration and rehabilitated by the CIA, but his charges against Golitsin — that he was *the* mole inside the CIA — left the CIA a house bitterly divided.

During that time, Angleton, on information supplied by Golitsin, had been searching for a Soviet spy inside the Soviet Division, and he demonstrated his confidence in Golitsin by making available to him the CIA files on the personnel of the main operating section of the CIA in the Cold War with Russia, the thousand-odd men and women of the Soviet Division. He settled Golitsin in an apartment in New York City, where he was permitted to receive and read the files. During this period — perhaps three years — many of the personal and operational files were delivered to him; and he began to trawl through them, looking for data that corresponded to his notion, obtained through conversations with KGB colleagues in Moscow, of who "Big Mole," as the suspected agent came to be called, might be — a man with "something Russian in his background" whose KGB code name was Sasha and whose real name might begin with the letter K.

Angleton devoted a very large proportion of the resources to the hunt for Big Mole, and a sense of intense disquiet began to infect the Soviet Division, especially when the chief of the division, David Murphy, became suspect. Many other consequences flowed from the hunt. As Ron Rosenbaum wrote in *Harper's* about the Angleton-Golitsin-Nosenko cases, the CIA had been rent by

> charges of treason, unresolved allegations against individuals at the very heart of the American diplomatic and intelligence establishment, some still in government service. We're talking about careers ruined, about mass resignations of counterintelligence people con-

vinced that the CIA has been irrevocably penetrated by KGB pawns, about men we thought were *our* moles in Moscow arrested and shot, and about schizophrenic distortions of our own perceptions of Soviet policy.

And, Rosenbaum continued,

at the heart of this continuing corrosive confusion, doubt, and ambiguity is the mysterious relationship between British master mole Kim Philby and America's master mole-hunter James Angleton. Although that has been a deadly serious duel that's stretched over three decades, the relationship has come to include elements of an incongruously intimate marriage: not unlike a real-life version of the deadly embrace between le Carré's Smiley and Karla . . .

On the surface, the outcome seems long established. There is Philby, generally acknowledged to be the most successful spy of the century, comfortably established in Moscow . . . now even more exalted by virtue of his long-time close collaboration with former KGB boss Yuri Andropov. And there is Angleton, the acknowledged genius of counterintelligence — spying out spies — in the West, whose brilliant career bears one ineradicable scar: his failure, by all official accounts, to detect or even suspect Kim Philby's true Soviet loyalties despite years of face-to-face contact with the spy of the century.[12]

Through Golitsin and his connection with Angleton, there had been allegations against the loyalties of persons of eminence such as Averell Harriman, Henry Kissinger, Harry Hopkins, Arthur Schlesinger, and two former chiefs of the CIA's Soviet Division. Nor was this amazing state of affairs confined to the United States. Golitsin had laid evidence in against major figures in the intelligence services of Britain, France, Canada, Norway, Germany, and Sweden. Rosenbaum wrote that these continued to "fester in the files, poisoning the perceptual apparatus of the West, paralyzing . . . the entire espionage establishment, making it impossible for us to trust what we know about the Soviet Union, or know what we trust."

But at some stage it was discovered that there were two KGB officers living in the same Manhattan apartment block as Golitsin. They were working under the cover of the United Nations and had their families with them, so it is said, as did Golitsin. When this proximity was discovered, Golitsin was evacuated suddenly to a farm in upstate New York. The files were sent to him there, but he never returned them. Nor did anyone else in the CIA, other than a small number of officers in Angleton's counterintelligence division, become aware before 1974 that Golitsin was being sent the files or that he kept them. When this was discovered, an operation was undertaken to retrieve them and, according to a senior CIA officer involved, "two vans were required to return them to the Agency — two van loads of our most secret files in the possession of a Russian in the boonies somewhere north of Albany! You can imagine what the FBI thought when they were told about what had happened to some of their most secret files."[13]

This and many other such excesses of his authority led inevitably to questions about the nature of the relationship between Angleton and Golitsin, although the questions were held within the Special Investigation Group, the core of Angleton's division, responsible for investigating reports of Soviet penetration inside the CIA. There one of the senior CIA officers investigating the many "serials" to Big Mole provided by Golitsin was Claire Edward Petty, an Oklahoman who had joined SIG in 1966 after working for eight years with a German organization in Germany working against Russia. An analyst with "a wonderfully clear mind," according to his chief, he had failed to establish any case for Golitsin's allegations against the two senior officials of the Soviet Division. And as he was to state, he began rethinking Golitsin's information; it was "at that point that I decided I'd been looking" at the cases "all wrong by assuming Golitsin was as good as gold." He went on:

> If you turned the flip side it all made sense. Golitsin was sent [by the KGB and Philby] to exploit Angleton. Then the next step, maybe not just an exploitation, and I had to extend [the reasoning] to Angleton. Golitsin might have been dispatched as the perfect man to manipulate Angleton or provide Angleton with material on the basis of which he (Angleton) could penetrate and control other services.
>
> Angleton himself must be the traitor, Petty decided . . . Angleton was a mole, but he needed Golitsin to have a basis on which to act.

Petty was "now sure he had unlocked the key to everything that had been going on inside the agency for the past decade" and added:

> Golitsin and Angleton. You have two guys absolutely made for each other. Golitsin was a support for things Angleton had wanted to do for years in terms of getting into foreign intelligence services. Golitsin's leads lent themselves to that. I concluded that logically Golitsin was the prime dispatched agent.[14]

Petty now found himself on exceedingly dangerous ground, for Angleton remained one of the most powerful men in the CIA, one who operated beyond the code of the agency and, sometimes, the law. Petty had concluded that Angleton was the mole and that his man Friday, Golitsin, was still under KGB control. Understandably, he looked about for someone who was himself powerful enough to serve as a confidant;

he found that person in James R. Critchfield, who had been Petty's chief in Germany and was now the chief of the Near East Division. Critchfield was himself disquieted by some of the things that were going on inside the CIA in the hunt for Big Mole, and he told Petty to go ahead with the investigation. As Critchfield would state:

> I had no doubt that there was a force in Moscow out to disrupt the CIA. Whether Philby was that force, or part of it, I do not know. But what I do know is that Angleton's part in defending the Agency was pretty bad. I was a supporter of his until I learned certain facts shortly before I retired.[15]

By late 1962, Golitsin's activities inside the CIA had taken on many of the aspects of a KGB disruption to destroy the agency from within. Yet Angleton continued to support him and to pay him large sums of money, mainly because he was satisfied that there was a monster plot. He continued to devote personnel, time, and money to it, causing disquiet in the agency and arousing suspicions about himself. But a fresh dimension began to emerge to strengthen the case against Angleton. Whether this came from Golitsin cannot be known, but the substance of the allegations was:

1. In 1962, the chief of the Western European Division of the CIA, Eric Timm, had formed a very adverse opinion of Angleton's conduct of office and let it be known that he intended to try to procure Angleton's relief from his duties. Timm died suddenly in his sleep shortly after he made his intentions clear.

2. In 1967, Desmond Fitzgerald, chief of the Far Eastern Division, a powerful figure inside the CIA, a leading Georgetown socialite, and hitherto Angleton's friend and colleague, also began to form an adverse opinion of Angleton's conduct of his office. He made out his case in writing before he left for a weekend at his estate at Haymarket, in Virginia, with the British ambassador, Sir Patrick Deane, intending to send the paper to the CIA management on his return. A man who had appeared to be the model of early-middle-age good health, Fitzgerald dropped dead while playing tennis with Dean.[16]

No suspicions were aroused by the deaths when they occurred; only later did it become known that both men had developed serious reservations about Angleton's conduct. But the disquiet did begin to develop after Petty's investigation, for it was noted that both Timm and Fitzgerald had constituted impediments in Angleton's attempts to obtain full access to the key officer at the CIA, Richard Helms. After the two deaths, Angleton obtained the access to Helms he required for his search for Big Mole. After that, too, the speculation against him became common currency.

At some stage Petty consulted William E. Colby, who was rising through the CIA to become its director in 1974, and Critchfield stated that just before he retired in that same year, "I conveyed that Ed Petty had told me of possible security problems in the CI Staff. Of course I mentioned Angleton. I did not want to walk out the door without bringing it to the attention of the director."[17]

When Colby became director, he was well aware that there was trouble in Angleton's branch. Angleton was called to Colby's office and was invited to stay with the CIA as a consultant in counterintelligence but not as chief. Angleton resigned from the agency effective Christmas Eve of 1974. Only twelve men inside the CIA were aware of the troubles, but his resignation — or, more accurately, his dismissal — did become known soon afterward in circumstances of considerable political effervescence.

President Ford named an eight-member commission, headed by Vice President Nelson A. Rockefeller, to investigate the CIA and the propriety of a wide range of activities, not the least of which was the Angleton-Golitsin-Nosenko affair and the murder of President Kennedy. Early in 1975, a major inquiry began in the Senate under Frank Church, the Idaho Democrat, with another in the House conducted by Representative Otis G. Pike, the Long Island Democrat. For the first time Angleton and his activities and responsibilities since the counterespionage branch was established in 1954 became known beyond the secret circle. Angleton made some unfortunate statements, not the least of which was that "it is inconceivable that a secret intelligence arm of the government has to comply with all the overt orders of the government," a statement he withdrew when questioned further about it. But even after his career was over, he remained convinced that there had been a mole in the CIA, as Rosenbaum wrote in *Harper's*,

> still among us, still a trusted figure operating at the highest levels of government, still burrowing even deeper into our most sensitive secrets, as embittered exiles from our espionage establishment, the losing side in the Great Mole War of the past decade, contend? Is he, even now, sitting in some comfortable Capitol district office and reading these words, chuckling contentedly?

Or, Rosenbaum wondered,

> Did he ever exist at all? Might he be a delusion engendered by the fevered fantasies of the hierophants of counterintelligence theory — a product of paranoid "sick think," as the complacent victors in the

Great Mole War, the current chiefs of the espionage establishment, have called it? Worse, might the entire twelve-year-long hunt for the American mole and the civil war within the clandestine world that it created have been a massive deception operation? Might Big Mole merely be a chimera craftily conjured up by the KGB of Kim Philby and Yuri Andropov in order to provoke and profit from the divisiveness and paralysis, the self-destructive finger-pointing that followed?[18]

Who knew?

And then there was the "most shocking and improbable of all the mole-theory heresies: the notion that Angleton himself *is* the Big Mole." The fact was, Rosenbaum went on, "the Great Mole Hunt" conducted by Angleton and Golitsin had, it could be argued, "done more to destroy the effectiveness of the CIA than any ten highly placed moles might have accomplished." Just what "was transacted between Angleton and Philby during those two years of long weekly lunches they shared at Harvey's restaurant in Washington, D.C.?" Was it possible that it was not Philby who was running Angleton but Angleton who was running Philby? That "Philby and even his KGB soulmate Andropov were our men in Moscow?" Rosenbaum went on in his delicious way:

> Wait, you say. How could that be? Angleton has been fired, exiled, and dismissed from intelligence work. Furthermore, Angleton and the Angletonians are constantly proclaiming the defeats the KGB has inflicted on U.S. intelligence. The Angletonian gospel insists that the brilliance of the KGB and the foolishness of the CIA ruling establishment have created disaster after disaster for our side, that it's practically run by the KGB.
>
> But look at it another way. What if Philby was our man in Moscow? Wouldn't we want his KGB associates to think he'd been a brilliant success, that he had even their archnemesis James Angleton on the run, that they'd dealt us grievous defeat after grievous defeat? Wouldn't we want the Soviet presidium to think that Yuri Andropov had been a masterful general in the complex war of moles and disinformation?[19]

Writers, filmmakers, poets, TV producers, began to dwell on the Philby-Angleton case as the debate about Big Mole entered the public forum. Was there ever a Big Mole, a traitor in the Russian service looking down from the management floor of the Langley headquarters, where sixteen thousand of America's best and brightest were said to be spending $4 billion a year to win the subterranean war with Russia? The CIA watchers in the press had fallen back, exhausted from the labors created by Angleton's departure and the Church Committee, when, in September 1978, the case was restimulated by a lurid event.

An empty sloop named *Brillig* was washed up on the shore of Chesapeake Bay. Coast Guardsmen found documents aboard analyzing Soviet military strength, along with "boxes of sophisticated electronic gear." The boat belonged to John Arthur Paisley, a Soviet analyst for the CIA. A week later, a waterlogged body was found with a bullet in the back of the head. According to the *New York Times* of January 22, 1979, the corpse was "hastily identified" as Paisley's and cremated. The director of the CIA, Stansfield Turner, put out the word that Paisley "possessed no secrets and his death was a simple suicide." As Turner declared upon learning that it was the view of the press that there were more sinister things behind the discovery of the corpse and its sloop: "I'm standing on the fine statement by the Maryland State Police that they see no evidence of foul play."

The case then came to the attention of the *New York Times*'s William Safire, who, noting that the name of the sloop came from Lewis Carroll's *Alice in Wonderland* wordplay, wrote an essay under the headline "Slithy Toves of C.I.A." As Safire asserted, the truth was that Paisley was the man in the middle of a great question dividing the U.S. intelligence community: Who was Big Mole? It then emerged, Safire recorded, that when he became director of Central Intelligence, Admiral Stansfield Turner brought Nosenko into the bosom of the CIA as a top analyst. He was befriended by Paisley, originally an Angletonian analyst. Now Paisley was dead and, as Safire wrote,

> the Senate Intelligence Committee wants to know whether Paisley was the mole, or whether Paisley learned who the mole was — and was killed before he could pass it on. Senators are furious at Mr. Turner's attempt to minimize Paisley's agency significance. An intelligence boss may have to issue a false cover story publicly, but it is against the law for him to mislead an oversight committee in secret session.

Safire declared that Paisley was the man who drafted a controversial report, warning of Soviet military buildups and expansionism, and then revealed:

> This schism in the world of U.S. intelligence — where only the hardliners have been getting fired, indicted or rubbed out — is no mere settling of intramural scores. Either view may be mistaken, but if it turns out that the old doubters are right — and not the "paranoids"

they are depicted as being — then our national security has been seriously weakened.

It then emerged that Turner, in the belief that Nosenko might spot Big Mole if he went through the Soviet Division staff records, had indeed turned him loose on the most secret of American secrets of state. This produced a further explosion in the Soviet Division. Tennant Bagley, a former deputy chief of the division, entered the lists, declaring that it was "irresponsible" of Turner to "expose clandestine personnel to this individual" and that Colby and the rest of the "current top brass are taking unnecessary chances to demonstrate contempt for their predecessors." Safire concluded his essay with a further bowdlerized extension of Carroll's wordplay:

> Beware the Family Jewels, my son
> The leaks that spring, the tips from Smersh —
>
> Taste not Nosenko's Plant, and shun
> The myriad Seymourhersh!
>
> Golitsen to the Bagley man
> Go find who serves another skipper;
> Promotion lies with those who can
> Win one for the Double Dipper.
>
> But high in Langley's ranks he stands,
> The Jabbermole, untouched is he —
> Kampiles' heel, a friend of Stan's,
> He snuckles in his glee.
>
> 'Board *Brillig* did the bearish spies
> Snatch Paisley's prints before he blabbed;
> All flimsey were the alibis
> While the mole laughs, ungrabbed.

There, for the time being, the case of Big Mole again rested, unproven. The reputation and the operating ability of the CIA were badly injured, as were the reputations of the British Secret Service and the British Security Service. Many investigations followed, some jointly on both sides of the Atlantic. But the question of whether there existed a KGB monster plot to split the Atlantic intelligence and political alliance remained, as did the question of Angleton's loyalties. Admiral Turner brought Cleveland Cram out of retirement to examine all the CIA files relating to Philby and Angleton as well as to Angleton's stewardship as chief of counterintelligence between 1954 and his retirement in 1973.

Among the matters that Cram found to be peculiar, and in contravention of all filing procedures at the CIA, was that Angleton had cleansed the files of every reference to his relationship with Philby. Under CIA regulations, Angleton had been required to dictate a memo after every meeting with Philby, as with all other foreign intelligence officers. This he had done, and there were, according to his secretary, thirty-three such reports. But when Cram went looking for them, they were not to be found. That was not all. Angleton never did a damage report on the Philby case. He had required all staff members to send a memo stating whether they had met Philby and what, if anything, they knew about him. Cram had replied yes, that he had met Philby. But as with everyone else there was no follow-up. No attempt was made to interview either Cram or anyone else who reported yes. There was a "rather shallow" attempt by Angleton at a damage estimate. Cram remembered (1) Volkov, (2) Albania, and (3) border crossing operations from Turkey into South Russia. But otherwise there was nothing in the CIA files that could have been used against Philby. Cram himself therefore prepared a damage estimate of the period 1949–1963. These included "twenty-five or so major *but* major disasters attributable to Philby."

Philby's file consisted of some sixty volumes in two parts: (1) his personal or 201 file, which contained all the reports about him, and (2) the CI operations file on him. Cram read them from end to end between 1977 and 1979 in order to prepare his official and secret history of the counterintelligence department. He discovered that Angleton had never permitted such a history to be done; he also found that Angleton had removed the Philby 201 and operations files from the CIA registry and placed them under his personal control in CI so that nobody could read them without his knowledge. When Angleton resigned, Cram returned the files to the CIA Central Registry, where they remained closely guarded as late as 1993. Cram stated too that when Philby's 201 files were recovered from Angleton's control, parts of them were missing. It is not known what these parts contained, nor why Angleton committed the administrative crime of mutilating official files. As to their sensitivity, the Philby files were still closed in perpetuity. Even their existence has never been officially acknowledged.

Cram, however, was in a special category as a CIA officer. His credentials gave him clearance to see all the files in order to enable him to fulfill his task. His work ran to eleven chapters or volumes, one of which concerned Philby. But in the end Cram asserted that he was not able to state definitely from the files, and his investigations based on them, whether Angleton was or was not a Soviet secret agent. Nor could he state definitely whether Philby and the Soviet Active Measures had run a monster plot against the American and British intelligence services. There was, quite simply, insufficient evidence one way or the other. Cram believed personally, based on his reading of the files and his other investigations, simply that many of Angleton's actions suited Soviet purposes.

Cram recommended to Admiral Turner that all CIA senior staff be briefed on the affair, and Turner duly authorized this unprecedented step. The briefings were remarkable in many ways, but the most surprising aspect was that, according to Cram, very few of the officers were aware of the problems, or even of the existence of Angleton. As to the monster plot, through the effective compartmentalization of the CIA, few officers who attended the briefings knew that there had been a problem at all or that in his search for Big Mole, Angleton had virtually negated the effectiveness of the Soviet Division.

The briefing lasted two hours. Cram told the executives the history of the monster plot and the parts Angleton and Philby may have played in it. He described the suspicions and controversies that had surrounded Golitsin and Nosenko and their evidence relating to the deaths of President Kennedy and his assassin, Lee Harvey Oswald; how Angleton believed that the KGB had sent many true and false defectors with the objects of (1) confusing the evidence being given to the Warren Commission and (2) disrupting relationships in the Soviet Division and thereby disrupting the work of the division as a whole. In all, Cram cited the cases of sixteen defectors as being sufficiently sensitive that it still remained "very important" to collect all available information, even though the cases had already been investigated many times, especially those of Golitsin and Nosenko. Cram was not certain that the truth had been established about the bona fides of any or all of these cases or whether they had not defected to the U.S. and the U.K. as part of some stratagem to disrupt the CIA.

But little emerged that would justify reopening the case against Angleton. The views of discredited men — all double agents except Nosenko were regarded as doubtful meat — could hardly justify such a step. Nonetheless, by 1991, in Cram's view, "substantial reasons" had come to light through his reading of the Philby-Angleton files "for suspicion to arise about the loyalties of Angleton." But this view was not shared by the investigation of Bronson Tweedy, another senior and distinguished figure in the CIA. Tweedy cleared Angleton of the allegations against him in 1976. But there was, nevertheless, an impressive case to be made that Angleton was either a fool or a rogue. But for internal CIA reasons, he was not brought before a security tribunal. However, much later a senior member of the CIA management did write an unofficial memorandum to assist Dr. Cram in the research of his history of the Angleton era. Such had been Angleton's conduct of great affairs that the official listed nine points that he thought would have warranted an investigation had Angleton still been alive.

His main charges were that Angleton had been "conspicuously aggressive, obsessed with tracking down the supposed KGB staff penetration of every defector's claim, yet he never found it." He had "wantonly intervened and embarrassed both internal and external Norwegian services. This was very detrimental to CIA and harmful to a generation of U.S. relations with Norway." He never questioned the highly dubious bona fides of General Reinhardt Gehlen, the chief of the West German intelligence service, and German liaison. If he was such a "responsibly dedicated anti-communist, why did he not erect a viable permanent organizational structure to carry on the work should something happen to him? When he left there was no organization at all. Without him it was nothing: all *sui generis* and *ad hominem*." In short, the Angleton agency had been a phantom, useless for the purpose it had been created. The CIA had been defenseless against the monster plot. But Angleton had nothing to say at the end. When in his last days his colleagues asked him "to come clean in the Philby case" at a "farewell luncheon" at the Officers' Club at Fort Myer, near Washington, he replied that "there are some matters that I shall have to take to the grave with me, and Kim is one of them." A week later he died of cancer of the lung, taking his secrets with him.[20]

Back in March 1967 Britain's SIS learned that a synopsis of memoirs by Philby was about to be circulated among Western publishers. This is what it said:

> This book, as sketched out below, falls into two parts.
>
> The first six chapters will contain a strictly factual account of the various developments in SIS, which are known to me at first hand. The thread of continuity will be provided by my own career in the service.
>
> The tone of the book should be moderate and cultivated. Yet, written in a vein of light irony, it should provide a devastating attack on SIS and other organizations with which it was associated.
>
> The attack will concentrate on such aspects of SIS as the social structure; internal intrigues; interdepartmental intrigue; coddling of

officers and ruthless handling of agents; breach of diplomatic usage; double-crossing of Allies, etc. The material available offers a rich field.

After the first six chapters the rest of the book will be devoted to a general survey of SIS and Allied services, bringing the material up to date.

The main thread of these chapters which I have sketched in only roughly will be an inquiry into how SIS and Allied services served the best interests of the British Government. The answer will, of course, be a steadily accumulating negative.[21]

Breaches of diplomatic usage, ruthless handling of agents, the double-crossing of Allies, internal intrigues . . . here indeed was an explosive mixture, one that, if Philby exploited his knowledge fully, might yet cause severe political trouble for Britain in NATO and the European Community.

Underlying Whitehall's concern, in part, was what Philby had revealed to his Russian masters, not only in current but also historical matters. World War II was only eighteen years in the past, and there were skeletons in Whitehall's closet — as indeed there were in the closets of all the powers involved in the war. Churchill had fought the war with his doctrine of force and fraud to restore what he called the prosperity, the power, and the prestige of England. The prosperity and the power had not yet been reestablished; the question of prestige was now imperiled. Philby knew as much about the secret war behind the scenes — with the Russians, the Germans, the French, and the resistance movements in general — as any officer of the British Secret Service. Such matters might serve to wreck Britain's chances of entering the Common Market or of maintaining its position in NATO.

First there was Philby's role in sustaining the communist underground in Europe during the war. There was no doubt, after his exposure, that he had supplied the ISOS intelligence at War Station XB to protect the communist movements in every country in Europe against German countermeasures. Dame Rebecca West, the British author, was particularly well informed about this aspect of Philby's activities; she wrote in her important *The Meaning of Treason* that there were in the resistance movements those who

> wished their movements to be wholly Communist, in order that [they] might become a revolutionary force at the end of the war and take over the government of all countries, as the partisans took over Yugoslavia. Such plotting for the future led in France to the murder of right-wing French parachutists who were sent over by the Free French

in London. It was widespread enough to lead to the quasi–civil war following the Liberation in France which accounted for deaths estimated at anything between 30,000 and 100,000. There was also at that time an ugly situation in the Low Countries which the Allied commanders had to meet by the forcible disarming of the resistance groups.[22]

How Philby got these highly secret decrypts from the War Station to the Soviet authorities would not become known. That he betrayed the trust in him by his chiefs is clear; it was the basis of the Soviets' trust in him. Nor can there be any doubt of his objective. He saw in the decrypts a method to facilitate the world revolution of the proletariat at the end of the war — a revolution that very nearly succeeded throughout Europe. His actions constituted a breathtakingly large attempt to alter the balance of power in Europe in the Soviet interest.

There was, too, disquiet at what Philby might have to say on that enduring issue in Poland, the death of the Polish commander in chief in World War II, General Wladyslaw Sikorski, in July 1943. His B-24 Liberator transport had crashed on takeoff at Gibraltar and all aboard were killed, save the pilot. A thesis had developed in which it was alleged that Sikorski was assassinated at Churchill's order because he had become a serious irritant in the relationship between Churchill and Stalin. And when it became known that Philby had been a Soviet agent in the British Secret Service, many anti-communist Poles were disposed to believe that he had had a hand in Sikorski's death. All this was troubling nonsense, but it was not without an element that might prove difficult to countervail. Philby had flown secretly to the Iberian capitals on April 16, 1943, on a special mission for the British Secret Service. His flight was intercepted by German long-range fighters and was damaged by their gunfire. Ten weeks later Sikorski was dead. When the crash was investigated, it was found that the aircraft had gone down in what was a mundane air accident: a British mechanic at Gibraltar left a haversack onboard the plane that had contained a light meal; the haversack slid aft on takeoff and jammed the controls. The very simplicity of the accident enhanced the notion of a conspiracy — Sikorski was killed at a time when the bodies of some twelve thousand Polish officers and bourgeois were found at Katyn Forest — and it did not evaporate with time.

Even as late as 1989, the former Polish ambassador to Washington, Romuald Spassowski, was sure Sikorski had been assassinated and that Philby had been the instrument. Spassowski's wife, a member of the Sikorski family, shared this belief. Sikorski's biographer, General Marian

Kukiel, made the same claim: the Soviet service, he insisted, had possessed the detailed itinerary of Sikorski's journey and "it had been provided to them by H. A. Philby." If Philby revived the Sikorski question in his memoirs, any number of embarrassments might arise in the official relationship between Britain and Poland, to say nothing of the North American Poles.[23]

This was not all that concerned the British secret circle when the contents of Philby's synopsis became known. There was concern about American operations in Eastern Europe during the war. Almost all in the Soviet sphere of influence had failed and all at the same time. These included the loss of Team Green (twenty-two men) in Slovakia in September 1944; the Soviet expulsion of Frank Wisner's mission to King Michael of Rumania in Bucharest in 1945; the Soviet expulsion of the OSS and the SIS missions in Bulgaria at the end of the war; and the loss of Operation Sparrow under Florimund Duke, who had had the task of arranging the surrender of Hungary before the arrival of the Red Army. In a fashion not as yet undetected, General Donovan's intention to insert secret agents in Poland was betrayed to the NKVD, which, acting through Stalin and the Soviet foreign office, succeeded in getting FDR and the State Department to forbid the operations. The extent to which Philby contributed to these disasters, if at all, never became clear; and the abrupt liquidation of the OSS at the end of the war ensured that the loss of these operations, and others like them, made it impossible to investigate them. Some parties were undoubtedly lost through incompetence and misfortune. But a fear arose that some unknown hand in London had betrayed them.

In his work as a Soviet agent — first as chief of the foreign counterespionage service, as station commander at Istanbul, and as liaison officer with the CIA in Washington — Philby was responsible for or a participant in all operations into White Russia, the Ukraine, Georgia, Armenia, Albania, Bulgaria, the Baltic states, and East Germany. All the agents in all these operations had to be considered as intercepted and destroyed, a consideration that was justified. Not only was there silence from almost all the agents involved, and few returnees, but Yuri Modin, Philby's Soviet controller in London at this period, would relate how the Soviet counterespionage authorities intercepted "very large numbers of Western agents" from the Baltic states down to South Russia and the Black Sea.[24] These losses were the cause of great distrust on the part of their CIA case officers in their relations with their British counterparts.

Beyond these casualties lay the unresolved matter of China's entry into the Korean War on the Yalu River in 1950, a dangerous impediment to the resumption of full relations between the American and the British intelligence and security services. This was becoming a running sore. Combat soldiers have long memories, and many in the Veterans of Foreign Wars were disposed to believe that they had been betrayed. When Truman relieved MacArthur from command in April 1951, one of the supreme commander's reactions was to claim that his "strategic movements" had been betrayed to the communists. William Manchester quoted MacArthur as stating: "That there was some leak in intelligence was evident to everyone. [The first commanding general of the Eighth Army] Walker continually complained to me that his operations were known to the enemy in advance through sources in Washington."

Manchester claimed — and he was right — that MacArthur's suspicions were justified, although at the time and since, both the Pentagon and the press took the view of Cabell Phillips, of the *New York Times*, who dismissed MacArthur's story as "far-fetched." As Manchester wrote:

> That fall the first secretary of the British Embassy to the United States was H.A.R. "Kim" Philby. The second secretary was Guy Burgess. And the head of England's American Department in London was Donald Maclean. Because the Commonwealth brigade was fighting in Korea, copies of all messages between the Pentagon and the Dai Ichi were passed along to the Attlee Government through the embassy on Massachusetts Avenue and the American Department in Whitehall. Philby and Burgess sat on the top-secret Inter-Allied Board, and Philby acted as liaison officer between the CIA and the U.K. Secret Intelligence Service.

Manchester then quoted Rebecca West, writing in *The New Yorker*, as having declared that "every secret they learned during their official lives was certainly transmitted to the Soviet Union." Secretary of the Army Wilbur M. Brucker "examined Defense Department files" and declared that "Burgess and Maclean had secrets of priceless value to the Communist conspiracy." General James M. Gavin recalled that "during his service in the last critical months of 1950, the enemy repeatedly displayed an uncanny knowledge of UN troop deployment." He also contended that:

> I have no doubt whatever that the Chinese moved confidently and skillfully into North Korea, and, in fact, I believe that they were able to do this because they were well-informed not only of the moves Walker would make but of the limitations on what he might do. At

the time it was difficult to account for this, [but I am] quite sure now that all of MacArthur's plans flowed into the hands of the Communists through the British Foreign Office.

As Manchester continued on the subject of what he called "the Philby conspirators," there was the troubled question of the orders MacArthur received forbidding him to bomb the Yalu River bridges over which the Chinese armies were crossing:

> In his *Reminiscences* MacArthur observes that after the war an official leaflet by Lin Piao published in China read: "I would never have made the attack and risked my men and military reputation if I had not been assured that Washington would restrain General MacArthur from taking adequate retaliatory measures against my lines of supply and communication."

Manchester then noted that Vice Admiral A. E. Jarrell had said of this pamphlet that Marshal Lin had learned of this decision through disclosures "by British diplomats Guy Burgess and Donald Maclean." Manchester tried and failed to find this pamphlet among Asian scholars at Harvard and Brown, and pointed to the possibility that "Lin was merely attempting to plant seeds of fresh discord between the United States and the United Kingdom." But Manchester felt compelled to add that "in the light of what is known about the Philby conspirators and the pattern of events on the Korean peninsula that autumn, it seems fair to suggest that the Chinese general may have been confirming what was already suspected."

Manchester took the matter to Dean Rusk, then assistant secretary of state, who felt that "the enemy knew the broad strokes of U.N. policy by reading American newspapers and following developments at Lake Success." But Rusk wrote to Manchester of the work of "the Philby apparatus": "It can be assumed that (1) Anything we in our government knew about Korea would have been known at the British Embassy and (2) that officers in the Embassy of the rank of these three would have known what the British Embassy knew." With that statement, Manchester then wrote to Philby in Moscow, inviting him to confirm or deny MacArthur's charges. In a letter dated April 7, 1978, Philby replied that he himself reported "no significant information about the Korean War" to the Soviets and doubted that Burgess and Maclean did. Kim added:

> Unfortunately, this leaves the general question unanswered. Was there a leak or wasn't there? I do not know, and, if I did, I probably could

not tell you. On the face of it, it is absurd that we three were the only possible source of leakage.

Manchester then commented in the *American Caesar:*

It is equally absurd to conclude, on the strength of this ambiguous statement, that the Philby apparatus bore no responsibility in this matter. Philby concedes that "the question is left hanging." So it is, but it seems reasonable to suggest that it hangs from his hook.

Manchester wrote by way of a conclusion to the affairs of "the Philby apparatus":

The key date is November 1, 1950, seventeen days after Wake [Island conference between Truman and MacArthur]. On that Wednesday Maclean was appointed chief of Whitehall's American desk. As an FO department head, his name went to the top of all distribution lists for classified material reaching London from Washington. With Philby and Burgess already in position, monitoring CIA and Defense Department developments, the three-man apparatus would have been able to tell the enemy, not only what the UN commander was going to do, but, as Gavin notes, what he could *not* do. For example a CIA memorandum approved by Truman shortly after the President's return to Washington recommended MacArthur make no moves against Chinese units which were entering North Korea to take up positions around the Sui-Ho electric plant and other installations along the Yalu. Philby and Burgess would have known of this vital decision a few hours after it was made, and a copy of the document itself would have been in Maclean's possession the following morning. The text could have been in Moscow within a week at the outside, and it might then have been sent straight to Peking and thence to Lin Piao's headquarters. On that assumption it is hardly surprising that Lin anticipated MacArthur's moves and was ready to foil them. Not until the UN rout reached disastrous proportions, and the General was improvising so fast that Washington and the Philby agents couldn't keep up with him, was he able to match the foe blow by blow.

This assumption seems shrewd enough, and there is independent confirmation for it. Robert Cecil of the Foreign Office, who knew Maclean well and succeeded him as head of the American Department, recorded in 1984 in a brilliant survey of the Philby affair entitled "The Cambridge Comintern":

Chinese intervention in the Korean War in mid-October 1950 had much intensified Cold War tensions, including tension between the USA and her principal allies. The wish of MacArthur to carry the war

to [Red China] led to fears in London that he might induce Truman
to employ the A-bomb. In December 1950 Attlee went at short notice
to Washington with the intention of averting this danger. Among the
secret papers, which I unearthed in Maclean's steel filing cabinet
after his flight [to Russia], was a copy of the Prime Minister's report
to Cabinet on his visit.

What would Philby have to say in his memoirs about this seepage of
suspicion about him in Washington? And how would the British authorities counter it? What would be the substance of his allegation that
the British Secret Service had engaged in the "ruthless handling of
agents; breach of diplomatic usage; double-crossing of Allies, etc." A
main fear was the belief, long held in Russia and alluded to from time
to time in her official histories, that in order to keep Russia in the war
in 1942, the British Secret Services had stimulated a battle of annihilation between the German and Russian armies in the spring of 1942.
The Russians had alleged that British policy had been to fight to the
last Russian. There were stories abroad in Whitehall and Fleet Street
of other such stratagems involving the French. One, the Prosper affair
of 1943, was particularly grievous in its outcome and rankled personally with the French leader, General Charles de Gaulle and the men
and women of the Resistance who had fought then and were in positions of power now. And the spokesman for the Media Committee,
Colonel Samuel Lohan, warned persons making inquiries about such
matters that "Philby and the Soviet government are engaged in very
large-scale deceptions to embarrass the British Government as much
as possible in his book."[25]

Now Whitehall reacted to defend its honor and prestige by directing
its full power to prevent another bullfrogs' chorus in the press, Parliament, and publishing, and to ensure that Philby did not become an
icon of the left in British politics, as seemed possible. A phenomenon
known as "treason chic" had begun to emerge in British politics. Of
it Richard Grenier, a writer on the cultural scene, wrote, "Treason is
in style. At least British treason when it is committed by Englishmen
with posh accents." Novels and films were in prospect about the Philby
case and about Burgess and Maclean, and "cultural despair" was "all
in style."

It was the era of a remarkable generation of English playwrights —
Alan Bennett, John Osborne, Harold Pinter — all leaders of the avant-
garde of the period, the New Young Turks come to write judgment on
the Old Young Turks, Philby, Burgess, Maclean, Blunt, and the still

unnamed fifth man. Alan Bennett had recently written and appeared in a powerful antiestablishment satire, *Beyond the Fringe;* in due course he would write one of the most brilliant plays of the era, *An Englishman Abroad* (about Guy Burgess in Moscow), *A Question of Attribution* (about Anthony Blunt at the Courtauld Institute and with the queen at Buckingham Palace), and *The Old Country* (which was thought to be about Philby in Moscow). The *New York Times* called his work an "unusually deep perspective on the juiciest and the most voluminously chronicled of modern espionage tales." *The Guardian*'s critic thought that the real fascination of his work "lies in the way it questions accepted notions of treachery." Bennett more than any other expressed the doubt of the new generation of young, working-class intellectuals about whether there had been a high treason — an attitude of mind that Whitehall found dangerous. As he wrote of his attitude toward the scandal:

> I find it hard to drum up any patriotic indignation over Burgess or Blunt, or even Philby. No one has ever shown that Burgess did much harm, except to make fools of people in high places. Because he made jokes, scenes and, most of all, passes, the general concensus is that he was rather silly. Blunt was not silly and there have been attempts to show that his activities had more far-reaching consequences, but again he seems to be condemned as much out of pique and because he fooled the Establishment as for anything that he did. It is Philby who is always thought to be the most congenial figure. Clubbable, able to hold his liquor, a good man in a tight corner, he commends himself to his fellow journalists, who have given him a good press. But of all the Cambridge spies he is the only one of whom it can be proved without doubt that he handed over agents to torture and death.[26]

Bennett went on:

> I think it's about time we stopped thinking of treachery as the crime of crimes. It suits governments to make it so and the sentences handed down by judges reflect this . . . The trouble with treachery nowadays is that if one does want to betray one's country there is no one satisfactory to betray it to. If there were, more people would be doing it.

Such was the attitude of one of the foremost writers of his time. It was to maintain the status quo in Whitehall, and to deflect the acceptance of such views, that the authorities in contact with the media began to suggest that Philby had substantially endangered the security of the state in its relations with the Soviet Union. But it was the Establishment press that undid the campaign.

In March 1967, the *Sunday Times,* a London newspaper with large resources, began a full-scale investigation into the Philby case. The services of four authors were retained to help in the collation of the information coming in, and in all eighteen reporters became involved under the direction of a new editor, Harold Evans. A peculiar story evolved of a man who had been a Soviet secret agent since 1934, who had been employed in high capacities by the British Secret Service, and who had, in the view of the team, been involved in at least one operation *against* the KGB, the Istanbul incident. The evidence that Philby had acted as a treble agent in Istanbul — that is, a British secret agent whose first loyalty was as a Soviet agent being employed to work *against* the Soviet Union — was strong. It was not long before the government knew that the *Sunday Times* knew, and dispatched its men to intervene. The former defense correspondent of *The Times,* Alun Gwynne Jones, who had recently been elevated to the peerage as Lord Chalfont and was a minister of state at the Foreign Office, warned the newspaper: "You must stop your inquiries. There is the most monstrous danger here. You will be helping the enemy." The investigation continued. An SIS man posing as a Foreign Office man, John Sackur, came looking for a job as a correspondent in Africa, and Evans told him they were investigating Kim Philby. "Philby?" said Sackur incredulously, "Philby? You'll never be able to print it. It'll get stopped. D[efense] Notices. It goes to the highest in the land . . . Philby was a copperbottomed bastard." Sackur, it turned out, had written the report on the damage done by Philby.

In due course the Services, Press, and Broadcasting Committee D Notice Committee sent a rare, perhaps unprecedented bulletin intended to show Evans that he was on thin ice in regard to the Official Secrets Act, that dread instrument of law with which the government seeks to protect its secrets. It said:

> You are requested not to publish anything about:
> (a) secret activities of the British intelligence or counterintelligence services undertaken inside or outside the United Kingdom for the purposes of national security.
> (b) identities, whereabouts and tasks of persons of whatever status or rank who are or have been employed by either [the Secret or the Security Services].

The notice had no power in law, but it was an official warning: woe betide the editor who ignored it.

But that is what Evans did. He ignored it and the inquiry continued.

He sent an Australian, Murray Sayle, to Moscow to find Philby. Sayle did so rather simply. He knew that Philby was keen on cricket (the season was still on) and went regularly to P.O. Box 609 at the Central Post Office in Moscow to collect his mail and *The Times,* which carried the cricket reports; sure enough, Philby appeared. Philby had his own reasons for talking with Sayle; he had finished his memoir and wished, he told Sayle, to trade it for two important Russian secret agents, Peter and Helen Kroger, who were serving twenty years in a British jail.

Philby and Sayle met at the Minsk Hotel on Gorky Street at eight o'clock that same night. The room held only a table with bottles of brandy, wine, and mineral water. Philby warned Sayle, who resembled a heavyweight boxer, against "any rough stuff," as there was an armed guard outside and Sayle would not "get ten yards if [he] tried anything." Philby declared himself to be an officer of the KGB; he referred constantly to "my superiors" and "my colleagues"; and he declared in regard to the Krogers, "Our position is that the Krogers are innocent of the charges on which they were convicted." They were being held under conditions that were "inhumanly severe"; Peter Kroger was "covered in eczema"; and they were not the top-level agents of the KGB they were represented as being in the court and the press. His offer to give the manuscript to the British government was his own idea, not that of "my superiors," and "I feel I would like to do whatever I can personally to get these people out." Perhaps it was a bad bargain, he said, "but we will just have to face the fact that the Western side always comes out worse in this type of exchange, for the simple fact that we have more and better agents than you have."

As to his own position, he said, "I love life, women and children, food and drink. I have all that and I want other people to be able enjoy it all to the full" — a statement that enabled Sayle to inquire how he felt about abandoning his own family. Philby responded, "I suppose I am really two people. I am a private person and a political person. Of course, if there is a conflict the political person comes first." When Sayle then made bold to ask him how he reacted to the charge that he was a traitor, he declared, "To betray, you must first belong. I never belonged. I have followed exactly the same line the whole of my adult life. The fight against fascism and the fight against imperialism are fundamentally the same fight." His book, he added, was some eighty thousand words long, but not more than eight pages were political, in that he discussed the merits of communism. Many young persons became communist in the 1930s; his objective in the book was to show why he had remained one, why he had "seen it

through to the end . . . through the Stalin period and everything else."
Of the KGB he stated, that "undoubtedly ours is the best intelligence
service there has ever been. Some really tremendous triumphs." He
would say nothing more "for operational reasons."[27]

By September 1967 the inquiry was complete. The first article appeared under a gigantic headline: INSIGHT REVEALS THAT TOP RUS-
SIAN SPY WAS BEING GROOMED TO HEAD BRITAIN'S SECRET SERVICE.
The cat was out of the bag. For years the Secret Service had remained
secure, secret, and anonymous. But now it stood exposed to the public
gaze. The matter touched the queen. When Richard Crossman, the
socialist minister, asked her whether she had read the Philby story,
which had dominated that Sunday's newspapers, she replied in a single
sentence that she didn't read that kind of thing, and Crossman realized that "this was not a subject which we ought to discuss." The queen
knew about the Philby case, of course, but as the supreme figure of
Establishment authority she stood above all politics and controversy,
a figure of probity.[28]

The articles caused a great sensation and were published by André
Deutsch, the London publisher, in book form late in 1968 as *Philby:
The Spy Who Betrayed a Generation*. The subtitle was apt; he had betrayed
his generation of Cambridge men who, in large numbers, had made
their way into Whitehall to lead the state and the empire during the
German war. John le Carré, a state spy with Old Etonian connections,
wrote the introduction. His thesis: "It is arguable that Kim Philby,
spiteful, vain and murderous as he was, was the spy and catalyst in the
ring of modern treason whom the Establishment deserved." Philby
was "a creature of the post-war depression, of the swift snuffing out of
the Socialist flame, of the thousand-year sleep of Eden and Macmillan."[29]

Tracing the distinct stages in the attitude of Stewart Menzies and
his colleagues toward Philby, le Carré accounted for his recruitment
in terms fashionably anti-Establishmentarian:

> *A decent, diffident boy, son of old St. John; Westminster and Cambridge; good-
> ish reports; plenty of guts and knows how to get on with intellectuals without
> being tarred with their brush.* And his left wing associations? Wild oats.
> *Open the door and let him in.*

The second stage, after 1944, saw Menzies and the Establishment
rejoicing in its collective judgment:

> *Kim is not only a good operator — fit to teach those rash Americans wisdom
> — but, when he wants to be, presentable. He rides hard, likes his drink and*

is a bit of a bastard with the girls; but he knows when to accept the bit. We were wise to choose Kim. And his left-wing associations? *All got up by MI5.*

The third stage, after the defection of Burgess and Maclean, is by far the most interesting, covering the mock trial and Macmillan's official clearance of Philby in the House of Commons and Philby's reemployment by Sir John Sinclair:

> *Kim has been monstrously misused. He has been playing a damned difficult game flushing out Russians and his actions have been misinterpreted by a lot of outsiders, including those lower class buffoons in [MI5]. He may have been a bit naughty but no more. We must get him back on the rails.* And, aside, the voice pleaded: *Kim, persuade us you are not one of them.*[30]

Savage literary fighting broke out. Hugh Trevor-Roper, Philby's old rival, was by now Regius Professor of History, a powerful post not only in academe but in other nations, including the United States and its literary capital, New York. He dismissed le Carré's views of Philby and the secret circle as "rich, flatulent puff."[31] Le Carré replied in the *Sunday Times* in 1968: "Writers are a subversive crowd, nothing if not traitors. The better the writer, the greater the betrayal tends to appear, a thing the secret community has learned the hard way."[32] Philby had the literati on the ropes.

The bullfrogs' chorus lasted many months, and it was expanded from time to time by declarations by one or another of the golden lads who had drifted into Churchill's games of legerdemain, force, and fraud. Dr. Goronwy Rees, a Fellow of All Souls and a friend of Guy Burgess's, was left with an "incurable disposition to doubt and suspect all impeccable authorities." The security and intelligence services seemed "to be a microcosm of that 'great capitalist class' now in the process of internal disintegration, whose structure and organisation, modes of behaviour and thought, I had found so alien when I first went to Oxford." Rees betrayed to MI5 the names of men and women whom he suspected of being spies, on the condition that he would be bothered no more. He denounced Anthony Blunt, Guy Liddell (the former chief of MI5 counterespionage), Robin Zaehner (an SIS counterespionage agent and Oxford don on active service in Persia), and Stuart Hampshire, who was in Trevor-Roper's circle of Canaris watchers during the war.

Rees's wife complained of the Gestapo-like tactics of MI5 when Rees was sacked from academic life and, blackballed and jobless, was hit in the street not by a Daimler or a Jaguar but by a Volkswagen minibus in what seemed to him an attempt to kill him, which very nearly succeeded. The golden lads who had surrounded Philby, Burgess, and Maclean were interrogated: Cyril Connolly, Tom Driberg, John Lehmann, Phillip Toynbee, W. H. Auden, Harold Acton, Brian Howard, Graham Greene, Malcolm Muggeridge, Claud Cockburn, Evelyn Waugh, Christopher Isherwood.

All the rogues and dandies were questioned while London society followed the hunt for the third man, the fourth man, the fifth man. Homosexuality in the Foreign Office was a persistent theme. Evelyn Waugh's second novel about the war, *Officers and Gentlemen*, came along, a tale of how Ivor Claire of the ruling generation abandoned his men on Crete and how his treachery and cowardice were aided and abetted by Julia Stitch, the wife of the British minister in Egypt, who pulls every string to save her friend from exposure and punishment. In *Unconditional Surrender* he dealt with English dandyism, homosexuality, and communist treachery. Martin Green, a social historian, wrote how — through Philby, Burgess, Maclean, and Anthony Blunt, that elegant figure in tails fresh from dinner at the Royal Academy:

> Britain became identified in the eyes of other governments as the country of dandies and rogues and not of gentlemen; the country of decadent *Sonnenkinder* [Children of the Sun], not men of maturity and responsibility. No doubt it was already known that the British diplomatic and secret services were infiltrated by such types, but by means of the scandal Russia brought home to America — another country in which such types were much more rigorously distanced from the seats of power — how dangerous this situation was. It thus contributed to the drama of temperamental conflict in America. The feverish McCarthy search for Communists in government circles was clearly a search for *potential* traitors as much as for actual ones, a search for security *risks,* for people of the wrong temperament to handle power . . . While in England itself the effect was . . . to crumble the image that the Establishment had always presented to the rest of the country — the image of a group of men so deeply and *a priori* "all right" that their undeniable eccentricities could be ignored or indulged.[33]

Each clever pen found the Philby case symbolic of the decrepitude into which England had sunk through two world wars — of the end of the greatest of the imperial powers. A literary furor developed, one without modern precedent that went on and on for years; a whole generation of journalists and whiz kids fed on it, married, raised families, bought houses, motor cars, on the public outrage. It became as much a trade as a cause. It was one noticeable for a single element. No one got through to the old C, the unknown dimension in the entire affair, the old fox.

Having read an article on the Philby case in the *Sunday Times,* Felix Cowgill, now in retirement in Dorsetshire, felt he had been libeled. He consulted lawyers and sought to enlist the help of the old C. Cowgill's resentment was not unjustified, for, under his command, Section V had defeated the German intelligence service as no intelligence service of a modern state had ever been defeated before. But that fact was not mentioned in the *Sunday Times,* which failed also, no doubt because of the Official Secrets Act or ignorance, to mention other matters that might have cast Cowgill in a better light — the triumph of Ultra, for example, and the still greater triumph of ISOS. Menzies, busily engaged in damage control at places where the high Tories met, twisted Cowgill's arm in the direction of silence. In a rare letter that hinted that he had used Philby, just as Philby had used him, the old C wrote:

Dear Felix,

The article which you found to be so offensive is not one that I should regard as one calling for action as unfortunately we are unable to defend ourselves & once one goes for the Press experience shows that one is unlikely to win. But what possible action could you take except possibly to write a defence to the "S.T." should they be willing to publish it. Again I do not know what the action would be of the "Firm." After all, the present incumbents have suffered more than we have & personally I intend doing nothing unless the . . . book forces one's hand. So far I have warded off 4 newspapers [and] 24 TVs. I am however trying to find out if there is any possible action for the likes of us, but I am pretty sure that the action will be to do nothing. What I think about Kim is beyond words & that he was seriously considered as the "top" is absurd as we all knew his weakness for drink. *But one could not have thought him to have been an out & out traitor.* But there are, alas, many such Englishmen, as witness the Communists in this country.[34]

Cowgill settled out of court for a trifling £50, about a hundred dollars, his legal costs. He might have got £50,000 had he stayed in, but he would also have been blackballed in the society he kept.

Then came the book. Philby's "devastating attack on SIS and other organizations with which it was associated" arrived in the West. It had existed in "provisional" form since the summer of 1967, he explained in a foreword, but, as dutiful as ever, he had given "long consideration to the desirability of publishing it" and concluded that it should be "shelved indefinitely" because "publication seemed likely to cause a rumpus, with international complications the nature of which was difficult to foresee." He explained further: "It seemed unwise to take action that might have consequences beyond the range of reasonable prediction." But this attitude had been "changed completely by articles which appeared in the *Sunday Times* and *The Observer* in October 1967." These articles, "in spite of a number of factual inaccuracies and errors of interpretation (and, I fear, gratifying exaggeration of my own talents), present a substantially true picture of my career." It was "immediately suggested, of course, by rival newspapers that the *Sunday Times* and *The Observer* had fallen victim to a gigantic plant." But this was "an absurdity," and "the consequences of the truth being disclosed are on us irrevocably, for better or worse. I can offer my book to the public without incurring charge of wanting to muddy waters." His purpose now, he said, "is simply to correct certain inaccuracies and errors of interpretation, and to present a more fully rounded picture."[35]

However praiseworthy Philby's intentions may appear, there was no doubt in the mind of the Cabinet secretary, Sir Burke Trend, or his intelligence advisers that Philby was out to make mischief, particularly in the frayed Anglo-American intelligence relationships. As Philby went on, administering what he trusted would be the kiss of death to many persons and several institutions of the state:

> Until quite recently, when the *Sunday Times* and *The Observer* let some large and fairly authentic cats out of the bag, writers who touched my case in newspaper articles and books thrashed around wildly in the dark. They cannot be blamed for their ignorance since throughout my career I was careful not to advertise the truth. But some blame perhaps attaches to them for rushing into print in that blissful state, and for their insistence on looking for complex explanations where simple ones would have served better. The simple truth, of course, was painful to a crumbling Establishment and its transatlantic friends. But the attempt to wash it away in words, whether ingenious or just nonsensical, was futile and fore-doomed to failure.

His principal concern during his youth was that "overt and covert links between Britain and Germany at that time were of serious concern to the Soviet Government."

Various mysterious individuals set about the task of muddying the authenticity of the work or of suggesting that publication would endanger the national security, and the book might have been torpedoed altogether but for the intervention of an Establishment editor, Robin Denniston. Denniston gave no reason for supporting a work intended, as the synopsis showed, to damage or demolish the reputation of an important institution. However, perhaps a reason lay in his background, for he was the son of Commander Alastair Denniston, the chief of C's code breakers for many years between the two world wars.

At that time, peremptorily but under the twin pressures of war and Churchill, C was compelled to improve the efficiency of Denniston's service during a period of extraordinary expansion that Denniston showed himself unable to manage. C relieved him, which left him bitterly distressed, and placed him in the lesser but still vital office of managing the attack against the enemy powers' diplomatic ciphers. Here Denniston did outstanding work, in which Philby himself played a major role. But he remained bitter at his removal, so bitter, indeed, that at a dinner of the diplomatic code breakers at the Café Royal just after the war, his advice in his afterdinner speech to those thinking of making code breaking their career was to find some other occupation, as government service was "not rewarding."

Robin Denniston's publishing house declined to publish the work, as did all other major London publishers. But as the *Sunday Telegraph* recorded, Denniston "felt so strongly that the book ought to be published that he took the unusual step of offering to act as London agent for the book in his private capacity and on a no-commission basis." Despite imprecations from the British government not to publish the book, Denniston found *My Silent War* a home with MacGibbon and Kee, a small left-wing London publisher. The North American rights went to Grove Press. Other rights were then sold worldwide, except for the Soviet rights, which became entangled in Soviet policy. Although it is claimed that the substantial royalties did not go to Philby, the sales were very large, and the work became an authentic world bestseller; in Moscow it is said that sixteen million copies were sold, mainly in paperback. How this gigantic figure was computed cannot be ascertained, for the work was not popular at the Central Committee and the International Department in Moscow.

In England, the book was regarded informally, by Sir Maurice Oldfield, the chief of the British Secret Service at the time, as "true — as far as it went." Which meant that Philby had not told all, as he had threatened in the synopsis. Or, more likely, that he did, but his KGB masters excised the parts they felt might cause them more trouble with MI6 than the propaganda value of the work was worth. But the work was important as the first view of the inner politics of a service that was then regarded as "the power behind the throne." It was also regarded as a considerable and successful operation in causing mischief between the chiefs of the service, and served to add to the already inflamed relations between the Atlantic powers' intelligence services. Its publication certainly contributed to Philby's reputation as a sort of Bolshevik James Bond, the one heroic figure of the Establishment, which had rotted from within after two centuries of ruling the world.

Philby left a couple of mysteries, one of which was probably important. In a preface dated 1958, he apologized for naming names — *infra dig* in the secret world — but did so in adroit fashion. He too, he explained, had "suffered personal inconvenience through my connection with the secret service" — possibly an allusion to his claim that C had attempted to use him, without his knowledge, as a deception agent against the Soviet service. He also alluded to the miasma of the double agency surrounding his name:

> Some writers have recently spoken of me as a double agent, or even as a triple agent. If this is taken to mean that I was working with equal zeal for two or more sides at once, it is seriously misleading. All through my career, I have been a straight penetration agent working in the Soviet interest. The fact that I joined the British Secret Intelligence Service is neither here nor there; I regarded my SIS appointments purely in the light of cover jobs, to be carried out sufficiently well to ensure my attaining positions in which my service to the Soviet Union would be most effective. My connection with SIS must be seen against my prior total commitment to the Soviet Union, which I regarded then, as I do now, the inner fortress of the world movement.

He sought to justify the path he had chosen in life with the statement:

> My persisting faith in Communism does not mean that my views and attitudes have remained fossilised for thirty years [as Trevor-Roper had written]. They have been influenced and modified, sometimes rudely, by the appalling events of my lifetime. I have quarrelled with my political friends on major issues, and still do so. There is an awful lot of work ahead; there will be ups and downs. Advances which, thirty years ago, I hoped to see in my lifetime, may have to wait a generation or two. But, as I look over Moscow from my study window, I can see the solid foundations of the future I glimpsed at Cambridge.
>
> Finally, it is a sobering thought that, but for the power of the Soviet Union and the Communist idea, the Old World, if not the whole world, would now be ruled by Hitler and Hirohito. It is a matter of great pride to me that I was invited, at so early an age, to play my infinitesimal part in building up that power. How, where and when I became a member of the Soviet intelligence service is a matter for myself and my comrades. I will only say that, when the proposition was made to me, I did not hesitate. One does not look twice at an offer of enrolment in an elite force.[36]

Philby dwelt briefly on the artistry he had displayed in concealing his politics for so many years from so many friends and enemies skilled in observing such matters. "The first duty of an underground worker," he wrote at the end of the book, "is to perfect not only his cover story but also his cover personality." By the time he reached Beirut, he had had "more than twenty years' experience behind me, including some testing years. Furthermore, I was baptised the hard way, in Nazi Germany and Fascist Spain, where a slip might have had consequences only describable as dire."[37]

Where the work succeeded, among those susceptible to him, was in establishing him as a man who had worked against the Atlantic powers, not through the prospect of gain or personal power, but out of conviction. This reaction was particularly marked by one of Philby's wartime colleagues, Graham Greene, who had emerged, in the view of his followers, as the foremost novelist of his time.

Greene always knew much more about Philby's game than he revealed. In 1963, after Philby's defection, he completed the manuscript of one of his most famous novels, *The Human Factor,* the story of a British Secret Service officer named Castle whom Boris of the Russian Intelligence Service in London (Yuri Modin?) recruits as a Soviet agent on an ideological basis. It is evident that the chief of the British Secret Service (Menzies?) knew of Castle's treachery but did nothing. Castle became the chief's plant in Moscow. But Greene did not publish the work until 1978, by which time he had reconnected with his old friend at Patriarch's Pond. According to Anthony Masters, the author of a biographical statement about Greene, he did not wish the public to conclude that he had drawn inspiration for the novel from Philby's character.

Greene himself alluded to this long delay in other terms. Explaining himself in a rare interview with the *Sunday Telegraph* in London on the occasion of the book's publication, he declared that he had liked Philby personally and had often asked himself what he would have done if he had discovered that Philby was a Soviet agent when they were together at War Station XB. Perhaps, he said, "I would have given him twenty-four hours to get clear, and then reported it." But, he said, Philby and the case in which he had been involved played no part in *The Human Factor,* and he abandoned the work in 1963 because of Philby's defection and his subsequent activities in Moscow. He had toyed with the idea of publishing it posthumously, again to avoid entangling himself in the Philby case—and also because from 1966 he had begun to rise to eminence. In 1962 he was made an honorary doctor of literature at Cambridge, in 1963 an honorary Fellow of Balliol. In 1966 he was made one of the fifty members of the Order of Companions of Honour, of which the queen was the first member; its motto was "In Action Faithful, and in Honour Clear." There was talk that he was a candidate for the Nobel Prize in Literature, and his work as a novelist was recognized by a number of important international awards. But Greene had enemies, some of them in important places in the press, so it was no time to involve himself publicly with Philby, who, in the American view, was the greatest British traitor since Major André in the Revolutionary War.

It fell to Greene to write the introduction to Philby's memoir, *My Silent War.* His thesis was that a man might betray his country but that he must never betray his friends. Despite his eminence, therefore, Greene wrote in a kindly fashion of Philby's activities as a Soviet spy. This was not, he declared, the book that Kim's enemies had anticipated:

> It is an honest one, well-written, often amusing, and the story he has to tell, after the flight of Burgess and Maclean, is far more gripping than any novel of espionage I can remember. We were told to expect a lot of propaganda, but it contains none, unless a dignified state-ment of his beliefs and motives can be called propaganda. The end, of course, in his eyes is held to justify the means, but this is a view taken, perhaps less openly, by most men involved in politics, whether the politician be a Disraeli or a Wilson. "He betrayed his country" — yes, perhaps he did, but who among us has not committed treason to something or someone more important than a country? In Philby's eyes he was working for a shape of things to come from which his country would benefit.

Philby's account of the secret service, which the ruling generation thought to be one of the four or five institutions that governed the world, was, Greene felt, "devastatingly true." Philby's character studies were "admirable if unkind." And if the work had required a subtitle, Greene felt it should have been *The Spy as Craftsman,* for Kim had been the best of them. As Greene acknowledged:

> The story of how, to attain his position, he eliminated Cowgill makes, as he admits, for "sour reading, just as it makes sour writing" — one feels for the moment the sharp touch of the icicle in the heart. I saw the beginning of this affair — indeed, I resigned rather than accept the promotion which was one tiny cog of the machinery of his intrigue.

I attributed it then to a personal drive for power, the only characteristic in Philby which I thought disagreeable. I am glad now that I was wrong. He was serving a cause and not himself, and so my old liking for him comes back, as I remember with pleasure those long Sunday lunches at St. Albans when the whole subsection relaxed under his leadership for a few hours of heavy drinking, and later the meetings over a pint on fire-watching nights at the pub behind St. James's Street. If one made an error of judgement he was sure to minimise it and cover it up, without criticism, with a halting stammered witticism. He had all the small loyalties to his colleagues, and of course his big loyalty was unknown to us.[38]

The old C, Sir Stewart Menzies, did not live long after the book was published. In it, Philby wrote, "I look back on the Chief with enduring affection," and there is evidence that he was sincere. Shortly before the book came out, Menzies had had a fall while riding with the Beaufort Hunt. He did not recover. Since so many of those connected with Philby died untimely deaths, or mysterious ones — and there was mystery about C's death for a time — C's death may be explained. The latest death, that of Frank Wisner of the CIA through a gunshot blast on his doorstep, warrants this.

After a funeral service at the village church, C was cremated at Bath. The next day, *The Times* published a notice by Sir Rex Benson, a relative, colleague, C's closest friend, and, as military attaché in Washington for much of the war, one of C's most trusted advisers. In surveying C's life at Eton, Benson recalled that their housemaster, the famous Edward Impey, "had a profound love and admiration for the works of Kipling and Co. and *Kim*." Had the book played its part in Philby's appointment to the secret service?

But of course C could not depart without an element of mystery. What became of his ashes? It is a sad story. His third and last marriage, which took place after the death of his second wife, had been badly clouded by the bullfrogs' chorus. Lady Menzies began to upbraid C in public for "having let the country down" through his employment of Philby. Thereafter they lived more or less separate lives. After the cremation, the ashes were delivered to the widow's home in the Manor House, Mayfair, but Lady Menzies banished the box of ashes to her cellar. There it remained for the next sixteen years. When it came out that C had no known grave, to use the official phrase, it served to nourish the rumors that there had been something strange about his death.

By 1984, with Stewart Menzies's ashes still in the basement of the Manor House, Lady Menzies was only rarely *compos mentis,* and it seemed that she could not live much longer. This caused considerable anxiety to Mrs. Ford, her secretary, who knew that the ashes of Sir Stewart were in the basement but had received no instructions about their disposal should Lady Menzies die. Fearing that they might well be thrown out and uncertain about what she should do, Mrs. Ford communicated her anxieties to C's family, and the ashes were recovered. On November 11, 1984 — Armistice Day — the remains of C were at last committed to hallowed soil in the churchyard at Luckington. The place is marked by a small stone plaque:

Sir Stewart Menzies, KCMG, KBE, DSO, MC,
Chief,
British Secret Service,
1939–1952

There thus passed the last of those who knew why C had employed Philby in his service and promoted him to its highest ranks. He left no public testament regarding the appointment, only a vast silence.

18

Endgame

1970–1994

I
N 1964, a fresh and agreeable face appeared at Patriarch's Pond. Thirty-year-old Lieutenant Colonel Mikhail Petrovich Lyubimov — his given name meant "the loved one" — had been with the KGB in London and was regarded by his masters as their leading British expert. He was influential in the KGB and considered an excellent example of the new Soviet man. His father had been a general in Stalin's counterespionage service, and this made him a member of the *nomenklatura*. He had been a diplomat but in 1959 was transferred to the KGB because he spoke excellent English. After two years of KGB training, Lyubimov was sent to London as the monster plot was breaking out and remained there until 1965.

His specialty was the Conservative Party, and he became a familiar figure at party meetings at all levels. Tall, good-looking, well-built, good-humored, by nature a poet, playwright, and novelist, Lyubimov became the KGB's man about town in London. He did experience much interference from the Security Service, but no serious action was taken against him, although it was known that another of his specialties was to make connection with the lower order — the secretaries and cipher clerks — of the Foreign Office and the Government Communications Headquarters. But in 1965 Lyubimov went too far. With an eye on the prospect of becoming chief of the KGB's Third Department, which was responsible for Britain and the British sphere of influence, Lyubimov gave his attention to no less a personage than the director general of GCHQ, Sir Clive Loehnis, one of the two most im-

portant men in the Anglo-American code-breaking operations against
the Soviet Union, the other being the director of the National Security
Agency in the United States.

Lyubimov succeeded in making contact with Loehnis and pressed
his case, because "to have recruited such a bird would have made me
a Hero of Soviet Russia at once," he later said. But Loehnis knew all
he needed to know about Lyubimov and laid a trap for him. When
the two men met in Shepherd's Market, Lyubimov made his impudent
proposal that "he assist us in our work." Loehnis replied that he would
think about it but first must visit the men's room. The moment he did,
Lyubimov remembered with great good humor, "two very rough men
approached me out of the crowd and announced: 'Mr. Lyubimov, Your
career is over.'"[1]

Locked up at a police station, Lyubimov claimed diplomatic immunity and was held until his embassy arranged his release. During that
time, Lyubimov was invited to collaborate against the KGB if he valued
his freedom. In due course, he was declared persona non grata —
*png'*d, as it is known in the trade. He left London for Moscow, re-
gretfully, for he was in the process of becoming an Anglophile; he
claimed he would have been much happier in the upper reaches of
Bloomsbury in Macmillan's London than in Khrushchev's Moscow.
But he was still a Marxist, and so he became first deputy and then
chief of the British desk of the KGB in Moscow — the job that Kim
still wanted. In that capacity he controlled all the KGB's British "assets"
— spies and informants — and operations in the British Isles and the
Commonwealth.

By 1965, the Macmillan government had been swept away by the
socialist regime of Harold Wilson. Having read Guy Burgess's main
work for the KGB, "The National Characteristics of the British," in
which Burgess argued that the British government was as corruptible
as any other, Lyubimov decided to call on Philby at Patriarch's Pond.
Philby, alone and lonely, was only too delighted to receive an officer
of influence in the KGB. Lyubimov was exactly the type of Russian
whom Philby liked most: a literary liberal communist with an unusually rich manner of speaking English. He had, too, an impressive presence, giving off the whiff of an English squire, although slightly more
English than the English themselves.

The KGB, hoping to make trouble between the British and American governments and thereby force the removal of the U.S. military
bases from England, encouraged a social relationship between Philby
and Lyubimov, and they began to talk, drink, meet, and eat, mainly at

Philby's apartment. Lyubimov had to assess whether Kim was a real defector or a British plant. It was his opinion, adhered to almost thirty years later, that Kim had not been "inserted by" the British. When asked how he knew Kim was not a British plant, he replied: "If it was a British plant it was a very far-fetched one and foolish. You cannot have a plant with a man with whom you have no contact at all. The British knew perfectly well that they could not contact Philby."

His view of Kim's flight was:

> Kim came here not as a sympathizer to Russia, not as an austere man seeking an austere home. Other reasons apart, he came here in the spirit of the old Comintern, of a world without frontiers. If you look at his soul it was the soul of the Comintern man, an absolute faith in Marx and Lenin, to work to make the world into a big paradise. That is why we called him the Robin Hood of communism. He did not come here in the expectation of finding the Marxist paradise.

But when asked whether Kim had found an evil empire, he replied:

> I think so definitely. He discovered it at once. He was not a fool. When he came here and saw all the monitoring of the KGB of himself, he understood at once that he was in a prison. That this was a totalitarian state. He himself had had no experience of our standard of living. He had read about it in the British press, but he had considered that press to be a bad one, and when he saw what was happening with his own eyes, the poverty, the conditions, he understood at once that the propaganda had been full of lies. It made a great impact on him. He saw that the administration entirely comprised cowardly bureaucrats. He found that everybody was afraid to say something. The KGB officers were very formal with Kim because he was a foreigner, and because there is a tradition in the KGB to treat a foreigner as a foreigner, as shit. I remember the deputy chief of the international department of the KGB telling me: "Look, these foreign communists are not real communists." The same applied to agents. Kim, I thought, had an illusion he would be considered an equal. You understand? But he was not considered an equal. He was considered an agent, a man to be used. Kim complained, "You are running me? You are running me as an agent!" He complained because, as he knew well, an agent is not an equal but dirt.

What did the KGB find in Kim that was so valuable?

The reason the KGB needed Kim, and why he made such a great name for himself in Russia, was because of his value to Active Measures. Ninety percent of our Active Measures was bluff to enable the

KGB to report to the Central Committee and the Government that it was successfully at work against "the main adversary" — the United States. Most of Active Measures — pamphleteering and rumormongering — was rubbish and a waste of money. Where they counted was "if one of our agents obtained a war plan" from the United States or NATO. There are such plans and it is known that the General Staffs create them every year. Then the great thing we can do with them is to publish them and make trouble for the other side. Similarly if we uncover a plot to kill someone we inject something into documents such as these that is very much compromising. This was the main work that Kim did after his debriefing. It was valuable work for this reason: As a trained and important officer of the British Secret Service, with great experience in the work, one who was absolutely loyal to Communism, Kim had great value. That is why he was "the unique spy." He was unique in this aspect of intelligence work because he was always there, ready to do what no Russian could do — place an informed and highly intelligent Anglo-Saxon mind at the disposal of Marxist-Leninism. In this he was better than Josef Goebbels because *he knew the mind of the other side.* He knew how the American and the British governments' documents were written. He could ensure the authenticity of the language and composition, for was he not a civil servant himself?

And asked what would have happened to Kim had he gone to the British Embassy or tried to escape abroad, he said:

There was nowhere for him to go and he stayed because he had to. Here, at least, he was the Honorable Prisoner. He never tried to go to England. He was not always content in Moscow and he did speak of "living abroad." But he understood that if he tried, he would be arrested. Do you think the KGB would have let him go? No! And for the same reason that they would not allow Sakharov to leave. Sakharov knew too much about the Russian thermonuclear bomb. Kim knew too much the KGB. If he had tried to live in one of the socialist countries, as the symbol of Western communists, he would, like Sakharov, have been exiled to Gorki. Here he was in the golden cage and had too much to lose by leaving — his flat, his dacha, his special privileges. He understood perfectly well that it was not necessary to have him shot. All that was necessary was to send him to the east of the Urals. A silver cage for Kim instead of a golden one.

In these circumstances, in May 1967, Philby learned that he had a new chief. Khrushchev and Semichastny were removed by Leonid Brezhnev, and Yuri Vladimirovich Andropov became the new chairman of the KGB. With Andropov came the longest period of stabilization and growth in the history of the KGB, one that would last until May 1982, when Andropov became secretary and then general secretary of the party. Born in 1914, Andropov was two years younger than Philby. A Soviet civil servant by trade, he had come to prominence in 1956 through his skill in tricking the Hungarian counterrevolutionaries into attending peace talks intended to end the Hungarian rebellion. But instead of talking when they were all assembled in one place, they were arrested by the Hungarian Secret Service, with the help of the KGB, and shot. Andropov was then appointed chief of liaison between the Communist Party of the Soviet Union and its fraternal parties in the Soviet bloc.

As Lyubimov related, in about 1968, after Andropov became chairman of the KGB, Philby became one of his advisers; and it was accepted widely that through Philby's advice the KGB stereotype of the Moscow hood vanished. Philby met with Andropov, not at headquarters, which would have given him great status, but at a special mansion in a side street just off Derzhinsky Square. Lyubimov remembered:

> Kim began to like Andropov not because Andropov was different from Brezhnev, who was a very boring man at the head of a very boring regime, but because Andropov was very clever. At one time all of us liked Andropov. At last, I remember thinking to myself, the Grand Master at the head of our service! His eloquent phrases, his ideas! But when a great liberal like Andropov began sending people to the psychiatric wards, it was much worse than Beria, who just shot people.

> Kim liked Andropov because he looked and talked like a progressive, clever, a man who had a positive democratic influence on Brezhnev. Kim was wrong. We were all wrong. We discussed politics with Kim but we never got into philosophy because Kim was not a great philosopher. He was a pragmatist. For him Marxism was an emotional thing. He gave me a very good analysis of the political situations in Great Britain because he listened to the BBC, we let him get *The Times*, and for him it was easy. He was not anti-British, definitely not. He was very attached to England, like his father. Kim's approach to England was as contradictory as his father's. He spoke of the Establishment in condescending terms. But at the same time, when I look at my correspondence with him, I noted that he always asked me to get him *British* goods, especially chunky Oxford marmalade.

So Kim had real power in the KGB? Yes, recalled Lyubimov,

> of course he had power. It was very nice for our chiefs to be able to say that they had been to Kim's flat, and that he had said, "We must take these, and these, and these measures against England." He was

manipulated. I myself discovered that this was an excellent method through which to get my chiefs to listen to my ideas. Kim was world famous, you see, and you know how prestigious it is to meet world-famous people. You can tell your wife, your friends. I myself keep a photograph of Kim in my study and people who visit me exclaim: "Kim Philby! Did you know him?" "Yes," I say, "I know him very well. He is my friend. We drink whiskey together."

"Oh!" they say, regarding me as a powerful man. I kept Kim's photograph in my office in the station in Denmark. It was inscribed "To the Danish Residentura." This was again prestigious for me, for my visitors would study the photograph and the inscription, and this gave me some flavor of being important. All my subordinates, my boys, knew that I was a personal friend of Kim Philby, that his portrait was on my wall. I made a special very good frame for it and when non-intelligence visitors called they used to say "Who is this? Keem Pheelby?" I would reply: "Yes it is. He is a great man." They would say "Yes he is" and feel that I was important and that they were more important for having talked with me, the friend of Philby. That is life.

According to Lyubimov, Philby was introduced to Andropov by V. A. Kryuchkov, who became Andropov's chief of the First Main Directorate, the secret intelligence service of the KGB, and, when Andropov succeeded Brezhnev as the first man in the Soviet Union, chairman of the KGB. As Lyubimov, who was a member of Kryuchkov's staff, related,

> Kryuchkov led Kim to Andropov, who used to see Kim from time to time or give Kim some decoration. You must understand the psychology of our bureaucrats. You want to show something to your superior. You want to involve your superior in some business all the time. If you do not involve your superior in some business all the time you get no promotion. So it was very pleasing for Kryuchkov to say to Andropov: "Yuri Vladimirovich, I think that you must meet this great man. If you do so it will support him morally.' So Andropov saw Kim, and not only Andropov but Kryuchkov as well and perhaps also the head of the department. All have a chance to be present when the head of the KGB is receiving Kim. So all people are interested in fixing up engagements with Kim, who was interested in being acknowledged as a Hero of the Soviet Union.

The relationship between Philby and Andropov, Lyubimov explained,

> was not as close as the Western press liked to think. He saw Andropov from time to time on various matters but of course Andropov had much more to do than pay court to an agent, however famous he might have been. But Andropov too was pleased to be able to say that

he had been talking with the world-famous spy, Kim Philby, and of course Kim was equally delighted. For one thing, Andropov could not speak English; for another, Kim could speak Russian only very badly. On the other hand, Kim's relationship with Andropov's protégé Kryuchkov was very good.

Secondly there was such a gulf between a graduate of Cambridge and a party functionary. I remember when Kim met the head of the KGB's Personnel Department, Ageyev, a stone-faced party man. Kim stuttered gratefully — he stuttered more when he was nervous in the presence of great man such as Ageyev. I remember that the conversation went like this. "What do you think we should do about our cadre work, to better our personnel? The people are not as Marxist as they once were. How can we better the ideological strength of the cadres?" The reaction of Kim was the same as yours would be if I spoke in such language to you. Ageyev and Kim were two different people from different planets, so to speak.

But in 1968, the year of the publication of *My Silent War,* the KGB management suddenly ended its relationship with Philby. They gave him no work, and he returned to the almost complete isolation of Patriarch's Pond. No reason was given for putting him back into the golden cage. He became lonely and despondent, he took to liquor again, and his health became as bad as it was toward the end in Beirut. Lyubimov thought that Kim might have become too outspoken at his apartment. To criticize could be dangerous to the critic. It could not fail at some stage to attract the attention of "the conservative orthodoxy." As Lyubimov related:

> Kim's criticism was in favor of a better communism, "communism with a human face," actually. We were not making criticism like Sakharov and Solzhenitsyn and so on. But making criticism against the party. We were idealistic here. It was possible to make the party clean, to make it correspond to the lofty ideals of Lenin and Marx. We never said we wanted a free economy or a free market. We never said we wanted to follow the liberal ways of the West — miniskirts and so on. At the Academy, I remember, we were forbidden to dance foxtrot and tango. We did that privately, of course, but not publicly. Women were still expected to be virgins. This was important; one of our generals declared publicly that at marriage his wife was a virgin and that there was blood on the sheets as evidence of that fact. Ours was a conservative Russian way; and jeans were forbidden.

Kim's advocacy was that

> first the Communist Party must rule and that fact must be admitted. Secondly some socialism must be permitted, like Lenin did. We wanted

freer discussion within the Communist structure. We wanted freer travel to the West. Nuclear war as a means of settling political questions should be excluded completely. We did not agree that war between capitalism and communism was inevitable. Capitalism, we decided, would decay without our help. Khrushchev said: "We shall bury you." Remember that. He meant it but not in a very serious way. But we would make a coup d'état or a revolution if necessary and in accordance with Karl Marx. It was a play. Nobody took it seriously at the Central Committee. Let us coexist was the advocacy, but it was an advocacy that was sauce for the West. However, there were troubles at Berlin, Budapest, Prague, Warsaw. Where were coexistence and communism with a human face?

Kim felt things like psychiatric hospitals, for instance, the Solzhenitsyn, the Sakharov affairs, all these affairs were blows against the great theory of communism. Here we were very close to you. If you cut off the bad part of communism, then you have communism with a human face. We had many social accomplishments, education, social security, health care, assistance from the government from the cradle to the grave. There were some social achievements done at the cost of exploiting our oil, but we were not so discontented economically. Also, Russians are accustomed to live rather badly. That is our way of life.

Kim wanted to hear different views. Let Sakharov speak. Let Solzhenitsyn get his books published. All he wanted, I assure you, was some scope for freedom within the Communist society. Less expenditure on armaments, of course. He was very proud of communist military power. He knew very little about it and never read about it very much. He was not very interested in it. He was a political animal, partly interested in history and literature — Johnson and Boswell, he liked to discuss these things. Kim was a *bon vivant*, I am a *bon vivant*.

There Philby remained, isolated and alone, at Patriarch's Pond, until Oleg Kalugin arrived from Washington, having discovered that the FBI in Washington was on his heels.

In April 1970, when Kalugin took up his new post as the deputy chief of Directorate K, the foreign counterintelligence branch of the KGB's foreign intelligence service — a very powerful post indeed in the Muscovy hierarchy — he wished to employ Philby as an adviser on the CIA and the FBI. He went to Patriarch's Pond and found Philby disillusioned with the Soviet political system under Brezhnev, with what were called in Moscow "the years of stagnation." But he had remained faithful to Marxism. As to his loyalties, it took somewhat longer for Kalugin to assess his man, but when he did he concluded "that there was no reason to doubt Philby's loyalty to the KGB, on the grounds of the record and common sense. He was an excellent man and we became good friends."[2]

Kalugin rendered Philby several important services; one of the earliest was to find Philby a companion in life. In 1969 or 1970 Philby met Ruffina Ivanovna, a handsome, lively woman who, according to Lyubimov, "moved in KGB circles." She was born in 1932 and was therefore twenty years younger than Philby, who in 1970 was sixty-eight. She declined to say that she was under the orders of the KGB. She also refused to discuss her private life, except to say that she had someone else in mind as a spouse when she met Philby. Nor would she reveal her maiden name, although a wire service statement by her later, about her attitude toward the Yeltsin government, would state that it was Pukhova. Her father was a Polish-born furrier working near Moscow. Having passed through the party system — the Young Communist League — she entered the Moscow publishing industry as an editor of books at the Central Economics Institute. There, she said, she did everything from fiction to economics textbooks.[3]

She was quiet, feminine, circumspect, well-bred, and far from being "Miss KGB" — strapping, booted, long-skirted, hefty-chested, chemically blonded. Politically she was a progressive, and she was by her own statement still under KGB control. During her shopping expeditions she displayed perhaps professional fleetness in working in dense crowds and shops; she was generally well dressed in the fashion of the *nomenklatura* and, in a demure way, strong-minded and determined. She was oddly like Aileen and Eleanor in manner but was politically conscious. She claimed in her first public statement, in 1993, that had Kim lived into the Yeltsin era, he would have been "horrified by the state of Russia," with "all these civil wars, by the millions who have been turned into beggars, by such wild capitalism." But in 1970, it appears, she was strongly anti-Brezhnev, a fact that was probably not known to the KGB management when it sanctioned a liaison between her and Kim.

She had, by her own account, met Philby through the wife of George Blake, the Soviet spy in the British Secret Service who had been caught in Beirut when Philby was there and who had been sent to prison at hard labor for forty-two years — one for each of the forty-two agents who had been killed through his treachery. Blake had escaped from Wormwood Scrubbs prison in London with the help of the IRA and, to the further embarrassment of the British government, had succeeded in reaching Moscow, where the KGB established him in grand style — an apartment in town overlooking the Moscow River, a dacha among the larches, a New Soviet Woman as a new wife, and considerable social status. Ida Blake, "a KGB cookie" and a friend of Ruffina's, had obtained tickets for the Ice Ballet, which was visiting Moscow from the United States. That first meeting between Ruffina and Philby led to a second during the summer of 1970, although Ruffina declared that she was reluctant to permit a friendship to develop too far as she preferred the company of younger men. She spoke little English and Philby little Russian, and she deplored Philby's suicidal drinking. A second meeting took place at the Blakes' dacha, outside Moscow.

On the first evening there, after dinner and some more of Philby's desperate drinking, Ruffina had retired to her room when the door opened quietly. The room was dark, and she remembered seeing "the light of a cigarette. The figure — Kim's — announced in poor Russian — 'I am Englishman.' 'Yes, yes,' I replied in poor English. 'You are gentleman. Okay, okay. Good night. I will see you in the morning.' He did not touch me. He tried to explain to me something. It was very late, maybe after twelve." The next morning at breakfast with the Blakes, "I thought to myself that Kim was very ashamed. He did not talk to me, but to Ida. We went to the forest for a walk and then I asked him why he had come to my room. He replied that he did not remember that he had done so."

On the occasion of their third meeting, Ida Blake invited Ruffina and Philby to visit the Golden Ring, the seven Old City fortresses around Moscow. Ruffina accepted, although "I thought little about him as he was a much older man. Ida told me he was a very interesting man. She told me, too, that he had a serious drinking trouble. We went for a walk in the evening and suddenly Kim took my hand roughly and said, 'Come with me!' He told me he was 'sick and tired of me talking all the time with Ida because this gave him no opportunity to be with me. We sat on a bench and he said in Russian, 'Cards on the table. I want to marry you.'" It was only a month since they had met, they had had little conversation because neither spoke the other's language, and as Ruffina recalled, she felt "so speechless" that she could not "take Kim seriously." Two weeks later, however, Ruffina moved into Kim's apartment, where they lived together "while we collected the necessary papers to marry." She denied that the marriage was forced upon her, and she became upset, when interviewed in 1992, at the suggestion that she was required to report to the KGB on his behavior and statements.

She maintained that Philby loved her and that she came to love him as a "a great man, a truly great man, a wonderful man, I never met such a man. He was the best man I ever met." She produced as evidence of his great love for her a Russian-English phrase book in which

Philby had written: "For my eternal Ruffina." But that love did not come quickly. She despaired of his bouts of self-destructive drinking, when he became "a very different man from the one who was sober." Ruffina threatened to leave him if he did not stop. There were visits to the KGB clinic for alcoholism. In due course, knowing nothing of Philby's nervous collapse just before he fled Beirut, she began to conclude that the alcoholism was caused by the despair Philby felt about the reality of Soviet life — "like Glasgow on a Saturday night in Victorian times," as Guy Burgess had remarked.

The moment of revelation came for Ruffina when, while standing at a window in the living room, he exclaimed, "This is our fortress against the world!" Philby now was in a state of "black despair" at his life in Moscow. "They have built communism for themselves," he also exclaimed. Ruffina Ivanovna had been brought up through the Soviet regime and harbored reservations about the society created by Lenin. She found herself in sympathy with the crumpling wreck before her. Yet she might have left but for a single incident at the Hotel Metropol on Karl Marx Prospekt, once the headquarters of the Comintern. It was here that, in her view, Philby demonstrated his love for her.

She was some fifteen minutes late for a meeting with him in the lobby of the hotel, and there had been some difficulty between them some days earlier. When she arrived, she found him leaning against a pillar with a wide, happy smile on his face. "At that moment I realized how deeply he felt for me. He was overjoyed." He said he had been afraid that she would not come and that she regarded their association at an end. Beaming, he took Ruffina in to dinner. Their marriage took place on December 19, 1970. It was a civil ceremony, and it could not have taken place without the approval of the Central Committee and the Collegium of the KGB. As a wedding present, the KGB sent a handsome Oriental light standard with a gold silk shade.

With Philby married, Kalugin's patronage developed in other respects. Although Kalugin did hear the rumors that Philby was suspect in important quarters in the party and the KGB, "that he was London's plant in Moscow," as Kalugin explained, "Having talked with Philby I realized that here was a good comrade, an officer, a gentleman, and a man with a very long history of outstanding service to socialism. He was a highly disciplined professional, and I felt he had much good work left in him. As to the suspicions about him in certain quarters at the KGB, these were commonplace. There were doubts about everyone who had had connection with the Western intelligence services, including myself."

The main source of Philby's dissatisfaction with the regime stemmed from the suppression of his memoir, *My Silent War,* in the Soviet Union. Few people knew who he was or what he had done for the party. When Andropov became Philby's patron, he was largely responsible for authorizing the publication of the memoir in the West. But he did not prevail in the USSR. The work was rejected on the grounds that the Soviet government did not engage in espionage against foreign powers and it did not wish to offend the Communist Party of Great Britain. As Lyubimov stated, the book was a KGB project that Philby had agreed to undertake because he desired public recognition in Russia. But in order to publish it in Russia, permission was needed from M. A. Suslov, the party's leading theoretician, one of the five members of the Politburo, and the head of the International Department of the Central Committee.

One of the most powerful and enduring men in the Soviet Union, Suslov did not grant permission because, the question of foreign espionage apart, John Gollan, the general secretary of the Communist Party of Great Britain, had protested to him personally before the book was published anywhere that it would give the impression that *all* communists were spies. Gollan failed to stop publication in Britain; as Lyubimov recalled, Suslov regarded the British party "as ideological shit." However, he saw Andropov's point that publication in the West would constitute a severe blow to the pride and the prestige of the British services — "the old enemy and the most dangerous one" — and one that was likely to cause a loss of confidence in those services at the CIA and the FBI.

As Lyubimov further related, "This matter went on and on and on for years — twelve years all told." The fate of his book was "a terrible shock. He wanted to become a famous spy in the Soviet Union. He wanted fame. He wanted recognition. But he never got it. For Kim this was a tragedy. When Andropov ordered the book published in 1980, it then had to go through a process in which much of what had been published in the West was deleted by the Military Publishing House in Moscow. It was poorly translated, poorly edited, and poorly published. Indeed, it was not really published at all in the Soviet Union. It was never sent to the bookshops, and its sales, in the main, were confined to party gatherings, where it was virtually given away for about eighty kopeks — less than a dollar. The book was buried, hushed. There were no reviews in the press. The first edition of thirty thousand copies was virtually given away in the Central Committee, the Foreign Office, the KGB, the Defense Ministry, and at official conferences. I know of nobody who bought a copy. Kim had a lot of copies that he autographed and gave away. Kalugin's foreword replaced Graham Greene's, a writing that faithfully reflected the party line and that in no way revealed Kalugin's growing alienation from the KGB."

By 1970, through Kalugin's power and patronage, a small circle of senior KGB officers grew up around Philby, a cabal perhaps. Kalugin himself named them: Mikhail Lyubimov; Victor Kolotov, Kalugin's case officer to Philby and later a KGB general; Ivgeny Ageyev, of the KGB's Personnel Department; Gennady X, who was with Kalugin at Columbia University and became, for the next ten years, the liaison officer between Philby and the Active Measures section of the KGB; Rem Krasilnikov, described by Kalugin as Philby's case officer at Beirut; Colonel Viktor Budanov, one of Kalugin's officers in Directorate K, a specialist in the British services; and Anatol Kireev, a staff officer of Kryuchkov's secret service, the First Chief Directorate. Only some of this group — Kalugin, Lyubimov, and Gennady X — met frequently at Philby's apartment; the others came as guests to parties given by Philby, usually on the occasion of one of the anniversaries he celebrated regularly each year.

These were January 1, Philby's birthday; January 28, the day he arrived in the Soviet Union from Beirut; May 9, "Victory Day over Germany and Fascism"; June 1, the anniversary of the day he was recruited into the Soviet service in 1934; September 12, the anniversary of his marriage to Ruffina. Occasionally, Gennady X remembered, Kryuchkov personally called at the apartment on one of these anniversaries, as did Viktor Fyodorovich Grushko, deputy chief of the First Directorate and responsible for operations against Western Europe. On at least one occasion in Gennady X's recollection, most of the directors and deputy directors of the departments responsible for operations against the United States, Britain, and the NATO powers arrived together and departed together. On one of these occasions there occurred a celebrated incident in which all the operational leaders of the KGB found themselves stuck for more than an hour when the electric elevator stuck about halfway down. There they remained until their cries rose over the chatter of Kim's party. Then they were rescued by a special squad sent from the Center.

Ruffina Philby was almost always present at these gatherings. Lyubimov and Gennady X were more frequent visitors than Kalugin. Politics was discussed, but, because the sitting room was bugged, the talk was usually in the kitchen with the water taps running. According to Lyubimov, Ruffina was herself a "sort of dissident or perhaps more accurately a critic of the regime and of the KGB." But Lyubimov — who became number thirty-five on the list of seventy of those to be arrested if the KGB's coup d'état of August 1991 had succeeded against Gorbachev — had words of caution about the use of such a term. Although Ruffina's father was but a lowly furrier, Stalin had had him arrested on unspecified charges back in the late 1930s. That had affected Ruffina and the rest of the family greatly, for their status was diminished. "Here one should not exaggerate," said Lyubimov. "During the Prague Spring I myself was in contact with people who were described as 'dissidents.' I myself might have been so described." But in 1991 "everybody says they were dissidents, especially everybody in publishing. I think a real dissident was a fighter. We did no more than gather in the kitchens, we drank and made parodies of Brezhnev, telling each other jokes about him, and trying to copy his rather superior way of talking. But this was not dissidence. Dissidents were political fighters. Rufa was not a fighter. But Kim shared her ideas, which were those of the intelligentsia speaking their views behind the noise of running water."

Gennady X had another view of Philby's attitudes:

> It probably could be true that in his last years Philby became disappointed about the paths down which socialism had taken him. During the years of stagnation, before *perestroika*, he certainly welcomed the changes toward democracy. But he was a diplomat, too, and he was thinking much of Rufa, who was very dear to him. Probably during the years of stagnation he abstained from speaking too sharply against the system, not because of his self-interests. He was thinking in advance about Ruffina's fate. I think that he did not wish to do or say something that would further damage Rufa's existence, her life, the privileges, the apartment, the dacha.

On the other hand, Philby remained active in the development of ideas for counterintelligence against the Western powers. The noteworthy element in these papers is the appearance, at least, of continuing animus toward the intelligence services of the Western alliance. Kim's "hatred" for the Brezhnev socialist doctrine — a word used by Ruffina Philby — had not diminished his desire to be of maximum service to the KGB.

It was against this background of considerable acceptance of Philby by important elements in the leadership of the KGB that Graham Greene began to write to and call on Philby in Moscow.

"Death makes cowards of us all," remarked John Waller, the high officer of the CIA who had been the inspector-general for much of the time of the Philby affair and the monster plot. "Kim Philby was no different from the rest of us. When that realization comes, it is in the nature of men to change somewhat in preparation for the hereafter." Waller was correct. In 1982 Philby turned seventy, three score years and ten, a life span, an age that gives some men pause about the future. Philby had suffered throughout his life from chest trouble, a sort of pneumonia, and that condition had become more frequent. He made his will with the office of the procurator general in Moscow in his spy name, Andrew Marpunc, in favor of Ruffina. Always quite rational about life and death, he never believed in the hereafter. You were born; you lived your life; you died. He made arrangements for his funeral. Unlike most comrades, he disliked the notion of cremation and asked to be buried in Russia, not England. He is said to have replied when asked what his great wish was: "To have Graham Greene opposite me and a bottle of wine on a table between us."

How the connection between Greene and Philby was reestablished is far from clear, but the initiative may have come from Philby. It seems that Philby made an approach to Greene in Paris through a young Soviet journalist, whose father, Genrikh Borovic, was a senior figure in the media with KGB connections. Would Greene come to Moscow to see his old friend? Nothing happened immediately. It may have been, as Evelyn Waugh suggested to Nancy Mitford, that Greene was under the orders of the Secret Service. "I think," Waugh said of Greene, "he's a secret agent on our side and all his buttering-up of the Russians is a cover-up."

But there is another, political reason a reunion could not take place immediately. As Gennady X, the KGB liaison officer between Active Measures and Philby, related, "Once he showed me a letter from Graham Greene. 'Look, Gennady; we are old-time friends. He wants me to come to Budapest for a reunion. What do you think of that?' I said he should go, why not? Philby said, 'Look here. If I meet Graham Greene I would like to be honest with him, but I would also like to be honest with the KGB. If I were to talk with Greene I would have to talk politics.'"

Philby spoke to Kalugin about a meeting with Greene. This presented Kalugin with difficulties. Would he repudiate Marxism? Might he not claim that he had committed a folly in his youth? Might he not say that he wished to go home to die and thereby to repent? Sure of his man, Kalugin agreed to the meeting.

In February 1984, the Old Guard at the Kremlin was dying off and Mikhail Gorbachev was coming to power. It was Gorbachev who eventually invited Greene to Moscow in September 1986. Greene accepted and visited Philby at Patriarch's Pond. There were further meetings in September 1987 and February 1988. Ruffina Philby was present throughout. She remembered: "It was a most moving reunion between comrades who had served together in World War Two. It was as if nothing had passed between them, there was much laughter and wine and good food. It went on for days." Afterward, letters began to flow between them, eight in all, according to Greene. They assumed that the letters were being intercepted "at both ends," as Ruffina recalled, so "they were cautious about what they said to each other." This exchange became known in London, and Chapman Pincher, a reporter with a London daily, quoted Sir Maurice Oldfield, the retired chief of the British Secret Service, as having said that Greene had passed Philby's letters to the Secret Service. Oldfield was the next in the long line of people who, having known Philby, died suddenly.

Greene spoke to the question of the correspondence in an interview with Anne-Elisabeth Moutet published in the *Sunday Telegraph*. He had had connections with Oldfield and with Philby. Greene never revealed whether the connection had any political purpose, but he did intimate that Kim's letters were given to him by Oldfield. The correspondence, he said, had been "largely on private matters." What the letters that were not about private matters contained, he did not say. Moutet recorded that Greene was "markedly evasive" and made mention that "if there was anything political in it, I knew that Kim would know that I would pass it on to Maurice Oldfield, so it was either information or disinformation."[4]

At a time of powerful speculation in London that great changes had begun in Moscow, Greene remarked to Moutet that he believed that "any change in the Soviet Union will have to come from the KGB" because "they take the youngest and the brightest and they train them and they send them abroad where they learn about the world. Whereas the army are really a bunch of Napoleonic old men."

Thus we find a conduit between Philby and his KGB cabal at Patriarch's Pond in Moscow and Sir Maurice Oldfield of the British Secret Service in London, via Greene. Whether the conduit extended to Nicholas Elliott, another of Kim's brotherhood at War Station XB, we do not know. But Elliott became what he himself called the "unofficial adviser in intelligence matters to Margaret Thatcher," the prime minister since 1979. She wanted information, especially about Gorbachev. Little or no interest had been taken in this obscure fellow in the West. Margaret Thatcher did what no other prime minister had done, and that was, without the knowledge of the Lubyanka, to consult Oleg Gordievsky, a KGB officer under British control in London. Who was this man Gorbachev? Could the West do business with him? Gordievsky's patron at the Lubyanka was Mikhail Lyubimov, Kim's friend and a member of the cabal at Patriarch's Pond.

As it emerged, Gorbachev's principal political adviser was Alexander Yakovlev, who had attended Columbia University in 1959 with Kalugin and Gennady X, and he had been on terms with them since. And as Gennady X vouchsafed in regard to the Yakovlev association:

At Columbia Yakovlev was around thirty-five and he was studying history at the Academy of the Central Committee. Later he came back to work as a section leader of the Central Committee's ideological committee, which was one of the leading committees within the Central Committee of the Communist Party.

Sometime in 1968 he became the chief of the ideological committee. He was an outstanding personality in his appreciation of reality here, and he was the head of the committee until 1973. Then he was sent as ambassador to Canada, where he worked for ten years up until 1983. On his return, through his work as the head of the Institute of International Economy here, he became an Academician and soon was promoted by Gorbachev to be the leader of the Communist Party during the *perestroika* period and then a member of the Politburo. He was one of the closest associates of Gorbachev. He was a member of the presidential council.

Yakovlev was never in the KGB but he, Kalugin, and myself lived in the same dormitory for a whole year. He did not know Kim personally but he knew about him; he had read his book and had a signed copy from Kim. Yakovlev was "communism with a human face," sure. I was close to Yakovlev in terms of human relations, yes. Of course, Kalugin new him very well, too. We had an association with the people who understood, probably, most about what was going on here in Russia and around the world. Kim was very sympathetic with the new movement, *perestroika*. He was a witness to the rise of that movement. He was fully one hundred percent to the movement and the changes it brought about.

Of course, Kim had the impression and conviction, along with leaders of the *perestroika* movement, that there are certain historical laws or objective conditions of changes that were imminent, and people could only facilitate those changes, or try to understand them. Those lines were in the direction of democracy. Kim was a democrat. He was against any sort of suppression of human individualism, though he was a very disciplined man. He was a man devoted to the cause he started to serve in his youth, in the early thirties. That was a different international situation; it was the struggle against fascism, for social justice. People talk of him in terms of adventurism and conspiracy. He was very consistent from the early days of his youth, and that's one of the early traits of his character that were striking in him. He remained consistent, probably, until his last days.[5]

KGB men talked worshipfully about men such as Kim, foreigners who had communicated with them from the inner tent of the enemy camp. But was Gennady X true? Had the man who had believed in Leninism now come to believe in *perestroika* as the best hope of mankind? The United States was pouring Pershing missiles into the NATO countries; these could strike the Kremlin in six minutes, and President Reagan had started the Star Wars program, which had frightened the Kremlin leadership into fearing that World War III might be inevitable.

Gorbachev leaped onto the world stage. He had been a member of the Soviet Politburo since 1980. Born in 1931, he was far younger than most of his fellow members, and according to reports reaching Mrs. Thatcher from the Foreign Office, he was an exceptionally able man. How these galvanizing reports reached Mrs. Thatcher is nowhere disclosed. Was Philby, the man seeking redemption, part of the connection? Kalugin thought not. "Kim was a disciplined man and it is not possible that he was turned again."

Hugo Young, Mrs. Thatcher's biographer, recorded, "It is to the credit . . . of the Foreign Office that they managed to discover this man before anyone else in the Western world."[6] Mrs. Thatcher invited Gorbachev to visit London, and in December 1984 he did, with a thirty-man delegation that included Alexander Yakovlev. Mrs. Thatcher's adviser was again Gordievsky. The visit was a triumph in the recent history of British diplomacy. At the end of the visit, Mrs. Thatcher told BBC-TV: "I like Mr. Gorbachev; we can do business together."[7]

It was the beginning of the end of the Cold War and of the Soviet Union. It emerged that Gordievsky, who had briefed the prime minister, had been a double agent in the service of Whitehall for sixteen years, having been recruited by the British Secret Service in Copenhagen in 1968. As he was to write in *The Times* in 1990, the most important factor was Gorbachev's selection of Yakovlev as his political adviser. That was "the first time in sixty years," Gordievsky recorded,

there was a man in the Soviet leadership who knew the West from personal experience and genuine academic study and whose vision was only slightly dimmed by the mists of Marxism. Thanks to Yakovlev, there was a complete change of character in the way in which the Kremlin was supplied with information from the diplomatic and intelligence services. They were not only allowed to report truthfully and objectively, they were instructed to do so.[8]

Norman Sherry, Greene's biographer, touched on the uncertainties that existed about Philby to the end when he wrote to Greene:

> The more I read about the game secret agents play, the more I feel that nothing, almost nothing, could be considered outrageous, so would it be too absurd to suggest that perhaps Philby's departure to Moscow was SIS arranged and that in the heart of Moscow the British had their own very private treble agent? I mean Philby operating on both sides of the Iron Curtain, perhaps even with the support and permission of Moscow.[9]

Graham Greene was dying of leukemia at a clinic in Switzerland when he received this letter. His mind was still excellent, and, according to Sherry, he raised enough energy to give instructions that certain books and papers be sent urgently to him by his family in various parts of the world. Evidently the questions that Sherry asked had touched an uncertain part of him and he wished to search the literature to see what had been said about Philby's affiliations. But the answer was not forthcoming. As he was about to set pen to paper he collapsed and died. The pen was there and so was the paper, but the thought was not, and so it was lost forever. And so was the question about redemption. But was a man who had spent forty years at the game of dirty tricks against the country he professed to love, England, likely to suffer any remorse about his actions? Lyubimov thought so. I spoke afresh with Lyubimov in order to elucidate further Philby's state of mind toward the end of his life with regard to the questions of guilt, remorse, redemption. Lyubimov stated, "Yes, these elements were in his character. At this time I thought he was a man who would have liked to make peace with his country. Whether he actually sought to redeem himself in the West I cannot say, for I was not in charge of his case at this time. But I can say that there was a correspondence with persons in the West; it was intercepted by the KGB, and this made the KGB very uneasy, very suspicious about him. It was one of the reasons why he slipped back into disfavor with the KGB toward the end" (telephone interview, May 14, 1994). General Kalugin addressed himself to this same question. He spoke again of Philby's great disillusionment, not with the communist ideal, but with the Russian way of communism. But had that disillusionment caused Philby to inform Whitehall about political conditions in Russia? Had he been doubled again by the British? "I cannot believe this," Kalugin replied very emphatically.

Philby's life with the KGB was always subject to the whim of the leadership, particularly during the long reign of Kryuchkov as chief and subsequently chairman of the KGB. In 1978 an atmosphere of what might be called uncertainty developed in Kryuchkov's attitude. By then Philby had become an untouchable, a socialist icon. A postage stamp of him was placed in circulation, one of six of the KGB's most famous spies since the 1917 revolution. None, however, was as famous, and the thought spread that Kryuchkov was attempting to reduce Philby's stature by including him in a group that had long since been forgotten.

In 1978 a reason began to appear for Kryuchkov: there might be a traitor in the KGB leadership. A KGB spy, an elderly secretary in the Norwegian Foreign Ministry, Miss G. G. Haavik, had been arrested on January 27, 1977, as she handed over state documents to a KGB officer in a dark side street of an Oslo suburb. Thirty-three years earlier, she had met and fallen in love with a Soviet prisoner-of-war whom she had nursed in the hospital when Norway was under German occupation and whom she had helped to escape to Sweden. In 1947 Miss Haavik was posted to the Norwegian Embassy in Moscow and reunited with her lover, although he had married. He was being used as bait by one of the Soviet security services, and to keep him she began to supply him with state documents. This continued for twenty-seven years, and at her arrest she confessed. In about June of 1977 she died of a heart attack before she had been brought to trial.

The Haavik case was of considerable importance to the KGB because Norway was a key NATO power with a common border with the Soviet Union. The country would become still more important in any naval operations against the Red Fleet by the United States and the North Atlantic powers. Haavik's case was examined minutely by the Third Directorate, which, under V. F. Grushko, was responsible for military counterintelligence. Grushko, one of the officers who had been stranded in the elevator at Philby's flat, decided to seek Philby's opinion. He sent the Haavik file to Patriarch's Pond, and Philby concluded that the only plausible explanation for her arrest, and that of her case officer, was that there was a mole in the KGB. There was, and Philby was present at a staff meeting when Grushko stated, "So, if Philby is right, there's a traitor right here in the department!"[10]

The mole was Oleg Gordievsky, the patron and friend of Mikhail Lyubimov — and former pupil of Kim Philby. But that fact did not become known at the Center until 1985, seven years later. Kim Philby lived just long enough to learn that a member of his circle at Patriarch's Pond was an SIS double spy and had been so since 1974. In the years between 1974 and 1985, when he escaped from Moscow while being questioned on suspicion of being a traitor, Gordievsky had worked on political intelligence in Copenhagen, the Center, and in London. Much of the time he had worked for Lyubimov or in close connection with him. He had been in a position to report on Philby to his controller in the British Secret Service. Philby had arrived in Moscow while Gordievsky was taking his training for service in the KGB in January 1963, and ten years later, on active service at Copenhagen, he bought a copy of Patrick Seale's and Maureen McConville's book *Philby: The Long Road to Moscow* and sent it to Philby. Philby read it and sent it back to Gordievsky with the inscription:

> To my dear colleague Oleg:
> Don't believe anything about me
> which you see in print!

Gordievsky had attended the first lecture Philby had been allowed to make at the Center, in 1977. There was an audience of three hundred, and Philby spoke in English. "This year," he began, "is a very special one. Not only does it mark the sixtieth anniversary of the Great October Revolution; it also sees the fiftieth anniversary of the Soviet Football Club." There were, Gordievsky said, two bursts of laughter: immediately from those who understood English, after the translation from the remainder. Gordievsky remembered his chief, Lyubimov, with affection, "as an expert in English literature and in Scottish malts." As a member of the KGB's inner circle, he could find out whatever he wished about Philby, and it is reasonable to assume that the SIS knew that most closely guarded secret, Philby's address, from 1974.

Counterespionage is unlike ordinary crime in that it commonly lasts for years, sometimes for a decade or more, and once in a while, as with Philby, for a lifetime. Gordievsky, a major case in modern history, had been a British control without its being known at the Lubyanka for eleven years, mostly in London. London had remained a vital KGB outpost, and he had won much praise for the excellence of his political reporting during Gorbachev's visit to London, when he was briefing both Thatcher and Gorbachev, with only Thatcher aware of what he was saying to the Soviet leader. In all, during his British service, he was paid, it is claimed, about a million pounds, $1.5 million. So highly was his reporting regarded by the Russians that in January 1985 he was called back to Moscow and appointed the chief of the KGB's London station, initiated into the special ciphers for his most secret communications with the Lubyanka, and sent back to London to take up his new duties.

But on May 17 he received another summons to Moscow. On its

face there was nothing suspicious about the telegram: he was required to attend a special meeting with the chief of the KGB, Chebrikov, who was a member of the Politburo, and Kryuchkov, still chief of the KGB's foreign intelligence service. He was briefed before he left by the Soviet ambassador, V. I. Popov. However, Gordievsky sensed that something was wrong, that a trap awaited him. But he left anyway for what he assumed would be a brief stay in Moscow.

What he did not know — what he claimed to have learned only in 1994, nine years later — was that the KGB had recently recruited what appears to have been a new agent in the CIA, a certain Aldrich H. Ames, who was one of Angleton's successors in the counterespionage department of the CIA in Washington. Gordievsky's British control-lers in London had been sending to their colleagues in Washington Gordievsky's instructions and orders from the KGB. As Gordievsky claimed, in some fashion that documentation had come to Ames's attention and he had warned his Soviet controller. The controller had, in turn, warned Chairman Chebrikov and Director Kryuchkov that the British evidently had a major source inside the KGB station in London. The nature of the documentation indicated, but did not prove, that the source must be Gordievsky. He was now in the gravest danger for his life.

When Gordievsky reached his apartment in Moscow, at 109 Lenin-sky Prospekt, he realized the apartment had been searched — the first ominous sign that he was under suspicion. The next day he was driven out to Yasenevo, the operational headquarters of the KGB on the Moscow beltway, to begin his meetings with Chebrikov and Kryuchkov, but encountered nothing but excuses. He waited there for a week. In the second week he was visited at his quarters by General Golubev and Colonel Gribanov of Directorate K, of the counterespionage branch. At that meeting he drank brandy with his guests and found that he had been drugged. Then he was directly accused of working for the British. On May 30 he saw Grushko, one of the highest officials in the service, who announced that his mission to London was terminated because the KGB now knew that "you've been deceiving us for a long time." With that allegation, Gordievsky realized that he had come under a suspended sentence of death. He was consigned to the KGB health clinic at Semyonovskoya, which Philby used from time to time. There he began to plan his escape through the agency of the British Secret Service in Moscow.

For reasons that are not clear, Gordievsky was allowed to leave the clinic on July 10, probably because the KGB leadership was awaiting further evidence of his treachery from Ames in Washington. He went to his home in Moscow and, as was customary, went out each day to jog, accompanied always, but at a distance, by KGB watchers. At 4 P.M. on Friday, July 19, 1985, he vanished. When next heard of, he was in London under an SIS guard. How he got there has never been disclosed. But against all the odds Gordievsky had escaped a certain death sentence. His wife and two young daughters were taken hostage. They remained in the hands of the KGB until, according to Lyubimov, Mrs. Thatcher intervened personally at her next meeting with Gorbachev. They were then allowed to join Gordievsky in London. Lyubimov also saw Gordievsky during a visit to London, and Gordievsky explained to him why he had acted as he did. As Lyubimov stated, "For the first time I experienced myself that dreadful sense peculiar to a person who had been betrayed personally by a friend and colleague."

The Philby case had almost come full circle.

On June 1, 1979, Philby celebrated the forty-fifth anniversary of the start of what he called in a letter to Lyubimov "my career of dirty tricks." To mark the date, the KGB leadership gave him a small banquet in a private room at the Prague Restaurant in Moscow. Kalugin was there, as chief of counterintelligence, as well as other prominent officers. Gennady X recorded:

> We congratulated him, of course, and wished him good health, success in his work, and the interesting thing was his response to all the toasts in his honor. He expressed his gratitude to the KGB for being here, for being allowed to work here, and the friendly attitude of his colleagues. Then Kim said: "When I started forty-five years ago I could never have imagined in any of my dreams that I would be celebrating my anniversary in Moscow. When I think deeply about it I feel that such a celebration here is very logical. Who am I? I was born in India; by background I am an Englishman; I was educated in England; but my first commitment from my youngest days was to the Soviet Union, to the cause of fighting fascism, of the struggle for socialism. I come to you as a man who has found my ideological motherland in the Soviet Union, and I am happy to be at the Prague Restaurant, which is the best restaurant in Moscow. Thank you, and let us have a drink."

Kalugin proposed that he be admitted to the Order of the Soviet Union, for those who had "performed outstanding feats contributing to the honor and material development of the USSR." But the proposal did not get beyond Chairman Kryuchkov. In 1982 Philby did, however, receive the Order of Lenin "in recognition of special services rendered to socialism through research, improvements, or otherwise, in industry, agriculture, trade, transport or work in State or co-operative enterprises generally." Ranked fourth in the Soviet order of seniority, the Order of Lenin was an important recognition of his services to the KGB.

The KGB sent him an ode:

> On the slippery slopes of alien Parnassus
> Not opening his heart to his own seclusions
> Not Argos' who could see everything.
> Not even the ears of the curious Midas!
>
> With years the secret curtain fell
> And your name all of a sudden was open to us
> In the radiance of glorious feats obscure,
> Available only to sacrificial hearts.
>
> On your jubilee of many years' standing
> We are not sitting around a festive table
> But we are honored on your jubilee by our greeting,
> Even if from afar, but with sincere warmth!
>
> No matter how far between Angarsk and Moscow
> We are together with you in this bright hour
> Raising toasts to the courage of heroes.
> For the Motherland, for Russia and for you!
>
> Without exhortation, fuss and long
> We are inviting you to Angarsk:
> Leave all your troubles near the fireplace
> And fly to our campfire.

This was mounted on a green plastic plaque with the badge of the KGB — a sword poised to stab a serpent — and Philby gave it pride of place in his study, on the shelves that lined the room.

At the turn of the decade, Kryuchkov began to take a stern view of the circle at Patriarch's Pond, probably part of a general tightening of security when he became aware of the spread of democratic forces inside the Center. In 1980 the estimates were that 10 percent of all KGB officers had democratic inclinations. Kalugin was posted as first deputy chief of the KGB in Leningrad — on its face a promotion. But when he took up his post he learned that it was in fact a demotion. He found himself under suspicion as a CIA double agent, and the Russo-American whom he had recruited at Morton-Thiokol was a CIA plant. The Russo-American was sent to a camp in Siberia and spent seven years at hard labor. Also, there was concern on the part of Kryuchkov about "wild parties" at Philby's apartment. Kalugin resigned from the KGB in 1982.

Mikhail Lyubimov retired in October 1980 after allegations of "immoral conduct" by Kryuchkov — Lyubimov had had two wives and wished to marry his third. This, according to the conservative social code of the KGB, amounted to an offense, so, recognizing that his career was at an end, Lyubimov left the Center and became an open critic of the KGB, a novelist, a playwright, and a poet. In this work he proved to be one of the most talented individuals among the Moscow literati. His autobiographical novel, *Alex Willkie: Spy,* was bought by a New York publishing house for a substantial sum, although he had not been published in the West before, his name was unknown in New York, and the work had not yet been translated from Russian. Lyubimov's hero indicted the world that Lyubimov left:

> I understood that I will never be able to engage in espionage, will not be able to lure an innocent person into a trap, will not be able to carry out work based on lies. After all intelligence is out and out lying! The filthiest kind of lie! How is getting secret information different from simple robbery, from shameful crimes? And paying people off? Isn't that bribery, a crime under our laws? And disinformation? Isn't that slander? All that is immoral, it all stinks of cheating and crime! Back then I still believed in a moral code and in the great future of the new society . . . But what does all that have to do with espionage? How can you assert great principles and secretly do dirty things? We're all like dumb, blond horses pulling a miserable cart into a far-off abyss, decorated, like a Christmas tree, with cheerful lights and stars.

The effect of Lyubimov's novel on the KGB old guard was menacing. General Kirpichenko told a Moscow newspaper that he was "disgusted." He said he could not finish it because it was about "a Soviet cloak-and-dagger knight leading the life of a superman, never parting with his pistol or his condoms." A KGB review dismissed it as a "phantasmagoric novel" with an "enormous number of drinking bouts and love affairs." The liberal press in Moscow, which was just beginning to bloom, hailed the novel as a "strong anti-Communist satire and as a serious look into the soul of a spy." A review concluded: "It's a long time since we have seen such a concentration of irony, satire, and sheer mockery of the KGB in Russian literature." Kalugin, however, described it as "a true picture of the life and work of Soviet intelligence" and wrote the preface to it. The *Workshop* declared:

> The plot of Mr. Lyubimov's novel is that of a thriller. A Soviet spy, living in London, infiltrates the CIA in order to murder a KGB defector. It is filled with suspense, intrigue and blood. But it's not really a thriller at all. The novel is, in fact, about the fate of a man who lives in a world where he has to tear himself into several pieces. It is the story of a man who serves his country but hates its rulers, loves his wife but doesn't live with her, and is betrayed by his friends . . . The style is always ironic, sometimes stylish — with overtones of Kafka — and is full of self-ridicule and the dramatic search for a God. The self-analysis reaches its peak as the story turns into the sincere confession of a spy, a unique work for our time.

Such was the hidden attitude of one of the KGB's star officers and one of Philby's most trusted friends, the man who gave Oleg Gordievsky his chance — Gordievsky, the British double agent at Philby's court for the last decade of Philby's life.

Lyubimov became a contributing editor to the new magazine *Top Secret*. As the Soviet Union and the KGB collapsed, there was a remarkable blossoming of magazines such as these, many of them devoted to exposing what had happened inside the Lubyanka. An early contribution was his article "The Two Faces of Kim Philby." In it, Lyubimov sought to address the question of whether, as Gordievsky had been in London serving both sides at the same time, Philby had been at Patriarch's Pond serving both sides with equal devotion. Lyubimov never really believed this, any more than Kalugin did. But he wrote it anyway and, as required, sent a carbon to the KGB. This immediately placed his pension at risk. As Lyubimov explained:

> When I dealt with that particular matter in my article on Kim Philby, Kryuchkov, the chairman of the KGB, ordered its deletion. But I repeated it. Again Kryuchkov's censorship ordered it out. I was interested in this question of distrust because how could they mistrust Kim?

Lyubimov was followed into retirement by Gennady X. As Gennady X related, early in 1978 Philby began to sense that the regime of the Shah of Iran, now a largely U.S. protégé, had become unstable and, through Gennady X, he wrote a paper to that effect for the chief of Active Measures. That was, according to Gennady X, General Vladimir Petrovich Ivanov. As Gennady X said of Ivanov:

As it happened, the head of the Active Measures was a man with very limited mentality. He was a slim man of small stature, he was a veteran of World War Two, and he was very proud of his part in that war, although he was little more than a clerk in some headquarters. He did not know English, he knew German, and as with so many people who know German, his outlook was limited, unlike people who could read and speak English and could therefore read newspapers and books.

In his intelligence and the span of his vision in foreign affairs Philby was "far ahead of most of the leadership" and:

After many successful operations with Kim by the late seventies or early eighties, I felt that Kim's line on the Shah was the right line. It became not only Kim's line but my line, too. I presented Ivanov with the paper for his consideration. Ivanov accepted the paper and said he would call me back. But a week passed, two weeks. When I queried him he replied merely that he had said that he would call me about this matter. The normal course with a good chief would be that when he has a good paper prepared by trusted subordinates he does not make alterations or corrections. But a bad chief with an inferiority complex makes unnecessary corrections. This is what Ivanov did; he began to alter Kim's recommendations and his paper in general. This meant that he regarded Kim and his proposals to be unnecessary. At times his alterations were contrary to the substance of the matter.

Then,

In time he began a maneuver to take me away from Kim as the liaison and to replace me with someone else. To do that he had to invent some pretext to do so. Kim felt this and asked me what I thought was the real reason for Ivanov's attitudes. I abstained from making critical comments about my chief. Kim thereupon wrote a letter to Kryuchkov, who was still the chief of the First Main Directorate, saying that "when he wrote about important matters like the Shah let it be considered by someone who knows about what I am writing about. Otherwise," wrote Kim, "I might reconsider my work in this field." I took the letter to Kryuchkov, who instructed me to give it to Vladimir Petrovich Ivanov. I said no, it should be handed over to you personally. I made a translation and then handed Kim's letter to Kryuchkov's secretary. I attached supporting documents.

So after a few days,

I receive a call from Ivanov. Ivanov said he had in his hand Kim's letter to Kryuchkov, and he, Ivanov, was returning it. Ivanov reacted quickly to clear himself of all possible charges concerning his handling of the Shah matter. He started to praise Kim. He was quite cunning, no fool. After that Kim went on working but I was gradually moved from Kim's side, with promotion to the rank of colonel, into academic research on international affairs from the intelligence point of view. After that I soon left the KGB in the middle of 1980.

Otherwise,

> Now, it also happened here that Kim had several KGB people who visited him on official business. These, too, began to be moved away from Kim. This left Kim very dissatisfied. At least three or four people were moved whom I knew. All were with the First Main Directorate. I was told also that since I was no longer working with Kim I was not to meet him socially as well. I questioned this on the grounds that Kim had my telephone number and he would call me and I would have to talk to him. Ivanov and his officers replied merely that I was to tell Kim that I was leaving Moscow on special business. I refused. While I agreed that I would stop talking with Kim about operational matters I could not refuse to see him when he wished to do so. I went to Kim and told him, he asked me whether I had come against orders. I replied that I had done so. He was silent. I left and called Ruffina to ask how Kim was. She said he was all right and asked whether I would not come and see him. Until now I had visited Kim on official business two or three times a week. After my orders to stop meeting with Kim I did continue to meet with him, but not as frequently. When Ivanov again ordered me not to meet with Kim I replied: "You can order me not to meet with the American ambassador but Kim is a Soviet citizen. I have constitutional rights to see somebody whom I want to see socially." Kim then saw me and told me that he, Kim, had been forbidden to see me. And therefore, to save everyone trouble, he would stop inviting his friends to his house for friendly occasions. After that we did not talk about official business, only about poetry, small talk. I enjoyed this, I enjoyed meeting a man of such stature as Kim. I then left the service because I had all my service years and I had an interesting job offer, deputy chief of Political Analysis in Tass.

As the isolation of Philby continued, he wrote to Kalugin that (using Westminster schoolboyese) "I will repeat my present theme song: Fings ain't wot they uster be." He had just had, he said, two and one half hours with Ageyev, chief of the personnel department and chairman of the Communist Party of the KGB, so that "something better [in the way of work] may be on its way." He added, "Of course, this last item is strictly between ourselves. In Byzantium, silence is golden!" Philby ended the note with the salute "All the best, old boy" — "old boy" being the ultimate bourgeois Britishism for affection and familiarity between equals. He wrote to Lyubimov more bitterly:

> We are going through unpleasant changes. Oleg [Kalugin] has left us for a northern point, a whisper is going on that Victor Pantalevich also could leave us and even Gennady spoke about leaving I think, although I should not write about it, that his boss is a son of a bitch who should be sent as a small clerk in a village, three hours away from Verkhoyansk. Well, each big organisation has its share of fools.

Late in April 1988, General Kalugin, by this time in Leningrad, called on Philby at the KGB clinic for senior officers just off the Leninsky Prospekt in Moscow. Philby had been taken seriously ill with the chest troubles that had beset him ever since his birth. Kalugin brought him flowers and fruit and looked about to ensure that he was comfortable. He also talked with the doctors to see what Philby's prospects were. They were good, they said, but would improve if Kalugin could obtain some Kagor. Kagor was a heavy Uzbekistani wine, not unlike port, and it was believed in Moscow that it contained properties that loosened the arteries and made the blood flow more easily to the brain. Kalugin agreed to see if any Kagor was available at the store for high-ranking KGB officers, but he found none. As explained to him, it was an altar wine reserved to the Archimandrite of Moscow. Perhaps the Archimandrite might give over a few bottles of the holy wine in order to sustain in life one of the heroes of the Soviet Union?

Kalugin went to see the Archimandrite and, he related, obtained three bottles of wine that he then delivered to the clinic, where the doctors began to give Philby a shot glass of it each day. Philby, it is claimed, improved greatly under its influence, and by the first week of May it seemed that he might be fit enough to be discharged. He was still there, however, when on May 9, 1988, Gennady X telephoned to congratulate Philby on an important anniversary — the forty-second anniversary of the surrender of the Third Reich to the representatives of the Soviet Union, Great Britain, and the United States. The Russians celebrated such anniversaries and so had Philby. They called it "the victory over fascism," which then had been the main enemy of Marxism. When Gennady X concluded his little speech, there was silence for perhaps a few seconds; then Philby uttered two words that showed how he regarded his life's work. "What victory?" he asked.

Those bitter words were, as far as we know, Philby's last to the little cabal that had grown up around him and was now entirely liquidated.

They were his political testament, for he died suddenly at about two o'clock in the morning of May 11, 1988, of, it was announced by the Gorbachev government in a communication to the Foreign Office in London, arrhythmia of the heart. His corpse was removed to the Hexagonal, the KGB's official funeral home. There it lay in state, alone in the middle of the room, with music by Mozart playing in the background.

The obsequies began. Tass announced Philby's passing to the world's press (but not to the Russian press, which virtually ignored Philby's death on the grounds that the KGB did not employ spies) during the night of May 12–13, 1988. The party and government press did publish a brief obituary, without a photograph, in which Philby was hailed as the spy who was "able to accomplish the impossible," "the unique spy," "one of the most important men of the twentieth century." *Red Star,* the newspaper for the military and the intelligence agencies of the government, announced that "the outstanding Soviet intelligence agent Kim Philby died on Wednesday in his 77th year." It described how,

> for a long time, he conducted exceptionally difficult work, or to be more precise, a direct battle against the special services of the capitalist countries, whose activity was directed against the Soviet Union, against the movement for peace and progress.

These were

> years of colossal nervous tension, years which demanded all of his physical and spiritual resources. Often, Philby was able to accomplish feats which had seemed impossible.

Signed by "a group of comrades of esteemed comrade Kim," it told how, "having carried out a new mission, Kim Philby came to Moscow, where he continued the work that had become for him the meaning and purpose of his entire life." He was a "remarkable intelligence officer" who possessed "a high sense of his internationalist duty." But as Lyubimov rated the importance of the space given to the obituaries, it was "stingy — similar to that given to a light earthquake, a small obituary by a nameless group of comrades. Oh, indeed, these modest, invisible comrades! Oh, these fighters on the invisible front!"[11]

And as Lyubimov also noted, there was argument about whether Kim was a traitor, although he did suppress, at Kryuchkov's repeated instructions, the KGB notion that he was a British plant in Moscow. Was Kim a traitor? "The history of mankind," he wrote in *Top Secret,* is not only of struggles between nations. It is a merciless struggle of religions. Communism demands Faith and that its followers should be burned at the stake. Sebastian, chief of the Guards to the Roman Emperor, secretly sympathised with the Christians, helped them. For that he was crucified by the Romans but was later made a saint. What appears to be treachery to some for others represents an heroic deed. That was Kim Philby's position in the world.

Overseas, the SIS and the CIA, of course, left his death unremarked, although Dr. Ray Cline, a senior CIA officer from Philby's days in Washington, did say, "I shall have a bottle of champagne — but first I shall need proof of his death." Philby's passing was world news with many echoes. But it was *The Times* of London, where Philby had once been the blue-eyed boy, which wrote a lead editorial about his life — an honor usually given only to kings, prime ministers, and other such personages. His lip curling at his task, *The Times*'s thunderer tapped out:

THE LATE THIRD MAN

The master spy from the English Establishment, who embraced the ideals and methods of the Soviet state and accepted its largesse, died as he might have chosen, a hero in his adopted country. Here, his epitaph will read: Kim Philby — murderer and unrepentant traitor. No less, and no more.

In coming months and years there will be no lack of people ready to plead in mitigation of Philby, even in the country he betrayed so lethally. It will be said that in his initial acts of treachery he merely conformed to the spirit of his age — an age in which intellectual internationalism was preferred to nationalism, and patriotism went out of fashion.

Such ideals, in a world barely recuperating from the savagery of the First World War and swept by the rise of Nazism and Fascism, had their place. They did not always produce traitors.

Philby's allegiance to the Soviet Union will find understanding among those who saw — and continue to see — Russia only as a valued wartime ally, and ignored its tyranny. Philby, they will say, remained loyal to his principles where others lost faith. And so he did, but what principles were those? A true believer might honourably exchange the country of his birth for another. There is no prior requirement to turn traitor.

The idealist, however misguided, will always be the most effective and least easily dissuaded traitor. Philby lived, to the end, apparently untroubled by the spiritual torment that afflicts less single-minded felons. He displayed none of the fleshly weaknesses which exposed his fellow traitors, Burgess and Maclean, to blackmail and subornation.

One may scour his strange upbringing for the origins of his future conduct, but psycho-history cannot excuse a conscious choice. Nor can it limit its damage.

The extent of the harm done by Kim Philby to Britain and the Western world may never be known. He had on his hands the blood of British secret servicemen and resistance workers. Alone, he tarnished the image of British diplomacy abroad and undermined the integrity of our security services. His activity eroded the trust which had enabled Britain and the United States to wage their common cause of freedom.

There is no need to go further than the claims of Mr Peter Wright to see how long is the shadow that Kim Philby cast across Britain's diplomatic and security services. Not only has valuable energy been dissipated in pursuit of the fourth man and the fifth, but the reputation and morale of many loyal servants of Crown and country has suffered by association with Philby and fellow spies.

If any benefit accrued from the case of Philby, it was minor. It was the lesson that impeccable Establishment credentials, a suave exterior and polished manner were no guarantee of loyalty. Philby, Burgess and Maclean taught that the right exterior and the right connections were no substitute for comprehensive vetting. But that is small consolation. Nor does it necessarily deter the determined and clever idealist.

There is a historical neatness about the death of Kim Philby. Even as he died, a new generation of Soviet leaders was preparing to shed some of the internationalist and egalitarian ideas that Philby had served with such devotion. To the end, the third man was also a lucky man. He did not live to see his dream shattered. But he did not see it realized either.

During the day, the Kremlin sexton, Georgi Kovalenko, and the Kremlin tombstone maker, Ilya Lipkin, were instructed to prepare a fresh grave in the cemetery at Kuntsevo, a branch of the Novodiverchy not far from Red Square, which was reserved for the greatest Russians, the ruling class of Moscow, the *nomenklatura*. Kovalenko selected a pleasant spot, close to the memorial for Heroes of the Soviet Union, but separate from the granite testimonials to the immortals. He dug Philby's grave next to those of Yakhov Solomonovich Kronrod (1909–1984) and Madame Serafima Mikhailovna Kronrod, Lieutenant General Georgy Dmitrievich Gorodetsky (1923–1988), and Lieutenant General Aleksey Viktorovich Vladimirsky (1904–1988). These were just down the row from the grave of Georgi Malenkov, Stalin's successor, and a certain Frank Jacson, alias Mercader, alias Jacques Mornard van Dendresched, who had murdered Leon Trotsky, Stalin's rival after Lenin's death. All about Philby's grave were heroic statues of Lenin's, Stalin's, Malenkov's, Khrushchev's, Brezhnev's, Andropov's, and Chernenko's most famous functionaries, generals, pilots with stone MiGs in flight on their tombstones, admirals, civil servants, academicians, a Kremlin physician, ambassadors, intelligence officers, and the like.

The new grave was covered with a blood-red and black mourning cloth as, at the headquarters of the KGB, the functionaries gathered at the KGB Club for the obsequies. A band played the Soviet national anthem and the Internationale, the hymn of the world revolution of the proletariat:

> Arise ye starvelings from your hunger!
> Arise ye prisoners of want!

By tradition, these secret obsequies — for they were indeed secret — opened in the following fashion: all the KGB management was assembled when the pallbearers slow-marched the coffin into the large room. All heads were bared. Then, in pairs, each executive went to and stood by the head of the coffin, head bowed. General Kalugin, Philby's particular friend, was first. But early in the procession a lady appeared. She was Madame Modrjrkskaj, who in 1948 had led an investigation into Philby's loyalties and had concluded that there were grounds to believe that he was guilty of treachery, that he was London's plant in Moscow.

The procession ended and the official eulogies began. The chairman of the KGB, V. A. Kryuchkov, flanked by his chief executives, V. A. Kirpichenko and L. E. Nikitenko, read this testimony to Philby's widow:

Respected Ruffina Ivanova!
   Accept our most sincere sympathy in connection with the death of your husband Kim Philby.
   Kim Philby's great and glorious life served as an example of selfless service to the cause of peace, for the struggle for peace and happiness on earth. Kim's noble impulse, his thirst for the struggle for establishing social justice, brought him into the ranks of Soviet intelligence, to which he gave fifty years of his life. Courage, firmness, loyalty to duty and high responsibility displayed by him, in his service to the security of the Soviet State, are marked by the high decorations he received from our Motherland.
   A man of great intellect, versatility and deep knowledge, a convinced Communist-internationalist and our devoted friend, he was and will be forever a good example of a steadfast person who gave

all his power and enormous experience in intelligence to the struggle which has such deep meaning. By his responsive, thoughtful and sympathetic attitude to the people, Kim Philby himself received the deep respect and love of the Chekists, who were drawn to him and always found good advice, help and support.

In his life and yours with him, as a faithful friend you shared with him the hard life and joy of victory.

We will always keep in our hearts bright memories of Kim, an oustanding Soviet intelligence officer, a man with a great soul and a friendly heart.

We share your immense grief in this sorrowful hour and we are together with you.

Kryuchkov's predecessor, V. M. Chebrikov, now the political head of the Soviet Union, then rose, and at the podium he, too, addressed Madame Philby:

The leadership of the Soviet State Security Committee expresses its sincere sympathy in connection with the death of your husband, Kim Philby.

For more than fifty years Kim Philby devoted his life to the struggle for the peace and security of the first Socialist State — the Union of the Soviet Socialist Republics. Neither numerous nor straight threats on his life could prevent him from reaching his noble goals. He always was and will remain an example of loyalty, courage and high responsibility. The personal merits of Kim Philby in the cause of the security of the Soviet State are marked by the high honors of the USSR.

His was deep respect and extraordinary self-sacrificing, a crystal integrity and generosity of soul, sensitivity and thoughtfulness for people.

Kim Philby will be preserved forever in the memory of the Soviet Chekists, as a steadfast and firm fighter, a convinced Communist-in-ternationalist, a man who devoted his life to the struggle and the ideas of Communism.

In our hearts we will preserve the bright memory of Kim Philby, a man of great soul and flaming heart, the Chekist-internationalist.

We share and understand your immense sorrow.

The obsequies at an end, the mourners filed out behind the pall-bearers into the bright spring day of Derzhinsky Square, which was silent and empty except for the shrill of KGB trumpets. All traffic had been stopped. A line of Zims, Zils and Zises drew up; the mourners entered the waiting cars, and the long line drew away toward the Kuntsevo cemetery. The foreign press were bused to the cemetery in yellow vehicles resembling American school buses. Crowds of cars pursued the cortège. There was a band, firing squad, eulogies. By Russian custom, the coffin was left open until the last minute before burial, and Kim was there for all to see. Some thought there was a slight smile on his face. In the opinion of attending journalists, Kim looked a good deal fitter in death than he had in life. The mortician had done his work well; moreover, a ruff of blood-red silk at his throat gave Kim's face a medieval aspect, as if he had been a cardinal. A guardsman from the Kremlin stood at the head of the coffin with Philby's medals on a crimson cushion.

With a last kiss on his forehead from Ruffina Philby and a final volley of rifle fire, the coffin was closed and Philby was lowered into his grave. All this was exceptional, politically a sign of the times; the usual manner in which the KGB buried its dead, however famous, was quick cremation and, at best, the lodging of the ashes in the Kremlin wall. A firing squad drawn from the Kremlin honor guard fired its Kalashnikovs into the sky to frighten away evil spirits, and Philby found his last resting place, almost within sight of Stalin's dacha. There was a short time of remembrance in which the mourners stood with bowed heads. It was all over now for Philby, except in one dainty respect.

In London, Philby's old comrade from the days of War Station XB, Nicholas Elliott, was in his club at St. James's at about this time, giving thought to a scheme to disrupt any attempt by the KGB leadership to iconize Philby posthumously, as indeed was their intention. The idea that formed in Elliott's mind was that the British Secret Service should comment to the Duke of Kent, the Grand Master of the Most Distinguished Order of St. Michael and St. George, that Philby be made a Companion of the Order. This was usually conferred upon British subjects as a reward for services abroad and often went to members of the foreign service. The Russians took such matters as honors and medals almost as seriously as did the British, and the award of a CMG to Philby posthumously might be expected to create a thought in the KGB's mind — and perhaps in the minds of official England and Foggy Bottom — that Philby had been Whitehall's man after all. But the idea came to nothing, although it is not clear why. Elliott leaked the idea to *The Times,* and some notice was taken of it. Philby therefore went into eternity unhonored in Whitehall.

The Kremlin's sexton, Georgi Kovalenko, was left to do him the final honors. The black sandy earth was shoveled back into the grave. He erected a small headstone, marked with Philby's Russian spy name, Agent Tom. But Madame Philby objected that it was "too commonplace," and, in any case, Philby had always regarded himself as a Soviet intelligence officer, not an agent. So in due course a slender shard of black marble replaced the proletarian stone. On it was inscribed in gold leaf, in Russian,

Kim Philby
1912–1988

That was all. There were many testaments to the master spy and disrupter. But the most telling of them all was that of Yuri Modin, the KGB's most famous secret agent, who had acted as steward of Philby's career from the 1940s through the 1980s. After luncheon amid the new Japanese bourgeois splendors of the Hotel Metropol, the old headquarters of the world revolution of the proletariat, Modin strode down the broad red carpet to the top of the marble steps leading out into the gray snowy evening on Karl Marx Prospekt. He paused for a moment, then uttered his conclusion in the Philby case: "I wonder whether Kim cheated us as he cheated everyone else."[12]

Notes

Chapter 1: The Approvers: 1885–1915

1. H. St. John B. Philby, *Arabian Days: An Autobiography* (London: Hale, 1948), p. 65. This recounts his life until the age of fifty.
2. Interviews, William E. Mulligan, lately of ARAMCO Research Division, Boston, N.H., July 1990.
3. Hugh Trevor-Roper, "The Philby Affair: Espionage, Treason and Secret Services," *Encounter*, April 1968.
4. Anon., "Classic Soviet Nets," *CIA Review of Intelligence*, declassified 1988.
5. KGB obituary of Kim Philby, May 1989.
6. Ibid.
7. Alistair Horne, *Macmillan: 1957–1986*, vol. 2 (London: Papermac, 1989), p. 465.
8. John le Carré, in Bruce Page, David Leitch, and Phillip Knightley, *Philby: The Spy Who Betrayed a Generation* (London: Deutsch, 1968), p. 9.
9. Hugh Whitney Morrison, *Oxford Today: The Rhodes Scholarships* (Toronto: Gage, 1958), pp. 56–57. All quotations about Rhodes and his principles are from this source.
10. In Elizabeth Monroe, *Philby of Arabia* (London: Pitman, 1973), pp. 19–20. All quotations about Philby's captaincy are from this source.
11. *Illustrated London News*, January 24, 1903.
12. In H. V. F. Winstone, *The Illicit Adventure: The Story of Political and Military Intelligence in the Middle East from 1898 to 1926* (London: Cape, 1982), p. 3.
13. St. John Philby, *Arabian Days*, p. 79.

14. In Monroe, *Philby of Arabia,* p. 24.
15. St. John Philby, *Arabian Days,* p. 4.
16. See Sir R. E. L. Wingate, *Not in the Limelight* (London: Hutchinson, 1959), p. 36. This was standard information given to all Indian civil servants in their preparation for their work.
17. Ibid.
18. F. C. Iremonger and J. Slattery, *Ghadr Conspiracy: 1913–1915* (Lahore: Government Printer, 1919), p. vii. All statements concerning the Sikh insurgency are from this source unless stated otherwise. This document may be found at the India Office Archives, London.
19. Monroe, *Philby of Arabia,* p. 30.
20. Ibid., p. 32.
21. In Patrick Seale and Maureen McConville, *Philby: The Long Road to Moscow* (New York: Simon & Schuster, 1973), p. 1.
22. Monroe, *Philby of Arabia,* p. 38.
23. Interviews with Sir R. E. L. Wingate, Bath, England, 1973.
24. The fact that young Philby's original name was Kimbo, not Kim, is recorded in his fathers correspondence constantly between 1912 and 1925.
25. Monroe, *Philby of Arabia,* p. 40.
26. St. John Philby letters, 1908–1961, St. Antony's College, Oxford; letter to May Philby, October 26, 1912. All personal correspondence between St. John and his family is from this source unless stated otherwise. The date is usually cited in the text.
27. C. E. Carrington, *The Life of Rudyard Kipling* (Garden City, N.Y.: Doubleday, 1955), p. 36.
28. St. John Philby, *Arabian Days,* p. 84. All quotations about the Jagadri incident are from this source unless stated otherwise.
29. Monroe, *Philby of Arabia,* p. 40.
30. Correspondence from Lyallpur, 1915 file.
31. Monroe, *Philby of Arabia,* p. 43.
32. Interviews with Sir R. E. L. Wingate. All information about Vivian and the Sikh uprising are from this source unless stated otherwise. See also Iremonger and Slattery, *Ghadr Conspiracy.*
33. Letters to Dora Philby, 1915 file.
34. Kim Philby Archives, Moscow, February 1992. All quotations about Philby's boyhood are from this source.

Chapter 2: The Ride to Fame: 1917–1919

1. Gertrude Bell, *Letters of Gertrude Bell* (London: Benn, 1927), p. 190.
2. Monroe, *Philby of Arabia,* p. 54.
3. Winstone, *The Illicit Adventure,* p. 180.

4. Ameen Rihani, *Ibn Saoud of Arabia: His People and His Land* (London: Constable, 1928), p. 7.

5. Monroe, *Philby of Arabia*, p. 50.

6. Ibid., p. 10.

7. In David Holden and Richard John, *The House of Saud* (London: Sidgwick & Jackson, 1981), p. 64.

8. St. John Philby, "Report on Najd Mission, 1917–1918" (Baghdad: Government Press, 1918), in the William E. Milligan files. All quotations about the treaty are from this source unless stated otherwise.

9. Letter to May Philby from Baghdad, November 11, 1917.

10. Letters about the deaths of his brothers are in the same package at St. Antony's College, Oxford.

11. Monroe, *Philby of Arabia*, p. 66.

12. Glubb Pasha, *War in the Desert* (New York: W. W. Norton, 1960), p. 220.

13. Letter to Dora Philby, May 1934.

14. St. John Philby official report.

15. Monroe, *Philby of Arabia*, p. 71.

16. Letter, January 1, 1918.

17. Monroe, *Philby of Arabia*, p. 79.

18. Ibid.

19. Ibid., p. 80.

20. Ibid.

21. Ibid.

22. Letter to May Philby, April 2, 1918.

23. Ibid., April 10.

24. St. John Philby, "Notes" in his papers at St. Antony's College, Oxford; all quotations about Ramadan are from this source unless stated otherwise.

25. St. John Philby official report.

26. Ibid.

27. Ibid.

28. Monroe, *Philby of Arabia*, p. 92.

29. St. John Philby, *Arabian Days*.

30. Ibid.

Chapter 3: Revolts: 1919–1924

1. Kim Philby, unpublished memoirs. Read in Moscow, February 1992, with the kind permission of his widow, Ruffina Philby. All quotations are from this source unless stated otherwise.

2. Monroe, *Philby of Arabia*, pp. 95–96.

3. Letter to Dora Philby, June 28, 1919.

4. Ibid., July 9, 1919.

5. Monroe, *Philby of Arabia*, pp. 138ff.

6. Ron Rosenbaum, *Travels with Dr. Death* (New York: Penguin, 1991), pp. 29–30.

7. In Monroe, *Philby of Arabia*, p. 104.

8. Ibid.

9. Ibid.

10. Ibid., p. 105.

11. H. St. John Philby, *Arabian Jubilee* (London: Hale, 1952), p. 56.

12. In Winstone, *Gertrude Bell* (New York: Quartet, 1978), p. 194.

13. Monroe, *Philby of Arabia*, p. 106

14. Martin Gilbert, *Winston S. Churchill*, vol. IV: *The Stricken World: 1916–1922* (Boston: Houghton Mifflin, 1975), pp. 490, 526.

15. T. E. Lawrence, *Revolt in the Desert* (Garden City, N.Y.: Doran, 1927), p. 24.

16. Winstone, *Gertrude Bell*, p. 249.

17. Ibid., pp. 217–18.

18. Gilbert, *Churchill*, p. 818.

19. Ibid., p. 512.

20. Monroe, *Philby of Arabia*, p. 105.

21. Gilbert, *Churchill*, p. 584.

22. Ibid., p. 523.

23. Winstone, *Gertrude Bell*, p. 235.

24. Ibid., p. 236.

25. Ibid., p. 237.

26. Monroe, *Philby of Arabia*, pp. 108–9.

27. Ibid., pp. 238–40.

28. Ibid.

29. Ibid.

30. Ibid.

31. Letters, St. Antony's College, Oxford.

32. H. St. John Philby, *A Pilgrim in Arabia* (London: Hale, 1943), p. 182.

33. St. John Philby, original ms. of uncertain provenance but in the private papers of William E. Mulligan, the unofficial ARAMCO historian.

34. Winstone, *Gertrude Bell*, pp. 240–41.

35. Gilbert, *Churchill*, pp. 810–11.

36. Ibid., p. 809.

37. Ibid.

38. Philby, original ms.

39. Ibid.

40. Monroe, *Philby of Arabia*, p. 116.

41. Kim Philby, unpublished memoirs.

42. Letter, November 4, 1921.

43. St. John Philby, original ms.

44. Gilbert, *Churchill*, p. 545.

45. Ibid., p. 572.

46. Ibid.

47. St. John Philby, original ms.

48. Monroe, *Philby of Arabia,* p. 119.

49. Correspondence, November 1922 file.

50. In Monroe, *Philby of Arabia,* p. 127.

51. "Memorandum — Mr. H. St. J. B. Philby, C.I.E.," Public Records Office, London: FO 371/24589, pp. 67–71.

52. Winstone, *Gertrude Bell,* p. 240, citing PRO London, CO730 (Air Staff Intelligence Summaries) and CO730/44 (Censorship, March 26, 1924).

53. Monroe, *Philby of Arabia,* p. 132.

54. Letter to May Philby, in March 1924 file.

Chapter 4: Renegade: 1924–1932

1. Monroe, *Philby of Arabia,* p. 187.

2. Ibid.

3. Letters quoted from the 1924 and 1925 voyages to Jidda are in the Philby-Dora-May files. Letters of particular importance are dated in the text, a practice followed by the author throughout these annotations.

4. H. St. John Philby, *Arabian Oil Ventures* (Washington, D.C., 1964), pp. 34–35.

5. St. John Philby, *Arabian Days.*

6. Ibid.

7. Ibid.

8. Ibid.

9. Ibid.

10. Information about Major Fisher derives from three sources: interviews with his daughter, Mrs. J. H. Farmer, at Haytor, Devon, 1990, 1991; Lord Hardinge's correspondence about the Fisher estate with his legal advisers, belonging to Mrs. Farmer; interviews with Mrs. Farmer's daughter, Denise Frieden of Paris; and the late Mrs. Martha Dresden, of Washington, D.C.

11. Monroe, *Philby of Arabia,* p. 146.

12. There is considerable correspondence about the stamps and pearls in the early 1926 Philby-Dora correspondence.

13. David Footman, *Red Prelude: A Life of A. I. Zhelyabov* (London: Cresset, 1944), frontispiece. It is noteworthy that Footman, an associate of both Kim's and St. John's and a future head of the Political Section of the British Secret Service, published this book with the help of his service's archives. It is also noteworthy that Footman's name is associated with the Philby case, although there is no evidence that would be worth anything in any court to show that he was a coconspirator. But, as will be seen, he was certainly suspected of being so in the British Secret Service. Yuri Modin, one of Kim's Russian controllers,

thought little of the opportunity presented by the Hardinge-Fisher connection for the penetration of Buckingham Palace. "There were much more important things for him to do," Modin stated. But Modin had forgotten his history. Among the most important political events of the mid-1930s was the Prince of Wales's admiration for the German Nazi Party. There was also his abdication in 1936.

14. D. Van Der Meulen, *The Wells of Ibn Sa'ud* (London: Murray, 1957), pp. 22–28.

15. Interview with Colonel Oleg Tsarev, a spokesman, conducting officer, and historian with the KGB, in Moscow in October 1991. He made several claims concerning the ubiquity of the agents of the Soviet Secret Service. In the context of his claim that St. John was a Soviet secret asset, his evidence for the statement was that at one time there was, in one of Kim Philby's KGB files, a note. This stated that a small file on St. John had been removed from this point in the file. This indicated, Tsarev declared, that the SSS had had an interest in St. John. The worth of such a statement is impossible to estimate. But it is noteworthy that Tsarev, when questioned, did not know the name Hassim Hakimoff Khan.

16. Sylvia E. Crane Papers: Leo Joseph Bocage, "The Public Career of Charles R. Crane" (Ph.D. dissertation, Fordham University, 1962). See also David Hapgood, "Charles R. Crane," Institute for Current World Affairs, Hanover, N.H., May 1986.

17. Letters, Charles R. Crane to Richard Crane, in Special Collections, Littauer Library, Georgetown University, Washington, D.C.

18. Letter, St. John Philby to Crane, December 27, 1929, in Charles R. Crane Archives, Woods Hole, Mass.

19. Dalton Papers, in the Philby Archives at St. Antony's College, Oxford.

20. PRO London: FO 967-38, November 14, 1930, letter from British Legation, Jidda, to Khan Bahadur Tasaddul Husain, M.B.E., Intelligence Department, Home Department, Government of India, Simla. In a file labeled "Mr. Philby."

21. Daniel Yergin, *The Prize* (New York: Simon & Schuster, 1991), p. 287.

22. PRO London: FO 967-38, November 14, 1930, letter from British Legation to Khan Bahadur Tasaddul Husain.

23. Ibid., letter from Hope-Gill to Rendel, Foreign Office, August 30, 1930.

24. "The Enigma of the Sands," *Times Literary Supplement,* December 7, 1973.

Chapter 5: At Court: 1930–1934

1. Ibrahim al-Rashid, *Saudi Arabia Enters the Modern World: Secret U.S. Documents on the Emergence of the Kingdom of Saudi Arabia as a World Power* (Salisbury, N.C.: Documentary Publications, 1980), vol. III, pp. 12–15.

2. Letter to Dora Philby, October 29, 1930.
3. Ibid.
4. Monroe, *Philby of Arabia*, p. 163.
5. St. John Philby, *A Pilgrim in Arabia*, pp. 38, 182, 183.
6. Ibid, pp. 103–5.
7. Ibid.
8. Correspondence with Dora Philby, April 27, 1931.
9. Ibid., 1931 file.
10. Ibid., 1930 file.
11. Ibid.
12. Ibid.
13. Ibid.
14. St. John Philby, *A Pilgrim in Arabia*, p. 112.
15. Ibid., p. 110.
16. Ibid.
17. Ibid.
18. Ibid.
19. St. John Philby, *Arabian Jubilee*, p. 170.
20. St. John Philby, *A Pilgrim in Arabia*, p. 105.
21. St. John Philby, *Arabian Jubilee*, pp. 170ff.
22. All information concerning Crane's visit derives from his papers and those of Sylvia E. Crane. They include Bocage, "The Public Career of Charles R. Crane." See also Hapgood, "Charles R. Crane."
23. Crane to Ibn Saud, September 9, 1932. Kindly provided by Crane's daughter-in-law Sylvia E. Crane from the Crane family papers at Woods Hole, Mass.
24. Bocage, "The Public Career of Charles R. Crane."
25. The author is grateful to Dr. Glen Brown, of the U.S. Geological Survey in Saudi Arabia, for this account of the outcome of Twichell's enterprise in Arabia. Also, interviews with William E. Mulligan, former deputy chief of the ARAMCO Research Bureau, New Boston, N.H., August 1990. And for Twichell's personal account of his search for water, gold, and silver, see his *Saudi Arabia* (Princeton: Princeton University Press, 1958).
26. For letters from Philby on his anguish at being thwarted in his desire to explore the Empty Quarter, see letters to Dora Philby, 1931 file.
27. Above letters also contain several accounts of his ride across the Empty Quarter, but for a consolidated account, see Monroe, *Philby of Arabia*, pp. 175ff.
28. Ibid.
29. Kim Philby's educational progress is discussed at length in St. John's letters to Dora Philby. See especially the 1927–1929 files for the record at Westminster.
30. For St. John's account of the letter from Luce concerning Kim's un-

truthfulness, see ibid. The correspondence shows that St. John knew Luce personally and held him in high regard.

31. Nicholas Elliott, *Never Judge a Man by His Umbrella* (Salisbury, Eng.: Michael Russell, 1991), p. 190. This is the memoir of a career officer of the British Secret Service and one of Kim's closest friends in boyhood and during their careers. Few men knew more about the Philby case in all its dimensions. When it became known in Washington that Elliott was publishing his memoirs, it was hoped among those CIA officers who had had to grapple with the Philby case that they would prove instructive. The men expected too much. Although Elliott devoted an antire chapter to Philby, he disclosed nothing. As one of the CIA men remarked, "Nick copped out." Elliott's curious title derives from a notice at Eton College: "Never judge a man by his umbrella. It may not be his."

32. These included Robert W. Headley, an officer of ARAMCO who read the letter while going through St. John's correspondence at Dhahran, Saudi Arabia. This letter, and others, was not in the correspondence when it reached St. Antony's, Oxford.

33. Correspondence with Dora Philby, 1931 file.

34. Kim Philby, *My Silent War* (New York: Grove Press, 1968), p. xvii.

35. Andrew Boyle, *The Climate of Treason: Five Who Spied for Russia* (London: Hutchinson, 1979), p. 84.

36. Andrew Sinclair, *The Red and the Blue: Cambridge, Treason and Intelligence* (Boston: Little, Brown, 1986), pp. 12–15. Small as it is, this is regarded as the preeminent work concerning the Apostles, Cambridge, homosexuality at Cambridge and in the London intelligentsia in the 1930s, and the moods of the times during the era of Philby.

37. Patrick Seale and Maureen McConville, *Philby: The Long Road to Moscow* (New York: Simon & Schuster, 1973), p. 45.

38. John Costello, *Mask of Treachery: Spies, Lies, Buggery and Betrayal* (New York: Morrow, 1988), p. 165.

39. Seale and McConville, *Philby,* p. 230.

Chapter 6: Little Son: 1932–1934

1. Monroe, *Philby of Arabia,* p. 201.

2. *The Times,* London, June 26–28, 1932.

3. Correspondence with Dora Philby, 1932 file.

4. Rebecca West, *The Meaning of Treason* (London: Virago, 1982), p. 257.

5. Correspondence with Dora Philby, 1951 file.

6. In Seale and McConville, *Philby,* p. 19. This first appeared in the *Trinity Magazine,* February 1932.

7. St. John Philby correspondence, 1932 file.

8. Ibid.

9. Ibid.

10. PRO London, FO file 371/16009, file labeled "Mohammed Amin Taminy," from Sir P. Loraine, Cairo, to Sir L. Oliphant, FO London, June 17, 1932. All quotations and facts about Tamimi are from this source unless stated otherwise.

11. See Subcommittee on Multinational Corporations, *Multinational Oil Corporations and U.S. Foreign Policy* (Washington, D.C.: U.S. Government Printing Office, 1975), p. 33, citing *Sperling's Journal,* August 1919; and 82nd Congress, 2nd Session, Committee Print No. 6, *The International Petroleum Cartel,* Staff Report to Federal Trade Commission Submitted to the Subcommittee on Monopoly of the Selected Committee of Small Business, U.S. Senate (Washington, D.C.: U.S. Government Printing Office, 1952). The worth of the facts in both these journals was challenged and found wanting in a special study of them by ARAMCO's Research Division. Nonetheless, they reflected the antagonisms of the times.

12. St. John Philby, *Arabian Oil Ventures,* pp. 77ff.

13. Ibid.

14. Ibid.

15. Dalton Papers, in the Philby Archives at the Middle East Center at St. Antony's College, Oxford. All pertinent documents are from this source unless stated otherwise.

16. PRO London: FO 967/38, November 14, 1930, from the British Legation, Jidda. In the file labeled "Mr. Philby."

17. Andrew Ryan, *The Last of the Dragomans* (London: Bles, 1951), p. 61.

18. Ibid.

19. All quotations in this passage are from Philby, *Arabian Oil Ventures,* unless stated otherwise. In particular, the statement "like a bird mesmerized by a snake" is on p. 126.

20. Ibid.

21. Ibid.

22. Statement by William E. Mulligan of the ARAMCO Research Department.

23. St. John Philby, *Arabian Oil Ventures,* p. xiii. This statement was written by Fred A. Davies in 1961, after Philby's death, in his foreword to the book.

24. For Ryan's reaction to Philby's news that Standard Oil had won the concession, see ibid., p. 125.

25. Ibid.

26. Seale and McConville, *Philby,* p. 52.

27. The personal information about Alice Friedman is in a letter from J. Edgar Hoover, Director of the FBI, to Admiral S. W. Souers, NSC director, at the Harry S. Truman Library in Independence, Missouri.

28. Telephone conversation with Nicholas Elliott in London, November 1992.

29. Alexander Orlov, *A Handbook of Counter-Intelligence and Guerrilla Warfare* (Ann Arbor: University of Michigan Press, 1962), pp. 108–9.

30. Monroe, *Philby of Arabia*, pp. 207–8, citing a letter from Kim to St. John. It is noteworthy that Dora's file in the Philby Archives was closed after Miss Monroe, one of the Philby family's friends, read them. They remained closed when this author asked that they be opened in 1990. Almost immediately they were transferred to St. John's literary executor, Diana Philby, by the custodian of the Philby papers, Miss Gillian Grant, on the grounds that "they contained much private family business." This included matters concerning Dora's ill health. Miss Grant declined to discuss what the files contained concerning Dora's knowledge of Kim's activities. Since Dora was Kim's closest confidante, it is probable that they contained much important information in the period between St. Aldro in 1919 and June 1957, when Dora died. Doubtless, too, they contained much about Dora's life with St. John and Major Fisher.

31. Muriel Gardiner, *Codename "Mary": Memoirs of an American Woman in the Austrian Underground* (New Haven: Yale University Press, 1983), pp. 50–51.

32. Seale and McConville, *Philby*, p. 65, citing Naomi Mitchison's *Berlin Diary*, and p. 66, Gedye's letter to the authors.

33. Correspondence with May Philby, 1934 file.

34. Monroe, *Philby of Arabia*, p. 209.

35. Kim Philby Papers, Moscow. All quotations about Philby's early meetings with Deutsch are from this source unless stated otherwise.

36. Christopher Andrew and Oleg Gordievsky, *KGB: The Inside Story of Its Operations from Lenin to Gorbachev* (New York: HarperCollins, 1990), pp. 203ff.

37. See Donald Robertson file in the Philby Archives.

38. Ibid.

39. Ibid.

40. See Correspondence with Dora Philby.

41. Monroe, *Philby of Arabia*, p. 209.

42. J. Costello and O. Tsarev, *Deadly Illusions* (New York: Crown, 1993), pp. 124–25, citing a statement to the KGB by Philby in 1985.

43. Ibid., p. 146.

44. Ibid., p. 419.

45. Interviews with Gennady X in Moscow, February 1992.

46. Julius Braunthal, *History of the International: 1914–1943* (New York: Praeger, 1967), vol. II, p. 75.

47. Anon., *Rote Kapelle: A Survey Report on Soviet Intelligence and Espionage Activities in Western Europe, 1936–1945*, vol. II (Washington, D.C.: CIA, 1973), pp. 444ff.

48. Costello and Tsarev, *Deadly Illusions*, p. 448.

49. Ibid., p. 146.
50. Seale and McConville, *Philby*, p. 73.
51. Kim Philby, unpublished autobiography.
52. Costello and Tsarev, *Deadly Illusions*, pp. 193–95.
53. All quotations relating to Burgess are from Kim Philby's unpublished autobiography.
54. See Costello and Tsarev, *Deadly Illusions*, pp. 226–28.
55. See ibid., pp. 235–38, for Burgess's encounters with Footman and Vivian.
56. All information and quotations relating to Wylie are from Kim Philby's unpublished autobiography.

Chapter 7: Lockhart and Haushofer: 1934–1939

1. Costello and Tsarev, *Deadly Illusions*, p. 158.
2. Interviews with Gennady X in Moscow, February 1992.
3. Costello and Tsarev, *Deadly Illusions*, p. 149.
4. Taprell Dorline, *Ribbons and Medals* (London: Phillip, 1960), p. 33.
5. Correspondence with Dora Philby, 1934 file.
6. This code name appears in Costello and Tsarev, *Deadly Illusions*, p. 156.
7. Ibid.
8. Ibid.
9. Ibid.
10. Ibid.
11. Ibid., p. 157.
12. Ibid.
13. Kenneth Young, ed., *The Diaries of Sir Robert Bruce Lockhart: 1915–1938*, vol. I (London: Macmillan, 1973), p. 97.
14. Ibid.
15. Adolf Hitler, *Mein Kampf* (New York, 1939), p. 960.
16. "Memorandum on the Bolsheviks or Communist Party in Russia and Its Relation to the Third or Communist International and to the Russian Soviets," National Archives, Old Naval Intelligence Archives, PD226-89, March 20, 1933.
17. Richard Griffiths, *Fellow Travellers of the Right: British Enthusiasts for Nazi Germany, 1933–1939* (Oxford: Oxford University Press, 1983), pp. 182–87.
18. Kim's official KGB biography, in Costello and Tsarev, *Deadly Illusions*, p. 161.
19. Ibid.
20. Ibid.
21. Anthony Cave Brown, *"C": Winston Chirchill's Spymaster* (New York: Macmillan, 1988), pp. 181–82, 184. The original source was *Documents on German Foreign Policy* (London: HMSO), Series VII, vol. IV.

All quotations regarding Coburg's talks with King Edward VIII are from this source unless stated otherwise.

22. Nigel Nicolson, ed., *Diaries and Letters: 1930–1939* (New York: Atheneum, 1966), pp. 272–73, entry for September 20, 1936.

23. Griffiths, *Fellow Travellers of the Right*, p. 215.

24. Ibid.

25. Nevile Henderson, *Failure of a Mission: Berlin, 1937–1939* (London: Hodder & Stoughton, 1940), p. 72.

26. Seale and McConville, *Philby*, p. 94.

27. Kim Philby's association with Lockhart and Haushofer is mentioned by General Kalugin in his introduction to the Russian edition of Philby's memoir, *My Silent War*. It is not mentioned in Graham Greene's foreword to the English edition. Kalugin's introduction was translated for the author by Gennady X in Moscow, February 1992.

28. Costello and Tsarev, *Deadly Illusions*, p. 454n.

29. Ibid.

30. Monroe, *Philby of Arabia*, p. 216.

31. Page, Leitch, and Knightley, *Philby*, p. 90.

32. Charles Grave, *Leather Armchairs: The Book of London Clubs* (New York: Coward-McCann, 1964), p. 45.

33. Kim Philby, *My Silent War*, p. 1.

34. Seale and McConville, *Philby*, pp. 99–100

35. Kim Philby, *My Silent War*, p. 1.

36. Seale and McConville, *Philby*, p. 100.

37. Costello and Tsarev, *Deadly Illusions*, p. 313.

38. Sotheby's sale catalogue, Philby correspondence, London, July 1994.

39. Correspondence with May Philby, 1938 file.

40. Tom Driberg, *Guy Burgess: A Portrait with Background* (London: Weidenfeld & Nicolson, 1956), p. 46. All quotations concerning Burgess's meeting with Churchill are from this source unless stated otherwise.

41. See FBI file 65-58785 on Anatoli Gromov.

42. CIA Survey Report, *Rote Kapelle*, vol. I, conclusions.

43. Costello and Tsarev, *Deadly Illusions*, p. 240.

44. Monroe, *Philby of Arabia*, p. 220.

45. William Roger Louis, *Imperialism at Bay, 1941–1945: The United States and the Decolonization of the British Empire* (Oxford: Clarendon Press, 1977), p. 50.

46. Flora Solomon and Barnet Litvinoff, *A Woman's Way* (New York: Simon & Schuster, 1984), p. 165.

47. Ibid., p. 172.

48. Ibid., pp. 165–72.

49. Peter Wright, *Spycatcher* (New York: Viking, 1987), p. 173.

50. Gordon Brook-Shepherd, *The Storm Petrels: The Flight of the First Soviet Defectors* (New York: Harcourt Brace Jovanovich, 1977), p. 159.

51. Solomon and Litvinoff, *A Woman's Way.*
52. A private statement to the author by a person who had good reason to remain anonymous.
53. Solomon and Litvinoff, *A Woman's Way.*
54. F. H. Hinsley and C. A. G. Simkins, *British Intelligence in the Second World War,* vol. IV, *Security and Counter-Intelligence* (London: HMSO, 1989), p. 22.
55. Solomon and Litvinoff, *A Woman's Way,* p. 22.
56. Kim Philby, *My Silent War,* p. xviii.
57. Ibid.
58. Ibid.

Chapter 8: War: 1939–1940

1. Pavel Sudoplatov and Antonio Sudoplatov, *Special Tasks: The Memoirs of an Unwanted Witness, a Soviet Spymaster* (Boston: Little, Brown, 1994), p. 231.
2. Malcolm Muggeridge, *Chronicles of Wasted Time,* vol. II, *The Infernal Grove* (New York: Morrow, 1974), p. 116.
3. Norman Rose, *Chaim Weizmann* (New York: Viking, 1986), p. 345.
4. Correspondence with Dora Philby, 1939 file.
5. The interdepartmental file on St. John's misadventures in Arabia and India in 1939–1940 is in the Public Records Office, London, file FO 371/24589. All quotations in this passage are from this source unless stated otherwise.
6. Monroe, *Philby of Arabia,* p. 229.
7. Hinsley and Simkins, *British Intelligence,* vol. IV, p. 20.
8. Ibid.
9. Brook-Shepherd, *The Storm Petrels,* ch. 12, 13. This work reflected considerable British official advice, which otherwise in cases such as Philby has been historically rare.
10. The Krivitsky File and attendant Washington, D.C., police reports are in the State Department Archives at the National Archives, Washington, D.C. See also, in the National Archives, Diplomatic Branch, File 861, 20200/6-1047 CS/A, November 6, 1947.
11. The two-volume file, which includes that of Henri Robinson, is in the declassified CIA study "Classic Soviet Nets: The Rote Kapelle [Red Orchestra or Red Choir]." This study was commissioned by the CIA's chief of counterespionage, James Jesus Angleton, from a CIA Soviet analyst, Don Pratt. Pratt was detached from all other duties to make this study, which included contributions from all NATO and other Allied intelligence services. It was hoped that the study would reflect something of the KGB as it fought the Cold War of 1945–1980. It

was never circulated by Angleton, one of the matters that were held against him.

12. Kim Philby, *My Silent War,* p. xxv.

13. Military Publishing House of the Ministry of Defense of the USSR, *Preparation for an Unleashing of the War of Imperialistic Powers,* vol. I, *History of the Great Patriotic War of the Soviet Union, 1941–1945,* translated by the U.S. Army (Moscow, 1960), p. 14.

14. Sir John Colville, *The Fringes of Power: 10 Downing Street Diaries, 1939–1955* (New York: Norton, 1985), pp. 40–41, entry for October 13, 1939.

15. Seale and McConville, *Philby,* p. 105.

16. National Archives, Washington, D.C., Diplomatic Brance: 862.002 Adolf Hitler 211. Telegram from the U.S. Embassy in Berlin to the State Department, November 9, 1939.

17. Ibid., f. 228.

18. Interviews with Frederick W. Winterbotham in Popham, Hampshire, U.K., June 1970.

19. Interview with Sir. S. G. Menzies, January 1964.

20. National Archives, Washington, D.C., Microfilm Reading Room, RSHA Records, T175: Sicherheitsdienst interrogation of S. Payne Best and Captain R. H. Stevens. See reel R649, frame 216, p. 87. I am indebted to Dr. Robert Woolff of the National Archives for bringing this invaluable document to my attention. There is also a translation of the article in *Deutsches Polizei* in the Director's Files of General William J. Donovan, chief of the OSS in the United States during World War II. This includes the *casus belli* between Germany, Holland, and Belgium.

21. PRO London, FO 371/24249.

22. Ibid.

23. Diaries of Sir Alexander Cadogan, Churchill College, Cambridge, May 17, 1940.

24. Braunthal, *History of the International,* p. 513.

Chapter 9: *"The Stupendous Double-cross": 1940–1942*

1. Winston S. Churchill, *The Second World War,* vol. II, *Their Finest Hour* (London: Cassell, 1949), pp. 197–98.

2. Christopher Felix, *A Short Course in the Secret War* (New York: Dell, 1963), p. 121. The true author is James McCargar.

3. Kim Philby, *My Silent War,* p. 2.

4. Hinsley and Simkins, *British Intelligence in the Second World War,* vol. VI. The grave problems inside the Security Index are well related on pages 68–69.

5. Ibid., pp. 82–83.

6. Kim Philby, *My Silent War*, p. 3.
7. Ibid.
8. Ibid., p. 4.
9. Bruce Page Etal, *Philby: The Spy Who Betrayed a Generation* (London: Deutsch, 1968), p. 64.
10. *Memoirs of Lord Glaywyn* (London: Weidenfeld & Nicholson, 1972), p. 101.
11. Kim Philby, *My Silent War*, p. 15.
12. Ibid., pp, 18–19.
13. Ibid., p. 17.
14. Ibid.
15. PWE's charter, marked Most Secret, is in the archives of Major General William J. Donovan at the U.S. Army War College in Carlisle, Pa. It was sent to him by the Cabinet Office, London, for his advice when PWE was established. This author has not discovered it in any British archive. At PRO London it is closed to the public until well into the next century.
16. Kim Philby, *My Silent War*, p. 18.
17. M. R. D. Foot, *Resistance: An Analysis of European Resistance to Nazism, 1940–1945* (London: Eyre Methuen, 1976), p. 140.
18. Foot, *SOE in France: An Account of the Work of the British Special Operations Executive in France, 1940–1944* (London: HMSO, 1966), pp. 13–14.
19. Interviews with George Begué, McLean, Va., July 1991. Begué was at Beaulieu at this time and was tutored by Philby in Nazi clandestinity. Then he became the first of several hundred SOE to be parachuted into France. He landed near Châteauroux during the night of May 5–6, 1941. When captured by the Germans, he was rescued by the exceptional U.S. officer Virginia Hall, of Maryland, who managed to operate effectively although she had only one leg. A wooden leg was dropped to her and, using it, she managed to escape across the Pyrenees to Lisbon and then England, where she was then employed as a secret agent in France by Donovan. Begué escaped from France about the same time and became the man in charge of clandestine communications between SOE headquarters and France.
20. Seale and McConville, *Philby*, p. 133.
21. Anon. (CIA: *Review of Intelligence*, declassified 1985), "Intelligence in Recent Public Literature" on the subject of classic Soviet nets.
22. Kim Philby, *My Silent War*, p. 22.
23. See H. M. G. Lauwers's epilogue in H. J. Giskes, *London Calling North Pole* (London: Kimber, 1953), pp. 175–205.
24. Louis de Jong, "The Great Game of Secret Agents," *Encounter*, January 1980.
25. Herman Friedhoff, *Requiem for the Resistance* (London: Bloomsbury, 1988), p. 180.

26. Interviews with W. E. Henhoeffer, June 1991–1992.

27. West, *The Meaning of Treason*, pp. 344–45.

28. All quotations by Kim Philby about Tomas Harris from *My Silent War*, p. 9.

29. Interview with James McCargar, Washington, D.C., July 1992.

30. Michael Howard, *British Intelligence in the Second World War*, vol. V (London: Cambridge University Press, 1990), pp. 8–9.

31. J. C. Masterman, *The Double-Cross System in the War of 1939 to 1945* (New Haven: Yale University Press, 1972), p. xiv.

32. James Douglas-Hamilton, *The Truth about Rudolf Hess* (Edinburgh: Mainstrean, 1993), p. 121.

33. Ibid., p. 129.

34. Ibid.

35. Ibid., p. 130.

36. Ibid.

37. Monroe, *Philby of Arabia*, p. 230.

38. St. John, letter to Dora, 1941 file.

39. Churchill, *The Great War*, vol. III (London: Newnes, 1934), p. 1263.

40. Ibid.

41. Kenneth Young, ed., *The Diaries of Robert Bruce Lockhart*, vol. II, *1939–1945* (London: Macmillan, 1980), p. 256, entry for September 4, 1943.

42. Letter, S. G. Menzies to Felix Cowgill, in the Cowgill papers.

43. Seale and McConville, *Philby*, p. 135.

44. Trevor-Roper, "The Philby Affair," *Encounter*.

45. Costello and Tsarev, *Deadly Illusions*, pp. 235–37.

46. West, *The Meaning of Treason*, p. 418.

47. Douglas-Hamilton, *The Truth about Rudolf Hess*, p. 150.

48. John Costello, *Ten Days to Destiny* (New York: Morrow, 1991), p. 436.

49. KGB, Moscow: 1991 declassification Philby documents; translations by the CIA.

50. Ibid.

51. Ibid.

52. H. Montgomery Hyde, *Stalin: History of a Dictator* (New York: Popular Library, 1971), p. 50, quoting the Soviet historian A. M. Nekrich.

53. Churchill, *The Second World War*, vol. III, *The Grand Alliance* (London: Cassell, 1950), p. 49.

54. *Washington Post*, July 15, 1941.

55. Kim Philby, *My Silent War*, pp. 23–24.

56. Hinsley and Simkins, *British Intelligence in the Second World War*, vol. IV, p. 3.

57. Leo D. Carl, *The International Dictionary of Intelligence* (McLean, Va.: Macen, 1990), p. 83.

58. Kim Philby, *My Silent War*, p. 25.

59. Ibid., p. 26.

60. Allen W. Dulles, ed., *Great True Spy Stories* (New York: Harper & Row, 1968), pp. 54–55.

61. Edward R. F. Sheehan, "Philby," *Saturday Evening Post,* February 15, 1964, and interviews with him. Sheehan has stated that the original source for this article was Miles Copeland, the representative of Gulf Oil in Beirut when Philby disappeared. Copeland claimed that part of his operating expenses were paid for by James J. Angleton, at that time chief of counterespionage at the CIA. Copeland had had associations with the CIA in Washington, and in Beirut he was widely regarded as a reliable and knowledgeable source in the Philby case. For a time during the Philby period he was a voguish source, but later his information came to be distrusted. "Charming but unreliable," commented Nicholas Elliott, with the British Secret Service in Beirut at the time.

62. Kim Philby, *My Silent War,* p. 154.

63. Muggeridge, *Chronicles of Wasted Time,* p. 125.

64. Dulles, *Great True Spy Stories,* p. 55.

65. Hinsley and Simkins, *British Intelligence in the Second World War,* vol. II, p. 61.

66. Patrick Howarth, *Intelligence Chief Extraordinary: The Life of the Ninth Duke of Portland* (London: Bodley Head, 1986), p. 164.

67. Alan Bullock, *Hitler and Stalin: Parallel Lives* (New York: Knopf, 1992), p. 717.

68. Anon. (CIA: *Review of Intelligence,* declassified November 1988), and CIA, *Rote Kapelle Survey Report,* Swiss Section and Swiss Personalities.

69. Elliott, *Never Judge a Man by His Umbrella,* p. 190.

70. SS Chronology, February 23, 1942.

71. Young, *The Diaries of Sir Robert Bruce Lockhart,* vol. I, pp. 143–46.

72. Kim Philby, *My Silent War,* pp. 46–47.

Chapter 10: War Station XB: 1941–1944

1. Hinsley and Simkims, *British Intelligence in the Second World War,* vol. IV, p. 180.

2. Muggeridge, *Chronicles of Wasted Time,* vol. II, p. 136.

3. F. H. Cowgill and David Pertrie, *Communism in India* (Delhi: Government of India, 1934), foreword.

4. Interviews with F. H. Cowgill, Dorset, England, April 1983.

5. St. John–Dora letters, 1943 file.

6. Phillip Knightley, *The Master Spy: The Story of Kim Philby* (New York: Knopf, 1989), pp. 118–19, citing interview in 1967.

7. Trevor-Roper, "The Philby Affair," pp. 28–29. All quotations by Trevor-Roper are from this source unless stated otherwise.

8. Kim Philby, *My Silent War,* p. 32.

9. Ibid. See the introduction by Graham Greene to the English-language edition.

10. This paper was found by the author in the director's files of William J. Donovan, chief of the OSS. Ten pages long, it constitutes the only paper that the author has seen in the public domain on the relationship between the decrypts, the large deception industry of the time, and grand strategy. Its internal evidence suggests that it was postwar in origin, written by a Briton for an American. It crossed the author's mind that it might have been a paper written by Philby in 1949 when he was advising the CIA on the creation of a counterintelligence section. It sounded like Philby.

11. Interviews with F. H. Cowgill, Dorset, England, April 1983.

12. Kim Philby, *My Silent War,* pp. 44–45. All quotations by Philby relating to the source books are from this passage unless stated otherwise.

13. Hinsley and Simkims, *British Intelligence in the Second World War,* vol. IV, p. 188.

14. Kim Philby, *My Silent War,* p. 53.

15. Diaries of David K. E. Bruce, June 1942, Virginia Historical Society, Richmond, Virginia.

16. Anthony Cave Brown, *The Last Hero* (New York: Times Books, 1982), p. 453.

17. Diaries of David K. E. Bruce.

18. Kim Philby, *My Silent War,* pp. 40ff for all information about Bodden unless stated otherwise.

19. Masterman, *The Double-Cross System,* pp. 1–3.

20. Interviews with Sir James Easton, Grosse Pointe, Mich., 1987.

21. Kim Philby, *My Silent War,* p. 39.

22. Trevor-Roper, "The Philby Affair," *Encounter.* All quotations of Trevor-Roper about Philby are from this source unless stated otherwise.

23. Kim Philby, *My Silent War,* p. 47.

24. These quotations are from the jacket copy of Anthony Read and David Fisher, *Colonel Z: The Life and Times of a Master of Spies* (North Pomfret, Vt.: Hodder and Stoughton, 1984).

25. Trevor-Roper, "The Philby Affair."

26. Kim Philby, *My Silent War,* p. 48.

27. Ibid.

28. The details about the arrest of Henri Robinsohn are in his biographical statement, CIA, *Rote Kapelle,* vol. 2. Felix Cowgill interviews provided the information relating to Vivian's investigation.

29. Cadogan Diaries, August 23, 1943, Churchill College, Cambridge.

30. Robin W. Winks, *Cloak and Gown: Scholars in the Secret War* (New York: Morrow, 1987), ch. 5 for Norman Holmes Pearson.

31. National Archives, Washington, D.C.: Modern Military Records, OSS

X2 London War Diary, vol. 2, Basic Documents. All quotations concerning X2 London are from this source unless stated otherwise.

32. David C. Martin, *Wilderness of Mirrors* (New York: Harper & Row, 1980), p. 12.
33. This paper is by E. Applewhite, a retired deputy inspector general of the CIA during the Angleton years. This question was still being asked as late as 1993. But in 1994 the Ames penetration of the CIA counterespionage seemed to provide a reason for the rehabilitation of Angleton's monomaniacal belief that the CIA was seriously penetrated by a KGB mole during the period 1954–1974.
34. Winks, *Cloak and Gown*, p. 325.
35. Kim Philby, *My Silent War*, p. 114.
36. D. C. Downes, *The Scarlet Thread* (New York: British Book Center, 1948), pp. 32–33.
37. National Archives, Diplomatic Section, File 841.44/7 PS Mel: "Denial of Exit Permit to Visit the United States," May 22, 1942.
38. National Archives, Downes OSS Papers, letter of July 24, 1942, to Colonel Ulius C. Amoss, "Arabia, Iraq, and the Minor Sheikhdoms and Sultanates of the Persian Gulf Country [sic]."
39. Ibn Saud and Hoskins files, FDR Library, Hyde Park, New York, and H. B. Hoskins File in William J. Donovan, OSS Director's Files, U.S. Army War College, Fort Carlisle, Pa. This file concerns Hoskins's travels in the Middle East and the demand for his court martial through his unauthorized contact with Arab and Jewish organizations in Palestine.
40. National Archives, OSS Records: Record Group 226, Letter Charles to Near East Section, Washington, D.C., June 16, 1944. The item cited is listed as document XL 995.
41. Robert Bruce Lockhart, in his Diaries, vol. 2, quotes Sir Orme Sargent of the Foreign Office as saying that, in the political mood of Britain in 1944, "the Common Wealth Party (the British form of Communism) might have startling success." See 2: 339.
42. Letter, Philby to Dora, 1944 file, at St. Antony's College, Oxford.
43. Letters about Aileen in ibid. All quotations by St. John about Aileen are from this source unless stated otherwise.

Chapter 11: Overlord: 1944–1945

1. These papers are unique in the public world. They have a significance other than their positive evidence of Philby's political and professional advocacy — had they reached the British or the American legal authorities when he was still an operational secret agent of the KGB they might have constituted a basis for an indictment in law under the various Anglo-American treachery laws. They are undated, as is most of Philby's correspondence, and their style reflect the toneless-

ness, an entirely ruthless spirit that came to mark all his professional correspondence in his later years in exile in Moscow. In this they resemble lawyer's business letters. His private correspondence with KGB officers is otherwise. These reflect ingratiation and servility which surprises the student of his character.

2. H. R. Trevor-Roper, *The Philby Affair: Espionage, Treason, and Secret Service* (London: Kimber, 1968), p.35. This work is a slightly revised version of Trevor-Roper's two essays on Philby and Canaris first published in *Encounter* magazine at a slightly earlier date. The revisions concern, mainly, the dates at which, in Trevor-Roper's view, suspicion of treachery first fell upon Philby, presumably in MI5. In *Encounter* the date is given as 1944, the time at which Philby became chief of the anti-Soviet branch of SIS. In an encounter, he gives the date as 1944, the year in which Philby became Chief of the anti-Soviet branch of the SIS. In his book, he gives the date as 1945, as, it is presumed, the consequence of the Volkov affair, which is related in Chapter 12. The question is, therefore, what caused suspicion to fall upon Philby in 1944? Why did Trevor-Roper amend the date? No explanations are available on this important point.

3. Muggeridge, *Chronicles of Wasted Time*, vol. II, p. 106.

4. The essay about Canaris is in Trevor-Roper, *The Philby Affair,* at the conclusion of his essay on Philby, see pp. 103ff. For Canaris's failure, see pp. 117ff.

5. Ibid., pp. 78–79.

6. The information by Cowgill re: Trevor-Roper's "trial" derives from two interviews with Cowgill in England in April 1983.

7. Interview with Sir S. G. Menzies, January 1964.

8. Knightley, *The Master Spy,* pp. 105–6.

9. Donovan Papers: Biography of Vermehren is Biography 440A in "U.S. Government Biographical Records, New York," February 11, 1944.

10. Brown, "*C,*" p. 561.

11. Trevor-Roper, *The Philby Affair.* Canaris section of the book.

12. Chester Wilmot, *Struggle for Europe* (London: Collins, 1965), p. 217.

13. Victor Rothewell, *Britain and the Cold War: 1941–1947* (London: Cape, 1982), p.125, citing exchanges between Churchill and Foreign Office between April 1 and 17, 1944.

14. Masterman, *The Double Cross System,* foreword by Pearson.

15. For texts of Garbo's messages see Sefton Delmer, The *Counterfeit Spy* (New York: Harper & Row, 1971). Other such texts are also in the British official history, *British Intelligence in the Second World War,* vol. V, by Michael Howard. This author had the privilege of a very long series of interviews with Sir Ronald Wingate, an old friend and colleague of St. John Philby, on the D-Day and D+4 deceptions, and with Delmer. He interviewed, too, many of the intelligence figures in the German

High Command during the Neptune period. Cowgill related the scene during the first period of Neptune during a series of interviews in 1983. The biography of Garbo himself also played its part. See Juan Pujol with Nigel West, *Operation Garbo: The Personal Story of the Most Successful Double Agent of World War II* (New York: Random House, 1985).

16. Interview with John Cairncross, St.-Antonin, France, April 1992.

17. "Otto John," four foolscap pages of handwritten notes, thought to be by H. R. Trevor-Roper, then with the Foreign Intelligence Analysis Bureau of Section V. They came to this author from the British author David Irvine, who obtained them originally, in the late 1960s or the early 1970s, from Trevor-Roper. This author is grateful to Irvine for his generosity in sharing this collection.

18. Otto John, "Some Facts and Aspects of the 20th July Plot Against Hitler," Operations and Plans Division, U.S. War Department, Modern Military Records, National Archives, c. 1944–1945. All quotations relating to Otto John's meeting with the British Secret Service, his journey from Madrid to Berlin just before the attempt on Hitler, and his presence at the HQ of the German Home Army on July 20, 1944, are from *Twice Through the Lines: The Autobiography of Otto John* (London: Macmillan, 1972).

19. Donovan papers, U.S. Army War College, Fort Carlisle, Pennsylvania: See "Breakers" file for telegrams between Dulles and Donovan July 13–20. "Breakers" was Dulles's code name for the attempt to kill Hitler. See also the official British history by Hinsley and Simkins, *British Intelligence in the Second World War,* vol. 3, part 2, Appendix 22, p. 895, "The July Plot."

20. Brown, "*C,*" p. 604.

21. David K. E. Bruce Diaries, Virginia Historical Institute, entry for July 28, 1944.

22. Donovan Papers: telegram 3423–31, Dulles to Donovan, May 13, 1944.

23. Donovan OSS Director's Files: memo from Deputy Director E. G. Buxton to Secretary of State Cordell Hull, May 17, 1944, File 14,825.

24. Sotheby's Catalogue, July 1994: "Books, Papers and Memorabilia from the Moscow Flat of Kim Philby."

25. Churchill, *The Second World War,* vol. VI, p. 495.

26. Anthony Cave Brown and Charles B. MacDonald, *On a Field of Red: The Communist International and the Coming of World War II* (New York: Putnam, 1981), p. 103.

27. OSS Director's Files: microfilm reel no. 125 OSS Ops., ETO memo of meeting of June 4, 1945.

28. Kim Philby, *My Silent War,* p. 69.

29. Interviews with F. H. Cowgill.

30. Kim Philby, *My Silent War,* introduction by Greene.

31. Boyle, *The Climate of Treason,* p. 258.
32. Kim Philby, *My Silent War,* pp. 73–75
33. Interviews with F. H. Cowgill.
34. Interviews with Robert Cecil, 1986.
35. Trevor-Roper, *The Philby Affair,* p. 40.
36. Muggeridge, *Chronicles of Wasted Time,* vol. II, *The Infernal Grove,* pp. 251–53.
37. Ibid., pp. 187–88.
38. Donovan Papers: memo by deputy chief, E. Buxton, to Joint Chiefs of Staff, "Nazi Attempt to Contact British," December 26, 1944. See "Breakers" file.
39. Ibid.
40. Ibid., "Breakers" file.
41. Virginia Military Institute, papers of George Catlett Marshall, Second Tripartite Meeting of the Argonaut Conference, February 6, 1945.
42. Brown, *"C,"* p. 656.
43. Ibid. See also Anon., *Stalin's Correspondence with Churchill, Attlee, Roosevelt and Truman 1941–1945* (London: Lawrence and Wishart, 1958), p. 210, March 30, 1945. Letter through Deane to Marshall.
44. Ibid., p. 656.
45. Public Records Office, London: Prem3 198/2. February 27, 1945.
46. Donovan Papers: OSS Director's Files Microfilm reel 67 (1 Germany 16,107), Armour to Donovan. No date available.
47. Anon., *Stalin's Correspondence.* The correspondence relating to the German surrender begins at p. 198 of this volume and ends at p. 214. All quotations in text are from that source unless stated otherwise.
48. Seweryn Bialer, *Stalin and His Generals* (New York: Pegasus, 1969), p. 621.
49. Loewenheim, *Roosevelt and Churchill,* p. 709.
50. Trevor-Roper, *The Philby Affair,* pp. 42–43.

Chapter 12: Suspicion: 1944–1947

1. Kim Philby, *My Silent War,* pp. 87–88. All quotations relating to the postwar reorganization of the SIS are from this source unless stated otherwise.
2. Felix, *A Short Course in the Secret War,* p. 121. The author is James McCargar.
3. Muggeridge, "Refractions in the Character of Kim Philby," *Esquire,* September 1968, p. 113.
4. John Bright-Holmes, ed., *Like It Was: The Diaries of Malcolm Muggeridge* (New York: Morrow: 1982), p. 198.
5. Boyle, *The Climate of Treason,* p. 258, and interview with Cohen, 1986.
6. Seale and McConville, *Philby,* p. 175.

7. Ibid.

8. Ibid., p. 176.

9. Ibid., p. 177.

10. Stated by a KGB officer, Moscow, February 1992.

11. Sudoplatov and Sudoplatov, *Special Tasks,* p. 231. This memoir and its main author have been severely criticized in the United States and Russia for statements claiming that Robert Oppenheimer, the "father" of the U.S. atomic bomb, was a Soviet spy. No such criticism has been made in regard to Sudoplatov's claims about Philby, Maclean, and the rest of the Cambridge Group. As will be seen, there is some additional evidence that the investigation of the group was carried out.

12. Ibid., pp. 231–32.

13. Private communication, 1994.

14. Harold Macmillan, *War Diaries: Politics and War in the Mediterranean, 1943–45* (London: Macmillan, 1984), p. 384; see also p. 584.

15. National Archives, Washington, D.C., Modern Military Records, War Diary OSS London, in OSS Entry 91, Box 32, Folder 81-81. All materials and questions relating to OSS X2 are from this source unless stated otherwise.

16. Dulles's Kappa message, Berne-Washington-London, no. 3465-3466, May 14, 1944, in OSS Director's Cables, Donovan Papers, U.S. Army War College, Fort Carlisle, Pa.

17. Ibid.

18. Seale and McConville, *Philby,* p. 179.

19. Donovan Papers: Report to 109 — Donovan — from Second Lieutenant James Angleton, January 2, 1945. All quotations are from this source unless stated otherwise.

20. Interview with James J. Angleton, Washington, D.C., 1983.

21. Donovan Papers.

22. Interview with James J. Angleton, Washington, D.C., 1983.

23. National Archives, OSS X2 War Diary, see conclusion of Report on Banana. See Donovan Director's Files for Banana, U.S. Army War College, Fort Carlisle, Pa.

24. Interviews with Cleveland Cram.

25. Letter, E. J. Putzell to author, November 9, 1987.

26. Seale and McConville, *Philby,* p. 178.

27. Kim Philby, *My Silent War.* See Volkov chapter, from which all quotations in this passage were extracted unless stated otherwise.

28. Interview with the late Peter Mero, a leading U.S. expert in clandestine wireless. Washington, D.C., 1986.

29. Interview with James J. Angleton, Washington, D.C.

30. Page, Leitch, and Knightley, *Philby,* pp. 170–78. The fact that this allegation was made by John Reed is recorded in Harold Evans, *Good Times, Bad Times* (New York: Atheneum, 1983), p. 54.

31. Trevor-Roper, *The Philby Affair*, p. 49.
32. Interviews with Sir William Stephenson, Bermuda, February 1986.
33. Kim Philby, *My Silent War*, p. 85.
34. Interviews with Sir James Easton, Grosse Pointe, Mich., July 1986.
35. Certain KGB documents came into the possession of the author during 1992. This excerpt is from one of them. Two others are given more space in the appendices to this volume.
36. Kim Philby, *My Silent War*, p. 97.
37. Carleton Coon's documents about St. John Philby and the establishment of an OSS secret service in Arabia are in a special file of the Donovan OSS Director's Files at the U.S. Army War College, Fort Carlisle, Pa. All quotations are from that source unless stated otherwise.
38. St. John–Dora letter, July 1945 file of the Philby papers at the Middle East Center, St. Antony's College, Oxford. All quotations relating to St. John's return to Arabia are from this source unless stated otherwise.
39. Monroe, *Philby of Arabia*, p. 247.
40. Kim Philby, *My Silent War*, p. 99.
41. Alan Bullock, *Ernest Bevin: Foreign Secretary, 1945–1951* (London: Heinemann, 1983), p. 249.
42. Trevor-Roper, *The Philby Affair*, p. 26.
43. Gordon Brook-Shepherd, *The Storm Birds* (London: Weidenfeld & Nicolson, 1988), pp. 46ff. All quotations relating to Akhmedov are from this source unless stated otherwise.
44. Ismail Akhmedov, *In and Out of Stalin's GRU* (London: Arms and Armour, 1984), pp. 191–97.
45. Page, Leitch, and Knightley, *Philby*, p. 192.
46. Ibid., p. 19.
47. Interview with Mikhail Lyubimov, Moscow, February 1992.
48. Seale and McConville, *Philby*, p. 190.
49. N. Bethell, *The Great Betrayal: Albania in the Secret War* (London: Hodder and Stoughton, 1984), p. 95.
50. Special source.
51. Elliott, *Never Judge a Man by his Umbrella*, p. 190.
52. Kim Philby, *My Silent War*, p. 110.
53. Interviews with Yuri Modin, Moscow and Washington, D.C.
54. Kim Philby, *My Silent War*, pp. 111–12.
55. Churchill speech, MIT, March 31, 1949.
56. Public Records Office, London: Air 2/12027 June 16, 1945.
57. Kim Philby, *My Silent War*, p. 112.

Chapter 13: Washington: 1949–1951

1. National Archives, Washington, D.C.: Central Decimal State Department files 45-59, R.G. 59, 701.4111/10-2149. Note from Franks, No 526.

2. POR London: ADM 223/107 92010, Laird to DNI, Admiralty, London, June 4, 1946.

3. Interview with Mikhail Lyubimov, Moscow, 1992.

4. Interview with Sir Patrick Reilly, Ramsden, Oxfordshire, U.K., April 5, 1986.

5. Interviews with Sir James Easton, Grosse Pointe, Mich., 1987.

6. Interview with Dr. Ray Cline, Washington, D.C., June 1993.

7. Special document. All quotations relating to this document are from this source. The extracts published will suggest a reason why the man to whom Philby addressed the paper does not wish to be named.

8. Letter to Phillip Knightley, in Knightley, *The Master Spy*, p. 154.

9. Interviews with Cleveland Cram.

10. Wilfred B. Mann, *Was There a Fifth Man?* (London: Pergamon Press, 1982), p. 65.

11. Interviews with Dr. Mann, Chevy Chase, Md., 1991.

12. Mann, *Was There a Fifth Man?*, p. 70.

13. Boyle, in ibid., p. 377.

14. Pearson, in Masterman, *The Double-cross System*, introduction.

15. *Daily Telegraph*, London, November 10, 1979, in Mann, *Was There a Fifth Man?*, pp. 117–18.

16. Ibid., p. 135.

17. William R. Corson, *The Armies of Ignorance: The Rise of the American Intelligence Empire* (New York: Dial/James Wade, 1977), pp. 327–28.

18. Interviews with General Edwin L. Sibert, McLean, Va., 1976, 1977. This statement was first printed in the author's *"C,"* p, 745. It was never challenged.

19. Walter Millis, ed., *The Forrestal Diaries* (New York: Viking Press, 1951), pp. 528, 537.

20. Donovan Papers, U.S. Army War College: Microfilm Reel 59 Memo William Harding Jackson to Donovan. "Coordination of Intelligence Functions and the Organisation of SIS in the British Intelligence System, June 21, 1945.

21. James McCargar, speech to retired U.S. intelligence officers, Kennebunkport, Me., 1989.

22. Chistopher Felix (McCargar), "A Second Third Man," *New York Times Book Review*, May 26, 1968.

23. Page, Leitch, and Knightley, *Philby*, p. 155.

24. Kim Philby, *My Silent War*, pp. 123–26.

25. R. J. Lamphere and T. Schachtman, *The FBI-KGB War* (New York: Random House, 1968), p. 127.

26. Ibid., p. 126.

27. Kim Philby, *My Silent War*, p. 125.

28. Lamphere and Schachtman, *The FBI-KGB War*, pp. 130–31.

29. Ibid.

30. John Newhouse, *War and Peace in the Nuclear Age* (New York: Knopf, 1989), p. 78.
31. Bundy, *Danger and Survival*, p. 217.
32. Newhouse, *War and Peace in the Nuclear Age*, p. 34.
33. Interviews with Dr. Mann, Washington, D.C., 1993–1994.
34. Kim Philby, *My Silent War*, p. 125.
35. Ibid., pp. 114–15.
36. Interview with James Critchfield.
37. Special information.
38. Ibid.
39. Interview with James McCargar, Washington, D.C., June 1993.
40. Interview with William Hood, Maine, 1992.
41. Ibid.
42. Ibid.
43. Ibid.
44. St. John–Dora letter, September 26, 1950.
45. Kim Philby, *My Silent War*, p. 126.
46. Ibid.
47. Ibid.
48. Ibid.
49. Ibid.
50. Ibid., p.127.
51. Ibid., p. 128.
52. Boyle, *The Climate of Treason*, p. 352.
53. Seale and McConville, *Philby*, p. 230.
54. FBI Washington Field Office, Summary Report on D. D. Maclean and G. F. de Moncy Burgess.
55. Boyle, *The Climate of Treason*, p. 354.
56. Mann, *Was There a Fifth Man?*, pp. 78ff.
57. Angleton interviews.
58. Noel Annan, *Our Age* (New York: Random House, 1990), p. 227.
59. Bethell, *The Great Betrayal*, pp. 35–39.
60. Michael Burke, *Outrageous Good Fortune* (Boston: Little, Brown, 1984), p. 145.
61. Dan Raviv and Yossi Melman, *Every Spy a Prince: The Complete History of Israel's Intelligence Community* (Boston: Houghton Mifflin, 1990), pp. 91–92.
62. Note to author from Cleveland Cram, July 20, 1993.
63. Robert Joyce, unpublished, untitled memoir.
64. Interview with Ambassador Hugh Montgomerie, State Department, Washington, D.C., February 1990.
65. Interview with John Mapother, Virginia, March 1990.
66. Mann, *Was There a Fifth Man?*, p. 70.
67. Interview with Dr. Mann, Washington, D.C., October 1991.
68. Interview with James McCargar, Washington, D.C., March 28, 1994.

69. George Kennedy Young, Foreword to Anthony Cavendish, *Inside Intelligence,* privately published in London, 1987.

70. Interviews with Sir James Easton, Grosse Pointe, Mich., 1987.

71. Kim Philby, *My Silent War,* p. 137.

72. David S. McLellan, *Dean Acheson: The State Department Years* (New York: Dodd, Mead, 1976), pp. 338–39.

73. Interview with Sir Patrick Reilly, Ramsden, Oxfordshire, 1986.

74. Kim Philby, *My Silent War,* p. 86.

75. Interviews with Yuri Modin, Moscow and Washington, D.C.

76. Henry Fairlie, "Political Commentary," *Spectator,* London, September 23, 1955, p. 380.

77. Kim Philby, *My Silent War,* p. 138.

78. Ibid., pp. 173–74.

79. Lamphere and Schachtman, *The FBI-KGB War,* p. 231.

80. Kim Philby, *My Silent War,* p. 134.

81. Easton interviews.

82. Kim Philby, *My Silent War,* pp. 137–38.

83. Easton interviews.

84. Kim Philby, *My Silent War,* p. 136.

85. Lamphere and Schachtman, *The FBI-KGB War,* p. 237.

86. Ibid., pp. 237–38.

87. Ibid.

88. Angleton's report on Burgess is available at the CIA as a declassification.

89. Interview with James Critchfield.

Chapter 14: London: 1951–1955

1. Letter (23 pages) from Sir James Easton to the author about the Philby affair, May 14, 1987.

2. Seale and McConville, *Philby,* p. 218.

3. Hinsley and Simkins, *British Intelligence in the Second World War,* vol. IV, *Security,* p. 288.

4. Kim Philby, *My Silent War,* p. 139.

5. Ibid., p. 140.

6. Letter from Sir James Easton to the author, May 14, 1987.

7. Easton interviews, Grosse Pointe Farms, Mich., 1987.

8. Letter, St. John to E. Reifenstahl, Brooklyn Museum, October 7, 1951, in St. John Philby collection, Hoover Institute of War, Revolution and Peace in the Twentieth Century, Stanford University.

9. Kim Philby, *My Silent War,* p. 141.

10. Ibid., p. 143.

11. Letter, St. John–Dora, February 25, 1952, in St. John letter files, Middle East Center, St. Antony's College, Oxford.

12. Interview with James McCargar, Washington, D.C., January 1, 1993.

13. Menzies private papers in the care of Mrs. Fiona Bell, Moreton-in-Marsh, Gloucestershire, U.K. Minutes of Joint Intelligence Committee Meeting, July 3, 1952.
14. Ibid., letter from J. Edgar Hoover.
15. Ibid., letter from Allen W. Dulles.
16. Ibid., letter from Anthony Eden.
17. Kim Philby collection, St. Antony's College, Diaries of John Slade-Baker, *Sunday Times* correspondent, Beirut, entry for January 27, 1957.
18. Kim Philby, *My Silent War,* p. 146.
19. Interviews with Yuri Modin.
20. Ibid.
21. Interview with William E. Colby.
22. Seale and McConville, *Philby,* p. 228.
23. Public Records Office, London, item Cab/29 CM (55) 36, October 20, 1955, p. 6.
24. Wright, *Spycatcher,* pp. 44–45.
25. FBI, Washington, D.C., Philby, Maclean, Burgess files, Section 9, serial 1–99, p. 93 and p. 15, serial 1–21.
26. Seale and McConville, *Philby,* p. 230.
27. *Sunday Times,* London, October 22, 1967, original italics.
28. Letter, St. John–Dora, October 14, 1955, St. Antony's College.
29. Letter, St. John to E. Reifenstahl, December 16, 1955, in Hoover Institute collection.
30. Tom Driberg, *Guy Burgess* (London: Weidenfeld & Nicolson, 1956), appendix.
31. S. Roskill, *Hankey: Man of Secrets,* vol. III, *1931–1936* (New York: St. Martin's, 1974), p. 639.
32. John Ranelagh, *The Agency: The Rise and Decline of the CIA* (New York: Simon & Schuster, 1986), p. 236.
33. Horne, *Macmillan,* vol. I, p. 443.
34. Seale and McConville, *Philby,* p. 234.

Chapter 15: Beirut: 1956–1963

1. Anon., "Classic Soviet Nets," *CIA Review of Intelligence,* declassified 1988.
2. Ibid.
3. St. John–Dora letters, September 1956 file, St. Antony's College.
4. Letter, Kim Philby to Dora, May 2, 1957, St. Antony's College.
5. St. John–Dora letter, September 1956 file, St. Antony's College.
6. Monroe, *Philby of Arabia,* p. 260.
7. Miles Copeland, *The Game of Nations* (New York: Simon & Schuster, 1969), epigraph.
8. Special information.

9. Miles Copeland, *The Game of Nations* (New York: Simon & Schuster, 1969), p. 28.
10. William Roger Louis, *Imperialism at Bay, 1941–45: The U.S. and Decolonization* (Oxford: Oxford University Press, 1977), p. 17.
11. Monroe, *Philby of Arabia*, p. 281.
12. Ibid.
13. Ibid., p. 290.
14. Ibid., p. 289.
15. Interviews with Gillian Grant, Oxford, 1987 and 1982.
16. Obituary of Nicholas Elliott, *London Weekly Telegraph*, April 21, 1994. All quotations regarding Elliott are from this source unless stated otherwise.
17. Knightley, *The Master Spy*, p. 206. All quotations are from this source unless stated otherwise.
18. Ibid.
19. Keith Kyle, *Suez* (New York: St. Martin's Press, 1991), p. 99.
20. Interviews with Mrs. Frances Farmer, United Kingdom, December 1990, 1991, 1992.
21. Interviews with John Farmer, Geneva, Switzerland, and Annecy, France, 1991.
22. Anthony Verrier, *Through the Looking Glass* (London: Cape, 1983), p. 158.
23. Ibid.
24. Interview with James Critchfield, Virginia, July 1993.
25. Interview with Sylvia Crane, Cape Cod., Mass., July 1991.
26. Wilbur Crane Eveland, *Ropes of Sand: America's Failure in the Middle East* (New York: Norton, 1980), p. 258.
27. Ibid., p. 260.
28. Copeland, *The Game of Nations*, p. 144.
29. Knightley, *The Master Spy*, p. 211.
30. *The Economist*, March 29, 1958, p. 1140.
31. Brookings Institute: "The Use of the Armed Forces as a Political Instrument. A Study for the U.S. Advanced Research Agency," December 31, 1976. See "Case Study on the Lebanon" by William B. Quandt.
32. Interview with Yuri Modin.
33. Seale and McConville, "Philby," *The Observer*, London, May 1968.
34. Interview with James Critchfield.
35. Eleanor Philby, *Kim Philby: The Spy I Loved* (London: Hamish Hamilton, 1968), pp. 31–33.
36. Said abu Ris, *The St. George Hotel Bar* (London: 1985), p. 78.
37. Eveland, *Ropes of Sand*, p. 319.
38. Interviews with E. Applewhite, 1993–1994.
39. Ibid.
40. Copeland, *Without Cloak or Dagger: The Truth About the New Espionage* (New York: Simon & Schuster, 1974), p. 146.

41. Ibid., p. 212.
42. Ibid., p. 146.
43. Ibid.
44. Copeland, *The Game of Nations,* p. 212.
45. Copeland, *Without Cloak or Dagger,* p. 189.
46. Joseph C. Goulden, *The Death Merchant, CIA Intrigue, International Terrorism, Multimillion Dollar Weapons Deals — The Violent and Shadowy World That Saw the Rise and Fall of Edwin P. Wilson, Master Dealer in Illicit Arms* (New York: Simon & Schuster, 1984), p. 374.
47. Trevor-Roper, "The Philby Affair," pp. 56–57.
48. Eleanor Philby, *The Spy I Loved.*
49. Boyle, *The Climate of Treason,* p. 428.
50. Seale and McConville, *Philby,* p. 239.
51. Carl, *The International Dictionary of Intelligence.*
52. Elliott, *Never Judge a Man by His Umbrella,* p. 183.
53. Ibid., p. 39.
54. Mary Barrett, "A Respectful Dissenter: CIA's Wilbur Crane Eveland," *Washington Report on Middle Eastern Affairs,* March 1990.
55. Elliott, *Never Judge a Man by His Umbrella,* p. 186.
56. Interview with Richard Storm, March 1990.
57. Letter, Kim Philby to Elizabeth Monroe, October 14, 1960.
58. Diaries of John Slade-Baker, Philby collection, St. Antony's College, entry for September 30, 1960.
59. Monroe, *Philby of Arabia,* pp. 295–96.
60. Interview with Ronald Metz, Washington, D.C., 1991.
61. Diaries of John Slade-Baker, p. 3238.
62. Ibid., p. 3239.
63. Ibid., p. 3241.
64. Wright, *Spycatcher.*
65. Horne, *Macmillan,* vol. I, p. 461.
66. Ibid.
67. Ibid.
68. Obituary of Nicholas Elliott, *London Weekly Telegraph,* April 21, 1994. A CIA source states that this statement was made by Elliott only to the *Telegraph's* obituarist and to no other newspaper. It therefore constitutes the only formal statement by Elliott concerning the circumstances in which he replaced Martin on the Philby mission.
69. Elliott, *Never Judge a Man by His Umbrella,* p. 44.
70. Wright, *Spycatcher,* p. 174.
71. Obituary of Elliott.
72. Wright, *Spycatcher,* p. 174.
73. Special information.
74. Knightley, *The Master Spy,* p. 215.
75. Wright, *Spycatcher,* p. 194.

76. Knightley, *The Master Spy*, p. 217.
77. Personal letter, May 1994.

Chapter 16: The Bullfrogs' Chorus: 1963–1964

1. Interviews with Yuri Modin, Moscow (1991) and Washington (1993).
2. Graham Greene, *The Human Factor* (New York: Avon, 1978), p. 280. The fact that Greene consulted Philby about the conditions he encountered on his arrival in Moscow is discussed in Anthony Masters, *Literary Agents: The Novelist as a Spy* (London: Blackwell, 1987).
3. Anon, *Moscow: A Short Guide* (Moscow: Foreign Languages Publishing House, 1955). This little volume was on Philby's bookshelves and was given to this author by his widow as a memento of his visit to Patriarch's Pond.
4. Andrews and Gordievsky, *KGB: The Inside Story*, p. 12.
5. Interviews with Mikhail Lyubimov, Moscow, February 1992. The author spent the better part of a working week in Lyubimov's company discussing Philby and his world in Moscow.
6. Ibid.
7. David Remnick, *Lenin's Tomb: The Last Days of the Soviet Empire* (New York: Random House, 1993), p. 172.
8. Juan Pujol and Nigel West, *Operation Garbo: The Personal Story of the Most Successful Double Agent of World War II* (New York: Random House, 1985), pp. 142–43.
9. Lyubimov interviews.
10. Modin interviews.
11. Horne, *Macmillan*, vol. II, p. 687.
12. Interviews with Gennady X, Moscow (1992) and Washington, D.C. (1993). Gennady X was probably Philby's longest and closest KGB associate in Moscow.
13. Ibid.
14. Mikhail Lyubimov, "The Two Lives of Kim Philby," *Top Secret*, No. 6, Moscow, 1990.
15. Lyubimov interviews.
16. Mann interviews, Washington, D.C., July 1992.
17. Interview with G. Torrie, lately of the CIA, 1990.
18. Said abu Ris, *The St. George Hotel Bar*, p. 3.
19. Telephone interview with Don Wykoff, Palm Springs, Calif., March 19, 1993.
20. Eleanor Philby, *The Spy I Loved*, provides all data and communications relating to the period in Beirut immediately after Philby's disappearance, unless stated otherwise.
21. Ibid.

22. Ibid.

23. Horne, *Macmillan,* vol. II.

24. Seale and McConville, *Philby,* p. xiv.

25. Eleanor Philby, memoir, p. 18.

26. Ibid., p. 56.

27. Ibid., p. 69.

28. Statements by Kim Philby, Moscow, to *Daily Express* and *Sunday Times,* London.

29. Horne, *Macmillan,* vol. II, p. 457.

30. David Leigh, *The Wilson Plot* (New York: Pantheon, 1988), p. 73.

31. Ibid., p. 75.

32. Horne, *Macmillan,* p. 462.

33. Ibid., p. 467.

34. Ibid., p. 576.

35. Ranelagh, *The Agency,* p. 254.

36. Eleanor Philby, memoirs, p. 35.

37. Ibid., p. 77.

38. Ibid.

39. Ibid.

40. CIA transcript of Canadian TV Program, "The Fifth Estate: The Story of the Wrong Man," March 30, 1993.

41. Eleanor Philby, memoirs, p. 82.

42. Ibid., p. 96.

43. CIA intercepts of Kim Philby–Eleanor Philby letters begin at this point in the text.

44. Ibid.

45. Interviews with Albert L Hennig, lately of the CIA, January 1993.

46. Interviews with Harrison Salisbury about Sam Pope Brewer and Kim Philby.

47. CIA letter intercept.

48. Ibid.

49. Ibid.

50. Ibid.

51. Eleanor Philby, *The Spy I Loved,* p. 155.

52. Ibid., p. 166.

53. Robert Cecil, *A Divided Life: A Biography of Donald Maclean* (London: Bodley Head, 1988), p. 177.

54. Eleanor Philby, *The Spy I Loved,* p. 171.

55. Ibid., p. 173.

56. Ibid., p. 174.

Chapter 17: The Monster Plot: 1963–1975

1. Eleanor Philby, "Two Traitors in Exile," *The Observer,* November 5, 1967.
2. Tom Mangold, *Cold Warrior: James Jesus Angleton, The CIA's Master Spy Hunter* (New York: Simon & Schuster, 1991), p. 380.
3. Interviews with General Oleg Kalugin, Washington, D.C., between 1992 and late 1993.
4. U.S. Government, Foreign Broadcasting Intelligence Service intercept SU/0798 b/5 June 23, 1990: "Former KGB official on future of *perestroika* in the KGB."
5. Kalugin interviews.
6. Interviews with Cleveland Cram.
7. Interview with Miriam Mann, Washington, D.C., 1992, and T. Mangold, op. cit.
8. Kim Philby, chapter of unpublished autobiography in his papers at Patriarch's Pond.
9. Senate testimony by James J. Angleton, October 5, 1978.
10. Mangold, *Cold Warrior,* p. 380.
11. Ranelagh, *The Agency,* p. 320.
12. Ron Rosenbaum, "The Shadow of the Mole," *Harper's,* October 1983.
13. Special information.
14. Wise, *Molehunt,* p. 253.
15. Interview with James Critchfield.
16. Special information.
17. Interview with James Critchfield.
18. Rosenbaum, *Harper's,* October 1983.
19. Ibid.
20. Special information.
21. Kim Philby archives, Moscow.
22. West, *The Meaning of Treason,* p. 344.
23. Interview with Romuald Spassowski, the former Polish communist ambassador in Washington, defected 1987.
24. Interview with Yuri Modin, Moscow, 1991.
25. Interview with Colonel Samuel Lohan, London, 1968.
26. Alan Bennett, *Single Spies and Talking Heads* (New York: Summit, 1988), introduction.
27. Murray Sayle, *Sunday Times,* London, interview with Kim Philby, December 17, 1967.
28. A. Howard, ed., *The Crossman Diaries* (London: Mandarin, 1991), p. 382.
29. Page, Leitch, and Knightley, *Philby,* introduction by John le Carré. Italics in original.
30. Ibid., p. 18.
31. Trevor-Roper, *The Philby Affair,* p. 59.

32. Masters, *Literary Agents,* biographical statement on Graham Greene.

33. Martin Green, *Children of the Sun* (New York: Basic Books, 1976), p. 369.

34. Copies of this exchange of letters between Menzies and Cowgill are (1994) in the files of Robert Cecil, who made a copy of them from Cowgill's personal papers.

35. Kim Philby, *My Silent War,* p. xii–xiv.

36. Ibid., p. xvi.

37. Ibid., p. 55.

38. Ibid., see Introduction by Graham Greene.

Chapter 18: Endgame: 1970–1994

1. Interviews with Mikhail Lyubimov.

2. Interviews with Oleg Kalugin.

3. Interviews with Ruffina Philby, October 1991 and February 1992.

4. Anne Elizabeth-Moutet interview with Graham Greene, *Sunday Telegraph,* London, 1994.

5. Interviews with Gennady X, February 1992.

6. Young, *The Iron Lady,* p. 392.

7. Ibid., p. 393.

8. Oleg Gordievsky, "Pershing Paranoia in the Kremlin," *The Times,* February 27, 1990.

9. Private information.

10. Andrews and Gordievsky, *KGB,* p. 567.

11. M. Lyubimov, "Two Lives of Kim Philby," *Top Secret,* Moscow, 1990.

12. Interview with Yuri Modin, October 1991. Did Modin really mean to say this? In November 1993, an opportunity arose to check whether he did. He came to Washington, D.C., and I asked him whether he remembered making this statement. "I remember it very well," he declared. "But what I said," he declared confidently in his excellent but deliberate English, was "I wonder whether Kim laughed at us as he laughed at everyone else." Was Modin having trouble with his synonyms? A further opportunity arose to check what he had said in May 1994. He was in Paris for the launching of his memoir. He lunched with Larry Collins, the novelist. During that lunch, as Collins reported, Modin remarked, "I wonder whether Kim tricked us as he tricked everyone else." And in his memoir, he wrote that while he trusted Blunt, Cairncross, Burgess, and Maclean, he had had no such confidence in Philby. Philby had a "mocking" side to his personality that left Modin uncertain about his devotion to Marxism and the proletariat. Modin of the sixth sense, an honest man, knew Philby as a Communist clandestine better than any other. What he said to me

was important, therefore. "He was so completely British, so completely the British Secret Service officer, that even now I cannot be sure of him." Of course, Modin had been paid to be suspicious and skeptical about his British comrades. So what had Modin really meant to say? The conclusion could only be that Modin had not had full confidence in Philby as a Soviet secret agent.

13. Applewhite memo, May 11, 1964. Presumably he meant May 11, 1994.

Index

Philby, Kim (*cont.*)

Abwehr desertions, 316; deception over Overlord plans, 317, 318, 320–21; and anti-Hitler conspiracy, 323–328; anticommunist activists betrayed by, 328; elimination of Cowgill and takeover of Section IX, 329–34; scene at Soviet embassy in Paris, 335–36; and withholding of MSS from Soviets, 336; and German peace overtures, 340–41, 342; Trevor-Roper on prominence of, 344; subverted Spanish OSS network (Banana), 360–61, 394; McCargar sees as "Young Turk," 404; and death of Sikorski, 567–68; and failed Eastern Europe operations, 568–69

IN BRITISH SECRET SERVICES (POST–WWII): horizontal reorganization accomplished, 345–47; bourgeois life, 347–48; and Angleton, 356, 358, 359–60, 394; and Volkov affair, 363–66, 369, 381, 387; and Gouzenko disclosures, 366–67; as station chief in Turkey, 368–69, 378, 379, 382–83, 574; and Edith Whitfield, 380, 384; and Akhmedov case, 380–382; and Korean War leaks, 569–72

AS CHIEF IN U.S., 391–99; selection, 386–87; preparatory briefings, 387–89; and Maclean disclosure, 389; and views on America, 393; and Angleton, 394–95, 400, 411–12, 419, 421, 423, 424, 560, 563–65; and Mann, 399–401; seen as manipulated to mislead Soviets, 401–3, 424; and CIA, 403–5, 411–12, 423; and FBI, 405–7, 410–11, 423; and Korean War crisis, 412–15, 426; Burgess arrives, 415–20; Kollek happens across, 420–21; in line for "C" post, 426; disastrous party given by, 426–28; and Maclean-Burgess escape, 428–33; summons to London and growing realizations, 433–37

INVESTIGATION OF AND AFTERMATH: and C's viewpoint, 438–39; White interviews, 439–40; colleagues' support, 441; Easton report to Washington, 441; Easton's ten points, 442–43; resignation, 443–44; Milmo's interrogation, 444–45; passport surrendered, 445; Skardon's questioning, 445–46, 450, 459; three-year period of quiet, 447; McCargar's visit, 447; unemployment and financial difficulties, 450; escape plan, 450; help from Soviets (Modin operation), 450–51; and ruling-class damage control, 452, 455, 456, 504; and Petrov revelations, 452–53; Macmillan on, 453–54; committee of inquiry, 454–55; Commons debate, 455–58; press conference, 458–59; and effects of allegations, 459;

Otto John's revelations, 460; vacation, 460–61; Elliott's support, 469–70; Flora Solomon's testimony, 502–3; confrontation with Elliott, 503; confession, 507; offer of immunity, 507–8; White on results of, 526

IN BEIRUT, 463, 464; re-employment, 462–63; and SJP, 464–67, 479, 491; White's plan to trap, 471–72, 491; and Elliott, 472, 490–93; and razor-bomb plot against Nasser, 475; and Eveland, 477–78, 494; marriage to Eleanor, 480–83; Soviet safe house for, 484; and Applewhite, 484–85; and Copeland, 486–88; and Barracks, 487; Trevor-Roper meets, 489–90; expansion of travels, 491–92; outrageous cocktail-party remark, 493; breakdown, 497–98; visit to look at SJP's papers, 498–99; new pressures, 502; confrontation by Elliott, 506–8; escape, 508–9

ESCAPE BY, 508–9; British motivations in, 504, 507, 509; and Elliott's complicity, 509–10, 621–22; reception in Moscow, 511; British-side response and consequences, 519–21, 526–32; letters to Eleanor, 521–23; Macmillan on, 523; and Angleton, 551

IN USSR: Order of Lenin, 511, 548, 609; debriefing, 511–14, 544, 546; first quarters, 513; Soviet suspicions toward, 513, 519, 545–46, 597; status, 514, 515–16, 589; permanent residence, 514–17; surveillance and control, 515, 536, 538, 589, 590; income, 516, 536; loneliness, 517; work, 518, 536–37, 545, 549, 590, 600; reunited with Eleanor, 519, 524–26, 533–35; and "monster plot," 532, 535, 549–50, 560 (*see also* "Monster plot"); Eleanor's interrogation, 534–35; and Macleans, 535–36; getting rid of Eleanor, 535, 537, 538–39, 545–46, 547; KP's value to Soviets, 537, 549, 589–90; Order of the Red Banner, 546–47; memoirs outlined, 565–66, 568, 572; memoirs offered, 575; Sayle interview, 575–76; and Lyubimov, 588–94; power and prestige, 591–92; work ceases, 593; and Kalugin, 594–95, 597, 599; and Ruffina, 595–97, 599–600; memoir suppressed, 597–99; cabal around, 599, 610; anniversaries celebrated, 599; arrangements for death, 601; and Graham Greene, 601–2, 605; forty-fifth anniversary of conversion to Communism, 608–9; isolation, 614; taken ill, 614–15; death, 615; obituaries, 615–16; grave and funeral of, 618–20, 621

Philby, May Duncan (mother of SJP), 2–4, 21–24, 46, 47, 75; hotel of, 4, 12; on